HISTORY OF MEDIEVAL & MODERN EUROPE

IN EIGHT VOLUMES

Volume VII

A HISTORY OF EUROPE

From 1715-1814

METHUEN'S
HISTORY OF MEDIEVAL & MODERN EUROPE

A History of Early Medieval Europe: 476–911
MARGARET DEANESLY

A History of Europe: 911–1198
Z. N. BROOKE

A History of Europe: 1198–1378
C. W. PREVITÉ-ORTON

A History of Europe: 1378–1494
W. T. WAUGH

A History of Europe: 1494–1610
A. J. GRANT

A History of Europe: 1610–1715
W. F. REDDAWAY

A History of Europe: 1715–1814
W. F. REDDAWAY

A History of Europe: 1815–1939
SIR J. A. R. MARRIOTT

A History of Europe

FROM 1715 TO 1814

W. F. REDDAWAY

M.A.

Late Fellow of King's College, Cambridge
and University Lecturer in History

BIBLIOGRAPHY REVISED BY R. L. GREAVES

LONDON: METHUEN & CO LTD
NEW YORK: BARNES & NOBLE INC

First Published May 14th 1936
Second Edition, Revised, August 1941
Third Edition March 1950
Fourth Edition September 1951
Reprinted five times
Reprinted (with new bibliographies) 1957
Reprinted four times
Reprinted 1964

4.6
CATALOGUE NO. 2/4356/10 [METHUEN]

PRINTED IN GREAT BRITAIN BY
BUTLER & TANNER LTD, FROME AND LONDON
AND BOUND BY JAMES BURN & CO LTD, ESHER

PREFACE

"THE eighteenth century," wrote Carlyle some eighty years ago, "lies massed up in our minds as a disastrous wrecked inanity, not useful to dwell upon." In the words of Edward Jenks, a generation later, it "lies like a nightmare on the imagination, and it is with a sense of relief that we see it disappear before the whirlwind of the French Revolution, in a cloud of full-bottomed wigs, hoops, patches and powder, sedan chairs, preposterous family coaches and heavy theological quartos."

To the later Victorians the eighteenth century seemed "too cold-hearted and hot-blooded, too bucolic, too bellicose, too dilettante, too dull" (Hutton). Yet who could deny that it was pre-eminently both the age of common sense, and, in modern times, that of widespread artistic excellence, "when it was wellnigh impossible to find a single absolutely ugly object" of daily use ? (Marcelle Tinayre).

The post-war age turns with sympathy towards that which the Victorians despised. The courage, the proportion and the simplicity in which the eighteenth century excelled are worshipped by many to-day. Imitation, indeed, cannot go far. The mould that shaped our great-great-grandparents is broken. Neither the economic conditions, nor the pre-revolutionary tradition, nor the social structure, nor the spiritual and intellectual postulates of that age can ever be reproduced. Despite the obvious resemblance between its Benevolent Despots and our Dictators, autocracy then came from a different source and wielded a far less comprehensive power. Both the likeness and the unlikeness between that century and this, however, have stimulated an interest which has resulted in a flood of recent publications.

My own book, which attempts to sketch almost a quarter of the lifetime of modern Europe, seeks a middle course between mere annals and a series of separate essays. "Bare events," as I think, demand some social background, and the Continent can best be understood if our own land is first recalled to view. A few full-length figures, moreover, characterize the century more vividly than a crowd of tiny busts.

Rousseau's indictment of history as a representation of actions rather than of men, showing man only in public life, cannot be wholly refuted. I have attempted to sketch some of the efforts made by the people to provide for the needs of mind and body, quoting, wherever possible, the language which contemporaries employed.

In the main, however, this book is a narrative of which collective Europe, not a group of separate nations, is the hero. Wherever possible, its political biography has been followed chronologically, but in some parts, notably those in which America or the Slavs are most concerned, some duplication has seemed unavoidable. The concluding chapters on Diplomacy and War may be read earlier by those to whom the outlines of political history are well known.

Footnotes, wherever possible, have been avoided. The index contains a few necessary references and an imitated pronunciation of some specially outlandish names. A general Bibliographical Note appears at the end of Chapter I. A new edition has enabled me to add to the Bibliographical Notes a few titles of recent works.

My grateful thanks for much zealous and skilful assistance are due to Mr. A. H. V. Welch, of Fitzwilliam House, and to Mr. T. F. Reddaway, of King's. I have also to record my indebtedness to Mr. E. V. Rieu and to Mr. G. F. N. Reddaway for valuable criticism and suggestions before the book appeared, and subsequently to the late Sir Richard Lodge, Professor G. R. Potter and Mr. W. J. Poynter. To my Wife and to Mr. Henry Reddaway I owe much gratitude for their labours on the index.

W. F. R.

King's College
Cambridge
16 *April*, 1941

CONTENTS

PUBLISHER'S NOTE

This edition is a straightforward reprint of the 1954 one, with the exception of the bibliographies which have been revised by Mrs. R. W. Greaves.

MAPS

CHAPTER I

ENGLAND IN 1715

IF a young English gentleman of to-day could awaken at dawn in the summer of 1715, his first impression would be almost wholly strange. Half stifled by the close-drawn curtains of his four-poster, he would strip the diamond-paned casement of its curtain, and fling open all that had not been structurally sealed against the dreaded night air. Daylight would disclose an uncarpeted chamber, a perplexing tinder-box, with flint and steel, a perforated canister containing a rushlight, and a tiny washstand on which hung a wig. The remaining clothes, the pleated and embroidered shirt, the cravat, whose name showed its Slavonic origin, the gay waistcoat, the stiffened coat which reached his knees, and finally the silken stockings and buckled shoes—all these he might don with pleasure. Bathrooms, however, lay several generations in the future. After stealing down the bare oaken staircase and escaping from the still shuttered house, he would find the dogs and horses less unfamiliar than the furnishings and clothes. Although Albania had sent the bulldog, no " peke " or " pom," no chow, Dalmatian or Alsatian had yet reached Britain. Intensive breeding, in dogs as in other animals, was still unknown. But spaniels and greyhounds, bloodhounds and mastiffs, sheepdogs, terriers and retrievers were already here, and the turnspit proved that a mongrel could be bred to help the women in their cooking. Foxes, which many countries shot, were in England hunted, though not with special packs. In the kennels at least the twentieth-century youth would find intelligible friends.

Contrast with the Present Day

The garden, though affected by Dutch formalism, was hardly less familiar than the church tower. The church itself lacked, often happily, its coloured glass; the churchyard, its Italian marble. Beyond lay the village street. Here surprise awaited the visitor at every turn. Cottages, perhaps whitewashed, straggled familiarly on either side. But the space between, unswept, unlighted and undrained, was a tract of foul and dusty ruts. Chapel, school, villas, post office, shop, village hall, and police station were missing.

While the horse and ass provided transport, smith and wheelwright must be within easy distance, nor, in spite of home-brew, did the village lack its inn. The eye turned gratefully to the inevitable mill, beautiful whether driven by wind or water. As the dew dried, smock-clad field-workers left their homes, glancing with respectful surprise at a young squire wandering on foot bareheaded. Their speech among themselves was beyond his comprehension, but in converse with them he need seldom fail in the end to understand, and to be understood. A Somerset schoolboy was heard to read " Chav a doffed my cooat, how shall I don't ? " with his eyes full on *The Song of Solomon*, chapter v, verse 3.

Men and women were shorter than their descendants, but less changed externally than the animals of the later scientific age. Small and bony sheep and beasts, pigs, in Arthur Young's phrase, " with mathematical backs," sinewy cows with tiny udders—such harmonized only too well with the light crops which covered the great open fields around the village, and with the wooden ploughs and feeble tools for cultivation. If chance brought the parson from his home, the youth might well be astonished both at the deference of his greeting and at its high-flown diction. When he returned to the manor house, where his great-grandfather's great-grandfather had ruled, he possessed the threefold clue to the life of contemporary Europe. Within an hour of waking he had savoured the general poverty or at least simplicity of life, the sharp class distinction and the local self-sufficiency. The last, emphasized in England by the victory of the squires over the crown, was everywhere made necessary by the badness of communications—a defect which long remained the basic fact of history. York might be reached in four days from London, " if God permit," as the pious advertiser did not fail to say, but London to Paris defied prediction.

Dwelling-houses

Further exploration would show more of the contrast between the house of 1715 and that of two centuries later. A certain bareness, less distasteful to the youth of 1941 than to his Victorian forefathers, arose from the absence of much that later ages have learned to take for granted. Carpets, wall-coverings and pictures, save a few portraits, were comparatively rare. Turkey rugs and tapestries indeed there might be, and soon the walls were to be covered by a kind of paper. Thermometer and barometer were there, the latter inspiring " an ingenious author " to observe that by its use men might " regain the knowledge which still resides in brutes, and which we forfeited by not continuing in the open air." Newspapers were meagre sheets, often written by a single author, and magazines infrequent. Books, though humorists were talking of a dry deluge, numbered a few dozen, usually bound in quiet leather. Anything made from rubber was as unknown as the camera or gramophone or wireless. Oil hardly counted, but candlesticks were everywhere, many with snuffers attached to them by chains. The candlestick, like the chair, was growing in simplicity and grace. Silver for the one, and for the other mahogany in place of walnut, offered new prospects of beauty which the century of Adam and Chippendale was amply to fulfil. Umbrellas had not yet been transplanted from the East. Riding gear and fishing tackle abounded, but implements for games seemed few. Weapons, on the other hand, were numerous. Gentlemen who carried swords practised with foils, and kept firearms both for sport and for defence. Holsters attached to their clumsy saddles were furnished with heavy pistols, without which few travellers, save the Quakers, took the road unarmed.

Reflection showed that in an age when men could journey but little and had few lucrative outlets for their savings, much would be laid out upon their houses. If peace brought a modest plenty, building must benefit. From Blenheim and Chatsworth, soon to be followed by Holkham and Stowe, down to the modest manor house and parsonage, dwellings were aiming at new dignity and space. Windows became larger, sash windows were introduced, and lighter rooms required new furniture and decoration. This our native craftsmen proved well able to supply. Though in design some foreign nations still led the world, the English were unsurpassed in execution.

" Many of our mechanics," a sober observer could soon boast, " excel other nations in their watches, clocks, locks, and edge-tools ; their cabinet work, also, is much admired; and the manufacture of glass is brought to great perfection, viz. coach-glass, looking-glass, perspectives, drinking glasses, etc. The goldsmiths and silversmiths, braziers, carpenters, and upholsterers, hatters, tailors and shoemakers, do not only furnish England with everything that is wanted of this kind, but vast quantities are exported to foreign countries, as well as to the British plantations."

Superficially, the most striking differences in daily life were, perhaps, the lower standard of cleanliness, the use of snuff in place of tobacco, the lack of effective illuminants, participation in two meals a day instead of four, and the practice of wearing wigs. In 1715 soap paid a heavy excise duty, and water must be dragged from wells and heated upon the kitchen hearth.

Contrast with Modern Habits

The spirit that had closed the Moorish baths in Spain and that forbade the exposure of her body to a modest female in her bath had left traces even in England. Probably no English lady would have made or kept for a year the vow of the Spanish princess not to change her shift until a besieged town should be taken. But Parson Woodforde, when his razor broke on Sunday, accepted the divine rebuke against profaning the Lord's day by shaving. Tradition, lack of variety in food, profusion of malt liquors and dependence upon daylight—all told against unnecessary meals. To rise at five, to dine at nine, to sup at five, to bed at nine, made a man live to ninety-nine, the more surely if after dinner he rested a while and after supper walked a mile.

Wigs

In general society, as in the law-courts of to-day, wigs marked off profession from profession, and the upper and middle classes from those who were too low and poor to wear them. The Freshman chose his colour, black, white or brown, a grizzled wig giving him the maturest appearance. Whether attributable or not to Charles II's baldness, "those accursed wigs, whether full or modified, were the undoing of every man's portrait for the best part of eighty years" (Fortescue). As the highwayman dangled from the gibbet, his mouldering scalp was decently covered by his wig. Wigs were costly to buy and to maintain, rising as high as £100 in an age when that sum might equal £500 or more in post war currency. As John Gilpin found, they were liable to accidents which made the wearer ridiculous. The Marquess of Granby, on the other hand, refused to be painted otherwise than wigless, in memory of that victorious charge when

Stanford, London

the cavalry had been guided by his bare and shining pate. When Pitt declaimed a moving appeal to the grey hairs of the elder Horace Walpole, that tough diplomatist laid bare his bristles and dissolved the House in laughter. Wigs, it may be safely said, contributed to that theatrical grace and courtly insincerity which tinged the eighteenth century, both upon the Continent and in this country.

The Squires and Jacobitism

In the manor-houses where local England found its leaders and the nation its chief source of strength, social unity prevailed but opinions were much divided.

The family almost certainly professed and believed Protestant doctrines, and save in rare cases, worshipped in the Church of England. Although they might have money in the funds or a stake in some trading or productive venture, their staple was almost always agriculture. But in politics, for a full generation, sharp disunion remained. The Glorious Revolution, like many revolutions, had been the work of the vigorous few. The Jacobites, as Lord Townshend could declare (May, 1716)

> "made such vast accessions of strength under the last four years of the Queen . . . (as appears by the conduct of both the universities and even of London itself till lately) that the confidence of their numbers encouraged them to enter into the rebellion . . . destitute of all successors from abroad, and still supports them in the same spirit and designs. . . . The fire . . . is rather smothered for a time than totally extinguished . . . and may break forth with fresh fury."

Apart from all questions of preference and interest, Divine Right troubled many, from George I downwards, in their sense of right and wrong. For thirty years to come, almost every European power might at some time be a patron of the Pretender, and any crisis might show that in England the Stuarts had it. The politics of the squire's parlour therefore swayed the fate of Europe, and for a time drove Britain into the arms of France. It is a divided and unstable people that the student of 1715 must survey.

The English People

In 1715 England and Wales, with their "twenty-nine cities, upwards of eight hundred towns and near ten thousand parishes," probably contained between five and six million people.

According to the guesswork calculations of an age that knew little of statistics, the young squire and his equals or betters comprised rather less than two in every hundred of the population. Landed gentlefolk numbered some 20,000 families. Merchants, in an age when at home or abroad a merchant often ranked as a pillar of the state, with the clergy, lawyers and civil servants were reckoned as some 40,000, or about the number of the more considerable freeholders. Officers and professional men doubled the numbers of the upper class. This comprised about 125,000 families, less than one-eighth of the nation. The tradesmen and artisans were computed at a still smaller fraction. Lesser freeholders and farmers each numbered more than all the gentry or than the greater freeholders or farmers. These in their turn were outnumbered by the labourers. Paupers, supposed to be some 400,000 families, formed the largest class of all. Of the five and a half million souls which England and Wales probably contained nearly five million were men working on the land or their dependants.

Where in Europe or in the world was a different distribution possible? Only perhaps in tiny Holland, with its vast trade, its numerous waterways, its fisheries, and its intensive cultivation could the balance between town and country hang more even.

Ages and Health of the People

In the early eighteenth century, however, a population of some 5,500,000 was divided between its constituent groups in a widely different fashion from to-day. Then, indeed, female births were believed to outnumber male. Statisticians ascribed it to Providence that one-and-twenty girls were regularly sent into the world to every twenty boys. But as between young and old the ratio has now completely changed. Many parishes in many countries swarmed, like Bemerton, with children. But so many died in childhood that Rousseau could mock the confidence of parents in the future. "Of all the children that are born," he declared, "only one half at most attain to fourteen years, and it is probable yours may not reach the age of manhood."

For those who grew up and shunned excess, however, the century afforded good hope of length of days. Patrick O'Neale, who lived on small beer and vegetables, served in the army from 1666 to 1740 and took his seventh wife twenty years later.

The Wesleys, Voltaire, Fleury, Marshal Münnich, and

Lord Kames, the Scottish judge, were but a few of those who produced admirable work when past fourscore. Fontenelle, seeing a lady drop her fan, wished to God that he were no more than eighty. Many a country churchyard shows at how great an age the rude forefathers of the hamlet fell on sleep. Yet it could be claimed that " the mean duration of life, the compendious test of social improvement," advanced in England between 1780 and 1816 in the ratio of five to four. Where the parents of the English children born in 1914 were warranted by the most careful calculations in expecting sons to reach on the average forty-four years and daughters nearly forty-eight, such ages would have been counted elderly two centuries before.

Causes of Mortality

The explanation of this terrible mortality cannot in England at least be found in war or famine or plague, or even in the horrors of the slums. England was in 1715 a rural country, never depopulated by wars on land, noted for good cheer, visited but seldom by Great Deaths. Overcrowding indeed played its part, favoured by the logical results of a benevolence in which England was unique. Here alone the destitute might call on their parish to maintain them. The parish, therefore, was reluctant to sanction new cottages. Housing shortage inevitably produced insanitary modes of life, and a crop of illegitimates doomed to neglect and peril.

It may be questioned, however, whether the worst enemies of life were not the methods taken to preserve it. In England, as upon the Continent, the most fantastic and tragic notions prevailed with regard to the care of children and the combating of disease. While Europe wasted time and brains in seeking some general key to medicine, the country-side, and not the country-side alone, was largely given over, in time of sickness, to old wives and quacks. One of Scott's admirers begged him to cure his ailment by lying on twelve stones gathered at midnight from twelve south-running brooks, and that prescription was mild compared with many. No superstition was more widespread than that the sick must be guarded against any draught of air.

National Character

What were the national characteristics of the English people in 1715? Like almost every nation in Europe, they were of mixed descent, and included many racial types. It has been claimed that, in Walpole's age, East Anglia, with its strong admixture of Danish and Flemish blood, dominated England. An English traveller in Normandy or Holstein might often observe that the people resembled closely Englishmen more than did his Welsh or Cornish fellow-subjects. But his very remark showed that an English national type existed, conscious of its own difference from foreigners, as they in their turn were conscious of its difference from their own. John Bull, at first a loutish rustic simpleton, grew into a stalwart farmer-patriot, who sucked in defiance to France with his mother's milk.

But a greater difficulty lay in the unbridged chasm which divided rich from poor, educated from illiterate, the vocal classes from the inarticulate. In England, where all were freemen, and where squire and labourer co-operated in the daily struggle with the land, the chasm was less wide and deep than in France or Poland. Yet it was of rustics akin to English that a kindly Hanoverian nobleman confessed himself unable to decide "whether or no they feel as we do." The English government, it may be maintained, knew nothing of "the masses," and those who brilliantly characterized "the Englishman" were voicing the ill-founded opinions of their own clique. When Addison styled him modest, thoughtful and sincere, he uttered a weighty judgment, and what he termed vicious modesty in speaking of religion might well be a genuine national trait produced by the anti-Puritan reaction. Rousseau, on the other hand, poured scorn upon the English claim to be good-natured and humane. "They may cry themselves up," he declared, "for this good quality as much as they please; there is nobody else will join with them." But no generalizations are more misleading than those which ascribe all the qualities of a race to its several members. "The public," "the people," "the nation," these are nouns which never cease to confuse history.

In the early eighteenth century as in the twentieth, Britain could not embark upon a war without the approval of "the nation." In 1743, as in 1914, her sword had not been lightly drawn. Yet in the earlier war a historic Briton went cheerfully "to fight for some damned queen or another," just as, in the later, one of his descendants set out "to fight the bloody Belgiums."

British Liberty

In sharp contrast with France, the subject knew his rights, and felt secure that he would enjoy them. Consciousness of liberty, " our own right divine," was well established many decades before " Rule Britannia." The rule of law, the independence of the judges, the supremacy of the civil over the military power and of the legislature over the executive, these and, above all, parliamentary control of taxation composed a birthright which roused growing envy across the Channel.

In 1715, the Tories might profess passive obedience, but they declared that Britons must not be enslaved. They, no less than the Whigs, feared Rome, for a Catholic monarchy would endanger liberty of thought and speech. The Briton's birthright found notable expression in the freedom with which he handled questions of faith and doctrine. Defoe reckoned 1,100 meeting-houses of the Independents and Baptists alone, and at Durham saw Catholics going to Mass with impunity. The *Spectator* regarded the Jews as " pegs and nails in a great building," holding together the economic structure of the world. Locke, a true representative of his age, rationalized the Christian faith, and secured enormous influence in lands less free than this. At the same time the tragedies of Charles I and James II, and the spectacle under Anne of a nation " torn with so many unnatural divisions," had given England the reputation and perhaps the consciousness of being " wild to hold," a King-killer and an unsafe ally. The attempt of the 'Fifteen to settle politics by force found its counterpart in not a few elections. The Whigs might in the long run make for moderation, harmony, and toleration, and the country might learn these virtues. But in 1715 they were an active minority ruling rather by wealth and skill and chance than as the chosen of the English people. Throughout the eighteenth century England ranked as " the classic land of mutiny (*émeute*)."

Novelty

Were the English prone to novelty ? The question, like that of their especial cleanliness, is relative and perhaps admits of no general answer. Lady Mary Wortley Montagu, an acute and travelled observer, declared that " we choose rather to neglect advantages than to try an unbidden path for 'em." Her instances, such as the scandalous opposition to bills for establishing a land register and for making rivers navigable, were to be outweighed by the speculative mania of 1720.

New fashions came readily from Paris to London and spread, though slowly, through the southern shires. By the time they reached Exeter, sneered a great lady, the imitation was more excessive than the original.

Efficiency

In the north of England life was still less affected by the capital. The rarity, the slowness and the cost of public conveyances prohibited any considerable Cockney invasion beyond the Midlands. In North and South alike, however, signs were already visible of that practical efficiency which was soon to make the Englishman the leader of the world. While in agriculture and in industry his most conspicuous inventions were yet to come, in strength, courage and aptitude he was already unsurpassed. Defoe, surveying much of England, found in the dockyard at Chatham and the cloth markets at Exeter and Leeds proofs of what organizing talent could achieve. In fitting out ships, he declared, "certain it is the dexterity of the English sailors is not to be matched by the world." At Leeds, in the most profound silence, ten or twenty thousand pounds value in cloth, and sometimes much more, would be bought and sold in little more than an hour. Before nine o'clock in the morning the clothiers had carried to the merchant's house or back to their own inn every piece of cloth which they had exposed for sale.

Conservatism

Organizing talent in 1715, none the less, had to contend with the natural conservatism of a rural nation and with the grave defects of its communications. A still more long-lived foe was the national distrust of ideas that were general, alien, or even new.

Cruelty

Nowhere is there a sharper contrast between Englishman and Englishman in 1715, or between England then and now, than in their treatment of the defenceless and of wrongdoers. Tender humanity and repulsive cruelty existed side by side, not seldom in the same person. The lady whose pity was roused by the hard work of the horses in dismembering Damiens could easily be matched here. In England whole towns shared in the pastime of beating a bull to death. To disturb an unpopular act of worship, men of Burton cut off the ears and tail of a young bull, and turned it against the congregation. If the rabble, it was said, could get nothing else, they would divert themselves by worrying cats to death. The supreme spectacle, more amusing than to watch the slaughter of tame ducks by dogs, or to mock lunatics in Bedlam, was the public execution of a man or woman. In 1715 the gallows waited for the thief of twelvepence farthing, and the stake for a wife who had been party to her husband's death. Witchcraft, though the scientists derided it, ascribing undue influence to "an ejaculation of the eyes," exposed scores of women to persecution. In 1715, cruelty and lust for gain mingled in the practice of luring ships to destruction upon rocky coasts, which was particularly rife in Cornwall.

The recital of these public and deliberate deeds makes it superfluous to comment on horrors due to individual cruelty or public negligence, those of the gaol, the hulks, the slaver or, in many cases, the man-of-war. Whitefield was told that if he had a mind to convert Indians, he might go among the colliers near Bristol and find there Indians enough. Even the parish cottages, which bore witness to a care for the poor which was unmatched in Europe, bolstered up a system of rural overcrowding, which could not but debase the population.

Position of Women in England

The treatment of women illustrates, though more faintly, the same curious inconsistency of practice.

Englishmen had never lost the reverence for the sex which Tacitus found among the early Germans. They gladly homaged Anne and remembered Elizabeth with pride. A woman yoked to the plough would not be seen in England as in France. But whereas in France female influence could be said to rule both society and the State, in England women took a lower place. Lady Mary Wortley Montagu, who had seen the world, declared that nowhere was her sex treated with so much contempt as here. Women might not vote or hold public office. The universities and the professions were closed to them. If they had property it passed on marriage to their husband, a law perhaps the less galling because marriage at fifteen was common. In their thirties many became mere backgrounds to their daughters and the more favoured males.

The English Scene in 1715

Between the accession of James II and that of George I, the face of England had been but little changed. South of the Cheviots, this island remained perhaps the most diversified and pleasant tract in Europe. One Englishman dwelt then where seven must congregate to-day, and as nine-tenths of them were rural workers the villages were as numerous and as populous as they are at present. London with its half-million was the only town that by modern standards counts as great. Bristol, Exeter, Liverpool and Birmingham, rising and important places, had only some 20,000 inhabitants apiece. Rivers and pack-horses were the chief conveyors of such goods as could not, like beasts and fowls, transport themselves. Canals and factories as yet were only dreamed of. Turnpikes, roads made in the hope that the tolls would provide a profit on the outlay, were only beginning to make travelling possible.

Comparison with 1941

Could such a land be recognized by a modern man as England ? Nearly a century ago Macaulay held that already the change had been too great. " We should not know one landscape in a hundred," he declared. Since the words were written the population has risen in the ratio of five to two, and new roads, railroads, buildings, telegraph poles, pylons, and all the apparatus of the new inventions have grown up. Beyond doubt since 1715 hundreds of landscapes have changed beyond recognition. Fens have been drained, reservoirs created, woods planted and cut down, heaths, meadows and grain-fields adjoining towns covered with works and houses ; above all the great " champion " tract between Yorkshire and the Dorset coast parcelled into fields within hedges or stone walls. For many years the favourite pastime of the rich was to improve the landscape. Bath, Woburn, Stowe and a host of similar creations prove their success. But wherever the scene comprises river, sea-coast or high hill, wherever a wide burst of country meets the view, in the thousands of quiet prospects which are made distinctive by a tower or steeple, probably in the great majority of cases we should recognize the landscape of 1715. What we cannot do is to realize what that landscape meant to men who crept over it, drew from it their sustenance, and looked in general not far beyond its bounds.

Obscurity of the Labourer's Life

To call up some vision of the country-side, then, may be no unhopeful task. It is far less possible, however, to penetrate that " dark and cavernous shadow wherein the common people move " (Morley), and to comprehend the hopes and habits of the masses who worked upon the land. When, in the eighteenth century, fashion dictated an enthusiasm for the rural worker, milkmaids and shepherds idealized into absurdity were the result. Gray's solemn *Elegy* may not convince readers brought up in the country. Tolstoy, the great realist, mowed with the peasants, and found the swing of the scythe and the triumph of resolve over weariness and thirst inspiring. Men who could not choose, however, regarded mowing as simply the most exhausting of all their unwelcome labours. When his rights were attacked, the rural worker might take up arms. In 1765 the East Anglian rioters against large workhouses declared that if the King sent a thousand men they could raise ten thousand and did not fear the issue. But his daily life seemed to him not worth describing, even if he had the power to describe it and if any cared to hear.

Peasant life, indeed, like the interior of the picturesque peasant dwellings, may well have escaped description because there was so little to describe. A two- or three-roomed cottage which sheltered man and wife, children and old people, lacked space, as its inhabitants lacked wealth, for any save the barest necessities. A home-made table, a few stools, chairs or benches, perhaps rude shelves and chests—these with some cooking and eating utensils and contrivances for sleeping formed the chief of their equipment. An upright settle, making a snug corner before the open hearth, was the greatest of luxuries. "The head of the family," wrote a traveller in Poland, "has a sort of mock bed: the rest lie on the floor, and the children that have the advantage to be small enough creep into the oven." It is possible that with regard to beds he was describing the state of his own country more nearly than he realized. Addison contended that but for Sunday "it is certain the country people would soon degenerate into a kind of savages and barbarians."

Towards a more precise idea of rural comfort, statistics help but little. About 1715 the standard price of wheat was forty shillings a quarter, and the labourer who earned his ninepence every day was normal in the west of England. Two centuries later, the State may intervene to secure a similar price to the farmer, and a minimum of more than fifty pence to his hired man. But in 1715 some cottagers lived "chiefly by commons and heath grounds," and the vast tracts of rough unfenced woodland helped many to fire and food. Many others doubled their wages by the spinning and weaving of their wife and children. In an age of wretched communications, industries were spread over the country, and much work was done at home. If a district were sufficiently industrial for a child of five to earn its living, everyone rejoiced. Even without such aid, a labourer's ninepence a day, if compared with a parson's forty pounds a year, might be found to afford almost equal satisfaction.

Stephen Duck

Fortunately for us, the rural masses at this time became articulate in the verses of the Wiltshire labourer-poet, Stephen Duck (1705–56). A born scholar, he earned four and sixpence a week for himself and his wife and children in the fields and barns, and at night-time studied Milton and the *Spectator*. The local clergy drew him on to describe his experiences. In 1736, *The Thresher's Labour*, a poem in the style of Pope, was published by subscription. Queen Caroline hastened to turn the rhymester into a court poet and official and rural realities became too low a theme for his pen. But he had already shown how thousands spent the winter in threshing with the flail, a labour equally noisy, dirty and monotonous. As the clumsy machine slowly dissevered husks and kernel, especially of beans:

> "The sweat, the dust and suffocating smoke
> Make us so much like Ethiopians look
> We scare our wives, when evening brings us home,
> And frighted infants think the bugbear come."

If his mate would tell a merry tale, both flails must stop and the silence brought the master upon them.

> "Rest never does but on the Sabbath show
> And barely that our master will allow."

When threshing gave place to winnowing

> "He counts the bushels, counts how much a day,
> Then swears we've idled half our time away."

Hay harvest brought a change which was welcome until the first morning's mowing made the labourers regret the shelter of their winter barn. The noontide dinner, the day's first meal, found them almost too spent to eat.

> "Nor can the bottle only answer all,
> The bottle and the beer are both too small."

The harvest dinner and Christmas cheer only made the unending character of the year's toil the more apparent. Stephen Duck himself was the one man in a million who was spared what must have weighed down his seniors—growing weakness with no prospect of emancipation.

Rise in the Standard of Life

In 1715, none the less, the hard lot of the villager was undergoing some improvement. While in many countries dearth not seldom became famine, in England food grew more abundant. The enclosure of open fields, the draining of the fens, the improvement of arable by turnips and of down-lands by pasturing sheep, the growth of landowners' capital—all these helped produce to increase more rapidly than population. In 1733, England could send 800,000 quarters of corn abroad, and thereby gain £1,000,000. At the same time the potato was becoming " a comfortable food for the low people . . . easily cooked and [requiring] neither kiln nor mill " (Lord Kames). As later with the blackberry, the English proved more willing than the Continentals to receive new food. The Prussian rustics defeated the efforts of Frederick the Great to introduce potatoes until taught better by the dearth of 1770–1. The French were slower still. Here the growth of industry provided wages for many of the cottager's dependants, and cheap goods which raised the value of the money wage. At Richmond in Yorkshire, Defoe found children's stockings of the smallest size selling for three-halfpence a pair or less. Slow as it was in operation, the movement towards improving communications could not but cheapen goods and increase men's chances of a change of occupation. In an island growing its own food, the rise of towns could not fail to furnish villages with a market, both for their labour and for their goods.

Influence of London

Men felt in 1715, and history deems them right, that the mainspring of the national life was London. " London, the metropolis of England and seat of the British empire," they boasted, was " the largest in extent, the fairest built, the most populous, and best inhabited of any in the European world." The *Spectator* saw in it " a kind of emporium for the whole earth." A cosmopolitan city, prominent in industry, supreme in banking, wealth and shipping, it offered by far the greatest market, the greatest centre of communications and the greatest fountain of ideas in Britain. To whatever shire the traveller might make his way he could not escape the influence of London. Newcastle sent thither coals, from heaps so mountainous that it seemed impossible that all should be consumed. From further north cattle walked to the fenland, there to attain the " grossness of fat " that made them fit for Smithfield. Norfolk and Suffolk despatched vast droves of geese and turkeys, until with the winter rains the roads became too sticky for their feet. From the Fens came wagon-loads of wildfowl. The southern counties supplied timber by water, or, despite amazing delays, by road. Purbeck shipped great quantities of stone for building. The east and the west of England alike found markets for their cloth in London. Wiltshire bacon and cheese, Hereford cider, great herds of black cattle from Brecknock—whatever any district could produce of special excellence—all strove to supply the wants of the favoured half-million in the metropolis. The shires, too, as the careers of Johnson and many another bore witness, also supplied London with men, and the city was likewise the goal of ambitious Scots and of fugitives from overseas.

London in return exported to the countryside, not only goods but also government, society, and culture. Bad as communications were, they were far better from London than from any other centre. If highwaymen made the approaches to London and its very streets unsafe, it was because the convoys and the persons to be found there were so rich. To some goods London gave the final processes—dyeing or printing the fabrics sent up from the country. Others, such as timepieces, she manufactured for this and other lands. Although Bristol, Hull and Liverpool were active ports, neither they nor the continental harbours could show anything like the wealth of the Indies pouring into London. Silks, chintzes, Chinese gewgaws and hangings, lacquer and porcelain came in plenty. Fashionable ladies went down to Blackwall to make their purchases on board the Indiamen, or met their lovers at the India houses, where kettles were always boiling, so that customers might taste the novel and costly tea. Oriental goods, with Turkey rugs and the like, were then transported at a walking pace into the houses of gentlefolk throughout the land.

As the seat of the court, the parliament, the chief law-courts, the supreme administration of the army, navy and civil service, moreover, the influence of London was felt in every parish. It was rivalled by the effect on daily life that is exercised by the source of fashion, politics and ideas. Without the three thousand coffee-houses of London the men of rural England would have been as much at a loss as the women without the great world that met about the Court. From London came the newspaper, the pamphlet and the treatise. In pulpit eloquence she had no monopoly, but her divines gained respectful attention here and abroad. The arts, save building, cabinet work and a few more, were at a low ebb in 1715, but when Handel, Gay and Garrick revived them it was from London.

Defects of London

In some ways, it is true, London was a public danger. Although less cramped and filthy than Paris or Vienna, and a gainer from the rebuilding after the Great Fire, it was in the main a city of narrow ill-paved streets and lanes " where doorside heaps afford their dubious aid "—a city covered by a cloud of soot and smoke and reeking with the filth of countless cows and horses. In London deaths habitually exceeded baptisms by a majority surpassing the number of baptisms uncounted because performed outside the Church of England. How far contagion spread from London to the countryside can never be fully known.

Like other great capitals, London threatened England also with a moral taint. There, and perhaps there only, the profligate could live in large groups without much to fear from the rest of the community. The desperate, therefore, turned their steps to London, and on more than one occasion set up mob rule. The Gordon riots of 1780 were presaged in 1716, when five rioters were executed for demolishing the " mug-houses " where the King's supporters met. With the mob, politics were, to an extent that could only be guessed at, a mere excuse for anarchism. Governments could seldom feel sure that society was firmly based, and constantly feared that, as Lord John Russell phrased it, " the whole thing would break up." Provincial mobs threatened anarchy only when that of London showed the way.

In actual fact, society in 1715 was in graver peril from vice than from riot, and here again London was to blame. In earlier days complaints were made on every hand that

England was being ruined by luxury. The old simple wholesome ways, moralists declared, were giving way to newfangled and costly indulgences, and to pay for these, men and women would cheat and thieve. Life was certainly becoming more complex, dress more elaborate, and food more variegated. To all this the example of France contributed not a little. The *Spectator* professed to dread the inundation of ribbands and brocades and the bad influence on female manners that the peace would bring. The days, indeed, were approaching when it could be said that society was one vast casino, and that the classic age of adultery had dawned in Britain. This moral decline may have been due to luxury, and certainly luxury spread from London. Almost every generation, however, brings the same charge against that which is about to take its place. The new age, however, was in very real peril from strong drink. In earlier days, home-brewed ale had cheered the two daily meals, and had also filled the place of the breakfast and tea of later generations. Now, however, at first under Dutch influence, spirit-drinking was spreading fast, with dire effects on health and morals. Gin (Geneva), French brandy, rum from the Sugar islands, all debauched the uncontrolled masses. Within thirty years the output of British spirits had been multiplied fourfold. In 1715, more than two million gallons supplied less than six million people of all ages. Twelve years later the supply had risen to over three million, six hundred thousand gallons, and was rising with ever-growing momentum. A nation in which respectable tradesmen, as at Lichfield, got drunk every day must reform itself or perish.

Britain and trade

While Anne still reigned, it had become a commonplace that we were a trading nation. Loose calculations seemed to show that Britain shared with Holland and Scandinavia some three quarters of the overseas trade of Europe. Many causes joined to make this pre-eminence lasting. Our seafarers and merchants lived in a small island with a dominant city as its greatest port. This made for ready information, swift decision, speed in finding the necessary capital, goods and men for a new enterprise, and the best market for what the ships brought home. Nobles and gentry, Catholics and Dissenters might trade, a tolerance which gave Britain a marked advantage over prouder and less tolerant realms.

" Raising estates for their own families by bringing in whatever is wanting and carrying out whatever is superfluous " seemed a clear service to the state. Trading ventures appealed to the appetite of the age for quick and large profits which would enable the lucky adventurer to become a landed gentleman in his prime. London, moreover, despite the staggering war debt, was beginning to hold an advantage that in an earlier generation had made Amsterdam invincible, a plethora of capital to be had on easy terms. This came but seldom from the standard industry of England, which was the cultivation of the soil. Successful farming usually meant greater flocks and herds, land purchased or reclaimed, and more building. Some of the refugees who fled to England brought their fortunes, and fortunes might be made from English mines and cloth. But the merchant had by far the best chance of enriching himself and his country. Although our naval supplies from the Baltic had largely to be bought with cash, other trades, particularly that with Portugal, gave a favourable balance year by year. The apparent profit of the nation was something like half as large as the public revenue. It entered England in the form of American gold and silver, which enlarged the stock of " money " and made it cheap. London thus served as the mainspring of British commerce.

Britain and Europe

Lucrative commerce, sea-power, which, as Richelieu found, opens the way into every state in the world, strong national feeling, freedom from some prejudices which hampered other nations—all these must help to maintain the great position which Britain had made her own. However unworthy her diplomacy, she had led Europe to victory in the war of liberation, and had imposed peace. Her abundant cash and credit would enable her to bribe foreign statesmen, and to hire fleets and armies without paralyzing her economic life. Her deeds and her resources alike made her a counterweight to France, which had more than twice her acreage and population with all the glamour inherited from the long European primacy of Louis XIV.

British Commerce c. 1715

To Voltaire, whose visit to England lay between the years 1726 and 1729, her produce seemed to be only " a little lead, tin, fuller's earth and coarse wool." A deeper student, Thomas Salmon, could declare that there were 'scarce any manufactures in Europe which are not brought to great perfection in England. And as to the woollen manufacture, it exceeds anything of that kind in other nations both in goodness and quantity. The silk manufacture also is equal to that of France or any other country. Our dyes are very numerous, and not exceeded by any other nation either in the beauty, or durableness of their colours: and the printers and stainers of cottons have brought that art to great perfection. And our printers of books print them as beautifully as the Dutch or any people whatever; but still books cannot be afforded so cheap here as in other countries, the workmen there taking less wages than they do in England."

Trade had already furrowed out the channels in which, with growing volume, it was to flow for generations. The object was to produce a surplus for sale abroad, and from every customer nation to receive, if possible, gold and silver in exchange. Failing gold or silver, it was not unprofitable to receive such goods as England needed, and could not herself produce. Two dangers must be avoided, those of accepting goods which supplanted our own, and of paying out gold or silver for no compelling reason. We had at our disposal (1) home products, including in some years "incredible quantities of corn," (2) products of our sugar-islands and plantations, notably tobacco, (3) other transoceanic products such as wrought silks and calicoes imported for resale, including if need be gold and silver, and, of course, (4) our manufactures. To enumerate British markets is to describe a great fraction of the trade of Europe and at the same time to indicate a leading factor in European politics. The most ancient of English companies was that of the Hamburg merchants trading on equal terms with Northern Germany, whence came particularly linen yarn. The Hudson Bay Company were forced by nature to pay in goods for the skins and furs that they brought home. The Russian merchants carried on a losing trade from the national point of view, since the Russians would not buy sufficient British exports to pay for our import of hemp, flax, linen, tallow, furs, and naval stores. Failing replacement from our colonies, however, these Russian products were indispensable, and bullion and coin acquired by other exchanges had to make good the loss. The Eastland Company supplied the remaining Baltic countries on like terms, and the Turkey merchants also had an unfavourable balance. Dye-stuffs, drugs, soap, fruit and oil were among their importations. Bullion was again required for the East India Company, whose purchases included china-ware and tea. The African and Guinea merchants, who bought negroes with British goods, and the Canary Company, who likewise tapped Spanish America, did something to redress the exchanges. The smugglers of our colonies and the absentee landlords of Ireland also helped to turn the scale, while trade with Spain and Portugal, so long as it could be kept from falling into French hands, was the most advantageous of all. Italy, whence came silk both wrought and raw, with wine, soap, olives, and dye-stuffs, produced an unfavourable balance, and Flanders, with her lawns and cambrics, did the same. French trade in "toys" and luxuries seemed to the patriots of more than one country ruinous, both to the purse and to the morale. "It were better we had no trade with them," complained the English critic, "but scarce anything is liked by the quality, either to drink or to wear, but what is French." Neither appeals to patriotism nor doubled duties checked the Englishman's demand for brandy, nor his wife's for velvet and brocade.

Luxury

"Luxury," wrote Davenant in 1697, "is deeply rooted in this nation,"—so deeply that to prohibit the existing import of unnecessary comforts merely causes them to be brought in from another source. "Our depraved manners," he urged, are responsible for the import of "wine, oil, fruits, spices, divers wrought silks, drugs for physic, perfumes, fine linens, jewels, etc."

Defoe in 1725 approved of pepper, drugs and diamonds, but regarded as "trifling and unnecessary" china-ware, coffee, tea and such goods as Japan exported. To him wrought silks, block tin and sugar seemed "injurious," like cotton, arrack, copper and indigo—probably because their import displaced our native labour. "This whole globe," sneered Swift, "must be at least three times gone round before one of our better female Yahoos can get her breakfast or a cup to put it in."

When America secured her independence, the Abbé Raynal admitted that Europe owed a few conveniences and a few luxuries to the New World. "But before these enjoyments were obtained," he demanded, "were we less healthy, less robust, less intelligent or less happy?" Every succeeding generation has asked the same question.

Religious differences, none the less, hampered friendship

between peoples at every turn. Only by slow degrees, in Britain not until 1751, was the Gregorian calendar accepted by dissidents from Rome. Foreigners might travel freely among those of another confession, but they could seldom become incorporated into their nation without a change of church. Heretical books might still be censored, or placed upon the Index, or confiscated by the Inquisition. A friendly censor, indeed, might accept a work on condition that it professed to come from abroad, usually from London or Amsterdam. A more usual subterfuge was to write the opposite of what was meant, doubly delighting the keen-witted reader. This device, which Montesquieu applied to politics, was dexterously utilized by Voltaire in his attacks upon "revealed religion." His *Philosophical Dictionary*, a series of ironical outbursts against priestcraft, tickled the palate of polite Europe, and deafened men to the thunders of the Church.

"All Asia, all Africa, half of Europe," jeered the article on Christianity, "the Dutch and English possessions in America, with the several unconquered parts of the vast continent, all the Austral countries, which make a fifth part of the globe, are left as a prey to the devil, in verification of that holy saying, 'Many are called, but few are chosen.' If, as some learned persons say, the number of all the inhabitants of the several parts of the globe is about sixteen hundred millions, the holy Catholic Universal Roman Church has within its pale near fifty millions, which amounts to more than the twenty-sixth part of the inhabitants of the known world."

"When once Fanaticism has touched the brain, the distemper is desperate," he declared, having himself seen the Convulsionists of Paris. "What can be answered to a person who tells you that he had rather obey God than men, and who, in consequence of that choice, is certain of gaining heaven by cutting your throat?"

In the whole world, declared Voltaire, there has been but one religion clear of fanaticism, which is that of the Chinese *literati*. As to the sects of philosophers, instead of being infected with this pestilence, they were a ready and pure preservation against it: for the effect of philosophy is to compose the soul, and fanaticism is incompatible with tranquillity. If our holy religion has been so often corrupted by these infernal impulses, it is the folly of men that is to be blamed.

BIBLIOGRAPHICAL NOTE

The lists of recommended books attached to this and the following chapters are, of course, by no means exhaustive. Section A comprises accessible books in English which many students may find suitable. In Section B are mentioned valuable but relatively inaccessible books, and books to which the text is specially indebted, although these may be in unfamiliar languages or not easily accessible. The titles of books in languages other than English, French or German have been translated and the country of origin indicated. In some cases the date of first publication, or of the edition used, has been added for guidance.

Among the printed books to which a student may turn at any moment may be mentioned :—

The Cambridge Modern History, vols. vi–ix (1903–9).

Lavisse et Rambaud : Histoire générale, vii–ix (1896).

Useful information and bibliographies may be found in the relevant articles in *The Cambridge History of the British Empire*, *The Cambridge History of British Foreign Policy*, *The Catholic Encyclopaedia*, *Chambers's Encyclopaedia*, *The Encyclopaedia Britannica*, and *The Oxford History of Music*.

G. P. Gooch : *Annals of Politics and Culture* (1492–1899).

Most of the constituent states of Europe are treated in the Cambridge Historical Series (1898, etc.), while for their mutual relations E. Bourgeois, *Manuel historique de politique étrangère* (1897, 1900), may be recommended. A small but well-chosen collection of illustrative documents is :—

Butterfield : *Select Documents of European History*, iii, 1715–1920.

The sober and informative works of Archdeacon William Coxe (1747–1828) and Thomas Carlyle's interpretation of many historical works extant down to *c.* 1858 must always throw much light upon certain aspects of the century. One of its most striking characteristics, the prominence of adventurers and charlatans, may be studied in biography, such as that of Casanova. For the diplomacy of the first half of our period, the studies by Sir Richard Lodge, several of which appear in the *Transactions of the Royal Historical Society*, are invaluable. The *Histoire abrégée des traités de paix*, 1648–1815, by Koch and Schoell, which became the basis of a later work, *Traités de paix*, by Garden, and the illustrated *Histoire de France des origines à la révolution*, edited by E. Lavisse, should give great assistance.

Much use may profitably be made of some of the many contemporary dictionaries and works of reference, especially those of Chambers and the *Grande encyclopédie* which Chambers' work inspired. From 1758, the *Annual Register* forms a valuable source. The larger collections, such as the correspondence of Frederick the Great and of Napoleon, the instructions given to the French ambassadors, and many more, have been mentioned only where special recourse has been had to them.

The following works provide a general introduction to the eighteenth century :

W. L. Langer (ed.) : *The Rise of Modern Europe.*

VIII. P. Roberts : *The Quest for Security, 1715–40* (1947).
IX. W. L. Dorn : *Competition for Empire, 1740–63* (1940).
X. L. Gershoy : *From Despotism to Revolution, 1763–89* (1944).
XI. C. Brinton : *A Decade of Revolution, 1789–99* (1934).
XII. G Bruun : *Europe and the French Imperium, 1799–1814* (1938).

L. Halphen and P. Sagnac (eds.): *Peuples et Civilisations.*

XI. P. Muret: *La Prépondérance anglaise, 1715–63* (3rd ed. 1949).
XII. P. Sagnac: *La Fin de l'Ancien Régime et la Révolution américaine, 1763–89* (3rd ed. 1952).
XIII. G. Lefebvre: *La Révolution française* (3rd ed. 1951).
XIV. G. Lefebvre: *Napoléon* (4th ed. 1953).

W. Goetz (ed.): *Propyläen Weltgeschichte.*

VII. W. Goetz [and others]: *Das Zeitalter des Absolutismus, 1660–1789* (1931).
VIII. A. Stern [and others]: *Die französische Revolution, Napoleon und die Restauration, 1789–1848* (1929).

M. Crouzet: (ed.): *Histoire générale des civilisations.*

V. R. Mousnier and E. Labrousse: *Le XVIIIe siècle: Révolution intellectuelle, technique et politique, 1715–1815* (1953).

L. H. Gipson: *The British Empire before the American Revolution.*

I. *Great Britain and Ireland* (1936).
II. *The Southern Plantations* (1936).
III. *The Northern Plantations* (1936).
IV. *Zones of International Friction, 1748–1754* (1939).
V. *Zones of International Friction, 1748–1754* (1942).
VI. *The Great Empire Before the War, 1754–1757* (1946).
VII. *The Great War for the Empire, 1758–1760* (1949).
VIII. *The Great War for the Empire, 1760–1763* (1954).

G. S. Graham: *Sea Power and British North America, 1783–1820* (1941).

G. S. Graham: *Empire of the North Atlantic: The Maritime Struggle for North America* (1951).

Indispensable bibliographies are:

J. S. Bromley and A. Goodwin: *A Select List of Works on Europe and Europe Overseas, 1715–1815* (1956).

S. Pargellis and D. J. Medley: *Bibliography of British History in the Eighteenth Century, 1714–1789* (1951).

CHAPTER II

EUROPE IN 1715—GENERAL FEATURES

England and Europe

HOW far may the state of England at the death of Louis XIV afford safe guidance to the state of Europe ? Both regions have since progressed so fast and far that to moderns their early differences may seem small. Both were then chiefly aggregates of villages, feeble, self-sufficing and unprogressive. Yet both contained cities and social circles which rank high in the history of mankind. Two errors at least may be avoided. Nations were then less uniform than now and less sharply differentiated from one another. The well-born and well-educated of all nations formed a class apart, while in an age of petty princedoms and rudimentary communications economic and national frontiers could by no means coincide.

In different regions, moreover, the same word signifies different institutions. A merchant, or a Jew, in France denoted a man of lower social standing than in Holland. In Germany, the noble caste with its sixteen quarterings was impenetrable, in contrast with France or Britain. Foreigners sometimes rejoice to find serfdom in eighteenth-century Britain because Scottish salters and miners were transferable with their saltings and mines. In their own countries, serfdom was then an outstanding reality, since it bound the rural masses to the place and the career to which they were born. Enclosures in England stood for an advance in cultivation, while when France made them the primitive routine went on. In different portions of the same country, as in England, agriculture might stand for widely different ways of life. Compared with the Irish bogtrotter the Flemish cultivator was a man of science.

Isolation of Europe

Since the Reformation, Britain had become a somewhat detached member of the western family of nations. An island lying on the flank of Europe, in Napoleon's phrase, a wart upon the nose to France, she possessed a language, a church, a constitution and, in many respects, a culture in which no other Europeans shared. But in 1715 British isolation was less conspicuous than five generations later, when Free Trade, voluntary enlistment and, above all, a unique Empire had estranged her from the Continental states. In 1715, Europe, deprived of the Balkan peoples and not yet assured of Russia, was still in great measure a world to itself, depending but little upon any other continent. French America, indeed, sent her furs; British America, tobacco; Spanish and Portuguese America, gold and silver. From Asia the tiny class of European rich drew many luxuries. Africa was still the home of the Barbary pirates, and Australia a land whose coastline had merely been sighted by Europeans.

The "Europe" of 1715

Regarded in the human sense, as a society of men rather than geographically, as a particular peninsula of the land-mass known as Asia, the Europe of 1715 covered an area somewhat smaller than that which its descendants occupy to-day. Could the Russians then be said to have entered Europe, and are they truly European at the present time? Our Estonia and Latvia comprise regions which Russia had then conquered, but their civilization remained unchanged. German barons still ruled there, the Lutheran pastors remained, and in the towns trade was in the hands of European merchants. Even if Archangel and Kiev were regarded as too Muscovite to be as yet European, the frontier of Europe could hardly be drawn further west than along a line stretching southward from Lake Peipus towards the mouth of the Danube. Such a line if prolonged would, however, include a vast region which had been ravished from the European society by the Turk. The power which now rules over hardly anything of Europe save Constantinople was then lord of the Balkan States, the Danubian principalities, the northern shores of the Black Sea and, by the close of 1715, the whole of Greece. Imperial Hungary, from which Buda had been torn, lay in peril, like those fertile regions near the western edge of Central Asia which may at any time be sterilized by drifting sand. Poland, a tottering bulwark of Europe, had begun to cede territory to the Muscovite in order to save herself by his aid from further losses to the Turk.

Area and Population of the European Society

From Ireland and Portugal, to the further boundaries of Finland, Poland and Hungary, Europe comprised some 1,870,000 square miles of land and perhaps some seventy or eighty millions of people. After 220 years, the same region is inhabited by about 335 millions and in each constituent country a yearly increase is expected. Apart from Paris and a few ports, London the chief among them, Europe then contained hardly any town that moderns would rank as great. There was "a kind of impossibility," held Hume, that any city could rise much beyond the 700,000 with which London was credited. Where great towns existed, their congestion and lack of sanitation made them heavy burdens upon the national vitality, for within their walls birth could by no means keep pace with death. In the countryside, moreover, although children were born at between twice and thrice the later ratio to population, no state showed rapid growth in numbers. Since rulers welcomed the increase of their subjects, and parents looked to offspring for support in their declining years, it is only to feebleness and ignorance that this terrible fact can be ascribed. The evils that have been described in London were surpassed in many of the great Continental towns. Urban populations, moreover, showed a resolute inertia in matters of hygiene that was worthy of their rural brethren. "Cities," declared a king who had ruled in Naples and Madrid, "are like children, who weep when they are scrubbed and cleaned." In such an age, Rousseau was warranted in exclaiming that mankind were not formed to be heaped together in shoals, but to spread over the earth for its cultivation. "The more they assemble together," he protested, "the more they corrupt one another. . . . Their breath is destructive to their fellow creatures; nor is it less so in a literal than in a figurative sense."

Weakness and pride of Europe

The full "Europeans" of 1715, counting those under Turkish rule as lost and ignoring offshoots overseas, were perhaps as numerous as the Frenchmen and Italians or as the Germans and Scandinavians who inhabit the Continent to-day. Although in an age of windmills and waterwheels, of horses and ox-drawn carts and ploughs, the power of man seems trifling, their leaders, proud of much that had lately been accomplished, were filled with a robust confidence in progress. Literature, through the untravelled Alexander

Pope, proved the fact while rebuking their presumption. "Go, wondrous creature," sneered the poet,

> "Go, wondrous creature, mount where science guides,
> Go, study earth, weigh air, and state the tides,
> Instruct the planets in what orbs to run,
> Correct old time and regulate the sun,
>
> . . . .
>
> Go, teach eternal Wisdom how to rule,
> Then drop into thyself and be a fool."

Class Divisions

In the conditions that then prevailed, the great majority of Europeans toiled, from seven to seventy, only to wring a scanty subsistence from the land. Except in Britain, the Low Countries, Switzerland, Norway and Sweden, most of the peasants were by law tethered to the soil. Those who were free to move had but little incentive and but little opportunity to quit their homes. No frontier might be crossed without a passport which might well be unprocurable. In towns likewise most men had their niche and left it seldom. A king or lord, of course, might summon men to make war. The Catholic Church favoured pilgrimage. Sailors, chapmen, merchants, ecclesiastics, students, robbers and beggars also moved about. Musicians, portrait painters, jugglers, gypsies masons and carpenters frequented the highways. Fairs were far more important then than now, and although almost anyone, given permission, could build a cottage, a great house or a church required more than local labour. But Europe as a whole, like England, mainly consisted of small rural communities plodding through life under the government of proprietor and pastor. Within their huts, they had only the taxgatherer to fear. Outside, they were hardly more consulted than the cattle. Even in Britain labouring men remained voteless until 1884. Illiterate, untravelled, unable to rise in life, the peasant of 1715 knew the traditional arts of the countryside and the teachings of Christianity, so far as Christianity had really dispossessed the older faiths. Above him were a small number of men who could not descend to his social level.

> "In all the states of Europe," complained the Abbé Raynal, "there are a set of men who assume from their infancy a pre-eminence independent of their moral character. . . . Being secure of a certain rank and station, they take no pains to make themselves worthy of it."

These men—"class and the dependents of class"—were for

the times educated, travelled, even cosmopolitan. A gentleman enjoyed the freemasonry of his rank all over Europe. A scholar, thanks to Latin, was at home in any university. Even Britons breathed this European air. Chesterfield declared that he felt no difference between France and England. Arthur Young was more than once sorely tempted to settle in France. Lady Mary Wortley Montagu declared that there were British or Irish settlements in every town. At Dijon she found no less than sixteen families of fashion (1739) who spoke no French. " France, Nice and Switzerland swarm with us," wrote Horace Walpole (1786), adding that half of these emigrants had been brought by the attraction of gambling. Still more convincing are the narratives of those who turned to the Netherlands and mixed easily with travellers of many nations. Spa, " a merry place, much like Bath," was already cosmopolitan, while Italy taught her guests to raise Palladian and classical structures beyond the Alps. Few great lords lived on their estates. The taste for travel, indeed, grew as communications improved, and wealth increased. Had it not been implanted early, however, and had not society been more friendly than were governments, one great characteristic of the century would have been lacking.

THE INFLUENCE AND IMPORTANCE OF RELIGION

Religion and Internationalism

This happy internationalism of well-born wits flourished in spite of the deep religious cleavage that still divided Europe. As the eighteenth century was to prove, the wars of religion ceased when Louis XIV finally made peace. Mutual suspicion and apprehension, however, long survived the King who had revoked the Edict of Nantes. Sincere co-operation between powers which upheld and which denounced the Pope was never easy.

To pass from a Protestant into a Catholic country or the reverse, moreover, was instantly to feel a difference in the tone and texture of men's lives. Racial distinctions apart, the Protestant abroad must wonder at the " objects of superstition," the wayside crosses and statues, the bells for ever calling the populace to pray, the priests and monks and nuns everywhere abounding, while the lack of all this chilled the

Catholic. Ecclesiastical celibacy, indeed, was so widespread as profoundly to affect the strength of nations. The Protestant priests bred up sound reinforcements for Church and State. Millions of Europeans existed, or owed strength of mind and body, to the sober married priesthood which Luther had authorized. From this point of view Catholic presbyteries were wasted. Catholics whose families were too large might, it is true, send daughters into religion, while discovery, teaching, nursing and agriculture owed much to the Religious. The drain upon the Catholic nations, however, remained enormous. It is attested by the fantastic estimates of clerical wealth and numbers which prevailed.

Catholics and Protestants

Although Catholic and Protestant powers rather feared new crusades than wished to lead them, new struggles were still expected for many years. " I have always apprehended a religious war," wrote William III to Heinsius in 1697, " fearing lest France and Austria should have a secret understanding."

While the following years saw the two Catholic states discordant, they proved their overwhelming military power as compared with any possible Protestant combination. Ripe judgment, indeed, pronounced France the equal of Austria and the Sea Powers combined. In 1715, when the Morea passed out of Christian control, the Pope's agent congratulated him upon the approaching conquest of the three Kingdoms of Great Britain.

Religion continued to help or to hinder alliances and was invoked in many wars. A league between France and Spain always roused Protestant suspicion, and when Austria and Naples joined them, diplomatists cried, " Church in danger." An archbishop drove 15,000 of his subjects from Salzburg for their faith. Spain persecuted almost as of old. Poland, once the most tolerant state in Europe, imitated Spain. The " blood-bath of Thorn " (1724) alienated Protestant Europe for half a century. No Swede might desert the Lutheran Church, nor might a Catholic live in Sweden. In Britain, Catholic emancipation was yet far distant, and " No popery " might still be a dangerous cry. In every country the people were compelled to present themselves in church on all days of obligation. Such, besides Sunday, were not numerous in Protestant lands, but Catholic festivals, both Roman and

Eastern (Orthodox), occurred so frequently as to hamper work. Fasts were as much lighter in Protestant than in Roman lands as these last were lighter than among the Greeks or Moslems. The rules for religious observance, of course, were liable to loose interpretation. Many Protestants slept while the preacher uttered his hour's discourse. Many Catholic men attended Mass without entering the church itself. At Cadiz during Lent a British footman fasted daily on a dinner of fish, salted, boiled, broiled and stewed in wine, sauce in plenty, eggs in various modes, potatoes, parsnips and spinach—a feast to a Londoner, as he observes. Catholic Europe was split by a huge wedge of men to whom its usages were superstition and its adherents in some sort enemies. A line from the Hague to Berne and thence along the frontiers of Bavaria and Bohemia to Reval (Tallinn) roughly encloses the Protestant mainland, to which Scandinavia and Britain must be added. Comprising, as it does, Cologne, and excluding those Huguenots who still contrived to live in France and the Catholics of Holland, such a line needs much correction. But it at least suggests how large a portion of Teutonic Europe was in some degree severed from its Catholic brethren and from the Latin races. The Roman Index, banning many works of learning, still diminished intellectual contact between the two camps. The Inquisition itself survived in several countries and its memory more widely, while Protestant preachers and consistories combated Rome with the energy that might better have been spent upon the devil.

"Europe" a Society

Europe, however, though far from perfect, was a true society. Some eighty million of the most vigorous people on the earth felt a certain brotherhood among themselves and a distinction from Africans or Asiatics. They were united by neighbourhood, by colour, by the practice of monogamy, by monotheism, by a degree of civilization, and by abjuring property in one another. No European wandered naked, or lacked some shelter, or made another his private slave, or kept several wives, or lived upon uncooked flesh. All save a few nomads were members of some state, and the states were grouped into a family of nations which recognized an international law. The right of every state to formal equality with every other and the instinct that none should become strong enough to dictate to the rest—these assets Europe had lately vindicated against the tremendous power of Louis XIV. It still remained, as when in 1707 Marlborough defined it to Charles XII, "not the object of England and Holland to lower France too much," lest the equilibrium between possible combinations should be destroyed. But the century continued, as it began, with a widespread determination to take from France, or from any other state, "the power of making offensive war daily and alone against all Europe, insulting her neighbours, invading their territories, and rendering the will of her King an universal law." None could deny that in the interest of Europe a balance between the force of her members must be maintained, or that every state had a right to question the undue aggrandizement of any other.

European Religion

In spite of the difference of the churches, perhaps the strongest European bond was still community of religion. Apart from the Jews and a few individuals, all Europeans were Christians, though Russia, America and the Balkans served as reminders that not all Christians dwelt in Europe. Church and State, still in some nations almost indistinguishable, were everywhere close allies. Rulers commanded and subjects obeyed with complete conviction that in so doing they were carrying out God's will and that this, like the rest of their behaviour, would be rewarded or punished in the world to come. An unbeliever, they held, could not be either a proper sovereign or a faithful subject. All morality must be based on piety. "Why," subjects would ask, "should we honour a sovereign who doth not pay due honour to one who is in a higher sense both his sovereign and ours ?" To deny God's existence was held by almost all the rising generation of philosophers, as by their predecessors, to be presumptuous and absurd. "Mere perception" would reveal even to savages that they would be called to account for their deeds on earth. Belief in rewards and punishments after death was the foundation of government, obedience and life.

Eternal Punishment

In one terrible doctrine, indeed, Catholics and Protestants agreed and every side of European life was thereby affected. To understand the eighteenth century, we must attempt to appreciate the contemporary idea of hell and the force of the authority which imposed it upon Europeans. Most Europeans in that day obeyed and imitated their parents; and, in general, parents everywhere yielded unquestioning allegiance to the established authority of Church and State. Enlightened men, a small minority, regarded the age as progressive. The vast majority, it is probable, disliked and distrusted the idea of change, but accepted such practical improvements as made their lives more pleasant. While, to the former, Newton seemed to have raised the stature and widened the horizon of man, the latter could be brought to make use of turnips and potatoes. In their view of the unseen world, however, men were governed by authority which it was difficult to challenge or disprove. If the Church spoke for God, who could contradict her? Scholars might, at their peril, attempt to prove that her interpretation was mistaken. A few secretly believed that God did not exist. In every church and country, on the other hand, there were saints whose lives were absorbed in the thought of Him. Between these extremes came the great mass of real or nominal Christians living traditional lives except when stirred by some powerful religious intrusion.

By far the most powerful practical weapon in the hands of the Church was the doctrine of future retribution. "Obey the will of God as we declare it," the priests could say, "or incur His wrath while you live unrepentant, and eternal punishment when you shall have died." All Christian churches taught that hell existed. The overwhelming majority of Europeans accepted their teaching. All Europe was therefore influenced in its thoughts and deeds by its belief in hell. With a clearness that can never be surpassed, a little pamphlet styled "Instructions for Children,"[1] and translated in great part from the French, expounds the doctrine to the young "as soon as ever they can distinguish good from evil."

"Lesson X and XI" treats, by question and answer, "Of Hell."

Q. Where do unbelievers go after death?

A. To hell . . . a dark bottomless pit full of fire and brimstone.

Q. How will they spend their time there?

A. In weeping and wailing and gnashing of teeth.

Q. Will both their souls and bodies be tormented?

[1] "Printed for M. Cooper, at the Globe in Paternoster Row, 1745. Price 8*d*. or 20*s*. a hundred to those who give them away."

A. Yes, every part of them at once.

Q. How will their bodies be tormented ?

A. By lying in burning and flaming fire.

Q. How will their souls be tormented ?

A. By a sense of the wrath of God ; by pride, self-will, malice and envy ; by grief, desire, fear, rage and despair.

Q. Who will be their tormentors ?

A. Their own consciences, the devils, and one another.

Q. But will they have no rest from torment ?

A. No, not for one moment, day or night.

Q. How long will their torment last ?

A. For ever and ever.

This doctrine was taught by every Christian Church to a Europe in which all save the merest handful of Jews and others were Christians. Like most else that is taught about the unseen, it was rejected by a few and by many more disregarded. But it can hardly be doubted that an overwhelming majority of Europeans throughout the eighteenth century believed in such a hell and in an unchained pervasive devil. "Good God," cried a drunken man of letters on awaking in the ashpit of a great engine worked by steam, "has it come to this at last ? " "You are of yourself nothing but sin," the *Instructions* continue, "and deserve nothing but hell." What were, what must be the social and political consequences of such a faith ?

Although no church claimed to possess the keys of hell, most churches could guide their adherents to the path of safety, and some claimed this as their exclusive power. All drew from the doctrine an enormous influence over men. An unsuccessful pastor was once advised to thunder. He did so and "more than a hundred members of his congregation were under deep impressions before the preacher himself began to think seriously at all." Many clung to the Church to escape from hell, and, at the bidding of the Church, meekly obeyed the King.

Social Consequences

It may be doubted, however, whether even the importance of hell in securing obedience to Church and State was not surpassed by its importance in influencing the character of high and low alike. If God, whose attributes were goodness, wisdom, and mercy, and who loved man above all, could punish unbelief by interminable torture, how should temporal rulers deal with crime? What limits—to take that which affected every family—what limits ought to be set to the severity with which parents punished sin?

It is impossible to avoid connecting the doctrine of eternal torment with the hardness and want of sympathy which consorts strangely with the exquisite tenderness which on some sides marks the age. The lady who pitied the poor horses straining to tear Damiens limb from limb epitomizes this disharmony. But Damiens had stabbed a king, and Eternal Justice doomed reputable folk to pains beside which this was nothing. Some, indeed, mildly questioned the teachings of the Church, while others jested among themselves. "Can anything be more uncharitable," exclaimed Lady Mary, "than damning eternally so many millions for not believing what they never heard?" A footman, having learned to read the Bible in the hope of escaping hell, argued that "if God approved of the conduct of the Rechabites . . . how much more shall He excuse those Gentoos (Hindus), who never had the Bible?"

THE PRE-EMINENCE OF MONARCHY

The majority of Europeans believed that monarchy was the form of rule which God had prescribed for His people. Many, of course, held also that His will designated a particular family and a particular rule of succession to the throne. Reverence for the Lord's anointed and respect for their oaths of allegiance to him were powerfully supported by the experience of recent times. A monarchy which became a republic was usually enfeebled, while nations which had installed strong monarchies were those which had done mighty deeds. What could be feebler than Poland or Germany, great countries where an elective monarchy formed a mere disguise for a loose aristocratic federation? Spain had risen with her monarchy, and had fallen when it decayed. Italy by her weakness emphasized the general lesson, as did France, and for a time Sweden, by their astounding strength. Denmark, like England in an earlier age and the Dutch whenever hard pressed, had fled to strong monarchy as a refuge. The Swiss and the Savoyard states taught the same truth by contrast. Russia arrived by instinct at a single

Tsardom. Britain as yet remained unique in establishing a strong central power while providing that the king should obey the people. Morley, indeed, has described her king as a "limited arbiter in the personal wrangles of the oligarchy." But just as a constitutional sovereign by personal astuteness might sway the State, so an autocrat by personal feebleness might sink below even the English level. In 1715, monarchy in Europe was far from uniform, or omnipotent, but it had no rival.

Monarchy and Progress

In the absence of any other agent of change, the king or prince occupied a position of special importance in men's lives. "A King's chief duty," declared Cardinal Fleury, "is the relief of his subjects," and to this doctrine every honest prince subscribed. Fénélon had even taught a royal pupil that kings were made for their subjects and that they could give presents only at their subjects' expense. Louis XIV, when attempting to teach his heir the trade of a king, insisted that, when he kept the State in view, the ruler was working for himself.

"The good of the one," he declared, "makes the glory of the other. When the former is happy, high and powerful, he who causes this is glorious, and therefore must surpass his subjects in the enjoyment of the greatest pleasure in life."

Though often less exalted, monarchy was almost universal throughout Europe. The Swiss, the Venetians and the Genoese had no kings. The Poles carefully spoke of "the Republic," and among the Dutch the House of Orange was something less than royal. With a few exceptions, however, the institution to which the masses turned for deliverance from aristocratic tyrants was that which the churches proclaimed as ordained by God for mankind. History and theology combined to make the prince demand, and the people concede, more power in return for less service than can easily be understood. "What fatherland ?", asked a Duke of Würtemberg with indignation, "*I* am the fatherland," and in 1914 Austria was still ruled by an Emperor who demanded "patriotism for Me." When Louis XIV died the idea that the monarch was merely the first servant of the state had made little progress among rulers, but that of royal magnificence was full blown. To possess the finest opera, ballet and stable, with castles everywhere—by the lake, on the mountain, in the forest and near the hunting-ground, as well as in the capital—such was the innocent ambition of many a prince. To gratify it he might impose tolls and taxes, despoil the Church, sell offices as well as timber, and hire out his conscript troops, all this not only without rousing rebellion, but often without forfeiting his people's love. "Great lords have their whims," they would murmur indulgently, and submit. Such human eccentricity was part of the price that must be paid for protection, or as some would say, for real freedom. "The greater share the people have in government, the less liberty, civil or religious, does a nation enjoy." Such was Wesley's creed and many of his contemporaries shared it. If "the people" comprised the ignorant, unprogressive millions who tilled the soil of Europe in 1715, the statement would be hard indeed to deny.

THE BACKWARDNESS OF THE COUNTRY AND THE POTENTIALITIES OF THE TOWNS

Even more than in England, throughout at least the north of continental Europe existence for most men was one long struggle with the land for shelter, clothing and food. The ordinary European went through life with his gaze fixed upon the soil, except when it was directed heavenwards by the Church. To fill the barns with the produce of the harvest and to keep enough animals alive through the winter to begin a fresh struggle in the spring—such was the lifework of rural man. He was struggling not so much with nature as with ignorance—with the traditional methods of misusing the land, and the failure to find out better modes and instruments of production. Towards Lady Day the men of 1715, fed through the winter on bread, salted fish or meat, and home brew, rallied such of their horses, oxen, or mules as had contrived to exist, often on straw or worse—and began the new campaign. Their ill-found attack aimed at breaking the stubborn glebe with a so-called plough of wood. Over a vast area in northern Europe the terrain was arranged on principles that had survived from ages too remote for history. The arable land around the village, sheltered by no hedge, was divided into three vast fields, one sown in spring, one in autumn and one left fallow. This last the villagers proceeded to plough in common, perhaps dimly aware that a year's rest could hardly have compensated it for the abstraction of two crops without return. In ploughing, they must leave untouched the balks or margins dividing off the several strips of land to which each family was entitled. Much soil thus escaped cultivation and sprouted weeds in plenty. Still more serious was the frustration of individual enterprise which the whole system imposed. If the crop failed or if their barns were emptied by a passing army, the villagers must migrate or starve to death. Hardly any means existed for transporting the surplus of some more favoured district to their aid. Goods were chiefly moved on horseback and on any but the shortest journeys horse and man would soon devour the load. If the stricken villagers lived near a navigable waterway, the tolls might well be prohibitive. On some of the French rivers payment must be made every seven miles or even less. In economic as in social life, indeed, the European village formed almost a world of its own. Its self-sufficiency extended to clothing no less than to food and shelter. While salt and fish must often be brought from afar, the main articles of clothing were made by the labour of the villagers from the wool and the skins of their animals, and from home-bleached linen. Country towns, like the villages, largely fed and clothed themselves from the surrounding fields. As the scenes of workshops, markets, inns and law-courts, and as the homes of lawyers, doctors and officials, the towns enjoyed a certain pre-eminence, but for the most part they remained small and poor. The countryside could not look to them for the leadership and innovation which it sorely needed. While its labour and capital barely sufficed to extract the accustomed quantity of food and clothing from the soil, ever greater demands were made upon it for men and money for the wars. When Louis XIV died, half the countries in Europe were less populous and less prosperous than in an earlier age. Portugal, Spain and France, Belgium and Ireland, many of the German states, Russia, Sweden and Poland—the enumeration of the impoverished powers excludes but few in Europe and is perhaps incomplete. It was the self-sufficiency of the units out of which each state was built up, that made possible the recovery and advance of Europe, after a century of almost unceasing war.

Lack of Communications

This cellular or atomic character of the European countryside was, of course, in great part due to the lack of such communications as later ages take for granted. Most men were peasants, and a peasant moving from his home must overcome every kind of obstacle, social, legal, and economic, as well as physical. The whole force of governments was directed towards settling and keeping settled the cultivators upon whom the finance and armaments of the State ultimately depended. To move more than a few miles was often to find a different government, a different dialect, different customs, different weights, measures and currency. A single German grand-duchy used some fourscore different weights called "pound," and still more measures called "yard." A serf could not move without his lord's consent nor could a subject cross a frontier without permission. If a different religion prevailed the imigrant might expect much discomfort and little or no security. Many villages lived in undying feud with their nearest neighbours. Movement indeed there was, both of migratory classes and of villagers in the weekly flux to and from the local market town. But it was the paucity and badness of the roads that made this traffic seem more than a trifle compared with the stationary habit of the mass. Millions doubtless lived and died without moving ten miles from the cottage in which they were born and without framing any notion of the world beyond that radius.

No newspaper, of course, disturbed their daily life, nor any save the rarest postal correspondence. In the absence of traders, their knowledge of the wider world must in general come from the priest or pastor, and from the conscript or veteran of the wars. So long as traders must themselves accompany their goods, and no capitalists existed who could buy surplus produce for sale elsewhere, the cultivator might hope in vain for progress.

The Towns of Europe

The hope of Europe lay in its towns, for there alone could either ideas or wealth make rapid progress. So far as size and numbers were concerned, the towns of 1715 were tiny, by comparison with what they have since become. A score of obstacles prevented the formation of modern aggregations. Manufactures themselves were on a small scale, and more often than not were carried on in rural districts. Toledo steel, Nuremberg iron-work, Zürich ribbons might be famous, but the main articles of use and wear came from nearer home. Communications were such that great inland towns could not easily be fed. Hygiene was worse, so that to increase the size of a town raised the death-rate among those who dwelt there. Although, in their government as in their situation, towns showed the utmost diversity, most of them enjoyed certain privileges and defended them against unwelcome immigration. Perhaps chief of all, towns needed defence against smugglers or armies and cowered behind barriers or fortifications. Their rank as fortresses coloured life in many ways, from the pomp and music of the garrison to the inordinate height of the houses, towering over the dark and filthy streets. Many of the workers toiled and slept in cellars, and few below the topmost storey could see the sun. Suburbs indeed might grow up at their own risk beyond the walls, and sometimes the fortress was extended to take them in. Normally, however, the citizen thought more of his purse than of his health, and made the utmost of the narrow site.

Both the military character of many towns and the walled-in state of many more conduced to their easy regulation. At night the gates were shut, and at all times those going out or coming in must satisfy the watch. Passports were always verified and imports often taxed. Local feeling was everywhere dominant, so that to the mob a man from the next town became a "foreigner." Their suspicion of him might be increased by some hereditary feud between the towns, while each might speak a different dialect which made the other hard to understand. Aliens lived under constant supervision; Jews, in many places, within a ghetto. Where, on the other hand, modern manufacturers and traders earnestly compete, they then lived in association. In some towns this association took the form of a single fraternity for all trades; in others, strictly-regulated unions of all the members of each single craft. Those who produced a particular class of goods lived side by side, above their workshops. Their apprentices and unmarried journeymen shared their home. If the town held a fair, they might dispose of extra products, and they would offer in the weekly market such goods as had not been made to order. Competition in the modern sense, however, hardly existed. Born with a definite social status, trained according to the regulations of the craft, producing goods of standard quality to meet a limited but stable demand, contented with the corporation which framed his life, the burgher of 1715 gave solidity to the urban life of Europe.

That life was in England presided over by a mayor and corporation, London and York alone having a Lord Mayor. The great towns of Flanders, Holland and Germany had burgomasters, whose duties included the appointment to town offices and the custody of the key of the town bank. Capitals were often governed by officials whom the King appointed. The presence of a court constituted a remarkable *imperium in imperio* for the civic organization.

Towns and Trade

As oceanic trade developed, seaports tended more and more to surpass the inland cities in wealth and size. Of the whole population of Europe, indeed, it may be doubted whether more than a quarter lived in towns, while the number of great towns was infinitesimal. Parts of a few small countries, notably the Netherlands and the north Italian plain, might be described as predominantly urban, and few states did not contain at least one important town. In general, however, the number of such hearths of progressive public opinion remained conspicuously small.

If Russia under Peter the Great should join herself to Europe, no great addition would be made to civic life. Among Muscovites, Archangel was familiarly spoken of as "town," but Peter the Great had cut the roots of its trade with the Dutch and English, thus dooming it to decline. Meanwhile, St. Petersburg, its favoured rival, was only painfully struggling into being. Some 60,000 houses had been built in obedience to the Tsar's decree, but by 1715 no true city adorned the bog on which they stood. Moscow, the most spacious of capitals, soon to be girdled by ramparts six-and-twenty miles in length, seemed, despite its palaces and churches, hardly more than a village hugely overgrown. Wooden dwellings and the indispensable farmyards, separated by lanes, housed a great part of its large, but shifting population. Although a centre of regional exchanges, it lacked the facilities afforded by the Volga below Nijni-

Novgorod for an inter-racial fair. Kiev, lately regained from Poland, had a great name in Christian history, but small political or economic weight. The German cities, Riga and Reval, which Russia had acquired by conquest, promised to remain minor European centres of commerce and art. At the moment, however, these Baltic capitals shared in the widespread ruin produced by the long Northern war (1700–21). In 1714 a German diplomat found that at Riga "the plague had carried off 60,000 persons and the houses there bore a melancholy aspect, by reason there had been 8,000 bombs thrown into the town by the Russians during the siege." Reval had likewise suffered, though the plague mortality of 55,000 was doubtless swollen, as in Riga, by deaths among the country-folk who had flocked within its walls for shelter from the devastating hordes of Russians.

On many of its coasts, however, the Baltic served as a reminder of the fickleness of trade. The route towards the Black Sea by the Dnieper had long ceased to be "the main street of the world," Wisby lay in ruins, and Lübeck's great days were over. Danzig, another German city, carried on a vast trade under the *aegis* of its Polish overlord, but half a century later, when Warsaw was approaching 60,000, French philosophers complained that Poland proper still possessed no town.

Vienna was an important capital, with more than 7,000 master craftsmen and all the dignity that the Habsburg Emperors could bestow. Still, however, she lay hampered and imperilled by the nearness of the Turkish power, a frontier fortress, rather than the centre of a Habsburg empire. Prague, her superior in majesty and romance, but in fashion only as Exeter to London, formed the heart of a province which had not yet recovered from the Thirty Years War. Leipzig, whose position at the meeting-place of several important roads made the fairs which she held thrice yearly events of international importance, was now a rising town. Frankfort-on-the-Main likewise owed much to its position, and perhaps more to the asylum which it had offered to Jews from Spain, and Protestants from Belgium. Many of the once famous German towns, however, had lost their old importance through war, the Turkish conquests, and the establishment of trans-oceanic trade. Berlin, indeed, had multiplied ten-fold the population of 6,000 which the Great Elector found there (1640), but for this expansion the court and garrison were the chief causes.

Swedish towns doubtless shared in the appalling loss of menfolk during the long Northern War. Stockholm, far the first among them, probably numbered some 50,000 people; Gothenburg, the second, 13,000 or rather more. In Denmark, Copenhagen may be credited with some 70,000 inhabitants, if the parochial registers may be trusted, but the disparity between the capital and any other town was greater even than in Sweden.

North of the Alps and east of the Rhine there were but three European cities which could claim to be rich, populous and progressive, and in each case the cause was commerce overseas. Danzig and Hamburg, with their magnificent combination of access to sea and river, were rivalled by Amsterdam, favoured as it was by the artificial denial of Antwerp's right to commerce overseas. South of the Pyrenees, the Peninsula was studded rather with great names than with cities that could now be reckoned rich or great. Madrid could not generate wealth or serve as the scene of copious exchanges. Lisbon, even before the annihilating earthquake of 1755, was in decline. At Seville the river had silted up, so that the wealth of the Indies was laboriously transferred from the ocean-going fleet to the ships of the northern nations at Cadiz. Oporto and Barcelona, which had suffered from the wars, could hardly rank high among trading cities. Between the Pyrenees and the Rhine as well as south of the Alps, however, towns abounded which remained considerable and promised to become great. There the accumulated wealth of earlier ages was not, as in Germany, reduced by the changed direction of the flow of trade. A fertile soil and easy access to the sea kept the cities of France and northern Italy rich and vigorous. Paris, materially and morally, ranked by far the first, and of French markets, that of Lyons, the supplanter of Geneva, stood second. Bordeaux carried on a great and increasing trade with the French colonies in America, while Marseilles was styled "Queen of the Mediterranean" from her profitable intercourse with the Levant. Havre formed her northern counterpart, and Nantes, La Rochelle, L'Orient and St. Malo shared in the ocean trade. The canal of Languedoc, which united Bordeaux and Marseilles, transformed the commercial geography of France, while the Channel ports, both by lawful trade and by smuggling, enabled her to profit by the neighbourhood of England, whenever peace prevailed.

Italy suffered from the changes which made the Turk the master of her former markets and Habsburgs and Bourbons of her fairest provinces. But Venice and Milan remained among the greatest towns in Europe, while Genoa, Leghorn and Naples were considerable ports. Rome was still a unique capital, and a dozen cities, with Florence at their head, served as magnets to attract the connoisseurs of Europe.

Commerce both joined and divided the nations of Europe. Posts While it promoted the general wealth and progress it proved a fertile source of war. Nothing, on the other hand, attested more clearly the growing unity of Europe than the progress of the posts. By this governmental institution, correspondence and passengers were forwarded as frequently, as swiftly, and as safely as the conditions in each country would allow. What Louis XI had established for his own security in 1464, the Holy Roman Empire had developed early in the seventeenth century and England under Charles II. In France, every important town had its own post, and the country was thickly studded with local stations. These were furnished with a tariff which guarded travellers against extortion, while the prescribed payments enabled the postmaster to provide good rooms, good horses and good postboys. Although inevitably impeded by frontiers, the post, like the ambassador, was sacred throughout Europe. International letters from and to the provinces, however, often went through the capital, and no postillion entered a foreign land. Inland posts naturally predominated, and England led the way. From London, letters set out for all parts of Great Britain thrice weekly, while from Kent and the Downs the post reached London every day. A letter of a single sheet was carried eighty miles for threepence. A passenger travelling post paid threepence per mile, with fourpence per stage to the postboy. Within a ten-mile radius of London the post conveyed packets not exceeding £10 in value or a pound in weight for a penny,—to the admiration of foreigners in England. In Holland the posts went by boat; across the mountains on mule-back; in northern Europe during winter by sledge, and in remote regions they might receive an escort of troopers. Where else could be found so clear a witness to the essential unity of Europe?

BIBLIOGRAPHICAL NOTE

See Bibliographical Note and Bibliography at the end of Chapter I. Some of the following works may be added:

A

R. Bayne-Powell: *Eighteenth-century London Life* (1937).

H. Belloc: *The Road* (1923).

M. von Boehn: *Modes and Manners. The Eighteenth Century* (trans. 1935).

J. B. Botsford: *English Society in the Eighteenth Century* (1924).

E. B. Chancellor: *The Eighteenth Century in London* (1920).

M. D. George: *London Life in the Eighteenth Century* (1925).

E. and J. Goncourt: *The Woman of the Eighteenth Century* (1862, new ed. 1901).

A. Goodwin (ed.): *The European Nobility in the Eighteenth Century* (1953).

H. G. Graham: *Scottish Men of Letters in the Eighteenth Century* (1901).

C. E. Kany: *Life and Manners in Madrid, 1750–1800* (1932).

R. S. Lambert (ed.): *Grand Tour; A Journey in the Tracks of the Age of Aristocracy* (1935).

W. E. H. Lecky: *History of England in the Eighteenth Century.* 8 vols. (1878–90).

R. B. Mowat: *The Age of Reason* (1934).

A. E. Richardson: *Georgian England* (1931).

W. Sombart: *The Quintessence of Capitalism* (1932).

A. S. Turberville: *English Men and Manners in the Eighteenth Century* (1926, 2nd ed. 1929).

B. Willey: *The Eighteenth Century Background* (1940).

B

A. Anderson: *An Historical and Chronological Deduction of the Origin of Commerce.* 2 vols. (1764).

C. B. Andrews (ed.): *The Torrington Diaries, 1781–1794.* 4 vols. (1934–38).

J. B. Beresford (ed.): *The Diary of a Country Parson: The Rev. James Woodforde, 1758–1802.* 5 vols. (1924–31).

R. Burton: *A New View and Observations on . . . London and Westminster* (1730).

W. Coxe: *Travels into Poland, Russia, Sweden and Denmark.* 3 vols. (1784).

C. Dreyss: *Mémoires de Louis XIV pour l'instruction du Dauphin* (1860).

J. Kulischer: *Allgemeine Wirtschartsgeschichte.* II (1928–29).

P. Lacroix: *Dixhuitième siècle, institutions, usages et costumes, 1700–1789* (illustrated) (1875 and 1876).

J. Macdonald: *Travels, 1745–1779* (1927).

C. Maxwell: *The English Traveller in France, 1698–1815* (1932).

Montesquieu: *Lettres persanes* (1721).

George Paston (pseud.): *Lady Mary Wortley Montagu and her Times* (1907).

H. Swinburne: *Travels . . . through Spain in the Years 1775 and 1776* (1778).

J. Townshend: *A Journey through Spain in the Years 1786 and 1788.* 3 vols. (2nd ed. 1792).

CHAPTER III

EUROPE IN 1715—CULTURE

The Pride of 1715 Europe

A MODERN schoolboy, glancing back across less than seven generations to the Europe of 1715, might think the men of that day rustic, ignorant and unprogressive. His own life has been so amazingly transformed by the discoveries made within the last four among the seven that to him eighteenth-century existence may well seem childish. The youth of 1715, it might be, would never travel, and without travel he could know but little of the life of his own nation, still less of any other. He must live in a society which believed in witchcraft, feared the corporeal presence of the Devil, supposed negro slavery to have been ordained by God, and women to have been divinely appointed a race inferior to men.

When perhaps four-fifths of mankind could neither read nor write, books were by modern standards rare, and daily newspapers almost unknown. Even the fine gentleman of the age carried no handkerchief in his pocket, used a far from perfect fork and bathed but seldom. In the proud society of Spain, intimates deloused one another in public. Everywhere, not least in hospital, several persons might be called on to share a bed. Life was lived, moreover, in a poisonous haze of superstition. One educated Puritan who ventured within a theatre fled in shocked amazement at the impiety of a stage thunderstorm, which seemed to mock the very voice of God.

History shows none the less that in their own eyes the men of 1715 seemed to be the proud heirs of a progressive civilization. Their pride, indeed, was warranted by the achievements of their age, both in science and in the arts. Posterity, it is true, finds that when Rembrandt and Murillo died the long line of great painters broke, and Kneller and Watteau no longer command enthusiasm. In architecture, however, Wren and his pupils were creating works worthy to adorn any age. The proportion, the dignity and the restraint of their creations were at once influencing and illustrating the achievement of the eighteenth century.

French and English Literature

Both in France and England, moreover, the men of 1715 were flushed with recent triumphs alike in prose and verse. The Augustan age of Boileau, Racine, Corneille, Molière and a score of names lesser only than these had effected in Holland that French conquest which the armies of Louis XIV had failed to accomplish, and had subjugated much of Germany and Spain. It had heralded the Augustan age in England, where French influence, as in Dryden, combined with native genius to produce a perfect instrument for expressing thought. And on both sides of the Channel the mighty march continued. Swift, Addison, Steele and Defoe, with Pope, from whose model would-be poets diverged at their peril, and Gray, the characteristic didactic of the age, these men might rank with Voltaire and Montesquieu, then rising into fame. Whether or no the triumphs of literature which belonged to an age of war would continue in time of peace, no man could foresee. War, beyond question, releases pent-up forces of all kinds, and contemporaries were not slow to mark the stimulus given to the French by Louis XIV, "their new deity, Jupiter-Bourbon." Peace, however, promised at least to enlarge the market for such wares as poets and prose writers might produce. The increase in every country of that class of wealthy amateurs who were eager to buy new books both enabled books to be written and influenced their contents. French, and in a less degree English, replaced Latin as the common language of educated Europe. Leibnitz of Leipzig (1646–1716), who was at home all over Europe and in all learning, the philosopher who "may be said to have founded in the course of his life the European commonwealth of letters," wrote in his later years in French.

Leibnitz

Leibnitz, who sought to serve Europe by suggesting to France the liberation of Egypt and to Russia Peter's new scheme of government, was a universal philosopher who left his mark on the society of 1715. Above all things comprehensive, he fostered the idea of a re-united Europe pooling its intelligence for the peaceful advancement of mankind. Restore the medieval intercourse between the universities, found new academies of science, re-unite, where possible, the churches, collaborate to solve questions which affect the human race—such was the advice which this benevolent prodigy offered in person to the educated in many capitals, and which found a ready ear. In 1715, when the Abbé de St. Pierre was advocating the establishment of a European Diet to secure perpetual peace, Leibnitz had stimulated into special activity the discussion of those great questions which were to absorb so large a share of the intellectual energy of the age. How was God related to man and to the universe? What is a miracle? What is meant by space, time, and the world of matter? Leibnitz' own answer, which finds a respectful echo in the modern world, was that all came from the Supreme Substance by the emission of monads of existence. These were endowed with the power of development, but their paths were predestined, so that in the long run all was for the best, in the best of all possible worlds.

Conversation and Progress

The challenge of such ideas developed what in the Europe of 1715 was an international art beside the arts of music, painting, literature and the rest—the art of conversation. Free from the trammels of the patron, the censor, and the publisher, men and women met systematically in the *salon* to formulate and discuss ideas. In a thousand cliques, from the coffee-house to the Royal Society and to its peers abroad, men likewise debated.

> "Paris," writes Sir Thomas Barclay, "is an intellectual Brighton. There the wind blows through your thoughts as at Brighton it blows through your clothes. There you may think aloud, and amid the *sans-gêne* of the French mind, have the glorious sensation of the open sea and the mountain-top."

Before the era of specialization, such an intellectual climate counted for much. In 1715, however, the French could not flatter themselves that in Paris "nine-tenths of the world's originality are centralized." Although the full tide of "Anglomania" had yet to flow, they must and did recognize that in philosophy, as in liberty, the Englishman was then the leader of the world. Within five years of the Glorious Revolution, Newton, Locke and Halley had taught mankind more about itself and the universe than the whole eighteenth century could discover.

Relics of Darkness in 1715

By 1715, it is true, not all was light. Many scholars clung to the Vortex theory, which Descartes (1596–1650) had devised to reconcile the demonstration of Copernicus that the earth moved round the sun with the official interpretation of the Bible that it stood still. If the earth remained at rest within a whirlpool of its own while that whirlpool was carried round the sun, science and conscience, he held, might both be satisfied. Alchemy still flourished. Locke, whom Gray styled "the second illuminator of our English race," obviously ranked with Newton as a philosopher, but his immediate influence upon the world could be but small. Halley's most famous deductions could not be verified until after the middle of the eighteenth century, when Venus should again pass between the earth and the sun, and until the comet seen in 1682 should return in 1758.

Oxygen was still known as dephlogisticated air, for men of science had come to the conclusion that a substance known as phlogiston was the raw material of fire. Fire, they now knew, could only burn in air, and they held that its effect was to draw from the substance burnt the phlogiston which rendered it combustible. Candles, they thought, were so rich in this imaginary element that when they burned hardly any residuum was left. Thus on a hundred sides men were bravely guessing the road to truth.

The Progress of Half a Century 1665–1714

Apart from Leibnitz and the great English trio, offspring respectively of a yeoman, a small squire and a bankrupt soap-boiler, thinkers in many lands had lately proved by their discoveries that humanity was on its forward march. Within a mere fifty years, man had learned much from these others about his body, about the world in which he lived, and what the keenest minds in Europe could divine about his soul. Robert Boyle (1626–91), an Irish gentleman with an European education, having satisfied himself that the circulation of the blood was real, went on to discover much of the necessity for air and many of its properties, facts long familiar to every modern schoolboy. The theory of spontaneous generation, with the authority of Aristotle behind it, still lingered on. Some men have always been found to believe that living organisms fully formed may arise from matter which is not alive. In 1668, however, the Italian Redi had struck at the most common source of error by screening meat from flies and showing that such meat bred no maggots. During the 'seventies the offspring of Portuguese Jews who had fled to Amsterdam, Spinoza, had stimulated all Europe and straightened the path of science by denying miracle, demonstrating the need of religious liberty and bringing the universe within the grip of reason. Bayle, a French Protestant refugee in Holland, produced a Historical and Critical Dictionary which became the great arsenal of freethinkers throughout Europe (1697). Before the seventeenth century closed, Petty and North provided statesmen with a new apparatus of statistics and a theory of commercial policy which held the field for many years. Meanwhile the Jesuits were mapping China, and the Somerset navigator, Dampier, was describing the world and exploring Australasia. The *Daily Courant*, founded in 1702, had become at least the pioneer of the modern newssheet.

In twenty years four great institutions had been founded to harness the forces of as many countries to the car of progress. The universities of Halle and of Moscow, like the academies of Berlin and of Spain, possessed the inestimable advantage of freedom from tradition if not from governmental interference.

Music in 1715

The state of two arts common to all Europe, those of music and of medicine, gives some further clue to the outlook of Western man in 1715. Two years before, a German work on music had distinguished between the Italians, who exalted music, the French, who enlivened it, the Germans, who strove after it, and the English, the best judges, who paid for it. Whether the characterization was right or wrong, it seems certain that music then filled a larger space in the life of Europe than is possible in the more crowded present, and that, in this field, Britain was not typical of Europe. The Puritans, indeed, had banished from their island that musical atmosphere which the Continent of Europe still enjoyed. They had struck hard at almost every source of harmony. While reducing its scope in public worship, they frowned on the alehouse, the theatre, and the dance. Minuet, gavotte, procession, cotillon, country dance, sword dance, morris dance—all demanded music and all were forbidden to the elect. A Puritan apprentice who loved music broke away from a choral group, because, as he wrote, "they began to sing catches and glees, and I knew not where it might end."

Lord Chesterfield's advice to his son in 1749 epitomizes a widespread opinion: "If you love music, hear it; go to operas, concerts, and pay fiddlers to play to you; but I insist upon your neither piping nor fiddling yourself. It puts a gentleman in a very frivolous, contemptible light."

In Catholic and Lutheran countries, however, music still occupied a great place in human life. After their work or on holy days, the masses could not go far from their own homes. They lacked bright light and the power or means of reading. Almanacs and chap-books of two dozen pages must be soon exhausted. Drinking, singing, dancing and gossip were their diversions. From the shepherd's pipe to the gradually developing pianoforte, a score of instruments were familiar to every considerable group of men. For the masses, musical education came chiefly from the Church. In the early eighteenth century, according to an expert, "the music of the stage was in all countries the most artificial, cold and formal that has ever existed." The vast majority of Europeans, however, could never witness a stage-play. Their music came first and foremost from Christian services, the only musical performance that was free and one which almost all were compelled by law to attend. "In church some muttering he doth make, well pleased when hymns harmonious rise, he striveth not to overtake the hurrying litanies"—such was no doubt the attitude of the elder generations in countless villages. But in Flanders, as Dr. Burney reported:

> "All the labouring people and *bourgeois* go to matins as soon as it is light on common days, and on Sundays and festivals two or three times in the course of the day; so that by their constantly hearing the priests, and singing with them, they acquire that kind of melody and expression which is used in the church, and apply it to their songs, in their work-shops and in the street."

This was indeed an epoch-making age in the advance of music, for Bach and Handel were raising the art to a higher plane. Their contemporaries, however, "thought of Handel as a fashionable opera-writer who with advancing years developed choral music as a pious fad; while nobody thought of Bach except people within coaching range of Saxony"

(Tovey). Music was the object of royal patronage: Louis XIV had performed the daily pageant of his royal life to the constant accompaniment of violins: Frederick the Great was to command an evening concert as long as he himself could lead it on the flute, and Maria Theresa moved her singing master to tears by the beauty of her voice. Since musical entertainments were largely a function of court life, their nature and history is fully known. It may be stated with confidence that from leaders of society some musical appreciation was expected; that rulers competed for the possession, permanent or temporary, of the finest singers; that in 1715 Italy still ranked as the metropolis of music; and that only as the century progressed did the Germans move towards pre-eminence. Lulli, the naturalized Florentine (1633–87), who had founded French opera and bequeathed to his sons the post of superintendent of the King's music, was the classic musician of the age, and English and German singers assumed Italian names.

Medicine in 1715

After two thousand years' experience, Europe remained astonishingly inexpert in combating disease. In some regions doctors were ridiculed as "the scythe" or as "the enemy of mankind." The *Spectator* professed to believe that in ancient times the north had swarmed with people because doctors were unknown. Now "like the British army in Caesar's time, some of them slay in chariots and some on foot." The doctor who could keep his carriage thereby gained mobility and did more execution.

D'Alembert (1717–83), the most sober and erudite of French philosophers, who became a medical student after taking a degree in law, judged medicine one of the three greatest absurdities that the human brain had devised. In 1750, none the less, when writing his preface to the great *Encyclopædia*, he, who was famous for speaking the truth even to princes, declared that Harvey had immortalized himself by discovering the circulation of the blood. He also named the epoch-making teacher Boerhaave (1668–1738) among the most notable of scientific men. His tribute to six medical and surgical Encyclopædists proves that, however absurd was the art of healing, it attracted some Frenchmen of ability. Taking Europe as a whole, however, the art was backward; progress slow; and able practitioners, but few. Lack of scientific knowledge was concealed by a jargon of pseudo-learned words. Purging medicines, for instance, were divided into Cholagogues, Phlegmagogues, Melanagogues and Hydragogues, carrying bile, pituita, melancholy and serosities respectively. A doctor in the early eighteenth century, none the less, possessed a considerable and increasing number of recorded observations of diseased persons both before and after death. Sir William Petty (1623–87) had taught him how to arrange them in statistical tables, and government kept records of disease in the army, navy and prisons. For diagnosis, on the other hand, his implements were hardly better than those of pre-Christian times. The eighteenth century was to bring him the pulse-watch and the stethoscope, in later times his inseparable tools for diagnosis. As " Jesuits' bark " (quinine) had testified for more than seventy years, Europe drew aid from other continents in healing.

Arab physicians enjoyed a great reputation among Europeans. The scourge of small-pox, so prevalent in England that a woman who escaped its pockmarks was deemed a beauty, was combated in the East by "inoculation," infection by deliberate contact with a patient suffering from a mild attack. The introduction of this treatment into Europe, and its replacement by vaccination, was to occupy the greater part of the eighteenth century and to constitute its chief advance in the struggle with any specific disease.

A profession in which a student could graduate M.D. at nineteen, in which the physician left surgery to the barber and obstetrics to the midwife or accoucheur, and whose chief remedy was to shed lakes of human blood—such a profession bore no hall-mark of progress. Yet the need for healing was so wide and some of those who responded were so able that progress, however spasmodic and irregular, was made. At Padua Professor Morgagni (1682–1771) had already begun the great advance associated with his name by introducing the " anatomical concept " into diagnosis. Within the next half-century he was to show that only a comprehensive knowledge of anatomical conditions could warrant the treatment of a patient.

It may safely be asserted, however, that in the Europe of 1715 most cases of disease were dealt with by guesswork, and that in many the doctor or the layman guessed wrong.

Medicine, indeed, suffered from the confidence and universality which stamp the eighteenth-century mind. Educated men knew perfectly well what the ancients had laid down. They also knew that the moderns had advanced and were still advancing. The faith in reason concealed from them how little was then known or how much it was possible to know about the mechanism of the human frame. In consequence, laymen believed in their own theories of disease and cure, while physicians made theory supply the place of experiment and observation.

Medical Jargon

"Suppose," wrote a high authority on purges, after destroying the sect of the mechanical physicians and other rivals, "suppose the humour which passes through the glands of the intestines to be composed of three or four several sorts of particles, that medicine, which will easily cohere to those particles, and cohering, increase their mutual attractions, so as they may unite in greater numbers at, or before they arrive at the intestines, than they would have done, if the medicine had not been given, must necessarily increase the quantity of humour which passes through the glands of the intestines; if the quantity of blood be not diminished in the same proportion as the quantity of particles is increased. After the same manner do diuretics, sudorifics, and medicines which promote all other secretions operate."

As late as 1793, the widowed vicar of St. Gluvias bemoaned the fact that the sudden fall of his wife's pulse from 85 (its usual beat) to 25 had not aroused the attention of either her apothecary or of her physician.

Surgical Practice

Surgical conditions were illustrated only too plainly when at Ochakov (July, 1737) Keith, afterwards Marshal, received a ball in the interior part of the thigh. The court physicians at Petersburgh only produced a swelling and increased the pain. At Paris, more than eighteen months after the injury, their colleagues consulted for three hours and voted by twelve to six for amputation. Keith, despite the pain and danger, demanded that the ball should be taken out. "I am prepared," he said, voicing the spirit of the age, "against all events. Gentlemen never fear." After eight days' treatment the swelling was reduced and the surgeons could operate.

"He held his thigh with both hands, and encouraged them to do their duty. They cut the flesh into the very bone for near an hand breadth, round the mark of the needle wherewith they had probed the wound; in which they detected some of the lining of his coat, sticking to the ball between two pieces of fractured bone which last they pared towards the extremities. After extracting the bullet, which was one quarter of an inch in diameter, they joined the bone."

Within seven months the patient walked on crutches.

Had Keith been sentenced to amputation on the battle field, the surgeon's knife and saw might have been followed by a styptic dressing of boiling tar, applied while an assistant was preparing to spend twelve or fourteen hours in holding the severed member with his hand. "Cutting for the stone" was so terrible that Robert Walpole refused to undergo it. Happily for the patients, surgeons, and in some degree physicians also, sometimes recognized the limits of their skill and knowledge. Deep-seated internal operations were not attempted. While the attribution of insanity to the direct influence of the moon was weakening, doctors admitted that the remedy lay beyond their art.

The French, regarding surgery as akin to butchery, refused to admit surgeons to their universities. A surgeon who had studied physic, however, was allowed to wear the gown which marked that art. The barber surgeon, on the other hand, was a barber who also drew teeth and opened veins when necessary. The vast majority of mankind, in all likelihood, passed their lives without a single contact with surgeon or physician. Traditional medicine dies hard, and while the learned world was beginning to disbelieve in witchcraft, in many countries mild sorcery continued to flourish.

Religious currents in 1715

In music, although every people had its own speciality and method, all Europe could unite. Medicine was likewise a weapon common to every nation in its fight against disease and death. Religion, however, still remained in one sense the great disintegrator of Christian Europe; in another, its strongest bond of union. The religious torpor of the age has been greatly overstated. A general lassitude had indeed succeeded to the tremendous religious wars of the two preceding centuries, while new sources of division, such as commerce, surpassed the creeds as a source of strife between the nations. Reverence for the ideal and contempt for all churches swayed various minds towards toleration. With Louis XIV, aggressive Romanism ceased to threaten the liberties of Europe, while in many lands the Huguenot refugees were strengthening the competitors of France. During his last forty years, none the less, the wars and persecutions had obscured rather than prevented many forward movements in religious life. Catholics and Protestants alike had made new efforts towards holy living. As early as in 1675, the so-called Pietistic movement in Germany was inspired by the teachings of the gentle Lutheran pastor, Philip Jacob Spener. Spener was reinforced by the vigorous theologian Francke (1663–1727), a Lübeck youth who read through the Hebrew testament seven times within a single year. Conspicuous as the benefactor of orphan children, Francke forbade them to seek pleasure outside religion by skating, swimming or such unedifying pursuits. A new spirit rather than a new sect, Pietism aimed at deepening spiritual life among Protestants by improved teaching, by study circles, by an increase of the share of laymen in church government, and, above all, by diffusing the assumption that greater fervour was to be expected from both priest and congregation. Its influence was wide enough to make it rank among the forces which produced the later literature of feeling. Its warmer atmosphere spread through all Teutonic countries and quickened not a few in every class before it faded away.

By stressing Christian feeling and Puritan standards rather than novel organization or dogma, Pietism naturally tended to promote union between the churches. The gap between Rome and Wittenberg had once more proved too wide, but that between Wittenberg and Geneva might perhaps have been bridged a century before their union in the Evangelical Church in 1817. The Prussian Frederick I (1688–1713), who as a Calvinist ruling Lutheran and Catholic provinces was compelled to be tolerant and to hope for Protestant reunion, was unfortunately succeeded by the narrow and aggressive "Sergeant King," Frederick William I (1713–40), and the dreams of union vanished. The Prussian army, however, stood ranked against Catholic persecution, while in Prussia herself a far-reaching campaign for popular education began. England at the same time took the lead in practical and fruitful toleration.

> "For modes of faith let graceless zealots fight,
> His can't be wrong whose life is in the right"

wrote the English Catholic poet, thus formulating what oft was thought but ne'er so well expressed.

Movement in Catholic Europe

Throughout the century, despite the resistance of some governments, the Protestants of Europe continued to establish new religious groups and sects. The fact testifies both to the inadequacy of the existing churches and to the lively interest of the Teutonic countries in religion. Among the Catholics, zeal could show itself only in new Orders, new devotional organizations and increased activity, but these were not wanting. Spener found a Catholic counterpart in the famous Quietist, Michael Molinos of Saragossa (1627–97). Although he died in the prison of the Inquisition, his teaching of passive self-surrender to the influence of God was diffused by Madame Guyon, the mystic, and by Fénélon, whose eminent wisdom and goodness caused Marlborough and Prince Eugene to spare his diocese of Cambrai. This great French pair, surviving until 1715, secured the religion of the heart from extinction in the foremost of Catholic countries.

The Jansenists

At the same time the vigour of Jansenism and the struggle of its followers with the Jesuits at least secured the French Church against stagnation. Although in 1715 no less than seventy-seven years had passed since the death of Jansen, bishop of Ypres, bitter controversy still raged round his doctrine of divine grace. Two years before, the papal bull *Unigenitus* had condemned 101 propositions associated with his name, only to divide the Catholics of France. Quesnel (1634–1719), the revered theologian from whose work the propositions were taken, survived, and claimed, despite the Pope, to remain within the bosom of the Church. Jansenists were eminent in education, in philanthropy, in literature. Secession from Rome formed no part of their design. They proposed from within the Church to restore it to its primitive purity of faith and order, and dreamed once more that a general council might reverse the verdict of the Pope.

According to their opponents, cautious Jansensists attempted to regularize their position within the Church by substituting " grace efficacious in itself " for the " necessitating grace " which had incurred the papal condemnation. Abandoning the heretical sense of the offending propositions, they remained " the fanatical preachers of a discouraging rigorism, which they adorned with the names of virtue and austerity." Under the pretext of combating abuses, they antagonized

" the incontestable characteristics of Catholicism, especially its unity of government, the traditional continuity of its customs, and the legitimate part which heart and feeling play in its worship. With all their skilful extenuations, they bore the mask of the levelling, innovating and arid spirit of Calvinism" (*Cath. Encycl.*).

To the whole-hearted Jansenist, the general acceptance of *Unigenitus* seemed nothing less than the apostasy which the Apocalypse foretold.

The Convulsionists

In Holland, the refuge of French firebrands, Jansenism was to lead to a definite severance. There the "Old Roman" Church retained the apostolical succession, the celibacy of the clergy and the use of Latin in public worship. In the French capital, on the other hand, the strangest of Catholic cults, that of the Convulsionists, owed its origin to the Jansenism of 1715. The devout ascetic, François de Paris, was born there in 1690. He beame a deacon in 1720, but found the path to the priesthood barred against him by his refusal to recognize the authority of *Unigenitus*. In 1727, a mere skeleton, he died and was buried in the little cemetery of St. Médard. Crowds flocked to his tomb, and miracles began to be wrought there by the holy soil. Many of the pilgrims fell into ecstasy or even into convulsions. In 1731 the Crown closed the cemetery, warning God, sneered freethinkers, that He must not work miracles in such a place. Devotions in honour of Deacon Paris, however, were privately carried on, and the convulsions which they provoked were sacred. During these fits the stricken person might prophesy or denounce the Pope and bishops. The Convulsionaries practised the most severe self-torment, extending in some cases to actual crucifixion. Soil from the Deacon's burying-place, or water which had been in contact with it, was credited with the power to render all such wounds harmless. On Good Friday, 1759, in the presence of two dozen priests and men of all ranks, an elderly sister was first severely beaten at her own request, and then, for the third time, crucified. For more than three hours she remained nailed by hands and feet to a cross which was inclined at various angles to the ground as she directed. Meanwhile, for about twenty-five minutes, a younger sister had endured crucifixion in a somewhat milder form. The Convulsionists declared that God directed them to submit to other tortures and made them invulnerable. Women predominated among them, and although the movement spread beyond the walls of Paris its adherents were never numerous. Its Jansenist origin did not prevent the condemnation of its alleged miracles by the doctors within the Jansenist ranks.

International Organizations

In the relatively simple conditions of 1715, it is possible to form a fairly accurate picture of how Europeans lived and how their states associated. Greater mystery, however, surrounds those international organizations which have woven glittering threads into the web of eighteenth-century life. The exploits of almost any of the amazing adventurers, from Görtz to Casanova, who played their part in the life and politics of the age usually made men say that behind such an one stood the Jesuits and Freemasons and possibly the Rosicrucians or the Jews. Some of these organisms played an undeniable part in history, and all are known to have influenced important statesmen. They represented, moreover, avenues of escape from the routine of a too inert and traditional world. Some study of them, therefore, seems indispensable to the story of a century to which they made an indeterminable contribution.

The Jesuits

A century and three-quarters had passed since Loyola's Company of Jesus first received the approval of the Pope. It remained an international force of marked activity and unquestionable power. Jesuits had incited Sobieski to save Vienna from the Turk and Louis XIV to drive heresy from France. They converted Augustus of Saxony. They educated the youth of many lands and organized the relief of the sick and poor.

> "The end principally proposed by this order," wrote an English observer early in the eighteenth century, "is to gain converts to the Romish Church; with which view they disperse themselves in every country and nation, and with amazing industry and address pursue the end of their institution. No difficulty so great that they cannot surmount, no danger so imminent that they will not undergo, no crimes so shocking that have not been perpetrated by them for the service of their cause."

In Protestant eyes, deluded by an honest mistranslation which suggested that his Superior might direct a Jesuit to commit mortal sin, they retained the secrecy, efficiency, pervasiveness and lack of scruple with which they had been credited in the sixteenth century. Their marvellous organization with its matchless economy of force, certainly survived. The Fathers still chose a General for life and endowed him, in name at least, with absolute power. At the same time nothing was neglected that might ensure the use of this power for proper ends. A residence in Rome was assigned to him with the attendance of five Assistants, representing Spain, France, Italy, Germany and Portugal. As of old, the chief security for the order lay in the practice of mutual confession and in the extraordinarily prolonged and careful training which every Jesuit received. The professed fathers, indeed, spent seventeen years in preparation and none were admitted at a lesser age than thirty-three. In 1715 the Order numbered some 20,000 members and its activities were world-wide. Distant missions at once bore witness to its zeal and drafted the most vigorous Jesuits out of Europe. Although driven from Japan, they were active in China, India and Persia and supreme in Paraguay. In Poland they had almost made the monarchy, the nobles and the religious policy of the State. There and in France, where they had sided with the King against the Pope, their influence was perhaps the most conspicuous. Their triumph over the Jansenists of Port Royal in 1710 had been signal and shocking. Their learning and devotion, their hold on education in the foremost state of Europe and their quiet influence over the princes and nobles of the Catholic world seemed to ensure their future power. At the same time, however, evil omens were not wanting. As the frenzy roused by Titus Oates had proved, a secret society may easily be made a scapegoat. The Glorious Revolution shut against them the doors of Britain. In 1705 their forty-five establishments in Holland were closed, and the exiles were stigmatized as disturbers of the public peace. None the less, internal decline formed their greatest danger. No written constitution can prevail for six generations against human nature. Although forbidden to interfere in politics, they did so ; although debarred from commerce, they engaged in it, for wealth and power ; and some broke their vow of poverty. As of old, moreover, their privileged position and corporate loyalty could not always be acceptable to bishops, cardinals or Pope. Meanwhile, the growing unity and vigour of the monarchies raised up a mightier rival. The Jesuit constitution, conferring unlimited authority upon the General, was not publicly known. Statesmen, however, might infer it from what they saw, and turn to crush an alien body in the State. No less dangerous to an authoritarian Order was the rise of a new literature of free thought, first in England and Holland, and now, though cautiously veiled, in France.

Jesuit Glory and Decay

These dangers germinated for half a century from the death of Louis XIV. During that time the existence of the Jesuits intensified the suspicion of the Protestant against the Catholic world.

The Freemasons

Freemasonry, another world-wide institution, resembles Jesuitry in its unquestionable influence and in the mystery which surrounds it. In the eighteenth century Frederick the Great and the sons of George III were prominent among its adepts, and it played no small part in the French Revolution. " A peculiar system of morality, veiled in allegory and illustrated by symbols," its basis appears to be the recognition of the Great Architect of the Universe, and its object union in promoting the general welfare of mankind. As a rival in the search after divine truth, unsectarian, upholding liberty of conscience, and a universal religion of humanity, freemasonry is a standing affront to Rome and no Catholic may join the order.

In 1715, the craft had a long existence if not a full history behind it. Connected perhaps by direct descent with Solomon and his temple, it had left its footprints even among savage races. In modern Masonry, the records of an Edinburgh lodge date back to 1599. A century later, the motto, " God is our guide," was supplemented by the words, " In the Lord is all our trust." The religious character of a movement often suspected of being subversive and even atheist was thereby emphasized. The refusal to initiate Jews may be ascribed to the wish to keep Masonry undenominational and Christian.

The next years were destined to contribute much to the organization of the order. Here England took the lead. The mother Grand Lodge of the world is said to be that founded in London in 1717. York followed in 1725 and remained a rival for two generations. Gibraltar, Calcutta, Ireland, the New England Boston and Jamaica possessed Grand Lodges by 1742. Meanwhile a fundamental question was being raised. Should brethren found new and independent lodges wherever they happened to be, or should Grand Lodges exercise some supervision ? The English favoured the unitary principle and other nations followed. Again, who should be admissible to membership ? Despite one notable exception, women were excluded, and by due regard to rank our eighteenth-century Masons displayed their elegance of mind. The French and Germans surpassed us, translating Gentleman by *Gentilhomme*, a less elastic term. Admission to the brotherhood, however, in itself conferred a kind of rank upon a Mason, and the order came to regard itself as closer to chivalry than to craftsmanship.

From its origins and nature Masonry was unlikely to attain to any quasi-Jesuit unity or elaborate organization. Non-masons criticized it as a set of mutual benefit societies for securing appointments and even verdicts in the courts at their expense. As the century progressed it became clear that the new force made for tolerance and cosmopolitanism and that it trained men for common action and for progress. Not a few of the French revolutionary leaders sat in lodge.

Rosicrucians

Freemasonry with its mystery and ritual undoubtedly did something to satisfy the widespread desire of man for brotherhood, for secret societies and for pomp. The deeper craving to possess superhuman powers and hidden knowledge prompted some to join the far less determinate fraternity of the Rosy Cross. As the century progressed, observers were discussing the relationship between the Masons and the Rosicrucians, both suspected of dabbling in the occult. Although some Rosicrucians may have influenced some masonic lodges, however, the two bodies have different origins, different histories and different natures. The Rosicrucians were not organized local benefit societies, but philosophers striving to imbue themselves with the mystic wisdom of the East, and to penetrate the deepest depths of the Divine Nature. Pseudo-history invented for them a fifteenth-century founder named Rosenkreuz, initiated by Arab philosophers in the Holy Land whence he brought back to Germany the key to knowledge. The sign of the Rosy Cross, symbol of the light hidden in all things, survives, however, in earlier monuments, Indian, Egyptian, Greek and Roman. In the eighteenth century the Rosicrucians constitute an indeterminate factor, powerful when it stirred the minds of thinkers or of grandees but unintelligible to the many. More universal than Masonry in its appeal, the doctrine claimed women and Jews as its adherents, and proved better suited to the East than to the West. It was naturally invoked by those charlatans claiming supernatural powers in whom the century abounded. When men and women believed in a miracle-working "east," the alchemist found ready credence. In one famous instance a woman paid large sums to an adventurer who was prepared to transmute her into a man.

The true Rosicrucians apparently believed that God created two original principles, Light and Darkness, from which arose the spiritual and the temporal worlds. The temporal world contained three spheres, the highest filled with the celestial fire and inhabited by nine orders of good angels. All things were produced by the struggle between light and darkness and in even the darkest object there survived a hidden light. Rosicrucians could pass and repass between their own world and the next, bringing thence such trophies as the elixir of life and the stone whose touch changes baser metals into gold. While the Christian expositor of hell poured scorn on the notion of "immaterial fire," the Rosicrucian claimed that with such fire he could "conquer the false knowledge and the deceiving senses which bind the human soul as in its prison." In his view the music of the spheres resounded when the sun crossed the planets in their paths. Earthly music, a faint memory of the heavenly, mastered men through their emotions. All nature, indeed, owed its form to "melodious combinations of the cross-movement of the holy light playing over the lines of the planets." Master of such mysteries and indifferent to the world of sense, the Rosicrucian was at once the proudest and the meekest of mankind.

The Jews

While Jesuits, Masons and Rosicrucians might pass unobserved, no one who scanned the face of Europe in 1715 could fail to perceive the Jew. His absence, indeed, was an index of the willingness of any country to be bound by medieval Church decrees. Thus Spain and Portugal refused to admit the enemies of Christ. In consequence the Iberian Jews, the best and ablest among the threescore Jewish tribes, had carried their unique financial acumen and culture to other lands, notably to Holland and to England. In those countries two generations of growing trade had made Jewish assistance indispensable. Even there, however, the Jews possessed no legal rights. In other countries they were secluded in the Ghetto, shut out from gilds and universities.

and compelled to wear their beards or a distinctive dress. The result was that the roads were speckled with peddlers belonging to the lower Jewish tribes, while the inborn talents of the race and the knowledge notably of hygiene and medicine which they had brought from the East were hardly tapped by Europe.

According to a tolerant Protestant, the Jews were still

> "among men what rabbits are among beasts, since they multiply with astonishing fertility and ruin the land which they inhabit. Useless for agriculture and all necessary arts, they may be tolerated, but never made the basis of a population. . . . Experience shows that a commercial state cannot altogether dispense with Jews, and that a moderate number, as in England, Holland or Hamburg, is useful, but that to have too many, as in Prague or Poland, is highly detrimental. . . . It is barbarous to treat them as does the Inquisition in Spain and Portugal, and unjust to overwhelm them with burdens as sometimes in Germany or Poland."

Jews and Taxation

As of old, the Jews were still used by Christian princes as a means of taxing their subjects without rousing resistance. Owing no allegiance to the Church, the Jew could not be bound by the papal condemnation of usury. He might therefore amass much wealth, for no Christian could ply his trade and high interest alone could compensate him for his special risks. Chief of these was that of a sudden levy from the prince, while the Christian subjects applauded the pillage of their tormentor, forgetting that the wealth he surrendered came from themselves. A Catholic prince thus circumvented the ordinances of religion, like a modern Jew who employs a Christian gardener to breed his pigs.

In 1715, then, the future of the Jew in Europe seemed to depend on the struggle between hereditary prejudice and the talent of a tenacious race. But the growth of trade, with its attendant merchanting and banking, must favour the superior tribes. A general rise in Jewish status, like the emancipation of Catholics ruled by Protestants and of slaves, awaited the growth of new thought about human rights.

BIBLIOGRAPHICAL NOTE

See Bibliographical Note and Bibliography at the end of Chapters I and II. The following works may be consulted :—

A

L. Cahen : *Les Querelles religieuses et parlementaires sous Louis XV* (1913).

M. Cheke : *Dictator of Portugal : the Marquis of Pombal, 1699–1782* (1938).

K. Clark : *The Gothic Revival* (2nd ed. 1949).

R. Clark : *Strangers and Sojourners at Port Royal* (1929).

J. M. Creed and J. S. Boys Smith : *Religious Thought in the Eighteenth Century* (1934).

A. Gazier : *Histoire générale du mouvement janséniste.* 2 vols. (1922).

R. F. Gould : *The History of Freemasonry.* 6 vols. (1884–87).

T. Kendrick : *The Lisbon Earthquake* (1956).

D. Knoop and G. P. Jones : *A Short History of Freemasonry to 1730* (1940).

L. von Pastor : *The History of the Popes*, vols. XXXIII–XL [to 1799] (trans. 1941–53).

E. Préclin : *Les Jansénistes du XVIIIe siècle et la constitution civile du clergé* (1929).

E. Préclin and E. Jarry : *Les Luttes politiques et doctrinales aux XVIIe et XVIIIe siècles* (1955).

P. Smith : *History of Modern Culture.* II (1934).

A. B. Yorke Long : *Music at Court* (1954).

B

J. L. de Azevedo : *O Marquez de Pombal e a sua época, 1699–1782* (1909).

C. Burney : *A General History of Music.* 4 vols. (1776–89).

C. Burney : *The Present State of Music in France and Italy : or, Journal of a tour through those countries, undertaken to collect materials for a General History of Music* (1771).

B. Dobrée (ed.) : *Lord Chesterfield : Letters to his son.* Vol. IV of the six-volume edition (1932).

Life of Lady Guion (1772). [Mme Jeanne Marie Guyon]. Her autobiography, in two volumes, was translated in 1897.

CHAPTER IV

EUROPEAN TRADE IN 1715

IMPORTANCE AS A FACTOR IN INTERNATIONAL RELATIONS

The Wealth of Nations c. 1715

IN 1719 a statistician endeavoured to assess the total value of the currencies which then circulated among the European peoples. Both the sum arrived at, £100,000,000, and its division between the several countries were highly conjectural, but they may serve as a record of contemporary reputation for wealth. Of the hundred millions, France was credited with eighteen, and Britain and Ireland with sixteen, figures attesting the high repute of Britain for individual riches, since the French were fully twice as numerous. The Low Countries came next with twelve million, followed with ten million by Italy, where the Venetians alone perhaps equalled the Dutch in population. Germany, Hungary and Switzerland were estimated as possessing nine million. To Spain, whither colonial gold and silver came without remaining, eight millions were ascribed, and to Turkey in Europe a like sum. Portugal and Russia had six million apiece ; Poland, four ; and all Scandinavia, only three. If combined with the amounts of their respective debts, the statement affords valuable hints as to the restrictions upon governments which desired to make war but could not afford the cost.

Trade and Politics

The poverty and weakness of the nations was far more important, however, because men were thereby impelled to seek wealth by way of trade. Trade, for reasons that will presently appear, meant chiefly distant trade by sea. Markets, in many cases, must be seized or stormed, and the approach to them guarded by fleets and forces. In seeking them, the governments of Europe competed, and even tended to become huge trading organizations. Hence sprang the most irksome limitations on their subjects' freedom. History, religion, seamanship, technical invention, arms and exploration all set in motion the kaleidoscope of European trade.

Utrecht and Trade

Trade considerations most of all rendered the peace of Utrecht an epoch-making settlement. In the general history of Europe it ranks with the peace of Westphalia, which ushered in modern times, and with the Vienna Congress, which prepared the nineteenth century. When the armies which had been fighting for the Spanish Succession and against French trading policy were sent home, no one could say that the roots of European strife had been destroyed. If indeed " no treaty between civilized states has ever embodied so many challenges to war," the interests of trade were largely to blame. Utrecht settled the immediate disposal of the Spanish empire, which was vital to every trading nation, but it left the general question of empire overseas unsolved. History had shown that neither Portugal, the Dutch, nor Spain could hold in perpetuity what each had gained. Utrecht left the prize more than ever alluring, and the French and British eager and competent to seize it. The history, so called, of Europe during the next quarter of a century at least has gained a name for unattractiveness because these underlying realities have found in it too small a place. Swayed by half-unconscious impulses to struggle for distant power and trade, the foremost nations indeed behaved somewhat absentmindedly in Europe.

Influence of Louis XIV

States, like people, change but slowly their notion of the framework of their lives and of the most appropriate way of living. The fifteenth-century man of taste, who would have been ashamed to own a printed book, finds a spiritual successor in the man who scorns " tinned music." Although eighteenth-century Europe was far from stagnant it was inevitably European, finding its world in one small and stable continent to a degree inconceivable to-day. Neither the French nor their neighbours could soon shake off the spell of generations of French ascendancy irradiated with the glory of Louis XIV. Aggrandizement in Europe, royal magnificence, religious uniformity, centralized government, standing armies, royal patronage of art and letters, watchful diplomacy, state self-assertion abroad—such was the legacy to Europe of the greatest " actor of majesty " of any age, the cynosure of Europe who " died standing on the pedestal of majesty."

For reasons of necessity as well as by personal preference, Louis had turned his back on the navy, overseas trade, and empire in favour of the army and hegemony in Europe. Meanwhile the world was moving towards a new imperial age. Navy and empire became more than ever the hen and the egg of politics. As a basis for transoceanic wealth and power, geographical situation counted for much, but ships and seamanship for more. In this the outstanding feature was the rise of Britain. During the War of the Spanish Succession it was commonly held that the French were stronger at sea than either the Dutch or British, but inferior to both combined. The peace left France mistress of a vast coastline, numerous ports, and fisheries which formed a fruitful nursery of seamen. She continued to build larger and faster ships than those of Britain. Colbert, long reputed the greatest Finance Minister who had ever lived, had set the fashion of fostering French shipping. Every war with Britain meant heavy loss by sea, but within twenty years of Utrecht, France was sending some six hundred ships westwards across the ocean and employing some nine hundred more in trade with the Peninsula and the Mediterranean.

Trading Competition French, Dutch, British

Holland, moreover, a power created and maintained by commerce, remained important at sea even when politically exhausted by her continental wars. The advantages of cheap money, cosmopolitan training, tolerance, and unrivalled experience were hers, with priceless possessions overseas. The jealous proprietor of Java and Guiana, furnished with trading stations extending from the Cape to the shores of Japan, herself admirably placed for navigation to the Rhine, the Elbe, the North Sea, and the Baltic, she remained for generations the foremost carrying trader in the world.

Britain, however, possessed rare advantages for the career upon which she had been launched by Cromwell. No competing nation enjoyed so central a position, so serviceable a coast-line, or so fine a supply of raw materials for ships. English and Scots, with their way to make, might well show more vigour than the Dutch heirs to their fathers' riches. British oak, again, was unsurpassed, and the hemp and tar, the flax and resin which she needed lay convenient across the North Sea or in her Atlantic colonies. She was already building warships whose length exceeded fifty yards and tonnage 1,500 tons, and which carried ninety guns. These were seconded by ships of forty guns and size proportionate, while armed merchantmen could easily be turned into commissioned ships of war. Numerous docks with gates had been built along the Thames and Medway, and Liverpool and Bristol were following suit. British navigation and seamanship developed hand in hand. Their concomitants were trade, wealth and empire. Thus the sea powers enriched Europe, widened her influence and at the same time reduced the relative importance of her domestic controversies.

Trade and History

That the Utrecht peace was largely inspired by trade, and that trade largely determined the history of the next generation—these are patent facts which cannot be gainsaid. Colonial rivalries and colonial wars take a leading place in the record of Europe for a century at least. If, since 1492, the European nations had sought colonies, their object had been chiefly trade. Trade had tempted the Portuguese to form a colonial empire and to monopolize its exchanges. Trade alone prompted the Dutch to rely upon native merchants rather than to multiply their own factories, or to form permanent colonies overseas. Some held that the true function of New England was to feed the West Indies in the interest of English trade. It was hopes of trade that had induced the French to form establishments beyond the ocean, and that tempted the Danes, the Swedes, the Brandenburgers, and even the Emperor to follow their example. To gain wealth by agriculture, nations must inherit or painfully create a large labour-force and a large area of fertile land. To gain wealth by trade, numbers and size were not essential. Sir William Petty declared that three-quarters of the trade of Western Europe was in the hands of the English, the Dutch and the Scandinavians. Scotland at the same time made a bold stroke for supremacy in world trade. Not long after the Darien Company had proved delusive, Britain was accused of striving to monopolize the commerce of the world. The Emperor hoped by tearing up a treaty and creating free ports at Ostend and Trieste to make Germany once more a great commercial nation. This all-alluring trade ran for the most part in channels worn deep by time. Nature and history had decreed that the chief of it should consist in exchanges between Western Europe and the regions which Europeans loosely termed the Indies. As the Abbé Raynal pointed out, the Egyptians had supplied India with the same commodities that had been exported thither ever since, namely

"woollen manufactures, iron, lead, copper, some small pieces of workmanship in glass and silver, in exchange for ivory, ebony, tortoiseshell, white and printed linens, silks, pearls, precious stones, cinnamon, spices, and particularly frankincense; which was a perfume the most in esteem from its being used in divine worship and contributing to the gratification of princes."

America, by providing gold and silver, made it possible for Queen Elizabeth Farnese to declare that the riches of the world passed through her husband's hands, but that the smallest part remained in Spain. Tea from the Far East, of which in 1734 the Dutch brought 415,970 chests and 369,577 lb., might stand for many other recent developments of the luxury class. Logwood (mahogany) alone was cut by the English to the annual value of £60,000. Rude as was the age, not a few surprising international exchanges had arisen. Great quantities of rubbed and moulded bricks came from Holland to English ports as far apart as Exeter and Lynn. Tallard complained in 1699 that France bought from England enormous quantities of horses, mohair, ribbons, lace, cider, beer, glass bottles, Spanish wine, cloth, lead and tin. The balance of trade, he held, was somewhat restored by the great number of English who visited Paris. The Moors of West Africa were eager to exchange their gum for blue Manchester goods, coarse brown sugar, sealing-wax, foolscap and munitions. French "toys" or "fripperies" commanded a ready sale as far away as Russia. All polite Europe adored the wares of China. As citations from contemporary treaties are advanced to prove, the governments of Europe were busily engaged in making their several dominions self-sufficient, in monopolizing colonial trade, and in finding out fresh manufactures for sale to non-Europeans.

Conditions of Trade c. 1715

SUBSERVIENCE TO POLICY AND NATURAL CONDITIONS

In many respects the policy of European governments towards trade resembled that to which they have returned in the years succeeding the Great War. Economic nationalism then demanded that a country should, if possible, buy from another goods of a less value in money than those which it sent there by way of sale. The balance, it was thought, would be paid in gold or silver, which would either set trade in motion at home or be laid by for use in war. Prussia thus stored up in the royal vaults of Spandau a treasure equal to a whole year's revenue. To send goods abroad, moreover, was to maintain the supply of workmen at home, and perhaps also the supply of ships and seamen. To this end there was a constant search for fresh markets and new trade routes. A passage to the Indies round the north of Asia or from Canada by an undiscovered river flowing west ranked with the discovery of a sub-Arctic continent whose inhabitants would be eager for woollen goods. Among lands already known, "that the nations that favour us most, ought to be most favoured by us" was held to be "a maxim in politics not to be denied." It was the more obvious because men still believed that in an exchange of goods one party must lose what the other gained.

A British view

The arguments employed in 1713, to determine whether Britain should favour trade with France, Italy, Spain or Portugal, show the ideas which influenced the commercial policy of the century. Spain, it was urged, sent us wool to employ our industrious poor, and oil to work up that wool. In return, she took from us great quantities of woollen manufactures, pilchards, herrings and salmon, with Irish beef, butter, hides and tallow. Better still, Spain received much fish from Newfoundland, wealth, as it were, mined from the sea, and that by men who were thereby made capable of serving in the navy. Portugal and Italy did the like, but sent us no wool. Portugal, however, furnished materials for dyes, and Italy raw silk, thus aiding the weavers of Canterbury, Norwich, and London. All three nations, being distant, gave employment to comparatively large ships with crews and guns fit for action in time of war. All three, moreover, took more goods from us than we from them, and paid the balance in precious metals.

France, on the other hand, actually deprived us of raw wool, and of dye-stuffs which helped her to rob us of the Turkey trade. She laid heavy duties on our fish and refined sugar. Her monopoly in tobacco enabled her to force down the price, so that Virginia and Maryland might well think of making for themselves goods that we were wont to send them. French linen and paper actually threatened the British manufacturer of those goods. French brandy competed with West

Indian spirit. French silks appealed powerfully to half a million British women, French wines to perhaps as many British men. Unrestricted trade with France, therefore, would drain us of money and render us inferior by land and sea.

Ere long, indeed, more virile and penetrating views on trade policy found expression.

> " The Grandeur of their Nation and of their Colonies leaning on the same principles," argued one British publicist, " Great Britain will always be the most formidable Power in Europe, while her subjects preserve their Freedom and increase their Trade. To both these Ends their Colonies exceedingly contribute, for the People are as free in them, or rather more so, than in their native Island. . . . The digging of Gold and Silver is a sickly and slavish business ; those who enjoy the profits of it are proud, lazy and timorous ; whereas such as cultivate Tobacco, raise Sugar-canes, or plant Rice are strong, robust People ; and as their commodities are bulky, so the transporting of them occasions an increase of shipping. . . . Hence it is evident that in proportion as the Spanish colonies flourish, the real power of Spain must decrease : whereas the increase of the English Colonies is the increase of the English power."

Man *versus* the State

Trade in the early eighteenth century, as in every age since history began, was conditioned by a struggle between the subject and the State. While the individual thirsts for riches, the ruler is determined to subordinate private comfort to the increase of the collective power. Except in moments of supreme religious or patriotic exaltation, men have always sought to satisfy their individual wants, and that with the least possible expense or trouble to themselves. Governments, on the other hand, have for ever interfered, crying that the expenditure which their subjects propose will be detrimental to the common weal. To eat, drink or wear this or that, they declare, will be anti-social, for it will weaken your mind or body, or deprive your neighbour of his livelihood, or enrich the foreigner, or fail to enrich your own State, or endanger it in time of war. Hence come heavy taxes on goods, prohibition, Navigation Laws, sumptuary edicts, commands to clothe corpses in woollen and the like, with grants of money towards substitutes produced at home. In 1715, the first object of the chief European nations was to safeguard their independent food supply; the second, to enrich themselves by commerce, particularly by commerce overseas. Small as it must seem to modern eyes, this commerce was then incomparably lucrative and vital. New trades, indeed, were stirring. The old and simple voyages by which wine was brought northwards from Bordeaux or millstones from Spain, while fish or amber or hemp or lead was sent in exchange were yielding in importance to ventures across the ocean. The chief potential customers lived in western Europe and southern Asia, with the Baltic and Mediterranean lands following them in importance. The desire of Europeans for spices, silks, the precious metals and other luxuries was boundless, but what could they offer in exchange ? Spices still came in ever-growing masses from the colonies, Portuguese, Spanish, Dutch, British or French. In the languages of the Continent, "colonial wares" signified primarily spices, with such luxuries as tobacco, tea, coffee, cocoa and sugar. With these were associated invaluable medicines, such as opium, ipecacuanha and quinine, and substances which, like cochineal and indigo, ministered to man's thirst for colour.

Defoe, indeed, did not hesitate to divide our imports from the East Indies into three classes, two of which he condemned. Such goods as china-ware, coffee, tea, Japan work, pictures, fans and screens were "trifling and unnecessary." Printed calicoes, chintz, wrought silks, block-tin, sugar, cotton, arrack, copper and indigo were "injurious." Goods necessary and useful included pepper, saltpetre, dye-stuffs, drugs, diamonds and raw silk. The criterion, of course, was promotion of British manufacture or its displacement.

Tradition and Careers

The "cherished changelessness" of the early eighteenth century was peculiarly inimical to trade. A prince, and hardly any but a prince, might disturb society, whether by calling men to the Colours, or introducing manufactures, or initiating great public works, or driving away his subjects on grounds of religion, or procuring colonists from other lands. Louis XIV had been the grand exemplar of all these modes of change except the last. How much the Protestant countries owed to him, alike in military and industrial power, can never be fully known. Perhaps the greatest boon conferred by the exiled Huguenots was educational, both by direct teaching and by the widespread inspiration of their model lives. Migrations like that which followed the Revocation were, however, rare. If, as in Scotland, population increased beyond the means of subsistence, men must find new homes or new callings to escape starvation. Man's chief hope, however, lay in the creation somewhere of an exchangeable surplus of goods and in its disposal by way of trade. Let one community anywhere produce more than its own needs required, and the impulse would be given to attempt the satisfaction of other needs by exchange of products. Capital might then be accumulated and the standard of life must tend to rise.

The Springs and Routes of Commerce

The accumulation of a mobile surplus anywhere, however, was checked by the conditions of human life. All through Europe, with less or greater ease as they spread from north to south, men fed and clothed themselves from the acres round them. Every man longed for the products of other climates. Nature and history had made it hard for some and far less hard for others to gratify their desires. The crofter could scarcely hope ever to gain an appreciable surplus. In any year, the vine-grower might be rewarded with a harvest which could be turned into desirable, durable, and portable goods far exceeding the value of what would have repaid his toil. The exchange of local surpluses within Europe followed familiar lines. Coals from Newcastle, wines from Oporto and Bordeaux, fashionable luxuries from France, cloth from England, dried fish from northern ports, corn from Poland, hemp and flax from Russia—such were standard exports. Regarding commercial Europe in the mass, however, it is evident that nature and history had combined to cramp her on every side save one. To the north lay frigid seas and barren countries. Fishing and whaling, indeed, brought wealth, and a few ships made summer voyages to Reykyavik or Archangel. On this side, however, no great commercial route could be devised. The vast, sparsely peopled and almost roadless plains of Poland and Russia likewise forbade much land trading from Europe towards the east. South-east and south, the Mohammedan powers reduced commerce to an affair of fitful favour. Only towards the west could Europe trade with freedom. The Barbary Powers, it is true, menaced her departing ships, while pirates, hostile nations and European rivals must be reckoned with further on. Voyages to Africa, India, America or the Far East demanded stout vessels, skilled navigators, sagacious statesmen and abundant capital, but they promised great returns. Both naturally and artificially, they were the exclusive right of a few European nations, and, within those nations, of a few persons and a few ports. The coast-line from Leghorn to Hamburg, or at furthest to Copenhagen, alone afforded a reasonable base for trading success beyond the ocean. Of the ports which it comprised, many were unsuitable through their aspect towards the wind, or their tendency to silt up or their lack of communications with good inland markets. It was remarked that when the impetus which Colbert gave had faded, Marseilles and Havre were left to themselves, Nantes became choked with mud and the free ports ceased to be free. Governments, moreover, were not prepared to leave in private hands enterprises which might yield vast profits and give rise to local wars. Nor would those governments which had secured new avenues of commerce submit, if they could avoid it, to the intrusion of new competitors. The European states which had overseas possessions were still less willing to share their trade with others. Such were the conditions of that struggle for colonies and commerce which largely determined the European history of the century.

Robbery apart, however, how could both the wealth of individuals and of the nations be increased ? It was, in theory at least, always possible that some new treasure, such as a copper mine, might be discovered. The migrations of fish or an improvement in the breed of sheep might enrich particular communities and stimulate exchanges. The German princes of the eighteenth century created a new export by hiring out their troops to Britain. Many nations profited by the slave trade. Normally, however, men were content if they could feed and clothe their families and lay by some small reserve against disaster. " Novelty spells calamity " seemed wisdom to millions outside Russia, whence that proverb came.

The first Europeans to grapple successfully with the obstacles which man and nature opposed to eastern trade had been the Dutch. They brought spices by unbroken voyages across the Indian Ocean to Amsterdam, " the magazine of Europe," and thence distributed them to other lands. The cheap capital and technical experience thus acquired survived the wars of Louis XIV, and for a generation from his death they remained the foremost commercial nation. In the Baltic, they almost defied competition. They, and the English also, imported goods from the Levant in French ships, the officials conniving at the breach of rule, although the

Marsellais could soon declare that a million Frenchmen were dependent on that eastern trade. In their own eastern islands, at least, they showed themselves "enemies to all Europeans but such as are under their own government, underhand dealers and destroyers of your trade and people." The justification for this exclusiveness and cunning appeared in an annual dividend on Dutch East India Stock averaging 24 per cent. since 1605.

The Dead Hand and New Endeavour

Powerful forces, gathering momentum as they advanced, were none the less changing the economic life of Europe. The gild system was breaking down, while banking, stock jobbing and trading overseas were growing fast. Both the individual and the State, however, found themselves obstructed by the survivals from an earlier age. The Church had frowned on the desires of both. Man risked his soul by heaping up riches, and the claims of Cæsar must be kept down. Privileged laymen, whether *seigneurs* or corporations, clung to their ancient rights. Inertia, tradition, custom opposed all change. Ignorance and suspicion, as well as lack of roads and waterways, hindered free movement about the globe. It was for the enlightened and the progressive, whether rulers or companies or private persons, to overthrow all barriers which did not protect their several interests. Within each state, both rulers and public usually profited by the substitution of taxes on exports and imports for the old internal dues on transit and by the establishment of uniform currency, weights and measures. Roads, canals, harbours, posts—such general benefits the State alone could bring into being, and all of them enhanced its power. The enrichment of its subjects enabled them to pay more taxes : the increased accessibility of its markets favoured its own international trade; and its economic beneficence won for it the support of the many against the few. To accumulate treasure, to form a strong fleet, to acquire colonies and to promote overseas trade —such was the duty of eighteenth-century rulers and by performing it they abased all their internal rivals.

Eighteenth-Century Aristocracy

It cannot, however, be too soon or too strongly insisted that to modern eyes such State activity bore anything but a democratic stamp. The workman doubtless benefited by the widened market for his work. But he was himself by no means free to quit his country, nor, in many countries, his employer. Treasure was often gained by harsh and arbitrary taxes, soldiers and sailors by the pressgang or by sentence of the courts, colonies by transportation or the slave trade. No truth was less apprehended than that the prosperity of one people conduces to the prosperity of its neighbour. Every state strove for monopoly of processes, markets and sources of supply. Not a few, rightly convinced that population gives the key to plenty, took strong measures to keep up their herd of men. Taxes on bachelors and prizes for families of ten or twelve ranked among the mildest. Colbert had tried to people Canada by sending out shiploads of girls and commanding the garrison to marry them. In Russia it became the custom for the serfs on a well-managed estate to be formed into couples at eighteen and marched to a collective wedding. The growth of Prussian power owed much to the skill of her Hohenzollern rulers in importing immigrants from other lands.

Food Supply In 1715, however, the day was still far distant when any considerable section of the population could be fed from overseas, or even by a neighbouring nation. If, by whatever means, an excess of births over deaths could be accomplished, more food must forthwith be grown at home. The eighteenth century was therefore predestined to be an age of agricultural improvement. Here Holland led and England followed. These kindred peoples were becoming close-packed, while among their gentry wealth was diffused and a scientific temper prevailed. Over their countryside "the economical and beautiful gradation of ranks," squire, farmer and labourer gave them a great advantage over bailiff-ridden France. Rejecting marvellous recipes for crop-production, they turned to clover, turnips and improved rotation. Soon England could both feed her own increasing numbers and export grain to France, sometimes to the value of a million in a single year.

Britain possessed only some 300,000 tons of shipping, the stowage space of half a dozen monsters of to-day. The total value of her exports and imports only slightly exceeded £1 per head of her population. Most Continental countries must in the nature of the case fall short even of this. Products of considerable bulk, such as grain and timber, reached their home ports with difficulty, and transport by sea was slow and full of danger. The Baltic might be closed for several months by ice and was entered by a tortuous channel. The more open seas possessed few harbours which were not often blocked by adverse winds. When Castlereagh crossed to the Continent for the final struggle with Napoleon he was forced to wait three days to embark at Harwich and three nights to land in Holland.

THE SHIPS EMPLOYED

Vital to Europe as was her trade, however, the modern student may seek in vain for some clear conspectus of its working. The first necessity for trade, it may be said, is a surplus product desired by someone else who in his turn can produce a desirable surplus. The second, in 1715, was government favour, which often developed into governmental trading. The third, which stifled many attractive ventures in the birth, was transport to some accessible place of deposit. The fourth, of course, was ships fit to make the double journey across the sea. The attention of naval historians has unfortunately been concentrated chiefly upon ships of war. Between these and merchantmen, indeed, the contrast was in the eighteenth century far less striking than in the ages of steam and oil. Both showed in their design that they were descended from the ancient galley. Although the port-holes in the merchantman were inconveniently small for taking aim, she was equipped with guns. Any ocean-going ship might leave home in time of peace and be unable to return until many months after the outbreak of a sudden war. Many ships were uneconomically rigged, the better to sail in convoy. The seas, moreover, swarmed with pirates, the greatest that Roberts who commanded three stout vessels of his own, the largest mounting forty guns. Apart from war, therefore, a safe voyage demanded guns, and the outbreak of war brought trading-ships by scores into the royal navy. It was war and preparation for war that conduced to progress in the design of all ships, to the maintenance of building and dockyards, to the supply of materials for hulls, masts and sails, and to such hygiene as could be found in their arrangements. The naval secrets of every power lay at the mercy of an enemy who captured its newest vessel, and Britain thus learned much from France.

Merchantmen

Of trading-ships the records are most imperfect, and some of those which exist were based upon designedly misleading information. To escape taxation, many ships were described as smaller than they were, while some were built for smuggling goods into and out of distant lands. A further source of confusion is that subjects of one state, particularly of Britain, were often responsible for the merchant enterprises of another which competed with those of their own land.

From such records as exist, however, it would appear that few merchantmen reached 600 tons, and that most were of half that size or less. Much of the trade of the world was carried by ships about 24 yards long and one-third as broad, drawing about 12 feet of water and bound to provide food, drink and quarters for a crew of several scores of men. To work the ship, and, if need be, to man the decks and guns, no fewer would suffice. As the depth of the hold was about that of a room in a modern house, an urgent problem of 1715 was to safeguard men, provisions and cargo by pumping out the bilge water and supplying untainted air. When Anson sailed in 1740, of the veteran soldiers who were assigned to him " all those who had limbs and strength to walk out of Portsmouth deserted." " Biscuit so worm-eaten it was scarce anything but dust," " beef and pork likewise very rusty and rotten," " scurvy . . . every day lessening our number by six, eight and ten "—such were the ills from which they fled. Within a year, more than one half had perished, and the survivors sometimes lacked strength to fling the dead into the sea. In the ordinary course, wastage might be made up in foreign ports, by shipping Lascars and derelict Europeans.

The East Indiamen, though neither the swiftest nor the most capacious among ships, ranked as the stoutest and the most secure. These were built and maintained for the Company by " ship's husbands " who counted on making a comfortable fortune from the six voyages for which a ship was usually chartered. When strict measurements came to be enforced by law (1784) the best of these ships somewhat exceeded 1,300 tons and their crew numbered 130 or rather more. In 1715, English exports and imports were each officially valued at about £7,000,000, and the ships, both English and foreign, which were cleared outwards amounted to some 448,000 tons. In 1696, Dutch merchant shipping had been reckoned at 900,000 tons against 500,000 for England and 200,000 for the rest of Europe. The reversal of this predominance by the British and their chequered progress towards maritime autocracy formed one of the chief factors in the history of 1715 to 1814.

Mediterranean Storms and Pirates

Statistics and general statements about ships and trade, however, give but a faint idea of the conditions which prevailed. Here individual narrative rightly claims a place. The dangers of travel in the western Mediterranean could hardly be more vividly epitomized than by the Strassburg merchant Zetzner when he recorded his journey of October 25 to November 30, 1718. Desiring to reach Marseilles, he took passage on the *Duc d'Orléans* at Cadiz. The ship carried thirty guns, and her cargo included cochineal, indigo, and an illegal consignment of piastres. A contrary wind kept her two days in Cadiz, and before she passed Gibraltar, she was first becalmed and then damaged by a storm. In sight of Ceuta, three pirates from Algiers hove in sight, gorged in a fortnight with five Dutch or Spanish cargoes and five hundred new-made slaves. The *Duc d'Orléans* hoisted her flag, which should have protected Frenchmen and lawful cargo, but fled to avoid search for Spaniards, Dutch and English, with the prospect of general massacre if the search party found the piastres. She was, however, overhauled and boarded, but a friendly interpreter saved those on board from slavery or death. Next a storm drove her back to Gibraltar. A fresh start was made, but two pirates from Fez appeared. Arms were dealt out and the captain undertook to shoot or drown all cowards. Again they took refuge in Gibraltar and reflected on the stories of Christian slaves bound naked to stakes as targets for the corsairs' sword and lance. None the less they set out once more and even sheltered in Algiers, where fifteen thousand Christians were supposed to live in slavery. After another severe storm, with all hands to the pumps, they reached Minorca, only to meet fresh storms in the Gulf of Lyons and to be once more becalmed. At last, after thirty-six days' travel, a journey which might have been performed within some eleven hundred miles reached its joyful close.

BIBLIOGRAPHICAL NOTE

See Bibliographical Note at the end of Chapter I.
Add :—

A

J. N. L. Baker : *A History of Geographical Discovery and Exploration* (rev. ed. 1937).

J. S. Barbour : *A History of William Paterson and the Darien Company* (1907).

J. C. Beaglehole : *The Exploration of the Pacific* (1934).

P. Bonnassieux : *Les grandes compagnies de commerce* (1892).

F. C. Bowen : *From Carrack to Clipper : Sailing-ship models* (2nd rev. ed. 1948).

J. B. Brebner : *The Explorers of North America, 1492–1806* (1933).

J. H. Clapham : *A Concise Economic History of Britain from Earliest Times to 1750* (1949).

J. S. Corbett : *England in the Mediterranean.* II (1904).

W. H. B. Court : *A Concise Economic History of Britain from 1750 to Recent Times* (1954).

W. Cunningham : *Essay on Western Civilization in its Economic Aspect.* 2 vols. (1900–2).

T. W. Fulton : *The Sovereignty of the Sea* (1911).

H. Furber : *John Company at Work* (1948).

G. C. V. Holmes : *Ancient and Modern Ships.* 2 vols. (1900–6).

J. W. Jeudwine : *Religion, Commerce, Liberty, 1683–1793* (1925).

L. C. A. Knowles : *Economic Development of the British Overseas Empire.* Vols. II and III (1930–36).

P. Leroy-Beaulieu : *De la colonisation chez les peuples modernes* (6th ed. 1908).

L. M. Penson : *The Colonial Agents of the British West Indies : A Study in Colonial Administration mainly in the Eighteenth Century* (1924).

H. W. Richmond : *Seapower in the Modern World* (1934).

F. P. Robinson : *The Trade of the East India Company from 1709 to 1813* (1912).

L. S. Sutherland : *A London Merchant, 1695–1774* (1933).

W. C. B. Tunstall : *The Realities of Naval History* (1936).

C. H. Wilson : *Anglo-Dutch Commerce and Finance in the Eighteenth Century* (1941).

J. A. Williamson : *The Ocean in English History* (1941).

A. C. Wood : *A History of the Levant Company* (1935).

B

P. Clément : *Lettres, instructions et mémoires de Colbert* (1861).

W. Dampier : *A New Voyage round the World* (repr. 1937).

C. Davenant : *Essay on the East India Trade* (1697).

J. Hanway : *An Historical Account of the British Trade over the Caspian Sea : with a journal of travels from London through Russia into Persia ; and back again through Russia, Germany and Holland.* 4 vols. (1753). (3rd ed. 2 v. 1762).

E. Levasseur : *Histoire du commerce française* (1911–12).

D. Macpherson : *Annals of Commerce, Manufactures, Fisheries and Navigation.* 4 vols. (1805).

Abbé Raynal : *A philosophical and political history of the settlements and trade of the Europeans in the East and West Indies.* I (trans. 1783).

R. Walter (ed.) : *A Voyage round the World in the Years 1740, 1, 2, 3, 4 : compiled from papers and other materials of the Right Honourable George Lord Anson* (1748, 16th ed. 1781, new eds. 1911 and 1928).

CHAPTER V

THE STATES OF EUROPE[1]

IF we turn from a survey of the European society as a whole to a scrutiny of the several powers between which Europeans were divided, our first inquiry may well be into the relationship between Britain and her continental neighbours. Because William III and Marlborough had marshalled Europe for many years, and because George I was a German soldier, Britain in 1715 stood in more than normal intimacy with the Continent, where Locke, the exponent of her Revolution, commanded an unusual respect for British thought. In the Baltic, in the Low Countries and in Portugal as well as in more distant continents she had vital interests to protect. What was to be her policy?

Insecurity of the Hanoverians

For thirty years at least, from the 'Fifteen to the 'Forty-five, a great factor in British policy was fear. A strong fleet and a full treasury could do little to cure disunion at home, and how far disunion extended no statesman could safely say. Throughout Europe, monarchy was the index of the success or failure of a State. Where the crown was strong so also was the nation, and no nation could be strong whose crown lacked power or skill. By her Revolution England had pointed the way towards a strong crown managed in the interests of the nation by others beside the King. Limited monarchy, however, was still novel and incomplete, while centuries had yet to pass before it could be based upon the will of the whole people. In 1715, a great section of the British nation believed that the Revolution had been a crime, and that by the law of God a Stuart could claim the throne. Such was probably the secret creed of George I. A section which was perhaps more powerful held that popery disqualified the heir, but that his rights revived so soon as he abandoned Rome and qualified for headship of the Church of England. A third section, threatening to include the great

[1] Compare map at end of book.

mass which felt rather than reflected, would at any cost rid the country of the Hanoverians. On the same side were groups with grievances or aspirations of their own, English Catholics, Scots detesting the Union, Irish remembering Cromwell.

The existence of all these people forced the King to rely upon the Whigs, and the Whigs to tremble. George himself was a veteran of the wars who possessed a safe retreat to his Electorate if London proved intolerable. An elderly autocrat, performing an unwelcome duty, he came with few illusions to a country which within fifty years had beheaded Charles I, hanged the corpse of Cromwell, exiled James II, and plagued William III to the verge of abdication. He had taken care, as he grimly assured his mistress, that the king-killers were on his side, and he honestly acted the constitutional sovereign, disappointing his expectant Hanoverians. But the guttural stiffness of the Guelfs enhanced the charm of the Pretenders, while the Whig domination could not fail to draw Tories and Jacobites together. For years after 1715, the insecurity of her government compelled Britain to strive for European peace.

Happily for George I and his Whig allies, the dynastic interests of France played into their hands. To secure the Hanoverians upon the throne it was before all necessary that the French should neither countenance the Pretender, nor exploit Spain. For both abstentions the regency of Orleans formed an ample pledge. Himself of ill repute and guided by his disreputable former tutor, Dubois, having gained power, moreover, by tearing up the testament of Louis XIV, he, like the Whigs, must at all costs avoid adventure. And, so long as Orleans remained a regent and Philip V a king, there was little danger from French influence in Spain. For even the supine Philip could be roused by the outrage which made a mere great-nephew of Louis XIV regent in place of himself, a grandson. Orleans in seeking British friendship committed himself the more deeply that a strong section of the French always hated Britain. By making them his enemies he became the more dependent on his novel friends. Spain at the same time looked to Britain rather than to France for those commercial services which she could not herself perform. Perhaps the most pregnant fact for Europe visible in 1715 was that the British, French and Dutch, who alone were normally capable of financing war, were driven by their several constitutional requirements to cling to peace.

Primacy of France

In numbers, wealth and pride no nation of the Continent could vie with France. Although her King ruled over Germans in Alsace, Northmen in Normandy, and Welsh in Brittany, her people ranked as a united nation. Her central position, it may be, rendered her alert, active, swift to judge and to act, a sharer in every great movement, wherever it might arise, and a unique popularizer of ideas. Frenchmen, it was said, talked eagerly and all at once, even if no one listened. Their gaiety and good humour were ascribed to different sources, but seldom if ever denied. In a couplet which eighteenth-century taste found most perspicuously condensed, Goldsmith wrote :—

> " They please, are pleased, they give to get esteem,
> Till, seeming blest, they grow to what they seem."

Mignet found his France logical rather than reflective, sociable rather than able, more impetuous than persevering, endowed with much good sense to remedy the excesses due to logic, enjoying unity in her territory and in the nation (*l'ensemble*), regularity in the language and systematic order in her institutions. " Our French fashion of seeing single where one ought to see double or triple " (Lavisse) had caused some blunders of policy and was to cause more. But her kings at least refrained from conquering what they could not assimilate. Louis XIV, resolved to be a king only to Frenchmen, had preferred aggrandizement through influence over Spain to the eastward extension of the French frontier, even when Lorraine might be acquired. Thanks to the politic restraint of France, it could be urged, time and again, that she was the only state by which Europe or Britain could be endangered.

Relations with Britain

When Louis XIV died, he left France the unquestioned head of continental Europe. As the Dutch, following the Italians and the Iberians, dropped astern, the French and British shared, and at times disputed, the leadership of western civilization. Despite nearly a quarter of a century of recent war, the two peoples were not yet the " natural enemies " that they had been in the later Middle Ages, and were again to be. The mild Richardson, indeed, came to regard Portsmouth as placed by Providence to bridle France, while the foremost of British diplomatists was to protest during peace-time against a Prince of Wales entering Paris save in the fashion of the Black Prince. But these outbursts were the product of later wars, which inspired the conviction that in every market and every continent France placed us in mortal peril. Before Louis XIV challenged Europe, his nation and ours had been natural allies against persecuting Spain. When communications were still rudimentary, the French were more exclusively our neighbours than to-day, and while neighbouring nations are often "too neighbourly to be friendly" they commonly find enmity inconvenient. The mutual use of ports, a fairly brisk mutual trade, the close association of "the wits" of both nations, and the habitual use of France as a high road and place of recreation—all these forms of friendly contact showed the advantage of harmony between French and British.

Every peace with France indeed opened to Britons the widest door of escape from their island. From Dover they voyaged by dozens to the only foreign country whose shores lay in their sight. "Fourteen hours for reflection in a vehicle that does not allow one to reflect" might bring them to Calais by mail packet or by private boat. For the former the basic charge was but five shillings, but the use of the master's cabin doubled it, and payments to the clerks of the passage, searchers, water bailiffs, landing boat-men and others, might make the total fifteen shillings. Lady Mary Wortley Montagu, to the disgust of her husband, paid £5 for a private boat. As well-to-do people from whom profit was certain, British travellers were received without hostility or reluctance. They might journey on by stage-coach, or on horseback, or in their own carriage, hiring horses according to a fixed tariff at every stage. By public con-veyance, a long journey probably cost not less than sixpence for every mile; by water, somewhat less.

Travellers

British travellers were likely to find the French people more sharply different from their own than France from England. Language, dress, religion and custom were all strange, though in some cases not unpleasant. The French might be less truthful, less clean and less efficient than the English, but they were also less moody and less splenetic.

If the parlours and stables of the inns were worse, the dinners and often the beds were better. The lack of romantic beauty in the scenery of northern France did not displease eighteenth-century English eyes. To them Norway was still "the land where after the creation the rubbish was laid on heaps," while in Lakeland the Honister offered a "fearful prospect" from which "we turned, afraid even of ourselves." What mattered more was that, thanks to the great central authority in Paris, a well-controlled road enabled them to approach the capital in safety.

Paris

Paris itself they rejoiced to find, both in size and beauty, inferior to London. "It is the ugliest town in the universe," sneered Horace Walpole, a young man who indeed had seen but few. Rousseau, with more experience, bade farewell to "that seat of noise, smoke and dirt, where the women no longer believe in honour nor the men in virtue." "Nor have they anything green but their *treillage* and window-shutters," Walpole went on. "Trees cut into fire-shovels and stuck into pedestals of chalk compose their country." Gray, in the same vein, declared the neighbouring Versailles "a huge heap of littleness." Paris, it is true, had come down from the Middle Ages through the sieges of the civil wars a mass of dark, crowded, and crooked streets, where citizens lived and died almost without quitting the precincts of their parish church. A royal town with little of self-government, its party questions were religious, and Jesuit and Jansenist contended for Parisian allegiance. Like London, however, the city contained diverse tribes who hardly knew of each other's existence. "The dread Bastille" was, in fact, an elegant place of detention for erring nobles. The men and women who stood for Paris in the reverent eyes of literary Europe met without the least popular attention in quiet gatherings which are famous in history as "the Salon."

The Paris Salons

There the most skilful hostesses in Europe held parliaments of wit, which served to inspire and to disseminate new ideas. The drawing-rooms of Paris became the real university of Europe, and the books on politics and morals which most influenced the world owed much to their inspiration. In distant capitals the institution was imitated, but Paris remained the spiritual home of countless foreign *savants*, refining their thought and language as French influence refined the taste of neighbouring lands in art, in dress and in dining. John Bull might sneer at "kickshaws" (*quelques choses*), but as a tribute to what he had learned across the Channel the menu gradually replaced his heavy bill of fare.

Although for the moment the Salon was the true glory of France, she was too powerful a state for her politics and policy to be matters of indifference in Europe. Who was to exercise in the name of the infant Louis XV the autocracy which Louis XIV had bequeathed? And, on the morrow of peace with Europe, what "system" was France to follow?

Strength of France

Since France had found in Marlborough a general whom she could not conquer, since she had suffered famine and lost millions of her population, it is well to remember that she remained potentially the strongest European state and still "marched at the head of civilization." Her greatness, indeed, seemed eternal. She still comprised the most fertile and well-knit country in Europe with the largest and most capable population, and no maladministration could wholly destroy her power. Touching many states by land, firmly established on the shores of the Atlantic and of the Mediterranean, she spread her influence far and wide. The interminable reign of Louis XIV had given her a tradition of glory, of victory, of primacy in literature and in the arts, which her partial defeat by united Europe scarcely tarnished. While British statesmen were accustomed to reckon France, in the field, as at least the equal of both their own state and any other, French diplomacy made it an almost unknown occurrence that France should take the field alone. The richest state in an age when bribery was widespread, and when troops could lawfully be hired from neutral rulers, France often gained victories either without fighting or at the sacrifice of merely alien blood. Since 1672, when Louis had attacked Holland, the old *protégé* of France, a new "system" had been built up which lasted far into the eighteenth century. On or near her own frontiers, France counted on the Bourbons of Spain, the House of Savoy, which kept the Alpine door into Italy, the Swiss confederation, and some at least of the German princes, especially Cologne, Bavaria and Lorraine. Further afield, her allies were one or both of the Scandinavian monarchies with their German possessions, together with Poland and the Turks. "Ludovicus decimus quartus," said the wits, spelt "Ludovicus, quid es? Sum turca"—and that truth was all-important for the French King. He was the traditional rival of the Habsburgs, whose Vienna the Turks had all but taken by storm.

Hostility to France

This formidable French "system," it is true, had not come into being without some other cause than the restless activity and the wealth of France. The mutual hatred between the French and the German races was already very old. For two centuries at least, since the election of Charles V to the Holy Roman Empire (1519) it had found expression in the ceaseless antagonism between the Habsburgs and the kings of France. In the constant aggrandizement of the Habsburgs they beheld a German threat to France, and "the throne of Charles V" became the classic formula for a power that France could never tolerate. To prevent Habsburgs from ruling at Madrid, to limit their power in Italy, to advance the eastern frontier of France at their expense, to encourage their rivals in Germany, to provoke revolts in their dominions, to keep the Turks aggressive in their rear—all this became the normal policy of Paris. "No enemy," said Loyola, "is so dangerous as having none," and it may well be that, in struggling against the aggrandizement of this German family, France braced her own muscles and served the cause of Europe. But the policy of Louis XIV and of Colbert had made a second enemy of Britain, a highly dangerous neighbour. France, the power with which Elizabeth and the Stuarts co-operated and with which Cromwell frankly allied, was portrayed by William of Orange as the traditional enemy of England and of the liberty of Europe. Enslaved, intolerant, false, coveting the trade of the world and compassing the conquest of Britain, the French might become the nation whom to hate was a religion. This mutual hatred would centre round two problems of policy—the Low Countries and the Protestant Succession. France must inevitably desire to extend her rule eastwards from Calais over an unbroken plain inhabited by Catholics whose fertile farms had never belonged to any powerful state. Dutch and English, however, were agreed that such a French extension would place them both in peril. Peace had been made at Utrecht on condition that the Netherlands were transferred from Spain to Austria, that a Barrier of border fortresses should be garrisoned against

France by the Dutch, and that Dunkirk should cease to be a fortress or a naval port. All this constituted a humiliation to France which her rulers could not ignore. At the same time the French had agreed to recognize the House of Hanover, whose loyalty to the Habsburg Emperor was well known, as lawfully entitled to the throne of Britain, thus sacrificing the Catholic Stuarts who had long been Louis' clients.

To these causes of future friction with Britain must be added that of the ever-growing rivalry in trade. During the seventeenth century British trade had become vital to a prosperity which impressed all observers and to which the products of the soil contributed but little. To build more ships and breed more seamen, to annex sugar-islands and profitable coast-lines, to set up trading-stations overseas, to discover new lands which would buy British manufactures and to gain fuller access to markets already known, to sell goods for gold and silver and to refrain from purchasing from a competing nation—such were British ambitions in the early eighteenth century. Each of them menaced France. Inspired by Colbert, the French had struck relentlessly at their competitors in foreign trade, and it was French attempts to close markets to British goods and to exploit the Spanish empire that had moved Britain to take up arms in 1701. Whatever politics might dictate in the way of Franco-British friendship, commercial and colonial rivalry must always threaten war. The true policy of France was plainly to preserve peace in Europe while she organized a strong fleet and an active commercial system for the struggle which was bound to come.

Unfortunately for France, however, her land tradition was likely to prove too strong. She could and did produce skilful seamen, brave explorers, devoted missionaries and able governors of dependencies overseas. Colonists, however, were hard to find, and for a French gentleman commerce was no fit career. Arms, on the other hand, formed his time-honoured profession, to be followed in the service of his country against her enemies in Europe. To renounce influence over Germany, where as guarantor of the Peace of 1648 she had an official status, to abdicate her unofficial protectorate of many of the smaller nations, to abjure her hopes of reaching her natural frontiers upon the Alps and

Rhine—these would be breaches with tradition such as few Frenchmen could conceive of or approve. Not even France could be pre-eminent both by land and sea, and, whenever her position in Europe seemed to require a choice, her instinct for the land would in all likelihood prevail.

French Finances

Since France had been for fifty years the mainspring of Europe, and since her strength was still so great, the particulars of her condition when Louis XIV died furnish a clue to a great part of general continental history. "Europe is quiet when France has need of rest" was more than a half-truth even in 1715. And certainly no true patriot could dispute the deathbed confession of the King that he had waged too many wars. To this the signs of lowered vitality in the nation may largely be ascribed.

The wealth and fame gained by those of the Huguenots who fled to other lands proves to posterity the loss sustained by France. If English glass and clocks and silk wares were bringing wealth to our nation in 1715 we had Louis XIV to thank for it. Some nine-tenths of the French Protestants, however, chose to renounce their religion and remain, with what detriment to the national morale no man can calculate exactly. It is certain that the strife between Jansenists and Jesuits distracted the Church in France and that the age is generally regarded as one of decadence in religion. The ruin of the French finances, on the other hand, can be proved by figures. The public debt exceeded 2,400,000,000 livres, of which one-third was due for immediate payment. This sum, stupendous in an age when the taxes might yield some 50,000,000 yearly, had been spent in the main on lowering the productive power of France. She had been forced to acquire manufacturing resources, it is true, by the imperative need for supplying the army with masses of goods. The Habsburgs, moreover, had been kept from securing the throne of Spain, while Strassburg and similar acquisitions were now assured to France. For the moment, however, these advantages seemed small in comparison with the inevitable waste of war. What was certain was that the gross revenue of many years had been expended and that 1715 and 1716 added 175,000,000 livres to the debt.

At such a crisis, leadership was everything. For more than fifty years France, the most monarchical of nations, had been wont to look for inspiration to her king. Now Louis XIV had given place to a child. His testament had been set aside, and Orleans, defying several competitors, had seized the post of Regent. In Orleans vice succeeded to decorum and mere opportunism to a mission from on high, while the uncontested right to rule which made the old King omnipotent had vanished. Until Louis XV reached manhood his kinsmen would dispute each other's title to govern in his name. But the very fact that the Regent felt insecure deterred him from adventure. His private interest, like that of France, demanded peace. He sought it in an understanding with the neighbour without whose friendship no French government has ever been secure. As soon as the House of Hanover had safely weathered the 'Fifteen, Orleans turned to Britain, and the Triple Alliance (1717) was the result. For the time being, at least, France and the Sea-Powers were leagued to uphold the peace of Europe.

Holland

The third member of the Triple Alliance and the next to be surveyed in Europe, was the Dutch republic, often compendiously spoken of as Holland, the greatest of the Seven United Provinces. During the two generations of their acknowledged independence (1648–1715) the Dutch had continued to show themselves " the teachers of Europe in everything, the university of the civilized world," and in commerce they were still the foremost power. Their trim plains, studded with thriving towns and intersected by busy waterways, the free and prosperous burghers with their world-interests and large patronage of art and letters—all this unique life made an ineffaceable impression on the visitor from other lands. Dugald Dalgetty's " mean, amphibious, twenty-breeched boors, unable to defend themselves by their own proper strength " had contrived to free themselves from Spain, to curb France, and to establish a rich colonial empire. Huguenots from France, Belgian Protestants, and Jews from beyond the Pyrenees strengthened their capacity and kept their outlook wide. Yet when Louis XIV died there were signs that the Dutch might share the fate of Portugal. They numbered only some 2,500,000 souls. Their country seemed too small to breed the manhood essential for an empire, and their vast exertions in the long struggle against France had left them over-taxed and seemingly exhausted. The natural timidity of capital was in their case accentuated by a singularly "crazy constitution." Perhaps because their greatest son, William of Orange, had been compelled to leave his own country for the defence of Europe, they emerged from the great War with the same imperfect union which had been hastily contrived for their uprising against Spain. Seven Provinces, of which Holland was too great to march easily in step with the rest, while Zealand might possibly become a dependency of Britain, formed a loose federal union, electing when in peril a prince of the House of Orange to act for the time being as a kind of king. Rich and timid, defending their trading empire by vigorous restrictions against other powers, they had acquired and kept throughout the century a remarkable unpopularity with their neighbours. "At gold's superior charms all freedom flies," wrote Goldsmith, declaring that the degenerate Dutchman of the upper class, though "vastly ceremonious" was merely an unpleasing imitator of the French. "The downright Hollander" he found "one of the oddest figures in nature. Upon a head of lank hair he wears a half-cocked narrow hat, laced with black ribbon, no coat, but seven waistcoats and nine pair of breeches," and a wife with twice as many petticoats. "Black teeth, white lips, unwashed toes" were the salient points of another British resident's description. Much of this animus doubtless came from the fact that the Dutch could not be trusted to court annihilation by defending Belgium as well as their own country against the French. The cool phlegm of what the elder Horace Walpole styled their "many-headed headless government, containing as many masters as minds" also proved peculiarly irritating at every crisis. The States-General changed their President every week, and their decisions, like those of the Polish Diet, must be unanimous.

From the frontiers of Switzerland, France and Holland to those of Poland, Europe was inhabited by the various tribes of the great German race. A single Germany, in the opinion of Machiavelli, would be the mightiest power on earth; in Palmerston's, a public nuisance. Before the rise of Bismarck the race seemed to be doomed to perpetual division and to endless party struggles, and this despite a valour which prompted one writer to derive "German" from *guerre*, and

Germany

a talent for governing attested by the presence of a German upon almost every throne in Europe. During the Thirty Years War German religious disputes had exhausted their ferocity, while the general misery caused the greater German princes to become even more pre-eminent than before. The peace which followed (1648) conceded virtual independence to the princes, and the Habsburg Emperors used the imperial office chiefly to increase that family power to which they owed their election. The rise of Habsburg Austria was paralleled by the rise of Saxony, Brandenburg, Hanover and Bavaria at the expense of the lesser German states. All these German agglomerations desired to complete their aggrandizement with a crown, and in the end every one of them succeeded. For centuries past the Habsburgs had been crowned in Hungary. The Elector of Saxony was chosen king by the Poles (1697). The Elector of Brandenburg, sometime a client of France, was bribed to fight against Louis XIV and Spain by the grant of a crown in Prussia (1701). The Elector of Hanover, largely for German ends, accepted the thorny crown of Britain (1714). The Duke of Bavaria gained an eighth electorate (1648) and aspired to rival his Habsburg neighbour and to remove the imperial crown to Munich.

Weakness of Germany

As the power of the great German princes rose, that of their overlord declined. While scores of German princes and imperial towns looked to the Emperor for favours of various kinds, the imperial Diet lay by no means wholly in his power. Besides the three Electors who filled thrones outside the Empire, the kings of Denmark and of Sweden held fiefs within its bounds, nor could the influence of France and of the Papacy be done away. To divide Germany and to rule there was, indeed, a permanent object of French policy. The time was yet far distant when she could not win German allies. Cologne, Bavaria, Prussia were hers by turn. Her task was the easier because Germany, by comparison with France, was a backward agricultural country lacking industries and towns, the foci of public opinion.

The first three centuries of modern times, it was clear, had done nothing to weld the German people into a national power. The German race, indeed, possessed a common language, ancient traditions and some sense of kinship. After untold suffering they had arrived at something like religious toleration. But their elected head and their parliament grew weaker with every generation: their army was an insult to a warlike people: and their nationality yielded readily to that of several of their neighbours. The Alsatians, Germans assimilated by France, gave but the most conspicuous example of what happened in countless individual cases elsewhere. In place of high national endeavour the Germans were perfecting particularism—the art of self-aggrandizement by princely houses and bodies corporate. Learning, music and the theatre offered the chief outlets for outstanding men who were not born to rule.

Scandinavia

Through its culture and by way of marriage, however, Germany deeply influenced its more backward neighbours. The three crowns of Scandinavia, now worn by the kings of Denmark-Norway and of Sweden, derived much of their lustre from the land which had given birth to Luther, to the Thirty Years War and to some of the most virile of their kings. The three Scandinavian peoples, however, were by no means German, and the Germans who served their needs in administration and in commerce incurred unpopularity unless they accepted assimilation. In Holstein and Western Pomerania, fiefs of the Scandinavian crowns, the inhabitants indeed remained German in speech and feeling, while in Slesvig Danes and Germans lived side by side for centuries with little fusion. Throughout Scandinavia itself the same religion, an intolerant Lutheranism, prevailed, and perhaps no Scandinavian native could have wholly failed to make another understand his speech. Although their subjects numbered only some 2,000,000, the two powers in sincere alliance could set in motion a considerable army and a fleet powerful enough to check all possible invaders. Their alliance, however, could seldom if ever be sincere. According to a Swedish legend, God made the fair and fruitful Denmark; Satan, their own barren and contorted land. To compensate, God made the Swedish people, but in fairness permitted Satan to make the Danes. Ancient rivalries, the enthronement of the Vasa in Sweden at the expense of the Danish dynasty (1523), the conquest of Norwegian and Danish provinces by the Swedish warrior-kings of the seventeenth century, a long series of inter-Scandinavian wars, the grasping policy of both states with regard to their water-ways—all these rendered Denmark and Sweden natural enemies and thereby commonly deprived them of influence over Europe. Since the King of Denmark and the Duke of Holstein were rivals in the German provinces to the south of the Jutland peninsula, the Duke became the ally of Sweden, and this small territorial question was destined to an importance comparable with the question of Gibraltar.

In both countries great constitutional changes had lately taken place, and more might be expected. Feudal Denmark had been suddenly transformed into an autocracy by the royal *coup d'état* of 1660. Given a series of wise kings, a condition rarely fulfilled in history, the Oldenburg dynasty might count on the support of a somewhat sluggish people, weary of the self-seeking nobles. A merely paternal government, however, must be jeopardized if the crown fell to a minor, an imbecile, a foreigner, or a tyrant, especially if the nation were attacked at such a time. In Sweden, on the other hand, the immemorial freedom of the peasants had been gravely impaired through the effects of the Thirty Years War, which, followed by misrule, by wars of conquest and by a long minority (1660–72), gave the great nobles overwhelming power. Before his untimely death in 1697, however, Charles XI had subjugated the grandees so drastically as, with the goodwill of the people, to bequeath almost an autocracy to his young heir, Charles XII. By 1715, the amazing victories and disasters of this "madman of the north" had so wrought that Sweden was half-ruined though still widely feared.

Prussia

No survey of northern Europe in 1715 can be complete without some account of the new military kingdom of Prussia. Berolinum, it was said, spelt *lumen orbi*, but to unprejudiced observers Berlin seemed the provincial capital of a straggling and undistinguished state. The agglomeration which three centuries of Hohenzollern toil had created sprawled across the map from Memel and Königsberg on the Baltic to Cleve and Wesel on the Rhine. Great wedges of alien territory severed its eastern and western wings from Brandenburg, the central mass. Accidents of its growth had given the state mixed blood and religious toleration. An unfruitful soil favoured energy and thrift; a well-placed river-system, commerce. The lack of natural frontiers had at once compelled the people to be *toujours en vedette* and had favoured that ceaseless territorial expansion which has been styled the inexorable law of Prussia's being. It is perhaps not merely fanciful to divine in Prussian docility the traces of the indigenous Slavonic population and to ascribe to the Teutonic conquerors her splendid officers and civil servants. But the creation of the state no less than the acquisition of its constituent provinces was the work of her South German ruling house. These Hohenzollerns maintained a consistent and resourceful policy of aggrandizement and produced from time to time rulers of outstanding energy and insight. Such a one, for all his repulsiveness of mind and person, was Frederick William I, who succeeded in 1713. The death of Louis XIV, of course, occurred before the new monarch had earned his title of "the Sergeant King," or reorganized the Prussian administration, or shocked Europe by urging the judicial murder of his greater son. But in the first moment of his reign he struck the chord which reverberated till its close—rigid economy, no futile aping of Versailles, everything to be ordered by the King, no arguing, no inconvenient scruples, five-sixths of the revenue for the army. In 1715, and for many years thereafter, Prussia ranked as a secondary state which might or might not count for something considerable in the event of war. Her bias was at once Protestant and Imperial, but Hohenzollern aggrandizement outweighed all else. The king, conscious that high politics were beyond him, took refuge in simple principles of conduct. What he had inherited must on no account be risked: no nonsense about "honour" must prevent him from getting more: in all domestic matters his will must prevail: he must himself be the foremost and most strenuous servant of the state. "All his life he toiled under the eye of an invisible taskmaster—the king of Prussia." The penetrating analysis of a foreign historian can thus explain a mode of life which amused, perplexed and irritated the contemporaries of the Sergeant King. By 1715, little more was clear than that Frederick William would not, like his grandfather the Great Elector, ally himself with France, and that he would of necessity play an important part in the long-drawn North European revolution, caused by the career of Charles XII.

Hanover

In Prussian policy, however, the local factor of Hanover could not be left out of account, for behind Hanover, since

1714, stood Britain. Hanover, of even more recent origin than Prussia as a state, comprised a fruitful and open country of perhaps one million people, with a well-found army more than 25,000 strong. Lying nearer to the main foci of culture, and connected by its rivers with the North Sea, in civilization it ranked above its eastern neighbour, and in military virtues and civil administration not far below. While the succession of the Guelf autocrats in constitutional Britain by no means brought the fortunes which some Hanoverians expected, it lifted their relations with the Hohenzollerns into the sphere of high politics. British statesmen could not be wholly insular while their king was a continental sovereign. However loudly they might complain that Britain had become a province to a despicable electorate, the logic of events tended towards making Hanover the axis upon which European, nay even world affairs must turn. If France and Britain were foes, the one supreme by land, the other by sea, then the French armies must strike at some British interest in Europe, and of such Hanover seemed naturally the first.

In 1715, however, France and Britain were at peace and the bond between Britain and Hanover was new and of doubtful strength. The princes of Germany, most of all the Sergeant King, were looking rather towards the Emperor and Vienna. As recently as 1683, Vienna, which throughout the nineteenth century lay in the centre of Europe, had suffered the perils of a naked frontier town.

"Austria"

No state has in modern times passed through more or greater vicissitudes than that which for two centuries at least has been known to Europe as Austria. To-day a German province, until the close of the Great War a dual empire, sometimes a single monarchy, for many centuries it was a shifting bundle of family estates glorified by association with the Holy Roman Empire. In 1715 it lacked its later *raison d'être*—to keep the peace between many jarring tribes. If Austria had then a European mission, it was to be a bulwark against the Turk and a counterpoise to France. Since Maximilian I succeeded his father in 1493, the lord of the Austrian lands and the elected Emperor had both been Habsburg, always united and usually a single person. While the Habsburg lands grew greater and more compact, the Empire as an independent institution faded. The Thirty Years War left the way clear for Leopold I (1657–1705) to use his Imperial office for the mere aggrandizement of Austria. When his son, Charles VI, came to both thrones (1711), Austria meant in substance the lands ruled by the Habsburgs of Vienna, who wore the Imperial crown. After the settlement of 1713–15 those lands were Austria proper, Silesia, Bohemia, Hungary (without Temesvar but with Transylvania), Moravia, Tyrol, Carinthia, Styria, parts of Slavonia and Croatia, together with Belgium, Sardinia, Milan, and Naples. The mere enumeration of the provinces suggests the manifold struggle in which their common ruler must engage. On all or any of ten fronts he might at any time be forced to battle. The Turks, hereditary foes of Austria, had almost taken Vienna in 1683, only to cede their portion of Hungary sixteen years later. All that could be foreseen was that the Turkish wars would be renewed and that unless the Austrian monarchs showed great skill they must face Hungarian risings. For two centuries the Habsburgs had been foes of France. They now held Belgium, like Hungary a coy possession, and a standing temptation to an ancient enemy, in this case France. The new Italian acquisitions promised trouble at least with Spain and with the House of Savoy. The neighbourhood of Venice, Poland and Bavaria, the last-named a constant object of Habsburg desire, enlarged the opportunities of strife. A power "whose basis was purely statistical" comprising seven major races bristled with challenges to strife. Split up by seas and mountains, with no unifying factor save the Danube, Austria depended for her strength upon her Germans, yet with these too the Habsburgs might find themselves at loggerheads, if they should give ear to the claims of their Magyar, Slavonic or Italian subjects. So long as Habsburg policy remained Catholic, the Roman Catholicism now common to all the Austrian dominions aided the monarchy both towards Austria and towards Europe. In 1715, however, the outlook for Austria was darkened by the defects of Charles VI himself. Mediocre and intolerant, he could not bring himself to accept defeat in Spain nor to conciliate any of his opponents.

The Pragmatic Sanction

In April, 1713, he had increased their number by his Pragmatic Sanction. This royal decree declared that all his provinces, though held by various titles, must pass undivided to his daughter if he failed to beget a son. As the hope of male issue waned, to secure the Pragmatic Sanction became more and more the main object of his life.

Prince Eugene

The inadequacy of Charles VI, however, was largely offset by the amazing qualities of his kinsman and servant, Prince Eugene. A Savoyard born in Paris (1663), through his mother Mazarin's great-nephew, Eugene had already avenged an hundredfold the injury done him by Louis XIV, who refused to employ him in the army. First and foremost a warrior who courted wounds and death, he was also a weighty diplomatist and an Austrian patriot of the highest order. Frederick William I, knowing that money and jewels would be refused, tried to buy his favour with wild horses from East Prussia for his private menagerie in Vienna. A hard man and regardless of women, he shone as a Maecenas and furthered science. Already he had fought campaigns in Hungary, Italy, France, Bavaria and Flanders, and at Zenta (1697) had given Austria her greatest triumph against the Turks. Made by his partnership with Marlborough a leading figure in Europe, he had become Governor of Belgium when the Turkish war broke out anew (1716). So long as his vigour continued, Austria might retain the European weight which her broad and fertile provinces seemed to claim.

Europe and Poland

Poor and weak as she had now become, and thereby an impediment to travel, the so-called Republic of Poland unquestionably belonged to Europe. Her religion was that of Rome; her polite language, Latin; the civilization of her leading circles, of the highest; her history, full of great achievements. Only two and thirty years before the death of Louis XIV she had saved Vienna from the Turk. Seventy years earlier, her princes had occupied Moscow and threatened to establish a Polish line of Tsars. Her population of perhaps eleven millions still almost equalled that of Russia, and her lands were fertile. But her government was such as almost to nullify her power. "Elective monarchies," said Döllinger, "are beacons of warning in history," and Poland surpassed even the Holy Roman Empire as a shining proof that his words were true. Egotistic and uncontrollable, the great landed nobles had brought all power and wealth into their own hands and used the Polish realm for their own enjoyment. While boasting that the "republic" united the advantages of monarchy, aristocracy and democracy, they had robbed it of every asset of a modern state. Social freedom, religious toleration, rational justice, an efficient army, an adequate revenue—all vanished that the power of the great nobles " as well in spiritual affairs as secular " might remain uncontrolled. Most of her kings were foreigners chosen through bribery, terror or intrigue. They inevitably used their life interest in Poland to aggrandize their own House, or their own Church. Native kingship, on the other hand, meant the strife of factions. The constitution, which aimed at the protection of aristocratic liberty, made progress impossible. Over a period of fifty-five years only seven of the annual diets succeeded in passing any law, all others failing before the *liberum veto* by which a single member could nullify the legislative labours of a session. The time was at hand when four Polish regiments were found to consist of officers alone, while not a single fortress was fit for service. With starveling serfs in the fields and Jews and Germans monopolizing city life, a fine land of ancient renown was nearing the state of " carrion fallen down upon the common highways of the world," a prey to neighbouring foxes.

The Saxon House in Poland

Since 1697, when France was prevented by her western war from interfering, Poland had been nominally ruled by Augustus II, the Elector of Saxony, who became a Catholic to qualify for the Polish throne. Having gained it twice over, he surrounded himself with courtiers of ninety grades. The chief powers which were wont to concern themselves with the fortunes of the Republic were France, Sweden, Russia, the Emperor, the Turk, and, with ever-increasing importance, the power which was now called Prussia. The Electors of Brandenburg governed autocratically a state as formidable as Poland, its neighbour, was weak. In 1660 they had gained full sovereignty over the province which gave their new monarchy its name—the eastern half of Prussia, a fief of Poland. The western half, often styled Royal or Polish Prussia, now formed a wider " Polish corridor " which cut off Königsberg from Berlin. Within its frontiers dwelt many Protestants and Jews, classes inclined to look to tolerant Prussia for protection against the growing intolerance of the Poles. Danzig, however, the most tempting morsel to the Hohenzollerns, strongly preferred the mild suzerainty of

Poland to the ruthless vigour which marked the Hohenzollerns of Berlin. None the less, as early as 1715, the situation was beginning to appear in which the continued integrity of Poland depended less on her own force or on that of her foreign monarch than on the reluctance of her neighbours to acquiesce in the aggrandizement of one of themselves at her expense. Her Saxon king, indeed, crossed the frontier from his electorate only when he must, and was prepared to exploit Poland even to partition for the profit of his own family.

Poland and the Russian peril

Saxony, and therefore Poland, could count on the protection of Austria. For half a century at least the immediate danger to the Republic had come from Russia. When two ancient enemies, one gaining strength and one declining, are neighbours on a vast plain where no third power can interfere, their mutual frontier can hardly be deemed secure. And Poland was the less sacrosanct against Russia in that she was a dual monarchy and that her eastern member, Lithuania, was largely inhabited by Russians. Lands lost by Russia in bygone ages stretched across Poland between points south-west of Moscow and south of Warsaw. White Russia, Black Russia, Little Russia, Red Russia—all were Polish, and White and Little Russia at least had many affinities with Moscow in worship, blood and speech. For half a century the disintegration of Poland had steadily contributed to the expansion of Russia. In 1667, a huge section of Lithuania including the fortress of Smolensk changed overlords, and in 1686 Kiev, the holy city, followed. Thenceforward Russia had no need to go to war with Poland. Northern Livonia with Riga, where German barons ruled, had been Swedish since 1629. Its conquest by Peter paved the way for the establishment of Russian influence over the German barons in Courland, which was still a Polish fief. Who could doubt that the upper Dwina and the upper Dnieper would in due course change their masters ? It was to ensure Polish obedience that Russia had placed and replaced Augustus on the Polish throne. Among the Polish factions there would always be some that looked to Russia. In 1717, with their consent, she assumed a real though vague suzerainty by guaranteeing the Polish constitution. Thenceforward the Republic must either miraculously regenerate herself, or find a stronger and less dangerous protector elsewhere, or submit to Russia. She had engaged with Russia that her army, or rather armies, Polish and Lithuanian, should not exceed 24,000 men and that her constitution should remain unchanged. Either of these provisions would have sufficed to make her impotent as against the Tsar.

Polish Disorder

Poland, indeed, was at this time chiefly renowned for two closely related features, disorder and the constitution. A German who witnessed a London election in 1710 reported that "the people behaved so wildly that one might have been in Poland." And the chief occasions on which the Poles went wild were those on which they met to perform their constitutional duties, in dietines for the choice of deputies, in the diet, or at the election of judges or of a king. All these were gatherings of armed gentry accompanied by their retainers, faced by their private enemies and reckless in their consumption of spirits and of Tokay.

The Polish Constitution

It was true, indeed, that the constitution showed traces of all three classic forms of government, monarchy, aristocracy and democracy. If the complete exclusion of the non-noble from political rights be consistent with democracy, Poland was certainly democratic. Every local noble voted at the dietine, and the deputy who represented him could break up the ensuing diet rather than submit to the majority on a single point. Dissatisfied nobles, moreover, either at the diet or in the country, were free to form confederations for the attainment of their desires. The marshal of such a confederation might even for a time practically supersede the king. The whole constitution, indeed, formed an elaborate machine for protecting the nobles against the King, and Lithuania against historic Poland. With the latter aim in view, all great officials had duplicates in Lithuania and one diet in every three met on Lithuanian soil. To curb the royal power, whenever the throne fell vacant the Primate of Gnesen became *interrex*. At his summons the state devoted all its energies first to determining the conditions which the next monarch must observe and then to the new election. All tribunals ceased to function. The national revenue was not collected. A "diet of convocation" prepared the way for the diet which should choose the king. Inevitably the whole realm buzzed with intrigue, and foreign powers intervened by negotiation, bribery and threat of force.

The Polish King

Once elected, the King found himself master of a small and inelastic revenue from which the expenses of the interregnum must be paid. He was tempted to take bribes from foreign powers and to sell those nominations to senatorships and high offices of state which were in his gift. Apart from such emoluments and the enjoyment of a pompous ritual of life, he could derive but little profit from his throne. The powerful hierarchy of Polish ecclesiastics looked to Rome. The great families, the real possessors of Poland, were in correspondence with foreign powers. A Great General controlled either army. A host of high-sounding officials hemmed in the King at every turn, and once a year he learned his impotence anew by presiding in the diet. He was indeed a King of Kings and a Lord of Lords, declared a witty Irishman, for he had no better than companions and equals for his subjects.

Italy in 1715

No region in Europe has changed its rank and character within two centuries more completely than the Italian peninsula. A modern student, surveying the physical map of Europe, finds Italy destined by nature to become a single state. It is effectively an island, encircled by the highest range in Europe and by the sea. Climate and situation, moreover, appear to qualify the predestined state for empire in one of the neighbouring continents, perhaps in two. A modern student, moreover, regards the Pope and Cardinals as men absorbed in directing a worldwide spiritual organization, to whom extensive temporal sovereignty would be a burden. Rome, again, appears as the city of the Cæsars, gaining in prestige from the papal residence, but the obvious capital of the Italian state.

In 1715, and even a century later, all this was totally untrue. Italy, a rich sub-continent stretching far into the sea, was still a geographical expression. History seemed to have decided that Italian sentiment lacked the power of Spanish, French or English to fuse a people into a single nation. Her governments resembled the medieval city states, "kissing and scratching by turns," more than the Great Power of Cavour and Mussolini. Rome with its 150,000 inhabitants still belonged to one of the chief Italian princes, the Pope, now always Italian by birth but a sovereign whose unique power and position seemed to frustrate Italian unity. Such unity, it has been said, was impossible either with the papacy, or without it, or against its will. Endowed with matchless artistic wealth and talent, the millions of Italians might be regarded as content to enjoy life without much political ambition. Remote as she was, for the only good road for immigrants ran across the Brenner, Italy formed the compelling lodestone to the polite of all the north. Her sons half-humorously complained of this new invasion. "Anciently they conquered the country; of late, they leave the inhabitants their lands and only take their learning"—for foreigners carried away Italian books as well as works of art. She was indeed "the pleasure-ground of cultured Europe." The English in particular declared that in entering Italy they felt as though they were coming home.

Italy in European Politics

Neither the goodwill of travellers nor the political inertia of the Italians, however, could keep Italy free from European complications. In 1714, indeed, the Turks had attacked the eastern empire of Venice, impelling the Pope to proclaim a new crusade. Far graver for Italy than the loss of such dependencies as the Morea, however, were the elements of instability in the Utrecht settlement which concerned her own peninsula and islands.

In substance, Italy had at Utrecht suddenly become Austrian. Cæsar then regained the birthplace of his title. The War of the Spanish Succession had led to the establishment of Austrian rule both in Milan and in Naples, placing the Pope between the hammer and the anvil.

In entrusting Italy to the Emperor, the allies had designed to compensate him for the loss of the Spanish Succession, to exclude the Bourbons from a fertile field for war and aggrandizement, and to favour their own trade both with Italy and with the Levant. They had therefore also assigned the distant island of Sardinia to the Emperor, who possessed no naval power. It remained to be seen how long all parties to these arrangements would remain content—Savoy and the Emperor to hold islands at the mercy of foreign fleets; France to witness the encouragement of her commercial rivals; Spain to abandon a country in which she had been predominant since 1559.

The Italian States

Within Italy there was hardly one considerable power. The Duke of Savoy, a state originally non-Italian, had profited by the war to advance his eastern frontier on the great northern plain and also to become King of Sicily. From him and from his successors an active though wary opportunism might be expected, since such was the necessary tradition of their House. Venice, with an empire of perhaps three million souls, as rich as Savoy was poor, and as famous as the Alpine duchy was obscure, was plainly failing in vigour. The scene of the greatest carnival in Europe and of incessant and widespread festivities throughout the year, she was bent merely on preserving her great estate without venturing the blood of her citizens. Austria now hemmed in the Venetians on the mainland and through Naples commanded the Adriatic. Genoa, like Venice an aristocratic republic, contained a vigorous and hardy population, but even endowed with unruly Corsica she must be accounted a minor state. Parma, Modena, Lucca—such duchies might produce able men, but they could hardly aspire to anything beyond neutrality when Great Powers fought. Tuscany, with wider boundaries than these, but impoverished by later Medici misrule, was faced with a succession question of her own. Was she or was she not an Imperial fief? And if the degenerate Medici died out, who should enjoy the dukedom? However such questions might be decided, it was certain that while Cosimo III (1670–1723) held sway, Tuscany would count for little. Substantially, the Papal states alone remained. Compact and fertile, inhabited by a vigorous population, this broad belt of territory, if well-governed, might have formed a respectable secondary state. Its effect upon the papacy was disastrous. Whatever power and prestige the Pope gained as a temporal prince was far outweighed by his consequent distraction as a spiritual ruler. A minor state must have allies, and whatever protector he might summon to his aid must gain undue weight in ecclesiastical policy. Several lay sovereigns possessed a right of veto in papal elections, and it was notorious that the calibre of the men elected had declined. Under the papacy the function of the Papal States was to supply the financial needs of an elective monarch, and one whose eyes were necessarily fixed on wider and more distant objects. Against the Austrian, Italy could hope for only one Italian champion, poor and backward Savoy. The peninsula, moreover, was still handicapped by conditions which progress has now largely swept away. Settled for centuries when beyond the Alps all was barbarous, her soil was wearied by incessant cropping without rest. When transport depended upon animals, the disproportionate length of the country and its innumerable hills kept Italians parochial. Poverty and ignorance made patriotism impossible. In the eighteenth century Italy could not be born.

Iberia (i) Portugal

For all their conspicuous weakness during the late war, the Iberian kingdoms had not yet wholly broken with their mighty past. Portugal, once the pioneer of European expansion overseas, was still important by reason of her earlier exploits. Her proud determination to resist the force which welded all the other peoples of the Peninsula into a state called Spain had survived sixty years of Spanish lordship over herself (1580–1640). The independence which France had helped her to regain she had now to defend against the Bourbons of both Spain and France. The great harbour of Lisbon and the vast empire of Portugal in three continents formed prizes which a small people with a long and weak land-frontier could not defend alone. England, so soon as she became the foe of France, became the natural friend of Portugal. Only sea-power could protect that Iberian Wales, while in return she could prevent the Bourbon coast-line from stretching unbroken between Calais or Antwerp and the Gulf of Lyons. Early in the last struggle against Louis XIV, therefore, England and Portugal concluded the Methuen treaty (1703) giving mutual preference to Portuguese wines and English manufactures. Port wine brought gout to British statesmen, but otherwise both allies gained, and their difference of religion proved powerless to rupture the alliance of the House of Hanover with the Most Faithful King. The political tie, it must be confessed, did not unite the peoples' hearts. "In this voyage among the Portuguese," wrote Defoe, "I learned particularly to be an arrant thief and a bad sailor . . . they are the best masters for teaching these of any nation in the world."

(ii) Spain

While Portugal remained obscure, Spain continued to show herself the land of astonishing collapses and recoveries. Her population, some eight million in 1600, had sunk by one-fourth before the outbreak of the Succession War. Great as had been her rulers and explorers of the sixteenth century and her soldiers and artists of the seventeenth, wide and rich as were her homeland and her empire, she depended, perhaps more than any other great power, upon vigour at the seat of government. Her almost African climate, her steep internal mountain barriers, the jealousy of the other Spanish kingdoms against Castile, the fanaticism of a race which scorned trade and abominated heresy—all this made for a swift decline whenever the king was weak. By removing the Netherlands, Italy, Sardinia and Minorca from her sway, the treaty of Utrecht had rendered the task of government less overwhelming, while the French administration which she had enjoyed since 1701 ranked as the best in Europe. A good understanding with France, moreover, removed her only dangerous enemy, and provided her with a friend whose energy and wealth would suffice for the development of her commerce and empire. A nation so backward that her current cash was reckoned at only some eight millions, but so honest that baggage could be left unguarded, might well be formidable under an inspiring king.

Philip, Elizabeth and Alberoni

Thanks to the strange chances of which eighteenth-century history is full, Spain found herself in 1715 under the dominion of three foreigners, each with a policy of his own. Philip V, the grandson for whom Louis XIV had accepted the bequest of Spain with the Indies, was in most affairs the most plastic and placid of mankind. "Younger brother of a violent and excitable prince," wrote St. Simon, "he was bred up in a submission that was necessary for the repose of the royal family." The darling of Spain for his constancy during the long struggle for her continued independence, he habitually obeyed his confessor and his queen. One prospect, however, no one could have brought him to sacrifice—that of future rule in France. As long as only his sickly nephew Louis XV had a better hereditary title to the French crown, so long Philip would regard any regent as a usurper, and himself, whatever treaties might lay down, as the rightful heir to the throne. In most other matters, however, he accepted the guidance of a low-born statesman whom neither race nor allegiance attached to Spain. Alberoni, a gardener's son and an ecclesiastic, came to Madrid merely to represent the minor state of Parma. With the industry and imagination of a Wolsey, despite his corpulence, he none the less galvanized Spain into activity both at home and abroad. From the discovery of quicksilver to the equipment of a fleet, every impulse came from him. As the patron of Philip's Savoyard queen and of the all-powerful Princesse des Ursins, Louis XIV had continued to dictate to the king of Spain. " Lose no time," he dared to write, " in carrying out my commands." But when the Savoyard died Alberoni chose Elizabeth Farnese of Parma to fill her place (1714). The first act of this " termagant " was to drive Madame des Ursins over the Alps, and thereby to seize an influence over the King which she exercised for more than thirty years. Detested by the Spaniards, the strong-willed Italian scold set herself, from private ambition, to regain what Spain had profitably lost, and in particular to establish in her native Italy the Bourbon princes to whom she now gave birth.

Gibraltar

Elizabeth's ambitions in Italy therefore influenced the course of European history for many years. Still more enduring was the ambition of the Spanish nation to win back Gibraltar from the British and to free the Mediterranean by driving them from Minorca. The Gibraltar question, indeed, formed the chief of those disputes about small but vital territories which swayed the movements of great states during long periods of the eighteenth century. The British occupation naturally aroused in Spain a resentment no less strong than that which would have been felt by France if Britain had continued to hold Calais, or by Britain if France had contrived to conquer Dover. Its importance to British trade with Italy and Turkey was enormous, and strategically it was to become a valuable safeguard of the West Indies. Yet so great was the danger of throwing Spain and her empire into the arms of France that more than one British statesman would have surrendered it, had not public opinion intervened. That for a long period Britain could keep both Gibraltar and Spanish friendship constitutes one of the most important facts of the century and not the least surprising.

Europe Overseas

No survey of Europe in 1715 could be complete if it ignored the " greater Europe " which was then being raised up overseas. Trading posts, dependencies, colonies, all attracted Europeans to themselves, and these must in turn influence both the social life and the political relations of the mother-countries. "Spain and the Indies," wrote Montesquieu, "are two powers under the same master, but the Indies are the chief." To subordinate the chief power to the secondary was impossible: the Indies, he declared, must draw Spain to themselves.

In judging thus, Montesquieu may well have been influenced by the poverty and shortcomings of European Spain, only too well-known in France, and by that idealization of unknown men and distant spaces which helped to bring his country into the war of American Independence. Of Spain, as of any other colonizing nation, all that was certain was that her colonies could not leave her unaffected. They might drain her of her best blood or reinvigorate her with their own. They might feed her or call on her for food, strengthen or weaken her economic system, expose her to fresh wars or help her in her own quarrels, multiply her sons, or confront her with a hybrid race, spread her ideas or attempt to convert her to their own. A glance at the colonies of Europe in 1715 reveals their utter diversity.

The French in Canada then reached the number of 18,000. The population of the English colonies in North America, swelled by some 60,000 negroes, had grown perhaps twenty times as great. At the Cape of Good Hope the Dutch for the first time armed a commando to pursue the Bushmen who had driven off the farmers' sheep. While the French were seizing Mauritius, from which the Dutch had lately withdrawn, English from Calcutta went to Delhi to demand new trading privileges from the Great Mogul. As the outcome of the Utrecht peace, the French in Nova Scotia were summoned to swear allegiance to King George or to quit the country, and they refused either alternative.

In Brazil the Portuguese were establishing a social life superior in many ways to that of the mother-country. There they showed more industry and less caste prejudice than at home, and negro slavery at least promoted Indian freedom. A vast area of fertile soil lay at their doors, with boundless hopes of gold mines. In 1715 Portugal overseas bade fair to outweigh Portugal in Europe. Spain too had retained the Indies when she lost much of her Old World empire. She was about to develop her administration overseas by adding a viceroy of New Granada to those of Mexico and of Peru (1718). But her system seemed already doomed by its defects. Her vast dominions in Latin America were exploited to enrich a few merchants and to provide the crown with treasure. The two small Spanish fleets which sailed each year across the Atlantic could neither supply her colonies nor take off all their exports. At Utrecht she therefore granted to the British for thirty years the exclusive right to export negroes to her overseas dominions. Besides this *Asiento,* Britain received permission to send annually to Cartagena a ship whose burden did not surpass 500 tons. It was certain that these concessions would be abused, and that they would prove galling to the competitors of Britain, above all others to the French. The inevitable friction must affect the politics of Europe.

Latins and British were not alone concerned. While the Portuguese, the Spaniards, the French and the British were true colonists, the Dutch had been driven by their commercial appetite to form a far-reaching colonial empire. In 1715 it was still possible to believe that in the East they were stronger than all their European rivals put together. Although they sent settlers only to the Cape of Good Hope, they were supreme in the Spice Islands, in Ceylon, and in the Malay Archipelago, and held trading posts in Bengal, on the coast of Coromandel, at Surat, in Siam, and in the Persian Gulf. Driven from New Amsterdam and from Brazil, they remained in Guiana and on the Guinea coast, and participated with every other naval power in the struggle for islands in the West Indies.

The bare recital of these facts suggests that in the years following 1715 the history of Europe would be powerfully influenced from overseas. The quest of colonies and commerce must enrich the life and broaden the horizon of every European people. From some it drew off the most active and enterprising of their subjects, from others, disturbing elements which they were glad to lose. "The Plantations" already suggested to some independent minds thoughts of a safe retreat, and the possibilities of social and religious experiments beyond the ocean were already taking shape.

Although the economic motive ranked by far the first, Christian missions formed an object always avowed and often practised by every colonial power. To seize or purchase Africans and carry them to the plantations was defended on religious grounds. It is true that many of them were slaves in Africa, and that the light of the gospel became to many a reality. Although Frederick the Great could declare that the traffic in negroes had always seemed to him a disgrace to human nature, few were shocked by the presence of black slaves in the capitals of Europe.

In the state of Europe overseas in 1715 a skilled observer could read much of the horoscope of eighteenth-century Europe—profits, adventure, capital, inventions, manufactures, new markets, jarring companies and colonies, colonial and European wars. And at every point in the cycle a fresh impulse must be given towards naval development and naval competition. In the decade which 1715 began, while the great colonial question quietly grew ripe, nearly ninety ships each year put into Table Bay. More than two-thirds of these were Dutch, outnumbering the British by more than three to one, while France sent less than two *per annum*. The figures might serve to point the way to the western powers for more than a generation.

Turning from forecast to recorded fact, we see that Utrecht had merely registered and advanced colonial changes which had been long in progress. Spain, following Portugal, was on the decline; Britain, following France, on the upward grade; the Dutch, struggling to preserve the monopolies which they had acquired; lesser powers, Swedes, Danes, Brandenburgers, eager to gain some profitable if restricted foothold overseas.

Along the eastern coast of North America the struggle had turned definitely in favour of Britain, the least distant power, and that which had most men to spare for settlement. The English settlers had ousted the Dutch, as these the Swedes, and by 1715 eleven sea-board colonies stood ready to assist the mother-country in any future struggle with France or Spain. The recovery of Hudson's Bay, and still more the cession of Nova Scotia and Newfoundland, might help to turn the scale, but the successors of Champlain and Colbert were actively penetrating the interior of the continent from Quebec. Before Canada had 20,000 inhabitants, the future encirclement of a British coast-line by a

Bourbon North American empire could be divined. European competition for the sovereignty of West Indian islands continued brisk, and its outcome impossible to predict. Without any violent revolution, the French, Danes and British were increasing their possessions, sometimes at the expense of pirates whose lairs it was hard to destroy. There was, indeed, a general presumption, evidenced by Spanish loss, that here sea-power would bring dominion. The islands, on the other hand, were too small and too near to the American continent for the factor of European sea-power to be completely decisive of their fate. This general rule likewise applied in Africa, where the Gum Coast, the Grain Coast and the Slave Coast bristled with European stations. In India, although the British had already gained a foothold near Madras, Bombay and Calcutta, while Danes, Portuguese and Dutch held important coastal stations, the sole dynamic power was that of France.

When Aurungzeb died (1707), the Mogul empire became the scene of a fratricidal war between his sons. At the same time the Portuguese and Dutch had plainly abandoned the race for dominion. The French and English Companies thus found India almost at their feet. To take it demanded vigour at home and on the spot and victory or agreement with their rival. For more than thirty years, until his death in 1706, François Martin had shown what could be accomplished. Thanks to him, Pondicherry had a population of 60,000. But his successors were not his equals, and in 1720 the bankruptcy of the Company took place. Next year Lenoir became governor of French India and in 1723 John Law reorganized the Company. A great forward movement was to ensue.

As the offshoots of Europe overseas grew in numbers, wealth and area they could not fail to influence old Europe more and more. The Emperor's struggles to establish an Ostend Company, and the outbreak of war between Britain and Spain in 1739 show how commerce and colonies made their way to the forefront of European politics. It must not be forgotten, however, that the feebleness and the remoteness of the colonies long prevented that intercourse and influence which a later age takes for granted. More than half a century after the death of Louis XIV Horace Walpole mocked at the powers which dethroned nabobs in the furthest corners of the Indies and prepared to fight each other for one of the extremities of the southern hemisphere. "It takes a twelvemonth," he declared, "for us to arrive and almost another before we can learn what we have been about. By next century, I suppose, we shall fight for the Dog Star and the Great Bear."

While the new England in America and the New Holland at the Cape quietly developed, and the French steadily fortified their Canadian dominion, the colonies did not come to the forefront of European history until France and Britain went to war in 1744. In that year Robert Clive arrived in India, where Labourdonnais and Dupleix had laid the foundations of a great French empire of the east.

BIBLIOGRAPHICAL NOTE

See the Bibliographical Note at the end of Chapter I. Add :—

A

W. H. Bruford : *Germany in the Eighteenth Century* (1935).

W. H. Bruford : *Literary Interpretation of Germany* (1952).

H. H. Dodwell (ed.) : *The Cambridge History of India.* V (1929).

C. J. Hamilton : *Trade Relations between England and India, 1600–1896* (1919).

G. B. Malleson : *History of the French in India . . . 1674 to . . . 1761* (1868).

A. T. Mahan : *The Influence of Sea Power upon History, 1660–1783* (1890, new ed., 1944).

H. Merivale : *Lectures on Colonization and Colonies.* 2 vols. (1841–42, new ed. 1861, repr. 1928).

W. Michael : *England under George I. The Beginnings of the Hanoverian Dynasty* (trans. 1936).

J. Sarkar : *The Fall of the Mughal Empire.* 4 vols. (1932–50).

L. S. Sutherland : *The East India Company in Eighteenth-Century Politics* (1952).

A. W. Ward : *Great Britain and Hanover* (1899).

J. A. Williamson : *A Short History of British Expansion* (1930, repr. 1931).

B

A. von Arneth : *Prinz Eugen von Savoyen,* II and III (1858).

CHAPTER VI

THE RUSSIANS AND TURKS (1715–25)

The Problem of Peter

PETER THE GREAT by his own desire became a member of the French Academy (1717), thereby earning the right to a funeral oration (*éloge*) on his death. The orator, Corneille's nephew Fontenelle, was a man who was said to profess two axioms—that everything is possible and that everybody is right. While the encomiums of such a critic must be received with caution, his admissions may be rated high. Frankly admitting that Peter was " not exempt from a certain moroseness, natural to his nation," that he was wont to unbend his mind by diversions " anciently used in Muscovy," and that he had made grave mistakes, Fontenelle amply proved by the enumeration of his deeds that he had raised the whole status of his realm.

" If Augustus," he summed up, " boasted himself that he had found Rome of brick and left it of marble, it is obvious how much, in this regard, the Roman emperor is inferior to the Russian. Medals were struck for him whereon he is called Peter the Great, and without doubt the name of Great will be confirmed by the consent of foreign nations."

During his eight years as an Academician he had successively put to death his eldest son, dismembered the Swedish Empire, and reorganized the government of Russia.

Since Fontenelle wrote, countless pens have endeavoured to depict the unique and amazing Tsar who changed the history of Europe.

To Lord Acton, the most learned and severe of historians, he seemed " undoubtedly the worst " of the great men who have influenced the course of Christian history. A hundred and sixty years after his death, Sir Richard Lodge declared that it was " as if a criminal of the lower classes were called upon to govern, and were found to be endowed with the highest qualities of constructive statesmanship." Subsequent Russian research has shown that his constructive statesmanship owed its being to long experience of the chaos that his own destructive barbarism had brought about. Many of his "crimes," moreover, were political, and ruffianly outbreaks that once seemed criminal are now regarded as the outcome of disease. By 1715, none the less, Europe was faced by the fact that an autocrat of colossal will-power had brought a new army into her midst, and that he seemed likely to wrest the hegemony of the north from Sweden. Since the downfall of Charles XII at Poltava in 1709, it had become clear that a Tsar who had studied Europe might shatter the most famous of European armies. Europe therefore must expect to find her area doubled by the intrusion of a race which, though Christian and white, was a byword for barbarism, and which in language, history and feeling seemed to be non-European.

The Problem of Russia

From her first rude contact with the west under Peter the Great, Russia had been, as she still remains, a misunderstood and even a mysterious power. For centuries she had been carefully shut out from Europe by her neighbours, who deemed her "the enemy of all free nations." She in turn disliked and despised their institutions, and, under Peter, consciously set out to profit by their ignorance about herself. European, she certainly was not. Although its founders had been Slavs and Northmen, the Russian state now comprised millions of Asiatic tribesmen, while Finns and Tartars had intermingled with her stock. More noxious still were the centuries of isolation from Europe and of subjection to the Golden Horde (1240–1480). The Russians, moreover, derived their religion from the non-progressive Eastern Church, which Rome regarded as schismatic. Their manners came from sources alien to the west. Their history contained none of the chapters common to European nations —crusades and councils, chivalry, free cities, trade gilds, the Reformation and the discovery of trans-oceanic lands. They knew little of the arts and sciences, the learning and literature of Europe. "In this country, where a book is a rarity," wrote a British ambassador half a century later, from the Russian capital.

Russian Separation from the West

The Protestants of Europe, indeed, might regard the Russian faith as purer than that of Rome, for it knew nothing of papal autocracy, of purgatory or indulgences, of confession-boxes, pastoral celibacy, Mariolatry or lay communion in a single kind. Most Russians, however, viewed Romanism and Lutheranism, Islam and Judaism with equal abhorrence. Christianity, therefore, was chiefly an estranging force, and Russians and Europeans, when Peter's attack on Charles XII brought them face to face, met with mutual contempt and loathing.

The Spanish Succession War, however, exposed Europe to the new and resolute Russian attack. Peter's Saxon and Danish allies at least diverted Sweden from the western struggle, and Charles XII was not a sovereign who invited western sympathy.

After fourteen campaigns, in which the Russian people denied Peter no sacrifice of blood and treasure, it was clear that the window towards the west which he had opened would not be closed by force. St. Petersburg, though all save Peter hated it, survived and grew, and Sweden could hardly hope to reconquer the lands which lay between Russia's new capital and Riga. The Tsar had proved himself the most forceful person in the world. By 1715 the real question was whether the victors of Poltava would or would not be able to dominate the Baltic and northern Germany. Russia, in a word, had forced the gates of Europe. In 1714 her Emperor's name for the first time was printed in the list of sovereigns issued annually in Paris. To win the war by borrowing from Europe, Russia had broken with her most cherished traditions. In 1714 she completed a long series of institutions copied from the west by adopting primogeniture in place of the division of a dead man's lands among his sons. More startling changes were soon to come. It was ominous for the future of Europe that expansion to the Urals represented not a victory for her civilization but a defeat for a great European power. Russia aped Europe not because she admired the west but from ambition. With western ideals she was less than ever in sympathy. The Russian Church while being forced to serve the government lost nothing of its hostility towards Rome. This lent a new significance to the fact that in Poland, now a zealous Roman Catholic power, lived many Eastern Catholics of Russian race. But the whole trend of Russian history was at this time opposed to that of Europe. In many western lands the tendency was towards social

Contrast between Russia and Europe

emancipation. In Russia it ran strongly the other way, and serfdom was climbing towards its height. While Europe granted more and more freedom to the individual, Russia was binding men ever more tightly into the commune (*mir*), a compulsory village association for collective farming and payment of taxes. In the west, notions of land tenure and government grew clearer. In Russia they grew more obscure, until peasants could say to their lord, "The land is ours and we are yours." In Europe, private property was becoming more important; in Russia, less. Of hereditary descent the same is true. Even the succession to the Russian Crown was now determined by no intelligible rule. Nowhere were local tyrants less controllable than in Russia, and yet nowhere was autocracy more complete. Peter subjugated the Church, established universal service, made war at will, taxed everybody and everything, and nationalized minerals, forests, fisheries, bee-hives and mills. Thanks to autocracy and to geographical remoteness, a poor and barbarous people, shrunk to some thirteen millions where Peter's father had ruled perhaps sixteen, now bade fair to sway for ever the balance of European power. This was done not by any moral intellectual or material contribution but by arming and drilling many thousands of unthinking but devoted men. Peter's improvements, wrote Adam Smith half a century later, "almost all resolve themselves into the establishment of a well-regulated standing army. It is the instrument which executes and maintains all his other regulations."

Prospects in 1715

In 1715, indeed, all that seemed certain was that Russia would win the Northern War. Too much hung upon the lives of Peter and of the no less incalculable Charles XII for a confident forecast of the terms of peace. But any possible settlement as compared with the pre-war position would mean closer contact between Russia and Europe in politics and in trade. In its essentials, the problem nearly resembled that which was posed by the triumph of Japan over Russia in 1905. Every important power must decide what attitude towards the intruder it should adopt. And for the family of nations, which in 1715 comprised those members of the great white race whose habitual co-operation far outweighed their occasional dissension, it became vital that the new-comer should be truly if gradually civilized on European lines. For this to be achieved, contacts between the peoples must supplement the efforts of the autocrat. Trade, books, travel and the pursuit of common aims might accomplish what lay beyond the scope of the most sweeping decrees. Russians could be forced by their Emperor to shave and to clothe themselves like Europeans, to assemble in salons and to instal foreign systems of administration. But unless they knew and respected Europe they could not effectively become European. And the least promising omen for the whole adventure was that while Peter knew Europe he did not respect it but imported the contrivances of civilization merely for the sake of power.

Could Europe assimilate Russia ?

If Russia remained hostile at heart to Europe, Europe, with less concealment, hated Russia. The ancient hatred which all his neighbours felt for the Muscovite, indeed, would not easily be overcome. Europe, near or far, would make small effort towards sympathetic assimilation. Such was, in fact, the course of history. Yet in spite of all miscalculation and reaction forces had been set in motion which drove Russia some distance towards Europe. Half a century later, Catherine the Great could declare that Russia was an European state and that Peter "introducing the manners and customs of Europe among an European people found the work easy beyond his own expectation." During that half-century, and for long afterwards, the transformation of the European system by the rise of Russia occupied a foremost place among the political problems of Europe.

Russia and European Trade

If Europeans were to have intercourse with Russia it must be, as of old, through the narrow gateway of Archangel, or through so much of the Baltic coast as might be wrested at the peace from Sweden. Gustavus Adolphus had boasted that without the consent of Sweden, the Muscovite could not launch a boat upon the Baltic Sea. For Dutch, British, French or Spanish ships to reach Petersburg or Riga involved the long and difficult voyage round the north of Denmark, a country which drew the utmost possible profit from their passage of the Sound. Ice, moreover, might reduce to seven months the season for navigation. Prudence therefore often dictated discharge at Danzig, which served as a distributing centre for Baltic trade. Land routes into Russia were largely blocked by the Turkish Empire, which comprised the lower Danube and the shores of the Black Sea, as well as by the vast plains of Poland. Moscow and Petersburg were separated from Breslau and Danzig not only by hundreds of miles of roadless Russia but by stretches of hardly more practicable Poland.

Even a Peter could not in a moment force Russia into the mechanism of European trade. What the last decade of his life proved that he could accomplish was to win a war of more than twenty years (1721) and to organize on the flank of Europe a powerful autocratic state.

Russian Policy

Peter's Russia, as M. Leroy-Beaulieu suggests, was neither of Europe nor of Asia, but a bridge flung boldly between the two. Peter himself rejoiced over the simplicity of western statesmen from whose eyes many things lay hid. Among these things not the least was that he himself was "Cæsar of all the Russias," and that several of these Russias—White Russia, Black Russia, Red Russia, the border-country or Ukraine—had not yet been regained. Already he had tasted defeat as well as victory, and no man could measure accurately either his power or his ambition. But for twelve years past St. Petersburg, built on a marsh newly captured from Charles XII, had given some clue to the measure of his imagination and of his strength of will. The sight of a Russian army in Mecklenburg with Peter at its head roused painful memories of Attila and Ghenghis Khan.

Assuming, as seemed most probable in 1715, that neither the invincible obstinacy of Charles XII nor the anti-Russian sentiment of the Poles and Germans could prevent Peter from consolidating his gains, how would Europe be affected? Sweden, it was clear, must either avenge herself or become a secondary power. From her Peter had taken not only Estonia, which flanked the southern shores of Finland, but also Livonia, the granary of Stockholm. At the same time his new capital was so situated as never to be safe while Finland remained Swedish. Against Poland he had fought no war. For nearly fifty years since Smolensk fell to Russia (1667), the inferiority of the Republic had been so obvious that she could safely be admitted to an alliance. Peter had, in fact, driven from her throne the puppet placed there by Charles XII, and had restored Augustus of Saxony, his

Stanford, London.

own ally. But the downfall of Sweden would remove the greatest check upon Russian progress westwards by the speedy subjugation of the Poles. The conquest of Swedish Livonia left Polish Courland much exposed. Many Polish subjects in Lithuania were Russian in speech and creed, and Kiev, to Russians a holy city and the cradle of their faith, had been regained only in 1686. No extraordinary powers were needed to divine that the Russian influence would permeate Poland until the Turks or the rulers of Prussia or of Austria took alarm.

Neighbour and latent enemy of Sweden, Poland and the Turks, the three accustomed client states of France, Peter, as a consummate realist, offered his sword to France in lieu of theirs. Allied with the strongest state in Europe, he could defy all other European powers. The French, however, declined the offer, not without contempt, and the political antagonism which naturally followed became one of the century's leading forces. Russia's task, however, would be lightened if the powers of Europe disagreed, and a shrewd Tsar might count upon the recurrence of the tension between France and Britain. The master of a strong army upon the European frontier would not always lack allies. At the moment, however, Peter's greatest victories were gained within the frontiers of Russia.

Peter and the Russian Church

The six years of European settlement (1715–21) closed with an achievement, little noticed at the time, which none the less was characteristic of the age and momentous for the future of Europe. This was the creation of a Holy Synod which made the Tsar dictator over the Russian Church. Throughout Europe, indeed, the drift of the age lay towards strong monarchies exalted at the expense of corporations. The resplendent example of Louis XIV showed what a state could accomplish by concentrating power in the hands of a single man. That of Britain went to prove that a group of men, guided by the national interest, might vie in effectiveness with a monarch. Poland and Germany as a whole might afford a convincing contrast. Among corporations which hampered the concentration of power the foremost was still the Church. More than a century had passed, it is true, since John Knox rebuked Mary Queen of Scots in public or the Pope excommunicated

" this bastard and detestable race of Bourbon." But no hierarchy could entirely abrogate its claim to speak for God; and, in every nation, church and state were still two aspects of the same society. What king could declare himself an atheist or forbid the practice of the national religion? In lands as far apart as Spain and Poland the people felt themselves to be a church more keenly than they felt themselves to be a state.

In no land did the Church more really constitute the nation than in Russia. History had decreed that the Russians should draw all their culture from Byzantine Christianity and that nowhere should inertia be more tremendous. A mob of Russians would be saluted as " Ye Orthodox," and a Russian's proudest boast was " I have kept the faith." The Russian Church centred in the Patriarch, and the dying wish of the last Patriarch (1700) was that all unbelievers might be burned to death.

To a Tsar resolved like Peter to gather all power to himself and to make his people Europeans, a church which consecrated immobility was a hindrance to be removed by force. In the Patriarch, whose ass the Tsar must lead on Palm Sunday, he saw a dangerous rival. As Prokopovitch, the Russian Lanfranc, plainly stated, the simple people, deluded by the splendour of the Patriarch, would support him against the Tsar, believing that they were supporting the cause of God. Peter therefore, while plundering and reforming the monasteries, refrained from naming a new Patriarch for twenty years. He then, in 1721, ventured on a new church organization under which no single ecclesiastic was authorized to speak for the whole. Henceforth the Church, like other state departments, was to be governed by a board of members appointed by the Tsar. In this the Holy Synod he was represented by a Procurator, who might be a layman and whose influence would certainly be paramount. Peter could boast that, surpassing the great Gustavus and Louis XIV, he had made the Church obedient. The Russians, indeed, regarded him as a changeling or a heaven-sent torment or even as Antichrist. Individuals went into the forests and burned themselves, but the nation did not resist. While " the stale and battered article of religion " forced Walpole to govern with one eye always on the

Jacobites, while it filled France with bitter strife and kept Germany on tenterhooks, in Russia, long reputed " the most religious country in the world," policy became almost completely free. Still, in the eyes of the faithful, " to pursue the Lutheran Swedes, the Romanist Poles, or the infidel Turks was to fight the good fight," but so long as every neighbouring power belonged to an alien faith Russian religious zeal only made it easier for the Tsar to wage opportunistic war. Of the six-and-thirty years of Peter's reign hardly more than two were peaceful.

Peter's work, 1715–25

In the short space that remained to him, issuing full fifteen hundred edicts every year, Peter completed and consolidated the autocracy which was the reward of his superhuman labours. The army and the fleet were developed, and upon them was spent three-quarters of a revenue swollen by every imaginable tax. That centralized administration by which alone the vast bulk of Russia could be held together was so organized that the Senate relieved the Tsar without menacing his power, while the great proprietors were made servants of the state. By their side were placed parvenus like Menshikov who could hardly become rival powers and whose presence showed that the Tsar formed the sole fount of honour. To frustrate those who would have returned to Moscow and the old seclusion, Peter decreed that the reigning Tsar might name his own successor (1722) and did not scruple to put to death his own reactionary son. Yet when in January 1725 this hard materialist died, many Russians mourned as for a father, and it was not long before their poets were acclaiming him as " a man like unto God himself." Under " the working-man Tsar," as the foremost of Russian historians can claim, Russia had accomplished more than any other nation in history within a single reign.

Russia and the Turks

At Constantinople a non-European power ruled both the Tartars, who threatened the Russian borders, and many coreligionists of Russia in the regions conquered by the Turks from Europe. Peter's long war with Sweden had been deliberately provoked. With Poland no struggle might be needed. But the Turk was the hereditary enemy whom many motives combined to urge a Tsar, whenever possible, to attack. The fertile lands of the south must be secured and widened for Russia's growing population. Her traders must be able to follow her south-flowing rivers to the sea. Moscow must vindicate her claim to be the "third Rome" by inspiring new crusades, while no Russian sovereign could forget that Oleg had hung his shield upon the gates of Constantinople. The Black Sea raised the question of the Straits. For Russia to conquer access to the Mediterranean would bring her far more profit and prestige than her conquest of access to the Baltic.

"The Turks" and Europe

Few political terms, indeed, are more ambiguous than "the Turks." The name is given to those sections of the human race which speak the Turkish language, whatever their physical form or culture or religion. In this sense a Yakut of Eastern Asia with his reindeer or a Central Asiatic nomad with his horses is a Turk. In the history of Europe, however, the term is restricted, just as "an American" often denotes a citizen of the United States. The Turks were for us those Ottoman tribes who adopted the Mohammedan faith, conquered Asia Minor, and set out to conquer Europe. When Constantinople fell to them (1453), Europe must admit that another Asiatic people had secured a colonial dominion within its bounds.

Other Asiatics in Europe

The Turks in the Balkans, however, contrasted sharply with any of the previous immigrants from Asia. The Lapps, the Finns and the Estonians had received or were ready to receive the religion, the social system and the education of their European neighbours. They retained their Asiatic speech, together with a sense of distinction from foreigners which in the future might serve as the basis for independent nationality. Substantially, however, they had become Europeans. The Jews, aided by their sacred literature, retained not only their language but also their religion. As Asiatics who felt themselves too widely scattered for a national home in Europe, many of them cherished hopes of one day regaining Palestine. Meanwhile they were prepared to co-operate with the nations which gave or sold them shelter. The Bulgars, on the other hand, had forgotten the time when they came from Asia. European in dwelling-place, language and religion, they commemorated their remote intrusion only by unceasing feuds with their alien neighbours. Among the Asiatic immigrants the Magyars seemed easily the first. Backward and divided as Hungary remained, they were the ruling race within a great European kingdom, proud of their language, their customs and their history. They alone belonged to the Roman communion, and they alone ruled over indigenous Europeans. Since 1526 their land had formed the battleground between the Turk and Europe.

Turkish Power in 1715

None of the Asiatics who had become Europeanized, however, could compare in power and numbers with the Turks, who regarded Europe as their predestined prey.

The Turkish Strength

In 1715 they still ruled over several European peoples and threatened others. South of the Save and east of Transylvania, their empire almost everywhere stretched to the sea, and northwards from Crete they held the islands. From Bosnia to Moldavia, Mohammedans, an armed minority, disposed of Christians, and the eastern Mediterranean remained a Turkish lake. The empire of Constantinople still shut off the Poles and Russians from the Black Sea. Despite the Franco-Turkish understanding, Christian Europe, as the war then in progress showed, saw a common enemy and menace in the Turk.

The Turks remained formidable for precisely the same reasons as those which had caused the success of their first assault on Europe. Theirs was still a military state based on religion. Despite its polygamy and slavery, their empire was wont to show astounding moderation. As it had no elaborate political organization, it could lose an outlying province without grave injury to the structure of the whole. The conquered Latins and Greeks, Serbs and Bulgars, self-ruled in Christian communities or converted to full brotherhood in the Moslem faith, fared better than downtrodden serfs in Christian Europe. Balkan races therefore strengthened the Turkish power, when if left to themselves they would have renewed their inveterate and senseless warfare. The Greeks of the Morea now cheerfully exchanged the Venetian dominion for the Turkish (1715). The conversion of a Christian to Islam brought him instant admission to the ruling race. When the Turks crossed to Europe, moreover, they had brought a breed of hardy fighting men and a fine feudal organization. Every Turkish peasant was a soldier, and, given peace with Persia, the army could draw from Asia an almost inexhaustible supply of brave recruits.

At the same time almost every crusade against the

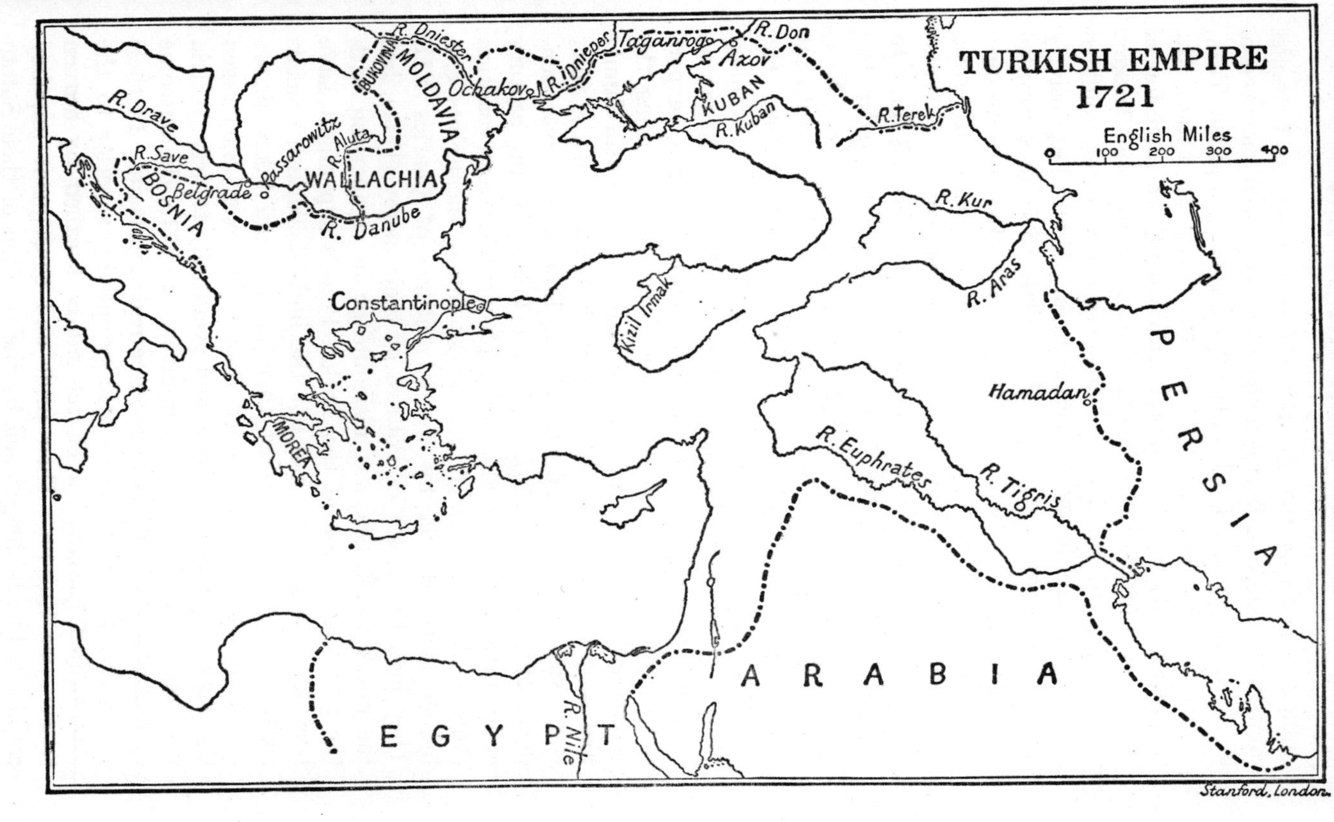
TURKISH EMPIRE
1721
English Miles
0
100
200
300
400
R. Drave
R. Save
BOSNIA
Belgrade
Passarowitz
R. Aluta
WALLACHIA
R. Danube
BUKOVINA
MOLDAVIA
R. Dniester
Ochakov
R. Dnieper
Taganrog
Azov
R. Don
KUBAN
R. Kuban
R. Terek
R. Kur
R. Aras
Constantinople
Kizil Irmak
MOREA
Hamadan
PERSIA
R. Euphrates
R. Tigris
ARABIA
EGYPT
R. Nile
Stanford, London.

infidel was frustrated by the cleavage between Catholics and Protestants, or between the Habsburgs and the French. With Hungary divided between the Emperor and the Turk, while France constantly urged the Turk to attack the Emperor, only a great Imperial revival or the intrusion of some new Christian power seemed likely to threaten Turkey.

The Turkish Weakness

These great advantages, however, were often nullified by grave defects in the Turkish system. Framed exclusively for war and conquest, it could do little to train statesmen or even generals. The military art, like other arts, is progressive; the Turks had no idea of progress. Removed from the soil they became effeminate and corrupt. Worst of all, an able Sultan was now almost past hoping for. In earlier days the Turks had conquered power under the guidance of an almost matchless series of great rulers. Now, to avoid being dethroned and put to death, the autocrat must murder or imprison most of his potential rivals. His successor in all likelihood would lack sufficient training even to choose a good Grand Vizier, if by chance a fit person existed. Upright governors, competent generals, expert naval men, qualified engineers—all were rare. During the latter half of the seventeenth century the Kiuprili family had shown how formidable a single firm hand on the tiller could still make the Turks. Prince Eugene, however, rendered the Austrians stronger in the field, and the century ended with the epoch-making triumph of an European coalition (1699). A decade later, the Turks found themselves embroiled with Russia by the adventures of Charles XII. They held the victor of Poltava at their mercy (1711), but the check to Russia was insignificant in comparison with the real humiliation of the Turk. Peter's slip might have been fatal to himself, had not the highest Turkish officials conspired with him against their master and taken bribes to let him go. Victory over Russia, however, encouraged the Turks to chastise Venice, and eventually to defy Austria with results disastrous to themselves. In 1715, the outcome of the new war with Venice remained uncertain. In their own eyes, the Turks were still essentially superior to the "unwashed giaours," a church militant called by heaven to conquer Europe. Their pride and consequent impolicy could not but be heightened by the position of their Sultan as Caliph, or head of the Mohammedan world. At a crisis in any negotiations with the unbelievers the Turkish ecclesiastics might declare that some course was the will of heaven, with dire results. In the eyes of the Mullahs of the capital, war with the infidel was a duty and God's help assured success. Such views defied experience, but more than half a century was to pass before the weakness of Turkey was realized by Europe. Well-informed statesmen still reckoned her as the equal of two European great powers in the field. Her northern frontier of some two thousand miles resembled a many-cratered volcano. While the Russians kept watch against the Tartars as the men of the Heptarchy against the Danes, the Poles must guard the Dniester and its northern fortress. Hungary, whence the Turks had been lately driven, was sheltered by a barrier of Croatian colonists. Behind the Save and Danube Austria could never feel secure. The Turks, it seemed, might at any time resume the advance which, two centuries earlier, had seemed irresistible. On the other hand, enough had happened to foreshadow a new phase of the question if the Tsar and Emperor should combine.

As the history of the nineteenth and even of the twentieth century has proved, Europe can seldom calculate exactly the strength or weakness of the Turks. Man-power, material resources, situation, character, religion—all give them a latent force which leadership may at any time rouse and magnify. During the reign of Achmet III (1703–30), the glories accomplished under his successor might well seem as unlikely as those which the Kiuprili had achieved.

> "The government here," wrote Lady Mary Wortley Montagu from Constantinople in 1717, "is entirely in the hands of the army. . . . When a minister here displeases the people . . . they cut off his head, hands and feet, and throw them before the palace gate, with all the respect in the world; while that Sultan, to whom they all profess an unlimited adoration, sits trembling in his apartment, and dare neither defend nor avenge his favourite."

A race from which in respect of temperance, fortitude, tolerance and medicine Europe had much to learn was largely ruled by the Janissaries, a mob of inefficient soldiers.

Yet the history of the Turkish Empire, like that of Spain, was a series of astonishing collapses and recoveries. In 1718, at Passarowitz, the disintegration begun by Eugene at Carlowitz (1699) continued along its northern and western frontiers. All Slavonia and Hungary was now in Habsburg hands, and Austrian power extended beyond the Save into Bosnia and deeply into Serbia. North of the Danube, Western Wallachia likewise changed its master. On the Adriatic side, Venice extended her dominion through Dalmatia towards Corfu, which remained hers. The rise of Russia, another hereditary foe, might well threaten to make the Turkish position in Europe untenable unless the two Emperors quarrelled. Yet in 1739, after fighting both of them at once, the Turks regained much that they had lost, and, twenty years later, a king of Prussia, almost conquered by both, looked to the Sultan for salvation. Thus within three centuries of taking Constantinople the mortal enemy of Europe, while rejecting her religion and culture, had fully entered her political system.

BIBLIOGRAPHICAL NOTE

See Bibliographical Note at the end of Chapter I.
Add :—

A

Lord Eversley (G. J. Shaw-Lefevre) and V. Chirol : *The Turkish Empire* (2nd ed. 1923).

S. Graham. *Peter the Great* (1950).

J. von Hammer : *Geschichte des osmanischen Reiches.* VII–VIII (1831–32, 2nd ed. 1936, Fr. trans. 1841–42).

V. O. Kluchevsky : *A History of Russia.* IV (trans. 1926).

J. A. R. Marriott : *The Eastern Question : An Historical Study in European Diplomacy* (4th ed. 1940).

B. Pares : *History of Russia* (rev. ed. 1955).

B. H. Sumner : *Survey of Russian History* (1944, 2nd rev. ed. 1947).

B. H. Sumner : *Peter the Great and the Ottoman Empire* (1949).

B. H. Sumner : *Peter the Great and the Emergence of Russia* (1950).

G. Vernadsky : *A History of Russia* (4th ed. 1954).

G. Vernadsky : " The Expansion of Russia," *Transactions of the Connecticut Academy of Arts and Sciences,* Vol. XXXI (July, 1933), pp. 391–425.

B

Baroness S. Buxhoeveden : *A Cavalier in Muscovy* (1932).

W. Foster : *The Red Sea and Adjacent Countries at the Close of the Seventeenth Century* (1949).

S. James : *Journey through Russia into Persia* (1742).

M. L. Shay : *The Ottoman Empire from 1720 to 1734 as revealed in the Dispatches of the Venetian Baili* (1944).

T. Thornton : *The Present State of Turkey* (1809).

R. Walpole : *Memoir relating to European and Asiatic Turkey* (2nd ed. 1818).

CHAPTER VII

EUROPE 1715–40

SETTLEMENT IN ITALY AND THE NORTH, 1715–21

Character of the Age

THE five-and-twenty years which followed the death of Louis XIV form "one of the flattest levels in the history of Europe," as history is commonly conceived. Bubbles and intrigues, short-lived treaties and still-born wars fill its records, with quacks and adventurers as the most stirring among its politicians. "A period dead in spirit and alive only in stomach" was the verdict of Carlyle, who saw in it chiefly the phenomena of putrid fermentation. It is true that the diplomatic dispatches upon which much of its history is usually based are often petty and sordid, and the biographies, in general, uninspiring. What nation save perhaps the Russian has shown pride in this chapter of its individual story by comparison with those which precede and follow?

The extraordinary character of the age has been accounted for in part by the coincidence that in almost every nation foreigners were in power. Britain was often swayed by Hanoverians; France, Holland and Portugal, by their British allies; Spain, by her queen from Parma; Austria, by the Spanish council of Charles VI; Sweden, by the Holsteiner Count Görtz; a host of minor states outside Germany, by Germans; while the names of Alberoni, Law, Ripperda and Biren emphasize this unusual feature. That foreign rulers and statesmen might be ignorant of the inborn feelings of their subjects cannot be denied. In modern times, however, few kings of unmixed native blood have reigned, and few nations have failed to assimilate their kings and statesmen of foreign birth.

An influence far greater may be ascribed to the lassitude and uncertainty that follow every great convulsion, and to the death of Louis XIV, who had shaped the history of

Europe for fifty years. The peoples needed above all things rest, and true statesmen might well be satisfied with securing the peaceful lapse of time. Peace in the Old World would permit of that development of the New in which one great task of that age consisted, as well as in that redress of social injustice to which the best minds in Europe were soon to turn.

Europe in 1715

In 1715, however, some wars were still in progress, and several unwise statesmen were in power. In the south of Europe the Emperor Charles VI had been compelled to take up arms against the Turks, and in spite of Prince Eugene's genius, and the absence of the western struggle, the issue was still doubtful. Four years earlier, the Turks had conquered peace with Russia, and in 1715 they expelled the Venetians from the Morea. At the same time in the north Charles XII was facing a formidable coalition of Denmark and Russia, Prussia, Saxony and Hanover, the first four being natural enemies of Sweden, and Hanover exerting no small influence upon the dispositions of the British fleet. To resist such a coalition might seem impossible for a mutilated empire drained of men and money by fifteen terrible campaigns. The Swedish gentry, it was said, were too poor to pay for lights during the interminable winter evenings, while the peasants maimed themselves to escape conscription. But the history of Sweden was the history of her kings, and when had a king of Sweden failed to defend her against invasion ? As a boy, Charles XII had shattered a seemingly invincible coalition. Now he was the most famous captain in a Europe which swarmed with disbanded fighting men. His subjects might dislike adventures in the Ukraine or even in Germany, but they had no illusions about the need to drive out the Danes from Sweden. Prussia and Hanover were merely seeking cheap conquests in Swedish Germany, and every German power dreaded the intrusion of the Tsar. At the same time men expected the general war to break out anew. The Pretender had not been subdued, nor Spain reconciled to the loss of her Italian possessions. In 1716 anything might happen.

Progress towards Peace

What actually happened seemed to bring Europe nearer peace. The Pretender and all the occult negotiations in his favour failed. The composite invasion of Sweden likewise failed, Peter perhaps remembering how 8,000 Swedes had put to flight his 40,000 men at Narva, and certainly distrusting his allies. Britain renewed her defensive alliance with the Emperor, who so far overlooked her desertion of his cause in the Spanish Succession war. Her nascent official friendship with France hardened into a treaty renewing that of Utrecht, while Louis XV abandoned the Pretender and gave Britain full satisfaction in the denudation of Dunkirk. In January 1717, their agreement developed into the so-called Triple Alliance between France, Britain and the Dutch. So long as this triple league subsisted, the best army in Europe, the most powerful fleets and the deepest purses stood united in the cause of peace. Finally Eugene, who had shattered the Turks at Peterwardein (1716), drove them out of Hungary. With the annihilation of the Turkish army at Belgrade (1717) the liberation of Serbia was begun. France, plunged by John Law into financial speculation and by her Jansenists into religious strife, rejected Peter's invitation to desert Sweden, but signed a treaty which recognized existing facts. This treaty, signed at Amsterdam between Prussia, Russia and France, guaranteed the Utrecht settlement in the west and the settlement which would eventually be arrived at in the north. It began regular relations between France and Russia, thus admitting to the inner circle of Europe the power which was dismembering the *protégés* of France. At the same time plans for a league between Charles XII and the Pretender received a violent check.

Spanish Aggression 1717

All this progress, however, was challenged by a sudden move on the part of Spain. In the autumn of 1717 a Spanish fleet seized the Emperor's island of Sardinia. This bold stroke, the outcome of many causes and the source of much light upon the age, demands somewhat detailed explanation. The Utrecht settlement, as we have seen, satisfied neither of the claimants to the Spanish empire. Charles VI continued to regard himself as the rightful king of Spain, and maintained a Spanish council which debated at Vienna in the Spanish tongue. Philip V, on the other hand, could not but resent the loss of that time-honoured dominion over great parts of Italy which his predecessors at Madrid had enjoyed. The Italians themselves abominated the rule of

Germans, and already felt that "the monstrous house of Austria" was "the poisoner of the Latin races." This feeling was shared to the full by the two Italians to whom chance had given vast influence over the policy of Spain—Alberoni and Elizabeth Farnese, the new queen.

Alberoni and Elizabeth Farnese

Alberoni, who in 1717 became Cardinal and therefore careless of papal favour, belonged to the class of low-born statesmen whose energy is vast but taste and discipline defective. While no grandee could equal him in breathing vigour into an administration, he was too imaginative for high politics, not knowing the limits of his own power or of the power of Spain. He saw that the Emperor had become the tyrant over Italy and that he was planning an insulting exchange of territories with Savoy. Sardinia, lately a Spanish island, was to be bartered for Sicily, to which Spain, the ancient possessor, still possessed reversionary rights. At a time when the Austrian armies were far away in Hungary, Charles' servants in Italy placed a Spanish Cardinal under arrest. In reply the fleet which Alberoni had assembled for Pope Clement's crusade sailed for Sardinia.

This Spanish attack upon the Emperor for an Italian aim began Alberoni's brief international career. It began also that of Elizabeth Farnese, which kept Europe in effervescence until 1738. Mediocre in mind and training, but endowed with an unbending will, this bright-eyed, passionate woman contrived to wield the sceptre of unwilling Spain. The people, it is said, hinted their opinion by roaring "Long live the king and our lady of Savoy" to Philip and that lady's successor, but they were compelled to carry out her plans. Since Philip, the most absolute of monarchs, was also the most uxorious of men, "the living oracle of His Majesty's most sacred mouth" spoke with the accents of the wife who never left his side. By passing her life in an interminable *tête-à-tête* with her husband, intercepting him when he left his bed to abdicate, and in the end allowing him to confess only in her presence, Elizabeth Farnese drove Spain to abandon its true interests for the sake of her Italian relatives and of her sons. Strong-willed rather than clear-headed, she made elementary political mistakes, challenging France and the Emperor together when success against either was impossible without the other's help, and omitting to make sure of Britain, which held the key to many situations. Yet her career proved no less notable than prolonged, and she became an ancestress of many royal Houses.

Charles VI

The Emperor, whom she challenged in Sardinia, and who must of necessity continue to be her main opponent, resembled her in mediocrity of intellect and in strength of will. As a Habsburg he was heavy where she was vivacious, and regal where she was shrill. Besides the inborn talent of his house for controlling men and women, nature had given him a handsome person, a well-knit frame and a human passion for the chase. A good husband and father, he sincerely held the family belief that Habsburg rule was the supreme blessing for mankind. Having daughters but no son, he had already secretly enacted that Habsburg family ordinance which became known to history as the Pragmatic Sanction. As hopes of male issue faded, it became the chief interest of his life to secure the execution of this decree by which all his dominions might pass to a female heir. His plans and those of Elizabeth Farnese gave a double impulse to the so-called history of Europe.

The Quadruple Alliance 1718

As a contribution to the peace and stability of Europe, the events of 1718 constituted a long advance. On all sides the adventurers suffered defeat and stable arrangements were prepared. In July, the Spaniards followed up their success in Sardinia by seizing Sicily with 35,000 men. This bold aggression threw the Emperor into the arms of the only group of powers which could act by sea. The Triple Alliance of 1717 thus became the Quadruple Alliance of 1718, a league of Britain, France, the Emperor and the Dutch to defend the Utrecht settlement. Savoy, hoping to gain Sardinia in exchange for distant Sicily, joined this league, which stood open to all powers desirous of an equitable peace. Spain, however, declined to accept the reversion to Tuscany and Parma as the price of her accession, and must therefore be coerced. In August, Admiral Byng destroyed the defenceless Spanish fleet off Cape Passaro, and the Sicilian venture lay in obvious peril of collapse.

War—Alberoni's Plans

With five powers arrayed against her, Spain must set Acheron in motion or submit. Alberoni toiled feverishly to unleash the forces of disorder. He planned to dethrone the Hanoverians by means of the Pretender, and Orleans by an invasion aided by high-placed malcontents in France. The Emperor, who was still occupied with the Turks, should be attacked by Peter and Charles XII in concert, while rebellion might be stirred up in Hungary, as of old. Portions of this programme may not have been impossible, but every item remained unfulfilled. Before July was over the Turks had actually signed a treaty at Passarowitz which yielded Hungary and strips beyond its frontiers to Charles VI. The Pretender accomplished nothing, but Britain resolved on war. The Tsar made offers to George I. The French plot merely caused France to declare war on Spain. Above all, in December, a chance shot ended the career of Charles XII, who was invading Norway. None save he could make Sweden an active factor in Europe, and all who had plundered his empire would hasten to secure their gains by peace.

In the new year (1719), none the less, Spain took the offensive by land and sea. Ormond with 6,000 men set sail for Scotland, but few arrived there. British forces sedulously destroyed the ships built and building in Spanish ports, and continued to isolate the victorious Spaniards in Sicily. In April, Philip, Elizabeth and Alberoni launched an army of invasion against France, while at the same time Berwick at the head of 40,000 French invaded Spain. Alberoni tried to end the hopeless struggle by diplomacy, but his own downfall was the price of peace. A modest but not unworthy career awaited him in Italy, and before his long life closed (1752) he saw the end of the Austrian exclusive domination.

Settlement of 1720

Early in 1720 Spain accepted the terms of the Quadruple Alliance and joined its ranks. By common consent, therefore, Sicily passed to the Emperor, who thus became a yet more considerable Italian prince. The schemes of Elizabeth Farnese had made no headway, but the Sea-Powers expected from her rival an improvement in their Mediterranean trade. In exchange for Sicily, the Duke of Savoy gained the new Sardinian crown. The Utrecht settlement had thus been reaffirmed in Italy, its most contentious sphere.

It remained for Europe to achieve a parallel settlement in the north after twenty years of warfare. To Sweden Charles XII, the hero who in Voltaire's phrase, "carried every virtue so far that it became the opposing vice," had left no obvious heir. Thanks to his father's confiscations no great nobles remained, but the lesser nobles now succeeded in grasping power. It was a strictly limited monarchy which was conferred by the Diet on Charles' sister Ulrica, and by her upon her husband Frederick of Hesse-Cassel (1720). Meanwhile, as the result of infinitely complex diplomacy under arms, most of the powers opposing Sweden had concluded peace. Hanover kept Bremen and Verden; Prussia kept Stettin. Britain, supporting Hanover and fearing to become dependent upon the Tsar for naval stores, found herself pledged to aid Sweden against Russia. She was successful in mediating a peace with Denmark based on the retention of Slesvig by the Danes, but to protect Stockholm against Peter's army was beyond her power. In September 1721, the last and greatest of the northern treaties was signed at Nystad. Ingria, Carelia, Estonia, Livonia, regions comprising the site of St. Petersburg and the granary of Stockholm, all were now given up. Sweden retained what she had conquered from Denmark on her own side of the Sound, and the ruins of her German bastion with a seat in the German Diet. As an imperial power, however, "the snow-king melted," and Swedish "great-power-time" was for ever at an end. Prussia with the mouth of the Oder, and Russia with all the ports between St. Petersburg and Riga, could forbid Sweden's future supremacy even in the Baltic sea.

European Progress

The continental empire of Sweden, like the continental empire of Spain, had lacked a firm basis of race or wealth or numbers or geographical situation. Both were replaced by structures whose foundations were less obviously frail, and to that extent at least the years 1715–21 had brought improvement. In the latter year signs were also visible of alliances which might prove lasting, on the one hand between the Emperor and the Tsar and between the two Bourbon houses on the other. While Britain looked on benevolently, France and Spain arranged a double marriage between their heirs. At a time when Europe was extending her influence overseas, when France gave birth to New Orleans and seized Mauritius, while the Spanish settlement at Pensacola and the Danish in Greenland coincided with the British advance in North America, it was a hopeful sign that France, Spain and Britain were in close accord, and that in Britain the pacific Walpole rose to power. It was something that since Louis XIV died Europe had had six years in which to grow richer and perhaps more wise. Besides this, however, her statesmen had done much for peace, and seemed likely to do more.

THE SPECULATIVE MANIA IN FRANCE AND ENGLAND, 1720-2

Financial Crisis of 1720

No account of Europe between the death of Louis XIV and the advent to power of Walpole would be complete without some reference to the French and English crises in finance. The operations of John Law in France and the South Sea Bubble in England combined to render 1720 famous as " the mad year." Its history reflects the general uncertainty that then pervaded Europe in economic theory no less than in politics and in religion. It also shows how wealth and credit had increased when there was small hope of profit from capital except through foreign trade. Many of the bubbles, it is true, were enterprises designed to be carried out at home, but the general cupidity was aroused, and by far the greatest schemes were created, by dreams of boundless gain from the Mississippi or the Southern Seas.

The mischief began in France, where public finance was in such a state that the Regent was ready to accept relief from any quarter. In 1716 John Law, an honest and brilliant Scotch financier, had set up a bank in Paris. Like other banks, it received money for safe keeping, used part of it to buy, of course for less than their face value, the promises of merchants to make payments at a future date, and gave as the whole or part of the purchase price its own promises, in the form of notes payable on demand. Since it bought judiciously and paid its notes in gold, it made large profits and gained a good reputation. Next year, having imparted to the Regent his own sincere belief that what the country needed was more money, Law was allowed to make his bank a government institution. Its notes could then be tendered in payment of taxes, and their issue was increased because the provincial collectors were instructed to use them instead of coin for remittances to Paris. There the Treasury paid them away for the goods and services which it required. Since money is what money does, the nation's stock of currency was thus augmented. The money which Law had at his command, since he had bought the use of it by exchanging it for paper, he sought to employ for the benefit at once of France, of French America and of his bank. His plan was to stimulate the development of Louisiana, the vast and largely unknown basin of the Mississippi. In 1717 he received permission to reorganize the great Company of the West. In return for a loan of 100,000,000 *livres*, the government granted to his Company a monopoly of the right to trade with Louisiana and to colonize it. His alliance with the Regent led next year to a great extension of the bank, and to a decree which rendered it difficult for large payments between Frenchmen to be made otherwise than by means of its notes. No right can be more profitable to a bank than the right to circulate its paper, or more dangerous to a government than the right to create cheap currency at will. As post-war experience has proved, millions may come to be bought and sold for the value of the blank side of the notes. Law and the Regent, however, went forward boldly with their policy of colonial rationalization financed by paper issues. By 1720, the Company had grown into a wider Company of the Indies, and had bought up all the overseas Companies of France. The French had now come to believe that fortunes were to be made by investing in enterprises hitherto unremunerative, and those who held shares were therefore able to sell them at a premium. With an investing public behind him, Law was able to purchase the rights of coining money and collecting taxes in France herself, a change from which both the Treasury and the taxpayer might expect to profit. The distinguished and deserved success of these flotations encouraged him to attack the enormous standing debt of the French state. Illustrating the truth, equally inexorable and simple, that the existence of more of anything tends to make men offer less of other things in exchange for it, the increase in French currency had lowered the purchasing power of every *livre*, whether the *livre* was paper signed by Law or silver minted by the King.

Law's Schemes

Those who had goods to sell therefore received more *livres* from those who bought them. With some of these they paid their creditors, and the creditors, unable to employ them profitably, would lend them to the State at lower interest than before. Law seized the opportunity for a vast conversion scheme. His Company provided 1,500,000,000 *livres* at 3 per cent. by selling new shares at ten times their nominal value. With this huge sum, contributed by the public, the State paid off its former creditors, who were in great part the purchasers of the new shares. The State had now one creditor, Law's Company, in place of many. It paid one-fourth less interest than before, and every *livre* that it had still to pay was handed to it by the taxpayer with less sacrifice than prior to the inflation. Its former creditors, who had been paid the full nominal value of their debts, might or might not have acquired a promising security by reinvestment in a genuine but untried undertaking.

Such an analysis, however, leaves out the factor of human nature. The bank lacked the experience and skill to finance these huge transactions by printing notes without unduly disturbing values. The public, not for the last time, lost its head, and scrambled for shares at almost any premium. Speculation in all its forms set in. Men bought shares without the means to pay for them or the desire to hold them, trusting to their ability to borrow the purchase money or to sell again immediately at a profit. Others contracted to buy shares from those who merely hoped themselves to secure them on better terms. Rogues profited by the temporary aberration of honest men. After the hot fit came the cold, and neither Law nor the Regent could prevent the collapse of credit. The bank, unable to redeem its notes, was abolished; Law quitted France; and early in 1721 the Company submitted to a drastic reconstruction by the State.

At the same time other countries, England chief among them, were attacked by the same disease. The war, like many wars, had left behind it vast public debts and considerable private accumulations, an appetite for gain without steady toil, and a distaste for quiet thinking. The lack of scope for profitable enterprise at home turned men's thoughts towards distant lands, and the mirages which they conjured up confused their nearer vision. During the year 1720, in England the classic year of "bubbles," shares in the South Sea Company were taken up at £1,000 apiece.

No more solid reason for this extravagance could be found than that the Company had contracted to pay £7,500,000 for the right to take over £31,000,000 of irredeemable national debt. The inevitable panic which followed burst many bubble undertakings and lowered the price of South Sea stock to £135. As in France, the collapse of credit ruined countless individuals and rendered necessary the intervention of the State. The storm which cowed ordinary statesmen revealed the rock-like confidence of Robert Walpole, and in 1722 his twenty years' ascendancy began.

EUROPE FROM NYSTAD TO THE WAR OF THE POLISH SUCCESSION, 1721–33

Robert Walpole

During the eleven years (1722–32) which preceded the war of the Polish Succession the outstanding figure in the history of Europe was a man who prided himself on being insular to the core. A Norfolk squire, whose delights were hunting hard and drinking deep, who left foreign affairs to others and at a pinch nodded his head and raised his eyebrows to emphasize his brother's eloquence in bad French —such a man seemed a strange arbiter between the proud Catholic Houses which reigned at Paris, Vienna and Madrid. The anomaly arose because Britain dared not let go the European balance and because Walpole by sheer ability always contrived to guide her hand.

Prominent among Whig statesmen since the accession of George I, Walpole (1676–1745) had reached the middle forties when the need for restoring public credit made him, in fact, the first Prime Minister of Britain. He gained and kept this great position by a rare combination of qualities—unbounded force of mind and body, unfailing industry and courage, quick perception and sound judgment, the power to act and to refrain from action. While he was at the helm, Englishmen could boast of a minister who did everything, but so easily and quietly that he seemed to be doing nothing. Service of this kind, by a politician who sneered at heroics, and who judged that his country would be best served if she kept him in office and avoided adventures, makes no spectacular appeal, especially when a Bolingbroke exists to rouse the Opposition with his fertile brain and lying tongue.

Hence it comes about that the most inspiring glimpses of England's foremost statesman date from his latest years, when he drank to the men who had proscribed him because they beat the French or when he drove a hundred miles in agony to serve his country. A supreme realist, he saw that for Britain a stable dynasty meant life or death. The nation, therefore, must be induced to accept the Hanoverians by domestic prosperity and lapse of time. Prosperity could not be arrived at without peace, and peace was three-fourths secured if Britain could escape war with France. If Walpole showed himself more zealous to preserve his own power than to make heroic use of it, if he chose to attenuate persecution rather than challenge the mob by proclaiming the rights of conscience, if he withdrew wise proposals in the face of factious opposition, he might have claimed with Pitt, who attacked him and afterwards repented, " I know that I can save this nation, and that no one else can." Successive kings and ministries found him indispensable, whether in or out of office, while the 'Forty-five and its collapse formed the supreme vindication of his career.

Schemes of Charles VI

The stolidity of British policy under Walpole sharply contrasted with the flightiness of continental powers. In 1722 the Emperor, relying on the capital and enterprise of British speculators, attempted to make his new possessions in the Netherlands the seat of an East Indian trade. In the interests of Amsterdam the Scheldt, which leads to the far finer port of Antwerp, had long been closed by treaty to ocean-going ships, but Charles VI held that Ostend might be made to serve his purpose. The impolicy of the Habsburg plan lay in its assumption that the Dutch and English would have installed the Emperor in the Netherlands to break into their own most cherished monopoly. Spain, they contended, had abjured such use of the Netherlands and the rights of the new sovereign of the Netherlands could not be greater than the old. Whatever his legal position, Charles and his Ostend Company were challenging an all-powerful and ruthless opposition.

Next year (1723), when the publication of the Pragmatic Sanction exposed the Emperor on another flank, dynastic changes opened anew the problem of the policy of France. Not every political problem could be solved by lapse of time, and a European Congress on Spanish claims in Italy was overdue. Departure from the moderation shown by the Regency since 1715 would further jeopardize the peace. In February, Louis XV, a shy boy of thirteen, came of legal age to rule. Orleans and Dubois remained in power, but before the year ended both were dead. As the King grew up, his own share in the government would be what he chose to make it, and his tutor Fleury, the modest and aged bishop of Fréjus, might come to influence policy. At his suggestion, Louis empowered the incapable Duke of Bourbon to succeed Orleans as First Minister. But France in the eighteenth century was usually ruled by women, and the gap between Madame de Maintenon and Madame de Pompadour was filled for a space by Bourbon's mistress, the less famous Madame de Prie. These personal changes, however, left the *entente* with Britain unaffected. France held to the same course, but the tiller was grasped by weaker hands. Next came a startling though short-lived change upon the Spanish throne. In January 1724, Philip V installed his son Louis in his place and, like Charles V before him, went into religious retirement. At the end of August, however, the boy-king died of smallpox, and Elizabeth prevailed with her husband to cancel his abdication. In the meantime the European Congress had assembled at Cambrai, and by its obvious inconclusiveness had changed the political situation.

Fleury

The Congress came into being as a sequel to the career of Alberoni. Europe assembled to settle questions, like that of Gibraltar, which the negotiations of 1719–20 had left unsolved. Considered as a European transaction its main object must be to safeguard the peace of Europe by contenting Spain. This, however, could hardly be accomplished save by concessions in Italy, and these Charles VI, a true Habsburg, was loath to make. By a supreme exercise of the obstructive pedantries of Vienna, a congress fixed for 1722 was prevented from meeting formally until February 1724. When King Louis died, it had been for a full half-year in session, suggesting to the young Voltaire that all the ministers of Germany had assembled for the purpose of getting their Emperor's health drunk, while the English delegates sent many couriers to Champagne and few to

Congress of Cambrai

London. Such a body was unlikely to persuade the Emperor to do justice to the claims of Don Carlos, Elizabeth's eldest son, nor would the other members of the Quadruple Alliance instal him in Parma by force and return Gibraltar.

Spain and Ripperda

Faced with the prospect of receiving nothing from the one party, the Spaniards remembered their old Habsburg connexion and determined to approach the other. With their vast colonial empire they could offer the Ostend Company a matchless chance of gain. They were likewise rich in potential bridegrooms, such as Ferdinand, the heir to Spain, and Carlos and Philip, the sons of Elizabeth Farnese. A marriage between Carlos and Maria Theresa, heiress of Charles VI, might eventually make the Emperor's grandson lord of a dazzling inheritance—Spain and Austria, Italy and the Netherlands, Hungary and the Indies. A second Charles V, he would thus be Holy Roman Emperor and Most Catholic King in one. The accomplished adventurer Ripperdá,[1] who was Dutch and Spaniard, Protestant and Catholic by turns, went on a secret mission to Vienna during the winter of 1724–5, only to find Prince Eugene too prudent for such fantastic projects.

Marriage of Louis XV

Early in 1725, however, a blundering stroke by Bourbon changed not only the basis of bargaining but the grouping of the powers of Europe for eighty years. Louis XV had now reached marriageable age; while his affianced bride, the Spanish Infanta, was a child of six, whom he delighted with the gift of a costly doll. Under Louis himself or his infant son, if he had one, Bourbon might hope to rule, but, if the King died without male issue, young Orleans would mount the throne. The Orleans family had therefore pledged Louis to a Spanish child, but Bourbon could not await the maturity of the Infanta. A list of a hundred eligible princesses was drawn up, each of whom, if chosen, would bring a different influence to bear upon the policy of France. The Russian Elizabeth, Peter's lovely daughter, was awarded the second place, and Catherine I, Peter's new-made widow and successor, was wild for the Franco-Russian alliance, which the great Tsar had failed to gain. Every moment, however, was precious, and Madame de Prie preferred a

[1] Cp. pp. 517 *et seq.*

humbler bride, whom she herself might dominate. Thus it came about that an exile in France was chosen, the daughter of the ex-King Stanislas of Poland, whom Peter had dethroned. As queen of France, Maria Leszczynska must stand for hostility to Russia. Heaping injury after injury upon Catherine I, Bourbon unwittingly drove her to the Emperor's side. The Russo-Austrian alliance of 1726 was dissolved by her death next year, but the tendency of Russia to prefer the Habsburg alliance to the French survived until 1807. The immediate injury to Russia, however, was as nothing beside the injury to Spain. Spain had performed part of her contract for a triple Franco-Spanish marriage, and a flighty Orleans princess had shared Spanish Louis' momentary throne (1724). Now the return of the Infanta by France was answered by the dismissal of the ex-queen and her sister the betrothed of Carlos, together with the Frenchmen who filled diplomatic and consular positions in Spain. Spain also threatened war, and permitted Ripperdá to accept the Austrian alliance on the Emperor's terms.

First Treaty of Vienna 1725

The treaty of Vienna (May 1725) pledged Spain to the Ostend Company, and foreshadowed an attack upon Gibraltar with the Emperor's consent. Madame de Prie seemed to have set all Europe ablaze. The strange alliance between Habsburgs and Spanish Bourbons was answered by a treaty of Hanover (September 1725) made between the French Bourbons, Britain and Prussia, and joined later by the Scandinavians and Dutch. The most convincing counter-demonstration, however, was given by the British fleet. The life-blood of Spain consisted in the treasure which her ships brought from Central America every year. In 1726, the treasure-ships were blockaded in Porto Bello, while British cruisers threw the Ostend Company out of gear. Diplomacy, indeed, sufficed to seduce the Sergeant King of Prussia from the Allies, but without Spanish subsidies the Emperor could not fight, even had he been as bellicose as the Spaniards themselves. Personal changes, moreover, made for peace. In May 1726, the Ripperdá bubble burst, and in June Bourbon and his associates were banished by royal orders. At the age of seventy-three Fleury found himself the master of France. What aims would this quiet ecclesiastic impart to his royal pupil?

Fleury and French Policy

The Fleury riddle has been answered by historians in many different ways. One finds him sly; another, mediocre and unfixed of purpose; another, hypocritical; another, a new Mazarin restoring France to greatness. If we decline to assume the complex until the simple has been disproved, and if we reject the folly of imagining unnecessary crimes, we may see in Fleury's policy the natural outcome of what he had previously appeared to be—a modest and blameless churchman. To perform the daily task without striving to increase it, to handle men and nations gently and with intelligence, to commit the issue to Providence and lapse of time—such was a rational conception of his duty. The most recondite system could not have served France so well. If Fleury could impart to her his own industry and quiet, her natural wealth and central situation would make her an unrivalled power. As the old Cardinal lived on to earn his nickname, "Your Eternity," much of this came about, despite the intrusion of unwiser rivals.

What is certain is that under Fleury "France and peace" became the watchword on one side of the Channel as was "Britain and peace" that of Walpole upon the other. But while the island power, like the United States until 1940, could view diplomacy somewhat coolly, France lay in the midst of a great group of states. To serve her dutifully, Fleury must make such international agreements that the balance should never again fall into English hands. In 1727 treaties were concluded as of old with Sweden and Bavaria, as well as in the post-war style with Britain. French diplomats toiled to lower the temperature at Madrid and at Vienna, and to break up the Austro-Spanish league. The Spaniards, indeed, could not be restrained from besieging Gibraltar, a fortress which many British statesmen would gladly have resigned had not public opinion tied their hands. The Emperor, however, intent on the Pragmatic Sanction, consented to suspend the Ostend Company for seven years, and generally to work for peace, pending a second Congress and an unhurried examination of the ancient treaties which fettered commerce.

Congress of Soissons

Early in 1728 it seemed that the pacific policy of Fleury and of Walpole had met with full success. In England a new Hanoverian had peacefully succeeded to the old, and the minister himself had found means to keep his place. An exasperating kinglet by comparison with his virile sire, George II could be managed by his able queen, and Walpole had only to manipulate the elections. On the continent France had not fought with Spain: the Emperor had escaped both war and Spanish marriages: and Spain, despite Elizabeth's Anglophobia, now accepted peace. For the convenience of Fleury, a convinced upholder of the notion of a league of nations, the European Congress met at Soissons (June 1728) within range of Paris.

As at Cambrai, however, the Congress method proved unequal to the needs of Europe. The Emperor steadfastly demanded, and Fleury no less steadfastly refused, that the accepted basis of negotiation should be the Pragmatic Sanction. By a secret treaty made in the previous year, at the Sergeant King's hunting-box of Wusterhausen, the Emperor believed himself assured of Prussia with her large standing army and well-filled arsenals and war-chest. His consequent contempt of his Spanish ally roused Elizabeth's facile fury. Forgetting Gibraltar, she demanded that the Italian duchies destined for Don Carlos should be garrisoned by Spanish troops. At the same time Louis' Polish queen was at last "brought to bed of a dolphin" (September 1729). This birth extinguished Philip's hope of being one day crowned in France and therefore favoured a sincere *rapprochement* between the Bourbons north and south of the Pyrenees.

Treaty of Seville 1729

The outcome in 1729 resembled the outcome in 1725. Despairing of the Congress, Spain allied with the power with which she had been at war. In the former year she had turned to the Emperor and had made the treaty of Vienna. Now she turned from the Emperor to the Hanover allies, and made with them the treaty of Seville (November 1729). By this, Britain, France and their associates guaranteed the succession of Don Carlos to Parma. In return Spain cancelled her concessions to the Ostend Company and resumed her former friendships. The Emperor replied by pouring troops into Italy, and to judge by the gestures of the two crowned adventurers the long-dreaded general war was imminent. Shrewd observers noted, however, that although the Emperor disposed on paper of vast forces, many of them were immobile garrisons in unruly provinces, while apart from France, the Sea-Powers and perhaps Spain, no state could pay for a protracted large-scale war. In 1730, indeed, the chief sufferers from the European tension were the royal family of Prussia. There the Sergeant King, always explosive in temper and confused in speech, found himself opposed by his Hanoverian queen and by Frederick, his detested heir. Himself a passionate Imperialist, both from aggressive Teutonism and from expectation of territorial favours in western Germany, he was driven to fury by his wife's adhesion to a plan for a double marriage with the other side. By this, four second cousins were to intermarry, the Prince of Wales with Wilhelmina and his sister Amelia with Frederick the Crown Prince. After suffering many public and private insults from his father, Frederick, at eighteen, resolved to flee to France. Arrested as a deserter from the army, he was forced to behold his confidant on the way to execution. Only the remonstrances of Europe and the refusal of the Prussians to countenance the judicial murder of their Crown Prince saved him from the fate which had befallen Tsar Peter's only son. At first imprisoned, then forced to live under rigorous restraint, and, at twenty, to marry the Emperor's insipid niece, Frederick endured an education which profoundly affected the after-history of Europe.

Crown Prince Frederick and his Father

Second Treaty of Vienna 1731

For the moment, however, Frederick's escapade merely inclined the Sergeant King to take part in the threatened general war. At last, early in 1731, the Duke of Parma died, and Don Carlos became entitled to succeed him. The Emperor, however, seized the duchy, Spain vainly summoning France and Britain to resist. War seemed inevitable, but Walpole resolved to avert it by paying the Emperor his price. A second treaty of Vienna brought the Emperor to satisfy both Spain and Britain. In return for a British guarantee of the Pragmatic Sanction, he consented to dissolve the Ostend Company and to admit Don Carlos to Parma and Piacenza, renouncing at the same time a Bourbon marriage for his heiress Maria Theresa. By the permutations of high politics and by her own persistence, Elizabeth had so far undone the Utrecht settlement as to reopen Italy to the Spanish line.

Spain and Britain

Not the least curious feature of this Spanish triumph was that it was won for Spain by a power with which she was on the verge of war. By the public law of that age, indeed, hostile relationships between states might be limited to definite portions of their forces or of the globe, without provoking a general war between them. But the race between Britain, France and Spain for colonies and commerce in America both North and South was so important as to imperil their good relations in Europe. With Britain under Walpole and Spain under "the Spanish Colbert" Patiño, commerce ranked very high, while commercial friction could hardly be avoided. The South Sea Company grossly abused their right to trade; unlicensed Britons smuggled on a great scale; and Spanish vessels, whether authorized or not, made indiscriminate captures of British ships. In point of time, the second treaty of Vienna coincided with the famous outrage upon Captain Jenkins' ear. The British public was roused by stories of their sailors done to death as heretics, while to such heretics the Spaniards ascribed fantastic crimes. The antagonism between the Emperor and Elizabeth was an affair of princes, that between Spain and England an affair of peoples, demanding still higher statesmanship for its restraint.

The Polish Succession

Throughout the year 1732, however, peace was maintained both in the Old World and in the New. While the Emperor lent all his energies to securing support for the Pragmatic Sanction, Britons were founding Georgia as a bulwark against France and Spain. But France, nursed by Fleury since 1726, and thrice as long a stranger to exhausting war, had accumulated stores of energy which must find vent in action. In February 1733 Augustus of Saxony and Poland died. In September, the father of Louis' queen found himself again, as in 1704, King Stanislas of Poland by election. France, ready, as Fleury complained, to ruin her own King in order to help his father-in-law, prepared for "a war of vanity" on his behalf.

1733–9—THE WAR OF THE POLISH SUCCESSION AND THE SUCCESSES OF FRANCE

So far as the Polish Succession itself was concerned, the war which took its name was for France a hopeless quest. Before the election of Stanislas, the Tsarina and the Emperor had chosen a new Augustus of Saxony to succeed his father in Poland, Charles gaining thereby the Saxon guarantee of the Pragmatic Sanction. Against the Emperor, France promptly declared war (October 1733). Poland, however, lay beyond her radius of action, except by the long voyage round the Skaw. Would her ancient clients, the Swedes, the Turks, or the Poles themselves obey her call to arms?

From Sweden, it was clear, no vigorous action could be expected. There the Diet ruled, and the Caps, favouring peace with Russia against the more war-like Hats, held the upper hand. The Turks, drilled by a French adventurer, were ready to ally with France, but to such an alliance Fleury could not consent. The Poles eagerly took French bribes and their leaders clung to Stanislas, counting on French reinforcements. As a born Pole in a nation which cried "Rather a gipsy than a German," the restored king, with his kindly bearing and real talent for rule, might well win popular support. In Poland, moreover, the fall of Warsaw has often been merely the signal for the national uprising to begin. The Emperor, as the sequel proved, might soon be forced to recall his army from the Polish frontier, while the Sergeant King firmly refused co-operation. But the splendid Russian army had defied the confusion which followed Peter's death and now, led by Scots or Germans, proceeded to enforce the will of Anne the new Tsarina (1730–40). Within a fortnight of the genuine election of Stanislas, a sham election had made Augustus king. Soon the Russians were marching on Danzig, the Polish fief which had received Stanislas within its walls.

France and Spain in Alliance

Fleury meanwhile was preparing to secure from the unwelcome upheaval the utmost possible gain for France. By rashly menacing Poland, the Emperor had exposed his Rhenish and Italian flanks to France and her allies. Before declaring war upon him Fleury had won the new Sardinian monarch, Charles Emanuel of Savoy, with a promise of the whole duchy of Milan. Early in November, by the treaty of the Escurial, France stepped into her natural place as the kinsman, patron and ally of Spain. The complete identity of policy befitting a family compact was attested, not for the last time, by bountiful promises made by France. Outside Milan, all conquests made in Italy should fall to

Don Carlos, whose prospects in Naples and Sicily seemed particularly bright. The treaty had necessarily an anti-British flavour, for Britain still held Gibraltar. While constantly embroiled with Spain in the South Seas, moreover, she was forbidding her northern colonies to trade with the French West Indies. But so long as the Stuart peril still hung over Britain, no throne in Europe seemed more secure than that of France. Fleury, confident in his power to prevent a rupture, could therefore act with greater freedom. If Britain stood neutral, France and Spain between them would command the Mediterranean, and southern Italy at least could hardly be defended by Charles VI.

Campaign of 1734

Thus prepared, the quadruple campaign of 1734 produced from remarkable confusion clear-cut and no less remarkable results. Much of the confusion arose from the dual position of the chief German princes. Charles VI was ruler of "Austria" as well as Holy Roman Emperor. In the former capacity he provoked France; in the latter, he prevailed on the Imperial Diet to support him. The decision of the Diet meant that Elector George marched Hanoverian troops towards the Rhine, while King George II observed the neutrality upon which Walpole had resolved. It meant also that while Frederick William as Prussian king stood neutral, as Elector of Brandenburg he sent 10,000 well-found men to the Emperor's aid. The state of the law of neutrality, moreover, permitted such phenomena as the march of a Russian contingent against France with whom Russia was not at war, and the presence of a French legation at Brussels, since the Austrian Netherlands were neutral.

A war so plainly opportunistic and professional was chiefly memorable for the bargains which brought it to a close. In its northern theatre, however, the Russian siege of Danzig led to one notably heroic deed. The French armada which the great city awaited proved to have merely three battalions on board, and these prudently returned to Copenhagen. There the ambassador, the Breton Comte de Plélo, seized the command, and sailed once more for Poland, to find a glorious death in a hopeless charge against the Russian lines. After 135 days, Danzig itself surrendered and Stanislas was driven to Prussian Königsberg for shelter.

The main French army, faced by the Germans, met with

its old success. Philipsburg, which guarded the road into the Empire, fell to Louis' troops, Prince Eugene proving impotent to save it. The Prussian King and Crown Prince were among the high-placed spectators of the campaign, and from this fact, perhaps, its chief contribution to history arose. Frederick beheld the triumph of indifferent strategy over Austrians under the most famous of commanders and over Imperialists under four commanders serving in turn, while 20,000 Russians marched to the rescue—a display of feebleness tempting to a realist prince who was sure of his army and of himself.

Meanwhile in northern Italy the success of French, Sardinians and Spaniards had been limited by their mutual jealousy, and the great fortress of Mantua remained in Austrian hands. Further south, Naples, and eventually also Sicily, fell to Don Carlos, the people aiding. In July 1735 he was crowned King of the Two Sicilies at Palermo. In all four theatres of war, the ineffectiveness of Austria had been displayed; and in 1735, with the Turks unquiet, Charles was inclined for peace. Fleury likewise thought it well to seize the moment before the English dislike of Spanish progress brought the nation to share their King's desire to strike for the Emperor against the French. In October, therefore, preliminaries of peace suggested by the sea powers were signed at Vienna, Fleury and Charles leaving the logic of the situation to compel Elizabeth's concurrence. Their terms had the merit of recognizing facts, and, by skilful compensation to individuals, of promoting their embodiment in law. Lorraine, though a fief of the Empire, had long been dominated and wellnigh encircled by France. Its Duke, Francis, was to marry the Emperor's heiress, Maria Theresa. Stanislas, on the other hand, might be regarded as a French prince and against Austria and Russia he had no chance of regaining Poland. The Emperor again could not recover Naples and Sicily, where his authority possessed no roots. A complex bargain might be made. Let Francis grant Stanislas the reversion to Lorraine, the heirs of Tuscany, the reversion of that duchy to Francis; the Emperor, Naples and Sicily to Carlos. In exchange the Emperor might secure the peaceful possession of the north Italian dominions, which he could reach by land, and an explicit

Third Treaty of Vienna 1735–8

guarantee by France of the Pragmatic Sanction—a momentous concession by a power which had been longing for the disintegration of Austria for more than two hundred years. These exchanges would leave Elizabeth baulked of Parma and Piacenza and Charles Emanuel of more than a strip of Milan, but their disappointment would not greatly distress their satisfied allies. Although this third treaty of Vienna was not finally signed until November 1738, nor accepted by Elizabeth and Don Carlos until eight months more had passed, the War of the Polish Succession ended in 1735. It left a new Bourbon dynasty in Naples and a Russian protectorate in Courland. Francis won Maria Theresa's hand next year, and in 1766 Lorraine fell finally to France.

Turkish War 1737–9

Before the War of the Polish Succession was legally disposed of, two further wars had broken out. Wars between Turks and Russians had hitherto been affairs rather of Asia than of Europe, but the march of Russians westwards in 1735 drew Austrians east next year. As auxiliaries under treaty they might have fought without embroiling their master with the Turk, but Charles counted on Balkan gains to balance his Italian sacrifice. Eugene, however, died that very year, and Bartenstein, a master of acrimonious dispatches, equalled him in honesty alone. Three campaigns (1737–9) under three successive commanders brought the ill-found Austrians a heavy balance of defeat. The Russians, meanwhile, had gained victories, but at an appalling cost in gold and human life. The desire of Münnich for the glory which had eluded him at Danzig did much to involve the German-led Tsarina Anne in war. The vigorous Münnich, indeed, regained Azov (1736), which Peter had won and lost. Ochakov, the key of the Dniester, also fell to him, and Moldavia followed. Then, however, the desert and the scorching sun came to aid the Turks, and the Russian losses mounted to some 100,000 men. Though a French adventurer, Bonneval, had armed the Turks, France had remained neutral. She could therefore mediate, and it now fell to an elderly French magistrate, Villeneuve, to negotiate for peace. Thanks largely to his skill, the Turks gained at Belgrade (1739) their last triumphant settlement. Although the Russians were to keep Azov, it was to be an open town, and the Black Sea must remain undefiled by Russian navigation. From Austria the Turks recovered what Eugene had gained in 1718. "'Tis Belgrade kills me," were the words ascribed to Charles before his untimely end in the next year.

Rise of France

Meanwhile, both in politics and in commerce, France had gained great success. In 1738, Sweden became her client. In Poland, and, socially at least, in Russia, her influence rose high. At Constantinople it passed all bounds. In May 1740, the so-called Capitulations were renewed, giving great commercial advantages to France, together with the right to protect the Catholic foundations in Turkey, and to guard the Holy Places. That commercial and colonial ambition, which was epitomized in the Indies by the great name of Labourdonnais, seemed thus victorious in the Levant. Britain soon felt the pinch of competition and was impelled to favour the anti-Turkish moves of Russia.

War of Jenkins' Ear 1739

While Fleury's France thus gained prestige all over Europe, the passions of the mob were forcing Spain and Britain into war. French diplomacy, it is true, helped to break down the honourable resistance to popular clamour which Walpole made in "the greatest party struggle since the Revolution." For French diplomacy had at last so far subdued the loathing of Elizabeth for Fleury that she accepted a French marriage for Don Philip, her younger son. The news of this may well have been decisive with the British ministry, who knew that such a match must inevitably draw Spain towards France, and that for the last nine years France had been secretly their foe. Within a week of its reception, the British squadron which had been recalled to England was ordered to continue at Gibraltar. This threat to Spain on the eve of a peaceful settlement meant that Britain intended war, that "public-house Protestantism," the braggadocio poetized by Pitt, the lust for galleons and ingots and for the free export of slaves had overborne Walpole's statesman-like moderation. Ripe judgment pronounces March 10, 1739, when the Gibraltar squadron was directed to remain there, the signal for a struggle only ended by the Monroe message of 1823. Until that day, Spain and Britain might possibly have collaborated in America, excluding France. Thereafter the combination must become Spain and France, excluding Britain, and Britain alone could not always defeat the two combined. Upon Fleury, who had by no means precipitated war, now fell the burden of reaping its harvest for France. If the war, which was declared in October 1739, should prove slow and indecisive, the gain to France was clear. The British navy must draw heavily upon British merchant-ships and seamen, while Spain, with the inferior fleet, must become dependent upon France. French commerce and prestige could be hindered from advancement only by the immediate victory of Britain, and victory in the tropics, against an enemy strong on land and elusive by sea, was by no means easy. Fleury therefore consented to French naval armaments for the eventual protection of Spain, and preserved a neutrality which qualified France to enjoy, as at Belgrade, the advantages of ultimate mediation.

For a whole year this expectant attitude was justified by events. Vernon, indeed, took Porto Bello one month from the formal declaration of the war. But thenceforward the laurels fell to Fleury and the English Opposition. Anson's amazing voyage round Cape Horn hardly did more for Britain than Plélo's splendid self-sacrifice had done for France. The "War of Jenkins' Ear" affected the immediate history of Europe chiefly by immobilizing Britain and by emphasizing the antithesis between herself and France.

BIBLIOGRAPHICAL NOTE

See Bibliographical Note at the end of Chapter I. Add :—

A

E. Armstrong : *Elizabeth Farnese* (1892).

J. O. McLachlan : *Trade and Peace with Old Spain, 1667–1750* (1940).

W. Michael : *England under George I. The Quadruple Alliance* (trans. 1939).

J. H. Plumb : *Sir Robert Walpole : The Making of a Statesman* (1956).

C. B. Realey : *Early Opposition to Sir Robert Walpole* (1931).

H. W. V. Temperley : "The Causes of the War of Jenkins' Ear," *Trans. R. Hist. Soc.*, 3rd ser., III (1909), pp. 197–236.

P. Vaucher : *Robert Walpole et la politique de Fleury, 1731–1742* (1924).

L. Wiesener : *Le Régent, l'Abbé Dubois et les Anglais.* 3 vols. (1891–99).

B. Williams : *Stanhope : A Study in Eighteenth Century War and Diplomacy* (1932).

A. McC. Wilson : *French Foreign Policy during the Administration of Cardinal Fleury* (1936).

B

John, Lord Hervey : *Some Materials Towards Memoirs of the Reign of King George II.* 3 vols. (edited by R. Sedgwick, 1931).

W. S. Lewis, *et al.* (eds.) : *Horace Walpole's Correspondence.* 19 vols. published to date (1937–).

CHAPTER VIII

1740–8, THE NEW AGE AND THE WAR OF THE AUSTRIAN SUCCESSION

Royal Deaths

IN 1740, as in 1715, it was the death of kings that changed the history of peoples. Again, in the courtly phrase of a contemporary, " death ventured upon many crowned heads " and a new era palpably began. Twelve months sufficed to prove that the cautious men must give place to would-be heroes, that diplomacy must wait on war, and that war in a corner of Europe might kindle almost all the world.

The physical decay of Fleury and the parliamentary decline of Walpole were changes no less momentous than many royal deaths. Of these, however, the three which fell within half a year could hardly leave Europe unaffected. Her enormous army might make Prussia formidable at any time and doubly so when France, Britain and Hanover seemed to be falling into opposite camps. The Russian army enabled Russia to act as a great European power whenever the Tsar judged intervention profitable. The Imperial office was still the most glittering prize in Europe and the Austrian succession the focus of diplomacy in recent years. At a time when the American war threatened to raise the question of Gibraltar it would be fortunate if Europe could replace the Sergeant King, the Tsarina and Charles VI without breaking the peace.

Accession of Frederick II

The first of the royal deaths, that of the Prussian King in May, surprised no one. Berlin was jubilant that its gloomy tyrant was no more. The English letter of condolence and congratulation to his heir had stood ready since 1734, when Frederick hinted to his sister that he meant to surprise the world as king. While general curiosity prevailed as to the conduct of a devotee of Voltaire on the throne, the serious Prussian succession question seemed to be that which the death of the Elector Palatine would raise when it took place. Claims to Berg-Jülich had drawn Frederick's father to the

Emperor's side and had given rise to several secret treaties. In the preceding year (1739) Prussia, conscious that the Sea-Powers as well as Austria and France inclined against her, had secretly engaged with France for a partition which should give her part of Berg. Her own guarantee of the Pragmatic Sanction, it could be argued, was contingent upon help from the Emperor in that duchy, but Charles had secretly engaged with France to support her rival (1739). The Berg question, however, was neither new nor urgent, and Prussia ranked in Europe as no more than a secondary state with a swollen and costly army which she was too timid to risk in battle.

Accession of Ivan VI

Anne's death in October punctuated for the Russians the loathsome tyranny which her " German " favourites practised in her name. Russia, however, seemed likely to be weakened, since Ivan VI, the new tsar, was a helpless infant and his Brunswick relatives commonplace as well as foreign. " Four light women, two children, two madmen, such were Peter's successors," and to contemporaries the death of the slothful Anne (1730–40) appeared merely to signify that the detested Germans would govern with even less restraint. *Coup d'état* followed *coup d'état* among them, but for a twelvemonth these merely concerned the administration and did not touch the throne.

Accession of Maria Theresa

The death of Charles VI in 1740, however, staggered Europe. Both the Imperial crown and the wide-flung Habsburg provinces had been his, and the foremost problem of politics at once became that of the Austrian succession.

The Pragmatic Sanction

The Empire, like the Papacy, could pass to any Christian man but to no woman. Since 1736, Charles' heiress, Maria Theresa, had been the wife of Francis of Lorraine. His accession to the Empire, followed by their son's, would effect the smallest breach in the immemorial series of Habsburg Emperors. Francis, however, was eminent neither personally nor in virtue of his possessions. Even for Austria, Vienna would have preferred another lord. Only the weight of an undivided and unchallenged Austria could give him any hope of success in the election. For twenty years Charles had made it his single purpose that Austria should pass undivided and unchallenged to his daughter. The Pragmatic Sanction, first approved by all his own dominions, had since been guaranteed by every important state, except Bavaria.

These guarantees had been bought by a long series of concessions—to Spain the recognition of the Bourbon rival at Madrid and of his son at Naples; to Prussia, not very honestly, the Berg-Jülich reversion; to the Sea-Powers, the abolition of the Ostend Company; to the Saxon house, the crown of Poland; to France, the reversion of Lorraine. Unquestionably, a well-drilled army and a full treasury would have been stronger than these parchment guarantees. But an estate which comprised Belgium and Milan, Austria, Hungary and Bohemia, with a score of lesser countries, might even gain in strength by a few judicious cessions. The long familiarity of Charles' subjects with the new law had won for the idea of Maria Theresa's succession a respect without which no queen of so many peoples could have been secure. Even those foreign guarantors who might forswear themselves would be hampered by their consciousness of guilt, while upholders of the Pragmatic Sanction must draw strength from the knowledge that they were acting in defence of law.

The Queen

In her hereditary states Maria Theresa assumed power unchallenged and declared Francis her co-regent. Like Isabella the Catholic in Spain and Victoria in England, she is conspicuous for uniting the characters of an imperious sovereign and a devoted wife. Foreign diplomatists found a difficulty in treating Francis so as to please his consort, who wished them to show him unbounded deference in intercourse but in politics to look to herself alone. A born ruler, however, she possessed in its highest form that power of pleasing which seems to be hereditary in the Habsburg house. In later years, she passed in night attire from her own rooms to the court theatre to tell the delighted Viennese that her son had fêted her on her birthday with a grandson. Dignity and sympathetic familiarity, unfailing courage and support for her advisers, complete devotion to her task and unfeigned confidence in God—these would in any age have made her an outstanding queen. In the eighteenth century and with such a task as hers, her lustre seems unique.

From the first moment of her reign, it was evident that she would be opposed. With the failure of male Habsburgs at Vienna, the day of the rival Wittelsbachs of Munich seemed to have dawned at last. Popular even in Vienna, always the ally of France, Charles Albert of Bavaria set out to secure

Excluding the Austrian Netherlands and Austrian possessions in Italy

for himself at least the Imperial and the Bohemian crowns. His wife, whatever her renunciations, remained the daughter of Joseph I, Charles' predecessor and elder brother; and, as Charles Albert held, a covenant made in 1546 gave Austria to his house if Habsburg male heirs failed. Augustus of Saxony and Poland, with Moravia as the bait, asserted the title of his wife, the elder daughter of the Emperor Joseph I. Elizabeth of Spain, coveting Habsburg North Italy for her younger son, prompted Philip V to declare that he himself, as heir to the Spanish Habsburgs, was the lawful successor to the Austrian Habsburgs also. Even Charles Emanuel of Sardinia trumped up a claim which merely disguised in legal language the hereditary longing of the Savoyard for Milan.

Prussian Repudiation

Some of these claims, however, obviously ran counter to one another, and none would be formidable if the strongest guarantors fulfilled their undertakings. Russia, Britain and Holland, though not at the moment free to give much assistance, could yet be reckoned friendly. France, the secular opponent of the Habsburgs, always tempted to acquire Belgium and to intrigue beyond the Rhine, could hardly repudiate a solemn treaty only five years old, while under Fleury she ranked as unaggressive. In December, however, the whole scene was changed by the tidings that the Prussian army had invaded Silesia, to which Frederick claimed to be the heir.

"That he might rob a neighbour whom he had promised to defend"—such was the use to which the young realist had put the great military machine bequeathed to him by the Sergeant King. His freedom of choice was such as few monarchs in history have enjoyed. His policy was hampered by no human weakness, for he was free from hampering affection or entangling vice, from traditional scruples or illusions. His ancestors had made the Prussian state in their own image, sneers a Frenchman, for it was they who had divided the land from the waters and had created even the spirit of man.

Power of Prussia

The Prussian state treasury was the king's, and no man or corporation dreamed of questioning his right to determine policy. None the less a fine band of civil servants and of field officers rendered him loyal service, among them many from other states who had chosen to serve in Prussia. A word from the autocrat sufficed to set the civil or the military machine in motion. The civil machine, indeed, was an auxiliary designed to make the army more effective. Since 1723, when the Sergeant King decreed that the ancient feudal dues and the new national taxation should be administered by a single board, the budget had been so shaped that now some six million dollars out of the total seven were devoted to the army or to its prospective needs. And the army, although born Prussians in the main commanded and many in the ranks were Prussian serfs, was largely composed of alien hirelings, who had been beaten with the rest into a coherent mass which blindly obeyed orders. From the first moment of his reign, Frederick had shown his eagerness to increase his already swollen forces. The Sergeant King had left a strength of some 80,000 at a time when France kept about twice that number under arms and Austria not many more than Prussia.

Frederick planned an immediate increase by some 10,000 men, and expanded the *cadres* so as to accommodate a still greater number. To the sixty-six infantry battalions no less than seventeen were added. Foreigners were to fill the ranks and with them contingents from other German states trained on the Prussian plan. The time might come when all Germany would in a military sense be Prussian, and Europe in self-defence would be forced always to stand to arms. With Hohenzollern persistence, using his queen to transmit his cajolery and threats, Frederick wrung from his brother-in-law of Brunswick two battalions which the Duke was loth to raise. All this and the tremendous strokes which were to follow have been ascribed by some to Frederick's peculiar wickedness.

Frederick's Personality

Nothing, however, can be more misleading than the common use of the proverb, "Like father, like son." Not seldom, environment counts for more than birth in forming character. In the case of kings and princes, the resemblance is often in great part due to the fact that the life-problems which father and son must face remain unchanged. It was Prussia that compelled the Hohenzollerns to be what they were—active, economical and realistic. In Frederick, indeed, there was far more foreign than Hohenzollern blood. The Sergeant King, his father, descended in the female line from the Houses of Hanover and Orange, while among his great-great-grandfathers was James I. Some three-fourths of Frederick might be accounted Hanoverian, for his mother was the daughter of our George I. On that side, however, he largely derived from France. The unfaithful wife whom George I immured in Zell, her father's capital, was by her mother the descendant of a line of French nobles. The share of Hanover and the Palatinate in Frederick's ancestry considerably surpassed that of the Hohenzollerns.

His language and "Kultur" were very far from German. A self-styled heathen, he had nothing but contempt for the religious camps into which Germany was still divided. Yet his modern admirers claim that his ideals were purely German and that his monarchy gave to the world a pattern of German perfection.

"The actual statesmanlike and heroic brilliance of his vision," it is declared in language which has no ready equivalent in English, "came from the holiest spheres of the German spirit. His idea of a king living in responsibility to the state and bound by the inmost laws of duty bore the purest and noblest imprint of German being in its political and spiritual discipline and its compelling spiritual strength. In this German . . . sovereignty lay dormant the power to resist without which the strokes of the Great War could not have been borne." (Berney.)

Yet the achievements to which this encomium is the tribute are those which at the same moment compel the grave indictment of Frederick as "really and wholly bad—the man who, seeing perfectly the choice between good and evil, coolly, deliberately, and after mature consideration chooses evil" (Mowat).

Frederick's freedom, however, far transcended the power to dispose at will of an enormous army. Fettered by no alliance, he was yet certain of allies when he had chosen his line of action. This certainty came from his observation of European politics since his journey westwards in 1734. As he read his world, its greatest political fact was the cleavage between France and Britain, a fundamental antagonism which Walpoles and Fleurys might disguise, but which no diplomacy could abolish. In a balanced Europe, each needed the Prussian army to turn the scale, and neither, he felt sure, would allow her to be subjugated by the other. Hanover, to protect if Britain were his ally, to conquer if his enemy, lay a helpless hostage at his doors. Courted by Britain, though his Guelf uncle, George II, hated the Hohenzollerns, he utilized her advances, as he paraded his own armaments, to impress Fleury with the value of his alliance. The Prussian representative at Versailles received written instructions from the King to describe him as a fiery youth whose lust for fame might easily kindle a world war. At a moment when the war of Jenkins' ear compelled her to throw her ægis over Spain, France might be willing to bid high for the sword of Prussia. At the same time Frederick instructed his representative at Hanover to declare in an outburst of jealousy that his colleague at Versailles was one of his master's bosom-friends who would not have been sent save on an important mission. Britain, he calculated, would thus be stimulated to outbid France, and the auction might bring him profit in the question of the Berg succession.

Prussia and Austria

The news which reached the sick Frederick on October 26, however, showed him that a far greater prize than the Berg succession might be won. The last business dispatched by the Emperor, a strong man suddenly cut off at fifty-five, had been an Imperial rebuke to Prussia for her violent behaviour towards Liège. Frederick's first comments on his death revealed his studied realism. The old political system, he divined, was dead. The Austrian colossus must collapse. His own machine had long been ready. As a Prussian king, he commanded his fever to begone and it obeyed. When veteran patriots wrote that the archives would disclose titles to Silesia, he answered that he had learned this from his father. He did not add that he himself had accepted parts of Silesia as security for a loan to Austria. It is probable that his eagerness for action was so great that to decline the Silesian adventure was beyond his power. For three days he debated with his confidant Podewils and with General Schwerin by which of three possible methods the province should be secured. One of the two European groups, that of the Sea-Powers and Russia, wished to preserve Austria as a check on France. They might therefore persuade her to yield Silesia in exchange for the Prussian alliance and various minor benefits. In that case, Frederick would gladly vote for Francis as Emperor, resign his title to Berg, and pay several million dollars to the Queen. Alternatively, France, Bavaria and Saxony might be induced to join with Prussia in a war of partition. The inducement to France would be unchecked ascendancy on the Continent, when the rival Habsburg power had fallen and she could sway a client Emperor in the Bavarian Charles Albert. But if negotiation with either group seemed too slow and its outcome doubtful, a third alternative remained. Prussia might grasp Silesia by a sudden spring and then make out the best case that she could and secure the largest profit that future negotiation or warfare might allow.

Invasion of Silesia

The secret conference closed on October 30. Eight days later Frederick ordered the mobilization of the invading force. On November 9 came the news that Anne was dead and Russia consequently out of action. Within six weeks of the mobilization order, on Friday, December 16, 1740, Frederick crossed the Silesian frontier with less than 22,000 men and 34 guns. Parvenu Prussia thus attacked the Austrian empire and with it the law and the morality of Europe. "The man is mad," cried Louis XV, and only the boldest thinkers dared to disagree.

Frederick, however, "crossing the Rubicon as it were in his sleep," was sane enough in his immediate calculations. However small his force, it far exceeded any that Austria could send to meet it, and the Protestants of northern Silesia welcomed it with open arms. Breslau, as an Imperial town, claimed the right to stand aloof from Austrian and Prussian quarrels. A few fortresses held out, but before spring had come, Glogau, the most northerly, had been taken by storm. Then at long last the Austrians under Neipperg intervened, though numbering almost one-third less than the army of Frederick and Schwerin. On the snow-covered

Mollwitz

plain of Mollwitz (April 10, 1741) the Prussian venture first endured the test of battle. The king was too inexpert to press home the advantage of surprise, or to realize that when his cavalry had been shattered the victory might still be won. But while he himself was riding more than twenty miles in flight, Schwerin and the infantry retrieved the day. Each side lost some 4,500 men, more than one-fifth of their total strength, and although the Austrians dared not risk another battle, they had manœuvred the Prussians out of southern Silesia. In diplomacy, however, Mollwitz proved one of the decisive battles of the world.

The vast effect of so small a victory arose from the position

Zorndorf
R. Havel
BERLIN
Cüstrin
R. Warthe
Kunersdorf
R. Spree
Schwiebus
R. Oder
Glogau
R. Elbe
Torgau
SILESIA
Leipzig
Rossbach
Liegnitz
Breslau
Hochkirch
Leuthen
Dresden
Pirna
Mollwitz
Hohenfriedberg
Maxen
Landshut
Schweidnitz
Glatz
SILESIAN WARS
English Miles
0 20 40 60 80
Prague
Kolin

of politics in France. Whether from honour, from indolence, or from calculation, Louis and Fleury were indisposed towards an anti-Austrian campaign. The increasing possibility that Francis might be elected Emperor, however, alarmed the new heirs to his former duchy of Lorraine. Tradition dictated an anti-Habsburg policy more than ever when the Habsburg was sustained by Britain. The Austrian Netherlands and Luxemburg might become the prizes of a timely intervention. Such considerations, which were not without influence even upon pacific statesmen, drove French hot-heads violently towards a war. The reigning mistresses of the lymphatic king, those nobles to whom a campaign meant martial sport in summer and Paris in the winter months, patriots who saw in Fleury only his almost ninety years—all these cried, Down with Austria, and whispered, Down with England. Unhappily for Europe they found a rallying-point in a veteran of two former wars, the Count, soon to be the Marshal, de Belleisle.

Belleisle and France

In 1740 the Parisians conceived a passion for Belleisle like that which kindled their successors for Boulanger in 1886. In Belleisle, however, they had found a real hero. Of giant strength, a fiery youth at fifty-six, brave, toilsome, abstemious and sincere, he merited and received the adoration of his family and of his friends. The policy of which he became the impassioned spokesman was in effect the ancient policy of France, hall-marked with Richelieu's mighty name. Abase the House of Habsburg, parcel Germany into secondary states; having divided, rule there; incorporate the convenient borderlands—was not this what Richelieu would have counselled France? The true answer was hardly what the French of 1740 supposed, for the century since Richelieu's death had transformed the problem with which he had to deal, nor had he been unmindful of the sea. Fleury's patience and non-aggression had brought within sight an *entente* with Catholic Austria which would have secured the peace of Europe and permitted France to throw her energies into rivalry with Britain overseas. Belleisle, with unfeigned patriotism, was urging France to abandon the principle of *suum cuique* for that which Frederick had already framed and followed, " If one has an advantage shall he not profit by it ? " Mollwitz, which proved that the Prussian infantry was not mad, brought Belleisle victory in France, and the outcome was to be the overthrow of public law in Europe.

Alike in diplomacy and in war, however, 1741 seemed to be Belleisle's year and that of resurgent France. Surrounded by everything that could dignify his mission, the Marshal made a majestic progress into Germany. Thanks to his advocacy, the chances of the Austrian candidate for the Empire paled before those of the Bavarian. At Nymphenburg, on May 18, a secret treaty was concluded which threatened to let loose upon Maria Theresa a separate enemy for almost every province that she possessed. There, in Charles Albert's castle, France, Spain and Bavaria agreed to partition her dominions, and Saxony and Sardinia soon became members of the league. The Prussian convention with France came nearly three weeks later, for Frederick long hoped to gain his ends by British mediation without further war. Britain, as usual, felt that the obvious duty of jarring German tribes was to compose their differences and to hold France in check. But Maria Theresa would face ruin rather than cede an acre to a robber, and Vienna held that George of Hanover would bring Britain to her aid. Frederick therefore bound himself to France, which guaranteed that northern Silesia should remain in his possession. Hastening back to Paris, Belleisle by sheer vitality forced Fleury into war. Soon came the welcome news of the costly British repulse from Carthagena. In August France brought in Sweden, where the Hats deemed the moment opportune for an attack on Russia, Austria's nominal ally. On August 15, French troops actually crossed the Rhine. The Bavarians, moving along the Danube towards Vienna, had already captured Passau.

Anti-Austrian Coalition

In this fashion began the so-called War of the Austrian Succession, the compendious title for the many wars to which the events of 1741 gave rise. "Not Dismal Swamp under a coverlid of London fog could be uglier," declared Carlyle. While the motives of most participants were sordid, and their diplomacy treacherous, the sinister figure of the Prussian king stands out triumphant, and the negation of morality between nations is consecrated by his success. The confusion of the narrative must be heightened by the fact that powers whose armies fought against each other were often technically at peace. Belleisle himself marched into Bohemia as a mere

War of the Austrian Succession

auxiliary of Bavaria, for France and Austria were not at war. George II in person likewise helped to beat the French at Dettingen while at peace with Louis XV. War between colonies compelled no rupture between the mother-countries, and if the Holy Roman Empire were not at war the area of hostilities in Germany might be dotted with neutral towns. As between the contending nations, moreover, war, judged by modern standards, was far less intense. Trading with the enemy was no crime, and outside the range of the half-professional armies men lived their ordinary lives. On the battlefield, however, the troops fought in close order and often hand to hand, with murderous results. Wounded who could not quit the field were more likely to be stripped than rescued. Pursuit was rare, but a defeated army might be almost annihilated, since its mercenaries often passed over to the winning side.

The World War

The history is further confused because as the war proceeded the Austrian succession yielded place to issues greater still. In 1741 the struggle was in the main compounded from the new desire of Prussia to rival Austria in Germany and the old desire of France to rival Austria in Europe. But even then there was perceptible the influence of a wider rivalry, that between Britain and the Bourbon powers for trade and for dominion overseas. As (by time and fighting) the problems of the Old World reached some solution the vaster problem of the New must necessarily develop in importance. The war between Prussia and Austria more and more became a war between France and Britain.

In 1741, however, the Austrian succession formed the prize, and it seemed as though Austria must be destroyed. Her few allies were occupied elsewhere—Britain, with Spanish America; Russia, with Sweden; Holland, with her own security. Under a young queen whose counsellors were feeble and her treasury empty, she had failed to hold a vital province against a single foe. Now she had suddenly to face six formidable powers—Prussia, Saxony, Bavaria, Spain, Sardinia and France—each coveting some of her dominions and well situated for acquiring it by force. How could she hope to resist?

Maria Theresa

What hope she had, rested on a twofold basis. In Maria Theresa she possessed a ruler whose very weakness was her strength, since it roused the chivalry in which her states were rich. The queen who could rally the Hungarians and defy the Hohenzollerns proved also an administrator of rare industry and no little tenacity and insight, a mistress whom all were proud to serve. That meant that the manhood of her wide empire flocked to her armies, the more willingly as they fought in a righteous cause.

On the other hand, the coalition was a league of mere spoliation, cemented by no great ideal, and conscious that many of its claims had no foundation. How could Saxony wish for Prussian success when northern Silesia blocked the road between herself and Poland, and when that ceaseless territorial expansion which has been termed the inexorable law of Prussia's being was likely to make Saxony or Poland its next victim? Prussia could as little wish to see the Saxons installed in southern Silesia and Moravia, thus encircling her new possession. In Italy, Spaniard and Savoyard pursued mutually conflicting aims. In Germany, few states would long exert themselves to secure the hegemony of France. Such a coalition would be equally disintegrated by success or failure. The successful would be tempted to slink off with their private gains, while failure would quickly show that they could fall back on no principle of right. If Austria could survive the initial shock, many ways of escape might open.

European Changes

The eight months which followed Belleisle's triumph, none the less, taxed all the courage of the Queen. Following the movements already named, Belleisle joined the Bavarians and captured Linz, a Danubian stronghold only three days distant from Vienna. A second French army entered the Netherlands, and George II, instead of bringing in Britain, agreed to Hanoverian neutrality. An attempt to buy off Frederick only revealed his incomparable treachery, and the provinces designed for Saxony fell cheaply into Prussian hands. Prague, centre of that Bohemia which has been termed the brain and heart of the whole Austrian empire, failed to resist the French (November 25). Ten days later, their diplomacy seemed to have been crowned by the installation of their *protégée* in Russia. There Anne of Brunswick had been regent for her infant son, prolonging the *régime* of the detested Germans. Now, counselled by the French ambassador,

Peter's beautiful daughter Elizabeth went to the Guards by night, bade them, if need be, die for her sake, as she swore to do for theirs, and flung Anne, Ivan and the Germans into prison. This stroke, it was erroneously supposed, would end the Swedish war with Russia and furnish France with two more ready tools. In January 1742, Belleisle's Bavarian nominee became the Emperor Charles VII, all eight Electors voting in his favour.

Austrian Progress

By January, none the less, the tide had turned and was already running strongly for the Queen. Her timely appeal to the Hungarians, the recall of troops from Italy, the mutual jealousy of French and Prussians, the rising loyalty in Austria, all added to her power. On the very day of his election Charles VII lost Passau, and soon Bavaria itself was overrun. Frederick was driven from Moravia and even in Bohemia he was attacked. The exchange of Carteret for Walpole, moreover, meant that Britain would side vigorously with Austria against France. British diplomacy, always active to reconcile the German powers, contributed also to draw Austria and Sardinia together. In February, by the Convention of Turin, Charles Emanuel actually changed sides. The astounding terms of this Convention, " which," says Sir Richard Lodge, " reads more like a labour agreement than a political transaction," bound him to defend Milan for the Queen against the Bourbons, suspending his own claims upon it, but reserving the right to reassert them on giving a month's notice in advance. In Italy, therefore, Austrians and Sardinians could begin a victorious campaign, while a British fleet gave Naples one hour in which to declare neutrality or face its guns.

Prussia makes Peace

The great event of the year, however, was the detachment of Prussia from the Coalition. Always the realist, Frederick was quick to see that even if the French could make a Tsarina and an Emperor they could not command success in Bohemia where he was. Victory in a confused struggle between Czaslau and Chotusitz, some fifty miles east of Prague, cost him over 4,000 men without driving away the enemy. He trusted neither the Saxons nor the faltering French. Britain meanwhile sustained her mediation and offered Austria help if she would come to terms with Prussia. In June, Frederick judged that he would gain more by peace than by continued war, and before July was over he had deserted France. The treaty of Berlin brought him the main body of Silesia, north and south. The region comprising the rich coalfields of after years was yielded to a Prussian negotiator whose instructions would have permitted him to let it go. By a mixture of sound and unsound calculations, by hardihood, efficiency and chance, Prussia had thus gained her end in eighteen months. The fertile basin of the Oder, if she could keep it, would almost double her consideration as a German power.

Saxony, on the other hand, was compelled to quit the Saxony follows
struggle with no compensation for the blood and treasure which she had poured out. With Prussia on her northern and eastern frontiers, she might in the near future be driven to look to Vienna for support against Berlin. In December, she joined Austria in a defensive alliance which boded ill for Prussian security in Silesia. Deserted by the Germans, the French must now extricate their forces from Bohemia as best they could. Belleisle's winter retreat from Prague was a costly feat of heroism, and the Bohemian failure for a time extinguished his prestige in France. The French success in Petersburg, moreover, had proved as illusory as their success in Frankfort. Elizabeth, the new Empress, showed herself wholly Russian, and her chief counsellor, Bestuchev, anything but French. Instead of a peace treaty favourable to Sweden, the year 1742 brought the conquest of Finland by the Russians and something like a diplomatic breach with France.

All this, however, and the spectacle of Austrian progress 1743
in Italy only roused the foremost military power in Europe to fresh exertions. Even before Belleisle's flight from Bohemia, Bavaria had been almost wholly reconquered for their Imperial *protégé* by the French. Like the fall of Walpole (1742) the death of Fleury in January 1743 meant that the party of action would gain control. Although the new campaign proved languid and its outcome everywhere unfavourable to France and her allies, the French, relieved of unhopeful adventures far afield, were braced to make war in earnest. Dettingen (June 1743) was lost by an accident to a mixed "Pragmatic" army: Bavaria fell once more into Austrian hands: in Italy the Spaniards were driven back: but France was being changed from an auxiliary into a principal in the war and the stage set for a new act in the clumsy tragedy of Europe.

It was Carteret, the statesman who accomplished little but won reverence from those who accomplished much, whose masterpiece marked the change. In September, after endless negotiation, a treaty was concluded before Worms, in the camp of George II. The signatories were Britain, Austria and Sardinia; the object, to weld together so vast a coalition as to compel a speedy peace and the evacuation of Italy by the Bourbons. Saxony, Russia and the Dutch came in and more allies might follow. The results of the treaty of Worms, however, were almost all the opposite of those which Carteret expected. Within six weeks the Bourbons united in a family compact, the treaty of Fontainebleau. By this Louis found himself pledged to support all the projects of Elizabeth Farnese with no equivalent advantage. France was stirred to meet the threat to her own soil by launching the Pretender against Britain, and to seek both defence and compensation by attacking the Netherlands. Austria, though encouraged to dream of reconquering Alsace and Lorraine, Naples and Sicily, resented the concessions to Sardinia which Carteret had exacted, and began to doubt the British system. Carteret himself paid the penalty for having pledged Britain to Austria far more deeply than the British public wished. London, it is true, was strong for the salvation of Austria as a bulwark against the aggressive Bourbons. But it was no less strong against a new Thirty Years War to gratify the Hanoverian
1744 pro-Habsburgism of George II. Austria had been duly saved, and London felt no desire to finance a new Grand Alliance for her aggrandizement. Carteret therefore fell like Walpole, and the less vigorous Pelhams came into power. Even Genoa resented Austrian concessions to her neighbour Charles Emanuel, and in self-defence favoured the Bourbons, who seemed less dangerous than the Queen.

The most fatal defect in Carteret's policy, however, was that his treaty destroyed the basis of the whole alliance, the neutrality of Prussia. An aggrandized Austria, Frederick knew well, would soon try to regain Silesia. Always aggressive in defence, he formed the Union of Frankfort to uphold the Imperial constitution, and in August marched into Bohemia with 80,000 men. The first success almost surpassed that of his seizure of Silesia. In mid-September Prague again capitulated, and, a fortnight later, all Bohemia was in Prussian hands. In allying himself with France before the move, Frederick had stipulated that he should keep the north-eastern section of that kingdom, thus buttressing Silesia and further encircling Saxony. Within two months this "second Silesian war" had changed the European situation. When Frederick struck, a Habsburg army had crossed the Rhine into Alsace. His stroke freed France from the invading Germans, whose need to regain Bohemia set Bavaria also free. But in Traun Austria had found a general, and, given generalship and subsidies, she could always prove herself a military power. In Bohemia Traun joined with the Saxons, whose neutrality Frederick had violated on his march to Prague. Being thus superior in numbers, the Austrian proceeded to give his opponent a costly lesson in the art of war. His Fabian tactics in a friendly country cost the invaders more than many battles. When December came, the Prussians found themselves across the mountains in Silesia and reduced to half their former strength. Of their foreign mercenaries, some 17,000 had changed sides, and Frederick's hold upon the rank and file was shaken. To save Silesia he urged France to sacrifice the Emperor and make peace.

Four other pregnant events had signalized the dying year. France had discovered a great soldier and lost a minister of mark. Maurice de Saxe,[1] bastard of Augustus II, a Protestant and a rake, now led the French army in the Netherlands with inimitable skill. In this campaign he began that career of conquest just beyond the threshold of France which was to influence French thought about the war until its close. In December, on the other hand, the strongest link between France and Prussia was severed by the capture of Belleisle. Arrested in Hanover while journeying to Berlin, the Marshal was haled to England, where he formed the opinion that a few thousand scullions of the French army would suffice to conquer the country. In his absence France declined to champion Prussia. Beyond the Atlantic French and British colonies were now at war, and Annapolis fell to France. At the same time the turbid course of Russian history had for a moment established Frederick's influence at Petersburg. He used it to recommend as a bride for Elizabeth's

[1] See also pp. 533 *et seq.*

chosen heir an obscure princess of Anhalt-Zerbst, the future Catherine II.

1745 The new year, 1745, began with the death of the hapless Emperor Charles VII, and went on to see both the area and the intensity of the war increased. While the Austrians overran Bavaria and threatened Silesia, the French and Spaniards gained the upper hand in Italy, and Marshal Saxe in Flanders. Fontenoy, his great victory of the 1745 campaign, was a murderous encounter lost largely through the failure of the Dutch. The Pretender's invasion followed, and for a moment the throne of the Hanoverians seemed to totter. The peril justified the quiet policy steadfastly pursued by Walpole. The fact that the peril was successfully dispelled forms the supreme tribute to his career. Meanwhile Frederick was restoring his own prestige and conquering peace. In diplomacy he cringed at once to Britain and to France, begging the one to plead with Austria and the other to invade Hanover " as an emetic." But in war his victory at Hohenfriedberg when pursued across the mountains on to the Silesian plain (June 1745) proved that both he and the Prussian army had become masters of their trade. Cool strategy, well-planned surprise, efficiency of every arm alike—all these were now achieved, and the mutual confidence of king and army formed a great factor in the history of Europe for many years. " The globe does not rest more securely upon the shoulders of Atlas," Frederick declared, " than Prussia upon such an army as she now possesses," and by Prussia he meant Prussia with Silesia. Three further victories beat back the invading Austrians and Saxons, and enabled him, again deserting France, to make peace at Dresden in December. The cession of Silesia was confirmed by Austria and guaranteed by Saxony, while Prussia recognized the new Emperor Francis I, who had restored the purple to Vienna.

American War

In America, meanwhile, the struggle between France and Britain had entered upon a most important phase. While King George's throne was tottering in the 'Forty-five, a vision of the future British empire was revealed. French North America depended on the mother-country far more than British, since it contained barely 50,000 Frenchmen, and their settlements were much less firmly based. Admirable as explorers and organizers, good soldiers, fishermen, hunters and traders in fur, the French did not turn readily to agriculture or handicraft overseas. Whatever possibilities the river route from New Orleans might contain, at present Montreal and Quebec could reach the sea only through British territory or by way of the St. Lawrence. The French must hold Cape Breton Island in force. Failing this, their access to the St. Lawrence might be cut off by the power which held Newfoundland and Nova Scotia on either side with eight hundred miles of settled coast-line to the south. In the quiet development of French colonies since Utrecht, therefore, the strengthening of Cape Breton had not been overlooked, and Louisbourg had been fortified at an enormous cost. In 1745, Old England and New, the King's ships and the militiamen from Massachusetts, combined to conquer Louisbourg. The local value of the capture was enormous. Cape Breton subdued, Nova Scotia prevented from revolting, the French fishing grounds commanded, Canada hemmed in, New England made secure—all this rendered Louisbourg an effective counter-stroke even to Fontenoy.

In 1746 the war spread to Asia, but in Europe the in- 1746
flamed area was reduced. While Labourdonnais took Madras and Dupleix routed the auxiliaries of Britain, Scotland ceased to be a theatre of war, like Bavaria, Prussia and Saxony during the preceding year. At the same time America was lost to the French, unless they could convey a fleet and army across the ocean. So long as Minorca and Gibraltar remained British, and Brest, the chief port of concentration, faced the prevailing wind, French Atlantic expeditions must be highly insecure. Early in July, moreover, Philip V died, and Elizabeth's bellicose influence at last came to an end. Barbara, said the wits, succeeded, and Barbara was Portuguese, which meant British. Her pacific husband Ferdinand VI, however, was impelled to follow his stepmother's policy in Italy, lest her son Don Philip should return to trouble Spain. Throughout the year Bourbon and British diplomatists actively negotiated for peace, though their labours had but little influence on the campaigns.

Of these the chief were two—that in the Netherlands and the Italian. By the Austrian House, north Italy was always far more highly prized than Flanders. Swayed by its traditional possession of the Imperial crown, Vienna felt itself a second Rome, and lordship over Italy a reality. To Germans, Italy is the magnetic south; the Flemings, dull half Germans. The north Italian plain lay at the foot of mountains which Austria firmly held, and she could therefore send armies for its defence. Her Netherlands, on the other hand, were distant and disconnected provinces assigned to her that she might protect the Dutch and English against the French. Maria Theresa therefore naturally used the relief that she had bought at Dresden to fling fresh armies into Italy, leaving Marshal Saxe to be dealt with by her allies. Hence in Italy the campaign of 1746 brought Austria success. Even the jackal strain conspicuous in Savoyard policy did not prevent the Austrians from conquering Lombardy and Parma and heavily defeating the Spaniards at Piacenza (June). The Bourbons withdrew beyond the mountains; the Spaniards, to Savoy, where Philip's dynastic fancy imagined for himself a new Lorraine. In September, Genoa paid the penalty for having allied with them. Stirred by the English, whose own raid on southern Brittany had failed, the Austrians invaded France, with Toulon as their objective. A Genoese revolt, however, compelled them to withdraw from both Genoa and France, almost before they had ceased to quarrel with Sardinia about the spoils of their September triumph. All three allies, including Britain, moreover, held discordant views with regard to their future policy. The Queen insisted that at Worms she had purchased the help of her co-signatories in reconquering Naples. To them such an enterprise spelt disaster in the north of Europe and subversion in the south; and, since their aid was indispensable to its success, the prospect before the Coalition was not bright. The gloom deepened when Russia showed signs of readiness to interfere. While in an emergency her troops might help the Coalition against France, the immediate effect of the Austro-Russian *rapprochement* was to kindle Maria Theresa's hopes of justice in Silesia. Frederick had already made Elizabeth and Bestuchev his enemies on private grounds, while no Russian patriot could fail to see in Prussia a public danger. Despite all this, it could not be denied that the campaign of 1746 had brought considerable results in Italy.

In the Netherlands, however, Marshal Saxe had won for France great glory and solid gains. Brussels in February,

Antwerp early in June, Mons, Charleroi, Namur,—these names signified conquests which the Dutch and British could not consent to leave in French hands but which they and the Austrians would find it hard to redeem by force. Cumberland, who at least possessed courage and the confidence of the British public, returned from the Highlands. Maria Theresa sent her husband's brother to command, thus dooming a fine army to failure in the traditional manner of the Habsburgs. A composite force some 80,000 strong took the field and in October met Saxe at Roucoux. Only nightfall, the French claimed, saved the allies from annihilation. The Bourbon triumph in the Netherlands equalled that of their opponents beyond the Alps.

The war had now raged six years, and what power, save 1747
perhaps Prussia, could be said to have gained by it in Europe or to stand a reasonable chance of substantial gain ? Several, including France, desired to end it ; Cumberland was of like mind ; but no statesman or diplomatist possessed the needful genius or persuasive power. Britain and France were steered by Newcastle or worse. Spain sent to a peace conference a pedant of seventy-seven, who thought that France might cede Franche Comté to Sardinia. Maria Theresa could therefore force her reluctant friends and enemies to begin a seventh campaign. An army of 140,000 men was to account for Marshal Saxe. While the Austrians recovered Genoa and invaded southern France, they hoped that the advent of the Russians would make victory more complete. Saxe's conquest of the Netherlands at least elicited unequivocal action by the hesitating Dutch. Although they had never been formally at war, they were widely suspected of intending to make a separate peace. Some even held that the pacific ministry in Britain wished their associates thus to force their hand. The seizure of border fortresses by France, however, silenced the Republican majority, and the country, as of old, turned to the House of Orange when in danger. Early in May, Prince William, namesake and grandnephew of the great English king, was placed in power by the States-General and by each of the seven United Provinces. At the English elections, the Ministers swept the country. Saxe, therefore, had to face a united Coalition.

It soon appeared that the campaign of 1747 would be

decided in the Netherlands, if at all. In Italy the discordant Austrians and Sardinians were opposed by the discordant Spaniards and French. The Austrians failed to capture Genoa: the French failed to force their way across the Alps. The invasion either of France or Naples thus became impossible. Saxe, on the other hand, resumed his career of conquest. Early in July, he knocked hard at Maestricht, the Dutchmen's eastern gate. After a desperate fight at Lauffeldt the covering force of Cumberland was driven off. The allies, however, crossed the Meuse and saved the fortress, only to hear that Bergen-op-Zoom, the "impregnable" western gate of Holland, had been stormed and sacked (September). Meanwhile the British navy prevented the French from garrisoning Canada, and cleared the seas of the French mercantile marine. Louis was nauseated by the purposeless and brutal war, while on the morrow of Lauffeldt Saxe made a striking peace-move of his own.[1] Without impugning the French king's nobility of motive, it may be remarked that France stood to lose her overseas possessions, that Maria Theresa and Elizabeth were strong in determination and in man-power, and that the British could never sincerely assent to French extension eastwards from Dunkirk. A French king who aped Louis XIV might provoke a standing Grand Alliance.

Progress towards Peace

End of War

Britain, on the other hand, could no longer hope for effective Dutch co-operation. Why should she ruin her finances and risk French conquest of the Netherlands to give a Habsburg Parma and Piacenza? As Saxe's peace move had shown, France had become more tractable since 1745. Her Foreign Minister was now the feeble Puyzieulx, who neither would nor could refuse to negotiate with Britain on the pretext that he could not tell who was her lawful king. Frederick, indeed, begged France to remember that her troops stood everywhere on foreign soil, that she had already made splendid conquests, and that no power on earth could hinder her from making more. King and people, however, were impatient to have done, and both took pleasure in a superb gesture of goodwill. France offered peace without annexations, and without indemnities except for her allies. Newcastle, to whom another failure would

[1] Cp. pp. 533 *et seq.*

mean collapse if not impeachment, hastened to grasp the proffered hand.

The long interval between campaigns was therefore utilized by France and by the Sea-Powers to frame a peace which they might force upon their several allies. At Aix-la-Chapelle a so-called Congress witnessed the enforcement of the French terms by a wily Italian diplomat first upon Britain and then upon the remaining belligerents. Britain sacrificed Austria, her ally, and advocated the claims of Spain, the ally of France. By securing Parma and Piacenza for Don Philip, she saved Gibraltar and Minorca and a fragment of her Utrecht trade concessions with regard to Spanish trade. Her action, however, deepened Maria Theresa's nascent belief that the British alliance spelt only sacrifice unrewarded. This conviction, strong since the Treaty of Worms and stronger because Britain seemed to be drawing near to Prussia, was already impelling Austria towards a separate accord with France if the French could be brought to consent to it.

By the close of April 1748, the preliminaries of peace had been signed, but the soldiers could not be wholly baulked of their campaign. To pacify the French army by victory and the Austrian royal circle by defeat, the French, British and Dutch diplomatists arranged that Maestricht should fall to Saxe. This farce, characteristic of the age, was duly played, and by midsummer all the warring powers were in agreement. Before the year closed, the treaty of Aix-la-Chapelle had ended the war of Austrian Succession.

Peace of Aix-la-Chapelle, 1748

Through eight campaigns, almost the twelfth part of the century, the fire kindled by Frederick in December 1740 had scorched the chief countries of Europe, spreading also to "lands in which the name of Prussia was unknown." While it lasted, it seemed to dominate the history of mankind. What were its actual results? "Mere end of war because your powder is run out, mere truce till you gather breath and gunpowder again" is a verdict which disguises the truth that great achievements were sealed at Aix-la-Chapelle. Few wars solve all the problems which provoke them, and this one left Prussia and Austria, like France and Britain, still enemies at heart. But the prime question, Shall there be an Austrian Empire at all? had been triumphantly answered

Results of the War

on the principles of Charles VI. His daughter's frontiers, indeed, had been compressed by the loss of Silesia and of part of Italy. But they now enclosed a loyal nation, united, for all its racial diversity, by tradition and common effort, and undeniably a great power. The goodwill of Russia towards Austria had been secured, that of Germany increased, that of France, the secular enemy, made possible. Europe henceforward looked on Austria as an indispensable portion of its frame. Even the Holy Roman Emperor remained Austrian.

Prussia, though far less securely, had gained the status of a great European power. All states which signed the Treaty of Aix-la-Chapelle guaranteed her possession of Silesia, and Silesia notably increased her wealth and man-power, her strategic advantages and her prestige. The rulers of Austria and Russia, however, had no dearer wish than to wrest it from her, and a situation had now been created which might bring to their side the King of France. Saxony, Hanover and Sweden, moreover, had losses to avenge or dangers to banish which made them potential enemies of Prussia. So long as a consummate general and statesman filled the throne, Prussia might defend herself, but the success of her unprincipled aggression was a dangerous basis for lasting power. The example of Sweden showed what might happen to a poor state made eminent by a great army and a vigorous line of kings. In this very war, the Swedish aristocracy had paid for the memory of her " great-power-time " by a rash move which lost her a part of Finland. The Dutch, by an exactly opposite route—for they exchanged aristocracy for monarchy and persisted in refraining from declaring war—had arrived at a similar humiliation. By the peace as by the war, they were taught to forget their days of greatness. The badges of Dutch inferiority, Austrian sovereignty in the Netherlands and the right of Holland to garrison barrier fortresses there, were duly re-established, the latter by a victory of Britain over Austria which left great bitterness behind. In Sardinia, Charles Emmanuel had used the traditional opportunism of Savoy to advance his house a stage further towards greatness. The coveted corridor to the sea at the expense of Genoa, indeed, was denied. But Savoy itself and Nice were returned to him by the Bourbons, and from the Habsburgs he gained an extension to the east.

Russia, though shut out by France from sharing in the negotiations, had drawn profit from the war. Under Peter's daughter Elizabeth, "whose education had been acquired in the servants' hall," and who believed that England could be reached by land, but who was eminently Russian at heart, the empire remained European. Not to withdraw to Moscow meant to advance in influence over Europe, since as against Europe Russia was a military despotism in an almost insular position. During the war, moreover, Elizabeth made a triumphant defence of what her father had won for Russia in the north. She also gained a close understanding with Vienna and acted almost as arbiter upon the Rhine.

France made both the war and the peace. She began by proclaiming the overthrow of the Habsburgs: she ended by accepting a Habsburg Emperor and the Austria of the Pragmatic Sanction. But the interval had been long enough to make the wisdom of 1741 folly in 1748. The line of natural enemies which expired with Charles VI seemed now to have given place to friends. Kaunitz, whose name stands for Franco-Austrian *rapprochement*, came to Aix-la-Chapelle as the representative of a dignified Catholic power whose overtures had already been half accepted by the Most Christian King. In the meantime France had proved her might by making Charles VII Emperor and Prussia a new great power. In the face of British, Dutch and Austrians she had burst their barrier of fortresses, won three great battles, and conquered all the Netherlands save Luxembourg.

In the peace negotiations, Britain and Austria had come to her secretly as rival suitors, and it was she who disposed of Spain. It seems idle to maintain that because she chose to give back the Netherlands and thus regain Cape Breton she lessened her prestige. Jesuit influence, the ascendancy of Madame de Pompadour, the acid tracts of the Philosophers, the degradation of Louis XV—all these were solvents of French glory, but in 1748 their action had only just begun. Only four years had passed since Louis' dangerous sickness at Metz had won him the title "well-beloved" from the devoted French, and none of those years had lacked a resounding victory. Montesquieu's *Esprit des Lois*, perhaps the greatest book of the century, and in its calm analysis the most fatal to the French *régime*, was contemporary with the peace.

Effects of the War on Britain

What effect, lastly, had the war exercised on Britain? It began by rescuing her from the effects of the apathy and opportunism which qualified Walpole's greatness. If in 1734, as he boasted, there were 50,000 men slain in Europe and not one Englishman, it was likely that when Englishmen came to slay and to be slain they would find few allies among Europeans. By 1739, Fleury's judicious participation in continental politics was triumphing over Walpole's mere abstention. The Spanish war, to which his political opportunism committed Walpole, might well have led to a great peaceful victory of France. Thanks to Frederick the Austrian war engulfed it, and in 1748 Britain emerged a vastly strengthened power. From Spain herself she gained a pledge that her pre-war privileges should be respected. She gained also the "benefit of time"—a decade more of her *de facto* sovereignty over Minorca and Gibraltar together with the replacement of Elizabeth Farnese by a pro-British queen. Most important of all, France had by no means endeared herself to Spain and French shipping had lost the power to compete immediately with British for transoceanic trade. War, moreover, had given Britain a strong and efficient navy and no little military training. For her, Dettingen, Culloden and Louisbourg were glorious victories; Fontenoy and Lauffeldt, perhaps more glorious defeats. Of equal significance was the final acceptance of the Hanoverian dynasty both by Europe and by the British people. France bound herself to banish the Pretender, and the cry of "Billy for Flanders" voiced the affection of the mob for Cumberland, a brave and outspoken prince. British security was further cared for by the French concessions in the Netherlands and by the surrender of the French right to fortify Dunkirk towards the sea. To secure Old England, indeed, Cape Breton was again allowed to threaten New, but French superiority in India was diminished by the British recovery of Madras.

On the Continent, some changes had taken place which might affect the British system of the future. The inefficiency of the Dutch had been made clear, and the connexion with Austria weakened. Sardinia, on the other hand, had proved a useful client, and, by way of trade, Britain was gaining influence in Russia. Perhaps the greatest change, however, was that which affected Hanover. By for ever tripping up British statesmen in peace, in war, in neutrality and in the transition between these states, the Electorate had generated a fury which Britons vented in bitter blasphemy against its White Horse rampant. " While Britain dared France the monarch was trembling for his Hanover " ; " We are become an insurance office to Hanover " ; " Make the Pretender Elector of Hanover, then no Briton will follow him "—such were the sneers of British statesmen, while one divine preached on the pale horse with its rider Death and hell following behind. Hatred of Hanover promoted indulgence towards her hereditary foe the King of Prussia. Frederick at a distance could pass for a Protestant ; he was certainly a hero ; his army was always ready ; he had no fleet ; his services to France had not been great ; and he showed signs of willingness to take a proper view of the antithesis between France and Britain. Thus were British statesmen and the British public prepared for one of those changes of system which are facilitated by the absence of a too clear comprehension of the proposed ally. The ripened fruit was plucked in January 1756.

BIBLIOGRAPHICAL NOTE

See Bibliographical Note at the end of Chapter I and bibliography to Chapter V.
Add :—

A

T. Carlyle : *Frederick the Great* (abridged and edited, 1909).
E. E. Charteris : *William Augustus, Duke of Cumberland, 1721–48* (1913).
W. L. Dorn : " The Prussian Bureaucracy in the Eighteenth Century," *Pol. Sc. Quarterly*, XLVI (1931), pp. 403–23 ; XLVII (1932), pp. 75–94, 259–73.
R. E. Ergang : *The Potsdam Fuehrer* (1942).
S. B. Fay : *The Rise of Brandenburg-Prussia to 1786* (1937).
G. P. Gooch : *Frederick the Great* (1947).
R. Koser : *König Friedrich der Grosse.* 4 vols. (1893, 7th ed. 1921–25).
E. Lavisse : *The Youth of Fredrick the Great* (trans. 1891).
W. F. Reddaway : *Frederick the Great and the Rise of Prussia* (1904).

B

A. Berney : *Friedrich der Grosse, Entwickelungsgeschichte* (1934).
Duc de Broglie : *Frédéric II et Marie-Thérèse, 1740–2* (1883).
Frederic II, Roi de Prusse : *Œuvres posthumes* (1788).
L. von Ranke : *Memoirs of the House of Brandenburg and History of Prussia.* 3 vols. (trans. 1849).
D. Thiebault : *Original Anecdotes of Frederic II* (1805).

CHAPTER IX

PROGRESSIVE EUROPE, 1748–55

The Contemporary Point of View

AFTER eight years of war the contending princes were exhausted, but the roots of their strife remained. Germany was not yet wide enough for Austria and Prussia, nor the world for France and Britain. Posterity knows well that the settlement of 1748 in fact amounted only to an eight years' truce, to be succeeded by a wider and bloodier war. Contemporary Europe, however, had no such sad prevision. To her thinkers it seemed that the great century which was their pride might now advance unhindered along the path of progress.

War and European Life

For eight years, beginning with 1740, the politics of Europe had centred in a tedious war. Wars form the most intense efforts of which states are capable, and they determine the conditions under which men are to live in time of peace. History therefore rightly finds its first landmarks in wars and in the treaties with which they end. In the eighteenth century, however, war while it lasted could seldom monopolize the life of a nation, as it does increasingly in modern times. Apart from sieges, wars were then wars of movement, and contending armies might manœuvre over a wide area and bring many villages to ruin. But with no transport swifter than the horse for men or tidings, war was a localized distemper, dominating contemporary life far less than it dominates the histories of the years during which it raged. When the Austrian Succession War broke out "a new generation had grown up which knew war only by its trophies." That generation, however, had had leisure to think fresh thoughts about other things than war, and war by no means vetoed intellectual progress.

Between the death of Louis XIV and the accession of Frederick II, Europe had been busy with schemes for religious reunion, for the improvement of agriculture, for the codification of law and for the exploration of the earth.

Science, in the widest sense, had given to man a deeper knowledge of mathematics, and mechanics, as well as the thermometer, the quadrant, the sextant, the flying shuttle, inoculation, the rudiments of electricity, and in chemistry and astronomy a notable advance. Frederick's Silesian foray could not halt progressive man.

European Progress 1748–55

The years 1740–48 were in fact peculiarly rich in non-military progress, alike in literature, in religion, in politics, and in the advance of knowledge. While Belleisle disposed of the lot of empires and kingdoms, and Saxe, a dying man, rivalled Marlborough's career, Swedenborg was recording mystic visions of heaven and hell, Linnæus creating botany and Richardson the novel, D'Alembert impressing his genius upon dynamics and Bakewell upon the breed of sheep. Religious toleration remained a battlefield where notable advances were made by the contending sides—in England towards practical non-interference; in Prussia, towards theoretical freedom; in France, towards persecution. Two schools or movements which may be called new form, however, the outstanding contribution of these years to the general harvest of the eighteenth century. Both were reactions against the inertia and materialism which followed the reign of Louis XIV, and which undeniably tainted the churches, Catholic and Protestant alike. Both were imbued with the assurance that they could not be wrong, and that it was theirs to widen the horizon of mankind. But while the Methodists, though they embodied German ideas and took the world for their parish, influenced mainly the Anglo-Saxon middle and lower class, the French Philosophers made an immediate appeal to educated men throughout the world. Methodism was the English form of a religious revival, visible in many lands, which demanded the more spiritual and energetic teaching of revealed religion. Warmth and zeal, not reform of doctrine or of establishment, was its desire. "Give me a hundred fearless preachers who hate sin, and I will shake the citadel of Satan"; "Orthodoxy is at best but a very slender part of religion . . . neither does religion consist in negatives, in bare harmlessness of any kind"—such were among Wesley's most characteristic pronouncements.

Methodists and French Philosophers

The Philosophers

The French Philosophers, men oppressed by the alliance of Church and State to compel them to accept what to them seemed absurdities in religion, vindicated the rights of intellect by satire, by anti-dogmatic argument, and by writings which quietly deposed theology by proving that there were other and more attractive fields of thought. Few of them were atheists, but none believed that what the Jesuits taught was true. With monarchy they had no quarrel, but, in France at least, Church and State were so closely intertwined that to attack the priests must ultimately shake the throne. Even to write educational works was to challenge the Church, for the Church controlled education at every stage. The creed of many Philosophers, frankly formulated, might have run, "I believe in God: I am convinced that I cannot know Him, or that He will concern Himself with me: I hold that those who profess to speak in His name are impostors: it is my duty to expose them, and I enjoy the task." Priest-baiting was perilous: a word to the King's confessor brought a *lettre de cachet*, that irresistible royal order for an indefinite sojourn in the Bastille: irreverence towards a religious procession might cost the scoffer his life.

The Salon, indeed, furnished the ardent Philosopher with a matchless safety-valve. Stimulated by his skilful hostess, he could there test, modify and proclaim his opinions freely. Ambitious men, full of their own superiority, however, wished to write, and then the censor and the Jesuits barred the way.

The cautious Philosopher would write so that only the astute could read between the lines, or court some high-placed protector, or attach himself to a religious order, or station himself near the frontier or abroad. His books perhaps found entry into France as so-called translations from the English published in Holland, and therefore passed the censor. Disguise heightened their charms, while the contrast between French fetters and foreign liberty could not but impress their readers.

The French Philosophers, it may be observed, were not philosophers in the modern sense of the term. Metaphysics they tended to rank with theology and medicine as the most useless products of the human brain. Voltaire, kinder than D'Alembert, compared them to dancers in a minuet, nimble but never moving an inch forward. *Les philosophes* were men of letters interested in natural science, and indeed in everything that concerned mankind. Montesquieu, the father of them all, ranking in politics with Aristotle and with Machiavelli, wrote first on echo, transparency and the renal glands. In that unlumbered age an educated man could know something of every study, and he might write on any topic if he expressed himself with point and grace. Swedenborg, an eminent engineer, produced works on metallurgy, natural philosophy, physiology and psychology, before turning to the spiritual world. Johnson did not hesitate to review Home's *Experiments on Bleaching* or Hales on *Distilling Sea Waters, Ventilators in Ships* and *Curing an Ill Taste in Milk.* Wesley wrote on whatever subject he believed instruction to be needed—grammar, logic, medicine, music or poetry, as well as on religion and philosophy. The salons in Paris, where incomparable women gathered around them bands of able men, united the Philosophers, and allowed their theories to be discussed and polished before they were stereotyped in books. Helvétius' slender treatise *De l'esprit* taxed his best energies for two dozen years, while Montesquieu's masterpiece demanded thirty.

Voltaire

Foremost among the Philosophers as among eighteenth-century writers of every kind stood and must ever stand Voltaire. In some fifteen million words, written between 1710 and 1778, he proved himself an unrivalled correspondent, a verse writer whom a good judge might place first, second and third among those of contemporary France, a careful original and brilliant historian, a consummate arbiter of taste, and a satirist whose pen etched away the wax mask with which tradition had disguised the lineaments of reason. Between his return from England in 1729 and the peace of Aix-la-Chapelle his rule was absolute, and he faithfully represented "the most subtle, ingenious, enquiring and prosaic generation that France has ever known."

Voltaire was rationalist to the core, impatient of all mystery and prone to underrate the strength that institutions have acquired or may acquire by gradual growth and long existence. But his rationalism contained a programme—mild government, even-handed justice, freedom of thought, religious toleration, the fraternity of liberal thinkers of all nations, and fraternal kindness of the rich towards the poor.

To the clerical advisers of Louis XV such ideas were poison, and the Philosophers found themselves denounced as enemies to France. Abroad, however, there were kings and ministers who lent them a ready ear and who used the power of absolutism to embody their programme in practice. During these years "the King-Philosopher" mounted the throne of Prussia, and a German girl who was to be ruler of all the Russias became an enthusiastic pupil of Voltaire.

Philosophy and Reform

In lands where Voltaire ruled by deputy, the inhabitants found the laws codified, justice improved, punishments made less barbaric and torture done away. There, so long as a citizen did not disturb public order, he might in general worship as he pleased or not at all. His house became sacrosanct: his pen gained greater freedom. Although the Philosopher deemed wars against barbarians like the Turks laudable, those between civilized nations were to be discouraged. A truly enlightened man, in his opinion, loved as his fatherland the country which for the moment gave him shelter, and instead of making war on neighbouring states an enlightened king would attack poverty, disease and degradation within his own.

The French *Encyclopædia*

During the decade which followed the Austrian War, the ideas of the Philosophers were to find popular expression in the *Encyclopædia* (1751–73). This vast tribute to the creative power of man was composed chiefly by the unbalanced genius, Diderot. At the same time, the reaction against excessive civilization appeared in Rousseau, whose teaching educated women were soon to find irresistible. Wesley regarded Voltaire and Rousseau alike as coxcombs; Johnson cared not to distinguish the proportion of iniquity between them; but to Frederick, Voltaire was the master mind; Rousseau, "the shame of literature." The Prussian king voiced the old order wounded by the new, rationalism by religion, the eighteenth by the nineteenth century.

Wesley

While Voltaire has few disciples and Diderot's *Encyclopædia* is no longer read, millions still owe to Wesley much of the inspiration of their lives. By 1748 his principles were formed, his Society organized, and its mightiest instrument, the hymn-book, lately published. More than forty years of unceasing labour lay before him, but all the missionary journeys which filled them were devoted to perfecting schemes already traced, while with their aid he called the multitude to salvation. As clear-sighted a realist as Frederick of Prussia, he saw that nothing on earth was of account in comparison with eternal life. And he was great enough to rank his own Society among things indifferent, provided that by any means the high goal could be attained. Although no latitudinarian, he was the friend of all who genuinely sought salvation. The Society, he proudly claimed, required but one thing from those who wished to join it—a desire to save their souls. Methodists might worship as they pleased. But the supreme object of Salvation must be denied to no man by vain tradition. As self-confident as any man in that self-confident age of reason, self-confident because convinced that he was the messenger of God, Wesley could respect no human ordinance that obstructed the salvation of men. Those who had the light must be allowed to spread it, whatever the tradition of the Church. Himself by birth, by education, and by cast of mind a champion of church and king, offering soldiers for the German War, esteeming George II, despite his mistresses, as the best of Princes, fulminating at eighty against any Methodist who should break away from the Church of England, he did not shrink from commissioning agents of his own to administer the sacraments and to ordain. He would obey no ecclesiastical law if such obedience meant that souls which stood in need of heavenly sustenance would thereby fail to find it. What church could accept the claim of one of its ministers to decide when its laws should or should not be kept? Only a saint on the one side and a tolerant hierarchy upon the other could have averted separation until after Wesley's death.

Eternal Punishment

It would be idle to maintain that the love of souls which so honourably distinguished Wesley was free from that theory of eternal rewards and punishments which was prominent in a robust and legalistic age. Hell was the supreme resource of every priest and the target of every philosopher. "An oyster," sneered Montesquieu, "is not as miserable as we: it is swallowed without being aware of the evil that hangs over its head, and there its sufferings end: but we live in daily expectation of being devoured, and we are made both to feel and to see that we shall be digested to all eternity." The official theory of life and death drove eminent men beyond number to take refuge in deism, which made God humane, but robbed them of intercourse with Him in daily life. Wesley used fear of punishment to terrify men into seeking the rapture of boundless love.

> "Nothing is worth a thought beneath
> Nothing but to escape the death
> That never, never dies"

sang the Methodist poet, and the preacher expounded the doctrine of the undying worm. Yet the habitual serene cheerfulness of the preacher was remarked by thousands, while the poet's visions of the "love divine all loves excelling" still enrapture millions. The Methodist could warble about the fire of hell to strains borrowed from the *Magic Flute*. Inspiration clearly transcended formulæ and logic, and the spirit of the Wesleys rather than their formulæ gave their Society enduring life.

The Methodist Policy

The spirit was in this case fortified and made effective by an organization unsurpassed since Loyola created the Company of Jesus. In the Methodist Society as in the Jesuit, the rules were framed so as to incorporate and discipline every possible recruit, lay and clerical alike. In both the aspirant to full membership must pass through many scrutinies and stages before the vocation that he claimed was taken to be fully proved. In both the members must frequently confess to one another, the Jesuit secretly to a director, the Methodist in "bands" of a dozen men or women meeting for mutual exhortation under an appointed "leader." The leaders themselves assembled before the preacher; the preachers in ordered groups and annually in a conference at which Wesley himself presided. Ordained clergy, lay evangelists, male members approved to conduct worship, leaders male and female, all had their appointed sphere. Soon, as the Society acquired funds and meeting-houses of its own, a new array of office holders came into being. Preachers, however, often delivered their message in the streets or fields, and by this and by the fervent use of hymns appealed to classes hitherto uninfluenced by religion.

The influence on the century which was exerted by the Wesleys and by the Calvinistic Methodists who derived from

Whitefield can never be exactly weighed. Religion, not politics, was their concern, and neither Parliament nor the Church had any pronouncement to make about them. Of some outcasts they made good citizens, and some good citizens outside their ranks they stimulated to play a nobler part. Their chief political contribution, however, was to increase the spiritual and philanthropic activity of inconspicuous men and women, thereby notably enriching the life of the nation. Thanks to their lives of quiet self-sacrifice, historic England could with a better conscience face the new and subversive gospel of the Rights of Man.

National Influence of Religious Movements

While missionaries and Philosophers aimed at distant goals, less ambitious practical men were striving to improve the machinery of government and thereby to raise the standard of life. The "average man" of the middle eighteenth century did not share the dissatisfaction of the Philosopher or of the Methodist with contemporary progress. At a time when the industrial revolution had barely begun, and when revolt in France seemed unthinkable, many educated men regarded themselves as the happy heirs of a progressive age. "We Europeans are proud, and with good right," sounded a representative voice from Denmark. "What a wealth of learning is ours, what morality and freedom! What a century is this eighteenth! Never was such brightness on the earth." The most progressive among women, Lady Mary, rejoiced that her daughter was born in such an age of enlightenment.

Government and Progress

Among contemporary optimists Baron Bielfeld (1711–70) takes a foremost place. Of gentle birth, bred among Hamburg merchants, a freemason, the companion of Frederick the Great before his accession, traveller, diplomatist, student, tutor to a Hohenzollern prince, ennobled, enriched by marriage, at once a Philosopher and a Christian, he touched life at many points and in some sort personified his generation. Frank, merry, naïve and shrewd by turns, he was one of those rare spirits who for an hour could make Frederick almost good-natured.

Baron Bielfeld on Europe

When the ogre Frederick William I died, and the courtiers of his heir were expecting ducats to rain upon them, "You don't know what I have lost in a father," said the young king to Bielfeld. "True, Sire," came the characteristic answer, "but I know what you have gained in a kingdom." "Be charitable to kings," wrote Bielfeld, "only God is perfect, and they are men. Criticize them only when they are dead. In tracing the ways of Providence, I note that all lead to the aggrandizement of the Prussian monarchy." Carlyle, who knew him from his *Familiar Letters*, deemed him a "rapid, clever creature of the coxcomb sort." Had he read the two thousand pages of the *Political Institutions*, written between the second and third Silesian wars, he might have done their author greater justice. Bielfeld there proves himself painstaking, straightforward and by no means vain. In the range of his survey, indeed, he is typical of a century whose sons were so confident in its destiny and in their own powers that they were ever ardent to instruct. Beginning with the laws that keep the planets in their radiant courses and ending with some precept deep for dressing eels or shoeing horses—such was the character of Bielfeld's manual for princes as of other contemporary writings. "All is art, all is system to-day," he cries, "except the most important of all, the art of reigning." "There is but one all-powerful cause that instigates mankind, and that is Government," echoed Arthur Young, a generation later. Politics, since Machiavelli, had been regarded as the art of over-reaching and deceiving. Bielfeld set out to prove from study and experience that this sinister view was false. His compendium of advice to rulers possesses no little value from the picture of life in town and country which it presents. As a manual of policy it was eagerly received by those to whom it was addressed, and it demonstrably influenced their reforms. No book can show more clearly the aims of the enlightened despots.

If the work of one who was neither a potentate nor a genius is selected for extended notice, it is because a plain and honest man surveying Europe for a special purpose, has left us a wholly truthful account of what he saw.

The Civil Servant

Politics, of course, were only for those born and equipped to govern. Bielfeld declares that there were more charlatans in politics than in medicine, especially in republics and free towns, and that the most insignificant Londoner read the public papers in his workshop and aped the minister, without the least influence upon the government. To qualify for a share in the government the first requisite was Latin. Holberg, satirizing *The Political Tinker*, makes his workingmen convict themselves of their incapacity to rule by failing to translate from Latin the language of laws and proclamations. Bielfeld insists that without it the aspirant must lack solid education and the power to read the treaties. His French also must be fluent, or he would be ridiculous. Logic, natural law and international law were indispensable, with public law, particularly the complex public law of Germany. This cannot be understood without history, "the soul of that science and of politics in general," and every aspirant must master the history of that state which he designs to serve. Geography, "pleasing in itself and needing only eyes and memory," and heraldry will supplement history, while genealogy prevents it from becoming dry. Thus equipped, the statesman may share in the government—the contrivance by which society protects its good members from the far greater number who are bad. Government must be carried on either by one man, or by several, or by all.

Forms of Government

Surveying Europe, Bielfeld finds in France, Prussia and Denmark three perfect monarchies, but their rulers are not despots like the Tsar and Sultan. Unlike the latter therefore, their monarchs need not fear revolt. Providence and his own interest, indeed, seldom allow a monarch to become a tyrant. England is a monarchy—aristocracy—democracy; while the Empire, the Dutch and the Swiss present associations of weak sovereign states. Government should be single and undivided. No sovereign should suffer another power to exercise within his dominions a legislative and coercive power. Posterity will cry shame on the eighteenth century for tolerating the Roman Inquisition.

Education

The first duty of the government is to civilize the people, that is, the whole people. Peasants, workmen, and common soldiers, some contend, should be looked upon as machines. Society, according to this view, needs their hands, not their heads, and education merely distracts them from their duties. Bielfeld on the contrary contends that every citizen has the right to be taught his duty towards God, himself and society, and to be instructed in the necessary arts. The smallest village ought to have its school and the school to be regularly inspected by the priest.

Luxury and National Wealth

Luxury, that is magnificent spending, he pronounces the chief source of a nation's wealth. To civilize his people, a sovereign must be magnificent, keeping a brilliant and imposing court. Politeness spreads downwards. A porter at the Hague is less rude than a porter at Amsterdam. The theatre, if purged as in France, is the best school of manners. Public festivals, like that at Venice when the Doge espouses the sea, stir the mind and encourage manufactures, at the expense of the foreigners who attend.

Human Rights

It is not for politics, Bielfeld holds, to inquire whether inequality among men is based on strict natural law. It exists: it is necessary to Society: the actual divisions may easily be changed. For the legislator that suffices. Justice should be equal and employment should follow next. European thought debars a nobleman from trade, thereby condemning many nobles to poverty, however carefully preferment may be reserved for the noble class. While Germany insists upon the purity of the sixteen quarterings, France, with greater wisdom, allows her nobles to enrich their caste by marrying outside it. Christianity has banished slavery, though the Barbary States still practise it, while in a sense all Turks are slaves. The Sovereigns of Europe may one day regret the fact that in their American colonies slavery survives.

Negro slavery, as regulated by the Black Code for the French colonies, is horrible, and the man who made the Code must have a soul as black as ink. But serfage as found in Poland, Bohemia, some German lands, Denmark and elsewhere, is of a quite different nature. A man who is born a serf must perform certain duties and cannot quit his lord's estate. He belongs, however, rather to the estate than to the lord, and in his person man does not hold property in man. The sovereign can call him up to serve in the army, however this may inconvenience his lord. He can sue his lord, and almost always successfully. His lord, again, is bound to provide him with the means of subsistence, to judge him according to law, and to leave capital charges against him to the State. None the less, Bielfeld opines, serfage might profitably be done away.

The Population Question

States, it is obvious, become strong by having many people. None ever had a population large enough to supply all its wants. Marriage should therefore be encouraged. In France, where politics are so well understood, they have begun to give a number of poor girls dowries—an admirable plan for raising up good citizens. Divorce should not be easy, but the marriage tie should not be too strong for human nature. The Foundling Hospital at Paris deserves imitation. Wise princes profit by the folly of those who drive out their subjects, but before such colonists are received, settlements should be prepared for them in advance. It is absurd to suppose that an exiled barber or tailor can reclaim waste land. It is no less absurd to denude the motherland, as did Spain, by sending colonists across the ocean. France and England act with much more caution. They carry to their colonies soldiers, sailors, and men of every nation, limiting the number to those required and bringing back some of the colonial born. To keep up the population, murder is terribly punished, and suicide made infamous. Duels, however, are tolerated. In France probably fifty take place every day. The Prussians forbid duels but cashier an officer who declines a proper challenge. The Russians with greater wisdom forbid them. The officer who has fought a duel should be broken with infamy, and insults severely punished. Orphanages and hospitals economize human life. The London Hospital, Bedlam, Chelsea and Greenwich do honour to humanity, though the money spent on making such institutions magnificent might be better used in increasing their endowment. No young and vigorous person should ever be allowed to withdraw into a monastery or a convent. Mendicants, whose life promotes idleness or worse, should be put down. Every town or village ought to fulfil the natural duty of man by supporting its own poor. These, concentrated in workhouses, may profitably be employed in such work as carding wool and cotton, cutting corks, preparing drugs for dyeing and other easily learned arts. Further, to reduce mortality, doctors and apothecaries should be supervised by medical colleges and quack medicines forbidden. By instructing midwives, one-twentieth of the human race could be saved from death. Small-pox is an ailment so world-wide that "we must believe that the Author of nature in His infinite wisdom has foreseen the need of it to cleanse the human body of evil humours acquired at birth." In his *Letters*, Bielfeld ascribes the Lisbon earthquake to the Devil. Inoculation is a hundred times less fatal than contagion. It should be ordered by the sovereign and supervised by the state. Although the Swiss must go abroad to find a living, over-population is a myth, for half the world remains uncultivated. The English, heaped one upon the other, enjoy every superfluity, while on the banks of the Dnieper, the inhabitants, being few, lack necessaries.

Religion and the State

Bielfeld agrees with the vast majority of thinkers that the first principle of good order is religion. Were there no hereafter, those near their end would act without restraint, and the wretched mass of the people lose all hope. However Hurons and Hottentots may have lived, no solid state has existed without a religious cult. Even if a sovereign had no religion, he should rigorously punish anyone who preached against it. Although Christianity is the purest, no religion which upholds morality should be put down. Superstition, however, leads to intolerance. Religion is essentially tolerant, although its ministers are almost everywhere prone to persecution. Of the Pope it had been said, "We must kiss his feet and tie his hands." As a Protestant Bielfeld has no doubt that the clergy must be respected but confined to the cure of souls. Matrimonial affairs, the building and maintenance of churches, and the distribution of alms he regards as outside their sphere. He would gladly see them, like their brethren in England, more highly honoured and better paid. Vice undermines a state, and Church, laws, police and sovereign should join to put it down. It is surprising that England flourishes in spite of public prize-fights, horse-racing, bull-fights, cock-fights, and habitual foul language, besides widespread prostitution. In England, moreover, the meanest claims the right to resent an insult by fighting with his fists in the street. All this is not the consequence of English liberty, for in many respects the free Englishman is remarkably subordinate to rules. He may not export an ounce of his wool or wear an ell of calico printed in England. On Sunday he is forbidden to trade or to have music or to play cards. But he knows what he may do and what he may not do, and is shielded by law against the caprice of his sovereign. His laws are the best in Europe, in so far as they have been made by Parliament, and not by legal experts.

Law and Codes

Every state should have its code of laws, published at such a price that every citizen can possess it. The military codes decide almost every case with admirable brevity. Why should not civil codes do the same? They should be written in the language of the country and the judges should be forbidden to remark upon them. Justice is simple, but lawyers have made modern jurisprudence artificial, complicated and doubtful. The legislator should proclaim his will, without giving reasons. Clear, brief laws, and simple judicial proceedings paid for by the litigants according to tariff would make an end of the ruinous chicanery and delay of the courts. Perquisites, indeed, should continue to accrue to the judges, lest they should become slothful and lest justice should be so cheap as to encourage litigation. The German practice of making one or more Universities the final court of appeal is excellent, since it is good jurists who pronounce judgment, while it cannot be known beforehand which University will be chosen. Corruption is thus avoided. England and Prussia have abolished torture without weakening the course of justice. It is strange that a nation so gentle as the French should continue to torture twice over a criminal who has been condemned to death. In cases of conspiracy and brigandage, indeed, it may sometimes be necessary to use such means of bringing accomplices to light. Justice should in almost every case be public. The Venetian Senate shocks the general conscience by the abominable secrecy of its proceedings.

Functions of the "Police"

In treating of "the police," Bielfeld throws much light on the life of the people and their relations with the agents of the sovereign. He declares that the nations desire not so much new laws as the proper execution of the old. From the police they expect protection for themselves, their honour and their goods. Libels and secret debauches are objects for police vigilance as much as theft and violence. Paris is patrolled by watchmen, both mounted and on foot. In London the watch proclaims the weather, so that in that great port the citizens may be guided in their commercial ventures. Hamburg is guarded and patrolled by armed men in uniform who give the alarm in case of fire.

In many towns, the police search the taverns every quarter and all houses every year, to round up suspects and to compute the numbers of the people. A great part of their duty is to guard against destructive fires. It is for them to see that the streets are wide enough to allow help to reach a burning house. A beginning has been made with compulsory solidity and safe design in building. The sovereign sets the example with his palace and with public structures, especially theatres. These have a great reservoir at the top with pipes which allow the whole building to be drenched by turning a tap. Every householder must keep six leather buckets, an axe, a ladder and a small portable extinguisher always ready. The police maintain a fireman with from six to ten men sworn to attend the public extinguishers which are now to be found throughout Europe, but chiefly in Germany. In each of the chief belfries watch is kept by day and night. When the watchman sounds the tocsin and indicates the direction of the fire, every householder sets a lighted candle in his window and every mason, carpenter or other building *employé* fulfils his oath to make for the conflagration. The English have an admirable system of authorized insurance companies, which receive annual premiums, take measures against fires and make good the damage. Failing this, it is best for the police to keep a register in which every houseowner declares the value of his premises. Loss by fire is then compensated by levying a rate. If a fund is formed by annual payments, the sovereign may seize it for other pressing needs, and in any case the citizens grow slack in averting and extinguishing the fires. The police must likewise guard against damage from flood.

Fire Prevention

Other "Police" Duties

Games of chance should be put down by the police, and private lotteries forbidden. State lotteries are beneficial, since they put money in circulation, attract it from abroad, and provide fortunes for some at a trifling charge to the rest. The state should do everything with the utmost probity and publicity, confining its gain to 10 or at most 12 per cent. of the value of the tickets. The police must keep an eye on the crowd of cheats who haunt fairs and prey upon credulous people.

Drawers of teeth are the only charlatans whom they

should tolerate, because these trust only to the skill of their hands. Astrologers, magicians, prophets, diviners and fortune-tellers swarm in Catholic lands. If all such were sent to the galleys, there would be as few ghosts and miracles as among Protestants. Those who claim to have found the philosopher's stone or to make gold should be driven out by the police. No one can change the first principles of things, nor will the elements unite until the day of judgment.

The police should also provide for the supply of good water, for the paving of the streets, for the removal of filth from cities, and for keeping herds of animals from coming in. A citizen, of course, may keep one or two cows in his stable, and a few geese or fowls in his yard. Noisy or foul-smelling trades, such as refining whale-oil, should also be kept at a distance. The dead must be well and promptly buried. Burial in church, though widespread, is an abuse. In Catholic churches, its effects are disguised by incense. In Protestant temples, especially in summer, it makes the air close, sepulchral and foul. Since few know the rudiments of architecture, and since gothic barbarism has long reigned in Europe, the police should control design, and the sovereign enlist, if possible, good architects. By proper town-planning and decoration, a smiling city may attract foreigners and gain a name in Europe. Lanterns to light the streets at night are the most necessary ornament of any town. Paris, London, Holland and Germany have different systems. That of London, a glass globe on an iron arm, is the best, but the glass is too costly. Where thieves abound, the police should fix an hour in winter after which no citizen may walk abroad without a torch or lantern. They should likewise control cabs and sedan chairs, fixing their stands, routes and tariffs, punishing the only too customary insolence of the cabmen, and seeing to it that the vehicles are in sound condition. In the big cities there should be boys at the crossways to cleanse shoes of dirt and after dark to light wayfarers to their homes.

Control of Prices

Having provided for the safety of the citizens and the cleanliness of the city, the police must attend to the need for cheapness. To them it matters little that a rich lord pays a *louis* for a bottle of Cape wine, or that an ell of cloth of gold is priced at twenty *livres*. But they must see to it that the populace can buy bread, meat and ordinary drink at reasonable prices. These determine the cost of labour, and so the dearness or cheapness of everything that the town produces. The police must therefore notify the countryside when any town lacks grain. They must control mills and millers, bakeries and bakers, slaughter-houses, butchers and sausage-makers. Drink must likewise be supervised, whether it be the water, small wine, cider, perry or country wine of the south, or the small beer, strong beer, mead or brandy of the north. The police should standardize measures, pay surprise visits to taverns and wine merchants' cellars, and prevent adulteration. In short, their duty is to see that every purchaser of drink receives the amount and the quality for which he pays. To protect the public health, every new distilled liquor should be notified to the police and examined by the faculty of medicine. In England not long ago the distillers found the pernicious secret of making brandy from all kinds of filth, and Parliament stepped in. Public control should also guard against the distillers' waste of grain.

Control of Production

Control of Prices

Salt is an object of prime necessity, but in the many lands where it is a royal monopoly or is heavily taxed the police cannot make it cheap. They can only try to keep it in good supply and to restrain the farmers of taxes. Grocers are still subject to the police, who can only see that they sell honestly and keep stocks of necessary goods at reasonable prices. Modern cookery needs oil, olives, capers, lemons, pomegranates, limes, figs, oranges, dried plums, dried grapes and the like. Herrings, butter, cheese, milk, lamp-oil and candles are indispensable, and the police must inspect their sale, especially in public markets. Fish must be inspected with special care and marketed as fresh as possible. On holy days the fish-shop should open immediately after divine service. In England, where Sunday is most strictly kept, herrings may be cried in the streets when they arrive on that day. Poultry-shops and those where game and venison is sold must likewise be frequently inspected.

Other Inspection

On the same principles, police supervision must be applied to every calling which is concerned with clothing, housing and providing for the citizens. Day labourers need special supervision. The want of it is manifest in Holland, where porters practise the rudest extortions upon travellers. The trade in old clothes which throughout the north is carried on by Jews demands specially rigorous supervision, since it may spread infection among the poor. Any outbreak of contagious disease gives the signal for stopping the sales and burning the stocks. Poisons must be forbidden when unnecessary, and when necessary must be distributed under supervision. The liberal arts, which are not indispensable to the public, lie beyond the sphere of the police. Manufactures which can be sold abroad, such as cloth, hats, thread, lace and linen, must be left to the department of commerce. The police, however, should complain to the sovereign if by the fault of the Minister of Commerce the town is suffering from excessive taxation or from dearth. Humanity suggests that they should form a fund of charitable contributions and apply it to redeeming the tools and furniture of ruined but deserving artisans.

Supervision in the Country

The countryside, where the majority of citizens produced those goods on which rested the well-being of the State, offered, in Bielfeld's opinion, less scope for the activity of the police. The sovereign himself and other proprietors—nobles, clergy, bishops, chapters, convents, even towns—owned estates and exercised over them many diverse rights. A state police, and that mounted, was urgently needed however, to repress beggars and brigands, while general supervision could do much to combat fires. Against wild beasts systematic war was necessary. In the interest of health, a surgeon should be established in every parish, supporting himself by acting as apothecary and barber. Midwives must be examined by the Medical Senate and quacks put down. Above all, roads should be repaired by the lord and kept clean by the peasants. In Catholic countries and in several Protestant, the number of holy days was highly injurious to rural prosperity. Marriages and baptisms, moreover, needed stricter control. On such occasions most of the villagers, and many other guests, spent several days in rejoicings which left them disordered in mind and body. The police should also control the dancing and gaming in the village inns.

National Economy

In dealing with the wealth of nations, Bielfeld shows how far enlightened common sense could guide the statesman a quarter of a century before Adam Smith's great work appeared. Although some attack the capitalist or *rentier*, it would be the height of imprudence, he contends, to forbid those who have toiled all their life to put out their savings at interest and thus enjoy a quiet interval between their active years and death. Take away their hope of doing this and you annihilate energy and enterprise, thus rendering manufactures faulty and trade wretched. As for national debts—those contracted for luxury or to pay ill-timed subsidies to foreign powers tend to inflict ruin on the people. But those incurred to spare them extraordinary taxes, or to increase their industry and commerce, or to avert the ruin of the state are highly beneficial. Subjects are bound to maintain their sovereign with filial gratitude, remembering that government costs great sums and that he has no gold mines of his own. Ministers of finance, however, constantly ignore the difference between the way in which a private person and a kingdom should manage their affairs. The private person sets down his income and then decides what he can spend and how. The minister, on the other hand, should reckon what expenses it is necessary and profitable for the State to incur, and then arrange to cover them by taxation. The resources of a private person are always limited, but those of a great and well-governed state are boundless. In finance, moreover, great ends are reached by the simplest means. When Frederick William I wished to establish new manufactures in Prussia, he merely forbade his subjects to export wool and removed the duty on wool from Spain. Soon his provinces abounded in wool, and as this wool must be consumed, the manufactures established themselves. France made herself a commercial nation and deposed the Dutch by a single ordinance of navigation. England perfected her agriculture not by coercive laws, but by putting a bounty on export. Such examples may well be followed. The finance minister must aim at increasing the numbers of the people, so that there may be more taxpayers, and their wealth, in order that they may pay more to the State. Surplus revenues should be circulated rather than hoarded. The expenses of a brilliant court, public and private building, luxury, fortifications, premiums for industry—all these cause circulation and so create national wealth. All history proves that poor nations are the most prone to revolt. A state without money will never be able to sustain a long and burdensome war. Thirdly, the natural products of the country must be encouraged. A foreigner in France questioned the villagers whom he found amusing themselves while the surrounding land lay waste. "Our fathers," an old man answered, "left us gay and poor, and so will we leave our sons. If we gained more by toil we should be forced to give it to the King." The English far more wisely give bounties on the export or import of grain as the price is low or high, and the Prussians welcomed Frederick William I by piling mountains of manure before their doors. Thus has the sandy desert round Berlin become admirable soil.

Rational Agriculture

The minister of finance must also study the soil and climate of his state with an eye to the introduction of new plants and animals and the improvement of all kinds of farming. The efforts of German princes to cultivate silk, for example, need closer calculations than have yet been made. Do the mulberry trees that it necessitates displace more grain than if sold would buy the silk required from Piedmont or Turkey? In Germany the cornfields suffer from the smallest shade, while in Piedmont the mulberries give invaluable shelter to the vines. The wife and children of the Piedmontese cultivate the silkworm, but the German peasant's busy wife has scarcely time to deal with the flax and hemp and wool that grow ready to her hand. If Germany needs mulberry trees, they should be planted on the ramparts, in burying-grounds and waste places, or along the highways, and tended by the orphans and the unemployed. Without forests, national independence is impossible: with too many, population is kept low. It is an accepted rule that never less than one-fifth of the soil nor more than one-third should be under forest. One man, if possible, should superintend both forestry and hunting. Although sea fisheries are far more important, carefully stocked fish-ponds, if possible with running water, furnish the land, to its great profit, with carp, pike, perch, tench and other fish, besides the salmon and sturgeon of the rivers. A general edict should be issued to prevent the extermination of the fish by unfair netting or by throwing into the rivers *nux vomica*, lime, and other drugs or bait.

Other Profits from the Land

Among the natural endownments which the minister of finance should develop are salt mines, salt springs, places for the evaporation of sea water, medicinal springs, quarries and mines. Although copper, iron, tin, lead and coal are far more useful to mankind than gold or silver, from which no tool can be made, every kind of mine must be vigorously worked. Marvels have been accomplished by mechanism for draining mines. In Hungary and in Scottish coal mines, the mere vapour of boiling water sets in motion wheels and levers of great size, so that enormous weights of water or of minerals are brought to the surface. For the inventors of such machines no reward can be too great.

Taxation

The State must be sustained by taxes, but by whom should these be paid ? In most European countries, lands which belong to the clergy or to the nobles are exempt from ordinary taxation. But the Church cannot reasonably claim to be dispensed from helping to support the State which favours it so highly. The sovereigns, indeed, request free gifts from the clergy and forbid them to acquire another inch of land. The lands of nobles, on the other hand, have enjoyed immunity for centuries, and this has raised their price when brought to sale. Throughout Europe they bear other charges. The nobles serve as officers, as courtiers and as ambassadors, careers which reduce their fortunes. Unlike the peasant, moreover, they consume great quantities of dutiable goods. Peasants' land bought by nobles gains no exemption from taxation. Adding all taxes together, a healthy policy would make each individual pay one-quarter of his income. This must support the sovereign, the civil service, the army and navy, the State representatives abroad, fortresses, clergy, churches and public buildings, police, hospitals, charitable foundations, the maintenance of crown lands, factories and ships, together with a reserve against public misfortunes.

Bielfeld's knowledge of Europe and his close connexion with its foremost prince lend no small interest to his statement of policy. " Live magnificently and the foreigner will pay," was a counsel which wise as well as unwise sovereigns were inclined to follow. Although Prussia comprised some Catholic provinces, Bielfeld evidently regarded their religion with imperfect sympathy. His criticisms are provoked, however, rather by the tendency of Rome to keep her sons poor and unprogressive than by any dangerous rivalry with the secular power. His indirect witness to the contemporary weakness of the Papacy supports the diatribe of Chesterfield (1749) against

> "that extraordinary government, founded originally upon the ignorance and superstition of mankind, extended by the weakness of some princes, and the ambition of others; declining of late in proportion as knowledge has increased; and owing its present precarious security, not to the religion, the affection, or the fear of the temporal Powers, but to their jealousy of each other. The Pope's excommunications are no longer dreaded; his indulgences little solicited, and sell very cheap; and his territories, formidable to no power, are coveted by many, and will, most undoubtedly, within a century, be scantled out among the great Powers, who have now a footing in Italy, whenever they can agree upon the division of the bear's skin."

Protestants and Philosophers at least had no doubt that Europe must look elsewhere for intellectual and material progress.

Bielfeld's general principle, that of the advancement of the commonweal by the energetic action of the central power, was that which dominated continental Europe between 1740 and 1789 whenever peace prevailed.

BIBLIOGRAPHICAL NOTE

See the Bibliographical Note at the end of Chapter I.
Add :—

A

C. L. Becker: *The Heavenly City of the Eighteenth-Century Philosophers* (1932).

H. N. Brailsford: *Voltaire* (1935).

E. Cassirer: *The Philosophy of the Enlightenment* (trans. 1951).

A. Cobban: *Edmund Burke and the Revolt against the Eighteenth Century* (1929).

A. P. D'Entrèves: *Natural Law* (1951).

F. T. H. Fletcher: *Montesquieu and English Politics, 1750–1800* (1939).

O. Gierke: *Natural Law and the Theory of Society, 1500 to 1800.* 2 vols. (edited by E. Barker, 1934).

F. J. Gould: *Thomas Paine* (1925).

P. Hazard: *La Pensée européenne au XVIIIe siècle.* 3 vols. (1946).

W. Mahrholz: *Der deutsche Pietismus* (an anthology), (1921).

C. K. Martin: *French Liberal Thought in the Eighteenth Century* (2nd ed. 1954).

D. Mornet: *Les Origines intellectuelles de la Révolution française, 1715–1787* (rev. ed. 1954).

D. Mornet: *La Pensée française au XVIIIe siècle* (1929).

R. R. Palmer: *Catholics and Unbelievers in Eighteenth-century France* (1939).

M. Piette. *John Wesley: sa réaction dans l'évolution du Protestantisme* (2nd ed. 1926, trans. 1937).

K. S. Pinson: *Pietism as a Factor in the Rise of German Nationalism* (1934).

W. R. Scott: *Adam Smith as Student and Professor* (1937).

T. B. Shepherd: *Methodism and the Literature of the Eighteenth Century* (1940).

J. S. Simon: *John Wesley and the Advance of Methodism* (1925).

R. Southey: *The Life of Wesley and the Rise and Progress of Methodism* (1820, new ed. 1925).

L. Stephen: *The History of English Thought in the Eighteenth Century.* 2 vols. (1876, 3rd ed. 1902, repr. 1927).

N. Sykes: *Church and State in England in the XVIIIth Century* (1934).

W. J. Warner: *The Wesleyan Movement in the Industrial Revolution* (1930).

B

N. Curnock (ed.): *The Journal of the Rev. John Wesley.* 8 vols. (1910–16).

J. Le Rond D'Alembert: *Discours préliminaire de l'encyclopédie* (1772).

P. S. Foner (ed.): *Thomas Paine: Complete Works* (1945).

Grimm and Diderot: *Memoirs and Anecdotes* (1815).

Montesquieu: *De l'Esprit des Lois* (1748).

John, Viscount Morley (ed.): *Voltaire, Rousseau, Diderot.* VII–XI 15 vol. edition of works, 1921).

J. Priestley: *An Essay on the First Principles of Government* (1768).

H. S. Reiss (ed.): *Political Thought of the German Romantics* (1955).

J.-J. Rousseau: *Du Contrat social* (1762).

T. G. Smollett: *Travels through France and Italy.* 2 vols. (1766, 2nd ed. 1772).

E. H. Sugden (ed.): *Wesley's Standard Sermons.* 2 vols. (1921).

J. Telford (ed.): *The Letters of the Rev. John Wesley.* 8 vols. (1931).

C. G. Tessin: *Letters to a Young Prince from his Governor* (1755).

H. P. Wyndham: *The Diary of the late George Bubb Dodington, Baron of Melcombe Regis, 1749–61* (1784, 1785, 1809, 1823, 1828).

Voltaire: *Dictionnaire philosophique* (1764).

CHAPTER X

THE EUROPEAN POWERS, 1755–63

DURING the eight years' peace (1748–56) which followed the eight years' war, the chief factors of European progress had been educational and social movements rather than political events. To one class the French Philosophers gave a new outlook upon life; to another, the Methodists; and each leavened a mass of future citizens. A more direct and signal portent of peril to the existing order appeared in 1755, when Rousseau's second treatise on the *Origin of Inequality* was published. In language which the age found irresistible, this errant Philosopher arraigned the wisdom of the age and its whole social structure. At the same time several European governments, most notably Austria and Prussia, were labouring to develop their resources, with results that soon affected the balance between the powers.

Progress and Politics

In international politics, however, two great and sinister problems were left by the Austrian war, to be solved if possible by Europe. Should France or Britain win the hegemony overseas? In India, and, more urgently, in America, this question was pressing for solution, and it could hardly be solved without disturbing European peace. But Europe itself was still agitated by the question which Frederick had raised in 1740, and to which the treaties of Berlin, Dresden and Aix-la-Chapelle had brought no definite solution—that of Silesia. As the plain man saw it, the question was whether or no, between organized nations, might should become right.

The Silesian Question

Silesia, indeed, dominated the politics of Europe from 1740 until 1763, and, as a bone of contention, has outlasted the settlement of 1919. As late as 1866, a pacific British statesman, Lord Clarendon, declared that what would please most people would be that Italy should get Venice; Austria, Silesia; and Prussia, a licking. In the decade following 1748, the Habsburgs had not yet been granted a century in which to grow accustomed to their loss. Maria Theresa, the most mettlesome of them all, would not believe that God could suffer Frederick to rob her with impunity. Declaring that she could never behold a Silesian without tears, she lent all her energies to securing restitution.

To regain Silesia, moreover, was an Austrian duty and not merely a matter of Habsburg pride. The addition of Silesia to Prussia raised up a formidable rival within the Empire and at the same time struck Austria in the purse, her weakest spot. In future wars it would give the Prussian legions a long section of the road towards Vienna, with the power to plan surprises against Bohemia. At the same time it separated Saxony and Poland, potential Imperial allies. The shock to public law, moreover, which a successful robbery involved was particularly felt at Vienna. If a power were allowed to train a vast army and snatch a neighbouring province on a trumped-up claim, how could the ruler of an empire so heterogeneous as the Austrian feel secure? Kaunitz, the rising Austrian statesman, had no doubt that at almost any cost Silesia should be regained.

Kaunitz

From the Congress of Aix-la-Chapelle, where he represented the Queen, down to her death in 1780, Kaunitz was her Essex and her Burleigh combined in one. The range of his ideas and the studied eccentricity of his behaviour suggest Disraeli, and Maria Theresa, like Victoria, rewarded his proved fidelity with unstinted trust. He affected inability to eat anything but boiled chicken or to tolerate the open air. He would summon the proud Viennese to his receptions and speak to no one, or reply in Council to the Queen's remonstrances on his way of life that he had come there to discuss her business and not his own. Like almost every Foreign Minister except the obvious fools, he was rated very variously by diverse judges, and Frederick's feline compliments may well be disregarded. When the King of Prussia declared Kaunitz a very great statesman and sat at his feet, Austria was then in danger. Some thought him *doctrinaire*, others held that with French levity he combined Italian penetration; others, again, citing his triumphs in diagnosis and negotiation, styled him an Austrian genius. His patriotism, his influence, his self-satisfaction and his powers of concealment at least are beyond dispute.

Early in his career, Kaunitz convinced himself that neither the traditional antagonism between Austria and France nor the long-standing connexion between Austria and Britain retained any real *raison d'être*. Without rancour against Britain, even though she was a Protestant power hiring Catholics to fight her battles, he questioned the possibility of profit from her alliance. Like more than one of her continental allies he complained that she tended to make peace at their expense as soon as her own objects had been fulfilled. Hanover was a useful henchman to the Emperor, but pickings for Hanover formed part of the price to be paid for every service to Austria from Britain. To recover Silesia Austria must disturb that treaty-Europe which Britain always upheld, and must divide those German powers which Britain always wished to unite against France. For Britain to side against Prussia, moreover, would be to venture Hanover—an unlikely policy for George II—and to attempt to force back the Protestants of northern Silesia under Catholic rule, which might shock British public opinion. If, on the other hand, Austria could gain the French alliance, she need not fear for her German or for her Italian provinces, nor for the Netherlands, while the Turk would no longer be incited by France to attack Hungary. France, reasoned Kaunitz, was influenced by two traditions—to humble the Habsburgs and to acquire the Netherlands. If Silesia could be regained by French goodwill, it would be profitable to cede the Netherlands, thus setting off one tradition against the other. The Queen, convinced of his wisdom, sent him in 1750 to Versailles, where he won over the all-potent Madame de Pompadour. Louis, however, was at this time deep in secret diplomacy of his own, with the chief object of ousting Russian and Austrian influence from Poland. For the time being, therefore, no such revolution as Kaunitz aimed at could take place. But Russia remained pledged to Austria by the alliance of 1746, which included, as a secret object, the recovery of Silesia. On personal grounds—Frederick, it was said, had styled her morals Mohammedan—as well as on grounds of policy and religion, Elizabeth was prepared to go to all lengths in order "to reduce the House of Brandenburg to its former mediocrity," and Saxony made a hesitating third in their alliance (1750). Britain, however, though eager to marshal

His system

continental powers against France, would not consent to action against Prussia, and in 1753 France proclaimed her intention of defending her untrustworthy ally. It was something that the Spanish and Italian Bourbons, together with Sardinia, had joined Austria in a mutual guarantee (1752), but no amount of safety for her rear could atone for the threat to her flank by France. Until Paris changed its mind, the recovery of Silesia would be impossible.

THE REORGANIZATION OF AUSTRIA

Recognizing that for the present a Silesian crusade was impracticable, Maria Theresa devoted herself to Austrian reform. In these years the work began which shaped historic Austria as the work of Charles V had shaped historic Spain. Its inspiration had a threefold source—necessity, imitation, and the personal impulse of the Queen. Strengthened by the Habsburg tradition and by the efforts of German ministers, the Government proceeded to give to the 250,000 square miles of " Austria " with all her miscellaneous populations the body and soul of a progressive state.

The necessity, indeed, had been revealed in 1740. Maria Theresa began her reign with an empty treasury and a faulty financial system. She ruled over a collection of feudal governments with a military power so slender that, as she declared in happier years, she knew not where she might bring forth her son in safety. Austria could not again trust to the chapter of accidents to give her time in the war itself to arm and to gain allies. She must become something more cohesive than the aggregate bequeathed by Charles VI. The example of the richest and of the poorest among the powers spoke loudly to the same effect. In France Louis XIV had shown not only how an incomparable " actor of majesty " could play his part, but how the State, personified in the King, could subdue every antagonistic corporation. Reaping, with Colbert's aid, what all the great French Kings and Cardinals had sown, he acted his reputed dictum, " *L'état, c'est moi.*" In Austria the Habsburgs possessed a still stronger dynastic claim, because it was solely by reason of Habsburg accumulation that the component parts of Austria had come together. Down to 1918 it was they who supplied the moral cement which united the ramshackle empire. Maria Theresa, living before the Revolution, had a stronger claim than Francis Joseph to stand for Austria. She could not but regard it as her duty to uphold the claims of monarchy and of the Catholic faith against provincial divergencies of every kind.

Austria and Religion

With regard to religion, indeed, what was policy for Austria might be impolicy for Prussia. Although Prussia was a still more sprawling state than Austria, her people, Germans or Germanized Slavs, were far more homogeneous than the great blocks of Germans, Czechs, Southern Slavs, Magyars, Flemings, and Italians of which " Austria " was composed. Reason of state, as well as conscience, impelled the Queen to support the Catholicism which most of these races had in common. Reason of state, however, made uniformity impossible for Prussia, where a Calvinist house ruled provinces devoted to the Lutheran or to the Catholic faith. But in all save religious tolerance and international bad faith Austria might profitably copy Prussia, and this she did. Neither was ripe as yet for the emancipation of the peasant-serfs. But Austria far surpassed Prussia in fertile land and population. Why should she not enjoy a greater revenue and a stronger army?

Austrian Progress 1748–56

If she was doomed to fail, it would be because Hohenzollern energy and thrift could not be improvised, nor self-abnegation taught in a moment to feudal estates and corporations. Much, however, was accomplished before the fateful year 1756. When the first Silesian war began, Austria found it hard to send against Frederick a mere 20,000 men. Sixteen years later, she could send 130,000, without undue exertion. At the same time her government was becoming centralized. A Council of State at Vienna supervised the whole administration. The provinces lost their ancient rights of voting and expending aids, and of controlling justice. Poll-tax and property-tax were doubled and levied on classes formerly exempt. The sources of revenue were cared for in the usual fashion of the age by the creation of new industries, cloth, china, silk and the like being subsidized and protected. These necessitated technical education, and from state creation and control of technical schools to state development and control of higher education the distance was not great.

Rise of Vienna

Vienna, in 1683 almost a frontier fortress, had long ranked as the German metropolis of fashion and of pleasure. " Who knows what you did, the last time you went to Vienna ?" was the rejoinder of Frederick, when Crown Prince, to a sermonizing tutor. Now its high renown in law and medicine began, while schools of Oriental studies and a hundred other necessary institutions were established. Theology at the same time was liberalized, and the Jesuit professors sent away. As a devoted Catholic, the Queen could secure from the Pope a drastic reduction of the festivals on which her subjects must hear Mass and refrain from working. As a masterful sovereign she taxed the clergy, controlled ecclesiastical revenues and restricted the number of monks and nuns. All this tended to increase the prestige of the crown. Like a host of other German rulers, Frederick conspicuous among them, the Queen homaged her office by building costly palaces, which, like the famous giant soldiers of the Sergeant King, seemed, on a superficial view, to squander the revenues painfully accumulated for the State. Before 1756, however, the genuine work of Austrian reform was well advanced. Maria Theresa, it is held, found a state hardly better administered than Poland: she left it as well administered as France, and although he inherited a fine civil service, it was from France that Frederick borrowed fiscal agents.

THE FRICTION BETWEEN ENGLAND AND FRANCE

The European Alliances

Of the three great questions which had produced the war of the Austrian Succession, two thus remained hushed if not dormant for several years. Between 1748 and 1756 Europe was not convulsed by the rivalry between Bourbon and Habsburg, nor Germany by the rivalry between Habsburg and Hohenzollern. But the world-question, France or Britain ? could never slumber. However conscious the two governments might be that from the late war they had "gained nothing but the experience of each other's strength and power," their subjects in distant continents remained active rivals whose rivalry must endanger European peace. When France and Britain should find themselves at war, all recent precedent suggested that other states would take up arms. In Paris and in London, however, the will-to-peace seemed strong. To dispel the boredom which increased with years, Louis XV turned to vice, to secret diplomacy, to dissipation, but both from indolence and principle, he turned away from war. Madame de Pompadour, whose power depended on humouring the King, had no quarrel with the English and no interest in the French navy, which in a war with Britain must take precedence of the army. As for the French ministers, if ever the taunt "transient and embarrassed phantoms" was deserved, it was by those who made the peace of 1748 and their successors. Across the Channel, power lay with a king who cherished Hanover and a minister who cherished office. Since France alone was to be feared, Newcastle's plain duty was to hem in France and her Prussian ally, and this he duly did. The "old system"—Britain, Austria, the Dutch, Sardinia, a Scandinavian power, Hesse and the like—was sedulously maintained, and strong hopes arose of adding Russia. In 1754, moreover, Wall, a friendly Irishman, was called to office in Madrid, and Spanish coolness towards France must thereby be increased. No one, however, who was acquainted with Newcastle or his colleagues could doubt that British diplomacy was directed solely towards defence, while the French proved by more than one concession that they were far from desiring war. Parliament had become the tool of ministers; and public opinion, though always anti-French, had found no hopes or grievances like those which in 1739 made it clamour for war with Spain.

French and British overseas

Beyond the ocean, none the less, it was hard to make French and British subjects refrain from fighting. No European treaty could compose Indian native quarrels, nor prevent the French and British Companies from taking sides. When six months must elapse before a communication could pass to or from the mother-country, control of the masterful men who served in India was impossible. In 1751 Clive held Arcot against Dupleix. This and the famous events that followed neither constituted war nor showed a will-to-war between France and Britain. But the French and British in India naturally called for help from the armies and navies of their states, and the conflict between them added to that general tension from which nations seek relief in war. Some grievances had been left untouched by the peace; others arose out of its execution; others again had sprung up since 1748. An ardent Englishman might say that, ever since the peace of Utrecht was signed, the French had been systematically attacking their new friends in Asia, Africa and America alike, that they had broken their promise not to fortify Dunkirk, and that while they kept up the farce of a commission on boundaries they were encroaching further still. An ardent Frenchman would deny part of the indictment and reply *Tu quoque* to the rest, adding that the British invented laws and titles to cover robbery by land and piracy upon the sea.

The Canadian Question

In North America a double collision was impending. At the gates of Canada, the foundation of Halifax (1749) threatened Louisbourg, while the French parried the thrust by intrigues in Nova Scotia. Further west, each nation was advancing at the expense of the Indian tribes. Boundaries might be vague, but the general trend was unmistakable. The British settlers naturally crept west; the French Canadians, south, towards the Mississippi, Louisiana and New Orleans. To British eyes, the deliberate movement of the military Canadian organization seemed an aggression designed with Indian aid to confine peaceful farmers to a seaboard strip. The French believed that their citizens, outnumbered twentyfold, were being hemmed in by land and sea at the instance of a power which disregarded treaties. In 1753, Duquesne, the new Governor of Canada, built two forts on lands to which Virginia laid claim. Britain prepared to vindicate the title by building Fort Necessity. On July 3, 1754, Fort Necessity was surrendered by a British agent, George Washington, to Duquesne's soldiers.

This startling act led only to negotiation, but Britain negotiated in the belief that France was hopelessly outmatched by land and sea. Lest she should merely temporize while consolidating her advantage in America and building a fleet, Newcastle and his colleagues planned strong measures for 1755. Braddock and a thousand regulars were sent to stiffen the colonial resistance. Fresh forts were built and measures taken to cut off French reinforcements. In Europe, new and promising efforts were made to protect Hanover against either France or Prussia by a subsidy convention with Russia. Meanwhile France armed by land and sea. She prepared to reinforce her Canadian army, and declared that vital points of difference must be excluded from the negotiation. War in America at least seemed unavoidable, and how could the

Atlantic highway separate the warlike from the peaceful zone ?

War overseas

In July, 1755, open war drew nearer still, but yet was not declared. Braddock, advancing with careless confidence through a forest, was routed and slain by the French and their savage allies. France succeeded in transporting reinforcements to the field of war. On their way, however, the collision which both sides thought probable had taken place. Boscawen and a naval squadron had engaged the French, and the *Alcide* and the *Lys*, with their freight of regulars and treasure, had been captured in time of peace. False charges of British treachery in the engagement increased the public rage in France. Her statesmen, however, still refused to court disaster by declaring war. Britain could only arm and negotiate with foreign powers. The struggle with France, it was clear, could not be long delayed, and Frederick, the ally of France, disposed of some 140,000 men. When Boscawen struck, the Prussian King protested to France against the treachery of Austria's ally and talked of an immediate seizure of Bohemia. Newcastle's counter-move was a convention with Russia for the defence of Hanover by 55,000 men. Frederick could hardly strike west or south until he was assured that the Russians would not march upon Berlin.

THE REVERSAL OF ALLIANCES

Convention of Westminster 1756

Austria, however, was at this time behaving ambiguously towards her old ally. While secretly longing for a French alliance against Prussia, she could hardly show ardour for the impending British struggle against France. Always resentful of the Dutch barrier in her Netherlands, which maintained at her expense a line of international defence against the French, she now flatly refused to fulfil her obligations on that side. Such evidence of decrepitude in "the old system" suggested to Frederick one of his most startling diplomatic moves. To him the enemy was the triple alliance between Austria, Saxony and Russia. Without the aid of a moneyed power, that is of either France, Britain or Holland, he calculated that its strength would be practically halved. Britain, he believed, could dispose of Russia as she pleased. Britain, he knew, feared above all for Hanover. If, then, he undertook to guard Hanover, and so won Britain, Austria and Saxony would lose Russia and British subsidies, and Prussia would be secure. For France under her then leadership he felt nothing but contempt. She had ceased, in his opinion, to be an ally of value, but her formal alliance need not be lost by his new move. It amounted, he could argue, to no more than the addition of another guarantee for Silesia to those which France and other powers had already given. In any case, nothing that France could do, or leave undone, ranked with the threat to Prussia which the British convention with Russia clearly implied. Early in December he offered Britain a mutual defensive pact. Newcastle and his master clutched at this new and conclusive guarantee. If Hanover were defended by three great military powers and several small ones, how could France attack it? Her armaments, indeed, were vast, but with a superior fleet victory should fall to Britain. Although a caviller might maintain that a bandit, whom all Europe detested, was not the best ally, the Prussian army proved too tempting a bait to be refused.

On January 16, 1756, Britain and Prussia signed at Westminster a mutual covenant to keep Germany free from war. The Holy Roman Empire, which Britain desired to shield by such a guarantee, would have comprised the Netherlands, but for them Prussia firmly declined to be responsible. If on any pretext, however, a foreign power should enter Germany, Britain and Prussia stood pledged to unite in her defence. Hanover and Silesia were thus covered, whether France or Austria should become the aggressive power.

The Revolution in Alliances

Frederick was not less proud than Newcastle of this triumph of the pen. He boasted that the grim league against Prussia was dissolved, and negotiated for a renewal of the French alliance. That France should join with Austria, or Russia with a group opposed to Britain, seemed to him equally absurd. Newcastle likewise saw "the old system" strengthened by an incomparable army, and the German powers duly aligned in restraint of France. But both the Prussian and the British statesmen, the supreme realist no less than the sentimental fumbler, had made a grave miscalculation. Neither had understood the sway that personal disgust may exercise over policy, especially in an age when policy was determined by the few, and when the few included several powerful women. To the disgust which Frederick aroused in the Queen and Kaunitz must be added that which Austria felt for the British system. To Elizabeth that system was acceptable, but what had made her Britain's ally was the belief that she would be paid to defend Hanover against Frederick alone. Madame de Pompadour, unlike her crowned contemporaries, had received courtesies and no insult from the Prussian King. The sudden conclusion at such a moment of an agreement directed against France, however, powerfully increased the influence with her and with her friends which Kaunitz already had acquired. In the smart of such an injury, ancient traditions lost their influence, and on May 1, 1756, Bourbon and Habsburg made a defensive treaty at Versailles. Thanks to the Convention of Westminster, the second and by far the more difficult portion of the revolution in alliances had been accomplished. While the world question had brought France and Britain to the verge of war, and while Austria hoped soon to win redress from Prussia, the ancient rivalry for the leadership in Europe was laid aside. France, Prussia's patron against Austria, had joined the Habsburgs. France, however, made the Versailles convention in no crusading spirit. She would be content to see Prussia lose Silesia, but no more: she would take no part in an attack: if Prussia attacked, she would send only 24,000 men: she would expect the Netherlands by way of compensation. Russia, on the other hand, was all for immediate invasion. The more cautious Austrian view prevailed, but in 1757 Frederick might have to face a storm like that which he and Belleisle had loosed upon the Queen sixteen years before. Austria, Russia, Saxony, Sweden, with France, as paymaster at least, and probably other German powers—against such a coalition he could count only upon his army, the gold of Britain and himself.

THE SEVEN YEARS WAR

British Disasters

Newcastle, meanwhile, saw his house of cards collapse. When the year 1756 began, Britain stood fully armed and buttressed by every conceivable alliance. By midsummer, she was at last openly engaged with France, and war had begun with the inept if not the cowardly failure of Admiral Byng to relieve

Minorca. The key of the Mediterranean thus passed to France, and Britain could count herself fortunate that when the French offered it to Spain as the price of her alliance it was refused. The disaster destroyed the country's confidence both in the navy and in the Government. Apart from the friendly neutrality of Spain, moreover, Britain found herself in fact as isolated as Prussia. Austria, though never hostile, was yet in league with France. Russia denounced the subsidy convention that she might free her hands against Britain's new ally. From the Dutch nothing was to be hoped; from Sweden, only mischief. Britain's first object must be peace on the Continent, avoiding the complications and fresh commitments of a general war. That the Netherlands were now in the hands of a friend of France, that Hanover was held by the grace of the King of Prussia, that in America the French were a military power and the British an agricultural, that the navy might prove unfit to keep inviolate the shores of Britain—all this was terrible, but not perhaps beyond remedy, if the struggle remained a duel. Gold could do much in Russia: Elizabeth might die at any time: without Russia, Austria's 80,000 could accomplish little: neither Russia nor Austria was preparing for a 1756 campaign. Frederick, Britain urged unceasingly, should give no provocation. In actual fact no league against him had been signed.

The ideas of a Newcastle with regard to Prussian policy, however, were not those of a military autocrat with a vast army in perfect preparation. Frederick held, and rightly, that if Prussia were doomed to invasion attack was the best defence. His superior speed might overcome the weight of the threatened coalition. If his swift blows did not paralyse its members, they would at least procure him territories which would nourish his army during war and serve as hostages, perhaps as compensations, in bargaining for peace. In August 1756, as in August 1914, Prussia struck at the associate of Russia before Russia could have time to intervene.

Prussia and Saxony

Saxony, rich, coveted, accessible, was the Belgium of the later war. The Saxons held the key to Bohemia, commanding with their fortresses the cleft made by the Elbe through the low mountain framework of the Bohemian plain. Frederick demanded freedom to use the country, promising full compensation during the war and restoration at its close.

Being refused, he seized Dresden, and claimed to have found there proofs of Saxon treachery. Having occupied the Electorate he hurried on the siege of Pirna. Pirna, however, held out long enough to save Bohemia from invasion, and although the Austrians failed to relieve it they proved themselves the equals of the Prussians as fighting men. Frederick's move had placed the revenues of Saxony at his disposal. He had also seized ten regiments of infantry and a base for future operations. But his violence towards Saxony had displayed him to Europe as the aggressor, and as a treacherous aggressor against the weak. Britain put the best face upon the misdemeanour of her ally. But in January 1757, the Imperial Diet declared war against him, and the Convention of St. Petersburg united France, Austria and Russia for mutual defence. Agreements of a more drastic nature preceded the next campaign.

Britain meanwhile was deprived by Frederick's move of any hope of his assistance. A King committed to a new Silesian war must denude even his Rhenish provinces of troops. Hanover was thus robbed of its sole defender. In August the fall of Fort Oswego removed the last obstacle between Canada and New Orleans. The general collapse of his system in Europe, in America and on the sea compelled Newcastle himself to retire from office. Diligent as he was, unrivalled as a parliamentary manager, ready to spend his private fortune for the public good, he could not rouse the nation, save to fury against himself. The national emergency was great enough to break the Whig monopoly of office which had lasted since 1714, and to compel George II to accept the one statesman whom the people reverenced as by nature a king of men. In William Pitt Britain incarnate took the helm of state.

William Pitt

Within five months, before gaining a single victory, Pitt had become to Britain what Frederick in the campaign of Hohenfriedberg had become to Prussia. As a war minister in a free country he has never been surpassed. Such an one must be conspicuous, that all may in some measure know him by eye and ear. He must be high-souled, feeling the cause sublime and seeing the sublime in all who serve it. He must speak to the people as to colleagues, shrink from no sacrifice, find nothing too great or too small for his attention, be ready to defy all precedent in his choice of means and plans. Above all, he must be inspiring, so that those who enter his presence may feel that his eye is always on them, and that, if they play their part, victory is sure. Gustavus Adolphus, Lincoln, Gambetta, Clemenceau, Lloyd George lend various lustre to the type, but Pitt is its perfection. Compelled to love the highest when they saw it, the nation condoned or even admired his defects—posing, dictatorial claims, bursts of passion, extravagance, choice of many bad generals and unprofitable plans. Rivalling Louis XIV or Canning in majesty, endowed like Frederick or like Gladstone with a compelling eye and a voice which could command every emotion, this free lance of forty-seven, broken in health and fortune, assumed the control of Britain as his natural right.

In some degree, indeed, Pitt's birth and training rendered him far more fit than the Whig oligarchs to lead the nation against France. His detestation of the enemy, it is true, was only more keen than theirs because his nature was more impassioned. Deist and parliamentarian, he felt with all his soul that France was evil—a land where men were forced to submit to the tyranny of priests and kings, itself corrupt, and eager to corrupt and to enslave throughout the world. But his descent from the governor of Madras had given him an outlook far wider than that of the great landed Whigs. Imperialism was in his blood, together with a just idea of the importance of the City, and he could rise above the party prejudice against the Tories as traitors born. Within five months, before the 1757 campaign began, Pitt rallied the British Empire for a united and world-wide struggle against France. For this supreme task all minor differences must vanish. Southrons and Highlanders, Whigs and Tories, British and Americans, friends of the reigning king and friends of the heir apparent—all were included in that moral union without which no free country can wage a successful war. His greatest failure, perhaps his only failure, was his attempt to inspire the King. In George II, the narrow vapouring Hanoverian, Pitt could revere the crowned majesty of Britain. When he entered the presence, sneered Walpole, he bowed so low that you saw his hooked nose between his legs. But the petty King deemed him merely an offensive adventurer whom the absurd constitution of an unpleasant

HANOVER
IN
1721
Hamburg
R. Elbe
R. Weser
Bremen
HANOVER
R. Aller
R. Ems
Herrenhausen
Hanover
R. Elbe
Magdeburg
MINDEN
Minden
R. Leine
R. Weser
R. Saale
Göttingen
English Miles
0
20
40
60
80

country had forced him to employ. He could not refuse to read to Parliament the King's Speech composed by Pitt, which made him declare that he relied with pleasure upon the spirit and zeal of his people. But when in April 1757 his favourite son Cumberland, Frederick's choice for the Anglo-Prussian defence of Hanover, demanded Pitt's dismissal as the condition of his own acceptance, he gladly complied and Frederick rejoiced.

The dismissal of Pitt showed how blind were George II, Cumberland and Frederick to what Pitt had already done, to what he could do, and to the natural response of a free people to such a blow. Despite his prostrating attacks of gout, the widespread curse of England in the later eighteenth century, Pitt had swiftly taught the country to rely on her own sons for home defence. He had reorganized the militia, raised Highland regiments for America, prepared a great American campaign, and taken thought for India, Africa, the West Indies and the Mediterranean. More vital still, he had accepted the strategy which in 1755 he had sacrificed office to oppose, and which meant everything to Frederick and to George II. He had consented to complicate the struggle with France for America by undertaking to defend Hanover, which constituted the defence of Prussia's western flank. Not only was Britain, for the first time without Dutch help, to engage France on and beyond the seas. She was also to fulfil the Convention of Westminster as though Prussia had been the power attacked instead of the aggressor. She thus undertook the immeasurable weight and cost of a continental war at a moment when her power in America and India was tottering and when she had lost the Mediterranean. Without Pitt, Britain and Prussia began the campaign of 1757 in Hanover, America, Bohemia and Eastern Prussia.

Britain and War in Europe

For Britain, despite the Hanoverian adventure, the war with France was primarily a war by sea. To her it could be fatal only if France gained such naval predominance as to permit invasion. Her victory, if it came, must come slowly, by rendering France war-weary as in 1748. If all went well by sea, the French coasts might be harried, French shipping captured, French commerce destroyed, French colonies conquered, but without a strong ally upon the Continent, France herself could hardly be invaded. If, on the other hand,

France could be drawn into any continental war save one of national defence, war-weariness might come more swiftly. If Britain could defend Hanover, she might distract and wear out France, while keeping from her hands a valuable pledge which would be used at the peace to regain what Britain might have conquered overseas. To defend Hanover was also, and that immediately, to save Frederick from destruction. Chance rather than calculation had restored Belleisle to power, and he had committed France to vast exertions against Prussia. While the army of the Rhine set out for Hanover, the army of the Main was to co-operate with Austria in freeing Saxony.

Campaign of 1757

Frederick, indeed, knew that he must win quickly if he was not to risk destruction. Besides the threat to Hanover and to Saxony, he had to face the main Austrian effort in Silesia, and the menace of Russians, Swedes and Imperialists on other fronts. Again, as in 1756, a swift thrust at Bohemia promised most, for to hold northern Bohemia would safeguard Saxony and Silesia, while weakening Austria and compelling her to dance to Frederick's tune. The Prussians, however, were well aware that to subdue Austria they must conquer Moravia and take Vienna, tasks which might well prove too great for their unaided strength. On the eve of hostilities, in March 1757, they were opposed by 133,000 Austrians, a force slightly outnumbering their own.

Trusting, not without reason, in Prussian mobility and skill, Frederick engaged at Prague on May 6, within three weeks of entering Bohemia. On that bloody day "the pillars of the Prussian infantry were cut down." The Austrians lost one-third of a force about 74,000 strong, but this was outweighed by the fall of some 18,000 Prussians. Still, the King believed, the capture of Prague and its garrison would end the war. His dear-bought victory had indeed terrified wavering powers, both France and German. To save Prague, the Queen must venture her last army, some 54,000 men led by the cautious Marshal Daun. Had Frederick shattered Daun, he afterwards declared, he would have led his victorious army into France. At Kolin, on June 18, he attacked the strongly posted Austrians with 30,000 men. So fierce was his onslaught that late in the afternoon only a bold stroke by two Saxon squadrons prevented an Austrian retreat. Then numbers told, and Prussians themselves began to talk of Charles XII, the iron-head who doomed his army to disaster. Daun's loss approached 7,000, but Kolin cost Frederick all but a fragment of his 30,000 as well as the Bohemian campaign.

Although none of their enemies knew how to press home an advantage, Prussians and British had still a series of ill-tidings to endure. From India came news that Calcutta had been lost in 1756, and English men and women choked to death in the Black Hole. The disasters in America continued, unrelieved by victory on the coasts of France or beyond the ocean. Cumberland, heavily outnumbered, was forced to yield Hanover to the French (September 10). By that time the Russians held the detached province of East Prussia at their mercy, and the Swedes, from their own territory of Western Pomerania, were preparing to regain what they had lost to Prussia forty years before. Pitt indeed had again been forced by the nation upon the King (July 29), but his offer of Gibraltar to Spain had failed to win her alliance. Berlin itself was held to ransom by a Hungarian force of cavalry (October 16–17). Many high-placed Englishmen thought that, at least for Hanover and Prussia, the war was lost. Frederick caught, as it seemed, between five victorious armies, in vain made overtures to France, and told Voltaire that he would not survive the ruin of his House. When October ended, he was endeavouring, almost without hope, to bring the would-be deliverers of Saxony to battle, while, far behind him, Silesia was welcoming back the forces of the Queen.

Rossbach and Leuthen

The last two months of 1757, however, made history with a speed almost beyond compare. Posterity is distracted by the spectacle of India where slender forces were producing vast results. By a single decision in the preceding year Clive, at thirty-one, had saved Bengal and made British India possible. At Plassey, with some 3,200 men, he now fought victoriously against odds of more than twenty to one, effecting in five months a solid conquest which for ten years had evaded the efforts of Dupleix. While Clive's great victory at Plassey (June) remained unknown, Frederick twice proved that in Europe also a small army could win as sweeping and as enduring a success. On November 5, protecting Leipzig, he routed with half their number some 43,000 French and Germans, of whom three-fourths were French. In this "ludicrous fight" at Rossbach, the Prussians lost 500 men and took 6,000 prisoners. Their moral victory proved stupendous, for they had rallied to themselves the rising Teutonic feeling against the luxurious, vain, marauding, desecrating French. In British eyes, moreover, a power that could beat the French stood absolved from bygone treachery towards its neighbour. Pitt promptly moved towards a far more liberal treaty with this glorious ally. Immediately, however, Frederick's presence in Saxony meant that in Silesia his troops lost a battle and 8,000 men, besides the capital and the great fortress of Schweidnitz. But while Silesia was thus being wrested from him, the victor of Rossbach was hastening to its relief. From Leipzig to the neighbourhood of Breslau, 200 miles as the crow flies, was covered between November 13 and 28. "I intend," he told his generals, "in spite of the rules of war, to attack the army of Prince Charles, which is nearly thrice our strength, wherever I shall find it." He found it, 70,000 strong, near Leuthen, on December 5. At a cost of 6,000 casualties among his own 35,000 men, he drove the Austrians from the field and took more than 21,000 prisoners. When winter brought them respite, only Schweidnitz remained in their possession. The most fluctuating of campaigns had left the Prussians almost where they had stood when it began.

Campaign of 1758

In April 1758, Frederick reaped the reward of his greatest conquest—that of Pitt. It was Cumberland who had spoken of "the improper spirit of economy," but it was Pitt who scorned to spare. His new treaty pledged Prussia to make no separate peace, but otherwise left her free. Britain stood likewise pledged, but undertook also to pay Prussia £670,000 for the year. A further £1,800,000 went to the support of a continental army under Ferdinand of Brunswick. Considerations both military and political kept a British squadron from the Baltic, where it would have been powerless against France and dangerous to British trade with Russia and Sweden. But, at the instance of Prussia, attacks were made upon the coast of France, in the hope of diverting reinforcements from her eastern armies. Ferdinand actually drove the French from Hanover, crossed the Rhine, won a victory at Crefeld (June) and attracted to himself the French troops intended for Bohemia. Although Belleisle's energy and vast resources afterwards reversed the position, the army paid by Britain protected Frederick against France throughout the year.

This relief was more necessary because the Russians now began to prove their value in the field. In 1758, as in the two preceding years, Frederick struck swiftly south before his enemies were all in line. In Moravia he failed, and during August the Russians victoriously approached Cüstrin which guarded the Oder crossing to Berlin. By Prussian standards they were ill found and ill led, and it was no secret that Peter the heir of their ailing mistress worshipped Frederick while his consort, Catherine, looked to Britain. Yet Zorndorf, where the King attacked them with an almost equal force, proved a most desperate and costly fight. Almost one-third of his 36,000 men were lost, but the Russians retreated and set him free to turn once more against the Austrians. At Hochkirch (October) he revealed both his strength and weakness as a general, losing 9,000 men through rashness and self-will, but wresting every consequent strategic gain from an enemy of twice his strength. In spite of Swedes and Russians, Austrians, Imperialists and French, Silesia and Saxony remained in Prussian hands.

Rise of Choiseul

Britain meanwhile had much improved her fleet, and had won profit from it in many distant fields. In America, where Louisbourg had fallen and Pittsburg had replaced Fort Duquesne, she gravely threatened Canada. Most ominous for Britain and for Prussia, however, was the advance to power in France of Choiseul, who was something of a Gallic Pitt. Famous, even among Frenchmen, for valour in the field, he showed such valour in office as to tame Madame de Pompadour. Choiseul, indeed, was a rake, whereas Pitt's life was pure: Pitt was the Great Commoner, Choiseul boasted that all save the Duke of his own Lorraine and the King of France were his inferiors or at best his peers. In spirit and enterprise as in personal integrity, however, Choiseul resembled Pitt, and as a patriot he was his equal. Louis and Madame de Pompadour had made French policy an affair of their own fancy, or at best a vent for vague idealism. How, save by living in a somewhat more moral world, could France benefit by making Conti King of Poland or Maria Theresa ruler of

Silesia? A full century later, only the very wisest could suppose that Prussia would ever menace France. Choiseul, a realist, saw that Britain, not Prussia, was the enemy, and checked the flow of French blood and gold to promote the interests of the Habsburgs. By his insistence, the treaties of Versailles gave way to a new Franco-Austrian pact (March 1759) which loosened the bonds of France. Though she still contracted to maintain 100,000 men in Germany, to finance the Swedes and Saxons, and to make no separate peace, she was free to devote more of her strength and energy to the overthrow of Britain. To this end, Belleisle drew up a vast scheme of invasion and aimed a blow at Hanover, while Choiseul sought earnestly to enlist the help of Spain.

Campaign of 1759

Britain, however, entered on 1759 in the full flush of victory following on despair. Inspired by Pitt, the nation faced invasion without modifying its own aggressive plans. While blockading and harassing the would-be invaders of England, Pitt sent no less than 52,000 British-paid troops to oppose the French in Hanover. No means for impelling France towards peace could be better than the signal defeat of her armies on the plains of northern Europe. At the same time her rich West Indian islands must be seized, Canada conquered, Clive's great achievements in India followed up, and Spain deterred from entering the war. The impending advent in Spain of Charles III, Elizabeth's son Don Carlos, King of Naples, must mean that Spain's considerable navy and resources would pass into more vigorous hands. The heir to Ferdinand the Pacific, moreover, was the son-in-law of the Saxon Augustus, Frederick's victim. He had himself suffered from British sea power in the Austrian war, when Admiral Matthews, watch in hand, allowed him one hour in which to declare Naples neutral. In both wars, like all neutrals, he had experienced the intolerable conduct of a nation which construed maritime law to suit its own superior strength, and commissioned privateers whose captains cared for no law at all. Alive to the danger, Pitt redressed many Spanish grievances and used much diplomacy, but safety, as he knew, lay only in an overwhelming naval force.

Victory for Britain and Prussian Decline

To Britain, 1759, the classic "year of victory," seemed to bring safety in every quarter of the globe. With August, her dazzling season of success began. Guadeloupe, deemed by many more valuable than all Canada, was already taken ; Quebec, hemmed in by Wolfe; the Havre flotilla, shattered by Rodney. On August 1, at Minden, the gateway into Hanover was firmly barred by Ferdinand in the faces of the conquering French. Minden was no Rossbach, but a military state like France could not but perceive that a promising campaign had been made futile. Sixteen days later, off Cape St. Vincent, Boscawen shattered the Toulon fleet, another blow to Belleisle's plan of invasion, and a timely hint to the new King of Spain. The Trafalgar of the war, a Trafalgar from which her neutrality shielded Spain, followed in November at Quiberon in southern Brittany. There the Brest fleet perished and the invasion plan disappeared. Meanwhile Quebec had fallen and good news from southern India was on its way.

But the success of Britain was offset and might well be in great part cancelled by Frederick's failure. Prague, Kolin, Leuthen, Zorndorf, Hochkirch—no army of 150,000 could endure such shocks as these, with as many more under Frederick's lieutenants, without losing something of its dash and fire. Winter quarters gave time for rest and training, fresh lads came of age to serve and mercenaries could be hired, but it was impossible that a population of five million should make good the waste of officers and N.C.O.'s. If these failed, how were the men to be trained to fear them more than they feared the enemy—the foundation of Prussian success ? " Dogs, would ye live for ever ? " Frederick once asked some who ran from certain death. In a fourth campaign, the answer threatened to be doubtful. The Austrians, moreover, were learning that, even against Frederick and the heavy guns which he would seldom part with, manœuvres amid woods, marshes and ravines might bring victory without the risk of battle. If only the Russians and Austrians could join forces, their superior numbers would make them safe, and they could devour Prussia as the Prussians were wont to devour Bohemia and Saxony. At the opening of the fourth campaign, Frederick could only hope for victory by chance, or for the death of Elizabeth or the intervention of the Turks or the sacrifice by Britain of her advantage in America for his sake. Instead, the Austrians denied him battle until the Russians, forcing their way to the Oder, seized Frankfurt, only 48 miles from Berlin.

There they were joined by more than 18,000 Austrians, the united forces, irregulars included, numbering nearly 70,000 men. On August 12, Frederick attacked them beyond the Oder with forces wearied by a long march under a broiling sun. At Kunersdorf, as at Kolin, the disciplined fury of the Prussians seemed, late in the fight, to have triumphed over numbers and position, but again disaster followed. Of the 48,000 Prussians who attacked, more than one-half fell and the remainder fled. The Queen, it seemed, had only to stretch out her hand to regain Silesia, whither the Russians turned their steps. The much-derided army of the Empire reconquered the greater part of Saxony, where Daun captured at Maxen a Prussian force almost 15,000 strong. Maxen, even more than Kunersdorf, lowered the prestige of Prussia and turned Russia away from thoughts of peace. But Austrian jealousy of Russian success and Russian fear of Frederick postponed, if only for a winter, that ruin of his House which was to be the signal for his self-destruction. The victors of Kunersdorf retreated to their several homes, the vanquished turned to negotiate for peace, with the warm support of Pitt. Thanks to Pitt's firmness, Britain refused a separate continental peace with France, and France found herself doomed to bleed further that Silesia might be regained by her ancient rival. Russia, moreover, insisted that the conquered province of East Prussia should revert to Poland, its former overlord, and that she should extend her own Baltic provinces to march with it on the north. Such aggrandizement of Russia would offend many European powers, but her co-operation was essential to the victory which seemed inevitable in the next campaign. In 1760, therefore, the contending alliances took the field unbroken.

Kunersdorf 1759

In the new campaign, Ferdinand's army, paid by Britain and strengthened with more than 22,000 British troops, completely occupied the armies raised by France. The offensive against Prussia, therefore, fell to forces whose chief talent was usually shown on the defensive. Although the Swedes and Russians attacked the northern coast, the main struggle was for Silesia and Saxony, where Frederick disposed of more than 100,000 men. His hope of beating the Austrians in Saxony before the Russians reached Silesia was foiled by their evasion, while the defect which he shared with Charles XII

Campaign of 1760

and Peter, that of regarding soldiers as mere machines, brought him yet another disaster. At Landshut, as at Maxen, a lieutenant was overwhelmed and 10,000 Prussians surrounded. Glatz fell, and only by brilliantly surprising the Austrians at Liegnitz (August) could Frederick save his army and Silesia. Austrian and Russian forces none the less made a momentary capture of Berlin, and the Austrians used their great superiority in numbers to reconquer Saxony. A desperate battle at Torgau (November) ended the campaign. Like Mollwitz, the first of Frederick's battles, Torgau, his last, had appeared to be an Austrian victory. When Zieten finally achieved the first Prussian triumph over Daun, each side had lost more than one-third of its fighting strength. Of some 33,000 casualties more than one-half were Prussian. Beyond all expectation, however, Prussia had survived the year.

George III 1760–1820

Frederick's survival was in itself a British victory, for his fall would have exposed Hanover and thereby made every conquest overseas hard to retain at the peace. Those conquests now included Canada, since a thrilling race for Quebec had been won by Britain, and her forces then closed in on Montreal. But Pitt's master, George II, died in October, and the new king might well aim at an independence which he could achieve only in time of peace. The negotiations which had filled 1760 still continued, and Pitt, already at issue with his colleagues, could no longer dominate as when he alone stood between Britain and defeat.

The Family Compact

In 1761, indeed, the negotiations gave Choiseul a victory worth many victories in the field. Fearing a Franco-British understanding, Charles III flung Spain into the arms of France. The Family Compact of August 1761 provided for an intimate union between all the Bourbon powers. Mutual defence, common foreign policy, even common citizenship were arranged for. Spain undertook to enter the war on May 1, 1762, and France bound herself to procure redress for the Spanish grievances against Britain. To curb Britain, indeed, both Pyrenees and Alps were to disappear, for Portugal was to be forced into this Latin union, and Sardinia invited to accede. The French armies, meanwhile, failed to use their numerical superiority to crush Ferdinand, while in India and in the West Indies the remains of the French

Fall of Pitt 1761

Prospects in 1762

empire were passing into British hands. In October, however, the fall of Pitt threatened to remove the mainspring of the great machine. When Pitt fell, the alliance between Britain and Prussia had existed for nearly five years. During more than four of them, both powers had been associated in a desperate struggle which raged within and without Europe. The European struggle, it might fairly be said, had been provoked by Frederick, and Britain had saved him from destruction. He had lost many provinces, but still held Silesia and part of Saxony. The extra-European struggle had brought Britain enormous gains, and to these Frederick had contributed, though indirectly. Was it the duty of Britain to fight on until he won back everything, or to redeem his losses with her own gains, or to adopt some intermediate course? Pitt stood alone in supporting his demand that Britain should make no peace which involved him in any sacrifice. Unless the Turks invaded Russia, the Prussian cause seemed hopeless. Without British help, or even with British help upon the previous scale, how could Frederick avoid destruction? Must Britain continue to spend half her revenue to oblige a madman?

The campaign of 1761, none the less, had again postponed Frederick's fall. While Swedes and Russians conquered Pomerania, Russians and Austrians joined forces in the south, but by able manœuvres the Prussians prevented them from reaching any vital spot. Both the invading armies wintered in Silesia and left the decisive stroke until 1762. They would no longer have to contend with Pitt, who had retired from office in October rather than be responsible for continued peace with Spain.

Peter III 1762

Early in the new year, Frederick, with an army of at most 130,000 deteriorating troops in an exhausted country, confessed to his brother that, if the Turks failed him, he saw no hope of prolonging the struggle. Without knowing it, he was already saved. On January 5, Elizabeth, dying "almost with a saucer of cherry brandy at her lips," had at last yielded the throne to her nephew Peter III, who promptly asked Frederick for the Black Eagle. "A strange knight," laughed the delighted King, "who feeds 80,000 soldiers at my expense." The new Tsar's "strangeness" soon proved itself to surpass anything that even Russia had ever known. The armies were recalled, eastern Pomerania and East Prussia simply given back to Frederick, and, at a price, the Russian alliance proffered. Frederick might have 20,000 Russians to serve against Austria if he would join Peter against Denmark for that recovery of his estates in Slesvig which was the inspiration of his life. The transfer of these estates in 1720 had been in part the work of Prussia. Britain and France had guaranteed them to the King of Denmark, and no German could relish the extension in the west of the family possessions of a Tsar. Frederick, however, did not hesitate, and at the end of June, Prussians and Russians were marching against Daun in Silesia. Sweden had already followed Russia into peace (May).

Revolution in Russia

No man of sense, indeed, could suppose that the mad anti-Russianism of Peter's policy both foreign and domestic could long be borne by Russia. To abandon all the fruits of a victorious war only to begin another for his private interest was but one of many insults hurled by the new Tsar at his subjects. At a state banquet he prostrated himself before Frederick's portrait, and he decreed that the army and the clergy should be shaved and clad like Prussians. A Holstein uncle received the chief command. That German yoke from which Elizabeth had freed her people seemed once again to threaten them. A few months made the impending revolution an open secret. The threads were gathered by the firm hands of Peter's German consort, Catherine, and without bloodshed he was brought to abdicate in her favour. Eleven days after the troops moved in Silesia she made her triumphal entry into the capital. For Russia, the Seven Years War was over.

Campaign of 1762

With their rear secured and their Baltic provinces restored to them, the Prussians proved that they could still take the offensive with success. While raids compelled the Empire to declare neutrality, two victories and the recovery of Schweidnitz brought the Queen to treat for peace. The failure of Turkish co-operation and the advent of a peace ministry in London wrecked Frederick's hopes of a resounding triumph. However strenuously the Hohenzollern might haggle, no dispassionate observer could see any other prospect for the treaty than that *status quo ante bellum* which mocks so many sacrifices and entombs so many hopes.

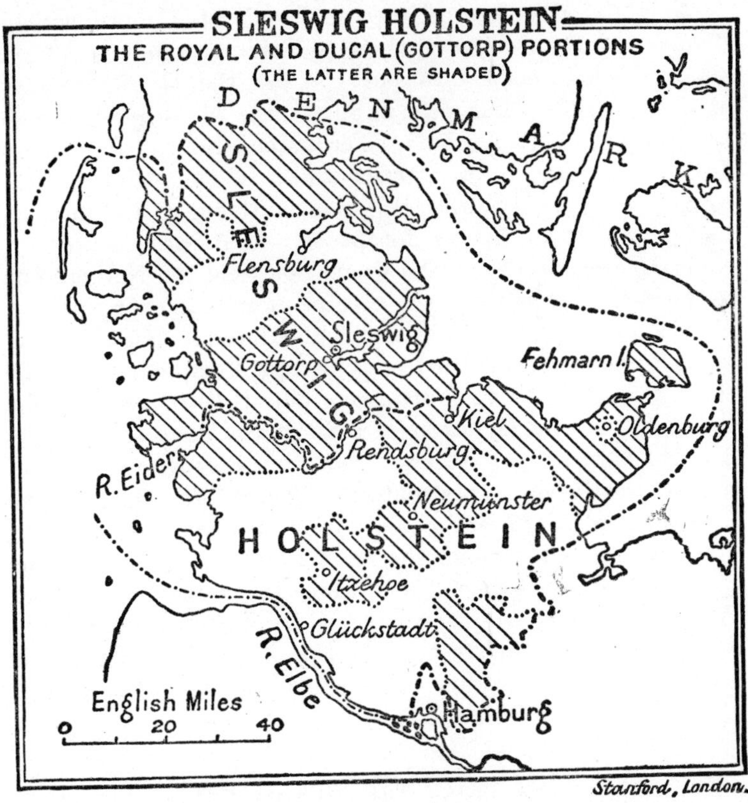
SLESWIG HOLSTEIN
THE ROYAL AND DUCAL (GOTTORP) PORTIONS
(THE LATTER ARE SHADED)
DENMARK
SLESWIG
Flensburg
Sleswig
Gottorp
Fehmarn I.
Kiel
Oldenburg
Rendsburg
R. Eider
Neumünster
HOLSTEIN
Itzehoe
Glückstadt
R. Elbe
Hamburg
English Miles
0
20
40
Stanford, London.

In 1762, therefore, chance had separated more widely than before the two wars which to Britain's profit had been almost compounded into one. While the Germans were moving towards a stalemate in Silesia, the world-question was being solved on distant seas. Ferdinand's intermediate army drove the French westwards towards the Rhine, thus emphasizing the severance between the struggles and increasing the thirst of France for peace. If Austria, moreover, could not regain Silesia, she would not yield the Netherlands to the Bourbons, and the war became more than ever pointless for France. Spain, it was clear, had entered it to no purpose. With French support, her troops invaded Portugal, only to be checked and foiled by Portuguese and British. At sea she found her enemy far stronger than in the days of Walpole. San Sacramento was taken from the Portuguese, but in August the Havana capitulated to Pocock, who took twelve Spanish ships of war and a booty of £3,000,000. Next month Manilla followed, though the news could not arrive in time to influence the peace. Meanwhile the remaining French West Indies were changing hands. By November Bourbons and British were in treaty, and the only question was the amount of compensation upon which the almost universal conqueror would insist.

THE PEACE TREATIES OF 1763

Peace of 1763

In February 1763, both the German war and the world war were brought to an end by treaties as nearly definitive as the incurable rivalries between the powers allowed. The Prussian and Austrian bargainers enjoyed the advantage of a clear principle and a sagacious King. Having accepted the principle that the peace should inflict no loss on either side, Frederick showed himself superior to the niceties of form in which Vienna took delight. He was prepared to send Hertzberg, his plenipotentiary, wherever the punctilious Austrians desired, and he accepted Hubertusburg, a damaged castle of his Saxon victim, as the scene of the negotiations. To favour a lasting peace, he promised to support Joseph as the successor to his father Francis in the Empire, while a few vexatious provisions of the earlier Silesian settlement were done away. As some slight compensation for evacuating Saxony he kept the Electoral revenue down to February 10, 1763. The substance of the treaty, however, was that "the third Silesian war" closed with the Austrian cession of Silesia and Glatz to Prussia.

Such was on paper the harvest of Frederick's youth and middle age as king, and of the unstinted blood and treasure of his subjects. "A good peace, but we must not let them observe the fact," were his words to Hertzberg, and for the Prussia of the Hohenzollerns he was right. Prussia had won beyond all question the rank of a great power. She possessed the most perfect army and the strongest monarchy in Europe, with high eminence in diplomacy and in administration. In her rise she had gone far towards transforming the public law of Europe to her liking, depressing the notion of legal right in favour of the right of demonstrated strength. If the rape of Silesia was just because Frederick could develop and defend the province, where need Prussia stop? The first partition of Poland was soon to demonstrate the historic meaning of the third Silesian war. Austria, on the other hand, remained irreconcilable at heart, and looked eagerly for an opportunity to treat Prussia in the Prussian fashion. While the great king lived, this would be dangerous, but for many years the news that his health was bad was wont to prompt an Austrian concentration in Bohemia. Prussia was therefore driven to court alliance with Russia, by nature an anti-German power. **Prussian Gains**

The Peace of Paris (February 1763) between Britain, France, Portugal and Spain, was necessarily far less simple. San Sacramento and Minorca must be bought back from their conquerors, but at what price? When Britain had the French overseas empire in her hands and the Spanish at her mercy, on what basis was she to yield or to retain the several portions? It was difficult to decide what could profitably be retained, even if former ownership were to count for nothing. If Canada, for example, passed to Britain, the French menace to New England would disappear and with it the chief reason for American obedience to the crown. Anything that France now lost would form a perpetual incentive for her to build fleets and sow intrigues in order to win it back. Yet to take from her everything seemed too bold a course for a nation far smaller than herself and one which desired to live at peace with her and with all Europe. To keep the Spanish **Peace of Paris 1763** alliance France must make sacrifices in compensation for the disastrous war. From these confused premisses emerged the substantial conclusion that France renounced her empire overseas. She recovered the island of Belleisle upon her own coasts, Goree in Africa, Guadeloupe, Martinique and St. Lucia, valuable units in the West Indies. The Newfoundland fisheries and five open towns in India likewise remained hers. But she agreed to leave Dunkirk unfortified towards the sea, to give back Minorca, to cede to Britain Senegal, four of the West Indies and North America as far as the Mississippi. Louisiana, the unknown land beyond that river, with New Orleans, passed to Spain. That power ransomed the Havana by ceding Florida to Britain and yielded at last the right to cut logwood in Honduras. Whatever the future might bring, the war had ruined the finances of France, disturbed her trans-oceanic trade and deprived her of valuable islands. It had left Britain deep in debt to her own subjects but foremost in trade and the unquestioned queen of the seas. On the Continent, it bequeathed to France the rule of Choiseul and the Austrian alliance, which Choiseul consolidated by marrying the future Louis XVI to the daughter of Maria Theresa, the future queen Marie Antoinette (1770). Although detested by the French nation, the Austrian alliance was a pledge of peace, and a boon to the Bourbons of Italy. France, however, neither needed it for defence nor gained by it either in Germany or in eastern Europe, where Austria acted independently. It therefore did nothing to restore the prestige of the crown, which the failures by land and sea had grievously impaired. At a time when French civilization dominated polite Europe, France became perhaps the least regarded of the five great powers.

BIBLIOGRAPHICAL NOTE

See the Bibliographical Note at the end of Chapter I and the bibliographies to Chapters VII and VIII.

Add (besides works named in the text) :—

A

C. L. Becker : *The Eve of the American Revolution* (1921).

E. E. Charteris : *William Augustus, Duke of Cumberland and the Seven Years' War* (1925).

J. S. Corbett : *England in the Seven Years' War.* 2 vols. (1925).

H. H. Dodwell: *Dupleix and Clive* (1920).
G. P. Gooch: *Maria Theresa and Other Studies* (1951).
D. B. Horn: *Sir Charles Hanbury-Williams and European Diplomacy, 1747–1758* (1930).
K. Hotblack: *Chatham's Colonial Policy* (1917).
Lord Ilchester and Mrs. E. Langford-Brooke (eds.): *The Life of Sir Charles Hanbury-Williams* (1929).
C. Jany: *Geschichte der Königlich-Preussischen Armee.* 4 vols. (1928–33).
J. W. Jeudwine: *Studies in Empire and Trade* (1923).
H. Kretschmayr: *Maria Theresia* (1925).
L. B. Namier: *The Structure of Politics at the Accession of George III.* 2 vols. (1929).
L. B. Namier: " The Monarchy and Party Government," in *Principalities and Powers* (1955).
J. B. Owen: *The Rise of the Pelhams* (1956).
R. Pares: *Colonial Blockade and Neutral Rights, 1739–1763* (1938).
R. Pares: *War and Trade in the West Indies, 1739–1763* (1936).
C. N. Parkinson: *Trade in the Eastern Seas* (1937).
F. Parkman: *Montcalm and Wolfe.* 2 vols. (1884).
C. H. Philips: *The East India Company 1784–1834* (1940).
H. I. Priestley: *France Overseas through the old Régime* (1939).
Z. E. Rashed: *The Peace of Paris, 1763* (1952).
A. von Ruville: *William Pitt, Earl of Chatham.* 3 vols. (trans. 1907).
E. Satow: *The Silesian Loan and Frederick the Great* (1915).
A. D. Schäfer: *Geschichte des Siebenjährigen Kriegs.* 2 vols. (1867–74).
A. Sorel: *The Eastern Question in the Eighteenth Century* (trans. 1898).
B. Tunstall: *William Pitt, Earl of Chatham* (1938).
R. Waddington: *La guerre de sept ans; histoire diplomatique et militaire.* 5 vols. (1899–1914).
B. Williams: *Life of William Pitt, Earl of Chatham.* 2 vols. (1913).

B

A. von Arneth: *Geschichte Maria Theresias.* 10 vols. (1863–79).
Duc de Broglie: *Frédéric II et Louis XV . . . 1742–1744.* 2 vols. (1885).
Duc de Broglie: *Marie-Thérèse, Impératrice, 1744–1746.* 2 vols. (1888).
Duc de Broglie: *La secret du roi, 1752–1774.* 2 vols. (trans. 1879).
Henri de Catt: *Memoirs 1758–60.* 2 vols. (trans. 1916).
Duc de Choiseul: *Mémoires, 1719–1785* (1904).
I. Mauditt: *Considerations on the present German War* (1760).
K. Waliszewski: *La dernière des Romanov* (1902).

CHAPTER XI

EUROPE AND PROGRESS, 1763–74

European Progress during the War

THE war, which for seven campaigns had taxed every great power and raged in every quarter of the globe, by no means checked the advance of man in letters and in the arts of peace. The years 1756–63 saw Hume and Burke in full activity beside Diderot, Helvétius and Horace Walpole. They gave birth to *Candide* and *Tristram Shandy*, to *Ossian*, the most amazing among literary forgeries, with its immense contemporary appeal, and to the *Contrât Social*, the bible of revolution. At the same time the Physiocrats were influencing Adam Smith, and Boswell was preparing to thrust himself on Johnson. Blast furnaces and flying shuttles, the Eddystone lighthouse and the Bridgewater canal symbolized a vast international activity in applied science. For both French and British *savants*, the war was hardly more than a remote convulsion, stilled every winter, which left their lives for the most part unaffected. When the gentry commanded and the peasants served in the ranks, the middle classes saw no service.

Fall of the Jesuits

In the religious sphere, the French Philosophers continued to undermine orthodox teaching, and the Methodists to give it a new vitality and application. Now, however, the statesmen of several lands joined in combating that quasi-religious rival of the state, the Jesuit Order. From their first foundation in 1540, Loyola's disciples had flourished most to the south of the Pyrenees, and in the middle of the eighteenth century their hold was strongest upon Portugal. There they opposed Pombal, one of those autocratic reformers who characterized the Age of Enlightenment. Pombal struck hard and without scruple, using the Inquisition to discover evidence of Jesuit plots, and breaking off relations with a Pope whom Jesuit influence had placed in office. In 1759, the Fathers were deported *en masse* to the Papal States, an example which Spain attempted to follow in 1767. The

Italian Bourbons likewise drove them out, and in their own domain of Paraguay their rule was brought to an end. In the meantime their trading activities had roused other states against them. In 1760 they were made responsible for a staggering bankruptcy in Martinique, which had been brought about by the activities of British warships. While Venice and Genoa cut down their privileges, the *Parlement* of Paris seized the opportunity to indict their constitution. A storm which had long been brewing was thus let loose upon them. Lawyers and Jansenists, Philosophers and anti-papalists, rival educationalists and Madame de Pompadour, to whom they had refused communion—all combined to overwhelm the lethargic King. Choiseul, himself indifferent to religion, lent his aid, for he owed his power to Madame de Pompadour, and felt that the whole current of the age ran counter to half-alien corporations which impaired the unity of the State. In 1764, the four thousand Jesuits in France ceased, by royal decree, to be a Society, and became merely four thousand ecclesiastics controlled by the local bishops. Nine years later, the Pope himself yielded to the Catholic princes, and declared the Order dissolved. As the Philosophers were not slow to mark, he thereby shattered a buttress of the papal power.

The Enlightened Despots

The quarter of a century which followed 1763 was pre-eminently the era of the Benevolent or Enlightened or Philosophical Despots. In many states of Europe, power was concentrated in the hands of a king who drew from philosophy the duty of using it for his subjects' good. Frederick the Great, Catherine the Great, Charles III of Spain, Gustavus III of Sweden, and above all, Joseph II of Austria were the outstanding exemplars of the school. In 1763, when Catherine was still a new-comer among sovereigns and Joseph merely an expectant heir, Frederick was by far the foremost among them. The French Philosophers had steadfastly acclaimed him as their own, assuring the victor of Rossbach that Europe had united to fight him and to admire. Fifty hard years and six terrible campaigns left him worn and bitter. Yet his administration, like his principles, remained unchanged, while his prestige and influence were enormous. "'Tis at present the Prussian century here," wrote his exultant minister from Petersburg a few years later. He might have said the same of most of Europe.

Frederick's Rule Frederick's Benevolent Despotism consisted in the strenuous application, by the least benevolent of men, of "enlightened" principles where they did not conflict with Hohenzollern sense. Like Peter the Great, he had an inborn perception not only of what would make the State more powerful but of what the common man would bear. No reverence for principle, no sympathy with suffering men and women, caused him to approve for one moment any reform that might weaken Prussia. In theory, perhaps, careers should be open to talent and the poor man's shilling might have more moral value than the rich man's pound. But the Prussian state and army were strong when the nobles commanded, the burghers supplied and the peasants fought, and these hereditary functions must remain. Serfdom, however anomalous, was sacrosanct, although nearly one-third of Prussia belonged to the king. Some abuses, indeed, might be done away, and on reclaimed lands free colonists were introduced. Hundreds of new villages on Prussian soil attested Frederick's vigilance and tolerance and insight in multiplying the taxpapers and infantry of the future. At the same time the nobles were repaid for their loyal service in war and peace by the preservation of their traditional monopoly of rank and office.

King and Civil Service Bureaucratic slackness and corruption, the avarice and dishonesty of tradesmen in their dealings with the poor—these were the objects of Frederick's unfailing and outspoken suspicion. Against these he recognized no duty of royal non-interference. By his orders "the police" were to show all the activity that Bielfeld had prescribed against fraudulent butchers, bakers and publicans. To spare the poor, Frederick did not hesitate to forbid changes in price, regardless of economic laws. At the same time he proved his willingness to make grants from the treasury to avert ruin through fire, plague or famine. The same principles prompted him to cheapen marriage and divorce, and to raise the standard of the provincial officers of health. Such "calculated humanity" profited the State. In legal matters, likewise, the King asserted his complete autocracy, but in general used it with moderation.

The strength and weakness of Enlightened Despotism were never more clearly shown than in one of the most renowned of lawsuits—the case of Miller Arnold (1778–9). Frederick then placed himself upon his trial, and with him Prussian justice, which had once defied his father and saved Frederick's life. In Europe justice itself, like the Church, was at that time much discredited by the long crusade of Voltaire against the French tribunals, which had erred conspicuously in the cases of Calas, Sirven and La Barre. The French Philosophers termed the judges cannibals, and in some other lands they were suspected. Frederick, ageing and gouty, deeply mistrusted judges and advocates alike. Reform of procedure, he held, might accomplish something; constant overhaul and exhortation, more; a sharp example, most of all, towards that swift and pure justice for the common man that he was determined to achieve. "Even a beggar," he declared, was, no less than the king, "a human being to whom due justice must be meted out." In his dominions, the rich should not oppress the poor, even if they could secure the complicity of lawyers. At the same time the King acknowledged the principle of the division of powers into legislative, executive, and judicial, and prohibited the use of cabinet orders to interfere with justice. By 1778 he had lost confidence in the then Chancellor and in the legal system, which judged rather on documents than on evidence given by word of mouth.

The Despots and the Judges

Such were the circumstances of the explosion of December 1779. Arnold, a country miller, had failed to pay his rent. His landlord therefore summoned him in his own court, secured an order for the sale of the mill and bought it from the purchaser. Arnold asserted that he could pay no rent because the landlord's new fishpond had deprived the mill of water. One vital and damning fact did not sufficiently appear,—that a sawmill between the pond and Arnold's holding had not suffered. On appeal, however, the provincial court upheld the landlord's court, finding no evidence of lack of water. Arnold petitioned the king, but the Ministry of Justice upheld the courts below. A new petition produced a special commission of two persons to inquire. One member, a military man, reported in Arnold's favour; the other, a lawyer, upheld the courts. The provincial court then affirmed its previous decision, and, on a fifth appeal, the Chamber Tribunal in Berlin rejected Arnold's claim. Then Frederick

The Case of Miller Arnold 1779

intervened. Infuriated that a poor man should be defrauded by aristocrats and lawyers in his name, he summoned the Chancellor and judges into his presence. With every circumstance of insult, he dismissed the Chancellor from office and flung the judges into the Berlin gaol. There they learned that, although the Minister of Justice and the Senate were on their side, they were to be confined in a fortress for at least a year, dismissed from office and compelled to pay Arnold compensation. Berlin society dared to show them sympathy, but the people and the Philosophers acclaimed the King. Frederick, indeed, was driven beside himself by the influx of petitions. On the other side "memorials and representations not much below the tone of the addresses of London and Middlesex" were presented, but it was left for his successor to do justice. The case of Miller Arnold had shown how the ablest and best-intentioned Despot might run amuck, and how little enlightened principles could avail to check him. Frederick, however, at least refrained from proclaiming new principles of law or drawing up new codes. Wheel and rack were reserved for specially dangerous criminals, sword and gallows for robbers and slayers of men. Thus punishing for the protection of his subjects, but no more, the King proceeded to rid society of the pest of antiquated civil laws and a clumsy legal system. His study of humanity taught him that an ill-paid judge would take bribes or multiply paid proceedings, and he learned from Montesquieu that the executive and judicature should be kept apart. Without sweeping changes, the legal system underwent manifold improvement.

The King-Proprietor

Frederick's autocracy could not but be heightened by the scattered character of his dominions. Although Berlin was growing fast and centralization had enjoyed an unbroken century of progress, Prussia still remained in some sense a miscellaneous bundle of Hohenzollern provinces. To the lands from Pomerania to Silesia Frederick avowedly showed most favour, since they were the kernel of the State. While hereditary ownership prompted the King to think of the State largely in terms of the nobles, just as to a great landlord his tenants personify their farms, it made it natural for him to act like the proprietor of Prussia. It was for him to sustain agriculture when calamity threatened, and for him also to take the lead in furthering industry and commerce. Silk, wool, linen, paper, cutlery, tobacco, sugar, salt and starch —such were the chief among the manufactures that he founded or developed. To such the State might give privileges and subsidies, while it demanded the maintenance of satisfactory quality and interfered in the organization of the trade. Its power to help industry in a backward agricultural country was perhaps most conspicuous in the importation of technicians from abroad. In this the religious tolerance which the long rule of Hohenzollern Calvinists over Lutherans and Catholics had ingrained in Prussia proved of the greatest service. As in agriculture, however, it was to the leaders rather than to their humbler instruments that the government paid first attention. As practised by Frederick, Benevolent Despotism meant that every subject might invoke the King, but that the King expected every subject to serve the State and to remain in that place and calling in which his service could be greatest.

Catherine II and Struensee

During the decade which followed on the Seven Years War, other north German statesmen shaped for a time the destinies of widely different states—Catherine II in Russia and Struensee in Denmark. Both gave the world most striking illustrations of that Enlightened Despotism in which the eighteenth century found its peculiar panacea. Struensee, almost the sole example of the physician-statesman, outdistanced all save perhaps Joseph II in translating Philosophy into action, and his public career illustrates beyond all others the confident application of the new ideas. Both Struensee and Catherine gained power untrained at thirty-three, and both—the princess hardly less than the " pill-maker "—rank high among the picturesque adventurers with whom the century abounds.

Catherine II

Catherine II was born in May 1729, the eldest child of Prince Christian Augustus of Anhalt-Zerbst and of his wife Elizabeth of Holstein-Gottorp. She was baptized into the Lutheran Church as Sophia Augusta Frederica, names redolent of north German and Danish history. The father sprang from the junior line of a most ancient ruling house: his wife, a mother at seventeen, had been brought up by the Duchess of Brunswick, whose daughters were renowned for brilliant marriages. Prince Christian, a travelled soldier, served Frederick of Prussia and rose to be commandant of Stettin. Despite her parents' poverty, their circle comprised a host of Prussian and other royal persons. Among them were Prince Henry, Frederick's able brother, with Ferdinand of Brunswick and that Duchess of Brunswick, born of an obscure house, who numbered among her grandchildren Maria Theresa, Tsar Peter II, and the queens of Prussia and of Denmark. For an ambitious girl-member of the princely caste, the one hope lay in marriage, but there the horizon was very wide. A Catholic canon who "occupied himself with prophecy and palmistry" once said to Sophia's mother: "I see crowns, three at least, upon your daughter's head." This prophecy the daughter neither shrank from nor forgot. Ambition, she believed, first stirred within her in 1736, when she heard that her second cousin, the mother of George III, was in train to be queen of England. Maturing early, she was soon conscious of her fitness for a like career.

"The cast of her features," wrote a lady who often observed her, "without being beautiful was very pleasing, and this impression was increased by the particular graciousness and friendliness which she always showed. Her education was conducted entirely by her mother, who kept a tight rein, and did not overlook the slightest expression of pride, to which she had a tendency. On the contrary she required her, from earliest childhood on, to kiss the skirt of the grand ladies who came to visit the Princess."

The influence of Stettin, her birthplace, though unconscious, cannot have been unimportant. Her father's duty had been to fortify this very recent acquisition of the Prussian state. A girl could know but little of the chicane by which the Sergeant King had acquired it, but she breathed in aggrandizement with her native air. The seizure of Silesia by her kinsfolk and its triumphant retention continued her education in politics and deepened her respect for Prussian power. When she sent Frederick her regrets that she had left Prussia too early to imbibe his wisdom, the tribute was as sincere as his compliments to her were hollow. Sincerity and determination to please, indeed, were the characteristics in which she particularly loved to excel.

Catherine's marriage

In her fifteenth year (January 1, 1744), chance offered her the possibility of a great career. The fitful course pursued by Russia after Peter's death (1725) had brought his daughter Elizabeth to occupy the throne (1741) with the Francophobe Bestuchev as her guide. The new

Empress summoned to Petersburg her nephew Peter, Duke of Holstein-Gottorp, whom she made her heir. To be his aunt's successor, this mediocre youth renounced the Lutheran faith and the proffered crown of Sweden. He remained, none the less, a fanatic for the claims of his own duchy upon Slesvig and for the worship of his idol, Frederick of Prussia. He came to Russia " irritable, stubborn, quarrelsome, underhand, mendacious and always artlessly convinced that his lies were true," and there learned nothing but hard drinking. The most grateful of contemporary diplomats can only belaud the goodness of his heart. His aunt, herself ignorant and debauched, could not fail to note his incapacity, but never actually revoked his nomination, which had been followed by the sworn allegiance of the people. To better him and to safeguard the succession, an early marriage was imperative, and the forces of intrigue in Russia and outside contended for the selection of a bride. At the decisive moment Frederick chanced to be able to sway Elizabeth's choice away from the Saxons whom he dreaded. Nine days after receiving the invitation to Petersburg, the Princess of Zerbst and her daughter were on their way. A Tsarina must be Orthodox, but between Lutheranism and Orthodoxy there appeared on inquiry to be " almost no difference." Within six months Princess Sophia had become the Grand Duchess Catherine, the daughter of Alexis, since Christian and Augustus were not Russian names. In the summer of 1745 she married her cousin, now the Grand Duke Peter.

At sixteen, therefore, Catherine began a new career which was also a new existence. Besides her new name, her new faith and her new status, language, climate and atmosphere were completely new. Her mother, prone to intrigue for Prussia, had been sent home. Prussia was now detested by the Empress, and by her minister: Catherine's attendants were creatures of Elizabeth: letters to her parents must be composed in the Foreign Office and only signed by herself. Her husband treated her with an indifference copied perhaps from Frederick's resentful neglect of his queen. The Empress was an incalculable despot rendered hostile by the non-appearance of an heir. The barbaric splendour of court life in Russia was mingled with much genuine privation. Religion involved interminable services, the congregation standing, and months of rigorous fasting every year. Travel was a torment: the wooden palaces, sometimes dangerous. However resolute to please, Catherine was an alien thrown back upon herself and driven to the verge of self-destruction. "For eighteen years," she declared, "I lived a life which would have driven ten others mad and twenty to die of melancholy." For relief she turned to dancing, riding, and above all to books. The Russian court contained no learned man or woman; the Russian nation, few. The Swedish minister, however, gave Catherine scholarly advice and she proved an eager and determined student. From 1746 she was counted among the ardent disciples of Voltaire.

Elizabeth and her Heirs

As the Empress, debauched and beautiful, refused to take a consort and seemed likely to prove short-lived, the political importance of the Young Court steadily increased. On the Russian side this led to an ultimatum—an heir to the throne or a divorce. Divorce meant sinking back into a Princess of Zerbst, with no future. In September 1754, Catherine gave birth to the future Paul I, whom the Empress immediately removed from her control. Sergius Saltikov, the child's putative father, was likewise sent away. From this time Catherine's attitude, as she expressed it, "became more regal." She guided her husband, especially in the affairs of Holstein, and gradually formed her own party among the Court and Guards. Unhappily for her reputation, she had learned to allow herself that intimate society which had always been denied her by her husband. For more than forty years her life was shared by a succession of favourites, and to supply a favourite became the object of more than one western government. The British minister, her friend Sir Charles Hanbury Williams, gave her his Polish secretary, Stanislaus Poniatowski. "He was amiable and was loved from 1755 to 1761," wrote Catherine to Potemkin. "I am sending Count Keyserling at once to Poland to make you king after the death of the present king" was her message to Stanislaus as soon as she reigned in Russia.

The War 1757–61

Between 1755 and August 1762 much more than a change of favourite had altered Catherine's life. While Russia fought against Prussia in the Seven Years War, Peter was at heart a Prussian and Catherine took British gold. As Russia never went to war with Britain, the British minister could remain at Petersburg, but the Franco-Russian intercourse which had been broken off in 1744 began anew. Early in 1758, therefore, Catherine found herself in deadly peril. The chancellor, Bestuchev, was charged with having conspired with her to paralyse the Russian offensive against Frederick, and, on the death of the Empress, to exclude Peter from the throne. Bestuchev was banished, but Catherine, though denounced by her husband, succeeded in cajoling Elizabeth. Thenceforward it was chiefly against her husband that she intrigued.

In love and politics the pair were far apart. For Poniatowski, expelled in 1758, Catherine found a successor in Gregori Orlov, a handsome soldier who, she wrote, " might have stayed for ever, had he not grown tired." In April 1762 she bore him a son, whose existence neither Peter nor his mistress divined. For Peter, generally believed to be impotent, had turned to Elizabeth Vorontsov, the coarse daughter of Bestuchev's successor. As Tsar, it was supposed, he would declare Paul a bastard, divorce Catherine, and marry Elizabeth Vorontsov. Catherine, on the other hand, kept in touch with several distinct sets of conspirators against her husband. Their projects were not the same, for the dethronement of Peter would by no means establish his German consort in his place. Gregori Orlov and his brothers were her passionate partisans, but Panin, the best head among the conspirators, meant to crown her young son, Paul, his pupil. In July 1762, however, chance gave the signal, and Catherine, aided by Dashkova, her high-minded romantic friend, guided the revolution. The Guards rallied to her side, while the people wept for joy. Peter, repulsed from Cronstadt, made an abject surrender of his crown. Eight days later, he was murdered by Alexis Orlov, whose crime Catherine condoned.

Catherine's Accession 1762

In Catherine, the boldest pupil of Philosophy mounted the Russian throne. From the moment of her accession, she showed a high-souled confidence both in her destiny and in her power of ruling. Refusing to regard her son as a potential rival, she made his tutor, Panin, her chief adviser. She did not affront the Russians by espousing Orlov, but continued to load him with favours and to play the wife. While fervently performing every religious rite, she seized the lands and serfs belonging to the Church and tolerated all religions. With Frederick, whom at first she had declared the hereditary enemy, she swiftly made an alliance, while towards France, the adored of Russian society, and her own intellectual home, she pursued an almost hostile policy. In little more than two years from her accession, she had disposed of Courland, won over Prussia, Denmark and Sweden, and given the Poles a king. The time then seemed to have come for great reforms in Russia. Projects Catherine had in plenty, from the education of noble girls to the substitution of Russian for French tobacco. But that which at the outset chiefly claimed the attention of Europe was her pan-Russian parliament for drafting a new code of law. In 1767 some 564 delegates assembled in the Kremlin at Moscow. They brought with them written statements of the grievances which their constituents desired to see redressed. Catherine, who sometimes listened unseen to the debates, had spent the leisure of at least two years in preparing a *Grand Instruction* for the assembly. Her *Instruction*, a manual of aphorisms drawn chiefly from Montesquieu and Beccaria, had undergone a drastic revision at the hands of her advisers. In substance, however, it still inculcated French "philosophy" as the basis of the future code of Russia. Guided by this treatise, which was read at every session, the assembly was to bring order into the chaos of more than ten thousand casual decrees to which the Tsars had given the force of law.

The Grand Commission 1767

As some of the foreign diplomats had advised their governments in advance, the task was far too hard for the Russians of that day. Sessions were numerous, committees laboured hard, but not a single statute came into being. The body which had begun by offering Catherine the titles of Great and Wise, the Mother of her country, ended with acrid criticism of many Russian institutions. The failure damped Catherine's enthusiasm, and in 1768 the outbreak of the Turkish war brought most of the business to a standstill. Catherine herself had been sincerely proud of her *Instruction* and sanguine of success. To secure this she had withdrawn the chapters which raised directly the vital question of ascription to the soil. But quick as were her sympathy and her apprehension, in four and twenty years at court she had had little opportunity to learn more of Russia than the society of Petersburg and Moscow as viewed from the steps of the throne. A few pilgrimages and royal progresses, one memorable visit to the Tartar city of Kazan—could these suffice to teach a German the mysteries of rural Russia? In 1773, the widespread revolt of Pugachev proved that she had been grievously deceived. Its failure, none the less, exalted her power and abased the nobles, whom it had shown to be powerless without the army of the crown.

Catherine's Rule

While Catherine's Philosophy was tempered by her common sense, and her parliament produced no code of laws, she proved herself an Enlightened Despot at every turn. The Church, the army, the bureaucracy, even the nobles were tactfully but firmly brought under her control. The prestige of the crown was raised by domestic triumphs as well as by foreign—by vast new palaces, new buildings, new towns, new industries, new societies and new forms of brilliant entertainment. To civilize the Russians and to convince Europe that they were civilized, Catherine spared no endeavour. The surroundings in which she received the western diplomats were a triumph of western art. She wrote plays and pamphlets, bought pictures, brought in foreign artists, set the example of inoculation, entertained and subsidized learned men and sent Russians into Europe. For Elizabeth's complete repudiation of the penalty of death, she substituted the best European practice, inflicting capital punishment only for crimes which hardly one Philosopher would term non-capital. Torture was effectively suppressed by the device of allowing it only with crown permission, which was invariably refused. The grossness of Russian society was combated by the example of a comparatively temperate and elegant court circle; the inertia of the peasants by the importation of thousands of provident Germans. The mental and moral effect of the Grand Commission and of the *Instruction* can hardly have failed to be considerable. Elections, debates, committees, above all the novel adherence of the crown to western principles—all these must have given Russia a salutary shock. Like Frederick, Catherine did nothing without an eye to the augmentation of the royal power, but like him she laboured incessantly to use that power for the advancement of the people. To make men comfortable, Bentham declared, you must appear to love them, and the best way to appear to love them is to do so in reality. Here Catherine, who could never have cried "Dogs, would ye live for ever?" to her troops, as far surpassed Frederick as in her true devotion to Philosophy. Lacking as she did the strength which comes from being born the unquestioned heir to a well-trained State, she achieved a success as notable as Frederick's in calling forth the energies of her people.

J. F. Struensee 1737–72

John Frederick Struensee, like Catherine, during his early years drank in the atmosphere of Prussian expansion and power. He was born in 1737 at Halle, a town which the Hohenzollerns acquired in 1680 and enriched with a favoured university. The second son of a pastor and professor, Struensee came of old Brandenburg stock, a vigorous family of clothmakers from the marshy country north-west of Berlin. As Lutheran chaplain at a minor court, his father had espoused the fifteen-year-old daughter of J. C. Carl, the court doctor and a famous Pietist. Dr. Carl was a man of considerable personality and position. His wife claimed descent from a Von Bülow. Their son-in-law rose to the highest rank in the Lutheran Church and his sons gained military, civil and academic posts with ease. Yet the whole family was thoroughly aware that they were "not born" and that the "great" world was closed against them. "How little would my life have been, and how few my pleasures!" ejaculated Struensee near the close of his days when charged with folly in contriving to enter the Danish court. The birthright of a Princess of Zerbst formed the almost unattainable goal of a Struensee.

As the son of a respected citizen, Struensee could claim the benefits of a Halle education. He studied first at the noted Pietistic Orphanage, where the hypocrisy of some of his schoolfellows disgusted him with religion, and then at the rising University. A quick-witted student in the backward and empirical faculty of medicine, he emerged a fully qualified doctor at nineteen. A year later, his father accepted the Lutheran equivalent of a bishopric in Holstein under the King of Denmark, whose affairs were at that time managed by the Hanoverian noble, Count Bernstorff. From the pious and gracious Bernstorff, the elder Struensee secured the appointment of the younger as town physician of Altona, a Danish town which adjoined the wealthy Imperial city of Hamburg.

Struensee meanwhile had turned libertine and had discovered in the writings of the French Philosophers a welcome justification for self-indulgence. It was not long before his father expelled him from his house, a severity which he always regarded as unjust. Young, gay and friendly, charming some men and many women, endowed with fine physique and no little talent, Struensee spent several years in a happiness clouded only by the jealousy of his fellow-practitioners and by debt. Hamburg was like a capital, and even in Altona interesting men were to be met with.

General Gähler, soldier, a would-be reformer of the Danish state, Falkenskiold, an adventurous and distinguished soldier. Enevold Brandt, a light-hearted young noble, and above all a scion of the first family in Denmark, of dubious repute but brilliant talent, Count Rantzau—such were his boon companions. Rantzau, a high-born and intellectual Falstaff, soldier, diplomatist and virtuoso, completely conquered the young doctor, whom he pronounced a genius in politics as well as medicine. Gähler and Rantzau, a born *frondeur*, were Danish nationalists hating the imported Bernstorff administration, and longing for a military monarchy with themselves and their hero, Marshal St. Germain, as its advisers. Learning from the witty Rantzau as easily as from Voltaire and his tribe, Struensee was soon ready to reform the world by the light of reason and to despise his own profession. His importance and his self-confidence rose when, by curing Madame Rantzau, he became the darling physician of the Holstein nobles. Through their influence with Bernstorff in 1768 he gained access to the King. He found in Christian VII a pallid dissipated boy, whose will had yet been firm enough to insist upon a tour in western Europe, and that without his queen, the sister of George III. As travelling physician, Struensee accompanied Christian and Bernstorff to Holland, England and France. The journey made him indispensable to the King, and he returned with him to Copenhagen. Christian, despite many accomplishments, was in the early stages of insanity, and Struensee, with admirable insight, detected and treated his disease. At court he pushed forward his fortunes with hardihood and judgment, for in a society where titles were everything he had none, and his slender stipend could not cope with his losses at the inevitable games of chance. His great achievement was the reconciliation of the King and Queen. As Christian's oracle and Matilda's paramour, the nameless underling soon became the veiled helmsman of the Danish state. In September 1770, Bernstorff was dismissed, and Christian, interpreted and inspired by Struensee, prepared to win the applause of Europe as a heroic reformer. To mark the change, the Press was granted freedom.

Benevolent Despotism in Denmark

During the eighteen months which followed, Danish history furnished to that age and to posterity an unexampled drama, displaying the political ineffectiveness of the honest doctrinaire. No autocracy could have been more complete. For a full century the Danish people had regarded the House of Oldenburg as their saviour and had obeyed like sons. A sluggish rural community with one great city, and that dominated by the court, had lounged through life with its traditions undisturbed, while the recent kings left policy to their council. Whatever the king signed, the people must and would obey. But history had given them a feudal society under a paternal king. They were strictly partitioned into classes, the cultivators being largely serfs and the condemned law-breakers slaves. The citizens took domiciliary visits by the police as a matter of course and the profession and practice of Lutheranism were compulsory. They were now exposed to a hail of royal " cabinet-orders " displacing every tradition which the new " philosophy " condemned.

Struensee's Coat-of-arms

In an age when heraldry formed part of a liberal education, the armorial bearings which Struensee adopted proclaimed to the educated public what Enlightened Despotism attempted as well as what the minister believed that he had done. As described by a contemporary traveller, his

" escutcheon (symbolical of the State) was divided into five fields, the centre one of which represented a sailing vessel (commerce) with a crown over it, typical of the monarch and the persons representing him. The first and fourth displayed four rivers (exports and imports) on a field *or* (Denmark, rich in corn, and Norway, abounding in metal, wood and fish). In the third and second quarters was a crown surrounded with palm leaves (peace and victory) and two crossed keys (authority and might) on a field azure, which allegorically typified fidelity and constancy. Below was the royal crown with the Matilda Order, surrounded by a laurel wreath (fortune, joy and honour) from which flowed two rivers running round the chief escutcheon (the State), supported by two bearers (architecture and industry) guarded by *bourgeois* helmets (national armament), counts' crowns, and an owl holding a key in its mouth (thought and wisdom). Above was displayed, between two eagle wings (power, strength and victory), a man-of-war in full sail (the navy), and above this, again, a suspended crown, surrounded by palm branches (the type of peace)."

Cabinet Orders

The principles of this Enlightened Despotism may be deduced from the decrees which dealt with individual cases as they occurred. The new *régime* proclaimed no programme and worked out no comprehensive plan. The ubiquity of the crown and its determination to make the people happy formed the ruling principle of the decrees. Nothing was too great or too small for its immediate and decisive action. Struensee had been deeply impressed by what he saw at Newmarket and Vauxhall, and races, military bands and gaming-tables were conferred upon Copenhagen. Humanity had its rights: the freedom of expression in print was followed by freedom with regard to public worship, and by the exemption of private houses from moral supervision by the police. To avoid both the spectacle of woe and the loss of labour from the attendant drinking-bouts, funerals were to take place before the day's work began. Foundlings were cared for; sanitation and hospitals, improved. In return, the needs of the State must be supreme over trade customs and religious requirements. The construction of warships, for example, abrogated Sunday rest and worship. In dealing with its subjects, the ubiquitous and benevolent crown showed no tenderness for caste. Denmark, like other western lands, was no stranger to those graceful petitions for favours of every kind which gave eighteenth-century statesmen the opportunity for so many exquisite replies. From Struensee these drew a curt endorsement, " follow the law," for posts must go to the fit, and noble birth with its pretensions was suspected of lessening fitness. An able prelate in remote Trondhjem was astonished by a summons to reform the University of Copenhagen. Struensee's counsellor had in fact suggested him in the hope that the inevitable delay would give the reforming ardour time to cool. It was an attack upon the Guards, the privileged within the army, that finally brought about revolt.

Foreign Policy

Such doctrinaire disturbance by the crown with no regard to the historic evolution of the State must necessarily wound the privileged in Church and State. The attempt to manage foreign policy in the same fashion was bound to fail. Denmark, however, offered a field for aggressive monarchy which was in some respects more favourable than those from which the Great Elector (1640–88) and Charles XI (d. 1697) had reaped a bounteous harvest. While the loyalty of the few would be diminished, that of the many might be increased. At the moment, moreover, the abjuration of a foreign policy exposed the State to no great danger. Russia, of late the chief source of danger to Denmark, was deep in distant war. The progress of the King's disease, however, destroyed the basis of the new *régime*. In 1771, Struensee was forced into the open. From pride or from necessity he abandoned the disinterested modesty of his early days of power to become a rich noble authorized by the King to sign ordinances in his stead. Thus the German parvenu concentrated on himself the discontent of all the aggrieved.

His education of the Crown Prince on the lines of Rousseau's *Emile* was construed as a design to cause his death so that Struensee might poison Christian and become regent for his own unlawful issue by Matilda. Early in 1772, a palace revolution was followed by unqualified reaction and Struensee was executed for high treason. Catherine, who had strongly protested against the fall of Bernstorff, tried in vain to save Matilda's lover from his fate. Frederick, though he owed much to his elder brother, mocked his career and fate in a brutal Dialogue of the Dead.

Benjamin Franklin 1706–90

Frederick, Catherine and Struensee illustrate the Benevolent Despotism which dominated Europe in the seventeen-sixties. Another dynamic of the age, rational democracy, was incarnate in Benjamin Franklin, printer, whom Oxford created Dr. Franklin in 1762. Born in 1706, tenth son of a Puritan New Englander from the Midlands, he was to show how talent and personality could influence history even when divorced from birth or wealth or office. Besides his unique share in founding a great nation, he earned the tribute of having added something to the art of living. Balzac ascribed to him three great inventions—the lightning-conductor, the *canard*, and the republic. Even in the eighteenth century, no man was more versatile. Journeyman, publisher, pamphleteer, popular educator, postmaster and city father, he was at one time most famous for studying electricity and at another for his feats of swimming. His life illustrated both the strength and the weakness of eighteenth-century Reason. As a boy he characterized himself by suggesting that, to save time at every meal, grace should be said once for all when the provisions were salted down for winter. In the same vein he decried the American eagle, urging that a turkey would be a fitter emblem of the United States. When the question of one House or two came forward he solved it by the analogy of two horses pulling the cart in opposite directions. A deist revering Socrates and Christ, he was proud of his "half mechanic ordering of life," assigning each successive week to the cultivation of one of thirteen virtues. Yet his natural children abounded, and—far worse—he counselled prudent adultery. "Throughout his whole public career, it was characteristic of Franklin to be at once temperate in the tone and unscrupulous in the substance of his arguments" (Doyle). Despite some stains, however, his resolve to be himself and to suffer no political theory to override plain sense made him a great world-figure. In Franklin Paris beheld America, and it would have been well if London had done the same. Having failed, though gloriously, to avert war between the Colonies and Britain, he did more than any man save Washington towards American success. As committeeman, propagandist, financier, diplomat, and above all as a figure around whom all could rally, he rendered incomparable service to the cause. No one but he could have captured the imagination of France at the crisis of 1776. In the robust old *savant*, plainly dressed, wearing his own hair but moving with serene self-confidence in the world of fashion, Paris saw Liberty incarnate, and passionately embraced the cause of one who had "plucked the thunderbolt from heaven and the sceptre from tyrants." Thus Franklin helped to establish a new dynasty, that of the patriot citizen. Throwing off her European fetters, America could perhaps save Europe by her example.

BIBLIOGRAPHICAL NOTE

See the Bibliographical Note at the end of Chapter I and add to the books named in the text:—

A

H. Boehmer: *The Jesuits* (1928).

V. W. Crane: *Benjamin Franklin and a Rising People* (1954).

M. Farrand (ed.): *Benjamin Franklin's Memoirs* (1949).

G. P. Gooch: *Catherine the Great and Other Studies* (1954).

E. A. B. Hodgetts: *The Life of Catherine the Great of Russia* (1914).

L. Krabbe: *Histoire de Danemark* (1950).

K. Larsen: *A History of Norway* (1948).

G. B. Nicolini: *History of the Jesuits* (1854).

W. F. Reddaway (ed.): *Documents of Catherine the Great: The Correspondence with Voltaire and the Instruction of 1767 in the English Text of 1768* (1931).

W. F. Reddaway: "Denmark under the Bernstorffs and Struensee," *Camb. Mod. Hist.*, VI (1909).

W. F. Reddaway: "Struensee and the Fall of Bernstorff," *E.H.R.*, XXVII (1912) pp. 274–86.

G. Scott Thomson: *Catherine the Great and the Expansion of Russia* (1947).

G. O. Trevelyan: *The Early History of Charles James Fox* (1899).

C. Van Doren: *Benjamin Franklin* (1938).

C. Van Doren (ed.): *Benjamin Franklin's Autobiographical Writings* (1946).

W. H. Wilkins: *A Queen of Tears. Caroline Matilda, Queen of Denmark and Norway and Princess of Great Britain and Ireland.* 2 vols. (1904).

K. Waliszewski: *The Romance of an Empress.* 2 vols. (trans. 1894) (fuller in the French original).

B

Baron von Bilbassoff: *Geschichte Katharina II.* (1897).

E. Holm: *Danmark-Norges histoire fra den store nordiske krigs slutning til rigernes adskillelse, 1720–1814.* 4 v. in 7 (1891–1902).

Lord Ilchester and Mrs. E. Langford-Brooke (eds.): *Correspondence of Catherine the Great when Grand Duchess, with Sir Charles Hanbury-Williams, and letters from Count Poniatowski* (1928).

J. J. Joubert (1754–1824): *A Selection from his Thoughts* (selected and trans. 1897).

B. Münter: *The Conversion of Count Struensee* (1773).

A. H. Smyth: *The Writings of Benjamin Franklin.* 10 vols. (1905–7).

N. W. Wraxall: *Historical Memoirs of my own Time from 1772 to 1784.* 2 vols. (1815; 4th ed. rev. with add. 4 v. 1836; repub. 1904).

N. W. Wraxall: *Posthumous Memoirs of his own Time, 1784–1789.* 3 vols. (1836).

CHAPTER XII

EUROPE, 1763–74

Character of the Age—The Philosophers and Religion

IN general, the 'sixties after the Seven Years War are notable rather for what they sowed than for what they reaped. If in 1774 America went to war to uphold a principle of unwritten law, it was because of the friction generated during these years between the Colonies and the mother-country. In like manner the Partition of Poland was consciously and unconsciously prepared for. In many states, and notably under Aranda in Spain, Enlightened Despotism was hard at work, raising ever higher the power of the crown and using it to reform abuses. "Philosophers," not French alone, continued actively to enlighten society, and their teachings were applied as swiftly as were Luther's in the first decade of the Reformation. Young Beccaria's treatise on crimes and punishments appeared only in 1764. Next year, Leopold of Tuscany, the Emperor Joseph's younger brother, applied its principles in his duchy, and two years later they were proclaimed from the throne by Catherine as the basis of Russian law.

At the same time the religious upheaval continued to spread far and wide. While Catholic powers were expelling the Jesuits as reactionary, non-Catholic Prussia and Russia were preparing to receive them in the name of toleration. While Britain was excusing herself from vehemently championing the claims of the Polish Dissidents on the ground of her own Catholic disabilities, Russia was allowing her Mohammedan subjects to build mosques. Febronianism, so called from the pen-name of Von Hontheim, suffragan bishop of Catholic Trèves, revived as living issues those questions of papal authority as against that of bishops and Councils which had been settled at Trent two centuries earlier. Gallican liberties, as a local claim by France, had always been dangerous to Rome. Now an anonymous writer invited all sovereigns to vindicate the rights of their own churches against ill-founded papal claims. In Catholic Germany and Austria his appeal aroused much anti-papal feeling, and Joseph II showed himself fully prepared to defy as an official the Holy Father whom he reverenced as a man. The vitality of the Catholic faith, however, was attested by the progress of new Italian orders, as in Reformation days. The Redemptorists of Naples went as missionaries to the countryside, and the Passionists called men to repentance in many lands. The worship of the Virgin grew. A new devotion, the celebration of the Sacred Heart, formed an outlet for intense religious feeling.

Its Protestant parallel may perhaps be found among the followers of Count Zinzendorf (1700–60), whose vivid sense of the merits of the blood of Christ led them to form communities at Herrnhut in Saxony and elsewhere.

Thus the classic epoch of rationalism was also an epoch of evangelism and mysticism—of many-sided revolt against indifference and stagnation in religion. Among educated men and women, however, the decade which produced the steam-engine and the spinning-jenny, Blackstone, the *Vicar of Wakefield* and the *Sentimental Journey*, Turgot, Lessing, and Captain Cook, that decade which Reynolds and Gainsborough painted and which gave Kant and Burke a special inspiration still ranked primarily as the age of Rousseau and Voltaire. Diderot was permitted to resume the publication of his great *Encyclopædia*: Voltaire gave a far more daring *Philosophical Dictionary* to the world: Rousseau with his irresistible rhetoric and weird self-martyrdom simply intoxicated thousands of men and women.

In politics, peace brought uncertainty and revealed exhaustion.

Uneasiness of the Powers

Britain, though inharmonious and deep in debt, was perhaps the only power that emerged from the Seven Years War with any apparent profit. France had experienced almost unrelieved humiliation. Austria, on the other hand, had shown new strength and vigour, while ridding herself of the old enmity with France and strengthening her hold on the Imperial crown. But she had failed either to retain the old Russian alliance or to remove the Prussian peril, and once again she had been forced to renounce Silesia. Prussia had kept her new frontiers and added to her prestige, but at what a cost! Her King, who had earned the hatred of all Europe, could look forward only to an old age spent in repairing the ruins of his backward State. Russia had won victories and made conquests only to fling all away, and she was baulked of her coveted share in drafting the terms of peace. Of the lesser combatants, Saxony, Sweden, Spain, Portugal, the German Secondary States, none could show anything but loss.

The year 1763 therefore ushered in a period of international uncertainty and discomfort. The Franco-British tension, like the Austro-Prussian, remained, but every power stood for the moment without a firm ally. The usual vague fears that general war would again break out pervaded Europe. The course of Russia under Catherine was incalculable, and the obsolescent Franco-Austrian alliance seemed the only safeguard against a fresh convulsion. Both in France and Britain leadership was conspicuously lacking, while few expected that the revolution of July 1762 in Russia would not soon be followed by another. Every European government regarded the German-born Catherine as a usurper, if not a criminal, and most foresaw the speedy advent of her son. Only by degrees did Europe discover that the Russian power was wielded by an Empress who equalled Maria Theresa in courage and Frederick or Kaunitz in ambition.

The Northern System

In the general uncertainty and exhaustion, every power sought allies. The suspected designs of the House of Bourbon, with Austria as its accomplice, gave rise to much diplomatic manœuvring for a counter-league. Panin, the leading Russian minister, strove honestly to promote a Northern System, within which Prussia, Poland, Scandinavia, Holland, Britain and several German states should be comprised. He failed, however, to surmount three fatal objections to the plan. While Frederick lived, Prussia would never again commit herself to Britain. In every war of the century Britain seemed to have sacrificed her German ally, and in the last Bute's correspondence had a flavour of that which preceded the French victory at Denain (1712). Britain, Frederick could say, was striving for distant objects with which Prussia had no concern. He would not shed Prussian blood that Portuguese rather than Spaniards should dominate Brazil. Britain, moreover, though Russia was her only possible strong ally, would never pay the Russian price for an alliance. If Russia was to bind herself to oppose France, must not Britain likewise bind herself to oppose the Turks? But this meant loss of privilege to British trade at Constantinople, and a complete surrender of the Turks to France, while a Franco-British war seemed remote and a Russo-Turkish imminent. Again, the Northern System failed to come into being because the Bourbon-Habsburg combination was not, in fact, aggressive. Choiseul, all-powerful from 1764, when both Madame de Pompadour and the Dauphin died, was indeed preparing for a possible war of revenge with Britain, but both military and diplomatic preparations demanded time. Austria did not share his antipathy, and she, no less than Prussia, was deep in domestic reconstruction.

The Polish Succession Question

Besides the familiar problems which had occasioned the Seven Years War, Europe was preparing in 1763 to face once again that of the Polish succession. Early in the year it was reported that Augustus III was breaking. The old man returned to his hunting and shooting, but in October his sudden death set countless wheels in motion. Poland, for two generations a mere appanage of the Saxon House, became a prize which every neighbour and some more distant powers desired to gain. A vast and fertile bundle of provinces, an elective monarchy with no aggressive power, Poland had long attracted interference whenever her throne fell vacant. Ever since Henry of Anjou had been her king (1573–4), France had felt a peculiar interest in the Republic. French need for an ally against Austria at last had ceased, but her ambition in eastern Europe died slowly, and Warsaw looked with reverent interest towards Parisian culture. Louis XV, moreover, dabbled in foreign politics for his own diversion, and took especial interest in the throne of which his father-in-law, Stanislas Leszczynski, had been deprived. France had it in her power to stimulate by arguments and bribes the interest which the Turks felt in a neighbour whose independence might well become the safeguard of their own. To Austria it was important that the power of the Polish crown, slender though it was, should be exercised in her favour, and not to jeopardize her position in Hungary and towards the Danube. Prussia must earnestly desire to break the link between Saxony and Poland. Apart from stategic considerations, which the late war had proved real beyond dispute,

Polish and Saxon lands stood high upon the list of those which the Hohenzollerns were resolved in due course to acquire. Western or Polish or Regal Prussia, so called to distinguish it from Eastern or Ducal, which had given Frederick's state its crown and name—this with its German ports and teeming population was actually the first entry which the Prussian King was wont to make when he wrote down instructions for the future advancement of his kingdom. To Prussia, moreover, it must be of high import that the "terrible power" of Russia should not be swollen by the addition—potentially the great addition—of the resources of the whole Republic. As the Russians confessed, an obedient Poland constituted a third part of their strength, and for a century they had been teaching her obedience.

Russia and Poland

Russia, of course, had the chief interest in the Polish question, whether this be regarded from the cultural, political, geographical or historical point of view. The Poles still occupied vast stretches of lost Russian lands and plagued vast numbers of the co-religionists of Russia. White Russia, Black Russia, Red Russia still lay within the confines of the Republic. For centuries Poland had been the gaoler of the Muscovite, barring his access to Europe. The reigning dynasty in Russia had been placed upon the throne to avert a Polish Tsardom (1613). Now that the scale had turned in Russia's favour, she counted on disposing of Poland at her will. For a century past, direct annexation or the extension of authoritative influence had been her course, if not her deliberate plan. Of the chief Russian towns half had been won or regained from Poland. Smolensk, Kiev, and Riga must point the way towards Vilna, Lemberg, and Danzig as the huge empire with "glacial certainty" drove its frontiers westwards. Meanwhile Poland must rank as a sphere of Russian influence and a buffer state against the military monarchies of Europe. From Courland, still in name a Polish fief, Catherine had lately expelled a Saxon prince and reinstated Biren, her own dependant. She now designed to replace Augustus by a *Piast*, or native Pole, and one whose dependence upon her should be assured by his own lack of resources. No nominee could be so suitable as a young member of the Czartoryski family, the powerful clan which possessed eleven castles and fifteen towns, and which for reasons patriotic though mistaken, was wont to lean on Russia. And among such Catherine dared to fix, despite his lack of consequence and popularity, upon her own discarded lover, Stanislas Poniatowski.

Candidature of Poniatowski

To secure the crown for Stanislas, however, Catherine must win over Russia, the Poles and Europe. The Russians, fearing that she would make a Catholic match, might not inconceivably revolt against her. The Poles, busy with a vigorous attempt to reform their institutions, could only regard so obscure a candidate as a badge of servitude to Russia. The powers collectively had strong reason to oppose the disturbance of the European balance which the addition of Poland to Russia would involve, while individually many of them favoured a Saxon candidate or some other. One power there was whose influence in Poland made it hard for Russia, unaided, to prevail and whose complicity would render it impossible for others to interfere. Let Catherine win Frederick and Stanislas might be sure of the Polish crown.

Prussia and the Polish Succession

Frederick, however, was the last man to be easy about his price. He, no less than Catherine, desired a weakling upon the throne of the Republic. Prussia's interest was best served by a feeble Poland, persecuting the Dissident Protestants so that they fled to her or invoked her aid, devoid of competing manufactures, inoffensive through lack of military power, anarchic with a sacrosanct *liberum veto*. For all this Frederick could stipulate as the condition of furthering Catherine's plan. But above all Prussia needed a friend to the north and east, so that never again should she be compelled to fight on two fronts at once. Whoever might reign in Petersburg, Frederick meant to have the soldiers of Zorndorf and Kunersdorf upon his side. Silesia, like Alsace-Lorraine after 1871, must be insured by every possible alliance. Russia, on the other hand, was of all powers the least open to attack and therefore reluctant to tie her hands by any permanent contract. Prussia, moreover, was an exhausted state, unpopular in Europe and traditionally "the deadly enemy of Russia." No other power, however, could serve her turn in Poland, and while Augustus still lived the negotiations with Prussia had been far advanced. A temporary *entente* would have been best for Catherine, but Frederick knew his advantage and firmly claimed his price.

Six months after the death of Augustus, Russia and Prussia became pledged allies (April 1764).

Russo-Prussian Treaty of April 176

The form of the Russo-Prussian pact was that of a defensive alliance for eight years. The substance amounted to an intimate association between Russia and Prussia both in Poland and elsewhere. Each guaranteed the territories of the other, Russia thus pledging herself to defend Silesia, and Prussia the Gottorp estates in Holstein, which had descended to Catherine's son. In Poland itself they undertook to secure the election of Stanislas and to defend it with 40,000 men. They agreed to maintain both the Polish and the Swedish constitutions, which notoriously doomed their neighbours to impotence and misrule. Among the secret undertakings, moreover, was one for the redress of those grievances of which the Greek and Lutheran " Dissidents " in Poland complained—a measure more certain than any other to convulse the ultra-Catholic population.

Stanislas Poniatowski Elected

The union of two well-placed military powers made French or Austrian intervention hopeless. The opposition of the Polish nationalists was paralysed by a show of force and by the distribution of some £300,000 from Russia. In September 1764, Stanislas was unanimously elected king. " Nothing seems to me more admirable," ran Frederick's congratulatory letter to his ally, " than your accomplishment of so many great deeds as it were without effort or resort to coercion or force. God said, Let there be light and there was light." Within eight years of the election, the first Partition of Poland had taken place.

Catherine could now flatter herself that it was she who really wore the Polish crown. During the next four years, however, the state of Poland went from bad to worse. Though well-meaning, liberal, handsome and a man of taste, Stanislas proved himself a *bon vivant* who lacked moral force. A king elected by bribery and intimidation had little claim to represent the nation or power of appealing to their patriotism. If he opposed his subjects' wishes he was denounced as a traitor sold to Russia. If he complied with them, Russia lectured him, cut off her subsidies and moved her troops. The situation was aggravated by two constant influences for evil. Catherine, like many rulers of Russia, deemed it her duty to maintain an almost superhuman dignity in dealing

Poland under Stanislas

with the weak. The "Tremble ye nations and obey, for God is with us" which a Tsar addressed to Europe in 1849 was no sudden improvisation. The application of this spirit to the Poles under Stanislas was the chief cause of all that followed. But the decrees that Catherine thus enforced owed much of their offensiveness to the studied malice of the Prussian king. Frederick, whose interest it was to embroil Russia and to exasperate the Poles, stood firm against any politic concession. Thanks to his counsels and demands, the Poles were compelled to abandon every new reform, and to resume the institutions which made Poland notoriously a weak, poor, and anarchic nation.

The limit of Polish endurance was passed when the Russian ambassador demanded that the Diet should restore the Dissidents to full political rights (1766). The political rights of a Polish gentleman were at this time so inordinate as to constitute the chief source of the Republic's downfall. In Poland, as French observers pointed out, no one could act but all could veto action, and the object of the laws was to secure the independence of every noble. Liberty destroyed itself by the measures taken to maintain it. At a time when Catholic Emancipation in England was unthinkable, the fervent Poles were called upon to give heretics a share in the mastery of the State. Many of them believed that to comply meant everlasting damnation. Stanislas, Philosopher as he was, declared that the Dissidents could only be granted redress by stages. To ask too much, he rightly opined, was to forfeit all. Catherine's dignity and Frederick's malice, however, were proof against humanity and reason.

Polish Resistance

Month by month, therefore, the Polish temper rose. One bishop dared to ask the omnipotent ambassador whether Mohammedans were also to be enfranchised. "Be silent," cried Repnin. "It behoves myself alone to know my sovereign's meaning. I will have only obedience." In vain, however, did Russian troops invade the country, seize the estates of members of the Opposition and deport bishops to captivity in Russia. No less vainly were Confederations of Dissidents organized to take the field. After three years' disturbance, Stanislas and the Russians ranked as the national enemies of Poland, and many Poles desired a National Confederation to drive both beyond the frontier. The leading families, however, failed to lay aside their divisions, nor could Polish troops face Russian in the field. In the autumn of 1767 the Diet broke up without satisfying the demands of Russia. Early next year a special session was summoned for this purpose and an unrepresentative body met. This "enslaved Delegation" yielded what Catherine could not be induced to forego—Dissident equality and the Russian right to guarantee the Polish constitution. As Kaunitz rightly held, this guarantee made Poland a Russian province. In Podolia, however, the malcontents formed the Confederation of Bar. Eight thousand Poles assembled to achieve the true will of the nation by force of arms. On all sides similar bands sprang up. It was impossible that a Catholic rising against Russia and Prussia should fail to command sympathy within Poland and without. In Warsaw itself Stanislas depended upon Russian bayonets. Austria, though the Queen clung to peace, sheltered the Confederates. France sent them money and trained leaders. In October, the Turks demanded that the Russians should evacuate the country, and failing compliance, declared war.

Russo-Turkish War

Catherine received the unwelcome Turkish declaration with her wonted gay courage. Thanks to the French, her pains to spare Turkish susceptibilities regarding Poland had been wasted. War, however, might bring the Russian frontiers to the Dwina and the Black Sea. The cat, she assured a correspondent, would spring upon the mouse, and "you will see what you will see." Europe in 1769 saw the Russians marvellously united and inspired by their Empress and engaged in a colossal plan. While five armies engaged the enemy over a frontier of some two thousand miles, a fleet was to rouse Greece against him and sail on to strike at Constantinople. Russia, however, lacked the numbers and the equipment to overcome in a few months the distance and the deserts which separated her from the Turks. Her senior native generals lacked skill and vigour, and Catherine dared not place foreigners in high command. While the summer passed, Galitzin displayed his incompetence upon the Dniester, and the Poles awaited a Turkish victory to rise *en masse*. Thrice did Galitzin cross and recross the river without taking Choczim, the key to Moldavia. Meanwhile the grand vizier had been beheaded and Ali, named

Moldavangi from his dealings in Moldavian slaves, succeeded him and crossed the Dniester. At last, in September, a rainstorm broke the bridges while his men were divided by the stream. Choczim fell without a blow. Fleeing far from Poland, the Turks abandoned Moldavia and Wallachia to Catherine, but too late for a Russian advance beyond the Danube. The Turk had lost the attack, but Russia had failed to win the war by a *coup de main.* Finance, recruiting, the jealousy of foreign powers—all would have a word to say before the next campaign. Russia accepted a few volunteers from foreign lands but hired no mercenaries and in general avoided foreign loans. Her troops were conscript serfs, patient and frugal indeed but ill-nourished and ill-supplied for marching through remote and poisonous countries. Wastage was therefore great, and to replenish it the landowners must be called on to send more conscripts from those who tilled their fields. At the same time the serfs who remained at home must be taxed still more severely to support the war. Thus every month that passed augmented Catherine's need for a victory which should bring a profitable peace. Her dignity, perhaps even her security upon the throne, admitted of neither a prolonged nor an inglorious struggle.

Austro-Prussian *rapprochement*

War at the same time cost her neighbours something, threatened to cost them more, and sharpened their appetite for compensation. A Russia threatening to absorb Poland and conquer Turkey made her rivals forget their differences. The Austrians ceased to gloat over despatches announcing that by the overflowing of Frederick's bile he often became frantic. In 1769, within conquered Silesia, Frederick received the young Emperor Joseph.

Joseph II 1765–90

In 1765 the death of the Emperor Francis I had been followed by the peaceful accession of his son, Joseph II, at the age of twenty-four. Although a Catholic and heir to the charm of his somewhat sluggish father, he proved himself the most radical of the Enlightened Despots of his time. Drawing from philosophy the duty of promoting the well-being of his subjects, material and moral alike, by the unwearied and unbounded exercise of royal power, he ruled with wellnigh unrivalled confidence in the efficacy of his ideas. "There has never been any epoch whose foremost men had such faith and hope in the virtues of humanity."

In sharp contrast to Frederick, Joseph showed himself the most doctrinaire among them, and for many years the most hopeful. While his mother lived, he was no more than co-regent of the Austrian States, and powerless against the Queen sustained by Kaunitz. He therefore attempted to make the Holy Roman Empire a reality. That task, perhaps not impossible before the Reformation, soon, however, proved itself beyond human power. His natural refuge lay in the domain of Habsburg foreign politics and he lived with the success of Frederick before his eyes. To reverence Frederick's success was not to trust him or to set "the patriotic German system" before an Austrian Revenge. But Joseph, still more than Frederick, was alarmed at the Russian movement towards the Danube. It was with no friendly feelings towards Russia that Frederick prolonged his alliance with her and at the same time raised his price. Catherine must now engage to fight, if need be, not only to defend Silesia but also distant Ansbach and Baireuth. As time passed, it became clear that Austria and Prussia would claim a large share in negotiating peace, and that they would oppose any considerable Russian gains from Turkey.

Recent Aggrandizement of France

France, moreover, might not indefinitely abstain from action. Choiseul had lately had the honour of uniting Lorraine with France when Stanislas Leszczynski ended his long career (1682–1766). His likewise was the dishonour of acquiring Corsica (1768) by what Freeman has stigmatized as "one of the most disreputable of juggles, without a shadow of right." The revolt of Paoli against Genoa, the mistress of Corsica, had roused the sympathy of young friends of freedom in many lands, and the crowned Philosopher at Petersburg dreamed of Corsican emancipation by Russian arms. In buying the island and crushing opposition, the French unwittingly altered the history of the world, for they turned into French subjects a Corsican noble family of remote Italian origin, to whom a son, Napoleone Buonaparte, was born in the following year.

In Poland, moreover, pacification eluded every Russian effort. At first, in the Ukraine, a war of extermination raged between Greeks and Latins, serfs and nobles. Later, Confederates or brigands made all the roads unsafe, while, to crown all, the plague began to decimate the countryside.

Anarchy and pestilence gave Austria and Prussia an excuse for sending troops across their frontiers to form *cordons sanitaires* against the Poles. This situation was in some respects only made worse by a breathless and astounding series of Russian victories. Within a few weeks "the Russian Turenne," Count Rumiantsov, and his small army had driven a huge host of Tartars and Turks into panic flight from the Larga and the Grand Vizier's main army from the Kaghul across the Danube. The Russians might count ere long on entering the Crimea, and on holding the lower Danube. Meanwhile their fleet annihilated the Turkish in the bay of Tchesmé. Dumouriez, the bearer of French aid, found the Polish Army reduced to some 16,000 jovial adventurers sheltering in Hungary. These dazzling successes, however, were far from bringing peace. Turkey was a vast military empire engaged in a holy war. The slaughter of tens of thousands of their fellow-subjects beyond the Danube could not induce the fanatics at Constantinople to cede provinces to the infidel. But without taking provinces from Turkey how could triumphant Russia recoup her loss? The fact that her actual conquests were regions which Austria would fight to keep from her, while, if Austria fought, reluctant Prussia stood pledged to fight for Russia, made the problem still more complex.

Russian Victories in 1770

Weakness of Russia

The Russian victories, moreover, did not delude foreign statesmen into believing her fleets and armies irresistible, or even strong. Frederick was warranted in styling this contest one between the purblind and the wholly blind. Some Turkish troops fought well, particularly against besiegers. Most of them, however, were untrained conscripts only intent on plunder. A rash vanguard of Rumiantsov's victorious army saw the plain between themselves and the Danube filled with a multitude struggling to escape from an imaginary enemy, attended in flight by 40,000 oxen, 30,000 camels and 100,000 sheep. More than once panic caused the garrison to flee from a fortress before the besiegers came. A Frenchman who could make shift to play the engineer was gratefully entrusted with the defence of the vital Dardanelles. Victory against such a foe might be expected, but in 1770 the victors were largely indebted to chance. No satire on Russia could be more biting than to dub Rumiantsov the Russian Turenne. Both the battles of the Larga and of the Kaghul were forced on the Russians by the German Bauer, backed by their fear of Catherine if the army should, as the generals desired, retreat. Tchesmé was won by British seamen. The Russian fleet, acclaimed and re-equipped in Britain, had sailed from the Baltic to Greece and roused the Morea to revolt. Alexis Orlov, who was now in supreme command, had neither force nor firmness enough, however, to defend the Greeks against their masters. He sailed on, and in the bay of Tchesmé, near Chios (July), his British officers gained a victory more complete than Lepanto (1571) or Navarino (1827). During the night fire-ships and red-hot shot wrought such havoc upon the Turks who were huddled together in the bay that of fifteen ships of the line only one escaped, and all six frigates were destroyed. "We are masters of the Archipelago," the victors informed their mistress. Admiral Elphinstone begged them to pass the Dardanelles and dictate peace at Constantinople. With his own ship he silenced the forts, but the Russians preferred retreat.

By land as well as by sea Russia in 1770 had alarmed Europe without proving herself a really formidable power. In 1769, moreover, Austria had occupied the county of Zips, a small pendant from Galicia which was almost surrounded by Hungary. Zips, indeed, was claimed by the Hungarian crown as having been ceded improperly in 1589. While an army of 50,000 men was assembled on the southern frontier of Austria, Zips was definitely annexed in December 1770. At the same time the fall of Choiseul removed a wise check on Joseph II. When winter fell the dwindling army was sick in mind and body, the fleet "ill-constructed, ill-commanded and ill-paid," the finances disordered and prices rising. Nothing less than Providence, held the British Ambassador, could preserve Russia from greater misfortunes. In the year of victory, Catherine's throne was still reckoned insecure.

Ascendancy of Prussia—Partition

All this inevitably increased the influence of the King of Prussia. In October 1770, Prince Henry of Prussia came to the court of Catherine, his old playfellow, on a four months' visit. Before he returned to Potsdam, Russia had resolved, if need be, to allow Prussia to advance in Poland.

At an evening party on January 8, the jocular suggestion was made to him that, as Austria had taken Zips, Prussia should take Warmia, which, like Zips, was dovetailed into her dominions. If Frederick's province of East Prussia were joined to the central mass of Brandenburg, Russia would in time be confronted with a more formidable neighbour, and her own prospective gain from dominating Poland would be reduced. It would be necessary, moreover, to allow Austria also to advance. But by paying Frederick's price Russia counted on some or all of a long list of immediate gains. Frederick, she might expect, would help her to pacify the Poles by force. Prussia, always at heart the foe of Austria, would ward off the threatened Austrian attack. Her carefully cultivated influence at Constantinople would be applied towards a good Russian peace. Prussia might even connive at conquests from Turkey, of which part would compensate the Poles. At the worst, Russia might annex as much of Poland as she pleased, and the line of the Dwina had long been her desire.

The Campaign of 1771

Russia, meanwhile, was fighting with varying success. On the Danube her efforts produced but little alteration, for neither side could hold much of what they might gain beyond the river. The Crimea, however, was subdued within a month. This proved the outstanding accomplishment of a disappointing year. Moscow was swept by plague. Austria, after the decline of French influence due to the dismissal of Choiseul from office, secretly sold her alliance to the Turks, and promised to defend Wallachia in return for Bukovina. The Russian fleet accomplished little. Poland defied pacification, and the Confederates shocked Europe by attempting to kidnap or assassinate the King. The death of Adolphus Frederick, Catherine's uncle, threatened to throw Sweden once again upon the side of France. The ambitious young Philosopher, Gustavus III, was not likely to acquiesce in the limitations upon monarchy which the Russian interest had maintained so amply that the successor of the great Gustavuses and Charleses could not refuse to have his name-stamp impressed upon a decree. Yet Russia would offer no peace-terms more moderate than that, while in deference to Austria the Turks should be allowed to ransom Moldavia and Wallachia, they must transfer the Tartars to her own protection. This meant that the Black Sea, that jealously guarded virgin of the Sultan's harem, might soon be ruled by Russia, a state of things intolerable to the Turks and to Austria but little better.

The Partition of Poland, 1772

On this basis negotiations were begun at Fokshani, and the armistice continued until the season was too far advanced for heavy fighting. The exhaustion of Russia and her fear of Gustavus III were alike attested by the concession of so long a breathing-space to Constantinople. Catherine even forbade her subjects by edict to speak of politics or of religion. Meanwhile the fate of Poland was determined. The Poles had proved incapable of defending themselves or of presenting any plan acceptable to Russia. Now the remaining Confederates surrendered to Suvorov, the rising Nelson of the Russian army. Their would-be saviours the Turks and Tartars were struggling to save themselves by negotiation. No help for Poland could be expected from western Europe. Britain, though she had always condemned Partition, had consistently declared that it was not for a distant commercial power to attempt to interfere by force. France, though perhaps willing for Poland's sake to form an *entente* with Britain, could not directly interfere. Sweden this year sacrificed her " liberties " to Gustavus, a king of twenty-six, whose irresistible appeal to the people foiled the plans of those powers who would have made her a second Poland. The Russian-paid oligarchy was cowed, but with no better ally than the Turks Gustavus dared not yet launch an attack upon Russia. If Russia, Prussia and Austria could agree, they could, therefore, work their will on defenceless Poland.

Early in 1772, the triple agreement, which Austria had refused a year earlier, came suddenly into existence. The failure of her crops made it impossible to fill her Bohemian magazines, the first condition of a Prussian war. In this year, at Kolin, Dr. Burney was happy to buy a pigeon and half a pint of sour wine for ten times the usual price. Frederick, knowing that he was safe, had exhorted Catherine to seize a share of Poland and with him defy the Habsburg. In January the Habsburg suddenly consented to share the spoils. Kaunitz and Joseph, the realists, overcame the reluctance of Maria Theresa to join Frederick and Catherine in trampling upon right. Frederick was apprised that

Austria would accept any of five specified territorial compensations for the Russian and Prussian aggrandizement in Poland. Of these five, two were Prussian, two Turkish, and the fifth, a part of Poland. In February, at Petersburg, a convention for Partition was signed. Its basis was equal annexations by the three powers, with no compensation to the Poles. For months many statesmen refused to believe that states whose interests clashed so obviously had thus far overcome their mutual distrust. Bargaining and encroaching, in fact, continued briskly, but the principle of roughly equal acquisitions was never given up. Through the spring and summer terrible reports gained currency of Prussian brutality towards the Polanders within the Prussian sphere. At last, in September, Europe was informed that Russia, Austria and Prussia were entitled to various Polish provinces, and that they proposed to take them. Russia, contenting herself with governing Courland by influence, advanced her frontier to the upper Dwina. and in White Russia seized a further portion of the Dnieper. Austria, whose portion was moved south of the Vistula so as to avoid threatening Silesia, seized a vast province in Galicia, including Lemberg and the rich salt-mines from which the Polish royal revenue was largely drawn. Prussia, though all Frederick's clamour failed to bring him Danzig, joined East Prussia to Brandenburg and Pomerania by acquiring West Prussia and other lands. He thus robbed Poland of both banks of the lower Vistula, and, except for Danzig, barred her firmly from access to the sea. He immediately claimed the port though not the town of Danzig, and set to work to ruin the town, if it should persist in clinging to the old *régime*.

The "First Partition"

Of the three partitioning powers, Austria gained the richest and most populous region; Prussia, that which she could make the most important, and Russia, the most easily digested. The new subjects of Austria were reckoned at 2,600,000, of Russia at 1,600,000 and of Prussia at 900,000, in all more than one-third of the Polish people. From the political point of view, Russia had reduced her chances of exclusive influence in what remained of Poland. Austria, by crossing the Carpathians and adding yet another race to her already heterogeneous mass, had violated the sound

POLAND
THE PARTITIONS
Partition of 1772
1793
1795
Windau
Riga
Courland
Libau
Mitau
Memel
Samogitia
Dünaburg
R. Düna
Polozk
Vitebsk
R. Dnieper
RUSSIA
Königsberg
Lithuania
Vilna
White Russia
Danzig
Elbing
Warmia
Marienburg
East Prussia
R. Niemen
Grodno
Minsk
R. Beresina
Mohileff
PRUSSIA
Bromberg
Thorn
Masovia
R. Narew
Bialystok
Black Russia
Posen
R. Warthe
R. Vistula
Plock
Warsaw
Smolensk
Kalisz
Poland
Podlachia
Brzesc
Pinsk
R. Pripet
R. Desna
R. Oder
Silesia
R. Pilica
Radom
Lublin
R. Bug
R. Goryn
Czenstochowa
Dubienka
Volhynia
Little Russia
Kieff
Cracow
Little Poland
R. Vistula
AUSTRIA
Red Russia
Lemberg
Tarnopol
Ukraine
R. Dnieper
Halicz
Bar
Podolia
Targowicz
Bracław
R. Dniester
R. Danube
R. Pruth
R. Bug
English Miles
0
100
200
Stanford, London

maxim of Kaunitz that any lands were preferable to the Polish. She had moreover abandoned, as Maria Theresa protested with the greatest grief, that "good right and the help of God" which had saved her thirty years before. "*Placet*," cried the Queen, "since so many great and learned men will have it so: but long after I am dead the consequences will be known of thus violating all that has hitherto been held just and sacred." Such was the protest of the old Europe against the new, of hereditary right and royal honour against realism and necessity of state. The century and a half which passed between the Partition and its undoing in 1919 were largely dominated by the Polish question, and the restoration of Poland was accompanied by the collapse of the Habsburg state. Partition was Frederick's triumph, and it "shook the political system, lowered the public morals and weakened the public law of Europe," as indeed the conqueror of Silesia desired. Tilsit in 1807 and Versailles in 1919, however, may suggest a doubt as to the reality of the advantage thereby gained by Prussia.

Poland and the Partition

In 1772, however, Stanislas and the Poles could oppose only a passive resistance to the seizure of one-third of Poland. Early in September, the three powers demanded the acceptance by king and diet of their demands. How could they be denied? The *liberum veto*, which Frederick and Catherine had made sacrosanct, empowered a single deputy to veto any measure. The self-deliverance of Sweden might perhaps inspire courage, while the Turks were bravely refusing Russia's demands. In 1771 they had broken off negotiations rather than yield the Crimea, and now a demand for the fortresses only, with Kinburn, led to the same result. The rupture, indeed, was ascribed to the impolicy of Gregori Orlov, who in his eagerness to quit Fokshani, proved less conciliatory than the interest of Russia required. His action was prompted, in part at least, by the news that after helping to enthrone Catherine and for ten years enjoying her indulgence, he had been replaced in her favour by an insignificant young lieutenant. Once again Europe vainly awaited news that the Empress had been forced from her throne.

Progress of the War

Progress of Partition

Although the Turkish war continued, however, the new peril from Sweden abated, Catherine kept her throne, and

Partition was carried out. Stanislas was no Gustavus, and Poland had no ally. In January 1773, under pain of further dismemberment, the three powers demanded that the Diet should delay no longer. Bribes and bayonets were used to overcome its resistance, and the *liberum veto* was evaded by turning the Diet into a Confederation. Although Rumiantsov failed to capture the Turkish fortresses, and in the Volga lands the rebellion of the Cossack Pugachev was gathering strength, the forces coercing Poland proved overwhelming, and more and more of her lands were filched away. In September 1773, King and Diet submitted. Poland found herself reduced to some ten million people and in substance cut off from the sea. Danzig, indeed, remained to her, but long before she yielded, Frederick had 6,000 men digging by day and night a canal designed to divert trade from Danzig to the newly-gained Prussian ports. In June 1773, he beheld the first freighted ships upon its waters. The next step was to cut off the water which filled the branch of the Vistula upon which Danzig stood in favour of the branch which he had gained by the Partition. In presence of such energy and of the immensity of Russia, while her own chief defects had been declared inviolable, how could Poland become regenerate ? A perpetual Council of State was established and a commission appointed to reform education, but the Russian Ambassador at Warsaw continued to act like a resident adviser at the court of a protected state. It was significant that while the normal stipend for a diplomat of his rank was 8,000 roubles, he received no less than 20,000, with a further 24,000 for the expenses of his household. In 1779, the Warsaw embassy cost Russia 51,500 roubles, against 14,300 for that in London.

Peace of Kainardji, 1774

In 1774, when Louis XV's long reign ended and the American Congress met, Catherine reaped the reward of her constancy since 1768. Rumiantsov, victorious in Bulgaria, threatened the remnants of the Turkish force in Shumla. A third peace congress, held at Kutchuk Kainardji, between Shumla and the Danube, reached agreement in a single day (July 21). Thanks to the Partition, Catherine could lower her demands and her associates could acquiesce in her aggrandizement. Repnin required only a moderate indemnity in cash and the concession of privileges and positions which involved no great immediate sacrifice by the Turks. The Tartars of the Crimea and Kuban received their independence, though the Sultan remained their religious head, and Russia acquired the fortresses of Kertch, Azov and Yenikale on their coasts. Kinburn at the mouth of the Dnieper passed to her, with a wedge-shaped hinterland between the Dnieper and the Bug. Parts of the Kuban and Terek region gave her also a footing in the eastern Euxine and in the Caucasus, and she secured exclusive rights of navigation with an outlet through the Straits. Extensive commercial and religious privileges, recognition as the second power in Europe, a vague right of intercession on behalf of Greek believers, free access to the Holy Places—all these formed additional compensation for those conquered provinces and islands which she gave back.

The Russo-Turkish War and Europe

The sudden collapse of the Turks in 1774 marked a permanent turn of the balance in eastern Europe. Henceforth Russia enjoyed a predominance over this ancient foe almost as clear as that which since 1667 she had achieved in Poland. The Empress began to dream of ruling, like Constantine or Justinian, a new Eastern Empire. She had reached the Black Sea and soon would threaten Constantinople, the Rome or Mecca of her Orthodox subjects. To Russian statesmen, moreover, Constantinople meant the gateway into the Mediterranean, which they designed to force. This long remained the most formidable Russian threat to Europe. Russia's momentary moderation was set off by the rapacity of Austria which demanded and received the Bukovina by way of compensation from the Turks (1775). The new realism, however, found such proceedings venial, and the way lay open for that collaboration between Catherine and Joseph II by which alone her " Greek project " might be achieved.

Rebellion of Pugachev

Before Catherine could attempt to endow her new-born grandson Constantine with a Greek empire worthy of his name, she must secure her own power in Russia. In 1773 and 1774 the Cossack Pugachev, professing to be Peter III, had spread a *jacquerie* over a vast area in the south-east, making even Moscow feel insecure. Such insurrections were no new thing in Russia, nor was Pugachev either the first or the last rebel to style himself Peter III. His followers burned mansions and murdered babies with the causeless cruelty and rapine of the half-savage desperado. But he represented Cossack and aboriginal discontent as well as peasant resentment at imperial taxes and proprietors' oppression. When such a rising could defy the Government for two years, it was difficult for the Empress to feel sure that her people were her own. At last, in 1775, Suvorov brought Pugachev in an iron cage to Moscow, where he confessed his imposture and bravely endured the amputation of his arms and legs before his execution. Catherine was now secure, but she had learned to depend upon her officials and gentry, not upon the inscrutable rank and file. The gentry, in their turn, took refuge with the Empress from the people. Whatever the French Philosophers might teach, Russia must be governed by her single will, working through a hierarchy of officials.

The Russo-Turkish War thus crippled Turkey, checked the constitutional advance of Russia and established that "communion in the eucharist of the body of Poland" which promoted despotism east of the Elbe down to the Great War.

BIBLIOGRAPHICAL NOTE

See the Bibliographical Note at the end of Chapter I.

From 1758, the *Annual Register*, founded by Burke, is of great value. Add :—

A

S. Askenazy: *Die letzte polnische Königswahl* (1894).

W. L. Blease: *Suvorov* (1920).

O. Halecki: "Modern Poland until the Partitions, 1506–1795," in *A Handbook of Slavic Studies* (ed. L. I. Strakhovsky, 1949).

D. B. Horn: *British Public Opinion and the First Partition of Poland* (1945).

R. H. Lord: *The Second Partition of Poland* (1915).

W. Michael: *Englands Stellung zur ersten Teilung Polens* (1890).

W. F. Reddaway (ed.): *The Cambridge History of Poland* II (1941).

W. F. Reddaway: "Great Britain and Poland, 1762–72," *Camb. Hist. Jour.*, IV (1934), pp. 223–62.

W. J. Rose: *Stanislas Konarski, Reformer of Education in Eighteenth-century Poland* (1929).

B

A. Brückner: *Katharina die Zweite* (1883).

S. O. de Falkenskjold: *Mémoires* (1826).

Diaries and Correspondence of James Harris, First Earl of Malmesbury: 4 vols. (1844).

Russian Imperial Historical Society: *Collections* (St. Petersburg).

CHAPTER XIII

EUROPE AND AMERICAN INDEPENDENCE

Lexington and the Colonial System

FOR Europe April 19, 1775, was probably the most momentous day of the whole eighteenth century. The first shot fired at Lexington shattered the moral basis of the existing system of colonial rule. That system was European. It embodied the belief that if some members of a state settled on lands which no government had previously claimed, they merely extended the area over which the monarchy of their home state held sway. Distance and local circumstances conferred no special rights on subjects. A king, like a husband, might keep the calf bred from his cow 'gainst all the world. This had held good in transoceanic Portugal and Spain and France and Holland. In all the colonies of those states, however, the motive-power had been governmental rather than individual, while the European settlers formed a small minority of the population. The same theory held good also in the no less distant colonies of Russia. These, however, were situated beyond the ken of Europe and merely expanded the frontiers of the parent state. No nation save the British had as yet sent out many thousands of its sons to settle in countries distant at least a month by sea and there to raise up communities like its own. In British North America, as in Britain, the English language and the English law prevailed. Each colony might have its own established church. The institutions of each resembled those of the mother-country. King, Lords and Commons of Britain found echoes in the Governor, Council and House of Representatives of every colonial State. Indians and negroes there presented problems which differed only in size from those of negroes, Jews, dissenters and unenfranchized whites in Britain. Colonial grievances were neither few nor silent, but colonial loyalty was strong. Although the British commercial system was irritating, prompting complaints that a New England blacksmith could hardly make a nail without infringing some monopoly, mutual adjustments were amply possible. The pamphleteer of 1776, who declared that 3,000,000 people rushed to the seashore to learn from each English ship how much of liberty was left to them, found that arresting statement too absurd to print. The Bostonian who wrote in 1774, "We have too great a regard for our parent state (although cruelly treated by some of her illegitimate sons) to withdraw our connexion," expressed the views of the First Continental Congress and of Washington. Sentiment apart, the British market and the British fleet could compensate for much annoyance. As the outcome of their controversies proved, trade between Britain and America was destined to increase, whether the two countries maintained or broke their union. Agricultural communities, new and therefore poor, with a fast increasing population could not dispense with British manufactured and imported goods. Economically, Lexington began no revolution.

American and European Politics

In political weight, however, 1775 surpassed every rival year. Utrecht restored the balance of power to Europe. 1740 and 1772 established the new immorality. After fourteen years, the lesson of America was to be applied in France, and through her to dominate for a quarter of a century the whole history of Europe. Lexington proclaimed that Britain had failed to solve her problem. It banished for many years the hope that a mighty and peaceful Anglo-Saxon union would grow up. Again, as in the days of Luther, it was decreed that if mankind were to progress it must be by revolution. American success would mean in time new demands on the part of every population for real self-government. But the revolution of 1775, like the revolution of 1917, must not merely overthrow. To be widely imitated, it must also convince the populations that the revolutionary sacrifice would lead them to a happier order. What could not fail to follow on American victory, however, would be the creation of a new state with an appreciable influence upon the alliances and wars of Europe.

American Unrest and Europe 1763–74

Such influence had in fact been clearly foreshadowed in the years between Lexington and the Peace of Paris (1763). For a full decade, the Colonies had been causing British diplomatic isolation. What powers, save such as lived by hiring out their troops for service, could wish for an ally who might at any time be paralysed by an outbreak overseas? Many sinister eyes were fixed upon the Yankees. French statesmen looked to them—and, as the issue proved, correctly—to give France victory in her next round with Britain. The Americans, argued Vergennes, had borne the British yoke only to gain protection against French North America. When as the outcome of the Seven Years War that passed to Britain, the Colonial System, founded on an absolute delusion, would soon make them rebel. Spain suffered constant depredations from the Colonists, and friction with the mother-country often arose concerning boundaries and rights. Prussia, through Frederick, was doubly resolved against collaboration with a threatened government. The King's reiterated warnings helped to influence Russia, a power from which Britain had the highest hopes of an alliance but which was naturally the most sensitive to the menace of rebellion. Austria was likewise strengthened by rumours of American discontent in her resolve to hold to the French alliance and avoid a return to that of Britain. Thus the Americans ranked with Wilkes as a force which absorbed the energies of British statesmen and at the same time lowered the international value of their country. In casting up the gain and loss of Independence this fact has too often been overlooked.

America burdens Britain

British statesmen, on the other hand, could not but feel that the Colonies were lowering our prestige and power. In December 1770, " our divisions and frenzy at home with the Colonies " were conjectured as the reason prompting Spain to attack the Falkland Islands. The costs imposed upon Britain by Colonial defence no one could gainsay. After war, as usual, economy loomed large, and it was easier to be more rigorous in collecting debts than to retrench expenses. In these years British diplomats not seldom met with difficulties in obtaining their salaries from home. The peasant, from France to Russia, found his dues increased or at least more stringently exacted. Such was the time at which the British Government was compelled by its recent gains to face fresh outlay on American defence. Besides the prospect of French revenge, Indian hostility over half a continent must be forestalled. Nothing could be more certain than that the Colonists would irritate the Indians and reject the financial burden of providing garrisons against them or their French allies. On the very morrow of the Seven Years War, a war which had cost her £90,000,000, Britain resolved to keep in America a standing army of 10,000 men and to require the Colonists to assist in its support.

Europe and American Resistance

Britain's resolve to tax America had thus its origin, in part at least, in Europe. Her famous efforts to carry out that resolve, epitomized as they may be in the Stamp Act, belong chiefly to domestic history. In that age, however, as may soon be the case in this, few taxes on commodities could be imposed without an eye to foreign politics. In 1764, indigo, coffee and molasses, wines and textiles were subjected to duties and prohibitions with the double object of raising revenue and hurting France. Then, in 1765, came the Stamp Act, and the Colonists claimed that taxation without representation was tyranny. To withdraw the Act in 1766 was not and could not be to expunge the fact that Parliament had been challenged. The Colonists turned from historic to natural law and found that rights which had never existed were graven in deep characters upon the heart of man. In 1774 Boston led thirteen colonies in combined revolt.

The Philosophers and America

American sentiment at the last moved swiftly from loyalty to separation, from monarchy towards a set of new republics. The change was the more startling because the Colonies, besides being weak and poor, were deeply divided. Scattered and heterogeneous communities sprawling over 800 miles of coast-line, their needs and interests often lay poles apart. Some states deemed slavery wrong; others, vital; some wished for commercial freedom; others, for state protection. Perhaps the only common sentiments were resentment against Britain and against any sacrifice of colonial to intercolonial rights. Their change of political belief could not have come so quickly had not the Philosophers of Europe sapped their hereditary creed. Within a dozen years (1750–62) Rousseau had issued treatises on Inequality, Education and the Social Contract which contributed far more than French arms and funds towards American resistance. Whereas Voltaire had ridiculed a church from which the Colonists did not greatly suffer, Rousseau, who shared their reverence for religion, taught that the civilization of their oppressors was absurd. The more we add to knowledge, he declared, the less we can study the most useful of all objects, the art of forming men. Intuition, not reason, should be our guide. Let us leave books of science, which teach us only to see men who have been made artificial, and meditate on the first and most simple operations of the human soul. All things as they come from the hands of their Creator are good, but all degenerate in the hands of man. In government society and education we should return to nature.

Influence of Rousseau

The reality of Rousseau's power is attested by the devotion felt for him by Kant and by his influence upon posterity. In him, it has been claimed, lay all the nineteenth century. Rational clothing, sun-bathing, the indulgent education of the child—such features of the twentieth century were his conceptions. No teaching could be easier to assimilate nor more conducive to drastic revolution.

"The true founder of society," Rousseau declared, "was the first man who enclosed a piece of ground, cried 'This is mine,' and found people silly enough to believe him. How many crimes and wars and murders . . . would have been spared the human race if someone had pulled down his fence or filled up his ditch, crying to his fellows 'Beware of listening to this impostor, you are lost if you forget that the land belongs to no one and its fruits to all alike!'"

Again, he did not shrink from ridiculing that *reductio ad absurdum* of loyalty to which the frequent child-kings or idiot-kings gave rise.

"If ever there was a sight, truly indecent, detestable, and ridiculous surely it must be that of a respectable body of magistrates, with their president at their head, in their robes of state, prostrating themselves before an infant in swaddling-clothes and addressing him in a florid harangue, to the pompous terms of which he returns a most gracious answer, by whimpering and bedewing his slabbering bib."

The Americans were human enough to apply the revisionist spirit which such words inspired to the historic institutions which they disliked and not to those which pleased them. As a society of freemen, remote from courts and armies, self-sufficing, educated and not yet crowded into cities, they acclaimed the philosopher of Geneva when he taught the sanctity of the general will. The most modern and the best opinion, they felt, favoured their rebellion. Rousseau thus did the American revolution the same service as Marx the Russian.

Rousseau and the Americans

Had Rousseau written to win the Americans, indeed, he could hardly have been more flattering. A rural people, they learned from him that cities depraved both mind and body.

"Mankind," he taught, "were not formed to be heaped together in shoals, but to spread over the face of the earth to cultivate it. . . . Man is of all animals the least adapted to live in herds. Flocks of men would swiftly perish. Literally, no less than figuratively, their breath destroys their fellows."

The Lisbon earthquake which shocked some Europeans into atheism he ascribed to human folly. "Nature never assembled twenty thousand houses six or seven stories high." Paris, he maintained, drove women to disbelieve in honour and men in virtue. From such a teacher the Colonists were ready to learn that man, born free, was everywhere in chains, and that at the moment when the government usurped the sovereignty the Social Compact had been broken and natural liberty regained.

The Declaration of Independence, 1776

On July 2, 1776, after bitter struggles, the Continental Congress declared the United Colonies free and independent states. Their social slavery grotesquely contrasted with their claims to freedom. One Pennsylvanian newspaper, which announced the great deed, advertised for sale "a Dutch servant girl, healthy, strong, and good-natured, has five or six years to serve." Another proclaimed three dollars reward for the recovery of a "negro named Ishmael, twenty-five years of age, colour between a mulatto and a black," who had run away. The Declaration was drawn up by the young Virginian *doctrinaire*, Thomas Jefferson, and approved by Franklin, Adams, Livingston and Sherman with no substantial change. In Congress about a quarter was cut out before the members signed unanimously, jesting among themselves that they must all hang together or they would hang separately (July 4). "At the time," wrote one American patriot to another two days later, "our forces in Canada were retreating before a victorious army," while he declared that General Howe with a large armament was then advancing towards New York. Many diverse currents had driven the public to dare to proclaim separation. Two years earlier the Colonies had " made their stand, not against tyranny inflicted, but only against tyranny anticipated." Since Lexington, however, hopes of reconciliation had had time to fade, while bloodshed roused men's temper. The Colonies found themselves outlawed by Act of Parliament, and confronted with the choice between slavery and independence. Anger is temporary madness, and they were angry men. The heady rhetoric of an English agitator, Tom Paine, could therefore pass for *Common Sense*, the title of his slender pamphlet. Its text came from the poet Thomson:

Paine's Common Sense

> " Man knows no master save creating Heaven
> Or those whom choice and common good ordain."

Reconciliation, Paine declared, had become impossible, for the English people were now presenting petitions against the Americans. " These are injuries which nature cannot forgive; she would cease to be nature if she did. As well can the lover forgive the ravisher of his mistress." The true interest of America, he maintained, was to steer clear of European contentions. This she could never do while bound to Britain. The British connexion had not a single advantage to offer. Europe and not England was the parent country of America.

Text of the *Declaration*

Paine's pamphlet, the logic of armed strife, resentment at the employment of German troops against the sons of Britain, the current notions of natural rights of man which must override the duties of allegiance, the need of claiming a status higher than that of rebels with whom no foreign sovereign could ally—all these contributed to determine the *Declaration*. As a manifesto it was superficial and ill-founded, but the claim that it embodied forms a landmark in the story of mankind.

" Perhaps a greater question never was or will be decided among men," wrote John Adams to his wife with true prevision on July 3. " It ought to be solemnized with pomp and parade, with shows, games, sports, guns, bells, bonfires and illuminations from one end of this continent to the other from this time forward for evermore."

Short as the *Declaration* is, it might, with advantage to mankind, have been shorter still. More than one-half is spent on proof that George III—Paine's " hardened, sullen-tempered Pharaoh "—was a prince whose character was " marked by every act which may define a tyrant," and his aim, "the establishment of an absolute tyranny over these states." From Jefferson's recital of the royal acts, a recital of which the repetition poisoned American opinion for five generations, Congress removed the indictment against the slave trade—a trade found profitable by the North and deemed by the South essential. "This piratical warfare, the opprobrium of *infidel* powers," Jefferson had written, "is the warfare of the *Christian* King of Great Britain, determined to keep open a market where MEN should be bought and sold."

The kernel of the *Declaration*, however, lies in five lines of the printed text.

Importance of the *Declaration*

> "We hold these truths to be self-evident," declared the rebels, "that all men are created equal, that they are endowed by their Creator with certain unalienable rights, that among these are life, liberty and the pursuit of happiness. That to secure these rights, governments are instituted among men, deriving their just powers from the consent of the governed. That, whenever any form of government becomes destructive of these ends, it is the right of the people to alter or to abolish it, and to institute new government, laying its foundation on such principles and organizing its powers in such form as to them shall seem most likely to effect their safety and happiness."

That, to defend these "human rights," the United States renounced an allegiance which had hitherto been accounted sacred by the laws of God and man, and that they won the ensuing war—these are perhaps the greatest of historic facts for Europe.

The importance of the issue has magnified that of the subsequent campaigns. Like the struggle for Dutch independence, the American war was small in scale. Hessians on the one side, French upon the other could not swell the forces into armies on the scale of Europe. In the summer of 1778, some 160,000 Prussians and Saxons marched against Austria. By that time, as three more campaigns sufficed to show, victory at Saratoga (1777) and its corollary French intervention had ensured American success. Yet Burgoyne at Saratoga led no more than 3,500 men, and only a dozen ships and some 5,000 soldiers arrived in 1778 from France. During the intervening winter, Washington and his ragged remnants had starved at Valley Forge, while in an army of volunteers it was doubtful whether any appreciable number would rejoin when their time was up. Britain, on the other hand, could supplement such voluntary forces as she could raise with 20,000 hired conscripts from Germany. Difficulties of recruiting, garrisoning, supply and transport, however, prevented her from marshalling for any action more than some 16,000 men. But for European aid, none the less, these small forces, if well managed, might have extinguished the rebellion.

The contribution of Europe towards that American success which influenced beyond all calculation its own future was prompted by mixed motives and took diverse forms. The decisive action came from France. Her resolve to intervene, fateful for herself, for America and for all Europe, was made in the face of no little opposition. Her new king, Louis XVI, sincerely loved peace. His ally, Charles III of Spain, refused immediate war. Necker and Turgot, the experts in finance, scouted the idea of costly and unnecessary intervention.

The French public, which adored Voltaire, was Anglophile to the point of Anglomania. At this time they imitated the externals of English life—manners, dress, gardens, field-sports—and revered English philosophy, English liberty and English parliamentary institutions. The year of the Declaration of Independence witnessed the publication of Shakespeare in a French translation and its immense success in Paris. Yet when France resolved to strike the nation applauded and for five years remained loyal to the American cause. This, it may justly be maintained, was the outcome rather of admiration for America than of hate for Britain. "Liberty, philanthropy, natural rights," claimed Ségur, "these were the magic words stirring not only writers and thinkers, but the very masses in France."

French action, first covertly aiding the rebels with money, arms and stores and then accepting their alliance, was prompted by political revenge. "England," declared Vergennes, "is the natural enemy of France, greedy, ambitious, unjust and false," and always aiming at her ruin. He urged that if France did not intervene, the Colonies would be reconquered and their commerce monopolized by England. If French aid gave them victory, he did not fear revolutionary contagion, but counted on the recovery by France of the ascendancy in Europe that she had lost by the Peace of Paris and by the Partition. The Franco-American agree-

Treaties of Commerce and Alliance Feb. 1778

ment, therefore, claimed for France neither conquests nor special privileges. Morally and financially, it saved the United States, and although Frederick was too cautious to interfere, other powers of Europe struck at Britain.

"In treating of trade to North America," wrote the British compiler of a gazeteer of 1782, "unhappily we are obliged to use the past sense . . . for since their unnatural alliance . . . they have been supplied by their new friends and by other nations neutral to everything but their own interest."

The forebodings of the British proved as baseless as the expectations of the French. Within six years of her American triumph, France, bankrupt, humiliated, and a prey to subversive notions, stood on the verge of revolution.

BIBLIOGRAPHICAL NOTE

See the Bibliographical Note at the end of Chapter I, the bibliographies to Chapters IV and V and the works named in the text.
Add :—

A

J. T. Adams: *Revolutionary New England, 1691–1776* (1923).
C. M. Andrews: *The Colonial Period of American History.* 4 vols. (1934–38).
C. L. Becker: *The Declaration of Independence* (1922).
G. L. Beer: *British Colonial Policy, 1754–65* (1907).
S. F. Bemis: *The Diplomacy of the American Revolution* (1935).
A. Cobban: *Rousseau and the Modern State* (1934).
E. S. Corwin: *French Diplomacy and the American Alliance of 1778* (1916).
D. S. Freeman: *George Washington: A Biography.* 6 vols. published (1948–).
L. H. Gipson: *The Coming of the Revolution, 1763–1775* (1954).
E. Green: *The Revolutionary Generation, 1763–1790* (1943).
J. C. Miller: *Origins of the American Revolution* (1945).
L. B. Namier: *England in the Age of the American Revolution* (1930).
R. Pares: *King George III and the Politicians* (1953).
J. B. Perkins: *France and the American Revolution* (1911).
J. F. Ramsay: *Anglo-French Relations, 1763–1770: A Study of Choiseul's Foreign Policy* (1939).
G. Stourzh: *Benjamin Franklin and American Foreign Policy* (1954).
T. J. Wertenbaker: *The Founding of American Civilization: The Middle Colonies* (1938).
T. J. Wertenbaker: *The Founding of American Civilization: The Old South* (1942).

B

J. P. Boyd, *et al.* (eds.): *The Papers of Thomas Jefferson.* In progress (1950–).
G. Hunt (ed.): *James Madison: Writings.* 9 vols. (1900).
W. S. Lindsay: *History of Merchant Shipping.* II. 4 vols. (1874–76).
S. K. Padover (ed.): *The Complete Jefferson* (1943).
T. Salmon: *Modern Gazetteer* (3rd ed. 1756; 10th ed. 1782).

CHAPTER XIV

EUROPE, 1774–92

REFORM AND REACTION IN FRANCE

Predominance of Peace 1774–8

BETWEEN the establishment of Russian superiority over the Turk (1774) and the assembly of the French States-general (1789) the vital history of Europe was chiefly determined by events beyond the ocean. Between 1774 and 1778 the American rebellion influenced the Old World more deeply than did anything hatched by statesmen nearer home. While Britain and her Colonies drifted into war, and Hastings built up a new empire in India, Europe changed but slowly. Austria added Bukovina to the gains which she had made from Turkey at the Kainardji peace. Spain failed against the Moors, but became reconciled with Portugal, where Pombal fell. The Swiss embraced a French alliance. France, in the last years of Rousseau and Voltaire and the first of Louis XVI, was turning with mixed motives towards colonial intervention and striving vainly for economy at home. In Russia a European monarch, at last secure upon her throne, was more than ever determined to dominate in Europe.

It was not until 1778 that the work of domestic organization, conspicuous in the three eastern powers and in Iberia, and by no means unknown in France, came to be interrupted by a great European war and by another round in the struggle between France and Britain. While Russia was conquering the Turk and Britain preparing to lose America, the march of civilization had continued on the paths already traced. Coke of Norfolk began to teach the world how to supply itself with meat, hides and wool, while Adam Smith exposed the fallacies which had hitherto obstructed the wealth of nations. The great name of Goethe stands for the new literature of many states, which at first copied the French and then reacted towards a nationalism of their own. Physical science became more than ever international, and new elements and new forces were discovered in various lands. The downfall of the Jesuits (1773) seemed to give the signal for an outburst of energy in education. For Europe, however, the outstanding question of the middle 'seventies was that of the future policy of France. In wealth and population she was slowly rising, but, for good or evil, her government was in the hands of a few men whose course remained highly uncertain. Choiseul and his successors had made the crown more than ever autocratic, suppressing the *parlements*, its ancient rivals, and leaving the royal agents everywhere supreme. The crying evils of France—the inequitable exemption from taxation, the tyranny of gilds in the towns, and the luxury on which absentee nobles lavished their rents—all this they had bequeathed to the new king, together with the Austrian alliance represented by his queen. Although France had enjoyed eleven years of peace, the deficit exceeded one-tenth of the revenue. Religion divided rather than united society, and the ill-paid parish priests hated their proud superiors in the Church. Louis XVI succeeded at twenty. He was a heavy youth with no French characteristics, devoted to hunting and locksmith's work, incapable of quick retorts or general ideas. No one could deny that his life was decent and his intentions excellent, and he sincerely proclaimed himself a liberal. "He was born to be a respectable mechanic." His brother compared the workings of his brain to the contact between oiled ivory balls. Conscious of his own inadequacy, he tended to obey his relatives, and finally his wife. Marie Antoinette, child of Maria Theresa, had inherited her mother's grace and beauty without her solidity and force. As the King could not and did not pretend to govern, the new ministers became all important for France. These were Maurepas as premier, Vergennes for foreign affairs, and Turgot for finance.

Policy of France under Louis XVI

Maurepas 1701–81

Maurepas, the choice of the King's aunt, was a choice to kill men's hopes of betterment under Louis XVI. Promoted, like Fleury, at seventy-three, he lacked every advantage that Fleury had possessed. Fleury was the King's confidant and tutor; Maurepas had been driven from the court by Madame de Pompadour in 1749. Fleury was hampered by no compromising past; Maurepas had a bad one, for he had been Minister of Marine in the war of the Austrian Succession, and had negotiated the treaty of Fontainebleau, which subordinated France to Spain. Fleury's strength had been to sit still, an admirable duty for a veteran; Maurepas was called in when France clearly needed reform, which only a fresh and vigorous brain could give her. A petty and reactionary intriguer, in love with the age of Louis XV, was perhaps the worst possible selection. This fact could hardly be disguised by the general applause which the dismissal of the dead King's ministers evoked, or by the delight of the *bourgeoisie* at the recall of the *parlements*. In them there reappeared a rival to the crown at a moment when it was all-important that the crown should be unfettered for reform. The rival, moreover, represented those selfish hereditary corporations which it was above all things necessary to overcome. A *parlement* was at best a judicial clique which claimed to interfere in legislation. In states where a confused and hasty despotism prevailed, such as Russia before Catherine II or Denmark under Struensee, it might be expedient that royal decrees should be approved by some independent body. But in centralized and highly developed France, the right of remonstrance which the *parlements* possessed had become a hateful class-survival. Its restoration presaged discord, for it was hateful to monarchists and strict Catholics, to Philosophers and reformers alike. Not the least severe among its critics was the statesman upon whom the hopes of France were centred, Turgot, the new Controller-general of finance. Turgot, awkward, modest and efficient, was summoned from the provinces by Maurepas, who hoped to strengthen his administration by including a strenuous and inconspicuous public servant. The conservative premier thereby unwittingly exposed his master to the influence of a man who was in himself a revolution. Turgot, indeed, no more than his fellow Philosophers, wished to restrict or to destroy the royal power. But his common sense, his economic knowledge, and his long experience as an *Intendant* had taught him that all else in France needed reform, and he felt within himself the force to satisfy her need. While quite prepared, if called on, to dictate a new constitution based on local democratic self-government, he was also ready to reform the existing organization in the interest of the common weal. He knew well that the vested interests would turn against himself and perhaps against his master, but he knew also his

Turgot, in power 1774–6

own fortitude, and he trusted in that of Louis. Deeply impressed by his personality, the King cordially endorsed his financial programme—" No state bankruptcy, no new taxes, no loans "—though this could only mean drastic economies at the expense of the privileged and influential classes. Turgot himself, when he received his *douceur* of 450,000 *livres* from the Farmers-general, handed it to the clergy of Paris for the poor.

Between September 1774 and May 1776, Turgot showed France what a Colbert could accomplish if he knew and loved the people and had mastered economic science. In spite of the deficit, he removed the most oppressive taxes, paid the arrears of pensions, and reduced the floating debt. By striking hard at extravagance and corruption, he made France pay her way, despite the Farmers-general. Proclaiming liberty to trade as the ideal, he began by establishing, at least within the kingdom, the unwonted liberty to trade in corn. Hitherto, for the sake of the royal monopoly, the sale of corn had been as jealously restricted as the sale of poison. Now all might import and sell, and the people were publicly invited to believe that it was their own business, not that of the State, to supply themselves with food. The harvest of 1774 was not abundant, and in the following spring bread-riots disturbed both Paris and some of the less favoured provinces. Turgot did not hesitate to put down the rioters or to repel the interference of the *parlement*. He was unable, however, to punish those nobles who had not scrupled to use the dearth to discredit him, nor could he check the rising hostile influence of the Queen.

In the summer, however, a good harvest strengthened his 1775
position, while his friend Malesherbes was called to office. Mild and conciliatory, an indulgent censor of the *Encyclopædia* for which Turgot wrote, Malesherbes stood for a liberal administration. He reformed prisons, favoured Protestant emancipation, mitigated the restrictions on the press, and indicted the financial maladministration. His presence at Turgot's side, none the less, tended to consolidate the opposition which nobles, lawyers and clergy were certain to set up. Worse still, since Turgot proved himself a disturbing rival, the opposition gained the sympathy of Maurepas.

Reforms in France

While the civil administration thus underwent far-reaching reforms, the services were not neglected. Sartine, though neither a sailor nor an enlightened man, was continuing the work of Choiseul and proving what energy and application could accomplish in the navy. The army was entrusted by Turgot to St. Germain, who was worshipped by the liberals in Denmark, but had grown old without making any deep impression upon France. Recalled from retirement on the strength of a memorandum, he proved himself a vigorous *doctrinaire* reformer, hostile to privilege, libertinism, and the slackness which had paralysed France in the Seven Years War. His personality, however, did not attach even those whom he promoted, and through him Turgot grew even more unpopular than before.

1776 Secure, none the less, in the support of the King, of the Philosophers, of many groups and—what with him outweighed all else—of his own conscience, Turgot began the year 1776 with a far-reaching programme of reform. The *parlement* was forced to register royal edicts attacking that privilege of certain classes which was the hall-mark of the *ancien régime*. The *corvée*, which threw upon the poor the burden of constructing and maintaining the highways, was to be replaced by a land-tax payable by privileged and unprivileged alike. At the same time the monopoly of handicrafts by gilds was done away, so that every man could enter upon what career he pleased. The storm raised by these edicts and heightened secretly by Maurepas caused Louis to remark that only he and Turgot loved the people. Turgot, indeed, urged his master to grant a constitution which should unite the nation on a basis of natural justice. Left to himself, Louis might have dared to comply, but his family took up the cause of privilege. The Queen avenged on Turgot his disgrace of a *protégé* of hers, well-merited though it was. Louis was turned against his minister by means of forgery. Eight weeks before America declared her independence, Malesherbes resigned and Turgot was dismissed. He did not live to see the close of a war which he would never have permitted France to enter.

Reaction in France

Turgot left a surplus of 11,000,000 *livres*, but with it a prejudice against reform and economy which was destined to cost France infinitely larger sums. The *corvée* and the gilds were at once restored, and free trade in corn abolished. Privilege, it was evident, remained sacrosanct. The direction of the finances was entrusted by Maurepas to a foreign Protestant, the Parisian banker Necker. A disciple of Colbert and of Law and an outspoken opponent of Turgot was thus invited to save society. As a Genevese, Neckar promoted economy; as a banker, he was skilful in promoting loans; as master of the finances, he overshadowed Maurepas and made the ministry seem his own. In quiet times he would have given France a balanced budget with an honest and competent administration and a system of provincial assemblies supervised by the Council, thus avoiding the interference of the *parlements*. Unhappily, however, foreign policy frustrated his designs as it had frustrated those of Colbert.

Necker and Vergennes

Seldom, indeed, in her history has the foreign policy of France reposed in hands more expert than those of her Foreign Minister, Vergennes. He had surveyed Europe from points as distant as Constantinople and Stockholm, where he inspired Gustavus' *coup d'état* of 1772. Convinced that the Peace of Paris had pronounced the doom of the British empire in America, since the Colonies no longer needed Britain for defence and disliked her commercial tyranny, he had watched for the moment when France might safely strike. Choiseul had accumulated reports on the resources of the future insurgents and on the most effective means of lending them French aid. Choiseul, moreover, had begun to build up a new French fleet. Vergennes continued his work, but determined to make sure of that Spanish co-operation which, in the Seven Years War, had been withheld until too late. His agents in America fomented insurrection. One motive for declaring American independence was that those who were otherwise mere rebels might thus qualify for the French alliance. In 1776, Vergennes prevailed against Turgot, and France decided to move cautiously towards war. Spain was approached, and the versatile dramatist Beaumarchais secretly conveyed to the Americans money, arms and munitions from the French and Spanish kings.

1777

When the year 1777 began, the shrewd Franklin appeared in France as the apostle of liberty and hope. The French gladly sent Lafayette and other volunteers, but Vergennes stood firm against open intervention except in partnership with Spain. When Burgoyne capitulated at Saratoga (October), however, he could no longer restrain the nation.

1778 In February 1778, France, recognizing the United States as independent, signed with them a commercial treaty. She further agreed that, if Britain resented this step by declaring war, the two nations should make war and peace in common, and that having achieved their ends they should mutually guarantee their possessions in North America. The Brest and Toulon fleets were immediately prepared for action, and, at a time when Britain must strain every nerve to wage war across the ocean, the latter sailed for America (April). France thus supplied the cordial needed to revive the hopes of the insurgents after a winter in which Washington's army had dwindled to some 3,000 effective men. Chatham's last speech demanded that Britain should take up the gage which her ancient foe had thus flung down. War was declared in May, and next month the Brest fleet proved that it could brave the enemy in almost equal force. The world-question, France or Britain ? had thus been put once more to the test of arms. With American assistance, the verdict of the Seven Years War might be reversed.

Franco-British War

At the same moment the question, Austria or Prussia ? was for the fourth time being put to the test of arms. On July 5, 1778, thirty-seven years after Mollwitz, Frederick marched into Bohemia at the head of more than 100,000 men. Joseph awaited him beyond the Elbe. With Russia and France the long-standing allies of the respective combatants, with a great maritime struggle in progress, with the connexion between Britain and Hanover still subsisting, Poland deeply hurt, Gustavus III adventurous, the Turks embroiled with Russia in the Crimea—with all this Europe might well be on the verge of a conflict greater than the Seven Years War.

THE AUSTRO-PRUSSIAN WAR OF 1778–9

The outbreak must be ascribed to one power—Austria, and within Austria to two persons only, Joseph and Kaunitz. Austria, as her acquisition of Galicia and the Bukovina had lately proved, was prepared to extend her frontiers without regard to physical barriers or to race. Almost surrounded by regions weakly held by Poland, Germany, Italy and the Turkish empire, she was constantly tempted to expand. Venice, projecting into her dominions on the south-west, like

Moldavia and Wallachia which flanked them upon the east, afforded a peculiar temptation. But the Habsburgs themselves, their Imperial throne and the dominant culture within the state were all German, and Germany attracted them the most. To regain Silesia or to incorporate Bavaria, the Queen would have sacrificed everything save honour, while her son and Kaunitz were realists whom her pious prejudices could not deter. At the close of 1777, a golden opportunity of expansion in Bavaria seemed to have arisen. The Elector then died; his line became extinct; and the Electoral dignity, a creation of the Thirty Years War (1623), came to an end. His remote cousin and heir, the Elector Palatine, was old and had no children born in wedlock. The Austrians, who could produce faint claims to portions of Bavaria, had been secretly but actively negotiating with him for recognition of these titles, which they interpreted as holding good for most of Lower (or Central) Bavaria. In return for this great aggrandizement they offered to provide for the Elector's bastard children. Frederick, whom few intrigues escaped, looked on so long as the Bavarian remained alive.

The news of the Elector's death reached Vienna on 1778
January 1 and Berlin two days later. On January 3 the Austrian terms, accepted by his representative, were sent to the Elector Palatine for ratification. The same night saw Frederick's emissary on his way to incite a collateral heir, the Duke of Zweibrücken, to resist, with the assurance that Prussia would make war rather than permit Bavarian partition. On January 14, the Elector Palatine ratified the treaty, breaking thereby a pragmatic sanction of his own. Even the pacific Queen thought that the game was won, and on January 16, 10,000 Austrian troops marched into her new province. On the same day, the Duke of Zweibrücken, supported by Frederick, appealed to the Imperial diet. German feeling and especially Bavarian feeling ran strongly against Austria, the more so that it was not a true-born German but a mere Lorrainer who dared to despoil the German heir and to partition a German duchy. The Catholic Bavarians, it was said, ceased to call on "Jesus, Mary, Joseph," and cried for aid to "Jesus, Mary, Frederick."

The breathless fortnight of action, January 3–16, was followed by five months of many-sided negotiation. Neither

Austria nor Prussia, however, would give way, though their rulers were not eager for a costly and toilsome war. Frederick, "as an old soldier, with probity and frankness," informed Joseph that by the treaty of Hubertusburg he had sanctioned the Peace of Westphalia anew, and therefore stood pledged to prevent an Emperor from disposing of Imperial fiefs at will. Joseph detected behind this pose the Prussian interests which, as Frederick confessed to Prince Henry, were his real care, and thought that Prussia would not incur the cost of battle. His mother, when the campaign had begun, brought herself for the first time to address "the evil man," asking him why he and she should tear the locks which age had whitened. Maria Theresa, indeed, negotiated behind Joseph's back as Prince Henry earlier behind Frederick's. Given a determined King and Emperor, however, the extent of the struggle turned on their allies. Catherine and Vergennes could veto or decree a new world war.

Attitude of Russia and France

Catherine had nothing to gain by assisting Frederick to overthrow the Habsburgs, on whose co-operation she counted in future dealings with the Turk. To hire out Russian troops as a Prince of Hesse hired out Germans was impolitic and beneath the dignity of an Empress. She had refused the urgent entreaty of Britain to send 20,000 men against the American rebels, and since that time she had become embroiled in the Crimea. She therefore resorted to dissuasion and delay. Towards the Austrian ally of France, Vergennes, a diplomatist of the old school, felt cooler still. All the Netherlands, he had declared to Louis XVI, would not compensate the nation for the smallest aggrandizement of the Habsburgs. To help them in Bavaria would be to dismember a most faithful ally of France, and to bring an aggressive German great power nearer to the Rhine. Participation in a continental war, moreover, would repeat the impolicy of 1756, and once more profit Britain. France, it was easy to argue, had guaranteed the Austria of 1756, not the aggrandized Austria of January 14, 1778. Marie Antoinette was impotent to move France against Prussia. To salve the wound, Vergennes promised a secret subsidy and protection for the Netherlands in case of need. The Austrian and Prussian armies therefore met in Bohemia without the distraction of a wider European war. Of secondary powers Saxony alone took part in their struggle.

The Elector, remembering the fate of his predecessor, and being himself interested in the Bavarian Succession, joined Frederick with some 20,000 men. The forces on both sides were larger than in the Seven Years War, but the campaign proved a fiasco. Frederick designed to seek a decision in Moravia, but he never reached that province. Although Prince Henry gained a strategic advantage in Bohemia by a fine crossing of the Lusatian mountains, he failed to press it home and the Austrians manœuvred too cautiously for either King or Prince to risk a battle. After spending two futile months in a corner of Bohemia, the Prussians had exhausted their supplies, and must retreat. The abortive operations had cost them some 25,000 men, but graver still was the loss of prestige which both King and army had sustained. For the victors of Rossbach and Leuthen to wage a " Potato War " was a damaging defeat of Prussia. Even among the generals voices ascribing to despotism the decay of discipline and of initiative were heard, while Prince Henry dared to say that he feared his brother's treachery more than the Austrian arms.

The Campaign of 1778

As in former days, Frederick strove to make good by diplomacy an adverse turn in war. He welcomed French mediation, insisted that Russia should participate, and drafted terms which Austria could readily accept. At the same time Catherine, whose Turkish difficulties were ending, called upon Austria to desist from violating the Imperial constitution. Joseph was obstinate, but the Queen was bent on peace, and peace was signed at Teschen on her birthday (May 13, 1779). Its terms did credit to the diplomacy of the six powers which had shared in the preceding congress. The Bavarian Succession passed to the Elector Palatine and his heir, but Bavaria gave both Saxony and Austria an appreciable compensation. Saxony received £600,000, and avoided any compulsory arrangement which would have transferred to Frederick the coveted Lusatia. Austria advanced her frontier to the river Inn, thus safeguarding Vienna and improving her communications with the Tyrol. France and Russia guaranteed the settlement, and, since it was expressly based on the peace of Westphalia, that fundamental pact of Germany and Europe was now placed under Russian supervision. Perhaps the chief result of the Austro-Prussian war was that the power which already dominated Poland and

The Peace of Teschen, 1779

Turkey had taken a long step towards future domination over Germany. If Austria, moreover, had no great reason for dissatisfaction with the war and peace, Joseph himself had received a severe rebuff. His natural course was to turn to fresh projects within and without the Empire and to seek the alliance of the other moving spirit in Europe, Catherine II. The death of his mother (1780) vastly increased his authority, and therefore qualified him still further to become the Empress's ally. The peace of Teschen was avenged by the Russo-Austrian alliance of 1781.

EUROPE, BRITAIN, AND THE AMERICAN WAR, 1779–83

Vergennes, in the meantime, had been reaping the harvest which he had skilfully sown during the affair of the Bavarian Succession. The peace of Teschen left France and America to fight undisturbed against Britain, and in the same year they were joined by Spain. The French party in Holland was already helping the Colonists underhand, like France before her treaty. The French navy, moreover, did credit to Choiseul, to Sartine, and to the nation. Gibraltar was besieged, two West Indian islands taken, and the French and Spanish flags flaunted in the Channel without disaster. Though Senegal was taken, it seemed that the British fleet, like the Prussian army, had lost its sting.

The least hint of British naval weakness sufficed to rouse disgusted neutrals against British tyranny by sea. Neutrality, under which a power claims to maintain friendly intercourse with both the parties to a quarrel, must always be an awkward and artificial relationship, as every great war proves anew. Its basis is a profession of inability to discern the justice of a cause for which the combatants are staking their existence. If the fact of neutrality be admitted by the combatants, the neutral must admit that his right to trade with them cannot override theirs to fight unimpeded by his interference. The limits of his right to trade, moreover, have never been generally agreed on. Powers weak by sea naturally claim that they should be very wide, while the strong narrow them down, and uphold their view by force. As a belligerent, Britain, being by far the strongest naval power, had given offence on all sides. Many classes of goods she prohibited as contraband,

and searched for them in neutral ships, compelling these to turn aside to her ports for inspection. The ports of her enemy she declared to be blockaded and confiscated ships and goods for breaches of her rules. Worst of all, she licensed privateers to exercise her jurisdiction, and to pay themselves by confiscating ships and goods with the sanction of her prize-courts. Neutrals, whose views as to the law were entirely different from hers, were compelled to submit. Their consolation must be that, as Britain captured many enemy trading vessels and turned her own merchantmen into warships, shipping became scarce and brought in extraordinary profits. In 1780, however, Catherine proclaimed principles of maritime law of which the strict observance would form a serious check upon British operations. Denmark, Sweden, Holland, Prussia, Austria, Naples and Portugal—almost every important state save those at war with Britain—joined Russia in an Armed Neutrality to defend their neutral rights.

The Armed Neutrality of 1780

The Armed Neutrality of 1780 formed a landmark both in the American and European war and in the attempt of the Family of Nations to provide itself with an enlightened legal code. As it amounted to a declaration that the Neutrals would vindicate by force rights which injured France far less than Britain, it was sincerely welcomed by the French. At the same time it gave Britain an excuse for war with Holland which might compensate her for her costs elsewhere. The British paid respect to the new alliance not by disavowing the grounds of their action but by modifying its abuses, especially as these affected Russia. In combating international anarchy by sea the Armed Neutrality was not without importance. At least it emphasized the lack of law, and united almost all the naval powers save Britain in a declaration of the rules which they wished to establish. These owed much to the work of Martin Hübner, which appeared in 1759. Hübner upheld the right of neutrals not only to continue their ordinary trade but to extend it to markets thrown open by the war. Neutral ships, he opined, were floating portions of their country, entitled to carry the goods of the belligerents, except contraband of war. Blockades, to be binding upon them, must be "effective," that is, maintained by enough ships to make access to the blockaded port or coast a matter of great danger. The right of search applied merely to the official papers of a suspected ship. All these propositions were strenuously denied by Britain. Two years of vain negotiation preceded their proclamation by the Armed Neutrality in 1780. Their weakness arose partly from difficulties of interpretation, but chiefly from the indisposition of the powers which proclaimed them to be bound by them when their own profit was at stake. What goods were contraband? and when could a particular blockade be termed effective? These questions offered difficulties as great as that of persuading British captains to accept the evidence of a ship's papers as equal to that of their own eyes. The principles of the Armed Neutrality could be enforced only by convoy, neutral warships thus protecting merchantmen against search by the warships of their belligerent friends. Such defeat of search by convoy obviously fell little short of war. Three-quarters of a century were to pass by before the principles of 1780 were adopted by all Europe.

1780

Despite these anomalies, the collective threat to British sea power combined with the Franco-American threat to her empire made 1780 a fateful year for Europe and for the world. Was France, despite the verdicts of 1713, 1748 and 1763, to become, with the aid of the Americans and of Spain, supreme

Europe and Rebellion

throughout the Indies? In Europe, moreover, were France and Russia to collaborate at last, and, linked by the alliance of each to Austria, to rule the continent? A third question, more momentous than even these, must force itself upon men's minds. It was clear that the Americans were rebels, defying their unquestioned sovereign. It was no less clear that the foremost kings in Europe were openly assisting them or at least hampering their brother George III. Could it then be true that rebellion was not "as the sin of witchcraft," and that man could claim those "natural rights" which the Americans had declared in 1774? An age fascinated by Rousseau might well draw from the American situation conclusions which would in Europe destroy legitimacy as well as privilege. The victory of France over Britain would cost Louis and the nobles dear if it meant the victory of the French people over historic France.

Britain and the War

For the moment, at least, the prospect of a French victory over Britain seemed greater even than in 1757. In 1779, the entry of Spain into the war had produced a new attempt at invasion, with the allied fleets double the strength of the British, and 400 transports massed in the Channel ports. Mismanagement and a Protestant wind had brought the attempt to nothing, and, early in 1780, Rodney had relieved Gibraltar. But the French and Spanish fleets still kept the seas. Gibraltar was still besieged; the Irish were arming to demand Home Rule; London was for six days dominated by the rioters named after Gordon; in southern India British power was tottering; the Americans remained unsubdued. If at this pass Europe united to dictate to Britain by sea, how could British power and prestige survive?

America and Independence

The most pressing problem was still that which had produced the whole situation—that of American independence. Some historians assert that the Colonies were ripe for separation, and that if they had not risen in 1774, their claim to independence could not have been long delayed. The connexion with the Mother-country, it may be answered, possessed many advantages to both, and thought was moving towards the removal of its drawbacks. The colonial system could not long survive the *Wealth of Nations* (1776). Again it may be urged that when the first shot was fired the moral basis of the British dominion was shattered and American independence thereby rendered invincible. "America," boasted Franklin, "increases faster than you can destroy her," since more children were born to her in a year than soldiers put out of action. Whether or no British statesmanship was adequate to following up victory, as in 1901, by imposing terms which the rebels could sincerely accept—this may indeed be doubtful. It is certain that the size of the Colonies and their lack of any vital point at which to strike made conquest difficult and slow. Town after town was seized without bringing about surrender. But it appears undeniable that, despite Saratoga, three campaigns (1776–8) had brought the Colonial forces near extinction; that the thirteen Colonies were by no means at harmony among themselves; that many Colonists were loyalists at heart; that few fought from pure goodwill; and that without the exceptional personality of Washington the whole rebellion would have foundered. The French alliance at least averted collapse during 1778 and 1789, and the presence of a French fleet in North American waters divided the effort of Britain. In 1780 while the Spaniards were conquering Florida, a British invasion of the southern states proved inconclusive. Time, a hesitating neutral, swung his scythe now against one combatant, now against the other. Without the intervention of some outside factor it was difficult for Britain either to conquer the Colonies or to yield her claims, and hardly less difficult for the Colonies either to expel the British armies or to submit.

The Campaign of 1781

When stalemate threatens, a new adventure often tempts the combatants. In December 1780, Britain, the patron of the house of Orange, declared war on Holland, where the Republicans, who looked to France, were now in power. The popularity of this step, which was followed by the conquest of the Dutch West Indies, helped to avert war-weariness in Britain, and to prolong her Colonial struggle. In October 1781, however, French intervention virtually secured American emancipation. After a victory in North Carolina, Cornwallis was awaiting reinforcements at Yorktown, on the shores of the Chesapeake. For one critical moment the French had gained superiority in the North Atlantic. De Grasse entered the river with twenty-eight sail of the line: the British admirals failed to dispossess him. French reinforcements appeared, and Cornwallis, with 7,000 of the best British troops, was forced to surrender. Not inappropriately, the land force which dealt this irreparable blow was an amalgam of Washington's army with Lafayette's and other French contingents. Although the British still occupied New York, Charleston and Savannah, and although the French predominance by sea soon passed away, Yorktown was one of those victories which, coming late in a war, break the will of a weary combatant. In March 1782, the House of Commons resolved without dividing that all who should contribute to the prolongation of offensive war in America were enemies to their country. Before the year was over, peace preliminaries had been signed (November).

British Recovery

The year 1782, none the less, witnessed the salvation of Britain from the peril which had menaced her existence. In spite of the Bourbon combination, the Armed Neutrality, the Dutch war and the American rebellion, Britain single-handed recovered her preponderance by sea and saved the relics of her empire. In April, thanks to Rodney's skill, Jamaica was freed from the French and Spaniards, and De Grasse himself made prisoner. Gibraltar, in the third year of siege, defied 50 warships, with floating batteries, and 40,000 troops, and received fresh supplies from Howe. Minorca, indeed, fell to Spain, but all the exploits of Suffren could not restore the French power in India. Britain herself, moreover, had been induced or enabled by the war to effect many salutary reforms. The King's prerogative had been quietly but effectively curtailed, legitimate grievances of Catholics and of dissenting ministers redressed, and legislative independence conceded to the Protestants of Ireland. Many indecisive battles indeed had been fought with French, Spaniards and Dutch, while Britain had suffered much from Paul Jones and other American privateers. Yet the navy had been reanimated and made twice as strong as those of France and Spain combined. Above all, thanks to the triumph of the pro-Americans in Parliament, the danger of a permanent Bourbon-American combination against Britain seemed to be averted.

The Peace of Versailles, 1783

Throughout the negotiations for peace Latins and Anglo-Saxons took opposing sides, and British distrust of France thus turned to the profit of the United States. Vergennes desired to compensate Spain with part of the territory between the Alleghanies and the Mississippi. Britain had privately agreed that the river should form the boundary, and so it was. The ocean, the great river, the frontiers of Canada and Florida—these were the limits of the new republic. France lost nothing. By abandoning India, she gained the right to fortify Dunkirk. Spain acquired Minorca and Florida. From Holland, on the other hand, Britain took Negapatam and the right to trade with the Dutch East Indies. Such were the main provisions of the peace of Versailles (September 1783).

THE BANKRUPTCY OF FRANCE

From a military point of view, the policy of Vergennes had been justified by success. France once again possessed a navy: she had protected her allies: she had changed the balance in North America and the Mediterranean to her rival's disadvantage. She had, however, patronized rebellion, and she had spent 1,500,000,000 *livres* upon the war. To make American farmers independent, she had overtaxed French peasants who were far less free and prosperous than they. Worse perhaps than all else, she had sacrificed her own reformer. Necker could raise loans as easily and cheaply as any man, but war, added to the extravagance of the Queen and Court, overtaxed even Necker's strength. In 1777, he had to borrow 106 million *livres* ; in 1778, to issue four millions of annuities ; in 1779, five millions of annuities and more than 53 million by way of loan ; in 1780, 36 million by lottery ; in 1781, nine millions of annuities. Early in 1781, he defied all precedent by publishing a defence of his administration, which disclosed many of the secrets of royal finance. Publicity following on reform alienated those who profited by the abuses, and in May Necker resigned. Reaction triumphed, and all save members of the old nobility were excluded from military command.

Fall of Necker, 1781

The death of Maurepas, following the birth of a dauphin, to some degree consoled the public, but France could find no fresh Turgot or Necker to cope with the aggravated evil in finance. Two respectable but incompetent successors preceded Calonne, the nominee of the Queen's party, who lightheartedly led France towards financial ruin. Calonne's gay confidence was exhausted within three years.

Europe 1783–6

Between the treaty of Versailles and the death of Frederick (July 1786), France, and indeed Europe generally, enjoyed a period of peace which hardly any untoward incident disturbed. In Britain, Pitt strove for reform. Frederick was searching for an ally, watching Austria, foiling her schemes in Bavaria, with the aid of the German princes, but resolutely avoiding war. Catherine, dreaming of new empires, annexed the Crimea and Kuban with the goodwill of every great power save Prussia (1783). Only Joseph showed himself a disturbing force, and his own dominions were wide enough to absorb his reforming zeal. Calonne therefore could fulfil his mission to restore financial equilibrium to France without interference from beyond the frontier.

Calonne and French Finance

Unhappily for the French monarchy and nation, Calonne proved himself an agreeable sciolist, no less rash than superficial. Spend and thereby gain credit, for credit creates wealth—such was his economic creed. To spend was easy : in 1785, at a time when the Queen was suspected of fraud for the sake of a diamond necklace, the royal family bought two palaces for 24 million *livres*. To pay, Calonne could only borrow, and for a time the public, infected with the virus of John Law, lent without question. By the end of 1784, however, the rate of interest had risen to 8 per cent., and next year the *parlement* protested. In September 1786, none the less, Calonne boldly defied both tradition and the deep-seated protectionist sentiment of the French. An Eden treaty with France imitated the Methuen treaty with Portugal, and Pitt and Vergennes thereby favoured the exchange of French claret for British manufactured goods.

The Franco-British treaty was signed at the time when Calonne had been compelled to confess his failure and to advise a desperate remedy. With a revenue from taxation far exceeding that of Turgot, he had borrowed 487 million *livres* during three years of peace, and the annual deficit now approached 100 millions. To the stupefaction of the King and the indignation of the Queen and nation, he now confessed to facts which even Necker had concealed. His remedy was that which his great predecessors had advised—tax all lands, without regard to privilege, establish provincial assemblies, allow free trade in grain, abolish the *corvée*, and so forth. The first step should be to summon, as Henri IV had done, a consultative assembly. In February 1787, hard on the death of Vergennes, some 144 notables, men with much to lose by reform, assembled at Versailles. Unable to dispute unpleasant facts, they attacked persons and procedure. Calonne was driven from office; Necker, banished from Paris; Brienne, a dissolute archbishop, but a friend of Turgot and reputed able, established in place of Calonne.

The Notables

The States-general

The Brienne ministry lasted nearly sixteen months (May 1787–August 1788). It profited only Brienne himself, who contrived to fill his pockets while the treasury became empty. The opposition to reform was taken up by the *parlement*, which resisted the universal land-tax adopted by Brienne from his predecessor. This led to a struggle with the crown, and this in its turn to an alliance between the *parlement* and the people. When funds for the salaries of the civil servants were lacking, the catchword became "the States-general," and *parlement* joined in the cry. The States-general had not met since 1614, but the meaning of the call for them was clear. Since the autocracy had led France into bankruptcy, it was for the people to find new taxation, and other matters might well come within their view. There were ominous murmurs against the interference of the Queen and against the King's use of *lettres de cachet* to break down opposition. Louis desired to postpone the States-general until 1792, and meanwhile to raise fresh loans, but the nation demanded earlier action. A Cromwellian blow at the *parlement*, its supersession in politics by a so-called *Cour plenière*, merely roused the provinces to legal and illegal resistance. When a special assembly of the clergy joined with the rest, Brienne gave way, and the States-general were summoned for May 1, 1789. He himself was driven from office by the storm, and the King could only recall Necker, whom he had exiled from Paris, and summon the States-general for New Year's Day.

Necker

In Necker the King had appointed as minister the one man who was not self-seeking, and who was trusted by the people. Beyond that fact and the frenzy for the States-general the situation was obscure. Necker himself was a foreign banker forced into a position which was too great for him. "The crown" meant a shifting compound of royal wills—those of the vacillating, well-meaning King, the flighty, aristocratic Queen, whom the mob styled "Madame Deficit" or "the Austrian woman," the King's brothers, who inclined to different sides, and the greedy reactionaries by whom the Queen was surrounded. To the privileged classes the States-general signified a safe assembly in which nobles and clergy counted for two and the third estate for only one. The masses regarded them as a national council in which noble and non-noble would be equal. When it appeared that the *parlement* desired for them the composition of 1614, its popularity was irrecoverably lost. Necker, naturally but unfortunately, called in the Notables to decide, thereby delaying the States-general. The Notables decided for the precedent of 1614. Necker so far deferred to public opinion as to grant a double representation to the third estate (December), a decision which has been deemed to have begun the Revolution. By a gesture characteristic of the irresolution of the government, the question of voting by orders or by heads was left to the States-general themselves. Male taxpayers over twenty-five were set to choose electors, whose duty was to elect deputies to represent their class.

In the France of 1789, as in the Russia of 1767, the *cahiers* of the electors informed the deputies of the grievances for which they must seek redress. On May 5, 1789, the States-general assembled at Versailles.

EUROPE, 1783–9

During the six years which had passed since the close of the war with Britain, France had perforce neglected Europe to make head against her own financial troubles. Britain, under a new and milder Pitt, was likewise absorbed in her own affairs. Rejecting or at least postponing domestic reform, she established a Board of Control for India, and brought Hastings to trial, while vigorously caring for her own debt, revenue and trade. Frederick, until his death in July 1786, avoided fresh adventures, though vigilant to prevent Prussian isolation from encouraging adventures at her expense. The active powers were therefore Russia and Austria alone, with Turkey, where Prussia was less powerful than in Poland, as their natural scene of action. Catherine's annexation of the Crimea and Kuban (1783) brought her in triumph to the Black Sea. A Russian secular ambition was thereby fulfilled, and the great fortress of Sebastopol, replacing a Tartar village, became a pistol pointed at Constantinople. Russia acquired and promptly utilized the long-denied opportunity to make her southern frontier safe and to civilize a great and fertile region. Odessa, founded in 1791, symbolized a change which substituted the rule of the Empress for that of Turkish dependants harrying the Russian borders and notorious for their trade in Russian slaves. Both in the Crimea and in the Caucasus, the Sultan felt the danger, and in 1787 war broke out anew. Joseph II joined in, fulfilling the terms of his Russian alliance, and an immense conflagration threatened. With Austria the ally of Russia, and France absorbed at home, who was to prevent the accomplishment in the Near East of the Greek or any other project that Catherine might devise? From the Bug to the Dniester and thence to the Pruth and Danube seemed a route irresistibly attractive to an autocrat with a map, and with Russians on the Danube, how could Turkey in Europe be maintained? Pitt sadly confessed that Britain

The Eastern Question

would not wage war for Ochakov, the fortress near the mouth of the Dnieper which Potemkin captured in 1788. In all this Catherine was using the preoccupation of some powers and the folly of others to advance the unquestioned national interests of her people. Her associate, Joseph, had been engaged for years in pursuing a policy which has become a byword for *doctrinaire* futility. After his mother's death in 1780, only eight years passed before he found himself helpless in a sea of troubles. The unhappy Emperor-King was repulsed by the Turk from Belgrade, confronted by the hostile alliance of Britain, Prussia and the Dutch, abandoned by France in Belgium, foiled once more by Frederick in Bavaria, and in both Belgium and Hungary brought to the verge of deposition.

Joseph II

Both the foreign and the domestic policy of Joseph, indeed, roused opposition which in view of his attractive personality and lofty aims seemed amazing. Handsome, gentle, witty and generous, simple in life and manner, unceasingly laborious for his people, the Emperor could charm most of those with whom he came in contact, from the Pope and the Empress down to the Belgians, whose petitions he read by the thousand. He had a mind unprejudiced enough to meditate making the Slavonic tongue the official language of the State. Faced with the crucial question of Hungary, he at least considered every possible mode of propitiating Magyar nationalist feeling. Many of his reforms have proved their worth, and although his championship of state authority against privileged corporations involved him in defeat, it tended to modernize a sluggish and backward empire as the usual half-hearted Habsburg measures could not do. He failed through the superficiality of a quick brain, undisciplined by solid education, and through that impolitic contempt for history and natural growth which was characteristic of the age. Of all the Enlightened Despots, Joseph ranks with Struensee as the most *doctrinaire*. Complete toleration for Christians and the equality of all men before the law were forced upon races where aristocracy and Catholicism had been from time immemorial the framework of society. Maximilian I (1493–1519), whom he resembled in versatility, simplicity and charm, had meditated becoming pope: Joseph, by a hail of edicts, substituted his own for the papal authority.

Reforms of Joseph II

"Josephism" signified an Austrian national church with bishops nominated by himself, and clergy educated under his direction, a church containing far fewer convents than heretofore and less hold upon the ritual of life, saying Mass in German and awaiting Imperial permission for priests to enter wedlock. Before the Emperor's death in 1790, this system had made considerable headway, and it left permanent effects. At the same time, earlier than in Prussia and fully two generations earlier than in Russia, the Austrian serfs were emancipated and measures for their education set on foot. Army reform and a free press came side by side. The administration was centralized and made symmetrical. The Austrian dominions, like the Russian, were divided into "governments," and these into "circles" each with its "captain," a royal officer on guard against feudal tyranny. Local courts for nobles and non-nobles respectively were created, and from these, as from the captains and governors, a system of appeals led up to the King himself. For such overthrow of their cherished local institutions and for the acceptance of German as the official language, neither Belgium nor Hungary was ripe. In the words of a great Hungarian, this world was not the world of Joseph II. He wandered through it like a ghost, the ghost not of a man long dead but of one too early born, a ghost out of the future.

The Triple Alliance of 1788

Upon the course of events in France, Joseph exerted a great influence, though indirectly. His vigorous efforts to benefit his Belgian subjects provoked a revolution which spread across the frontier into Holland. There, in 1786, the "Patriots" who looked to France had wrested the command of the army from the Stadholder, William V of Orange, who looked to Britain. Next year, the new King of Prussia, Frederick William II, combined with the British to restore his sister's husband William V, and France tamely acquiesced. This acquiescence, even more than Rossbach, robbed her monarchy of its prestige at home. In 1788, Prussia, Britain and Holland united in a triple alliance to maintain the peace of Europe. On every side, the nations dared to act without regard to France.

Frederick William II and Hertzberg

Britain, Austria and Russia were now familiar factors in the European situation. Since Frederick's death in 1786, however, Prussia had greatly changed. Frederick William II,

Frederick's nephew and successor, had received no systematic training in affairs and showed little of the usual Hohenzollern force. A bulky sentimentalist of over forty, susceptible to mistresses and to the occult, he must rely upon others for the initiative, if Prussia was to have any policy worthy the name. His own preferences, of course, coloured the administration, infusing into it a personal kindliness which Frederick lacked, while a king who twice committed bigamy was notable for enforcing Christian orthodoxy upon his people. With all his weakness, he was a soldier and no spendthrift, a well-meaning and a fairly active king. For Prussia in 1786, however, something more was necessary, if a straggling country of some six million people "with nature sunk in sand and mankind in slavery" was to remain a great power. Frederick had left a treasure of £7,650,000, about two-and-one-third years' revenue of the State. But he had often lamented that when he was gathered to his fathers, Prussia, with no ally, would be powerless to parry the Emperor's intended thrusts. Besides the Prussian army, the inspiration of his own great deeds and the German League of Princes, he bequeathed to her a still more shadowy Russian alliance, a Turkish question, in which she might find her surest shield, and one trained familiar, Count Hertzberg.

Hertzberg, like Joseph II, had long looked forward to Frederick's death, since a weak successor would give him his opportunity. In spite of an association of more than thirty years with the great King, he felt perfect confidence in his own power to aggrandize the Prussian state. Although pre-eminently a master of diplomatic documents and forms, he, like Napoleon III, thought that skilful negotiations sufficed to win territory or to keep it safe. In 1756 and 1778 Prussia went to war against his judgment; while the peace of Hubertusburg and the peace of Teschen were partly of his making. In 1772, negotiation had gained West Prussia. Why should not similar strokes of statecraft bring Posen, Western Pomerania, Saxony or whatever Prussia might desire? Always the foe of Austria, he none the less stood firm against the war party at Berlin, which would have struck at her in February 1788, when Joseph joined Catherine against the Turks. Leaving the rearrangement of Turkish territory to future negotiation, he preferred the bloodless triumph in Holland, with its corollary the Triple Alliance of 1788. He thus realized the benefit for which Frederick had hoped, the redemption of Prussia from isolation through the conduct of her Imperial neighbours towards Turkey.

Sweden and Russia

At the same time a new and incalculable factor threatened to turn the scales in Europe. While Gustavus III (1771–92) disposed of Sweden none of her neighbours could feel safe. Her secular antagonism towards Denmark had not been driven out by two generations of resentment against Russia. Norway, weak and far distant from her Danish sovereign, formed a standing temptation to conquest. Her royal commander-in-chief had been absent fifteen years and half the guns were useless. In 1783 Gustavus had vainly endeavoured to persuade Catherine to countenance a sudden attack on Denmark. Five years later, when she was embroiled with the Turks, she found herself cast for the part of victim. So long as Finland remained a province of Sweden, the power whose capital was Petersburg was no less hampered than the power whose capital was Copenhagen, now that the Swedes held the further shore of the Sound. The recovery of Swedish provinces from Russia tempted Gustavus both for their own sake and for further strengthening his power at home. He had armed without rousing Catherine's suspicions, and in July 1788 he launched a seemingly irresistible attack. When the armies of Suvorov and Potemkin were on the shores of the Black Sea, how could the road from Helsingfors to Petersburg be held against the Swedes? A sea-fight off Hogland, however, proved as effective in 1788 as Tchesmé in 1770, while the Swedes themselves aided Russia by a stroke which the Turks would have abhorred. Denouncing as illegal a war which had not received the consent of the Estates, the rebel officers invited Catherine to become the protector of an autonomous state of Finland. Unable either to advance or to retreat, Gustavus was on the verge of losing his crown and perhaps his life. He was extricated by the intervention of the Danes, in whom every Swede saw the natural enemy, and by his own address. In face of the Triple Alliance, Denmark could not declare war. Under the then law of nations, however, she could fulfil her treaty obligations to Russia by attacking Gothenburg with 10,000 men. The Danish stroke saved Gustavus. With all the inspiration of his name, his office and his personality, he appealed to his people against the rebel nobles and the loathed Danes. The Dalesmen rallied to his standard; Gothenburg was saved; the Danes, expelled; and the Estates, convened for the New Year. Before the States-general assembled at Versailles, the Diet at Stockholm had abolished many of the privileges of the nobles and entrusted all initiative to the King. Gustavus, whose insight and experience showed him that the summons to the States-general would cost Louis at least his throne, and whose adventurous spirit prompted him to intervene, was left during two more campaigns to struggle with the autocrat of Russia. He emerged uncrushed, but before the Russo-Swedish peace of Verela (August 1790), the civil constitution of the clergy had been decreed in France.

To every reader of history, May 5, 1789, seems the signal for an age of boundless strife, and a great landmark in the ascent of man. To contemporary statesmen, the meeting of the States-general seemed rather an incident in the domestic difficulties of France, difficulties which blotted her out of the map of Europe and thereby simplified their tasks. On February 17, 1792, Pitt ventured to reduce the estimates, declaring that unquestionably there never was a time when we might more reasonably expect fifteen years of peace. During the first years of the Revolution, the foreground of Europe was mainly filled by the eastern struggle, which thus had no small share in determining events in France.

The Eastern War 1788–9

The campaign of 1788 closed with one of those sudden victories which render the calculations of a Hertzberg vain. For many months Ochakov, the key to the lands between the Bug and Dniester, had withstood the Russian siege. In December, Potemkin, formerly Catherine's giant paramour, and once a sergeant in the Horse-Guards, attacked it with half-savage fury. The Russian troops showed their characteristic willingness to say "It is an order" and to comply, when commanded to attempt impossibilities. Ochakov fell, and had not Gustavus moved, the Russian fleet might again have kindled a Greek rebellion. Next year, against a new Sultan, both Austria and Russia gained successes. The Austrians took Belgrade and other cities in their lost lands beyond the Danube; the Russians pressed on towards the

Dniester. Defying the Triple Alliance, the two powers extended their compact of 1781 for eight years more. Prussia, on the other hand, had now become the patron or ally of all the powers hostile to Russia—Sweden, the Poles, the Turks and Britain. Such were the groupings and preoccupations of the active powers of Europe while France was publishing the Rights of Man. According to Hertzberg's calculations, they were to lead to the aggrandizement of Prussia in return for her services in procuring peace. In 1790, however, the whole scene changed.

Europe in 1790

In February Joseph untimely died. At that moment a treaty with the Turks awaited ratification by which Prussia bound herself to coerce a Russia exhausted by two campaigns. With the Belgians and Magyars in rebellion, Austria was paralysed. Britain, indeed, was at issue with Spain about the newly-discovered Nootka Sound, and France was linked to Spain by treaty. But British goodwill and that of several other powers would have been with Prussia in the war, while Catherine could not hope for a single ally. In return for Austrian Galicia, Poland might have rounded off West Prussia by yielding Danzig and Thorn, and Turkey could hardly have refused to compensate those who saved her from the Russians. Joseph's death, however, brought to the Imperial and the Austrian thrones his brother Leopold II, a cautious reformer who had been schooled in Tuscany for five-and-twenty years. While he withdrew sufficient of his brother's innovations to restore harmony everywhere save in Belgium, he appealed to Frederick William to negotiate a moderate peace with Turkey. The transfer of Danzig and Thorn he could not sanction, but in this, as soon appeared, he was at one with Frederick William's own allies. The Prussian king gave way; the Hertzberg policy collapsed and with it the prestige of Prussia. By the treaty of Reichenbach in Silesia (July 1790), Prussia ceased to support the enemies of Austria and of Russia, while Austria agreed to restore what she had conquered from Turkey and to abolish Joseph's reforms in Belgium.

Meanwhile Suvorov, who understood his Russians perfectly and taught them that they were invincible, took the key-fortress of Ismail on the Danube. On the side of Finland, the Russians suffered a signal defeat at sea (July), but in

August both sides consented to restore the pre-war frontier. Next year, indeed, Gustavus returned to the old practice of accepting subsidies, and on those terms became Catherine's ally. But the *rapprochement* with Sweden coincided with an estrangement from Poland, where Hertzberg was endeavouring to supplant Russian influence by Prussian. Not unaffected by the example of reform in Austria and France, the most enlightened Poles drew up a programme which was designed to remedy the notorious defects of their constitution. The *liberum veto*, intolerance in religion, the right of confederation, and the immunity of the nobles from taxation were all to be abolished; the succession to Stanislas was to be vested in a Saxon dynasty with a responsible ministerial council. What Frederick had guaranteed was thus to be done away under the auspices of Frederick William.

Europe 1790–2

The treaty of Reichenbach was soon broken, for next year the Hungarian frontiers were rounded off as the price of the peace of Sistowa (August 1791). After the fall of Hertzberg, Russia, unhampered by foreign intervention, continued to conquer peace. The lands between the Bug and the Dniester rewarded her exertions. Her treaty with the Turk was signed at Jassy (January 1792). That she had to wait twenty years for Bessarabia was due to the Polish reformers and to the course of events in France. In 1792 statesmen learned that a state in revolution was not necessarily a blank space upon the map of Europe.

BIBLIOGRAPHICAL NOTE

See the Bibliographical Note at the end of Chapter I and the bibliographies to Chapters XI and XII.
Add :—

A

L. A. Atherley-Jones : *Commerce in War* (1907).
H. Belloc : *Marie Antoinette* (6th ed. 1928).
C. Bergbohm : *Die bewaffnete neutralität, 1780–1783* (1883).
D. Dakin : *Turgot and the Ancien Régime in France* (1939).
M. de Germiny : *Les brigandages maritimes de l'Angleterre* (1879).
A. Goodwin : "Calonne, the Assembly of French Notables of 1787 and the Origins of the Révolte Nobiliaire," *E.H.R.*, LXI (1946), pp. 202–34, 329–77.
O. G. de Heidenstam : *La fin d'une dynastie, 1774–1818* (1911).
P. Jolly : *Calonne* (1949).
P. Jolly : *Necker* (1947).
S. K. Padover : *The Revolutionary Emperor : Joseph II* (2nd ed. 1938).
J. H. Rose : *Life of William Pitt* (1923).
H. W. V. Temperley : *Frederick the Great and Kaiser Joseph* (1915).

CHAPTER XV

THE REVOLUTION AND EUROPE, 1789–92

ON May 5, 1789, the States-general met at Versailles. France, which had not experienced a Joseph II, a Peter, or a Sergeant King, was still in many ways a synthesis of feudal provinces. Her national consciousness, none the less, was keen, and the nation was now united by a general desire for liberty and a great hope of regeneration. Save by the King and a few about him, the fifth of May was recognized forthwith as an outstanding landmark in French history. As the years passed, it came to be regarded as no less a landmark in the history of mankind. Although America was emancipated and the eastern question continued to loom large, it was the French capital that for full ten years seemed to sway human destiny. Posterity, therefore, follows with unfailing interest the events in France, almost from day to day.

The States-general

The name and the form of French States-general were old: the spirit and composition of the assembly were entirely new. Between 1614 and 1789, a new nation had been born, and its representatives had been summoned to repair the failure of its rulers to give it appropriate institutions. Impatient of history and avid of Philosophy, the ninety-eight non-noble Frenchmen in every hundred had no desire to perpetuate the predominance of the remaining two. Of the 1,214 members, slightly more than one-half represented the Third Estate. In the absence of thirty noble Bretons, the First Estate, with 308 members, outnumbered the Second, and of these 308 two-thirds were ill-paid parish priests who hated the privileges of the nobles. The "nation" therefore could count on a majority of two to one in Estates and, if the voting went by heads, of rather more. It was significant that lawyers, a class trained to controversial tenacity, formed more than one-half of the representatives of the Third Estate.

The *cahiers*

The 1,214 members, however, were deputies bound by solemn oaths to make known the grievances of the electors, and to follow the instructions recorded in the *cahiers* which the electors had drawn up. Since Louis and Necker had refrained from influencing these instructions, while the reformers issued standard forms, the *cahiers* comprised certain opinions which were sufficiently widespread to be regarded as those of the nation. Louis XVI had shown a sincere desire for reform, and from time immemorial the growth of the monarchy in strength had formed the criterion of French well-being. The republics of the Old World—Poland, the Swiss, Venice, Genoa—stood for ineptitude and decay: in the New, Washington was now first taking up the burden of office. Religion, good taste, and caution alike forbade any questioning of the royal title. The 24,000,000 inhabitants of France, through the 600,000 who had the right of voting, seemed unanimous for the continued rule of the House of Bourbon. The sufferings of France and the example of Britain, however, argued for a limited or constitutional monarchy, and this many of the *cahiers* demanded. Outside the monarchy, there was hardly an institution that the *cahiers*, at least those of the Third Estate, were not prepared to abolish or to reform. Everywhere privilege stood indicted, in the manors, in the army, in taxation, in judicature, in the civil service and in the Church. To cure the deficit, they advised direct taxation; to cope with the debt, the sale of the crown domains. Nobles and clergy alike, it appeared, would renounce their immunity from taxation, but both these Estates, and especially the latter, stood by their other privileges. In 1789, the French Church desired a monopoly of public worship, of education and even of civil rights. When "a new assembly of untrained men was set between a weak, discredited and bankrupt government and a people rapidly passing beyond control," it remained to be seen whither such ideas would lead them.

French Political Theorists

Unhappily for France and for mankind, the men of 1789 were not merely untrained but deluded, deluded by the most eminent French writings of the age. By the side of Montesquieu and Rousseau, the upheaval set Sieyès, the ex-priest "whose scheme of things found no place for the Church and no place for God," as a perennial fountain of ideas and guidance. Montesquieu had warned the thinking aristocracy that—

> "When the legislative power is joined with the executive power in the same person or magisterial body, there is no liberty, since it is to be feared that the same monarch or the same senate may make tyrannical laws to carry them into effect tyrannically. . . . The executive power should take part in legislation by its right to prevent the execution of laws, without which it would soon be despoiled of its prerogatives. . . . It should not take part in debating business."

In contrast to such refinement Sieyès, as sweeping and persuasive as Rousseau, who had taught that the people is infallible, put his rhetorical questions to a public far wider than that which welcomed the *Esprit des lois*.

"What is the Third Estate ?" asked Sieyès, and answered, "Everything."

"What has it been up till now in the political order ?—Nothing."

"What does it ask ?—To be something."

He then set out briefly to determine what it remained for the Third Estate to do in order to take the place which was its right.

His words produced on the France of 1789 an effect like that of Luther's theses on the Germany of 1517. His treatises influenced the elections and opened a political future for Sieyès himself when the States-general met.

Evolution of the National Assembly

In May 1789, twelve hundred deputies, for the most part mutually unknown, met at Versailles, in the neighbourhood of the King and Court. Were they, as the name States-general implied, three feudal assemblies summoned to draft petitions to the King, or were they, as the spirit of the age dictated, one national assembly destined to set France free ? The crown declined to give any effective guidance. Necker produced an uncandid balance-sheet, with suggestions that proved him to be no statesman. The King greeted the Estates with the etiquette of 1614, but left them to determine their own procedure. From the very morrow of their meeting, the Third Estate, leavened by its lawyers, demanded that all the Orders should sit together, and showed that they regarded themselves as speaking for the nation. The principle of joint session was disputed for six weeks, while day by day in eager talk the Third Estate developed its corporate consciousness, and leaders rose from among the mass. By June 17, when the first revolutionary step was taken, Mirabeau, a noble from the south, towered head and shoulders above his fellow-representatives of the Third Estate. An adventurer now forty years of age, of which years three were spent in prison for abduction, Mirabeau was at war with his father, and therefore with his father's caste and with the whole *ancien régime.* Reckless, warm-hearted and unscrupulous, repelling and fascinating by turns, he forced all the deputies to attend to him by surpassing all in bodily and mental stature. A French equivalent of Bolingbroke, Chatham and Wilkes compounded into one, he dominated by his oratory a race moved by oratory since the time of Cæsar. Aristocrat, traveller and student of human nature, he, far more than *doctrinaires* like Sieyès or even than Lafayette, was capable of distinguishing sense from nonsense and of changing for the better the worn-out régime of France.

Mirabeau

Revolution in June 1789

On June 17, guided by Sieyès, the Third Estate overcame the obstructive tactics of the other two by a formal breach with the old States-general. Its own members, with other deputies who cared to join them, declared themselves the National Assembly of France. Reason and justice, in a word, were to override tradition. Pressing the Revolution further, they decreed that no taxes which lacked their sanction should be levied after they had ceased to sit. The King's slow preparations to recall the States-general to their duty caused the Third Estate, which had taken refuge in the tennis-court, to swear that they would not break their ranks until the constitution had been solidly established (June 20). On June 22 the majority of the clergy and a few nobles rallied to their side. Next day the King solemnly admonished the three Estates, at the same time promising far-reaching reforms, and commanding them, each in its separate chamber, to deliberate upon others. His admonition came fifty days too late. The Third Estate had now learned to look not to the King, but to themselves, and, with Mirabeau as their spokesman, they unanimously refused to disperse. More nobles joined them, the Duke of Orleans, a descendant of Louis XIII, among the number. On Louis' birthday (June 27), at his express request, many of the remaining clergy and nobles followed, and the plan of a single assembly thus prevailed. Arthur Young declared that the revolution was complete, and the King doomed to become a mere spectator.

At this point the aristocratic party, with the Queen and Louis' brother, the Count of Artois, at its head, procured measures which could not fail to widen the breach between crown and people. On the pretext of numerous riots, including those for bread, an army of 40,000 men under the veteran De Broglie closed in on Paris. On July 11, moreover, Necker and his partisans were dismissed, and friends of the Queen established in their places. The Baron de Breteuil, a veteran diplomatist, became chief minister of France at the crisis of her fate. **Fall of Necker**

The fall of Necker flung Paris into revolution. Paris, with its 700,000 people, was vast enough to unite several cities into one. Its narrow winding streets with their lofty and overhanging houses were still the home of a teeming *bourgeois* population of which successive generations seldom quitted their own quarter from birth to death. United in parishes and in gilds, ministering to the Court and to the rich, both French and foreigners, lightly taxed and little interfered with by the officials whom the crown appointed, middle-class Paris was by no means disaffected. On the other hand, the elements of a mob such as terrorized London in the Gordon riots, or murdered Fersen at Stockholm, were swelled in Paris by thousands of ruffians from the provinces whom want or greed had driven to the capital. Workmen were there in force, students, needy men of letters soaked in Rousseau, and all these and other elements so crowded together that a catchword might swiftly kindle thousands to rash adventure. The news of Necker's fall was so manipulated as to begin a riot; this, being tolerated, grew: a bloodthirsty mob seized arms and terrorized the city: on July 14 they stormed the royal prison, the Bastille. Necker was hastily replaced in office: Artois, Broglie and others of the Queen's friends fled: the Parisians and the National Assembly fraternized, and Lafayette became commandant of a new National Guard, 48,000 strong. With Louis' sanction, Paris had thus thrown off his control and established an unpaid army of volunteers. The tricolour, compounded of the red and blue of Paris and the white of the House of Bourbon, symbolized the new liberty, and also the new **Paris in July 1789** disorder. For the example of Paris was copied throughout France: hasty improvisations replaced the ancient institutions, and savage *jacqueries* proved the decay of order. A turbulent debating society had in effect become the government of France, and Jacques Bonhomme quenched his hatred of the landlord in blood and fire. Having no experience and little constituted authority, the Assembly could not withstand gusts of popular passion and often took its orders from the Paris mob. Even in 1789, two tendencies became visible which may be termed laws of revolutionary science. Having broken with the past, the men in power for a time moved forward, "towards the Left," with ever-increasing speed, the bold thought of yesterday becoming the commonplace of to-day, and perhaps the outworn formula of tomorrow. In the France of 1789 this law worked with peculiar force. A logical race swayed by *doctrinaire* treatises laboured in an unreal atmosphere of sensibility which made no ideal seem impossible. The *ancien régime* had few practical merits to set against its theoretical and practical defects, while contact with the King and Court only revealed the well-meaning ineptitude of the one and the malevolence and treachery of the other. At the same time, the reformers were exhausting themselves by prolonged excitement and overwork, while one by one the moderates and reactionaries quitted the Assembly and perhaps the country. This leftward drift was accompanied by a phenomenon conspicuous in the revolutions of February 1848 in France and of October 1917 in Russia. While the capital remained excited and irresolute, a determined minority, however small, could bend it to their will, and through the capital the nation.

The Constituent

From the moment at which it was resolved that all three Orders should sit together in perfect equality (June 23), the National Assembly had before it the duty of devising a new constitution. When this work was completed, it styled itself the National Constituent Assembly, a title by which posterity knows it throughout its course. On July 6, the "Constituent" appointed a committee to advise it about procedure, and until September 3, 1791, when the constitution was enacted, constitution-making formed its chief task. In the meantime France enjoyed external peace. The Belgian democrats actually proclaimed a republic, but the provinces returned to their allegiance without a struggle and without affecting France.

From the first, however, a not unlikely difference of outlook appeared between the Constituent and the nation. In modern parlance, the people stood far to the leftward of the politicians. While these were absorbed in such problems as that of the division of powers, the plain man cared chiefly for his calling and for his pocket, and demanded social and economic betterment without delay. While the Constituent struggled with the theory of the Rights of Man, the peasants in the north withheld their rents and labour-dues. In the south their brethren slaughtered nobles and sent *châteaux* up in flames. On the night of August 4, the reaction of the Constituent to these tidings threw a strong light upon the mood and competence of those who were seeking to regenerate the nation. Nobles and clergy led the way in proposing the abolition of privilege; towns and provinces rivalled them in self-sacrifice. In its essentials, feudalism was abolished at a sitting. The institution of property was undermined, and thousands of proprietors beggared. By the decree of the Assembly a *Te Deum* was to be sung, a medal struck, and the title of Restorer of French Liberty bestowed upon Louis XVI.

The King none the less hesitated, as well he might, before sanctioning the sweeping decrees of the Assembly. His hesitation and the widespread suspicion that the Queen was plotting armed reaction had their effect upon the outcome of the following debates. Declaring that France had co-operated in securing liberty for America and was now learning from her how to preserve her own, the Constituent proclaimed the Rights of Man and of Citizens as a preliminary to the forthcoming constitution. On November 3, 1789, in the presence of the Supreme Being and under His auspices, "the natural inalienable and sacred rights of man" were proclaimed to the government and people of France and of all other nations.

The Rights of Man

"Men," ran the foremost article, "are born and remain free and equal in rights." These rights, which every political association should preserve, were defined as being liberty, property, security and the right to resist oppression. Sovereignty, it was explained, can have no other source than the nation. Liberty consists in the power to do anything that does not harm another. Its limits can be determined only by the law. The law cannot forbid acts which do not harm society. It is the expression of the general will. All citizens share in making it: all are equal before it. All therefore are equally admissible to every dignity and public service, as talent and virtue may decide.

No man may resist the law, but none may be indicted or detained save as the law prescribes. Those who solicit or resort to arbitrary orders must be punished. Since every man is presumed innocent until he is declared guilty, all violence against him, save such as is necessary to secure his person, must be severely repressed by law. "No one may be disturbed for his opinions, even for those about religion, if their expression does not trouble public order established by law."

Every citizen may freely speak, write and print his thoughts and opinions, but is answerable to the law if he should abuse this freedom.

The public forces are necessary to secure the rights of man. To maintain them and the administration there must be a common contribution. This is to be levied equally upon all according to their power to pay. All may pronounce upon the levy at every stage. Every public servant must give account when called on.

"A society has no constitution," so runs the sixteenth article, "if rights are not guaranteed nor powers separated." The seventeenth and last declares that—

> "As the right of property is sacred and inviolable, no man may be deprived of it save by evident public necessity, lawfully determined, and on condition that a just indemnity has been paid."

Such was the "single page of print, not the work of superior minds" which yet, in Acton's judgment, "outweighs libraries and is stronger than all the armies of Napoleon." A hurried and half-hearted creed, it is better than some of the criticisms levelled against it. Those who objected that the Duties of Man should rather have been proclaimed, were doctrinaires, not propagandists. Sermons are seldom war cries. The Assembly showed practical wisdom in emphasizing at the outset the supremacy of law. The Declaration, indeed, is vague with regard to citizens who object to the levying or disposal of taxes. A moment's reflection upon previous French taxation, however, will sweep away all doubt of the immense advance now made. The concluding article may seem bourgeois to the contemporaries of the Russian revolution. The Constituent retained God, the King and the landowner, the family with its Roman paternal power, and the right of the individual to amass wealth. Locke, indeed, had taught them that property was older than society, while Sieyès, who once styled it "the God of all legislation," had learned how lack of it can be oppressive. The Declaration, however, did not secure equality of sacrifice by graduating taxation, nor equality of opportunity through education. As a creed, it lacked the vision and grasp of principle which could make it a perennial source of inspiration. But as a demonstration in favour of the unprivileged, its sincerity and its strength were unmistakable. The Rights of Man might be ill formulated, but France told the world that man had rights. Her own conduct best explained her ideas. Although a property qualification for voters and deputies was soon established, while manhood suffrage had sixty years to wait, with the assertion that men were born free and equal the lawfulness of serfdom vanished. Meanwhile freedom of worship, of the press and of the person were secured and punishments made more humane. The old *régime* was over.

The Constitution

As the framework of the Constitution, it was resolved that the new legislature should consist of a single chamber, and that the King should have no absolute veto upon its decisions. Two successive legislatures, with an interval of four years between their votes, could make laws without regard to any other body. While the Constituent at Versailles spent August and September in debating the Constitution, the absence of any effective government favoured violence of every kind. Riots continued both in Paris and in the provinces, and Orleans intrigued on all sides in the hope of becoming king. His residence, the Palais-Royal, had long been a focus of debauchery, advanced thought and criminal conspiracy. Thanks to his machinations, on October 5 a mob of women, accompanied by many men, marched to Versailles in quest of food and attempted to assassinate the Queen. Lafayette and his National Guard saved the Court, but the cry of "the King to Paris" proved irresistible. Louis, a virtual prisoner, migrated to the Tuileries, and the Constituent followed. While Orleans, suspected but not convicted, accepted a mission to England, a new emigration carried off many of the moderate deputies. With dearth and disorder certain, since the old government was destroyed and the Constituent palpably ineffective, the outlook for the winter months grew dark. The Court began to meditate an appeal to foreign force, but the King remained sincerely anxious to co-operate with the Assembly. So long as she upheld the Bourbon monarchy and the Catholic Church, France could regard herself as engaged in reform, drastic indeed, but stopping short of revolution.

Mirabeau and the Jacobins

At this point, while the depleted Constituent toiled on in Paris, two new forces intervened. Mirabeau, the outstanding figure in the Assembly but never its master, felt himself impelled to save the crown. He had vainly advised Louis to find safety in flight. On November 7 he was precluded from entering the King's service by a decree of the Constituent that no deputy might become a minister. He therefore became the secret mentor of the Court. His debts of more than 200,000 *livres* were paid, and he received a monthly allowance of 6,000, but his paymasters always viewed him with distrust. Although, like the elder Pitt, he could do anything with the Assembly except command their votes, his unrivalled abilities, knowledge and inspiration qualified him to be the hope of the monarchy, perhaps its last. On the other hand, a new influence was rising, that of a club of Breton deputies which met in the convent of the Jacobins. The "Jacobins" added many democrats to their numbers, and had affiliations in the provinces. Their great importance, however, lay in the future, while Mirabeau profoundly influenced current constructive work. Before the year closed, a symmetrical system of local government had been devised. In every town, borough, parish or rural communalty, an elective municipality invested with wide powers was to be set up. The electors, to the number of nearly 4,300,000, were taxpaying males of twenty-five years and upwards; while the elected must be men of substance. The communes thus created numbered some 44,000, and the communists of later days aimed at making them almost

New Local Administration

independent units in a national federation. The unity of France was emphasized, however, by the creation of eighty-three departments, named, save in the case of Paris, from the rivers, mountains, capes or lagoons which they comprised. Although almost every department lay wholly within the bounds of an ancient province, the nation now put itself into the place which such historic states as Brittany and Alsace had formerly possessed. A further consequence of the reform was that nearly three in every hundred Frenchmen became government officials. The characteristic French weakness for posts, however ill-paid, in the civil service was thus encouraged.

Progress in 1790

In 1790, the work of reconstruction went on without a break. The *parlements* and the judicial rights of the nobles had vanished, and punishments became milder, as Beccaria had advised. The new system of law-courts corresponded with the new divisions of the State. From the justice of the peace in the commune to the *Cour de cassation*, or court of appeal in Paris, an ascending series of tribunals was set up. Judges became elective, and in criminal cases a jury was to be employed. The army remained a royal force, but all titles of nobility and badges of rank were abolished. The question whether France should or should not support Spain against Britain in the dispute about Nootka Sound led to an important change in the King's position. Henceforward he was to be " King of the French," not " King of France," a national official, not the owner of the realm. He remained the directing head of French foreign relations, but to declare war a decree of the Assembly was required. Of still greater moment was the civil constitution of the clergy. Having dissolved the monasteries and encroached upon the wealth of the Church, the Assembly proceeded in May to construct an ecclesiastical organization like those of local government and of the law-courts. Leaving doctrine and worship untouched, they gave patronage to the electors, and limited the numbers of bishoprics and of benefices according to the supposed needs of the people. Stipends were fixed by the State, and when a bishop wished for leave of absence it was to the directory of the department that he must apply. This measure, however logical, was destined to wreck the peaceful movement of reform. King and nobles had accepted the work of the Constituent, so far as it concerned their own rights. But the civil constitution of the clergy wounded the consciences of pious Frenchmen, made the Pope an irreconcilable foe of the new *régime*, broke the union between the parish priests and the Assembly, and finally estranged the King. The anniversary of the fall of the Bastille (July 14, 1790) was celebrated by a splendid *fête* in Paris at which Talleyrand celebrated Mass on the altar of the fatherland, and Lafayette swore the magnates to be faithful to the constitution. "I, King of the French, swear to use all the power committed to me by the constitutional law of the State to uphold the constitution which I have accepted"—so ran the oath taken by the infinitely patient King. But as his religious feelings asserted themselves, he realized that the breaking-point had come.

The Flight to Varennes

In September 1790, Necker quitted France, and in April 1791, Mirabeau died. Louis, more than ever isolated, was prevented by the mob from spending Easter at his palace of St. Cloud, within two miles of Paris. Mirabeau had long urged him to regain his liberty by quitting the capital. On June 20, he fled in disguise by night, but was arrested at Varennes, a small town in the Argonne, when seven-eighths of the journey had been performed. Louis returned to the Tuileries as a recaptured prisoner, and the Jacobins and Orleanists declared that he had forfeited his crown. Provincial France, however, was still strongly royalist, while to the Constituent the King remained the keystone of their long-laboured constitution. Monarchy, therefore, dragged on, but Jacobin opinion inevitably gained ground and Robespierre's influence increased.

The most serious outcome of the flight to Varennes, however, consisted in the suspicion that it denoted an appeal to foreign powers. Coblenz, the *Confluentes*, where the Moselle joins the Rhine, was at this time the scene of a shadow court of France, with the King's brothers as regents and Calonne as premier. Among the Queen's brothers were the Emperor, who had lately suppressed the Belgian revolution, and the powerfully placed Elector of Cologne. Gustavus III longed to be the saviour of the monarch and of monarchy: Frederick William II was not unwilling to do in France what he had done in Holland. Spain and Naples had Bourbon sovereigns,

Foreign Powers and French Monarchy

and the King of Sardinia, whose daughter Louis' brother the later Charles X had married, took the same side. Cautious as was the Emperor Leopold, he could not but feel that the French were handling a kindred dynasty on principles that would make every dynasty insecure. Early in July, from Padua, he invited the powers to demand the liberty of the French King and, failing compliance, to take up arms. France scorned the threat, and Leopold, having made peace with the Turks, drew closer to the King of Prussia. At Pillnitz, near Dresden, the two German monarchs declared that restoration in France was the concern of Europe, and that if the other powers would join them they would intervene. Their declaration was not designed as a menace to the French, for they knew that Russia was unlikely to co-operate, and that Britain was bent on non-interference. It was accompanied by condemnation of the actual "aggression," the armaments by French emigrants on German soil. Its immediate result, indeed, was to raise prices on the Stock Exchange in Paris, since moneyed men regarded it as a pledge of peace. About a fortnight later (September 14) Louis accepted the new Constitution. The epoch-making character of this step was attested by the dispatch of special missions to notify foreign powers, even including so doubtfully sovereign a State as Danzig. Leopold withdrew the Declaration and the Constituent dissolved. Next day (October 1) the new Legislative Assembly came into being.

The Legislative Assembly

The body which within its year of office brought about war with Europe and shut up the King consisted of 745 inexperienced and for the most part well-meaning men. The fatal idealism of Robespierre had brought about a self-denying ordinance excluding members of the Constituent from election, and the Jacobins, exploiting the apathy of the country, had gained far more seats than their numbers warranted. Yet the *Feuillants*, or strict adherents of the Constitution, outnumbered them by nearly two to one, and behind these moderates stood the middle-class, hitherto all-powerful in the movement for reform. Youth and inspiration, however, formed the strength of the Jacobin Left, and particularly of that eloquent southern band known as the men of the Gironde. "Filled with the noblest spirit of Greece and Rome, these dreamed of making France strong and beautiful by a revival of antique virtues." Republicans, none the less, were in a clear minority within the Assembly, and probably formed a mere handful of the nation.

Difficulties of France

The raw Assembly, in which oratory was not likely to be on the side of sense, had many outstanding difficulties to encounter. In spite of all the toil of the Constituent, no one could doubt that the constitution required revision. Its defects might be less grave than those of the American federation and less palpable than those of the Second Republic, but they were conspicuous enough. An omnipotent Assembly was exposed to the dictation of the mob, while the King's Ministers were entitled neither to persuade the Legislature in person nor to issue decrees of their own. Over the municipalities the State possessed no effective control. The fine navy, uncoordinated with the new democratic system, was fast disintegrating. No other class could yet replace the gentry as officers. In Catholic France, the basis of public order was threatened by the civil constitution of the clergy, which produced disaffected and seditious non-juring priests and bishops. The King counted on foreign intervention, while the Queen frankly informed Leopold that in accepting the constitution they were merely tricking their opponents. The emigrants, disobeying both the Emperor and the King of Prussia, continued their warlike preparations. Above all, there were in every section of the Assembly men who turned to war as the remedy for ills which they felt themselves powerless to cure. The nascent war-fever was soon heightened by a constitutional crisis. In November the Assembly decreed under heavy penalties that the emigrants and the non-jurors must submit. The King vetoed these measures, as being laws. The Assembly replied that they were not laws and therefore not liable to veto. If, however, the Assembly were free to issue executive decrees, the separation of powers became an illusion and the King a shadow.

The War of 1792

Before the end of the year, France was stirred by the censures of Vienna to challenge both the emigrants and Europe. Avignon and other papal lands were declared to be incorporated in France. No redress was offered for the destruction of Imperial feudal rights within Alsace. Three armies were placed upon the frontier, and on April 20, 1792, Louis read to the Assembly a declaration of war against

Francis II, who had succeeded to his father Leopold. War with Austria meant war with Prussia also, if their recent defensive alliance were observed. Gustavus III had been struck down by an assassin, but Sardinia might be counted an enemy so far as her own security allowed. What of Britain and of Russia ?

The war of 1792, a war in which " both sides were the aggressors," arose from the conflict between the new revolutionary faith and the old historic Europe. All the miseries, self-seeking and intrigues in France should not wholly obscure the fact that the Constituent believed itself to be legislating for the human race. Followers of Rousseau, like followers of Martin Luther and of Karl Marx, honestly regarded the new doctrines as self-evidently true and the war as a crusade on behalf of natural right and reason. That the inevitable struggle came in April 1792, however, was due to fleeting and mutually contradictory causes, backed by the national instinct to resent dictation from abroad. Some desired war to restore the King; others, to dethrone him; some, to emancipate the peoples; others, to conquer Belgium. Brissot, the Girondin leader of the ministry, calculated that Louis at war could be indicted for assisting the enemy, and that thus France might free herself from the traces of the old *régime*. The soldier, Dumouriez, one of the last of the masterful adventurers of the eighteenth century, hoped to win over Prussia and to gain the Netherlands for France.

Campaign of 1792

Although the French field-armies had lost their officers by emigration, and their discipline through the habit of debate, they attacked on the classic battle-ground of Tournai and Mons before the Prussians could arrive. The result was a fiasco which caused every foe of the new France to regard her as defenceless. Repulse, murder, and panic flight in Belgium brought down the Brissot ministry and made Dumouriez for a moment royalist minister of war. Encouraged by Lafayette, the King asserted his authority, expecting thus to regain his normal power. Assailed and insulted by the mob (June 20), however, he failed to profit by the consequent reaction and to ally himself with the moderates in the Assembly. Seven weeks later, when the threats of foreign armies had roused the revolutionaries, and the *Marseillaise* had been shouted in the capital, he had to flee to the Assembly, while in the Tuileries his Swiss guards were done to death. The fatal August 10 brought the mob-orator Danton and Robespierre into power, and Jacobins swayed the commune of Paris as they pleased. These men confined Louis in the Temple, summoned a National Convention to revise the Constitution, and procured the establishment of a supreme tribunal to try the enemies of the people. The property of emigrants was confiscated and non-jurors banished from France.

Meanwhile the army on the frontier had been divided and paralysed by the news of August 10. Brunswick and his Prussians invaded France, and on September 2 captured the key-fortress of Verdun. Only the weak lines of the Aisne and Marne lay between them and Paris. At this juncture, the Commune of Paris seized the supreme power. Danton, with his motto "Be bold, be bold, again I say, be bold, and the fatherland is saved," and his lieutenant, Marat, exploited the anticipated tidings from Verdun to make a blood-bath of suspected persons. In Paris 1,400 royalists perished, including many priests, while the provinces were urged to follow suit. The massacre was skilfully used by Robespierre to secure the election of extremists to the National Convention, a body chosen by some 6 per cent. of the French electors in defiance of the rules laid down by the Constitution. Although Robespierre carried Paris, however, less than 7 per cent. of the 782 members were the extremists who filled the higher benches of the "Mountain." The Girondins formed more than a sixth part of the Convention. Fully 600 members occupied the "Plain" or "Marsh," and for their suffrages Mountain and Girondins contended. The first act of the Convention, however, was unanimous. On September 21, 1792, France became legally a republic, and the year I began.

The French Republic

The new republic was baptized with victory, for the Prussians were unexpectedly in retreat. The strategic skill of Dumouriez and the courage with which the new levies bore the cannonade of Valmy had saved France. In a dazzling and many-sided campaign of ten weeks, the whole scene changed. One army carried the French frontiers to the crest of the Alps, conquering Savoy and Nice. Another seized Mainz, the great bulwark of the Empire upon the left bank of the Rhine. In Belgium, Dumouriez turned upon the Austrians and defeated them at Jemappes, near Mons. As a counterpart to the French flight in April, the Austrians now retreated more than a hundred miles, while the Belgians welcomed the French in Brussels. The new doctrines proved the best allies of France. The challenge to historic Europe, incarnate in its " legitimate " emperors and kings, was equally clear and comprehensive.

> "The National Convention," ran their decree of November 19, 1792, " declares in the name of the French nation that it will grant brotherhood and aid to all the peoples who shall wish to regain freedom. It charges the Executive to give the generals the necessary orders for bearing aid to these peoples and for protecting the citizens who have suffered or who might suffer for the cause of freedom."

No such protectorate over Europe had ever before been proclaimed, and until the Bolshevists declared the *bourgeoisie* incapable of organizing the collaboration of peoples no parallel arose. Holding that war is a relation of state to state, and not of individual to individual, proclaiming " war to the palace, peace to the hut," the armies of the Republic posed as liberators of the peoples among whom they came. At the same time it was to the occupied territories that they must look for pay and plunder, while the rapacious Jacobins swooped down upon Dumouriez' conquest, to fill their own pockets and the empty treasury of France. In November the Convention declared to all the world that it would grant brotherhood and succour to every people wishing to regain its freedom. In December it pronounced all nations which preserved their princes or privileged classes to be enemies of France. At the same time the Girondins were proving themselves too timid to resist the clamour of the Mountain and of the Paris Commune for the condemnation of the King. Under the Constitution, his person was inviolable, but Robespierre argued that Louis must die because the fatherland needed to live, and that the events of August 10 had sentenced him already. Doomed by an absolute majority of one in a body terrorized by a few determined men, he suffered with no less dignity than Charles I. The " Son of St. Louis, ascend into heaven " of his confessor was a viaticum of which his death was not unworthy.

Europe and the Rights of Man

Historic Europe was now confronted with an evident and appalling danger. "What is the fate of our first Charles in comparison of this!" cried a representative voice from the English people. "How dangerous it is to make concessions, or to relinquish any part of power. One thing leads to another, till the whole fabric is subverted." Europe's strongest member had declared war upon the constitution of every state, and had already shown how swiftly some states could be overthrown. The Rights of Man in 1793, like Bolshevism in 1919, constituted an explosive force of which no man could estimate the power. They made a strong appeal, it was clear, to the educated, and Holland and the west German towns seemed likely to follow Belgium in welcoming the French. Apart from the danger from propaganda, moreover, French armies on many frontiers stood ready and eager for pillage and for conquest. "We have 300,000 men in arms," confessed a French agent. "We must make them march as far as their legs will carry them, or they will return and cut our throats." How could the threatened sovereigns fail to join hands against such cut-throat hordes? Prussia, Austria and Sardinia had done this in 1792. Now Dumouriez was opening the Scheldt, and Britain, driven from her neutrality by the threat to the Low Countries and to monarchy, was about to strike. And, although Valmy had proved the worth of the royal artillery, Jemappes, that of the new levies, and the sequel, that of the revolutionary propaganda, France herself was still far from unanimous. Lafayette, commander of an army, had already left the country. The campaign of 1793 witnessed Dumouriez changing sides, *la Vendée* in revolt, all officers of noble birth cashiered, and the Girondins subjected to proscription. Could not and should not historic Europe give victory to the moderate majority in France? Historic Europe, however, was not united, and the key to her disunion lay in Russia. Catherine, the high-priestess of autocracy, was combating a revolution on her own frontier, and her victory would involve an aggrandizement which her neighbours could not behold unmoved. That revolution raged in Poland, where the progressives had made use of the chances of high politics to establish a national constitution (3 May 1791).

BIBLIOGRAPHICAL NOTE

See the Bibliographical Note at the end of Chapter I. Add :—

A

Lord Acton : *Lectures on the French Revolution* (1910).

F. A. Aulard : *Political History of the French Revolution.* 4 vols. (trans. 1910).

P. Bastid : *Sieyès* (1939).

M. Bloch : *Les Caractères originaux de l'histoire rurale française* (rev. 1952).

C. C. Brinton : *The Jacobins* (1930).

J. H. Clapham : *The Causes of the War of 1792* (1899).

J. H. Clapham : *Abbé Sieyès* (1912).

G. L. Dickinson : *Revolution and Reaction in Modern France* (1892, rev. ed. 1927).

J. Egret : *La Révolution des notables : Mounier et les monarchiens* (1950).

G. Lefebvre : *The Coming of the French Revolution* (trans. 1947).

M. B. Garrett : *The Estates General of 1789 : The Problem of Composition and Organization* (1935).

A. Goodwin : *The French Revolution* (1953).

L. Gottschalk : *Lafayette.* 4 vols. published (1935–50).

A. Mathiez : *La Révolution française, 1787–1794.* 3 vols. (1922–27 ; trans. 1928).

R. R. Palmer : *Twelve who Ruled* (1941).

A. Sorel : *L'Europe et la révolution française.* 8 vols. (1895–1904 ; 23rd ed. 1942).

J. M. Thompson : *The French Revolution* (1943).

J. M. Thompson : *Leaders of the French Revolution* (1929).

B

E. Burke : *Reflections on the French Revolution* (1791).

J. M. Thompson (ed.) : *French Revolution Documents* (1948).

Arthur Young : *Travels in France and Italy.* 2 vols. (2nd. ed. 1794).

CHAPTER XVI

THE EASTERN FACTOR IN EUROPE, 1772–93

THE four years which followed the meeting of the States-general set royalists against republicans in France, while historic Europe took up the challenge of the Revolution. But for the eastern question, the year 1793 might well have witnessed the triumph of the Powers over the regicides. But Poland, a country in sympathy with the revolution, was fated to be sacrified anew, and France escaped. To understand why Prussia turned aside at the moment when all Europe seemed to be joining in her crusade we must survey twenty years of Polish history.

Progress in Poland after the First Partition

The Partition of 1772 had left Russia unchallenged mistress of Poland, which, though mutilated, was a vast country still. Her *protégé*, Stanislas, was now the undisputed king, and her ambassador at Warsaw the unquestioned power behind the throne. With the lopping off of territories where Lutherans and Orthodox most abounded, the question of the Dissidents automatically shrank in importance. While Frederick could not but desire further acquisitions, above all Danzig and Thorn, he valued peace still more, and his energies were largely diverted to the consolidation of his recent acquisitions. Austria stood consistently for the integrity of Poland, a buffer-state between herself and Russia. It seemed, moreover, that blood-letting and lapse of time had solved the problem which from 1764 to 1772 defied solution—that of pacifying a Poland in which Russia guaranteed the constitution. Some changes, indeed, Russia had permitted or even prescribed. From 1773 onwards, a Permanent Council of thirty-six was chosen by the Diet in alternate years to advise the King. The old tyranny of the Great General and the other high officers of State was thereby done away. At the same time the Poles renewed their reforming efforts of 1764. The national revenue was notably increased, and the army, small as it was, became efficient.

After the suppression of the Jesuits in 1773, a new national system of education was introduced. "The Poles," if by the term is meant that part of the nation which counted in politics, themselves were changing. Under the new *régime* the selfish grandees who had commonly been regarded as "Poland," began to give place to new and ardent liberals, and a middle class appeared.

During the twenty years which followed the First Partition, moreover, Poland became enriched. Like France, whence at this time she eagerly received a flood of new ideas, she was naturally so fertile, spacious and prolific that, given peace, only the worst government could keep her poor. Now, the long chaos having ended, the imperative need for reconstruction aroused energies which carried Polish agriculture to a higher level than that of earlier times, and evoked a capacity for manufactures. Warsaw, expanding rapidly to a city of 100,000 people, formed a fitting emblem of this peaceful revolution. Before 1793 Poland contained the elements of a progressive European state amid the remains of feudalism.

Polish Prospects

What might have been achieved by the Poles if left to themselves almost defies conjecture. Their mud and marshes still impeded centralization, and the dynastic question remained unsolved. The success of Partition, moreover, made it almost impossible that they should never again be molested by the Powers. They had been sacrificed to ease a European tension which still survived. At bottom, Austria and Prussia remained incurably hostile. Both viewed Russia with jealous alarm, which Catherine's designs on Turkey must increase. Although the Russo-Prussian alliance was prolonged as a reality until 1780 and a Russo-Austrian alliance followed, the future for peace, and consequently for the Republic, was dark. Statesmen, among whom Hertzberg was conspicuous, talked of territorial rearrangements, and in 1786 the visionary Frederick William replaced Frederick the realist at Berlin. In August 1787, the Turks once again declared war on Russia. Austria stood by her ally, and Prussia hoped by diplomacy to secure for herself a part of Poland. In May 1788, the allies bound themselves to oppose such aggrandizement, while Catherine proposed to secure Polish support by a Russo-Polish alliance—the lifelong dream of Stanislas. At the same time Potemkin was buying vast estates in south-eastern Poland and recruiting Cossacks with a view to some independent principality of his own. For this he was willing to cede Polish lands to Prussia.

The project of a Polish alliance, if realized, would make Poland more than ever dependent upon Russia. This challenge to her ambitions provoked an immediate and startling response from Prussia. By threatening Denmark with invasion she favoured the attack on Russia which Gustavus of Sweden had actually launched (1788). She also secured the abandonment of Catherine's project and substituted for her courtship of Russia an attitude of watchful suspicion. When the thieves fell out, Poland enjoyed something like a momentary independence. Russia might need her army, while Prussia must pay in advance for the hope of acquiring Thorn and Danzig. The easiest mode of payment was to make Poland her ally.

European Alliances and Poland

In October 1788, the Diet met at Warsaw with the highest hopes. As usual, party divisions turned on Russia. While Stanislas and the "Parasites" counted on an increase of the army with Russian goodwill, the enlightened Patriots and the Die-hards looked for the abolition of the old subservience to Russia. When Prussia offered Poland her alliance and declared that the triple guarantee of 1773 did not preclude reform, the enraptured nation flung itself into her arms. Russian institutions were done away, and the withdrawal of the Russian troops demanded. Whereas in the Seven Years War Elizabeth had been free to march through Poland against the Prussians, Catherine was not to cross a corner to repulse the Turks. The statesmen at Berlin calculated that she would violate Polish soil, that the Poles would appeal to Prussia and that Polish territories would form the price of Prussian aid. They were foiled by the influence of Austria, which induced the indignant Catherine to give way. A Prussian alliance and a new Partition were talked of, but in May 1789, the Russians marched out of Poland and the Austrian alliance was renewed.

The Polish Patriots seized the opportunity to work for a strengthened and hereditary monarchy with Prussia as its ally. It was with Prussian encouragement that they began the slow process of constitutional reform. They might well hope that Prussia stood for the Triple Alliance of 1788, and that through the Triple Alliance they would enter a new League of Nations for the protection of weak states against Austria and Russia. Thanks to the crisis in France and in Austria, and to the desire of Frederick William to settle with his natural enemy the dying Emperor, Poland was in fact admitted to the Prussian alliance along with the defeated Turks. In March 1790, Prussia thus made ready to lead a coalition against the successor to Joseph II.

Death of Joseph II 1790

That successor, Leopold II, however, adopted a rational and conciliatory policy of peace, while Prussia moved uncertainly between the plans of Hertzberg and the plans of Frederick William. If Austria was to become her friend, the Poles would merely burden Prussia. Pitt laboured to avert war, and the Prussian mobilization revealed serious defects in the organization of the army. At the same time both Russia and Austria were prepared to buy off Prussia by a fresh Partition. While more than 300,000 Austrians and Prussians ranged themselves on either side of the Giant Mountains, and the Poles longed to invade Galicia, the Convention of Reichenbach reconciled the two powers, and the Turkish war ended on the basis of the *status quo ante bellum*. Within three weeks, Russia and Sweden concluded a similar agreement at Verela.

The Ochakov Question

The war between Russia and the Turks had still to be brought to an end. Both the balance of power and common fairness to Austria forbade Britain and Prussia to permit Russian aggrandizement at the peace. Catherine, on the other hand, with eight-and-twenty years of glorious rule behind her, was determined to gain Ochakov, a fortress which meant security for southern Russia and her Black Sea trade. The year 1791, therefore, began with an east European tension which was paralleled by the growing tension in the west. Should one league of states fight Russia or another the French Revolution? Prussia, without which the answer to both questions must be "No," negotiated with all parties, being ripe for adventure but uncertain what adventure might bring the greatest gains. Britain, meanwhile, had gained a diplomatic victory over Spain regarding Nootka Sound, and could not but enjoy the temporary self-extinction of France. She zealously pursued the notion of a great European league which should defend the smaller powers and Turkey against Russia. Poland, thus made secure, might replace Russia in supplying those naval stores which British sea-power needed. Thanks to most active if secret diplomacy, the spring of 1791 saw Russia threatened by Prussia and by Britain, while the new Emperor had shown himself disposed to accede to the Prussian overtures for an understanding. Catherine declined to give way before British threats of force, and Pitt appeared as the organizer of an anti-Russian coalition.

At this point, however, British public opinion intervened. The nation, as Pitt ruefully confessed, was not prepared to go to war in order that Ochakov might remain a Turkish fortress. Deserted by Britain, Prussia also yielded. In January 1792, by the peace of Jassy, the Turks surrendered Ochakov to Russia. Poland had thus been prevented from taking up arms against Russia in the company of powerful allies, while Prussian hopes of aggrandizement had been disappointed.

The Polish Constitution

The Poles meanwhile had astonished Europe by their bloodless revolution of May 3, 1791. In 1772 Sweden had availed herself of a Turkish war to throw off the yoke of Russia. Poland now followed her example. After long and largely secret discussion, King and Patriots, by a surprise vote in the Diet, carried a far-reaching plan of reform. Hereditary succession in the Saxon family, a truly national legislature, a strong executive, renunciation of privilege and of the *liberum veto*—all this dignified Poland as a power. While Poland was to remain Catholic, she proclaimed religious freedom. Frederick William was effusive. Kaunitz saw that reform would emancipate the Poles from Prussia. Leopold endeavoured to commend it to other powers. " Here is a revolution," cried the liberals of Europe outside France, " wnich is truly moderate and patriotic." The Russians gnashed their teeth but temporized until their Turkish war should end.

France and the Eastern Question

Meanwhile the mutual relations between Prussia, Austria and Russia had been altered by the course of events in France. When Louis resolved to flee from Paris, the cause of monarchy and order plainly stood in need of their united intervention. This helped the German powers towards an alliance and one that should if possible bring in Russia. Austria and Prussia included in their compact an undertaking to respect the integrity and the free constitution of Poland. They abjured the future candidature of their own princes for the Polish throne and invited Russia to accede to their convention. In August the Austro-Turkish war definitely ended with the peace of Sistova, and the Turks and Russians agreed on terms of peace. The battles in north and south had changed almost nothing, but the negotiations had effected a startling revolution. Leopold, though reluctantly, was to join Frederick William in a French crusade, while Catherine, the most vehement in denouncing the western rebels, intended at the earliest possible moment to deal with the eastern—the Poles who had thrown off her yoke. She would keep her rivals embroiled with France until she had reduced Stanislas and his subjects to obedience. As she knew full well, the new cordiality between Austria and Prussia would be short-lived.

Prospects for Poland

With regard to Poland, no written compacts could remove the fact that of the three neighbouring powers one, for her own purposes, wished well to the Revolution and two did not. Austria saw in a reformed Republic with a Saxon succession a future ally of her own, secure against Russia or Prussia and helping to safeguard Austria against either. Prussia, on the other hand, found the new Poland a bar to her acquisition of Danzig and other Polish lands and to her recovery of the Russian alliance. Russia had no mind to buy the Austrian alliance at the price of an emancipated Poland. Prussia foresaw, not without a secret satisfaction, that the situation of 1772 would in all essentials be reproduced. Russian ambitions on the Black Sea coast would compel the Emperor to accept territorial compensation, and then Prussia must follow suit. For her, this meant the further partition of Poland, and in this sense she spoke of the Second Partition on August 1, 1791. It was, therefore, not surprising that before the Austro-Prussian alliance could be signed, in February 1792, Austria must consent to reduce the proposed pledge in favour of "*the* free constitution" of Poland to a pledge in favour of "*a* free constitution." The French crusade was thus preceded by an understanding that Polish liberties were not, as Austria had intended, sacrosanct.

Catherine and Prussia

Eight days later, the tidings reached Prussia that Catherine intended to occupy Poland with a vast army and, if the allies opposed her, to offer compensation or a new partition. In October 1791, three Polish magnates had met at Jassy, invited thither by Potemkin just before his death. These men represented the natural reaction of the Die-hards against the breach made in their " liberties " by the Polish Revolution. They were prepared to form a confederation in defence of that older constitution which both Russia and Austria had guaranteed. The Russian plans were favoured by the death of Leopold II on March 1, 1792. Neither Francis II, young, honourable, stiff and mediocre, nor the ageing Kaunitz could give the Austrian factor its due weight in Europe. Prussia could and did seize unhampered the bait which Catherine offered. She was aided by the fact that in April France declared war on Austria. Prussia, whose policy had brought about the war, was confident that the indemnities which she coveted could be found on the Vistula if not beyond the Rhine. Catherine, delighted that the German forces should be removed from the east to attack her enemies in the west, organized with the Polish Die-hards the so-called Confederation of Targowicz. This purported to be the Polish nation calling in its protectress to fulfil her guarantee of its " liberties " against Revolution. In May, while the Germans marched against the French, an immense Russian army entered Poland. A fortnight earlier, with brilliant festivities, Warsaw had been celebrating the Third of May. Now the " Four Years " Diet placed the national resources at the disposal of Stanislas and closed its session.

Polish Resistance and Collapse

The Poles, of course, appealed to their Prussian ally for aid and turned also to Austria and Saxony. One month sufficed to show that they stood alone. Lacking experience, everywhere outnumbered by more than two to one, their troops could only fall back on Warsaw, fighting occasionally a rearguard action. Kosciuszko, a brigadier in the American army, proved himself a hero in the field, but from his cabinet the elderly sybarite Stanislas wrote secretly imploring Catherine for mercy. At her demand, King, government and army joined the Confederation of Targowicz, while many Patriots fled the country. Once again, Catherine found herself mistress of Poland. Austria and Prussia competed for her favour, and became separately her allies.

Possibilities of Partition

The First Partition had been brought about by the difficulty of ending a war with Turkey without compensation to Russia for her exertions and without compensation to Austria and Prussia for her aggrandizement. Austria and Prussia were now engaged in a war in which they expected to defeat France, but not to gain compensation at her expense. Austria might perhaps be rewarded in Germany, but Prussia and Russia could only look to Poland. While Austria was torn by doubts and Francis II at last decided for Alsace, Prussia drew closer to Russia and, as in 1771–2, with ever-increasing appetite. On September 20 the fate of Poland turned upon one of the most grotesque of battles—Valmy. Within six weeks the Prussian invasion of France had ended in tragic failure, and Frederick William was impelled to erase its memory by some success. His method was to declare to his ally that Prussia would fight on only if she were allowed at once to indemnify herself in Poland (October 25). If Austria consented, she was willing to join her in demanding that Russia should permit Partition. Frederick William would even countenance the Austrian occupation of a Polish province until the coveted Bavaria could be exchanged for the Austrian Netherlands. In January, Prussia had inherited Ansbach and Baireuth, while Austria demanded that in exchange for her Belgian provinces she should receive a Bavaria enlarged by these two principalities. To carry out this arrangement, the first task before the allies in 1793 would be to recover Belgium from the victorious French. Austria, harassed and uncertain, distrustful of her two allies and suspicious of the new interest shown in the Continent by Britain, negotiated as feebly as she had fought. At one and the same moment she was urging on Partition and secretly inciting Russia to restrict the Prussian share.

Danger to Russia

The military failure of the allies which began at Valmy threatened to expose not only Germany but Russia to the Revolution. Stockholm, Warsaw and Constantinople became danger-spots for Catherine. To reward those who, with such results, had bungled the military promenade to Paris seemed preposterous. But while Austria remained silent, Prussia threatened to quit the war if she were not indemnified at once in Poland. The rich Ukraine, lands stretching from the Dwina to the Dniester and linking Minsk with Ochakov —such formed an almost irresistible bait to Russia. But the eighty miles of common frontier with Austria which it involved would be by no means to Austria's liking. Early in December, therefore, the Empress resolved to arrange the Partition with Prussia. Austria was given fair words, while her allies swiftly rounded off their dominions by vast appropriations. On January 23, 1793, Russia and Prussia agreed on the Second Partition, basing their treaty on the peril of Europe from Revolution and their own expenses in contesting it. The Poland of 1792 was halved, and four-fifths of the confiscated area fell to Russia. These, it is true, were ancient Russian lands and hardly vital to Poland. Stanislas was to remain the nominal ruler of a buffer-strip stretching from Courland to Cracow and containing four or five million people. Danzig and Thorn, Posen and Gnesen, each a terrible loss to Poland, were chief among the Prussian gains. The people of Danzig alone sang the *Marseillaise* and made a vain defence of their ancient freedom. Early in April they surrendered. The rank and file of the garrison were forced into the Prussian army.

The Second Partition and Europe

The Poles, it was clear, could themselves do nothing to avert Partition. Britain, though outspoken in her condemnation, was impotent even to save Danzig, since Russia and Prussia were agreed and France on the verge of war with her. On March 25, 1793, she concluded an alliance with Russia. In Austria the shock resulted in the transfer of power to Thugut. The new minister demanded a foothold in Poland, sympathized with the Poles, and obstructed the transfer of the Prussian portion to Frederick William. These manœuvres, as might have been expected, only helped to withdraw Prussia from the war in the west in order to secure her share of Poland. Catherine, meanwhile, urged Austria to seek her compensation in France, where the only hope of conquest lay in Prussian help. For a time indeed it seemed as though the French might strike back by reviving their old alliance with the Turks, Sweden and the Poles, but in their hour of victory, they thought rather of winning Prussia to oppose Austria and Russia. Early in 1793, however, the tide of battle turned against them. In March, the

Austrians relieved Maestricht, and on the 19th Dumouriez was beaten at Neerwinden. Hating the Jacobins more than the enemy, he evacuated the Low Countries and attempted to swing his army to the anti-revolutionary side. He failed, but the French, exposed at once to invasion and to civil war, lost both desire and opportunity to oppose Partition. Robespierre was not the man to pursue an adventurous policy for such a nation as the Poles. Until August 1793, moreover, France was struggling for her own existence.

The Partition Completed 1793

Abandoned thus by all Europe to their own feeble resources, the Poles could only hope to delay their own complete subjugation by Russia. Their Diet, indeed, did little more than manifest the skill with which Catherine had made her plans. Of the seven-score deputies who met at Grodno in Lithuania, the majority, like Stanislas himself, were already sold to Russia. They debated under the control of the Russian ambassador and in the midst of Russian troops. A party of "Zealots" none the less spoke out boldly for their country, and much theatrical oratory came from less honest and determined men. The drift of the Diet of Grodno was towards frustrating the detested Frederick William by propitiating Catherine. The Russian demands were accepted; the Prussian, vehemently opposed. Catherine was therefore able to show her ally that without her aid the Poles would cede him nothing. At the same time she pleased the Poles by reducing his dishonest extra claims and by redressing their commercial grievances against Prussia. Even so, it was only *sub silentio* that the famous Dumb Session sanctioned the Prussian share in the Partition. The Poles then entered into a treaty which made their state a mere protectorate of Russia (July 1793).

BIBLIOGRAPHICAL NOTE

See the Bibliographical Note at the end of Chapter I and the bibliographies to Chapters XII and XV.

Add :-

R. N. Bain: *The Last King of Poland and his Contemporaries* (1909).

Lord Eversley: *The Partitions of Poland* (1915).

J. Fabre: *Stanislas-Auguste Poniatowski et l'Europe des lumières* (1952).

M. Gardner: *Kościusko: A Biography* (1942).

H. M. Hyde: *The Empress Catherine and Princess Dashkov* (1935).

CHAPTER XVII

FRANCE AND EUROPE, 1793–5

France in Peril 1793

THE death of Louis XVI was followed in France by eighteen months of peril, of unbridled passion, of devoted effort and of alternate failure and success. No Frenchman could predict in January 1793 that intrigues regarding Poland were destined swiftly to save the Revolution. When the campaign began, France was confronted by the armies of three great powers, with Russia inflexibly condemning regicide and sedition. Behind the invaders stood almost all Europe. The Swiss and the Scandinavians remained neutral, but Holland, Portugal and Tuscany joined the coalition, and Spain and Sardinia were in the field. More dangerous than all the secondary states was the discord within France herself. The *emigrés*, brave amateurs without an army, rather hindered than helped the Allies. The Non-jurors and Girondins, on the other hand, were to prove more deadly than the Prussians.

Conscription and *La Vendée*

In Western France the sons of the Church launched an army of the Cross against the Convention. The revolt of the Poitevins in the department of *La Vendée* coincided not only with defeat in the field and Dumouriez' treason, but also with a manifest flagging of the revolutionary effort of 1792.

> "The French people," wrote one of their constitutional historians, "has a hidden spring which works unexpectedly and restores the state when prostrate and seemingly moribund. 'Tis the mass of the nation, sober and toilsome, simple and loyal, standing aloof from party, which . . . at a bound drives off the sophists and rhetoricians and restores the glory and vigour of France" (Hélie).

Such had been the triumph of the preceding year, but now the war had become too big for anything short of general compulsory service. At the same time, disunion had begun. In February the Convention voted 300,000 men, to be enrolled by lot. In districts which regarded the Revolution with horror this demand provoked rebellion.

Such districts were numerous in the west.

"Barbarous peasants, no bourgeoisie; above the peasants, petty rustic gentlemen living almost as they did; and in the parishes well-beloved priests. It is not surprising that . . . there the Civil Constitution of the clergy had marred all . . . This monstrous Revolution, not satisfied with expelling the good priests, would ravish away 'the boys' to make them soldiers of the devil. If they must fight, they would fight the devil" (Madelin).

Revolt on the Atlantic sea-board opened the way to British invasion. Meanwhile French subjects surrendered Toulon and Corsica, while Lyons called in the foreigner and Bordeaux and Caen threatened to do the same. Class war naturally followed. Commanders of noble birth were executed and all nobly-born officers dismissed. Civil war, chaos in the finances, paper money discredited, the ports blockaded—with all this, famine threatened fertile France. When Dumouriez was defeated at Neerwinden, indeed, his army refused to join him in deserting to the Austrians. Their refusal formed the first revolutionary success of what was to prove a chequered and fateful year. It was counter-balanced in July, when the new French conquest, Mainz, surrendered to the Prussians. Five days later, Valenciennes fell to the Austrians. These fortresses, however, had been defended with a firmness which promised well for France. The Austrian bombardment and the hunger to which the Prussians trusted had been almost beyond endurance. The commandant at Mainz, before surrendering, regaled his staff with a cat garnished with a dozen mice. The loss of Mainz, Valenciennes and Condé threw France open to the land forces of the Prussians, Austrians and British, for in the field the French troops were now proving themselves inferior to their opponents. The Revolution, it seemed, had destroyed the old army and had failed to create a new. A reduced and regenerated monarchical France now represented Pitt's ideal and it seemed to be attainable by force.

French reverses 1793

The eighteen months which followed Louis' death, however, showed France and the world how simultaneous war and revolution could transform both men and nations. The Committee of Public Safety and the Reign of Terror, twin products of the national peril, are both for ever linked with the name of Robespierre. Robespierre, a provincial barrister of thirty whom the States-general brought to Versailles, was a blameless follower of Rousseau, destined in normal

Robespierre and the Terror

times to be a leading citizen of Arras but hardly more. Among the Jacobins, his high character, his talent for debate and his whole-hearted devotion to republican principles gained him influence, while the atmosphere of revolution turned him into an unqualified fanatic. At first obscure, he became the pivot upon which every internal battle seemed to turn—the Committee against the Paris Commune, moderates against extremists, atheists against believers, followers of Hébert against followers of Danton. His growing ascendancy cannot easily be explained on grounds of talent, personality, connexion, or even manipulation of the revolutionary machine. Essentially respectable and middle class, a fairly able advocate and writer, he had, like Lenin, the strength which comes from a clear and simple creed, in his case the verbal inspiration of Rousseau's *Social Contract.* No thundering Danton, he could yet compose speeches which mastered those to whom they were addressed. His tepid personality prevailed with bodies of excited men, such as the Jacobins, and with abler and firmer colleagues, such as Couthon and St. Just. He disbelieved in capital punishment and resigned a judgeship rather than violate his conscience. Yet it was he who doomed the King to death, and who was soon to prolong and widen a reign of terror which France neither needed nor approved.

A more typical revolutionary was Marat (1743–93) with his foreign origin, his wandering life, his dubious morals, his shallow versatility and his delight in violence. The publisher of *L'ami du peuple* and of many less famous journals, he declared that 260,000 aristocratic heads must fall to safeguard the revolution, and that with two hundred Italian bravoes he could conquer France. His triumph over the Girondins was swiftly followed by his own murder in July 1793.

Renaissance of France Aug.–Nov. 1793

During the earlier months of the campaign, Danton and the Committee of Public Safety had been labouring to build up a new French power. In July, Danton's place was taken by Robespierre. The next four months (August–November 1793) sufficed to transform a moribund France into a France upon the point of achieving domestic unity and international success. These months are classic in the history of revolution, and the principles which gave the Revolution victory are borrowed by revolutionists to-day. Inspired by Carnot, France taught the world what power lay in a nation whose government, unhampered by vested interests and rival corporations, could dispose of the wealth, the labour and the life of every subject. Her almost incredible resurrection, it is true, was rendered possible by the disunion between the invading powers. Prussia and Austria were severed not only by the tragedy of Poland, but also by their historic jealousy, and by divergent views about Alsace. While the Austrians hankered after Bavaria, the Prussians sought a French alliance. Yet Carnot, "the organizer of victory," who joined Robespierre's Committee of Public Safety in August, was neither a politician nor a statesman, but just what his sobriquet implies. Aided by that sense of peril which impels a nation to become a camp, he created within a year fourteen armies comprising some 1,200,000 men and supported by new fortifications. Barère's decree (August) provided for a *levée en masse* which extended to the whole nation. While men from eighteen to forty were placed at the disposal of the fighting force, the aged were to inflame their courage, and to spread hatred of kings and love of the Republic. Carnot's inspiring personality made it easy for men of the old royal army to assist him, while he himself provided and superintended sound plans for the campaign. The cruel excesses which disgraced France in the autumn were due not to Carnot but to more political members from among the Fourteen who governed France. Robespierre, the incorruptible *doctrinaire*, with his lieutenants Couthon and the young St. Just, regarded terror as a logical necessity of state; Collot d' Herbois and Billaud-Varennes, as a pleasure. Violence reached its climax in October, when Lyons fell. The Convention decreed that the name of Lyons should be erased from the roll of towns and all the houses of the rich demolished. The prisoners were shot down by seventies until thousands had been destroyed. During the same month of October, the Queen died bravely on the scaffold. The martyrdom of this Austrian princess, on an indictment which included incest with her son, horrified Vienna and turned Austrian opinion against France for many years. Twenty of the Girondin leaders were next done to death, then Philip of Orleans and many more.

Reign of Terror 1793–4

While the Terror raged, victory attended the new army, both on the foreign and on the domestic front. The Duke of York was driven from Dunkirk (September 1793), the Austrians defeated at Wattignies south of Maubeuge, and Strasburg freed from the Austro-Prussian menace. It was highly significant, moreover, that French victories were being won by young revolutionary generals such as Hoche, Jourdan and Pichegru, and by new methods adapted to the Revolution. To improvise troops capable of the elaborate manœuvres of the Seven Years War was beyond even Carnot's power. But to launch upon the enemy a mass of brave and intelligent fighters inspired by the *Marseillaise* to despise his black-powder musket-fire—this could be done, and the nation in arms became victorious. In December, the widespread revolt of *La Vendée* was quenched in blood, and barges filled with men and women roped together were sunk in the river Loire. While France was witnessing such scenes and the foul blasphemy of the Feast of Reason was polluting Notre Dame, an artillery lieutenant, Napoleon Bonaparte, regained Toulon from the English.

Reaction in France

Neither France nor any other western nation could long endure unmoved such a reign of terror as that which disgraced the year 1793. By its close, France with her vast and growing army seemed secure, and the people had abolished every shred of privilege to make her so. Peace and a milder government formed their secret aspiration, but, for all the theoretical democracy of France, they were powerless to influence the government. To proclaim democracy, indeed, the most elaborate efforts were made to break with the historic past. When the rule of the nobles was justified by right of conquest, the Third Estate invited them to go back to the day before the conquest and try again.

The New Era

With the foundation of the French Republic on September 22, 1792 (the autumn equinox), a new era had begun. The new era was now emphasized by a new calendar (October 6, 1793) which implicitly deified the Revolution. The four seasons had each three months of thirty days, three decades replacing the former weeks. At the end of the year, five supplementary days in the season of primeval feasting were dedicated to Genius, Labour, Actions, Recompenses and Opinion. The February 29 of Leap Year was replaced by a sixth supplementary day, that of the Revolution. Saints' days gave way to days of natural products and rural instruments. This propagandist insult to human habits and tender associations lasted for more than twelve years. Then France once again accepted fellowship with western nations, and the Day of Opinion of the year Thirteen was followed by January 1, 1806. Along with the revolutionary calendar the *doctrinaires* presented France with a completely democratic constitution which was approved by local votes. It was claimed, indeed, that more than 1,800,000 had voted "Yes" and less than 12,000 "No," thus condoning the violence previously offered to the Convention. The new constitution lowered the voting age to twenty-one, made the Assembly annual, allowed the voters to protest against new laws, and provided for the selection and renewal of an executive of twenty-four by a combined effort of voters and Assembly. In October, however, it was decreed that until the peace the provisional government should remain revolutionary.

Religion Restored May 1794

When the new year began, both votes and victories had convinced Robespierre that he was indispensable. He accompanied his rule of blood by an extraordinary restoration of religion. For fully five months, with all her churches closed, Paris had lived under a law which practically condemned to imprisonment or death the citizen who asked that one might be reopened. Meanwhile commissioners were spreading the worship of reason through the provinces. Robespierre at once protested against making atheism a religion. Soon he secured from the Convention a vote which, in name at least, set worship free. Early in May, he caused the vague deism of Rousseau to become the established faith in France. Dogma was comprised in a sentence, "The French people recognizes the existence of the Supreme Being and the immortality of the soul." Morality was summed up in the duties of detesting tyranny and ill-faith, punishing tyrants and traitors, succouring the unfortunate, respecting the weak, defending the oppressed, doing the others all possible good, and being unjust to no one. To every "decade" or ten-day week, Robespierre assigned a *fête*, of the human race or of some edifying idea. His supreme moment came when in a superb festival he figured as the pontiff of the new religion (June 8). Fifty days later, his own tyranny and the French victories had brought about his fall.

Kosciuszko in Poland

During the spring and summer of 1794, indeed, the foreground of history is filled by three inseparable forces—French politics, the revolutionary war and the Polish insurrection. It was Kosciuszko who gave victory to the French army and thereby procured a more moderate government for France. Before the close of 1793, the Russians reduced the Diet of Grodno to obedience, and procured a decree limiting the Polish army to 15,000 men. They then left an army of occupation, controlled by their ambassador at Warsaw, and prepared for a new struggle with the Turks. But the shameless Partition of 1793 had roused the Polish nation, indignant that while the French were overthrowing tyranny, Poland should be dismembered. As in 1768, they rejected what an "enslaved delegation" had allowed. Regiments refused to serve their new ruler. A great secret committee was formed within Poland and her lost provinces, and in April 1794 the nation suddenly rose. Kosciuszko, whose sword had helped the Americans to win Saratoga, and who had received the honorary citizenship of France, returned to Cracow. Thrusting aside the King, he appeared as the active head both of the rising and of the State. The valour of the peasants gave him victory over Catherine's veterans in the south-west. Warsaw flung out the Russians, who lost more than 4,000 killed or captured. The third capital, Vilna, joined the movement, and even Stanislas ventured to rebel. Soon, however, the partitioning powers were in line, and the prospect, save of glory, became hopeless. The Poles had the honour of repulsing the Russians from Vilna, and Frederick William himself, supervised by the Russians, from Warsaw (September). But Catherine soon sent Suvorov, with the army which had tamed the Turks, and Kosciuszko, more than thrice outnumbered, was wounded and made prisoner (October). Suvorov next stormed a suburb of Warsaw, massacring some 20,000 people, and the capital submitted (November). For a century and a quarter Kosciuszko's fall signified that "Finis Poloniae" which he did not say. In the first days of the new year, 1795, Austria and Russia agreed upon the Third Partition. Prussia gave her consent in October, and a year later the apportionment of the short-lived buffer-state among its neighbours was finally determined.

Poland aids the French Revolution 1794

If the object of the Poles had been to advance the cause of revolution, they had at least achieved it in the west. Their inopportune revival of the Polish question completed the detachment of Prussia from the common cause of Europe. Apart from the distraction of Poland, Frederick William found it hard to fight on in the west as the sincere ally of Austria. Only a special effort of the greatest of British diplomatists, Lord Malmesbury, procured a convention in April by which Prussia was to provide 62,000 men at the cost of Britain. The news which followed immediately from Poland drew every available Prussian towards the Vistula. At the same time, Thugut indicated clearly that the Austrian interests lay not in the Netherlands but in the east. Carnot therefore found no directing brain pitted against his own. In June the fall of Charleroi opened the road to Brussels, and the Austrians, hastening to regain the fortress, lost the hard-fought battle of Fleurus.

Fleurus and the Fall of Robespierre

Fleurus may rank with Rocroi, Denain and the Marne as a battle on which the destiny of France was staked. Its issue changed both the political and the strategic situation. A fortnight earlier, Robespierre had used French fears to sharpen the Terror by the law of 22 Prairial (June 10). This law empowered the Committee of Public Safety to send any member of the Convention to practically certain death. The accused would be allowed no counsel, and the jury must condemn or acquit them collectively. In seven weeks, 1,376 persons were put to death at Paris. But when the news came that the British were retreating northwards and the Austrians eastwards towards the Rhine, the troops refused to obey the Commune leaders. Within a month the Convention had freed itself and sent Robespierre and a hundred of his friends to the guillotine.

The Low Countries overrun

Meanwhile the French army reaped the rich military harvest of Fleurus. Without the protection of a mobile force the Belgian border fortresses could not hold out, and soon the French gained Antwerp. Pressing on further in a winter campaign, they were acclaimed by the republicans of Holland and conquered the whole country. French cavalry, crossing the ice, even seized the Dutch fleet off Texel. Thanks to Poland and the Rights of Man, a single campaign had extended France to her "natural frontiers" and even beyond them. After Fleurus the Austrians retreated across the Rhine, and the French seized Cologne, Bonn and Coblenz, towns on that left bank which marked the limit of Roman Gaul. Savoy and Nice were theirs, with strips beyond the Alps and Pyrenees. Geography or race, or both, might give some reason for annexations as far as the Alps and Rhine, but to justify wider extensions the French must invoke their new principles.

Prospects of French Expansion

If subjects everywhere in the world had a natural right to expel their sovereigns with French help, Paris would assume a position like that of the Turk in the sixteenth century or of Moscow under the early Bolshevist *régime*. A system hostile to that of historic Europe would be championed by armed missionaries eager to replace the existing governments by a dictatorship of their own. To meet such a danger, three courses, and no more, were possible. The first and most natural, to defeat the new enemy, whether by foreign armies or by its own dissidents with foreign help—this had already failed. Failure to win the victory, indeed, did not imply failure to limit its results. If British sea power proved overwhelming, as in some earlier wars, the Revolution might be confined to the European mainland, and hampered even there. The revolutionaries, it was clear, had damaged the discipline of their fleet and had destroyed or alienated many of its officers, while, as the event proved, Britain possessed a dozen great admirals in the making. But for some time, under the aged Lord Howe, British superiority was only slight, and his victory of June 1, 1794, did not cut off American food supplies from France. Next year the wretched fate of an emigrant invasion proved anew that the Revolution could not be destroyed in its birthplace. Signs of royalist reaction had increased. In the south, a White Terror avenged the Red. The armies of *La Vendée* had been crushed, but a guerilla warfare followed. Thus encouraged, the *emigrés* landed at Quiberon, but the Breton rebels would not co-operate heartily with Frenchmen who came in British ships. The Committee, completely victorious (June 1795), heartened themselves with the slaughter of prisoners by hundreds.

Privilege and the Rights of Man

The second course open to the sovereigns was to make revolution unattractive to their subjects, both by rousing their detestation of the French and by themselves governing well. Russia, it has been contended, was at this time impervious to revolution, because she lacked the conditions essential to its growth. Unlike pre-revolutionary France, she possessed neither a privileged and powerful nobility, nor a strong and ambitious *bourgeoisie*, nor a system of peasant proprietors. Just as in 1920 the labouring classes in states bordering on the Soviet Union refused to bring across the frontier the tyranny and misery which they believed to prevail on the other side, so in 1795 the pious Tyrolese abhorred the murderers of a Habsburg queen, and the destroyers of the Church of France. But the Revolution stood for the emancipation of the serfs, whom Kosciuszko had not dared to free, as well as for religious equality, general taxation and a host of institutions prescribed by reason and contradicted by the very being of a hundred German princes. Save in France, and in Austria so far as Joseph II had had his way, Privilege everywhere prevailed, and the privileged formed a small minority of the population. The revolutionaries therefore held a strong hand, but it would have been infinitely stronger had they not broken with the Church. The dictates of reason lost much of their attraction when men believed that to obey them led straight to hell. To denounce the French as foes to morality and religion while removing all possible abuses was a policy which promised some success.

Opportunism

A third course, and that which mediocre rulers often find most attractive, was to give the revolutionaries rope and trust to time. To assume that human nature seldom changes, and that new and violent ideas will find their level, was harder in the unhistoric, optimistic eighteenth century than among those who know more of the long ascent of man. Even in 1795, however, the fact that as conquerors Jourdan and Pichegru had surpassed Condé and Turenne could not disguise the fact that for years French politicians had been slaughtering each other by hundreds, and that the Commune and the Jacobin Club, which inspired the recent victories, had been suppressed by Sieyès and the moderates. France, it seemed not improbable, would be taught by her own sufferings to modify her unsocial attitude, and armed Revolution would cease its threats against Europe.

Increase of Toleration

The new year, 1795, afforded innumerable proofs of the altered mood of France. In spite of bread riots in Paris, and the impetus which dearth gave to advanced ideas, the Convention always contrived to maintain itself as the government of the country. Purged of its most violent elements, and recruited by the recall of moderates formerly proscribed, it now acted almost as a ministry of reconciliation. While the scoundrel who had massacred the prisoners of *La Vendée* was guillotined, the rebels themselves received a reasonable settlement. In the midst of a great foreign war, the freedom of worship and exemption from military service for which they had taken up arms were substantially conceded (February). Immediately afterwards, for reasons of state, men who hated all religion set men of all religions free to worship unostentatiously in France. At the same time, royalist opinions proved less dangerous to those who expressed them than did the opinions which had been dominant in the year II. The *salons* once again drew social Paris together, and there republican deputies learned to smile when graceful hostesses jested about the Revolution. The "Gilded Youth" played the Fascist in the capital, while in some of the more distant provinces the White Terror was destroying extremists whom the people loathed.

Louis XVIII

A landmark in the history of royalism was passed on June 10, when the child known as Louis XVII succumbed to the rigours of his imprisonment in the Temple. The Louis XVIII whom French royalists must now acknowledge was his uninspiring uncle, a glutton, an *emigré* and a foe to France. Louis XVI had been King of the French and a reformer, Louis XVIII declared himself King of France and champion of the old *régime*. So long as he and his brother, the future Charles X, represented the monarchy, the white cockade of Bourbon would challenge the tricolour, the recent transfer of lands would remain a robbery, and no French peasant could feel secure. Thus favoured by fortune at home, as well as by the glorious results of the war, the Girondists of the Convention drew up a new constitution, to supersede that democratic constitution of 1793 which extremists now demanded. Doubt of democracy was the keynote of the plan of 1795. Manhood suffrage for tax-payers was retained, but in the legislature two chambers were established. These were based on indirect election with high age-qualifications. They were to be renewed by one-third each year, and in the first instance chosen as to two-thirds from the Convention, rules fatal to swift democratic change.

Constitution of the Year III

The executive was a Directory of five, chosen by the elder chamber from among the nominees of the younger, with one member retiring by lot each year. This timid challenge to the sovereignty of the people was at once taken up by the Paris "sections," or city wards. A *plébiscite*, indeed, affirmed the Constitution by 914,000 votes against 95,000, the army having been brought in to vote. With regard to the "two-thirds" provision, however, the majority was less than two to one, only some 263,000 voting. Royalists and Terrorists united against the self-perpetuation of the Convention, and on 13 *Vendémiaire* (October 5) its 5,000 armed defenders found themselves hemmed in by four times their number. But the skill of Napoleon Bonaparte, who secured cannon and fired grape-shot, disposed of the insurrection with the infliction of only some 100 casualties. By sheer competence, a soldier who was not technically in command had saved the Convention, just as he had regained Toulon. Only two executions followed. Three weeks later, the old Convention was dissolved, and the newly-devised Directory gave its name to the government of the two chambers, the "Ancients" and the "Five Hundred," which succeeded. Among the five Directors, Carnot found a place, but only because Sieyès declined to serve.

France Victorious

That a moderate though anti-monarchical government could be established in October 1795, and that Carnot could occupy an almost secondary position, meant that victorious France now felt itself secure. The war with Austria and Britain, indeed, continued, but the campaign of 1794 had substantially disposed of the remaining enemies of the Republic. The Dutch had been conquered with their own consent and now formed the Batavian Republic. This ceded (May) the lands south of the Meuse except Zealand to France and entered the war against Britain. The

Emperor's brother in Tuscany had laid down his arms (February). Prussia, thanks largely to Poland, followed suit in April, and Spain, buying peace with her half of San Domingo, in July. By that time the Bretons were in train to be pacified, the *emigré* invasion had been crushed, and, on the German front, the republican armies were moving towards conquest. Of these achievements, by far the greatest was the peace with Prussia, which was signed at Basel on April 5. Without Prussia, the Allies might wound France but could never lay her low.

Treaty of Basel 1795

The treaty of Basel, however, was momentous in European history rather for what it implied than for what it stated. Prussia, indeed, made peace with France, but during the previous campaign she had not substantially made war. Until October, she had kept troops on the Rhine in return for British subsidies, but when these ceased, the show of force ceased also. But at Basel the mighty Triple Alliance of 1788, between Britain, Prussia, and Holland, made end with Holland a French client-state and Prussia a French accomplice. Seven years earlier, Prussia had turned away from the firebrands of Europe to join the pacific and conservative powers. Now she accepted the Revolution in order to press her claims in Poland. Prussia, moreover, promised France to cede her own lands on the left bank of the Rhine. In return, she was to gain secularized Church territories upon the right bank and the neutrality of the French in northern Germany. These harmless provisions, however, marked a Franco-Prussian treaty of partition. France, in effect, was to annex the Austrian Netherlands and to reach the Rhine, while Prussia was to dominate North Germany. In northern as in eastern Europe she thus pursued her own aggrandizement by abandoning her allies. Such treason can admit of no defence, but two extenuating circumstances may be cited. France, the Prussians might argue, had proved that she could not be coerced, and that she had ceased to be a crusader against historic Europe. Without a monarchy, she was returning to the old monarchic path—a reasonable measure of practical tolerance at home and normal diplomatic relations with other powers. Her conduct towards the Dutch, which reached its climax in the following month, was far less oppressive than that of Louis XIV. Prussia, moreover,

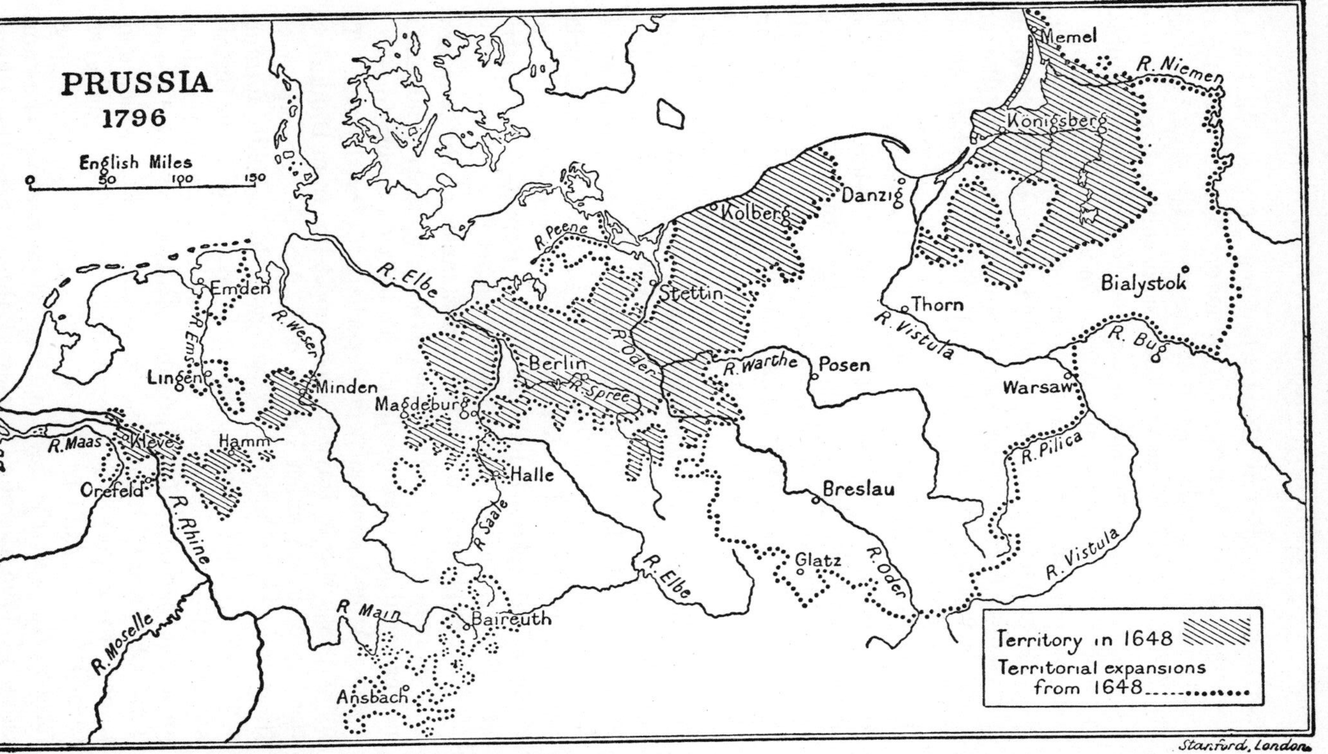

All territory west of the Rhine, except Neuchâtel, was surrendered by the Peace of Basel 1795.
(Neuchâtel is not shown here.)

betrayed her allies at Basel when one of them had lately betrayed her in Poland. In January, Austria and Russia had agreed not only to trisect the rest of Poland,[1] but also to force Prussia to accept their contemplated partition of Turkey. Thugut actually consented to make the Danubian principalities a Russian appanage. In return for this dangerous concession, for Austrian sacrifices in the war, and for the exclusion of Austria from the previous Partition, he demanded, indeed, an enormous compensation. In Poland, Austria was to extend northward to the Bug, and to hold the Vistula from Cracow almost to Warsaw, Prussia curving northwards to the Niemen with a smaller share. But the main reward was to be sought outside Poland. If France could not be despoiled, Austria might turn to Venice or gain suitable acquisitions elsewhere, presumably within the Empire. The eternal Bavarian and Silesian questions thus seemed once again to press on Prussia. Once again Austrians massed in Bohemia, with Russia this time their ally. Prussia did not discover the whole agreement, but she felt its effects in 1795. Almost the whole year was spent in compelling her to accept the Third Partition as Austria and Russia had designed it, and in bringing the monarchy of Stanislas formally to an end. Meanwhile the Bourbon powers and many others acknowledged the French Republic, but Austria and Britain maintained a hostile coalition.

War without Prussia

The responsibility for the continuance of the war now rested upon Pitt, since without British gold Austrian manpower could not take the field. To fight on meant to risk a second Armed Neutrality and perhaps defeat by sea. To make peace was to leave the long coast-line from Dunkirk to the bay of Frisia under French control, with Antwerp, freed from the old prohibition to navigate the Scheldt, forming a naval and commercial threat to London. In May, Britain and Austria drew closer their alliance, while Sardinia remained an active partner. In September, Russia concluded a new Triple Alliance with the other two Great Powers which continued to oppose the Revolution. Catherine, however, turned from Poland to Persia, rather than attempt to perform in the west the duty of the western states. The campaign of 1795 therefore possessed three faces—the Rhine, the southern Alps, and the sea.

[1] See map, p. 273.

In June, after a long siege, the great fortress of Luxemburg fell to the French. One road to Paris was thus closed to possible invaders, and more than one road from Paris to the Rhine laid open. Jourdan and Pichegru operated successfully on both sides of the river, but Pichegru, following Dumouriez into politics, nullified the advantages of the campaign. Politics, in this as in many other cases, meant the acceptance of a bribe to change sides, openly or in secret. Pichegru stood to win high power and honours and enormous wealth if the Royalists triumphed. It remained to be seen whether in 1796 his army would, or could, overthrow the Directory and restore the King. Meanwhile the struggle in the south against Sardinians, Austrians and a British fleet was bringing new men into command—Augereau, the son of a fruiterer, and Masséna, a Niçois orphan who had risen from the ranks. After much indeterminate fighting, the Allies were almost destroyed and the road to Piedmont opened, but the advantage was not pressed. This fault was exposed by Bonaparte, whose memorandum proved far more weighty in history than the victory of Loano or the Austrian loss of 7,000 men. For its hall-mark of strategic mastery caught Carnot's eye, and the memories of Toulon and 13 *Vendémiaire* outweighed the young soldier's evasion of his task in *La Vendée*. In March 1796, Bonaparte, who now cast off the Italian spelling of his name, arrived at Nice to command the army of Italy. For Italy, for France and for Europe a new age had begun.

Campaign of 1795

BIBLIOGRAPHICAL NOTE

See the Bibliographical Note at the end of Chapter I and the bibliography to Chapter XV.

Add :—

A

A. Goodwin : "The French Executive Directory—A Revaluation," *History*, n.s., XXII (1937), pp. 201–18.

F. A. T. Hélie : *Les constitutions de la France* (1875–79).

G. Lefebvre : *Les Thermidoriens* (1937).

G. Lefebvre : *Le Directoire* (1950).

A. T. Mahan : *The Influence of Sea Power upon the French Revolution and Empire, 1793–1812.* 2 vols. (1893).

P. Rain : *La Diplomatie française de Mirabeau à Bonaparte* (1950).

J. M. Thompson : *Robespierre.* 2 vols. in 1 (1939).

B

W. J. Temple : *Diaries, 1780–1796* (1929).

CHAPTER XVIII

BONAPARTE, 1796–1802

TO the year 1795, famous for the collapse of Holland and the rise of Bonaparte, for the extinction of Poland and the "April fools' day trick" which Prussia at Basel played on Europe, must be ascribed a maritime significance worthy to be ranked with those events. Three years of warfare had made it clear that the new revolutionary power of France was to be applied to the realization of her old aggressive policy. The Netherlands had been won; Germany and Italy were more than threatened; Spain was in process of reconversion into an ally; the Dutch, who had defied Louis XIV, were now a client state. Victory over Britain and the creation of a new and more glorious French empire overseas must inevitably become the object of the Directory, or of whomsoever else ruled France. The indispensable requisite was French superiority by sea. Could this now be hoped for?

France and Sea Power

After nearly three years of warfare the answer remained uncertain. The British had gained no signal victory, nor had they denied the Atlantic to the enemy. Their administration was palpably corrupt. They had mismanaged the Mediterranean. They had alienated Spain and the neutral powers, among which the United States might assume considerable importance, and the Dutch had entered the war against them. On the other hand, they had done much damage to the French fleet: they had captured several of the French Indies: the Dutch intervention had given them Ceylon, Malacca and the Cape of Good Hope, upon which French power further east depended. At the same time the war had strengthened their fleet and trained its *personnel.* Above all, the higher command was being changed. As in the French army, so in the British navy, efficient youth was gaining power. Jervis, indeed, was to prove that half a century of service had not drained him of his force. But

Nelson, still in the thirties, could form and carry out the principle of the annihilation of the opposing fleet, and the future lay with him. None the less, at the end of 1795 British superiority by sea was not great enough to discourage French projects of invasion.

The Campaign of 1796

The main campaign of 1796 consisted in an effort by the Directory to storm Vienna and thereby crush their only serious enemy on land. To this end, three armies were to converge upon the Austrian capital, two marching down the Danube, while the third, that of Italy, struck north-eastward from Venice. Jourdan, commanding the most northerly, left Mainz besieged in his rear, and pressed victoriously up the river Main to the Bohemian border. Thence he detached the young southerner, Bernadotte, to make contact with Moreau, once a law-student and now Pichegru's successor. Moreau had likewise marched eastward in triumph, and the spectacle of German princes toadying to the French in the hope of receiving ecclesiastical territories had already been witnessed in the south. Moreau, however, neglected Jourdan for the army of Italy, and Austria was saved by an unusual chance. The Habsburgs, though brave men, have seldom been distinguished soldiers, but at twenty-six the Emperor's brother Charles proved himself perhaps the finest Austrian general since Eugene. Being royal, moreover, he could escape the usual court jealousy of its commanders and lessen the pedantic deliberateness which traditionally cursed Austria when at war. The Archduke Charles defeated Bernadotte and Jourdan, and drove the northern army across the Rhine—a movement to which Moreau could not but conform. His retreat was magnificent, but the fact was plain that in Germany the campaign against Austria had failed.

In Italy, meanwhile, Bonaparte had taught the world the difference between genius and mere talent, however great. When all his campaigns were over, he declared that his sixty battles had taught him nothing that he had not learned at school. His campaign of 1796 ranks as the finest of his career, the more so since he was then a little-known semi-foreigner in the twenties commanding senior colleagues and a tattered and half-starved force. Two of his lieutenants, it is said, lived for some time with a single pair of breeches between them. Himself for years a needy student, he knew how to make the poverty of his men their greatest incentive to conquest, while his own meagre visage and shabby uniform only strengthened the spell of his compelling glance and words. From the first his fire and charm forced soldiers to give him gladly of their best, and soon they were ready to lay down their lives to shield the General.

Napoleon Bonaparte in Italy

Bonaparte had studied deeply the history of earlier campaigns, both in the Alpine regions and wherever the Austrians had fought. His 36,000 men were twice outnumbered by the enemy, but the enemy had two commanders and a tradition of routine. Within a month of his arrival, he had won four victories, divided the Austrians from the Sardinians, and brought King Victor Amadeus to wish for peace. More than once, indeed, defeat had seemed inevitable, but the general never failed either to command success or to draw from it inspiration for his army.

> "Soldiers," he declared on April 26, "in a fortnight you have won six battles, taken twenty-one standards, fifty-five guns and several fortresses, and the richest part of Piedmont is yours. You have won battles without guns, crossed rivers without bridges, made forced marches without boots, encamped often without food. Soldiers, I thank you."

Such were the accents to which all Europe was soon to give ear, and which were to determine European history for nearly half a generation.

Napoleon

History, indeed, plainly records that from an obscure family in a remote island there had been born the ablest of historic men. The Revolution gave him his opportunity; and France, the necessary tools; but he was the offspring neither of the Revolution nor of France. "Your Rousseau," he declared, "was a madman," and for equality he had nothing but contempt. His genius, like his name, was rather Italian than French, and Italian formed his natural vehicle of expression. But one who, as Goethe said, widened the bounds of human consciousness and will cannot be comprised within the bounds of any national type. He was in reality as contemptuous of racial differences as of religious, treating both as human weaknesses which made men easier to rule. Only the year before his birth in 1769 had France acquired Corsica, which had belonged to Genoa and might have belonged to Britain. His genius indeed was universal. Not

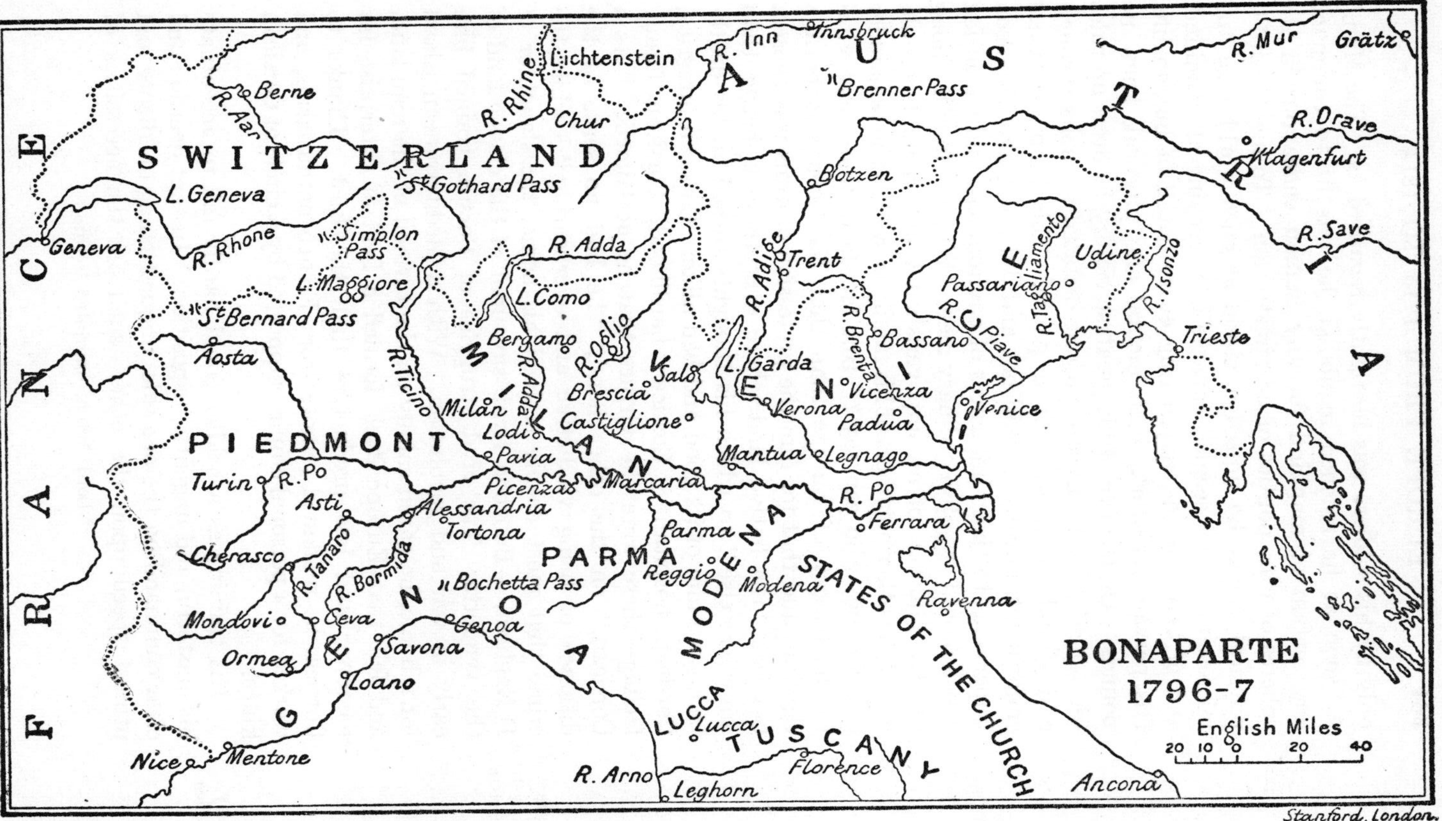
BONAPARTE
1796-7
English Miles
20 10 0 20 40
FRANCE
SWITZERLAND
AUSTRIA
PIEDMONT
MILAN
VENICE
PARMA
MODENA
GENOA
LUCCA
TUSCANY
STATES OF THE CHURCH
Berne
R. Aar
Lichtenstein
R. Rhine
Chur
R. Inn
Innsbruck
Brenner Pass
R. Mur
Grätz
R. Drave
Klagenfurt
R. Save
L. Geneva
Geneva
R. Rhone
St Gothard Pass
Simplon Pass
L. Maggiore
St Bernard Pass
Aosta
R. Adda
L. Como
Bergamo
R. Oglio
Salò
Brescia
Castiglione
R. Ticino
Milan
Lodi
Pavia
Botzen
R. Adige
Trent
L. Garda
Verona
Mantua
Legnago
R. Brenta
Bassano
Vicenza
Padua
Venice
Passariano
R. Tagliamento
R. Piave
Udine
R. Isonzo
Trieste
Turin
R. Po
Asti
Alessandria
Tortona
Picenza
Marcaria
Cherasco
R. Tanaro
R. Bormida
Bochetta Pass
Mondovi
Ceva
Genoa
Savona
Ormea
Loano
Nice
Mentone
Parma
Reggio
Modena
Ferrara
Ravenna
Lucca
Florence
R. Arno
Leghorn
Ancona
Stanford, London.

only by his soldiers was he rightly regarded as "The Man." As soon as he reached manhood, he was fit to command any section of mankind for any human endeavour in the spheres of war, politics or administration. To inexhaustible physical vigour he united a vision at once world-wide and microscopic. He seemed capable of surveying all mankind, and of knowing and re-ordering every detail of human life. His passion for work, both mental and physical, knew no bounds. On the eve of his greatest victory he drew up rules for a girls' school: in captivity he dictated memoirs through a day and night without a pause. This unique natural endowment, however, could not and did not make Napoleon impervious to those influences of environment and education which mould or polish ordinary men. Why the fourth among the ten children of an impoverished Corsican noble should dwarf the other members of his family as well as the remainder of mankind, who can say? But few facts were more vital to the history of Europe than that Napoleon was born a Corsican and that for him the profession of arms was chosen. Corsica, "the native land where everything is better than anywhere else" to which his thoughts turned on his death-bed, gave him of its good and bad alike. Corsican integrity, Corsican hospitality, Corsican hardihood, Corsican family feeling—these were the virtues that he acclaimed. "As a Corsican," on the other hand, "he had no sense of the disgrace of being vindictive and overbearing," [1] while the crime that most deeply stained his name, the slaughter of D'Enghien, a Bourbon rival, savoured of the classic land of the vendetta. The civil struggles of Corsica trained him early in war and revolution. With a Mediterranean island for a home, he gazed calmly on the turmoil of the mainland, and felt that Europe itself formed a field of enterprise far narrower and less productive than the East. Thanks to Corsica, he remained remote from French enthusiasms, and worked for a personal empire supported by a circle of Corsican kings.

Influence of Corsica upon Bonaparte

Military Influence

His training as a soldier could hardly fail to accentuate his masterful and ungentle disposition. Instant decision and clear command on the one side, unquestioning obedience and utmost speed upon the other—such are the necessities of

[1] Lord Acton, unprinted lecture.

war, and the soldier naturally conceives of them as the necessities also of government. The democracy of the Revolution might demand the temporary aid of a Napoleon, but in the long run democracy and Napoleon must be incompatible. If it be true that " of all men who ever lived, he was the greatest cause of suffering and wrong," [1] the cause lay rather in the times than in himself. Trained to command as a soldier, he came to be entrusted with civil rule, and for any form of civil rule save despotism he was by nature and by training unfit. Peace was to him a state in which his own profession had but little scope. When told that certain islanders had no wars he found it monstrous and unnatural.[2]

For a decade and a half (1799–1814), as never before or since in human history, the record of western civilization was to be predominantly the biography of one man. The four campaigns which divide Bonaparte's first triumphs in Italy from his achievement of authority in France appear in retrospect as the prologue to this stupendous drama. To those who were fighting for and against the Revolution, however, the old antagonists France and Britain still held the centre of the stage. In 1796, as in many earlier years, the French attempted to strike down their enemy by an invading force and to jeopardize her empire by seizing Portugal. Once again both endeavours failed. Hoche, who had pacified the royalist rebels in north-western France, sailed from Brest in December with 15,000 men to establish an Irish republic, which, the Directory hoped, would proclaim pure deism as its faith. With such an Ireland, a secure base against Britain would be theirs. The forty-five ships of this new and dangerous Armada, however, lost thirteen of their number and accomplished nothing, while a minor descent on the Welsh coast ended in the capture of the invaders (February 1797). The threat to Portugal, which had seconded Spain in combating the Revolution, was made through the medium of Spain, which had but lately made peace with France at St. Ildefonso (August). Godoy, the unworthy Spanish minister who was derisively surnamed " Prince of the Peace," found no alternative to taking sides against

Campaign of 1796

[1] *Ibid.*

[2] Captain B. Hall, R.N., *Times*, September 6, 1933.

Britain and her Portuguese ally. The disastrous results of his action, which for the moment promised to turn the scales of sea-power, appeared in 1797. In the meantime, Portugal remained unharmed. All fluctuations of fortune elsewhere, however, even the death of Catherine of Russia in November, yielded in obvious importance to the triumphs of Bonaparte in Italy. These were twofold, over the Austrian armies and over the Directory of France. Sure of his soldiers after their victories in the spring, Bonaparte firmly refused to divide the command, as his government decreed. The Directors, hoping for further spoils from Italy, overlooked this insubordination and allowed him to remain. Soon they were compelled to accept his strategy in preference to their own, and to console themselves for their impotence with the spectacle of Italian paintings and statues pouring into Paris. Before July was ended, Bonaparte could report that Italy had been drained of nearly 2½ millions sterling, and that the King of Sardinia had ratified the cession of Savoy and Nice to France. It was impossible to insist that such a victor should negotiate when he showed himself determined to march upon Vienna.

The strength of the Austrian fortresses and armies, none the less, made the latter half of the campaign of 1796 arduous and uncertain. Victories continued to punctuate Bonaparte's progress as he advanced across the north Italian plain towards Mantua, the transalpine gateway of Vienna. At Arcola, however (November 15–17), a French defeat and the death of Bonaparte himself were narrowly averted, and Mantua remained untaken. But the activity of Masséna and Augereau, the martial fervour of the troops, and above all the genius of their commander procured a series of successes which were skilfully exaggerated in the bulletins. The Cispadane Republic came into being as a proof of French victory and of Bonaparte's ascendancy, for the Directory would have left the Duke of Modena on his throne. The creation of a revolutionary republic in place of four feudal states may be ascribed to many causes, the Italian strain in Bonaparte, his ostentatious adhesion to the Revolution, and the clarity of his political thought perhaps foremost among them. What is certain is that the creation of the Cispadane Republic inaugurated both his amazing career as a maker of new states, and also that movement for Italian unity and independence which triumphed half a century after his death.

Bonaparte's Campaign of 1797

The new year, 1797, continued without a break, indeed almost without a pause, the movements which Bonaparte had begun in 1796. Subjugation of Austria, revolutionary transformation of Italy, progress of Bonapartism and threat to Britain—all these characterize that memorable campaign. In January, the French defeated the relieving armies at Rivoli, and on February 2 Mantua fell into their hands. Within three weeks the intriguing Pope Pius VI had been forced to accept the peace of Tolentino. The terms which Bonaparte dictated revealed a new aspect of his unchanging mind. Though in facing unknown perils he proved himself as embarrassed as he was contemptuously bold against the known, he lacked all feeling of religion. In the general human impulse to bow before a higher power he did not share. As a statesman, however, he recognized its value, and in his library he placed the Bible and the Koran in the section entitled Politics. As ruler of the Papal States, the Pope was forced at Tolentino to pay indemnities, to cede lands to the new body and to recognize an Italian Republic. As head of the western Church, however, he received the assurance that Bonaparte would protect him against the anti-religious fervour of the Directory.

Having thus secured his rear, Bonaparte set out upon the long and perilous march towards the Austrian capital. He now disposed of more than 70,000 men, including a division brought by Bernadotte from the army of the Rhine. But Italy lay behind him, and it would be nothing new for Italians to unite against the invading French. Before him might be massed the main army of a great military power, commanded by a royal and victorious general, while on his flank were the mountain homes of several virile German tribes. Not even the Archduke Charles, however, could wholly overcome Austrian bureaucratic slowness, and before March was over he had lost many fine positions and more than 20,000 men. Early in April, the French were within 80 miles of Vienna. Both to them and to the Habsburgs the risks of a decisive battle seemed enormous. Bonaparte must stake his army, his conquests, and his whole career, while in revolutionary times none could foresee what consequences signal defeat might bring to a composite dynastic empire. In the heart of Europe, Britain was powerless to protect her ally. Prussia had proved herself at best a doubtful friend, while with the half-crazy Paul I (1796–1801) upon her throne, Russia became unaccountable. There were therefore strong reasons for following the Polish precedent—Partition. France might gain and Austria could scarcely lose if a fund for their compensation were found in the empire of Venice.

Peace with Austria 1797

Such was, indeed, the basis of the preliminaries of peace which were signed at Leoben on April 18. The Emperor Francis II, whose habitual rectitude won warm tributes from the conscientious Aberdeen, agreed to receive all the mainland territories of Venice between the frontier of Milan and the furthest limits of Dalmatia. Venice, it is true, was to be compensated, as Poland never was, with lands taken from another lord, in this case from those lately surrendered by the Pope. France would gain Belgium and Milan, prizes which had evaded her mightiest kings, while the Emperor as saviour of the left bank of the Rhine could plume himself on having checked French expansion over Germany.

Bonaparte's Negotiations with Austria

The agreements made at Leoben, however, were no more than preliminaries, arrangements needing confirmation by both parties, and which both hoped to improve by change of circumstance and by negotiation. Five months must be spent by General Bonaparte in securing the partial reorganization of Europe which he had dictated at the age of twenty-eight. Helped by the massacre of the French garrison by the Venetian patriots of Verona, he treated Venice with the same contempt for decency and justice that had distinguished Frederick's dealings with the Poles. Thugut, as he knew well, was pulling every diplomatic string in opposition. The mob broke Thugut's windows when Vienna fell, and his adversary warned him that they would hang him. Joining Lombardy to the Cispadane Republic, he created a new "Cisalpine" state, and endowed it with a constitution like that of France. Pending annexation to France, Genoa was forced to become a republic. Bonaparte's most dangerous opponents, however, were to be found in France, and not unnaturally in the ranks of that Directory whose prerogatives he had so flagrantly usurped. Throughout the summer, Carnot and Barthélemy stood out for the continuance of that new moderation in revolutionary France which had made it possible for Britain to offer terms of peace. They were strengthened by the election of one-third of the Legislature, which gave conservative results. Again, however, Bonaparte used the army of Italy to carry out his design. On 18 *Fructidor* (September 4) Augereau, his lieutenant, occupied the Tuileries with 12,000 men. In defiance of the constitution, Carnot, Barthélemy and their friends were overthrown and replaced by violent Jacobins. "*Fructidor*" immediately affected the negotiations. The deliberateness and pride of the Imperial court, with the skill and insight of its experienced diplomats, proved insurmountable to Bonaparte so long as official France was secretly against him. Confronted with an extremist government in Paris, however, the Austrians gave way, while Bonaparte was piqued by the appointment of Augereau, a potential rival, to command the army of the Rhine. In these circumstances an agreement was hurried on, and peace signed at Campo Formio on October 17. Bonaparte trusted, and rightly, that the joy of the nation at a triumphant ending to the six years' war would force the Directory to ratify his treaty.

***Fructidor* and Peace 1797**

The ending to the so-called War of the First Coalition was, indeed, triumphant. Revolutionary France, more than ever revolutionary since *Fructidor*, had vindicated against historic Europe her right to depose the nobles, to defy the Pope, and to execute the King and Queen. Having proclaimed the Rights of Man, she had reorganized her own structure on that basis, and had made it the basis also of the client republics, Batavian, Cisalpine and Ligurian. Prussia, Iberia, Sardinia and Italy had been subdued. Now, at Campo Formio, Austria was forced and bribed to cede Belgium, to acknowledge the French title to the Ionian Islands, and, by secret articles, to partition Germany with France. By suppressing Venice altogether, France could purchase her "natural frontier" upon the Rhine. From the Swiss frontier to a point beyond the great fortress of Mainz, the left bank was to be French, while the dispossessed rulers, like the Stadholder of Holland, were promised compensation in Germany. The aggrandizement of France at their expense entitled Austria to that westward extension to the Inn which she had long coveted. Thus Austria followed Prussia in selling Germany to France, disguising the transaction by providing that a congress should meet at Rastadt. This congress, however, would be merely Franco-German, to bargain, not to determine European right. With Belgium and the Rhine within her borders, Holland and northern Italy her clients, Spain and Prussia seemingly impotent and Austria her accomplice, France far surpassed the glories of Louis XIV. The thrones of Gustavus Adolphus and Catherine were occupied by madmen. For the Directors as for the Great King, it remained only to vanquish Britain.

Britain and the War

Across the Channel, the situation had become far worse than the imposing list of British conquests might suggest. France and her allies indeed had gained no success by sea, and their overseas possessions had therefore been steadily acquired by Britain. In 1794, Martinique and the Seychelles; in 1795, the Cape; in 1796, Ceylon, Santa Lucia, St. Vincent and Grenada; in 1797, Trinidad—these profitable conquests had been made and probably could be retained. But no true statesman would regard Britain as the gainer by a war which had brought her these at the cost of a depleted treasury, a mutinous Ireland and a Europe in which France, towering over all other powers, ruled the coast from the Ems to the bay of Leghorn. How could Britain hope to save the world from the triumphant Revolution? In 1796 the Mediterranean fleet was withdrawn. In 1797 the Bank was forced to suspend cash payments. Despite victories over the Spaniards off Cape St. Vincent, and over the Dutch off Camperdown, widespread mutiny in the navy seemed to threaten national collapse. Before the downfall of Austria Pitt had sent the resourceful Malmesbury to ask for the restoration of Belgium as the price of peace (October–December 1796). The Directory returned a stern refusal. By what road could Britain reach either peace or victory in 1798?

The Situation in 1798

In the new year, the forces familiar in the old continued to furnish like results. Her improved and improving navy gave Britain Minorca and British Honduras. The Irish rose and failed, in spite of feeble and belated help from France. The French, on the other hand, made some progress with the only strategy that they could follow—the exclusion of their enemy from Europe. They overthrew the Swiss and Papal governments, replacing them by the Helvetic and Roman Republics. Such conquests were prompted in part by a restless disharmony in France, arising inevitably when neither the civil government nor the army is unquestioned master. French expansion became easier, however, because the Rights of Man disguised the old aggressiveness of conquest. Seventeen years later, indeed, a British diplomat reminded Alexander of Russia of the conduct during their Republic of the ephemeral parties in the direction of affairs in France. However violently opposed with respect to the interior, the exterior policy of war and plunder had uniformly been the same under all. The armies came, none the less, with professions on their lips that disguised their motives from those who had little to lose, while the autocrats who were attacked dared not at first appeal to so democratic a force as nationality.

The year witnessed the incorporation of Geneva, of Mülhausen, and of the left bank of the Rhine. France seized also the treasure of Berne, which was needed for Bonaparte's new and astounding venture. This, the outstanding achievement of 1798, was none other than an amazing onslaught upon Egypt. At the moment when an army had been assembled to invade England, and when improved Franco-Turkish relations had made the turban fashionable in Paris, France suddenly attacked Cairo. The Revolution and the appearance of the foremost military adventurer of all time, however, had turned European history into a kaleidoscope. On every side governments and boundaries were being swept away. The Pope was a captive exile. None could tell where the next blow might fall. In May, when Bonaparte sailed from Toulon, it was conjectured that his destination might be the Crimea, or Lisbon, or Ireland, or Naples, or Jamaica. The truth seems to have been that, finding the invasion project impracticable, he had resolved to strike at Britain's Empire overseas and at her trade. Talleyrand, the far-seeing Machiavellian French patriot, approved the scheme. First Egypt, and then perhaps India, would be the goal. For Bonaparte, born a Mediterranean islander and brought up on Cæsar and Alexander, the East possessed a glamour far surpassing that of Europe. "Only in the East," he declared, "is achievement on a great scale possible."

The Egyptian Expedition

Nothing less than some such achievement could appease

his titanic impulse to create. As a rival power to the Directors, he shared their desire that the utmost distance should be placed between himself and them. If his military objective was Britain, his political objective was an independent empire, perhaps including France. In the pursuit of such designs, a ramshackle armada of some 335 ships and more than 50,000 men braved Nelson over 2,000 miles of sea. Shielded by fortune, sustained and consolidated by Bonaparte's faith and courage, the expedition reached Egypt at the end of June, having captured Malta from the Knightly Order of St. John. There Bonaparte merely bribed the defenders, but in Egypt, after storming Alexandria, he revealed himself as the complete statesman, ready if he captured Jerusalem to become a Jew. None the less he conquered the Mamelukes, then the masters of Egypt, by inspiring his troops and handling them with supreme skill rather than by serving up extracts from the Koran which he judged convincing to a Moslem. The victory of the Pyramids on July 21 gave Cairo to the French, but ten days later their fleet was annihilated by Nelson in Aboukir Bay. Thus marooned in Egypt, Bonaparte had at least an opportunity of displaying his talents without the Directors' interference. The Sultan's declaration of war (September) brought a new enemy of France within his reach. Before the year was out, he had cowed the rebels of Cairo, set in motion a vigorous Institute of research, explored the isthmus of Suez, and planned the invasion of Syria.

French Difficulties in 1799

This display of energy and skill was to be continued and even surpassed in 1799. None the less Bonaparte's actions cost France dear. The firstfruits of the adventure was the downfall of Wolfe Tone and the Irish rebels with their French allies, and the collapse of the invasion project. Bonaparte had already made an Italy which he alone could handle and a Germany which could not be handled by those whom he left behind. By seizing Malta he baulked the desires of Russia, already hostile, and by invading Egypt he made the Sultan and the Tsar allies. Britain, for whom every extension of French dominion meant a loss of markets, could only hope for a second coalition against France. For the Habsburgs, again, it was impossible either sincerely to acquiesce in the loss of Belgium and Milan, or in the spoliation of the Church, or in the substitution of French influence in Germany for their own. To Austria, therefore, the peace of Campo Formio must be a mere truce. As a wholly dynastic state, she could make no sincere agreement with the Revolution. Early in 1799, France gave her further provocation by forward movements in Italy. There the rash onslaught on Rome inspired by Lady Hamilton and the Habsburg queen of Naples was answered by the establishment of a Parthenopean republic beside the Roman (January). The rulers of Sardinia and of Tuscany were deposed. If the French remained masters of Italy they would assuredly not leave rich Venice in Austrian hands. Their violence, however, was rousing an Italian revolt which threatened their position. The possibility drew nearer that Italy would once more become the Frenchman's grave. At the same time France gave equal provocation to the Germans. Favoured by the greedy passivity which Prussia maintained under a third Frederick William (1797–1840) France was revolutionizing the German lands which she had already gained at Rastadt and expanding the area demanded at the Congress. Austria therefore had every reason for joining a new coalition, if a strong one could be formed by Britain.

Growth of the Second Coalition against France

At the close of 1798 this condition was in process of fulfilment. Paul, the new Tsar, was a capricious and irresponsible tyrant but as yet his word was law. In Suvorov he possessed the most eccentric of generals, a grotesque Bayard whom the army adored and for whom they performed miracles. His prestige may be measured by the legend that at the Last Judgment the Knights of St. George will rise in their numbered rank with Suvorov at their head. Britain, linked with Russia by strong bonds of trade, now secured her intervention in the west, and this in turn gave Austria courage. The restoration of British sea-power in the Mediterranean, moreover, profoundly modified the situation. The Sultan's declaration of war opened the Straits to Russia and brought the North African powers into a state of enmity towards France. Aboukir and the Spanish loss of Minorca isolated Bonaparte, promised to check the French in Italy, assured to Austria the command of the Adriatic, and guaranteed Europe against those naval ambitions of Russia which always made her a dangerous ally. Early in 1799, therefore,

Austria could join with Britain, Russia and Turkey in a league which also included Portugal and Naples. To finance this second Coalition, Britain had resorted to the income-tax; to meet it, France introduced a new conscription. Every Frenchman was declared a soldier, and five "classes," from twenty-one to twenty-five, were forcibly enrolled.

The Campaign of 1799

The war of the Second Coalition began with the assault by the forces of historic Europe upon a revolutionary frontier which stretched from Holland into Italy. French armies of the Rhine, of Switzerland, and of northern Italy marched in concert under Jourdan, though Bernadotte and Masséna were also in communication with Paris. Despite the conscription, they could not hope to equal their opponents in numbers. No longer were the French armies supported by a Carnot, and in the absence of Bonaparte, Suvorov and the Archduke Charles could cope with any French commander. Masséna, indeed, reached the Inn, but the Archduke foiled the plan by overwhelming Jourdan at Stockach, near Lake Constance, and by driving him across the Rhine. Victory brought the Austrians to Rastadt. The Emperor's proclamation annulling the Congress had failed to dissolve it, and his soldiers now murdered the French envoys (April). Austria, it seemed, hated the Jacobins more than she respected the most sacred public law. Meanwhile the ruin of the French structure in Italy was begun by the Austrians and brilliantly continued by Suvorov. The British brought back the exiled King to Naples, where Nelson played a lamentable part in the White Terror which ensued. While Masséna was reduced to a precarious defensive in Switzerland, British and Russian troops landed in Holland, and the Dutch fleet hoisted the Orange flag. Inevitably, the French nation turned against the corrupt and inefficient Directory, and inevitably they longed for the symbol of victory, Bonaparte.

Bonaparte's Return from Egypt, 1799

Early in August, Bonaparte resolved to return with a few picked officers to France. During his isolation he had done wonders, but in vain. Foiled at Acre, largely by British sea-power, he had effected an amazing march back to Egypt. His crushing victory over the Turks and Mamelukes at Aboukir made his conquest safe. Even under Bonaparte, however, a dwindling garrison of Egypt could exert no important influence upon the fate of Europe or of the world. The news of the French disasters which he read in the journals sent him by Sir Sidney Smith were the cause of his landing at Fréjus on October 9.

The home-coming of Bonaparte sent a thrill of rapture through the French nation. For his own ambition no better moment could have been found. The tide of disaster, indeed, was already on the turn. Once again Austrian egotism and contempt for Russia had frustrated a seemingly victorious coalition. The function of the Russians, as seen at Vienna, was not to invade France but to restore Italian towns to Austria, and in Switzerland to spare the Austrians all exertion. Thanks to Austria, Masséna defeated them at Zurich (September) and it needed all the heroic ingenuity of Suvorov to save them from annihilation in the mountains. On this, the veteran returned to Russia. Meanwhile the Anglo-Russian army under the Duke of York had been fairly driven out of Holland. In his disgust Paul at heart renounced the whole enterprise. Thus the union between Austria and Russia, the basis of the Second Coalition, was shattered while Bonaparte was still upon the sea. Masséna's victory at Zurich forced the Archduke Charles to fall back from the Rhine. But their own government was too unpopular for Frenchmen to do it justice, while in Italy the enemy's success continued until only Genoa remained to France. The Directory was bankrupt; politicians, divided; royalists, aggressive once again. The nation would condone the crime of Bonaparte if he could seize the helm.

Bonaparte and 18 *Brumaire*

This he did on 18 *Brumaire*, "in its immediate political consequences the most important revolution in modern history" (Temperley).

Bonaparte owed his triumph rather to force and chance than to any clear plan or display of talent. In the course of a prolonged and bitter crisis, the Jacobins passed laws of panic violence which banished all security from those whom they might accuse of counter-revolution. Moderate men in desperation turned to Sieyès, a constitution-maker whose silence convinced chatterers that he was a sage. A far-seeing politician, but too professional to govern, Sieyès desired to guide some man of action who would satisfy the longing of France to be rid of a corrupt and ineffective clique. Joubert, a blameless and brilliant soldier, at first seemed cast for the part, but in August he was defeated and slain by Suvorov and the Austrians at Novi. France, therefore, turned to Bonaparte at the moment at which Bonaparte was resolving to rescue France. Before he could arrive the government was paralysed by intrigues and the deputies fought with their fists at public sittings. His landing seemed to promise victory, order and a glorious renaissance of the Revolution.

Within a week of his landing (Oct. 9) Bonaparte was studying the ground in Paris. He came as a citizen, not as a soldier, and the gazettes duly noted that he had exchanged his uniform for a frock-coat. He courted all parties with success, but a few days' intercourse with Sieyès sufficed to make the two men partners in a plot to transform the constitution. For this it was necessary that, on the pretext of a Jacobin conspiracy in Paris, both Councils should transfer their sittings to St. Cloud, whither the Parisian mob could not easily be summoned to defend the constitution. In the Council of the Ancients, Sieyès ruled. That of the Five Hundred had Lucien Bonaparte as its president. Among the army the plot found strong support, though Bernadotte remained a doubtful factor and picked republicans composed the Guards. Financiers, always eager for strong and moderate government, lent money to the Sieyès-Bonaparte combination. An incalculable element of strength was brought to the conspiracy by the adhesion of Talleyrand, perhaps the supreme diplomat in all history. Rake and ecclesiastic, subtle, far-seeing and tenacious, all that he did was marked by superhuman calm. This he accounted for by asserting that his heart missed one beat in every four, giving him rest without the ordinary need for sleep and promising to prolong his life indefinitely. In the actual *coup d'état*, Fouché, as chief of the police, proved an even more valuable ally.

On the 18 *Brumaire* (Nov. 9) itself all went according to plan. The assent of the Ancients to the transference of both councils to St. Cloud was secured by the simple method of omitting to summon those who were likely to disagree. By the end of the day the legislature was temporarily suspended, and Bonaparte with the local troops had been placed in charge of affairs. Next day, however, hot resistance, both corporate and individual, was encountered. While the figment of a Jacobin plot faded away, the reality of a Bonaparte plot drove the Councils into angry opposition. Bonaparte himself lost his head when attempting to intervene. After a scuffle, he was rescued by his men; but the Assembly prepared to vote him an outlaw, and their guards might well have carried out the decree. Thanks, it may be, to the coincidence of three accidents, however, the attempted revolution did not end in a scuffle which must have changed the history of Europe. Lucien Bonaparte, the untried president of the Five Hundred, was found to be a master of obstructive tactics. The deputies, heated and egotistic, foolishly seconded his efforts to gain time. The sight of their general bleeding from a casual scratch fired Bonaparte's troops against the palaverers who, they supposed, had wounded him, and they obeyed the order to drive out the Five Hundred. Lucien then successively prevailed with the Ancients to grant all that the conspirator desired and with a remnant of the Five Hundred to concur. During the night the Directory was thus abolished, the Legislature purged and adjourned, and Bonaparte made First Consul, with Sieyès and Ducos as colleagues.

The First Consul and France

Although force, fraud and lies had installed this triumvirate in power, France gladly accepted a seemingly national government. As the man of the Revolution, Bonaparte immediately enlisted the revolutionary energy of the French to cope with the colossal tasks that confronted him on every side. A strong executive, an orderly administration, a united nation and victory abroad—these he must have, and by a unique display of intelligent will-power all were swiftly achieved.

The first task must be to gain an authority such as the Enlightened Despots had been wont to wield. To this end Bonaparte ruthlessly tore asunder the doctrinaire cobwebs of Sieyès. To prevent impulsive changes, that theorist had drawn up a constitution, known as that of the year VIII, in which the principle of indirect election was carried to unprecedented lengths. Half a million men chosen for ten years by manhood suffrage formed a *corps* from which all local officials must be drawn. The half-million themselves selected fifty thousand who alone were eligible as officials of the Departments. The fifty thousand in turn declared five thousand to be qualified for governmental and legislative service. All appointments lay in the hands of the government. Laws were to be proposed by a Council of State, discussed by a Tribunate, accepted or rejected by a Legislature. Even if accepted, they might be vetoed by a permanent Senate as being incompatible with the Constitution. As the Senate had previously chosen the Councillors, the Tribunes and the Legislators, and as its own members were designated by Sieyès himself, harmony between the head and the members of the government was made trebly secure. All this suited Bonaparte excellently well, provided that he were himself the unquestioned head. Sieyès, however, had provided that a Great Elector responsible to the Senate should, like an English king, appoint and dismiss prime ministers, in this case one consul for peace and another for war. Trenchantly comparing Sieyès' Great Elector to a hog fattened on many millions, Bonaparte substituted a First Consul with two others as advisers. He himself became First Consul with full monarchic power. In Cambacères, a cool and able lawyer, and Lebrun, an inconspicuous moderate, he found colleagues who could assist him without detracting from his fame. The function of Sieyès was to form and to inspire the Senate. Thus disguised, military despotism, incarnate in the greatest of adventurers, began to dazzle France and Europe.

Bonaparte's Reorganization

In the first months of the Consulate, Bonaparte proved both at home and abroad that his energy was equalled by his insight. As a despised Corsican cadet, he had taken the measure of the French, and found them proud and fickle as in the days of Cæsar. Like his nephew Napoleon III, he was compelled always to pose as the delegate of the Revolution, and to work with the knowledge that when he ceased to dazzle Paris he would fall from power. But foreigner as he was, he shared with the French their love of order, and this he secured by institutions so perfectly adapted to French needs that for a century few laws were needed to amend them. "Every institution which a law-abiding Frenchman respects," wrote Mr. Bodley in 1898, "from the Legion of Honour to the Bank of France and the *Comédie Française* was either formed or reorganized by

Napoleon." And it was as Consul, when the need was most obviously urgent, that he gave most to the reconstruction of France. On Christmas Day, 1799, he installed the new-born Council of State, "the great central laboratory of government" (Fisher). The enthusiasm aroused by a dower of institutions unmatched since Augustus was naturally greatest when the Consulate was new. For a few years after 18 *Brumaire*, men could not but contrast the orderly and economical administration of the First Consul with the chaos which the Directory had brought about. For a time, moreover, France enjoyed a centralization more perfect than any that even she had ever known without losing the illusion that she had made herself a democracy free from the tyranny of king, of nobles and of priests. In foreign affairs likewise the skill of Bonaparte and Talleyrand persuaded a nation which longed for peace that the continuance of war was due to the wickedness of their opponents.

Peace Overtures by France

Tearing asunder what the citizen always regards as the cobwebs of diplomacy, Bonaparte wrote to Francis II and George III as man to man, inviting them to put a stop to bloodshed. After a struggle which had lately gone against her, France thus invited historic Europe to accept her Revolution. Whether any historic monarchy could be safe in a Europe of which revolutionary France was a member might perplex the statesmen of 1800 as acutely as like problems regarding Russia and Germany perplexed their successors in 1920 and 1938. Austria, often courteous when others are offensive, elicited the fact that to her the price of peace was the surrender of what she had gained in Italy while Bonaparte was conquering Egypt. Britain, which had twice rid herself of the Stuarts, seemed to demand that France should restore the Bourbons, and in Egypt required evacuation. Bonaparte, to whom no coalition without either Prussia or Russia seemed formidable, merely used the negotiations to justify further war. At the same time with unsparing force he suppressed both actual rebellion and the outspoken press. By war or by diplomacy he was determined to regain Italy and to strengthen his hold on Egypt.

The Campaign of 1800

Aided by fortune in the field, and sustained by a re-animated France, Bonaparte broke the Second Coalition in the campaign of 1800. His strategy was designed to subdue the Austrians and to reserve the laurels for himself. To Moreau's great army of the Rhine was therefore assigned the limited objective of preventing Austrian reinforcements from crossing the mountains into Italy. Bonaparte himself used Genoa as a bait to draw the Austrians in Italy towards the south-west. By a triumph of staff work, he then crossed the Great St. Bernard (May) and thus took the enemy in the rear. At Milan he restored the Cisalpine Republic. Melas, the Austrian commander, must either cut his way through the French or retreat on Genoa, which was now his own. At the moment when Bonaparte had detached Desaix to prevent this, Melas attacked him with a far superior force. Marengo, the scene of the encounter (June 14), promised to be the tomb of the Consulate and of the Consul. Desaix, however, suddenly returned, drawn thither by the booming of the guns. His unexpected attack shattered the victorious Austrians and his death enabled Bonaparte to claim all the glory. No other event was of the same weight in his career. Marengo (June 14) conquered Italy to the Mincio for France and enabled Moreau to lead the northern army into Munich.

At this stage hostilities both in Germany and in Italy were suspended. Bonaparte returned to Paris, hoping by negotiation to end the Austrian war and to save Egypt from the Turks and British. As always, his own position claimed his first attention. Marengo, however won, had recovered northern Italy, thus helping the First Consul to conquer the *emigrés* by glory. Louis XVIII, now a fugitive in Courland under Paul's protection, was bluntly told that a hundred thousand Frenchmen would die to debar him from the throne. Fouché taught innumerable agents of the administration to spy ceaselessly upon the disaffected. Soon the only hope of the dwindling Opposition seemed to lie in Bonaparte's assassination. A few genuine conspirators, however, only provided the Government with a pretext for indicting anyone of whom it disapproved. The France on which Bonaparte thus strengthened his hold, moreover, was becoming day by day more powerful. The end of civil strife and the existence of a strong and stable administration would alone have enabled her people to draw vast wealth from her bounteous soil. Their taxes amounted to hardly more than a quarter of those payable under the Bourbons, since Privilege no longer intercepted some three-fourths of what they paid. Five or six thousand revenue officials replaced some two hundred thousand. Population was rising fast, and it included a new class, perhaps 1,200,000 strong, which looked to Bonaparte to secure its possession of the national lands purchased after the Revolution. Although no government could have remedied in a moment the chaos left by the Directory, the First Consul swiftly convinced the French that in activity, boldness and intelligence, no government could vie with his. The Bank of France and Marengo appeared simultaneously.

Bonaparte and Europe

Although peace was denied by intransigent Britain, Bonaparte made great progress in redeeming France from isolation. Few could resist his personal fascination or the magic of his renown, and in his written appeals he often showed himself at once adroit and regal. By captivating Godoy he won Spain, and by captivating Paul he bade fair also to win Russia. From the degenerate Spanish Bourbons he received by the Treaty of San Ildefonso (1800) the vast domain of Louisiana. Half North America was thus obtained at the price of a secret undertaking to make its monarch's son-in-law King of Tuscany, a region which France did not possess. Through Spain, Bonaparte could strike at Portugal and thereby at Britain. But higher hopes for the overthrow of Britain and for the achievement of world-power were raised by his relations with Russia. The year 1800, indeed, furnished a counterpart to the year 1762, when Paul's reputed father suddenly forced Russia to change sides in time of war. Bonaparte, in whom this second half-demented Tsar rightly discerned a foe to the Revolution, delighted him by releasing the Russian prisoners. Britain, on the other hand, refused to return her new conquest of Malta to the Knights, who had elected Paul Grand Master.

The Second Armed Neutrality

Hence arose a most formidable combination, which placed Britain's maritime supremacy in peril and therefore made possible a boundless triumph for France. This, the Second Armed Neutrality, was formed between Russia, Sweden, Denmark and Prussia in December 1800. It revived and amplified the principles of law already formulated in the

First, and lately adopted by the French. The right of a neutral power to continue its trade with any belligerent, except in contraband, was again asserted. It was claimed once more that a blockade, to be binding upon neutrals, must resemble a real siege, and that those charged with breaking it should be arrested without violence. Prompt and judicial trial must follow, with appropriate damages to shipowner and State in case of error. The four associated neutrals now further demanded that the declaration of the commander of a convoying ship that the convoy carried no contraband should exempt the ships composing it from search. The fundamental reasonableness of these doctrines was to cause them in the main to become part of the Law of Nations in 1856. Within ten years of the Second Armed Neutrality, however, the exigencies of the life and death struggle between France and Britain would make their enforcement the wildest chimæra. At the moment they gave Bonaparte the opportunity of publicly blessing them as sacred and of declaring that until Britain had acknowledged that the sea belonged to all nations France would not treat for peace. This proclamation (Dec. 7) followed hard on Moreau's crushing victory at Hohenlinden, which exposed Vienna. The French army of Italy was joining in an advance upon that capital when, on Christmas Day, the Archduke Charles concluded an armistice. Austria, it was clear, must make peace without regard to her ally.

France and Europe 1800

The result of the year 1800, therefore, was to accentuate the struggle between France and Britain. Broadly speaking, the Continental powers had accepted the new France, or were on the point of doing so. At Paris the Bourbons had been dethroned, but the Family Compact seemed to be reviving. A Republic extended to its "natural frontiers" and buttressed by a system of client republics existed in virtue of the Rights of Man. Yet monarchs by divine right gave it recognition and accepted favours from it. Many dispassionate observers held that the freedom of the seas must be a myth until British naval preponderance was ended. France, which had most to gain from it, now found that view upheld by the masters of four considerable fleets. She could also count upon a fifth power, Spain, while the United States, neutrals by principle in the quarrels of the

Old World, had joined with her in a commercial treaty (Sept. 30).

Position of Britain

Britain, on the other hand, could draw consolation from the fact that her fleet was now not only large but experienced, that she stood committed to no expensive wars on land, and that sea warfare brought her many prizes and much profitable trade. She hoped to be stronger from the work of the dying year in Ireland, which the Act of Union had drawn closer to herself. She could reflect that the First Armed Neutrality had enriched her at the expense of its members, that the Second could not abolish the ancient feuds of Sweden with Denmark and with Russia, that Austria, though beaten, must remain a great power, and that the reign of a mad Tsar who betrayed his nation was likely to be short. In Egypt, moreover, she seemed certain to achieve her ends. Kléber, Bonaparte's brilliant lieutenant, had been stabbed to death by a fanatic, and his successors were lesser men, faced with a mutinous land and with Turkish and British armies. France none the less had acquired a deep interest in Egypt, and the hope of continuing to hold the tiny historic country swayed Bonaparte's political designs. If he could gain Austria and Russia, the Turkish Empire and India might be partitioned like Poland by an irresistible combination of three.

France and Russia

The first business of the new year, 1801, was therefore to overawe or overthrow Britain; the second, to net the profit from the decisive Austrian campaign. As in 1762, the technical enemy of Russia received a series of welcome proposals from the Tsar. " End our war, attack England, include the Portuguese and the Americans in the Armed Neutrality, join in invading India "—such were Paul's exhortations to France. Early in February, the Austrians signed at Lunéville a peace which in private they rightly styled terrible. In Italy the Adige now marked their boundary and Tuscany paid the price of Bonaparte's gains from Spain. In Germany, Austria must consent to see the French installed upon the Rhine, while Belgium became French, and the Batavian, Helvetian, Cisalpine and Ligurian republics received the guarantee of Austria as well as that of France. The evicted princes could only be compensated by secularizations, and to these the Holy Roman Emperor must consent.

As a dynast, Francis, however resentful against the French, could not fail to be tempted by their scheme for compensating him at the expense of Turkey.

The restoration of French power in Italy at Lunéville had caused the Cisalpine and Ligurian republics to reappear. The Parthenopean, however, was sacrificed to Paul, the new ally of France. Thanks to Paul's powerful intervention, the Bourbon at Naples, Ferdinand IV, kept his throne. He must consent, however, to close his ports against the British and to open them to the French, who counted on thus securing bases for their future eastern expedition. With the Pope, Bonaparte was bargaining hard for a Concordat which would rally the French Catholics to his side. At the same time the Catholic question in England brought about the resignation of Pitt, the centre and symbol of the war with France. It was under a King trembling on the verge of madness and the feeblest of premiers, Addington, that Britain entered on the campaign of 1801.

The Campaign of 1801

In 1801 Britain fought for peace, the more sincerely that she had lost every hope of measuring swords with France in Europe. Even if her fleet remained supreme, the contest had now become that of the elephant against the whale. The monstrous power of France upon the Continent appeared at every turn. Prussia occupied Hanover; Spain obediently attacked Portugal; Portugal, after a few weeks of stage warfare, capitulated early in June and closed her ports against Britain. Turkey alone resisted, and for her the fate of Poland and of Venice had been prepared. The acuteness of the peril nerved even a feeble and pacific British ministry to action. Britain treated the Armed Neutrality as a league against herself, and sent Parker and Nelson to the Baltic. At the same time she launched a great triple attack upon the French in Egypt. Every enterprise succeeded. At Copenhagen the Danes fought well, but Nelson, ignoring the signal to retire, compelled them to quit the Armed Neutrality (April). Meanwhile, in the Mediterranean, memories of his victory of the Nile were helping to make the French admiral cautious in the transport of reinforcements to Egypt. In military matters Bonaparte was no adventurer, but even he sometimes ignored the fundamental differences between warfare by sea and by land.

His admirals, however, must move as the wind allowed them, and might at any moment find their own persons under fire—considerations which affected their exact fulfilment of his plans. In 1801 the remains of his army of 1798 capitulated and their return from Egypt was effected in British ships.

Deposition of Paul I

The decisive event of the campaign, however, was the replacement of Paul by Alexander on March 23. The Tsar's capricious tyranny had given his capital the aspect of a penitentiary and convinced all educated men that he was unfit to rule. A regiment which displeased him on parade was ordered to march to Siberia: a Cossack force, to go to India and take it. Amiable and well-meaning by nature, he was popular with the soldiery and with many who had not suffered from his blind and ready rage. But in addition to the insults and cruel decrees which he dealt out daily, his breach with Britain robbed many of the nobles of the sole outlet for the produce of their estates. In Alexander, Russia possessed an heir of the highest promise, whose nickname in court circles was "The Angel." A plot centering in the Commandant of Petersburg, Count Pahlen, was formed to place him on the throne. To save himself and his family from his father's violence Alexander gave his consent. In 1762 the deposition of Peter III had been swiftly followed by his death. In 1801 Paul was wakened from a drunken sleep by the assassins, and it is said that his words proved that he suspected a younger son. The horror of succeeding by a crime of which he had never dreamt clouded the whole of Alexander's momentous reign.

The news of Paul's death was instantly recognized as the equivalent of peace between Russia and Britain. Nelson with twelve ships-of-the-line actually sailed into the Russian port of Reval as a friend (May).

Collapse of the Armed Neutrality 1801

In June, while the French power in Egypt was collapsing, a convention signed at Petersburg recorded the substantial triumph of Britain over the Second Armed Neutrality. Those demands of Russia and her associates which vindicated undoubted principles of law or indicted obvious abuses were courteously conceded by Britain. But Russia renounced the important claims that the commander of a convoying ship might forbid a belligerent warship to search his convoy, that the neutral flag protected innocent enemy merchandize on the high seas, and that blockade by cruisers was invalid. Deprived of Russian aid, her associates had no option but to concur. The result was that in a war with France Britain remained free to capture upon the high seas any French ship, any French goods upon a neutral ship, and, as contraband, all the tar and hemp, the sail-cloth and timber, the horses, saltpetre and munitions generally which were consigned to a French destination by any route. Provisions and clothing intended for the French armed forces were likewise contraband, and the list might at any moment be extended to include any article capable of warlike use. Bulls' hides, for example, when shipped to Algeciras to protect the hulls of ships intended to besiege Gibraltar, might lawfully be seized. A competent British authority, moreover, might heighten the inaccessibility of French ports to neutral traders by issuing a proclamation of blockade and sending cruisers from time to time to seize disobedient ships. Any neutral ship which wilfully defied such a proclamation rendered itself liable to seizure upon the high seas either in going or returning. The shippers were tempted to break these laws by the high prices which the French were prepared to pay, while to the British seamen a rich prize might mean a fortune. Speculators, therefore, fitted out privateers, whose profits largely depended upon their success in seizing contraband. It could hardly be expected that such units would observe the niceties of law as carefully as the king's ships, and neutrals regarded them as little more than pirates.

The United States and Europe

The power which was interested beyond all others in the respect for neutral rights was the United States. Its members owed their origin to a desire to escape from the delusions and quarrels of the Old World and were essentially neutral and commercial. France had helped them to become independent, and France had now adopted the view of human rights and the form of government for which they had fought as pioneers. To them Bonaparte naturally looked for aid in any struggle, whether military or commercial, against Britain. He had eased that tension caused by Talleyrand's intrigues which drove the Americans to sing "Hail Columbia" in place of the *Marseillaise*. At the moment he was intent on restoring the French colonial empire, and had therefore regained Louisiana from Spain. His American policy, however, would remain subordinate to his needs in Europe.

Prospects of Peace in 1801

Throughout modern times the outbreak of war has usually been popular with the combatants. This popularity has, almost without exception, soon given place to a deep desire for peace. The war of the Second Coalition had now dwindled into a war between France and Britain. Both nations were bearing the burden of a ninth or tenth campaign. Fundamentally, indeed, the two powers still remained opposed. France lived in the year IX, Britain in 1801. The Revolution championed by France still challenged historic Europe, which Britain still defended. From a less theoretical and more insular point of view, France dominated the coast of Europe from Holland to Italy in a manner which British statesmen must always regard as fatal to British security and British trade. But time, which by 1914 had brought Britain to accept the standing peril from the German fleet, had by 1801 convinced her that there were worse evils than an expanded France. Her traditional dislike of the French and contempt for their institutions helped her to tolerate their political and social reorganization. In the First Consul, moreover, many saw the saviour of France from the excesses and horrors of the Revolution. Britons were not slow to admire his military genius, even when displayed at the expense of their own allies. When Bonaparte declared that if he won his way to London the mob would rise in his favour, he was probably misinformed. But, as the street scenes of 1802 were soon to demonstrate, if he came as the friend of Britain the people would welcome him as their grandsons welcomed Garibaldi. Britons are unsurpassed in believing what they wish to believe about foreign nations, and to them the First Consul seemed to be a saviour of society as well as a military hero. He had at least driven from office those who had murdered their king and queen.

The British and Bonaparte

This popular feeling helped on the negotiations which, on a hint from Britain, took place in London during the summer of 1801. Nothing in Bonaparte is more astonishing than the speed with which he could accept an untoward fact, replacing the clear-cut and detailed plans which it disturbed with others equally practical and far-reaching.

Before the death of Paul his watchword had been the overthrow of Britain. Europe was to be closed to her commerce; her shores were to be threatened with invasion; French troops were to march by the shores of the Caspian into Egypt; the British hold upon the east was to be destroyed. Now that the Russian alliance and the army of Egypt had been lost, peace with Britain and the reorganization of France and her dependencies became the objective which Bonaparte used all his energy to attain. Two years earlier, with that ringing rhetoric which he could always command, he had invited George III to abandon their suicidal strife.

> "For eight years our war has ravaged the four quarters of the globe. Must it go on for ever? Our two nations are the most enlightened in Europe, mighty beyond what their safety and independence require. Do they not feel that peace is the prime need no less than the prime glory?"

Two years of further war had made Britain supreme by sea and France by land. One must regain access to Europe; the other, to the wider world. Immediate necessity, the present futility of struggle—these blinded their peoples to the unlikelihood of lasting concord. Throughout the century it had proved difficult for the world to contain them both. With Bonaparte at the head of France it was impossible.

In both countries the needs of the moment prevailed. By October 1, a provisional bargain had been arrived at. Paris illuminated at the news, and the London mob, believing that the envoy of Bonaparte was his brother, drew him in triumph through the streets. Six months of negotiation at Amiens gave them time to cool, and when peace was signed in March 1802, the lack of real concord was already evident.

Bonaparte's Supremacy 1801

The year 1801 was that in which the will of Bonaparte became beyond all question the will of France. As First Consul he already held her foreign policy in his hands. He now used his power over appointments and his rising popularity with the masses to root out all possible opposition, personal and constitutional alike. Royalist banditti infested the countryside and a royalist planned to murder the First Consul. Bonaparte replied by deporting his Jacobin opponents, by creating special tribunals to safeguard his authority, and by reducing the powers of the Tribunate. The negotiations with the Pope for a Concordat which would make the clergy Bonaparte's allies and agents were actively pushed on. Finally, since Bonaparte no less than Louis XIV realized that if he were supreme abroad France would the more devotedly obey him, the reorganization of western Europe was hurried on. This was, indeed, imperative, since France, revolutionary and aggrandized as she was, stood in grave risk of isolation. Whither could she turn for an ally ? Even a century later it was hard for a Tsar to ally Holy Russia with the Revolution. In 1801 it needed a madman on the Russian throne. Alexander, though he sincerely believed himself a republican, was a sentimental autocrat who saw in Bonaparte a militant Jacobin usurper. Austria, it was clear, could only wait her opportunity to avenge her Lunéville humiliation. Prussia, though willing to sell her neutrality at a high price, was wholly unworthy of trust. From Britain Bonaparte needed and expected only a truce. Provided that she acquiesced in the French overlordship in Europe, the truce might be prolonged until a great French navy had been built, and a great French colonial empire restored. Such acquiescence, however, was improbable. France must therefore enlarge and buttress herself at once so that when the British war broke out anew no hostile combination could bear her down.

France and Europe, 1802

Before peace was signed at Amiens (March 1802), Bonaparte's reorganization in France and Europe was already far advanced. The new Batavian republic formed a bridgehead beyond the Rhine and a sally-port for the advance to Hamburg and the lordship of the Elbe. French influence in Germany was sedulously maintained by controlling the secularizations, for which the German princes courted Talleyrand with indecent greed. In Switzerland, a vast natural fortress on the frontier of France, the Helvetic republic was a child over which Bonaparte claimed full parental rights. Between the Swiss confines and the sea, the House of Savoy had toiled for centuries to build up that dynastic state of which the names Savoy, Piedmont, and Sardinia record the evolution. This Bonaparte prepared to sweep away, and to give France her " natural frontier " of the Alps with the Italian plain at their feet. All Italy, indeed, must become in some form his appanage. A like fate was reserved for all Iberia, perhaps at a more distant date.

The Peace ill-founded

Before the treaty was signed Bonaparte's manifest intentions dimmed the joy with which Britain had received the news of peace. To some provisions, indeed, she consented at Amiens with no more sincerity than Austria at Lunéville. The nation could hardly believe it necessary that of all her conquests only Ceylon and Trinidad should be retained. She consented, however, to surrender the Dutch East Indies and the Cape, Minorca, Guadeloupe, Martinique and other lesser acquisitions. Thanks to Bonaparte, George III now ceased to style himself King of France. A far more solid concession was his tacit renunciation of the right to defend the balance of power in Europe. In ten years the nation with which Britain went to war in 1792 had wholly or partially absorbed six neighbouring nations, and this the Peace of Amiens implicitly condoned. In return for all these advantages, the French were to evacuate Portugal, Egypt, Naples and the Papal States, while the Ionian Islands became an independent republic. As the new Tsar renounced all claim to Malta, while both France and Britain knew its importance for the eastern Mediterranean, its future became the subject of an elaborate compromise. The powers agreed to guarantee its neutrality under the Knights of St. John, employing if necessary Neapolitan troops for its defence. Paper guarantees upheld by Neapolitans, whose military reputation was that whether dressed in red or in blue or in green they would always run away—these would form a frail rampart against Bonaparte, with his Corsican gaze fixed firmly on the regions to which Malta formed the key. This fact entered more deeply into British consciousness when it was realized that Amiens did nothing to remove the fierce French prohibition of the importation of British goods. The notion that, under Addington or any other, eighteenth-century Britons would wait meekly while Bonaparte closed their markets and created a fleet greater than their own appears fantastic. Amiens in 1802, like Aix-la-Chapelle in 1748, was a conscious and obvious truce.

The Concordat

If Britain used the breathing-space to husband her resources, Bonaparte made a far more spectacular advance. Both in France and beyond her frontiers, he gained fresh conquests day by day. Concurrently with the Peace of Amiens he achieved the Concordat with the Pope, which placed the power of his government upon a higher plane. When he styled it the vaccination of religion and predicted that in fifty years there would be none in France, he merely exposed the limits of his understanding. The papal blessing, none the less, gave Bonaparte's administration a new title to the allegiance of the majority of Frenchmen, and a set of disciplined and powerful supporters in the clergy. By the Concordat, Catholicism became the official faith of France, as it had been before the Revolution. Prelates were to be nominated by the First Consul and confirmed by the Pope. Parish priests were to be nominated by their bishop and confirmed by the First Consul. To rid France of the effects of the civil constitution of the clergy, which had cost Louis XVI his head, all sees were declared vacant and the Concordat procedure immediately applied. Thus where the Catholic autocrat Louis XIV had combined with his clergy to repel the Pope from France, Bonaparte, proud of having no religion, combined with the Pope to discipline the French Catholics.

The Consulate for Life, 1802

The peace and the Concordat naturally made Bonaparte more than ever the darling of the people. This he cleverly exploited to augment and to consolidate his power. In August, by one of those *plébiscites* for which Bonapartism became famous, he gained the Consulate for life. More than three and a half million Frenchmen were qualified by age to vote, and it was held that all favoured the proposal except those, numbering less than nine thousand, who openly voted "No." Thus supported, and having rallied many *emigrés*, though Louis XVIII remained obdurate, Bonaparte drew nearer to formal monarchy. He secured the right to appoint his successor, reduced the Tribunate, and instituted the Legion of Honour, which attached the *élite* of the nation to himself. To preserve the semblance of limited monarchy while freeing himself from the restrictions of a parliament, he increased the powers of the Senate, but secured to himself the nomination of a majority of its members and the right to summon it and to preside. Such was the constitution of the year X, by which Bonaparte and a majority of Frenchmen practically broke with the Revolution.

French Hegemony in Europe

In Europe, the new France took rapid steps towards supremacy. Before the Peace of Amiens the Cisalpine republic had given place to a so-called Italian republic, with

Bonaparte as its president and a constitution made by him. Soon the Ligurian republic was transformed into a similar dependency. Bonaparte's rule in French northern Italy, indeed, was far superior to that of the Austrians whom he had driven out, and to that of the remaining princes. Local laws and local tyrannies gave place to the institutions and to the administration of a great progressive power. In Holland, French rule was less successful, but the Prince of Orange renounced his claims and the people were apathetic. On both sides of the Rhine, the power of France was gaining at the expense of the Germans. On the left bank the inhabitants of the annexed regions profited by their transference to a rich and vigorous republic. On the right, princes and prelates courted French interference in the redistribution of Church lands and imperial cities. Prussia had secured ample compensation by the treaty of May 1802. Meanwhile the internal dissensions of the Swiss afforded a pretext for French intervention and Prussia and Austria declined to interfere. The French hegemony upon the Continent, it was clear, might go far before any power dared to oppose it. By the treaty of October 1802, France actually associated Russia with herself in the settlement of Germany and Italy. Britain alone was to be feared.

BIBLIOGRAPHICAL NOTE

See the Bibliographical Note at the end of Chapter I and the bibliographies to Chapters XV and XVII.
Add :—

A

H. C. Deutsch : *The Genesis of Napoleonic Imperialism* (1938).
H. A. L. Fisher : *Bonapartism* (1909, 2nd impr. 1914).
H. A. L. Fisher : *Napoleon* (1924).
L. Gershoy : *The French Revolution and Napoleon* (1933).
A. G. Macdonell : *Napoleon and his Marshals* (1934).
L. Madelin : *The Consulate and the Empire.* 2 vols. (trans. 1934–36).
L. Madelin : *Histoire du Consulat et de l'Empire.* 16 vols. (1937–54).
M. Reinhard : *Carnot.* 2 vols. (1950–52).
J. H. Rose : *The Revolutionary and Napoleonic Era* (7th ed. 1935).
E. L. Woodward : *French Revolutions* (1934).

B

F. Meinecke : *Das Zeitalter der deutschen Erhebung, 1795–1815* (3rd ed. 1946).
H. V. Treitschke : *History of Germany in the Nineteenth Century.* I (1886).

CHAPTER XIX

EUROPE FROM AMIENS TO TILSIT, 1802–7

France and Britain after Amiens

PEACE between France and Britain had been signed at the end of March 1802. In August, the two countries were again in bitter controversy. Britain harboured the irreconcilable *emigrés*, whose overt hostility was perhaps less dangerous than the disaffection of some who accepted the Consul's invitation to return. The free press of London irritated Bonaparte as the free press of Amsterdam had irritated Louis XIV. Failing to secure satisfaction from the government, he pressed on the aggrandizement of France in time of peace by measures which dwarfed the *Chambres de réunion* of the Great King. Britain was powerless to deliver the Dutch and Swiss, but she could cling to Malta, while Bonaparte's proceedings taught the British public that they must face a further war. In place of a new fraternity of nations they beheld the France of Louis XIV under a ruler who in military genius far outshone Turenne. Twelve years before, Burke had declared that in scanning the map of Europe he had found a great space empty—the space occupied by France. Now Sheridan could assert that if they looked at the map of Europe they would see there nothing but France. And no one who judged Bonaparte rightly could suppose that he would leave Britain mistress of the seas and of the old French colonial empire. Such a surrender was impossible for any vigorous ruler of France and for any great French soldier. He had used the armistice and peace to send a fleet and army to San Domingo, and to subjugate its negro republic. Although failure followed this first success, the adventure showed his bent. When Britain, early in 1803, further increased her armaments, kept Malta and demanded the evacuation of Switzerland and Holland, Bonaparte preferred to fight. Posing as mediator, he had already turned the Helvetic Republic into a Swiss Confederation of nineteen sovereign cantons, all powerless to resist the guardianship of France. Now he insulted the British envoy, Lord Whitworth, and left no doubt as to the insincerity of his renunciation of Egypt. In May, Whitworth quitted Paris, and Bonaparte embittered the new struggle by an act which long rankled in British minds. Cooped up for ten years in their own island, the class which looked to the grand tour rather than to school and university for education, flocked on the morrow of the Peace to France. Bonaparte professed that they belonged to the militia of their country, and flung some 10,000 civilians into prison. Visitors to Switzerland were equally affected by the decree. Defying the treaty of Basel, by which France conceded to Prussia the neutrality of the north German States, Bonaparte seized Hanover, and Prussia dared not intervene. Like Bavaria, Würtemberg and Baden among the chief secondary German States, she had lately been loaded with the spoils of the ecclesiastical foundations and France had made her more than ever the rival of Austria in Germany.

Campaign of 1803

The first campaign of the new war, indeed, consisted chiefly in movements in regions where opposition must be futile. The revived camp of invasion at Boulogne impressed France more than Britain. While the British seized Tobago, St. Lucia and British Guiana and conquered the Mahrattas, the French sold to Spain the right to remain neutral and themselves entered Naples. The Royalists in France and the Catholics in Ireland vainly planned insurrections. A characteristic and important step was taken by Bonaparte when he sold Louisiana to the United States for some fifteen million dollars, or, when interest payments were included, about twopence for every acre. Such an alienation of the national patrimony drove his brothers to remonstrate with him in his bath, but the autocrat scorned even to give them reasons. He doubtless calculated that the transfer would deprive the British of a conquest which France could not defend. It might well embroil them with the Americans, thus strengthening the prospect of a Franco-American alliance.

Sale of Louisiana

Death of d'Enghien

A war in which geography prevents the combatants from meeting must necessarily be languid, and Britain's weapon of blockade is seldom swift. Even a sluggish war, however, quickens the national pulse and hastens certain tendencies, notably that towards the rule of a dictator. In France, the Royalists, underrating Fouché's skill and Bonaparte's hold upon the nation, were plotting a Restoration. In February 1804, the government seized the conspirators, but no Bourbon pretender lay within their reach. Bonaparte's Corsican instinct prompted him to strike at the rival clan without regard to law. The Comte d'Artois, younger brother of Louis XVIII, had been privy to the plot; their nephew, the Duc d'Enghien, was not involved in it. But d'Enghien lived in the bishopric of Strasburg, only a few miles beyond the Rhine. Believing him guilty of conspiracy, the government had him kidnapped on March 14 and brought to Paris. Investigation proved him innocent beyond a doubt. Bonaparte, none the less, demanded his execution, and on March 21 he was shot. D'Enghien's death, like that of Nurse Cavell, was one of those crimes which rouse the conscience of mankind and which therefore in the long run help the enemy more than many battles. Of the real conspirators, but few were put to death, though Moreau, the victor of Hohenlinden, was banished, and Pichegru, one of the foremost soldiers of the Revolution, died in prison.

The Empire Established, 1804

The immediate consequence of the conspiracy was the First Empire. Carnot alone opposed the resolution of the Tribunate in favour of declaring Napoleon Bonaparte hereditary emperor of the French. On May 18, the senate saluted His Imperial Majesty, and in November the nation was declared to have confirmed the new constitution by a majority of about 1,390 against one. Only 2,569 Frenchmen recorded their opposition. France, it was clear, was prepared to fight in defence of her new *régime* of social equality, centralization, Catholicism and aggrandizement, under a despotism thinly disguised. How long social equality under an Emperor would survive, and how far French aggrandizement would proceed, the future alone could show. But it did not require the political vision of a Sieyès, one of the four opposing Senators, to see that a hereditary empire meant the succession of some Bonaparte far less talented than Napoleon. Joseph, the heir apparent, might have made a tolerable constitutional king but could never dominate the French. Napoleon's Corsican clannishness perhaps blinded him to the defects of his family, whom he promoted as though nature's monarchs one and all. But others could not fail to see that by crowning Napoleon France saddled herself with two tribes of quarrelsome mediocrities, the Bonapartes and their connexions the Beauharnais. Josephine Beauharnais, now Empress, brought Napoleon two step-children, Eugene and Hortense Beauharnais, but no child of their eight years' union. The Pope, summoned to Paris for the coronation in December, insisted that a secret religious marriage must be added to the civil ceremony, thus rendering more difficult a dissolution of the bond, should the interest of the dynasty require it.

At the very outset of the Empire, indeed, its incompatibility with the social equality of the Revolution made itself felt. Like several of his predecessors on the throne of France, Napoleon regarded himself as the heir of Charlemagne, the Emperor of the west. He brought from Aix-la-Chapelle the insignia and the sword which in some sense added a thousand years of history to his new title.

Likewise he turned to Germany, the home of formal dignity, for the human trappings with which the imperial dignity had been adorned. The second and third consuls became the arch-chancellor and arch-treasurer of the French Empire and sixteen marshals replaced the Princes and Electors. As the Holy Roman Empire was tottering, Francis II styled himself Francis I, Emperor of Austria. Napoleon's title he accepted, whatever it might portend, and burned the protest against it which he received from Louis XVIII.

Russia and Britain

While Austria thus avoided fresh adventure, and Prussia schemed for fresh expansion without recourse to war, Britain and Russia were uniting against Napoleon. War brought back Pitt to power, while the murder of d'Enghien made it easier for him to find allies against France. Of these Russia was by far the chief. The young Tsar, although no soldier, and a baffling mixture of suspicious autocrat and sincere idealist, was at this time impelled by many forces to oppose Napoleon. The protector of Louis XVIII in exile, he regarded himself as the champion of legitimacy against usurpation. Swayed by Adam Czartoryski towards the deliverance from German rule of the Poles, whose king he wished to be, he found France in the way of the necessary combinations. A Russian Tsar, German by descent and marriage, he resented the new influence of France in Germany. France, moreover, clearly coveted power in the Near East, always Russia's cherished sphere of influence.

The Third Coalition

Napoleon's crime helped to drive Russia into the arms of Britain, who could pay her armies and make the seas safe for her trade. The *entente* between Britain and Russia which preceded their alliance in turn influenced Austria, which had failed to displace Prussia and Bavaria in Napoleon's system. Austrian policy proved as hesitant as Prussian, but in 1805 Napoleon turned the scale by his treatment of Italy. There he made himself King, and the Habsburgs judged that with Napoleon King of Italy they must draw the sword or abandon Venice. The Emperor, indeed, seized Genoa in the midst of his negotiation. Thus the Third Coalition came to comprise three whole-hearted great powers and appeared more formidable than the two preceding leagues of Europe.

The Third Coalition came definitely into being in August 1805, when Austria acceded to the Treaty of St. Petersburg made between Britain and Russia in April. A minor member, Sweden, added only 12,000 men to its armed forces, but removed a standing threat against the Russian rear. Prussia declined to commit herself to either side, though insulted by the French occupation of Hanover. The allies proposed to restore the former boundaries of France, and so to rearrange the border territories as to fortify Europe against a future French irruption. With the internal government of France they declined to interfere. More than 400,000 men were to be mustered by the continental powers at an annual cost to Britain of £12 10*s*. for every man.

Prospects of the Third Coalition War

The pay-roll was enormous and the numbers great, but the Coalition suffered from obvious defects. The Russians must fight far from home; the Austrians would think more of annexations than of hard fighting; and composite forces were to operate on either flank. Napoleon, on the other hand, disposed of a force nearly half as numerous, much of it drilled to perfection at Boulogne and all moved by the single will of a consummate strategist and inspector-general. He could double its numbers by conscription, while in Spain and the south German states he possessed obedient allies. None the less, his campaign of 1805 staggered Europe. In July the stage seemed to be set for the invasion of Britain. Calder, however, met Villeneuve in the Bay of Biscay and was not defeated. Without superiority at sea, the French could not hazard their army in an island.

Campaign of 1805

Early in August, Napoleon offered Hanover to Prussia in return for neutrality, undertaking to make its cession by George III a *sine qua non* of peace. Prussia did not scout the offer, and the French could therefore strike at Austria unperturbed. Before the month was out, the army of Boulogne was marching towards the Danube. In six weeks they reached the river. By October 19 they had enveloped Mack, a paper strategist, at Ulm and captured some 50,000 men. This brilliant success, indeed, was soon in some degree offset by Trafalgar (Oct. 21) which proved that even under Napoleon the Revolution was not invincible. Prussia, moreover, had now armed to defend a neutrality which Alexander respected and which Napoleon treated with contempt. At the end of October, Louise, the beloved Prussian queen, descended with her husband and the Tsar into the crypt of the garrison church at Potsdam where the great Frederick rests. There, by his coffin, the two rulers swore mutual fidelity, and soon a Prussian ultimatum to Napoleon was drawn up. Ulm had not crushed the Austrians; in Italy they were partially victorious; the Russians were coming up; 180,000 Prussians might well turn the European scale.

This fair prospect, however, was banished by Napoleon's skill and speed. In mid-November he marched into Vienna. Although his armies might soon be hemmed in by a vastly superior coalition, he would neither offer terms which Francis could accept nor consider those which the allies demanded. As a soldier he looked on battle as the true source of profit. Negotiations were a form of tactics to gain time and weaken his opponents' will. Now as always, moreover, the feeling that he was an upstart, not like Louis XIV the inheritor of France, shaped his course. He must keep the throne as he had won it, by unbroken and dazzling success. At Austerlitz (Dec. 2) on the first anniversary of his coronation, he gained the most dazzling victory of his career. Having convinced the enemy that he dared not face the Austrian and Russian armies, each with an Emperor at its head, he trapped and destroyed them both, and with them the Coalition. His greatest conquest, however, was over the Tsar himself.

Peace of Pressburg, 1805

During the Empire, the history of Europe was often shaped by the moods and prejudices of two or three high-placed persons. Among these the Tsar was second only to the lord of France. Russian policy was determined by the conflict within his complex soul. "Mysterious being, mixture of strange impulses, with something baffling in his purposes and unpredictable in his actions," Alexander felt that Napoleon was his superior long before his policy bore witness to the fact. "In the Russian mind above all there seem to be mysterious fervours and subtle workings and strange broodings; and in Alexander himself there was a curious interweaving of German transcendentalism with all this" (Butterfield). At the same time Napoleon was ever more completely sacrificing France to his own dynastic aims. All initiative and all glory must be ascribed to the Emperor, with the inevitable result that the national initiative waned and the source of glory was drying up. Napoleon's methods and behaviour could not but alienate great Frenchmen and stunt the growth of those who might have filled their place.

Austerlitz, indeed, decided but it did not end the war. Abandoned by Russia, which retreated, and by Prussia, which allied itself with France, Austria could only sue for peace. This she obtained at Pressburg, but at a terrible cost. The Habsburg dominions north and south of the Alps, the Habsburg authority in Germany and Italy, the Habsburg exchequer and administration—all were disposed of by Napoleon. Venice passed to the Italian kingdom, Tyrol to Bavaria, Swabia to the other south-German allies of France. These allies also gained independence of the Emperor, Bavaria and Würtemberg becoming kingdoms and Baden a grand duchy. In return for Hanover, Prussia acquiesced in what was done, and made some smaller cessions. Her ports upon the North Sea were to be closed against the British. Terms due to the panic of his envoy Haugwitz, after Austerlitz, King Frederick William dared not disavow, and Prussia became the nominal ally of France.

Britain at once replied by seizing some 400 Prussian merchantmen within her ports.

The Campaign of 1806

The new year, 1806, opened with the brightest prospects for Napoleon. The Revolution, it might well appear, had done its work by installing a new and greater Louis XIV as the lawgiver of Europe. The claim that, led by France, humanity had broken with its past was now implicitly renounced. On New Year's Day the year XIV was abandoned and the Gregorian calendar resumed. Trafalgar, it was true, had crippled the French and Spanish fleets. But Nelson had perished: French sea-power might yet revive: the master of the Continent could press other fleets into his service: the United States would fight to maintain their trade to the West Indies: Britain, Napoleon determined, should be starved or impoverished into surrender. Austerlitz had killed Pitt, who left no heir to his name and inspiration. For a full year, under Grenville and the Ministry of All the Talents, Britain was governed by a discordant coalition and a mentally unstable King. Until his death in September, the most conspicuous minister was Fox, whose passion had been peace with France. At sea, indeed, Britain remained supreme, but how could sea-power alone bring victory?

Napoleon's Pomp of Power

The hero of Austerlitz was now free to remould at his will the countries upon his borders. On the morrow of the Pressburg Treaty he proclaimed to the world that the Bourbons of Naples had ceased to reign. Ferdinand fled from the peninsula, to be maintained as ruler of Sicily by a British fleet. The throne of Naples, like thrones old and new on all sides, was filled by one of Napoleon's relations. There his brother Joseph was proclaimed King of the Two Sicilies. In Holland his third brother, the docile Louis, became king, with Hortense, Napoleon's stepdaughter, as queen. Eugene Beauharnais, her brother, already served as viceroy in Italy, where a dozen new duchies dowered Napoleon's marshals. Murat, the incomparable dragoon, became his brother-in-law and Duke of Berg. The sisters Bonaparte received Italian principalities. Within the family Napoleon would not suffer the marriage-tie to check his designs. Jerome obediently divorced his wife and became a prince, the husband of a Würtemberg princess. Lucien, Napoleon's saviour on the 18 *Brumaire*, refused a like compliance and thereby fell into disgrace. In this triumphal year, Napoleon styled himself the Great and made a national festival of August 15, his birthday. His mother, who received the strange title of Madame Mère and an ample income, remained undazzled by the new splendours and hoarded against the hard times which she expected when the bubble burst.

Napoleon and the new Germany

While in Italy and Holland, as in France, 1806 continued a transformation previously begun, the face of Germany was in this year completely changed. At Napoleon's bidding, the Holy Roman Empire passed away. It was replaced by a tripartite Germany in which Napoleon could govern. The western third with some eight million people formed a Confederation of the Rhine under French protection. French military and civil administration was introduced and French foreign policy became supreme. For federal business, a diet, presided over by a prince-primate, was to meet at Frankfort-on-the-Main. This was to consist of the representatives of states of a moderate size, in contrast with the minute principalities which rendered Germany a laughing-stock. By an act of mediatization, some fourscore petty princes, hitherto subject only to the Holy Roman Empire, were absorbed by their stronger neighbours. Bavaria, Würtemberg, Baden and the prince-bishopric of Mainz were the leading members, together with Berg, two branches of the House of Hesse and the southern Hohenzollerns. Within their dominions serfdom vanished and the French freedom of career was introduced.

According to Napoleon's plan, the Rhenish Confederation was to have for neighbours Prussia, which gained Hanover, and Austria, which lost Swabia and Venice. Whatever Prussian gratitude might be worth, France could safely count on Prusso-Austrian friction. In such a Europe she needed only peace with Britain to defy Russia and partition Turkey. Failing this, by agreement with Russia she could destroy all save a fragment of British trade and perhaps dominate the east. To buy Britain she offered Hanover with which she had just bought Prussia. As Britain refused, she turned to Russia, but met with a decisive check. Early in July, Prussia had undertaken not to fight against the Tsar. A month later, the news of Napoleon's treachery concerning Hanover caused a Prussian mobilization.

Prussia and the Fourth Coalition 1806

Deluded by memories of Rossbach, Prussia challenged France with unwary haste. Napoleon vainly appealed to Frederick William for the peace which at that moment he required. Spain, as he knew, was on the verge of a revolt against him, and Pitt, before he died, had prophesied that in Spain the deliverance of Europe would begin. The Emperor's immediate tasks were to partition Turkey, to embellish France, and to expand the Rhenish Confederation. But he divined that, if Prussia challenged him, she must be sure of Russia, and that his only course was to break the Fourth Coalition, like the Third, before the Russians could arrive in force. Again with lightning speed French forces turned the opposing army. Marching through hostile Saxony, they cut off the Prussians from the Elbe, and overwhelmed them at Jena and Auerstädt. At Jena—for Auerstädt had been won against colossal odds by Davoust and was belittled by Napoleon—the Prussian army collapsed far more completely than the Austrian at Austerlitz. Blücher, indeed, fought on with conspicuous valour, and the King, fleeing as in the Thirty Years War towards Königsberg, refused humiliating terms of peace. But the great structure reared by Frederick tumbled at a blow. The fortresses surrendered almost on demand, Magdeburg, the precious key to the barrier of the Elbe, containing twenty generals whose united ages numbered some 1,370 years. Stettin and its 5,000 defenders capitulated to an empty wagon on a hill. On October 25, the eighteenth day of the campaign, the French entered Berlin. Soon Napoleon harvested the fruits of Jena. Prussia had proved unworthy of her destiny—to be the watch-dog of France against Vienna: if suffered to survive, she must be crippled and hemmed in by hostile states. On the west, therefore, the French frontier was moved forward to the Elbe, while Hesse-Cassel and Brunswick were seized to form a new kingdom of Westphalia. South of Berlin lay Saxony, a member of the Fourth Coalition, but of old Prussia's victim or her rival. She, like her southern counterpart, Bavaria, was admitted to the Confederation of the Rhine and raised into a kingdom, while Saxon zeal against Prussia might find a rich reward in other portions of their long-disputed plain. Finally, on November 21, Napoleon marked the conquest of Prussia by issuing from Berlin the

French Reorganization of Germany

decree which was to conquer British sea-power on dry land.

The Continental System

The Berlin Decree inaugurated the so-called Continental System, a gigantic reprisal against the maritime claims of Britain. The Armed Neutrality had been forced to accept blockade by cruisers as part of the Law of Nations. Napoleon now declared every British port in a state of permanent blockade. Neutrals had long desired a fixed list of contraband. Napoleon gave them a list which was short and comprehensible—all British goods by land or sea and all goods destined for Britain. British civilians, moreover, were to be seized and imprisoned if found in the dominions of France or her allies. Before long, luxuries from the East were entering France by way of the Baltic, Odessa and the Danube, at prices proportioned to the toil and risk involved.

The Campaign of 1807

The campaign of 1807 was begun early by the Prussian and Russian armies, but earlier still by the ministry of Britain. Napoleon's attempt to cut off the nation's food and to annihilate its trade had the inevitable result of rendering it immaterial which party was in office so far as concerned the continuance of the war. The Whigs, indeed, were about to give place to the Tories, since they would not abjure Catholic emancipation, the bugbear of George III. But it was they who, in January 1807, launched the first of those Orders in Council with which Britain fought the Continental System. In substance these declared the ports which obeyed Napoleon to be blockaded and forfeited the property of nations which seized British goods. Reversing the usual course, they prohibited the sale of neutral vessels to belligerents. By the combined action of the Berlin Decree and the Orders in Council, the United States found their trade with Europe practically forbidden by law.

Such were the opening moves in the campaign of 1807. They were soon followed by the clash of arms on land. For all his brilliant triumphs, Napoleon was still confronted by Prussian and Russian armies. He wintered some 700 miles from Paris.

Every march eastwards placed dubious Austria further in his rear and exposed a further stretch of flanking seaboard to the British fleet. The obvious remedy was to detach Russia by battle or by negotiation. If by battle, common prudence dictated a swift attack before the Baltic ice should thaw, or the Coalition widen, or Napoleon's enemies in Spain and Paris rise. Common prudence no less demanded that for a campaign on or beyond the Vistula he should if possible enlist the co-operation of the Poles.

Napoleon and the Poles

Excepting eloquence and martial valour, indeed, Napoleon and the Poles possessed no quality in common. Religious, chivalrous, insubordinate, unpractical, the Polish nation was everything that he despised. Its partitioned state, indeed, was a standing contradiction to the doctrines of the Revolution. But in Napoleon's eyes liberty and equality, democracy and nationality were folly. No revolutionary nonsense could warrant an unpardonable affront to three strong states for the sake of one that must at best be weak. To restore distant Poland in the face of Prussia, Austria and Russia would be far more dangerous than to create Italy at the expense of Austria alone. No man ever understood better than Napoleon, however, the art of appeal to instincts which he did not share, and in making and breaking promises no man was bolder. Whatever he thought of the Revolution, he could always quote its creed. To rally the Poles for the campaign without permanently alienating Russia—such was the problem which he solved with brilliant success. Polish legions already fought for France. Napoleon, through Polish leaders, summoned the Poles to join them and thus prove to him that they deserved to be a nation. Kosciuszko, set free by Paul I, demanded a binding promise. Napoleon merely used the hero's name without his consent. He thus gained thousands of recruits and the affection of the Polish countryside and gave nothing in return.

The campaign of 1807

The closing months of 1806 had shown that the Prussian army was a shrunken remnant and that Napoleon's marshals could outwit the Russians. The Emperor passed a few pleasant weeks at Warsaw, the eastern Paris, before Bennigsen brought a new Russian army to protect East Prussia. Napoleon must therefore give battle in the midst of snow and ice. He hoped for a new Ulm or Jena, but at Eylau he found his Zorndorf. Bennigsen, indeed, retreated, but the strength of his position, the skill of his gunners and the stubborn valour of his troops had cost Napoleon dear. As on a more famous field, the advent of a Prussian *corps* decided the issue. Napoleon, victorious on paper, moved from Poland into Prussia and offered the King his kingdom for a separate peace. Hardenberg, however, succeeded in maintaining the alliance, and the valiant defence of Colberg showed that the Blücher spirit was abroad. In March, domestic politics in England brought back the Tories into power and Pitt's disciple, Canning, became Foreign Secretary. Next month, though the siege of Danzig promised to hamper the British fleet, Prussia, Russia and Sweden bound themselves at Bartenstein to fight on and to make peace in common. Defying Austerlitz and Jena, a Fifth Coalition was in being. Before Britain could strike, however, Napoleon, on the anniversary of Marengo, crushed Bennigsen at Friedland, and entered Königsberg, Frederick William's second capital (June). With the Russians driven across the Niemen, Prussia had suffered such a conquest as Austria never knew.

Friedland and Tilsit 1807

The fate of Prussia and of Europe now depended on a conference between Napoleon and the Tsar. On June 25, the two men met at Tilsit on a raft moored in mid-stream. They emerged as allies, pledged to impose upon the Coalition the settlement which they had there drawn up.

As in 1762 and 1801, Russia had suddenly changed sides in the conflict between France and Britain. At Bartenstein on April 26 Alexander had pledged himself to free Prussia and in many respects to restore historic Europe. At Tilsit, less than two months later, he arranged the details consequent upon the decision which he had made a week before—to ally himself with Napoleon. Peter III and Paul I had not equalled their descendant. Yet Alexander, though superstitious and emotional, was no madman. He seems rather to have been one of those rare and dangerous statesmen who can believe at will that in seeking their own advantage they are practising an altruism inspired from on high. Despite his German blood, his character was Russian, and Russians are notoriously prone to despair and to sudden action. Russia, he realized, was faced with ruin. Prussia was conquered; Austria might join Napoleon; Britain had found troops for several distant expeditions but as yet no Russian loan and nothing for the Baltic. The French stood at his gates, with armies in every way superior to his own. They had already roused the Poles and Persians against him, and the Turks might follow. Was Holy Russia to be dissolved or the Tsar murdered for a scruple about keeping faith with Europeans? The easier course of accepting an enormous bribe might well seem truer patriotism.

The German settlement of Tilsit

Napoleon's bribe included concessions to Prussia which enabled Alexander to feel himself Frederick William's saviour. Brandenburg, Silesia, and East Prussia were to remain intact, while a broad Prussian corridor still passed south of Danzig. The remainder of Prussian Poland, however, went to form a duchy of Warsaw under the King of Saxony. With the Rhenish Confederation and French forces at their back, the Saxons thus gripped Silesia and gained the right to march across it. Prussia west of the Elbe was included in a new kingdom of Westphalia under Napoleon's brother Jerome. This, with all Germany save Austria and Prussia, entered the Rhenish Confederation. The Germans would in future look to Paris for leadership, rather than to Vienna or Berlin. Halved in territory and population, largely disarmed, surrounded by French dependencies, herself garrisoned by 100,000 French, on the pretext that impossible arrears had not been paid, Prussia was forced to join France and Russia against Britain.

Tilsit and Russia

To Russia, though defeated, Tilsit was worth many a victorious campaign. At the price of recognizing what Napoleon had done and of promising to join in what he meant to do, the Tsar saved Prussia, averted a formidable invasion, and actually gained the region of Bialystok, which since the Third Partition had been Prussian. Alexander might hope that, as in 1801, Britain would come to terms when no land-power remained to fight against the French. But even if war continued, Russia was almost unassailable by sea, and on the land rich booty offered. Finland might easily be hers, and the Danubian principalities or other parts of Turkey. With such hopes she accepted the French alliance. Her duty was to coerce Britain by joining the Continental System and by helping to bring Denmark, Portugal and Sweden within its ranks.

Napoleon in Paris

At the end of July, Napoleon returned to Paris. He was losing Talleyrand from the department of Foreign Affairs, while his Corsican enemy, Pozzo di Borgo, was gaining influence at Vienna. These were important changes at a moment when he had taken on his shoulders little less than the management of Europe. But Paris revelled in the unwonted peace and novel splendour, while Napoleon's energy seemed adequate to any task. "I am always working," he declared, "at dinner, at the theatre, in the night. My destiny is to change the face of the globe." Now his hand was everywhere. He suppressed the Tribunate, decreed vast public works, bound Würtemberg to himself by Jerome's marriage, forced the Pope and Tuscany into the Continental System, fortified Corfu and Cattaro in the Adriatic, and prepared an invasion of Portugal which would strengthen his hold on Spain. At the same time, from the Atlantic to the Baltic coasts, he was vigorously arming against Britain. Sweden still obeyed the madman Gustavus IV, whose cult was legitimacy and whose model Charles XII. His notion of a neo-Carolingian masterpiece was to renew the struggle with Napoleon after Tilsit. The French promptly deprived him of Stralsund and prepared to launch the Danes against Sweden. At this point, however, Canning intervened.

Britain and the Danish Fleet 1807

Denmark, where a madman reigned, and a narrow-minded crown prince governed, now found herself in a most perplexing situation. Her strength had been to sit still while the great powers fought, and with swollen commerce and soaring prices, to enjoy the profits of neutrality. The Berlin Decree and Britain's reply to it inevitably changed the scene. Soon France took in Hamburg and threatened Holstein. By land the Danes could not cope with the French, nor by sea with the British. A trading nation whose capital lay on an island, their fear of British sea-power would probably decide their action, but Canning did not wait. To assist the Coalition, a belated British force had passed the Sound, and reinforcements were on their way, when Canning received false news that the Danes had become the tools of Napoleon. The danger to the expedition and to Britain was forestalled by an act of violence which with that of 1755 earned for Albion the enduring epithet *perfide*. Having in vain demanded the custody of the Danish fleet, she seized it after bombarding Copenhagen. The capture of Heligoland, the key to the Elbe, followed. For a time the moral scales turned against the lawless power. Denmark joined Napoleon, Austria acceded to the Continental

System, all nations suffered it more readily, and in November Russia declared war. At the same time Napoleon sharpened the Continental System by ordering that on the southern coast of the North Sea any ship which had touched at a British port should be confiscated. In reply, a new Order in Council declared that any ship which had not touched at a British port should be good prize. Napoleon's rejoinder, known as the Milan Decree, denounced as confiscable any neutral vessel which had done so.

Britain in 1807

The confused and violent history of 1807 ended with the flight of the royal family of Portugal to Brazil and the British blockade of a Russian squadron in the Tagus. Portugal, in Napoleon's eyes, formed a southern counterpart to Denmark. By conquering her he furthered the blockade of Britain. Britain, however, secured the escape of the Portuguese fleet, thus further lessening her own peril from a composite Napoleonic navy. But while the French campaign had expanded land-power from Kovno to Lisbon, sea-power had conquered only Curaçao and Heligoland for Britain. In the Baltic, the eastern Mediterranean and South America she had failed. At any moment, moreover, the United States might join her foes. For the time being, Jefferson, the pacific President, merely laid an embargo on the ships of both the powers which were trampling on neutral rights. In the life-and-death struggle between them, however, it was unlikely that such an attempt "to make war without bloodshed" would succeed, or that Britain, as the stronger at sea, would not appear the chief offender. Shut out from the Old World and menaced in the New, how could she avoid defeat?

Prospects in 1807—Russia

The counter-question inevitably posed itself. Could the Tilsit system prove enduring? The partnership between the autocrats of eastern and of western Europe could flourish only if each remained secure at home and continued to attain his ends abroad. From internal disruption Alexander had little to fear. No part of his gigantic empire possessed the means or perhaps even the will to break away. In language, religion and social custom, the true Russians were the most homogeneous of peoples, while of their subject races few were formidable. Even the Baltic Germans loyally served the Tsar to his advantage and to their own.

The Lithuanians and White Russians annexed by Catherine had gained by the exchange. On the other hand, Russian history since 1682 bristled with proofs that the Russians could find means to rid themselves of rulers of whom they disapproved. Although the gentry loved French culture, they knew well that only by trade with Britain could they find money with which to gratify their tastes. In commerce as in politics, France had always failed them. Would Napoleon serve them better than the Bourbons? Moldavia and Wallachia, Constantinople, Greece, the Straits, islands in the Mediterranean—all these stood high on the list of Russian aims. Moldavia and Wallachia, as Danubian principalities, were hardly tenable without the consent of Austria, the chief Danubian state. Could and would Napoleon always bend Austria to his will? Would the Rhenish Confederation and the new Warsaw serve France in place of dismembered Prussia as a lever upon Austrian policy? Austria had become a compact as well as a powerful state: her gaze had been turned from Germany and Italy towards the east: she had always regarded the advance of Russia to the Danube as fatal to her power. As to more distant goals, Napoleon deemed Constantinople the natural seat of a world empire and merely masked his own ambitions by proposing to leave it to the Turks. His interest in Egypt was well known. At his bidding Alexander had withdrawn from the Mediterranean, where French fortifications pointed to a pending French advance. Stripped of romance, and with Alexander romantic ideas usually yielded to his inborn egotism, the partnership with Napoleon dwindled into a temporary expedient to escape from an awkward situation. "What need," Panin once asked, "has Russia of an ally, for who would dare to attack her?" In 1807, thanks to events almost beyond belief, the answer became "Napoleon." Russia astutely countered the blows of fate by making Napoleon her ally, for as long as suited her convenience. "The Angel" could not suppose Napoleon proof against his high idealism, intelligence and charm. Napoleon, of course, meant to make Russia his tool until their interests clashed. A greater soldier than Frederick and a far greater politician, he might well count on dazzling Alexander as Frederick had dazzled Peter III. With Russian aid he could swiftly close the north to British trade and at the same time withhold essential supplies from the British navy. The alliance, therefore, would remain for some time a pillar of his system. But, Russia apart, was that system securely based?

Prospect before the Empire

The answer must largely turn upon "a force difficult to marshal but irresistible when marshalled," which in the twentieth century was to re-draw the map of Europe—the force of Nationality. In 1807 that force was powerful in some countries, notably Russia, France and Britain; in others of doubtful strength, as in Spain, Italy and Prussia; in others, among which Germany was most conspicuous, plainly weak. How far a people with a strong national sense could absorb others was as yet little known. In modern times Bretons, Alsatians and Lorrainers had become Frenchmen. The same assimilating process might well go on within the "natural boundaries" of France—the Rhine, the Alps and the sea. Since the Revolution, moreover, the French could offer a new social equality which attracted many of their client peoples, while the Empire provided a system of administration which was clear-cut and intelligent beyond all others in Europe. Where the French were least hampered, as on the left bank of the Rhine, in Italy or in the new kingdom of Westphalia, the masses were the most grateful for their emancipation. There the feudal relics, tithes, *corvées*, absurd divisions, the tyranny of churchmen and of antiquated laws, all yielded to the orderly rule of prefects and sub-prefects, the concordat and the civil code. If taxation and conscription were heavy they were not capricious, and as a set-off the government made roads, established industries and instituted public works. The wars, moreover, set money in circulation and could be justified as distant defensive operations necessary for a lasting peace. Like Italy, Germany both north and south gained from the example and the ideas of France, and began to rise from the local outlook towards the national.

It was unlikely, however, that all western Europe could be comprised in France, or that the mixed team of Bonapartes, Bourbon and German princes could work in harmony with an all-potent Emperor. Napoleon shared the fatal foible of Louis XIV—intolerance of other men's opinions. While his best years lasted, he would doubtless retain his crown and surpass the Romans in developing his dominions. But since Louis XV died the most stable monarchy in Europe had become the most insecure. Of the six French sovereigns who followed Louis XVI all save one were driven from the throne, and that one was the nominee of foreign powers. Napoleon, as he well knew, reigned in defiance both of the Bourbons and of the Revolution. With peace, he feared men would claim liberty, and in his own capital the Emperor would be in danger. Only in "necessary" wars could he remain indispensable.

Regeneration of Prussia

Immediately, however, the Empire was threatened rather from without. Britain was bound to fight for her existence. Though her debt was huge, it was hard to say that either her financial or her maritime power was failing. To Napoleon, moreover, Austria might well become as dangerous as Russia. In Metternich, Francis had secured a minister who, like Talleyrand, faced Napoleon's thunders with a pitying contempt for his ill-breeding. In Prussia a marvellous regeneration had begun. "I should as soon have expected a resurrection of the Romans," wrote Scott a few years later, "as of the Prussians." The year which followed Jena proved, however, that Prussia had her pride, and that her greatness under Frederick had not emanated wholly from the King. Guided by enlightened ministers from non-Prussian Germany, the Prussian people embarked on an arduous course of training and reform. In October 1807, Stein, by his Edict of Emancipation, went far towards abolishing that horizontal cleavage between the classes which had hitherto seemed vital to the Prussian state. No longer were the Hohenzollerns to rule over an empire organized, like the Turkish, wholly for war and conquest, with the noble caste commanding the peasant rank and file and the burgher caste acting as commissariat. Henceforth Prussian subjects were to be citizens who might purchase any land and enter any calling. As Napoleon had limited the army to some 42,000 men, Scharnhorst, a peasant's son, planned a short service system with a large trained reserve and strong militia. The national power was to be developed by new systems of education, finance, and urban government. While every year brought some great and wise reform, Prussia shared in the new spirit which was kindled by the Romantic School of British writers. A host of creative artists, Schiller and Goethe foremost among them, were signalizing the German genius and gilding the German past. By their eminence if not by their exhortations, they made men proud to be Germans. Among wide sections of the people, pride in their fatherland dictated the eviction of the French, the classic foes of Teutondom for at least three hundred years. Throughout Prussia, hatred of Napoleon and ambition to lead Germany against him spread like a fever. It was at least probable that among the many races lately subdued by France, others no less disaffected would be found.

BIBLIOGRAPHICAL NOTE

See Bibliographical Note at the end of Chapter I and the bibliographies to Chapters XV, XVII and XVIII.
Add :—

A

H. Butterfield : *The Peace Tactics of Napoleon, 1806–1808* (1929).

G. S. Ford : *Stein and the Era of Reform in Prussia, 1807–1815* (1922).

W. F. Galpin : *The Grain Supply of England during the Napoleonic Period* (1925).

C. de Grunwald : *Baron Stein* (trans. 1936).

E. F. Heckscher : *The Continental System* (1922).

E. W. Lyon : *Louisiana in French Diplomacy* (1933).

F. E. Melvin : *Napoleon's Navigation System* (1919).

J. R. Seeley : *The Life and Times of Stein.* 3 vols. (1878).

P. F. Shrupp : *The European Powers and the Near Eastern Question, 1806–1807* (1931).

A. D. White : *Seven Great Statesmen* (1927).

B

E. Botzenhart (ed.) : *Freiherr vom Stein : Briefwechsel, Denkschriften und Aufzeichnungen.* 2 vols. (1931–37).

CHAPTER XX

NAPOLEON AND THE CONTINENTAL SYSTEM, 1808–12

THE events of 1808 suggested that Napoleon might find a troublesome stumbling-block in Spain. That year, indeed, afforded the curious spectacle of a deadly war ending its seventh campaign with only a minor and indecisive battle. Britain could array no great army against France: France could array no great navy against Britain. Some unforeseen conjuncture and Napoleon's scheme for defeating sea-power on the land offered the only hope of peace. Time, which disarms the superman, might in the end frustrate Napoleon, but could Britain hold out for another ten or twenty years? King, parliament and society indeed stood firm, and no ministers could be abler or more resolute than Castlereagh and Canning. But British organization, both political and military, showed grave defects which could not be repaired in time of war, nor could the mob be trusted. If Europe made no move against Napoleon and the Americans took his part, Britain might be forced into a second peace of Amiens or worse.

The Year of Crisis 1808

Early in 1808 the new allies began to reap the harvest sown at Tilsit, a process which continued throughout the year. In February, Austria joined the Continental System. Napoleon therefore urged that while Britain could not interfere Turkey should be partitioned between France, Austria and Russia. To occupy and to conciliate his dubious ally of Tilsit, he was ready to concede him Sweden. He himself strove to secure the Mediterranean and planned to invade India. Alexander promptly seized what lay within his reach and merely negotiated about more far-reaching schemes. The Finns, though Swedish since the fourteenth century, were in origin and language as foreign to the Russians as to the Swedes. Their cousins the Estonians under the German baronial conquerors had belonged successively to the Danish, the Swedish and the Russian states. While the sea was frozen, the Tsar's troops easily vanquished the Swedish garrison in Finland. The Finns themselves were prepared to resist conquest but willing to accept autonomy from Russia. Alexander chose this path, and by midsummer the grand-duchy was in his hands.

Napoleon and Spain

Napoleon, meanwhile, had met with an unexpected obstacle to his designs. For every reason—prestige, spread of good government, control of Portugal, maritime power, the Continental System—he must strengthen his hold on Spain. If, as he intended, he was to lead in the autumn a great expedition to the East, he must leave no shadow of insecurity in his rear. The Bourbons of Madrid, like those of Naples, must cease to reign, and a Bonaparte must take their place. In Spain, as often, all was dynastic strife. The Spaniards loved their king, Charles IV, but hated his minister, Godoy. Charles and his son, Ferdinand, were at feud. Were Charles to quit the throne, it might without difficulty pass to a nominee of the outgoing King and of Napoleon. On pretence of reinforcing the army in Portugal, Murat and several bodies of French troops therefore entered Spain. The King prepared to take flight: his son forbade it: the mob rose against Godoy: the King abdicated in favour of his son, whom the Spaniards took to their hearts as the enemy of Godoy. Murat, who supposed that Napoleon intended the crown for him, then seized Madrid, and the King secretly withdrew his abdication. Napoleon had Spain at his feet, but he failed either to come in person or to designate a successor to Charles IV. Instead he lured Ferdinand to Bayonne, confronted him with his father and demanded his renunciation of the crown. Meanwhile, early in May, the indignant mob of Madrid had risen against the French. Murat ruthlessly suppressed the rising, and Napoleon utilized the news to frighten both Charles and Ferdinand into abdication. The reluctant Joseph was forced to accept the throne of Spain, and Murat found himself King of Naples in his stead. By the end of May, Napoleon described Spain as quiet and loyal to himself. He could now arrange to meet Alexander with a view to arranging for their great adventure in the East.

The Spanish Rising 1808

Early in June, however, tidings reached Bayonne which proved that all Spain was blazing in furious revolt. Cut off from Europe by the Pyrenees, forced to wring subsistence from bleak mountains and arid plains, nurtured on seven centuries of crusade against the infidel, then placed at the head of Europe in warfare, wealth and empire, the Spaniards were no ignoble cravens, to be disposed of by a Corsican like sheep. The constitution which Napoleon had foisted upon their so-called notables at Bayonne provided the same benefits which France had conferred upon the Rhinelanders and Prussia upon herself. It considered Spanish feeling, for in the dominions of the Most Catholic King the Catholic faith alone was to continue lawful. Priests, peasants and townsmen none the less joined in guerrilla warfare which no French victory could quell. July, indeed, brought a resounding French defeat, when more than 20,000 French capitulated at Baylen amid the southern mountains. Joseph was driven from his capital and Napoleon forced to give up the eastern expedition. Both within and without the Peninsula, the Spanish rising shook the Napoleonic Empire. Spain herself, according to military calculations, called for 200,000 men. Napoleon could find them, but only by contracting his designs beyond the Elbe. To quell the Spaniards he must relax his hold on Prussia. Austria, moreover, saw that where the Spanish government had failed, the Spanish people had succeeded. Austrian emperors, ultra-dynastic as they were, did not always shrink from invoking racial feeling. In 1808, the devoted statesman, Count Stadion, vied with Stein in organizing public service, and an Austrian militia included all fit civilians between eighteen and twenty-five. The Austrian statesmen, indeed, differed from Stein in holding that the time was not yet ripe to strike. But 1808 seemed to herald the dawn of a future German war of liberation.

The Peninsula

In Iberia, the war of liberation spread more quickly. The Portuguese rose and appealed to Britain, thus restoring contact between the French and British armies. In August, Wellesley, north of Lisbon, triumphantly repulsed Junot at Vimiera, and the French were glad to be allowed to quit the kingdom. Portugal thus became a base from which Britain could support the Spanish rebels.

His own victories against the Swedes and Napoleon's embarrassments in Prussia, Austria, Portugal and Spain all

Napoleon and Alexander at Erfurt 1808

now combined to make the Tsar master of the situation. At Tilsit he must propitiate Napoleon. At Erfurt, fifteen months later, Napoleon must seek to propitiate him. Real harmony, indeed, could not be looked for, since Alexander's thoughts were fixed on Constantinople and the Straits, which Napoleon was determined not to give. But nothing could be of more service to a threatened empire than a demonstration of its own power and of its friendship with a powerful ally. In September, Napoleon humbled Prussia. The French agreed to quit the country, but they exacted a large indemnity, to be paid before they gave up the Oder fortresses. The Prussian army of 42,000 men was to provide 16,000 against Austria in case of war. In October, at Erfurt, Napoleon welcomed Alexander with an unrivalled display of pomp and friendship. Whatever their bargainings in private, it was made clear to all the world that the Tilsit alliance was renewed. Before parting they joined in a solemn warning to George III that if Britain persisted in contesting what they had done, worse would follow. This proved to be no barren threat. Before the year was over, Napoleon had forced Stein to take refuge in Bohemia and Sir John Moore to retreat into the furthest corner of Spain. The Spanish army, paralysed by a corrupt and incapable government, had been destroyed. Joseph reigned at Madrid with the support of 300,000 soldiers.

Napoleon and Europe in 1808

It would be difficult to decide, however, which of his brother monarchs, Spanish or Austrian, Neapolitan or Prussian, Napoleon had most deeply wounded during the year. Ill behaviour, which contributed to the downfall of the German Empire a century later, helped to make the Napoleonic intolerable. One sovereign, whose fate appealed to millions outside his own small domain, was conspicuously oppressed in 1808. The Pope, Napoleon declared, must be taught his place as bishop of Rome under Charlemagne's successor. Pius VII, as befitted a divinely appointed champion of law, declined in many ways to act as Napoleon's accomplice. He refused to interpret the concordat as Napoleon decreed, or to recognize the Bonaparte at Naples, or to quash the American marriage of Jerome. He would neither acquiesce in the loss of some of his estates nor apply the Continental System in the remainder. In February, therefore, Napoleon seized Rome itself. The Papal States were

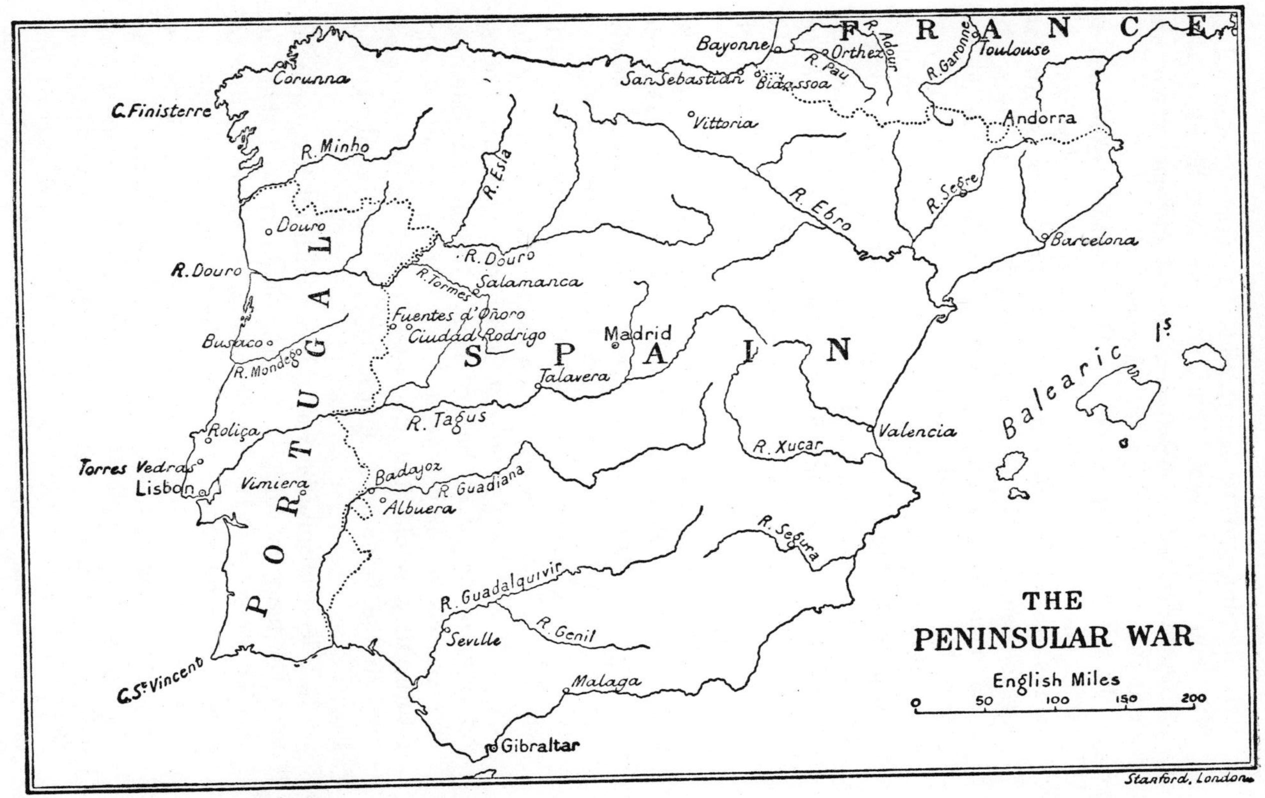
THE
PENINSULAR WAR
English Miles
0
50
100
150
200
FRANCE
SPAIN
PORTUGAL
Balearic Is
Bayonne
Orthez
R. Adour
R. Garonne
Toulouse
San Sebastian
Bidassoa
R. Pau
Vittoria
Andorra
Corunna
C. Finisterre
R. Minho
R. Esla
R. Ebro
R. Segre
Barcelona
Douro
R. Douro
R. Tormes
Salamanca
Fuentes d'Oñoro
Ciudad Rodrigo
Madrid
Busaco
R. Mondego
Talavera
R. Tagus
Roliça
Torres Vedras
Lisbon
Vimiera
Badajoz
R. Guadiana
Albuera
Valencia
R. Xucar
R. Segura
R. Guadalquivir
Seville
R. Genil
Malaga
Gibraltar
C. St. Vincent
Stanford, London

virtually annexed to Italy, and the papacy subjected to Napoleon's supervision. Pius, none the less, by his passive resistance helped to swell that moral current which was beginning to undermine the Empire.

Napoleon and Europe in 1809

In the new year, 1809, the Tilsit partners continued to exploit their union. While Alexander, however, had received at Erfurt freedom to follow the natural lines of Russian aggrandizement, Napoleon had already gone too far. In Finland and on the lower Danube a politic Tsar would not encounter such obstacles as those perceptible in Austria and Prussia or in Portugal, Spain and Rome. Although no man ever proved more brilliantly that attack may be the best defence, Napoleon in 1808 had been placed on the defensive, and 1809 found him struggling to maintain his colossal power. Britain, he realized, could be dealt with only when the disaffected elements in Iberia, Germany and Italy had been overcome.

The Peninsula

In Iberia, the first three months of the year seemed to complete the work of 1808. Moore, indeed, defeated Soult at Corunna (January), but his victory and death merely secured the safe departure of his battered force. Saragossa rivalled Haarlem and Leyden in the desperate valour with which its inhabitants endured a siege, but in February the city fell. In Portugal and in southern Spain the French for a time carried all before them. Lisbon and Badajoz, however, could not yet be attacked. If the British should return, they would find the Tagus open, armies of some kind in the field, and the countryside still hostile to the French.

Germany: the Austrian War 1809

Napoleon meanwhile was striving with all his might to keep Germany in subjection. Austria knew well that she was threatened with the fate of Prussia, as soon as the Iberian revolts were quelled. Unfettered by the natural reluctance of a Habsburg to trust the people, Stadion urged that a national war against the French should be undertaken without delay. Although the Archduke Charles proved less enthusiastic, Stadion, helped from Paris by the reports of Metternich and by the intrigues of Talleyrand, carried the Council for war. The Austrian Emperor appealed to the German nation. With no ally and no reasonable hope of any ally save Britain, Austria planned to attack Napoleon's

Empire in Italy, in Warsaw and in Bavaria. War with France, moreover, meant war with much of Germany and with Russia. The heroic effort failed. In April, the Archduke found himself in Bavaria, supported by superior numbers, but opposed to Napoleon in person. Five days' fighting near Ratisbon sufficed to break up his army and to open the road to Vienna. In May, Vienna fell, while the Archduke was moving from Bohemia to its aid. At the villages of Aspern and Essling a desperate battle was fought, the French striving first to complete their crossing of the Danube, and later to regain a place of safety. Aspern was the Eylau of this campaign, and the Austrians fought as stubbornly as had the Russians. While Napoleon thus failed to conquer, his Bavarian allies were confronted with the loyal peasants of the Tyrol, who refused either to accept their transference to Bavaria by the Peace of Pressburg or to admit defeat. Andreas Hofer, the heroic inn-keeper, was soon to defy both the Bavarian and the Italian armies, and to become a living symbol of resistance to the Napoleonic empire.

Austrian War of 1809

Meanwhile a seven-weeks' armistice enabled Napoleon to renew the attack with numbers greater by 30,000 than those of the Archduke. At Wagram, early in July, another murderous struggle won him the war. Again a triumphant treaty, signed in the palace at Schönbrunn, transferred great tracts of Austria to France and her allies (October). Napoleon himself acquired the Illyrian provinces, thus excluding Austria from the sea and making the French Empire march with Turkey. New (northern) Galicia, which Austria had gained at the Third Partition, passed to the duchy of Warsaw, which now included Cracow. In the rise of Warsaw, the Poles could not fail to see the promise of a restored Poland, and their enthusiasm lent Napoleon new strength. Meanwhile Russia received parts of Eastern Galicia. Salzburg and Tyrol became Bavarian, though Hofer still resisted. The Austrian army, like the Prussian, was limited in numbers. A force of 150,000 would be harmless for offence, since Austria was broken up by mountains and hemmed in by the French Empire, its dependencies and its great ally.

Napoleon Victorious in Europe 1809

The Schönbrunn terms were imposed by Napoleon because he had been victorious also beyond the Austrian frontiers. They were accepted by Francis in part from calculation of what the future might shortly bring. Before Austria struck, Gustavus IV, Napoleon's sworn foe, had been deposed from the Swedish throne, which passed to his feeble and childless uncle, Charles XIII. When Napoleon reached Vienna, he trampled on Pope and Emperor alike by annexing Rome. Meanwhile the forlorn hopes led by Prussian officers in northern Germany failed. On the very day of Wagram, the Pope suffered arrest. At the same time Britain seemed to give ample proof that, while she might annex distant French islands, in Europe her blows were idle. For in July she struck in Iberia, and, with infinite expense, in the Low Countries. Wellesley, indeed, drove Soult from Portugal, marched up the Tagus and defeated Victor at Talavera. Lack of Spanish support, however, compelled him to retrace his steps. Meanwhile the troops which might have brought victory in the Peninsula or in northern Germany were wasted in a fatuous attack on Antwerp. Chatham's Walcheren expedition accomplished nothing but the lowering of Britain's power and reputation. It was an Austria both isolated and defeated that Napoleon despoiled at Schönbrunn. But Austria, steered by able statesmen, accepted Schönbrunn in the hope of future gains. Stadion, of course, quitted office, but he left behind him something like an Austrian nation. Thugut, the aged patriot, had counselled any sacrifice to avoid destruction, since the Napoleonic empire, as he judged, must soon break up.

Napoleon's Austrian Alliance

Metternich, who knew Napoleon well, now took the Foreign Office. He was confident that by skilful diplomacy he could gain and exploit a French alliance. Within six months of Schönbrunn, indeed, Napoleon was speaking of Louis XVI as his uncle, for he had espoused a grandchild of Maria Theresa, and a niece of Marie Antoinette. Thus the Peace of Schönbrunn was transformed into an Austrian Peace of Tilsit—a compact which might perhaps expect a longer life.

Turn of the moral tide in Europe 1809

The year 1809, in which Napoleon reached the age of forty, thus saw his authority vindicated by triumphant force wherever it was challenged by armies. At the same time armed force had not yet proved strong enough to vanquish Britain or to repress the risings in Iberia and in Tyrol. There were signs that in many regions men were unwilling to break with the past at Napoleon's dictation, and he could offer them no fresh inducement to accept the Napoleonic system. At Schönbrunn, indeed, he had abjured every design of restoring Poland. The blockade could not but disturb all economic life and reduce men's pleasures.

"The French," writes Mr. Fyffe, "were themselves compelled to extract sugar from beetroot, and to substitute chicory for coffee. . . . Germans proof against all the patriotic exaltation of Stein and Fichte felt that there must be something wrong in a system which sent up the price of coffee to five shillings a pound, and reduced the tobacconist to exclusive dependence upon the market-gardener."

Russia, moreover, had now exhausted her immediate gains from Tilsit. Finland and a strip of Galicia were hers by treaty, Moldavia and Wallachia by force of arms. For her continued support of the Continental System she would at least demand Constantinople, which Napoleon deemed vital to himself. On the whole, therefore, the year of Walcheren and Wagram rather thickened than dispersed the clouds that hung over Napoleon's path. If only Britain were weakening, however, all might yet be well, at least so long as his health and strength remained unbroken. The very violence of the Orders in Council showed that their authors were apprehensive. As market after market was closed to Britain by the French, the pressure on her manufacturers increased, and Tilsit threatened them with ruin. The Spanish rising, however, brought some relief and promised more, since Central and South America were mainly Spanish, and their trade of vast importance.

In January 1809, Britain found a new ally in Turkey, and the fear of Anglo-Turkish action in the Black Sea soon embarrassed the Russians on the Danube. On the other hand, British arms had failed on land, and the failure cost Britain one of her foremost statesmen. The Walcheren fiasco brought about an exchange of pistol-shots between Castlereagh and Canning, and in September Canning quitted office. His eclipse might ruin Britain, since the sternest trial of the national courage was imminent and in rousing the masses he had no living rival.

Britain and Napoleon in 1810

From its opening, indeed, the year 1810 was one long strain on Britain. In January, Sweden approached the hostile coalition. Having previously made peace with Russia and with Denmark, she now made peace with France. From

Napoleon, as from Louis XIV, she regained Swedish Pomerania, this time at the price of acceding to the Continental System. This Napoleonic triumph was followed by abundant proofs of French mastery over the Continent. In February the Spaniards were defeated in the south, and the Tyrolese repressed. While Spain was divided into military fiefs and threatened with partition, Andreas Hofer was shot at Mantua as a rebel. At the same time the depapalization of Rome was completed. The city was formally proclaimed the second city in the empire, and the seat of the Prince Imperial, henceforward to be King of Rome. The Pope was to become a well-endowed imperial official, with palaces in Rome and Paris, but without domains or real independence. In March, Napoleon raised himself yet higher in the scale of human dignity by his marriage with the Habsburg Emperor's daughter.

The Austrian marriage

In many aspects of Napoleon's history, human, dynastic, ecclesiastical, military, diplomatic, his espousal of Marie Louise stands prominently forth. Dynastic ambition triumphed over his love for Josephine and his pride in Corsican fidelity. The bride, as a loyal Habsburg, sacrificed herself to a man whom she detested and despised. She played her part so well that Napoleon's advice became "Marry a German," but in later days she would cross herself at his name. The Church found means to obliterate from its memory a marriage upon which it had insisted less than six years before. The new union was of course a stroke of policy, internal, since it offered hope of issue, and external, since it renewed the old Franco-Austrian alliance. If Austria were an outpost of France, Napoleon must be more secure in both Germany and Italy, while in the eastern question he could bid defiance to the Tsar. By calculating thus, however, he was exposing himself to a power which of all powers was perhaps the most unlikely to bestow favours blindly. The fact that Francis had honoured an upstart with his daughter's hand was not in the least likely to cause himself or Metternich to neglect Habsburg dynastic interests. Austria joined France after Wagram as Russia had joined her after Friedland—to gain advantages. Failing these, she would embrace any safe occasion of changing sides. Meanwhile she was the better assured of her ally that by his

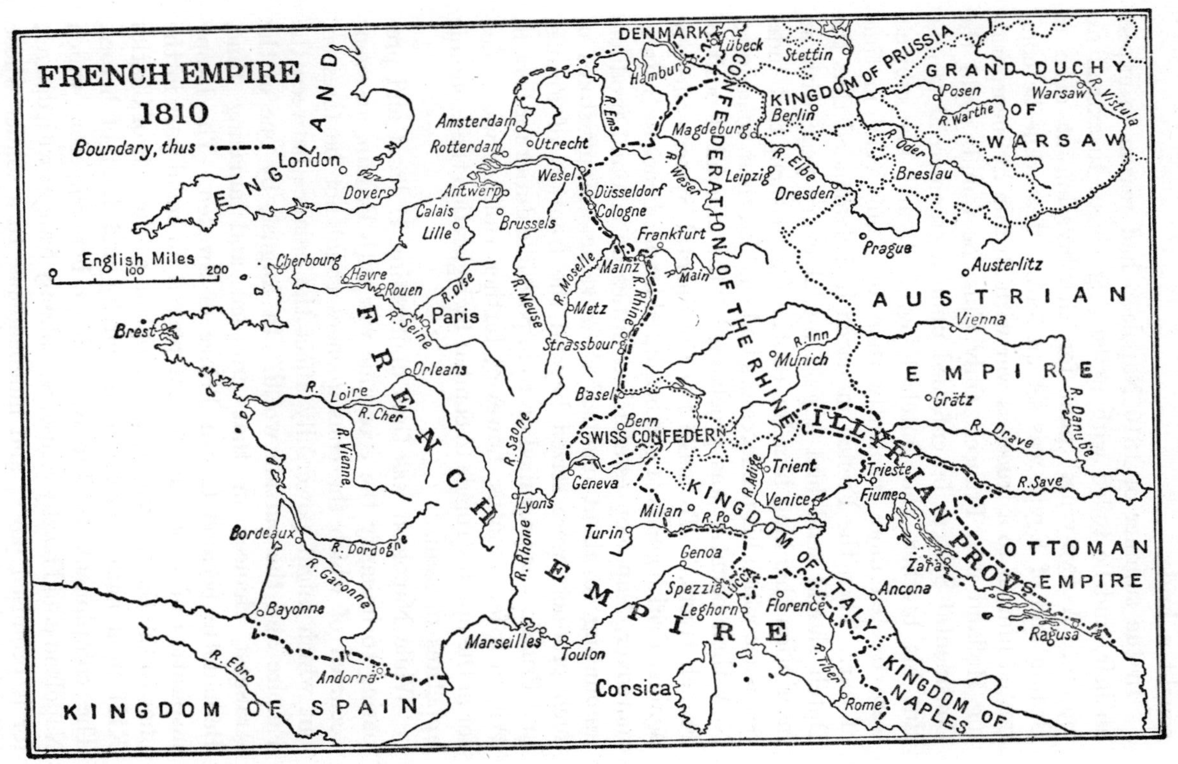

FRENCH EMPIRE
1810
Boundary, thus
English Miles
100
200
ENGLAND
London
Dover
DENMARK
KINGDOM OF PRUSSIA
GRAND DUCHY OF WARSAW
CONFEDERATION OF THE RHINE
AUSTRIAN EMPIRE
OTTOMAN EMPIRE
ILLYRIAN PROVS.
KINGDOM OF ITALY
KINGDOM OF NAPLES
SWISS CONFEDER.
FRENCH EMPIRE
KINGDOM OF SPAIN
Corsica
Lübeck
Stettin
Hamburg
Berlin
Magdeburg
Leipzig
Dresden
Breslau
Posen
Warsaw
R. Vistula
R. Warthe
R. Oder
R. Elbe
R. Weser
R. Ems
Prague
Austerlitz
Vienna
Grätz
R. Danube
R. Drave
R. Save
Ragusa
Zara
Fiume
Trieste
Ancona
Rome
R. Tiber
Florence
Lucca
Leghorn
Spezzia
Genoa
Milan
R. Po
Turin
Venice
Trient
R. Adige
Munich
R. Inn
Bern
Basel
Geneva
Frankfurt
Main
Mainz
R. Rhine
Düsseldorf
Cologne
Wesel
Utrecht
Amsterdam
Rotterdam
Antwerp
Brussels
Calais
Lille
Metz
R. Moselle
Strassbourg
R. Meuse
R. Saone
Lyons
R. Rhone
Marseilles
Toulon
Paris
R. Oise
R. Seine
Rouen
Havre
Cherbourg
Brest
Orleans
R. Loire
R. Cher
R. Vienne
R. Dordogne
R. Garonne
Bordeaux
Bayonne
Andorra
R. Ebro

marriage he had affronted Russia, where he had previously sought a bride.

French Imperial Expansion 1810

In the summer of 1810 Napoleon had reason to expect an heir, and he toiled with unflagging vigour to extend his empire. A two-years' plan for the invasion at once of Britain and of Egypt was set on foot. Meanwhile he committed himself to a truceless war with Britain by incorporating Holland into France. Only thus, he found, could the Continental System be enforced upon a commercial people. But his brother, the Dutch King, fled, and his subjects were treated more insolently than by Louis XIV in time of war. Then the French monarch had demanded that the Dutch should send him a gold medal every year with an inscription thanking him for continuing to them that independence which his predecessors had enabled them to acquire. Now their country was proclaimed "the alluvial deposit of French rivers." To make the Continental System effective against British goods or goods tainted by obedience to Britain, moreover, Napoleon established duties on colonial products amounting to about one-half their value. Many stores of such products were seized beyond the frontiers of France, and Prussia was prevailed on to impose like duties for herself. Within a few months, however, further violence was called for in the uphill struggle to combat by legislation the economic appetites of man.

Bernadotte and Sweden

While Napoleon was thus maltreating Holland and preparing to intensify the economic war with Britain, an event occurred of which the consequences could not be foreseen, but which might powerfully affect the balance between the Empire and the outside world. In August, by one of the strangest chances in that crowded and amazing time, Bernadotte became Crown Prince of Sweden. The happy inspiration of a mere lieutenant played no small part in the offer to the Gascon marshal of adoption as the heir of Charles XIII in a nation prone to monarchy and fond of heroes. The compliment to France and to her emperor, which Napoleon could hardly refuse, was plainly fraught with danger, for it promised power and independence to a soldier whose ambition was to succeed or supplant Napoleon. One by one the degenerates or madmen who had lately reigned in Europe were giving place to men of vigour, and the task of a European dictator became yearly more complex. For the moment, however, the Empire was apparently advancing. In Spain resistance seemed to be almost limited to parts of Catalonia and Cadiz, while, to keep a gateway into Portugal, Wellesley must create "the triple works, the vast designs of his laboured rampart-lines" at Torres Vedras. To end the Peninsular War and to secure his rear before marching into Turkey, Napoleon made a gigantic effort and sent some 370,000 men. Masséna, though punished at Busaco for rashly attacking the strongly-posted British and Portuguese, swept on towards Lisbon in October, hampered only by the self-devastation of the countryside. At this point Sweden declared war on Britain.

The Empire checked and extended

At this point also, however, the Empire received its most conspicuous defeat. Between Masséna and Lisbon lay the unsuspected lines of Torres Vedras, manned by a force which at Busaco had both proved and increased its value. For months the French refused to admit their impotence to force the lines, though hunger, sickness and marauding guerillas thinned their numbers day by day. But as autumn gave place to winter, Napoleon could conquer only the unarmed, and that by way of proclamation. In December, the Valais, on the French side of the main Alpine range, was incorporated into France. The Tyrol on the Italian side was incorporated into the Kingdom of Italy. The Prince-Primate of the Rhenish Confederation found himself ruling a new Grand Duchy of Frankfort, modelled on French lines and controlled by France. By a far more arresting display of power, the coast of northern Germany as far as Lübeck was annexed to France, which thereby touched the Baltic. The French towns of Hamburg, Bremen and Emden thus sealed the Elbe, the Weser and the Ems against British trade. It was unlikely, however, that rich Hanseatic cities would either prosper under the new conditions or willingly accept their fate. But a greater immediate political effect was produced by the seizure of Oldenburg, where Alexander's uncle was Grand Duke. Crossed in Poland, Turkey, Oldenburg, Austria, and the Russian ports, Alexander retaliated by deserting the Continental System. Russia proclaimed her readiness to admit neutral ships and imposed duties upon many French products. Nothing could have insulted Napoleon more deeply nor given greater encouragement to Britain.

The strain of 1810 in Britain

Despite her successes in the Peninsula, the revolt of Spanish America and the capture of more French islands, Britain had suffered keenly in 1810. The harvest failed, after a poor yield in 1809. Had Napoleon realized that to his enemy food was more necessary than bullion, he might perhaps have starved her into peace. To drain her of gold, however, he licensed exports of grain, and the appetite of Europe for cheap goods enabled her to recover the gold in return for smuggled manufactures. Bankruptcies, however, became numerous, and in the Baltic many British cargoes were seized by Napoleon's allies. While French land-power was employed to tax her vassals and infuriate them by insane decrees, Britain's sea-power brought her many confiscated cargoes, but also a powerful foe. Madison, who succeeded Jefferson as President in 1809, abandoned the policy of embargo which had almost put an end to trade, and offered exclusive trading rights to either combatant in return for the revocation of its decrees. France ostensibly at least accepted, and Britain found the American market closed against her, with an increasing probability of strife.

Prospects in 1811

The year 1811 was for Europe a year of patient endurance and painful anticipation. While the British remained able to feed themselves and Napoleon retained his vigour, neither France nor Britain seemed likely either to win the war or to seek for peace. General dearth, indeed, heightened the sufferings which the war and the Continental System brought about. But the impotence of popular uprisings had been proved in Germany by the campaign of 1809 and in the Peninsula by that of 1810. Although Britain held firmly to her doorway into Portugal, it was more likely that the French would close it against her than that she would drive them from Portugal and Spain. Once again the fortunes of the west turned on Russia.

Russia and the Empire

Russia began the year entangled as of old upon the Danube in a long and fruitless struggle for Constantinople. Since 1806, as in many earlier wars, the river, the fortresses, the deserts and the mountains had intervened to redress the balance between Turks and Russians. Provided that the Turkish armies remained south of the Danube they could escape disaster. With the phlegmatic Kutusov in command the Russians made no bold move, while Alexander was preparing to meet the peril from the west. As the year 1811 advanced, Turks and Russians contended for a lesser or greater cession in Moldavia, and French and British strove to gain the Turks for war or peace. Throughout the year, therefore, the Turkish war formed a distraction for Alexander like that in the Peninsula for Napoleon. Having failed, as his grandmother had failed forty years earlier, to conquer Turkey, the Tsar turned for compensation to Poland, this time by undoing the Partition. Meanwhile in March, a year after Metternich had dared to toast "The King of Rome," Napoleon rejoiced in his longed-for son. The birth of an heir could not but hearten the father, and, since the father was Napoleon, it stirred him to fresh adventure. At many points the Tsar now crossed his path. Napoleon's dearest objects were unchallengeable primacy and the subjugation of the east. In each of them he was now, more or less openly, defied by Alexander. The Tsar had deserted the Continental System, and now regarded Napoleon's Warsaw as a standing incitement to the Poles. His armaments pointed to a movement on the Vistula which could only be hostile to the Empire. Were the Empire diminished, Napoleon always felt that France would dispense with himself. For a Corsican adventurer, foe of the Revolution which had brought him power, she would fight no Malplaquet. To defend himself and the King of Rome, therefore, he must marshal his unrivalled military resources and dispel the Russian peril. Thus it came about that through the autumn of 1811 French, Germans, Dutch, Swiss, Poles, Spaniards, Portuguese, Italians, Croats, Dalmatians—all the races of the Empire were marching towards Danzig and Warsaw to wrest the initiative from the Russians.

Wellington in the Peninsula

With this mighty enterprise on his mind, Napoleon naturally demanded relief from the teasing war and rebellion beyond the Pyrenees. That relief, however, was denied him, thanks to his own unpopularity in the Peninsula, and to Wellington's military skill. Napoleon's genius, indeed, the British commander could not rival. But he was the incarnation of well-trained sense, and his natural sagacity had taught him that against steady men the French tactics were unsound.

An enemy which sought a quick decision by bewildering the army and terrorizing the civilians could have found no greater obstacle than "the Duke." The Peninsula campaign of 1811 opened with a tardy confession of the French failure in 1810. Masséna was at last compelled to retreat from the mountains of Portugal into Spain. His seven months' fruitless invasion had cost France some 25,000 men—no unimportant fraction of the reserve of that Grand Army which Napoleon was marshalling against Russia. While the French kept 300,000 men beyond the Pyrenees, however, it was impossible for Wellington with 50,000 British and Portuguese to conquer Spain. But his force proved sufficient to win sectional victories and to defend Portugal, since whenever the French garrison was reduced the Spaniards rose in arms. When the year ended, Napoleon was still compelled to choose between keeping 300,000 men in Spain and hazarding the loss of the Peninsula.

European Peaceful Activity

Thus in 1811, on the eve of the vast offensive with which Napoleon proposed to defend his empire, the peace of the Continent remained unbroken, save on the Danube and beyond the Pyrenees. It is noteworthy that at this crisis in the fortunes of humanity, science and literature made great advances entirely unconnected with the war. Goethe, whom Napoleon admired and who admired Napoleon, published his *Theory of Colours* in 1810 and the first part of *Dichtung und Wahrheit* in 1811. While the great German thus continued his production undisturbed, Jane Austen, with the fidelity of a Van Eyck, painted the most tranquil of social scenes. The creation (in 1810) of Berlin University was but the coping-stone of a gigantic structure of education whose base the National Society in England was widening. Chemistry, physiology and physics could boast, not indeed of their greatest names, but of concurrent discoveries by *savants* in many lands. Some advances were even occasioned by the war. To injure Britain, Napoleon himself caused sugar to be made from beet, and enforced a home-grown substitute for indigo.

1812

After an almost tranquil period since the Austrian revolt (1809) came 1812, the classic year of fate. When it opened, Britain and Russia were still nominally at war, while in name the bond of Tilsit still united Napoleon and Alexander.

FRENCH EMPIRE &
CENTRAL EUROPE
1811
English Miles
0 50 100 150 200
DENMARK
Copenhagen
SWEDEN
Swedish Pomerania
Kiel
Holstein
Lübeck
Mecklenburg
Pomerania
Danzig
PRUSSIA
Königsberg
Memel
Kovno
R. Niemen
Grodno
Graudenz
Thorn
R. Vistula
Stettin
Brandenburg
Berlin
Frankfort
Posen
R. Warta
Warsaw
R. Bug
WARSAW
Lublin
Sandomir
R. San
Cracow
Galicia
Silesia
R. Oder
Breslau
Hamburg
Bremen
R. Weser
R. Ems
R. Elbe
Hanover
Münster
Westphalia
CONFEDERATION OF THE RHINE
Magdeburg
Halle
Saxony
Leipzig
Dresden
Jena
Coburg
Baireuth
Prague
Bohemia
Moravia
Brünn
Amsterdam
The Hague
Antwerp
Brussels
Lille
Namur
Liège
Cologne
Wesel
Berg
Düsseldorf
Marburg
Frankfort
R. Main
Mainz
Trèves
R. Meuse
R. Moselle
Havre
Rouen
R. Seine
Amiens
Compiègne
Rheims
Paris
R. Aisne
Verdun
Metz
Heidelberg
Nürnberg
Ratisbon
Stuttgart
Wurtemberg
Ulm
Baden
R. Rhine
Strassbourg
Fontainebleau
Orleans
Auxerre
Chatillon
R. Loire
Dijon
FRANCE
R. Saône
R. Rhône
Basel
Schaffhausen
Bavaria
Munich
Innsbruck
R. Inn
Passau
R. Danube
Vienna
AUSTRIAN EMPIRE
Buda
Pest
R. Theiss
R. Maros
R. Drave
Illyrian Provs. (French)
SWISS CONFEDERATION
KINGDOM OF ITALY
Stanford, London.

All Europe, however, knew the real situation, and the weight of British diplomacy and arms was promptly thrown upon the Russian side. Wellington was the first to feel relief from the eastward movement of the French and the first to hamper Napoleon's expedition. By storming Ciudad Rodrigo and Badajoz, where his troops committed horrible excesses, he opened both roads from Portugal into Spain, and a victory at Salamanca enabled him to seize Madrid (August). When Joseph fled to Valencia his brother was already deep in Russia and in sore need of every man and gun. The Empire, it might well seem, could not recover Spain.

Two Camps in Europe

Meanwhile the struggle for alliances, inevitable on the eve of war, had been waged with diverse fortune. In February, to the despair of Prussian patriots, Prussia threw in her lot with Napoleon. In March, Austria promised him at least a show of aid. In April, however, Bernadotte brought Sweden secretly to ally herself with Russia. His new country had before her only a choice between two thorny paths, for her neutrality in the coming struggle would be regarded by the victor as a crime. By joining Napoleon she might hope to be rewarded with Finland, which Alexander had lately taken from her. Napoleon, however, dwelt far from Sweden, while the Tsar must always be a formidable neighbour. To Napoleon Sweden would be a pawn; to Alexander, an ally. As a maritime nation, Sweden might well court Britain, Napoleon's arch-enemy, while to her the Continental System meant ruin, perhaps starvation. Above all, Denmark since 1807 had been Napoleon's willing *protégé*, and Denmark, always Sweden's rival, ruled Norway, which with Russian goodwill Sweden might hope to gain. The balance of Swedish hopes and fears thus turned in favour of Russia, in conformity with Bernadotte's own desires.

End of the Russo-Turkish War 1812

A still more signal service was rendered to Russia by Britain in May, when the Turkish war was finally disposed of. Young Stratford Canning, forty years later the most dangerous among Russia's foes, cleverly procured from the Turks the Treaty of Bucharest. Russia consented to restore all that her six campaigns had taken from the Turk in Asia, and to content herself with acquiring Bessarabia and the frontier of the Pruth.

Napoleon and the Poles

Napoleon, however, secured an irregular ally which was likely to help him in the war far more than timid Prussia or diplomatic Austria. The Polish people, fettered by no jackal government, burned to reconquer their independence. They numbered several millions, and inhabited wide regions through which the invaders and defenders of the Russian capitals must pass. Poles by thousands were in the service of the Tsar; Adam Czartoryski, among his intimates. On the other hand, the Grand Duchy of Warsaw had already been triumphantly defended against the Austrians by its Polish army (1809), and had received an augmentation and a constitution from Napoleon. The greatest of Polish poets, the Lithuanian Mickiewicz, saluted him as the liberator sent by heaven. Although the great lords feared revolutionary principles and many peasants came of Russian stock, Poland as an active force answered Napoleon's summons. With his native astuteness he convinced the Poles that he intended what could never have squared with his political plans—a Polish restoration. A revived Poland, he was well aware, would be a standing challenge to the three partitioning powers and a state too proud, too vast and too remote to be his docile vassal. But he could represent the campaign of 1812 as the defence of Warsaw against Russia; he could enrol in the Grand Army more than 80,000 Polish soldiers; and he could permit the Warsaw Diet to decree the Restoration (June 26). While the Tsar, in a mood of spiritual exaltation, stood forth to defend Holy Russia against Antichrist, Napoleon, with nearly forty sovereigns as his vassals, moved the armed west for a cause which without Poland was reduced to personal ambition. The defence of Napoleon was in truth the aim of the vast offensive. If five years of the Continental System had failed to humble Britain, it was clear to all save himself that his plan had failed, and that for himself alone he sacrificed the general peace.

The Invasion of Russia, 1812

Napoleon's great adventure began at midsummer, when he crossed the Niemen into Russia. His proclamation of June 22 to the army declared that Russia had broken her vows of 1807—eternal alliance with France and war with Britain. Fate had drawn her on: her destinies must be accomplished. Did she think that the French had ceased to be the men of Austerlitz? This second Polish war would be as glorious as the first, which had ended at Friedland and Tilsit. The peace would deliver Europe from the evil influence which Russia had exercised for fifty years.

These were brave words, but Napoleon knew that Britain was Russia's ally in all but name, while Sweden might join her in striking some blow on the southern Baltic coast. In substance, however, Russia stood alone to confront an unprecedented coalition. Her most effective though invisible ally was widespread discontent in Europe. To garrison Iberia, Italy and France absorbed no less than half a million men. Yet the Grand Army could muster nearly 700,000, of whom less than one-half came from historic France. The bulk were divided into eleven army corps, of which one was stationed on the Elbe and another on the Oder and Vistula, while two guarded either flank. With the Imperial Guard and the cavalry led by Murat, some 400,000 men and 1,000 guns were available to conquer Russia. Of trained men Alexander could bring less than 150,000 to the scene of action. It was certain, however, that the further the invaders penetrated into his dominions, the more the climate and the lack of provender would lower their fighting strength. Reasons of strategy compelled Napoleon to march eastwards upon Moscow, nearly 850 miles as the crow flies. More than half the road lay through historic Poland, but to reach Vilna was to discover the difference between the indifferent Lithuanians and the enthusiastic Western Poles. Every march through the poverty-stricken country brought the invader into a more hostile countryside and one stripped barer by the Russians. Lack of roads and abundance of woods and marshes tended to reduce even the Grand Army to a mass of slow-moving individuals.

The Contending Plans of Campaign

Even westward of the Niemen it had already become clear that the time-tables by which armies moved in central Europe were impracticable further east. Ambassadors and princes travelling light and spending freely were wont to find beyond the Vistula that nothing on wheels could be relied on for swift transport across the sandy and marshy plains or through the unending forests. To stagger along under arms in the summer heat taxed the hardiest. Conscripts by thousands went sick or decamped by night. As he grew older, Napoleon everywhere sought quick advantages from battle, in preference

THE RUSSIAN CAMPAIGN OF 1812
RUSSIA
Livonia
Courland
Lithuania
PRUSSIA
WARSAW
L. Peipus
L. Ilmen
R. Lovat
R. Volga
Tver
Moscow
R. Moskva
Borodino
Mojaisk
Gjatsk
Utitza
R. Nara
Borovsk
Velichevo
Viazma
Kaluga
R. Oka
Smolensk
Lubina
Krasnoi
Mogileff
Riga
R. Dwina
Dünaburg
Drissa
Polotsk
Memel
Glubokoie
Kamen
Vitebsk
Ostrovno
Sventziany
R. Viliia
Lepel
Senno
Orsha
Borissoff
R. Dnieper
R. Berezina
Tilsit
Kovno
Danzig
Königsberg
Vilna
Oshmiany
Molodetchno
Minsk
R. Niemen
Grodno
R. Vistula
R. Nareff
Bialystok
R. Bug
Warsaw
English Miles
0
50
100
150
Stanford, London

to those which manœuvre might ultimately yield. The Russian country made him still more eager to meet the Russian armies at the earliest moment. From the purely military point of view, therefore, those armies must aim at weakening his force and perhaps his determination by delaying battle. Strategically, Russia possessed no heart at which a mortal blow could be struck. So long as the Tsar willed war and his subjects supported him, Russia remained unconquered. Alexander in 1812, like Lenin in 1918, declared that if need be he would retreat to Kamschatka rather than submit. This was, on a far grander scale, the strategy that had served in the Peninsula and it must have cruelly embarrassed Napoleon. Victory in battle would have been denied. Russia held little to plunder or to destroy. The invaders could hardly have lived on the country or made stable conquests. But Alexander was neither wise enough nor strong enough to impose such a sacrifice of goods and pride upon those about him. The length of the Russian retreat was not determined by pure strategy or by Alexander's will. When Napoleon turned towards Moscow he compelled a proud nation to give battle.

Barclay de Tolly

July and August, however, were consumed in the vain quest for victory by threats or blows. Vilna, the capital of Russian Poland and the headquarters of the Russian army, formed Napoleon's first objective. He reached it on June 28, only to be disappointed. To move quickly forward or to crush either of the two Russian armies before their union or to overawe the Tsar—all these lay beyond his power. While he halted for eighteen days at Vilna, the Russians corrected some of their early errors. Their vast defensive camp at Drissa, a mere death-trap, was abandoned, and Alexander brought himself to leave the supreme command to soldiers. While he retired to Moscow to animate the nation, Barclay de Tolly, a Baltic Scotchman, took his place. That change in the Russian command probably wrecked the Empire.

Barclay, suspected by the Russians for his race, had the strength of mind to avoid disaster by retreat. At Vitebsk, on the Dwina, which he reached in spite of Napoleon's efforts to cut him off, he might have fought, if the second Russian army could have joined him. As, however,

Davoust drove it back from Mohilev to Smolensk, Barclay again baulked the invader's hope of battle. Smolensk, the key of the Upper Dnieper, had been Russian since 1667, and lay within 260 miles of Moscow, the metropolis of Russia. There Barclay mustered both armies and the garrison, in all more than 130,000 men. But wherever French and Russians met, the French had proved victorious, and Barclay once more desired retreat. His Russian colleagues forced his hand, with the result that two bloody engagements cost him some 20,000 men. Smolensk was lost, but by a timely retreat Barclay again preserved the army.

Napoleon, who had declared that in crossing the Niemen he was beginning the second Polish war, found himself in six weeks master of all Poland save Austrian Galicia. While he was driving the Tsar's main forces beyond Smolensk, his lieutenants struck north and south and even captured Riga. Should he not now consolidate the huge gains that he had made, leaving to Alexander the thankless choice between accepting a dictated peace and striving to dispossess him? Russia, indeed, was vast, but her population outside the French lines was smaller than that of France and far less warlike. Napoleon was master of the Tsar's most wealthy provinces. The wastage in the Grand Army had been terrible indeed, but from the Pyrenees and the Straits of Messina to the Dwina and the Dnieper the manhood of Europe could be summoned to make it good. Every month brought thousands of young men to their eighteenth birthday, and the French could collect and train them with unrivalled speed.

Napoleon's Dilemma at Smolensk

On the other hand, it was hard for a soldier who had pursued his enemy from Vilna to Smolensk to cry halt in summer, when he might hope to destroy him a few marches further on. Three weeks at most should bring Napoleon into Moscow, as indeed they did. It would be strange if the Russians did not fight for their hallowed city; strange if he failed to rout them; strange if their rout and the fall of Moscow did not bring the Tsar to reason. Napoleon, moreover, always felt the need of ruling by prestige, especially in France. What feat in modern history could compare with a progress from Paris, at the head of Europe, to dictate peace in Moscow? The Continental System would be saved, the Peninsular rebels doomed, and the road to India kept open. To pause at Smolensk, moreover, would be to face the Polish problem before the war was over. That problem, complicated as it was by the vital interests of five nations, must tax the statecraft of Napoleon even with Russia at his feet. To attempt it when Prussians, Austrians and Poles were his allies and Russia still unconquered would be madness. Although he might pose as a demi-god to awe mankind, however, Napoleon remained the most practical of soldiers. When, midway between Smolensk and Moscow, the rains of early autumn began to melt central Russia into mud, he promised his staff to break off the march, if the next day proved no better. Next day (September 4) the sun shone out and the advance towards Moscow was resumed.

Borodino

On the morrow the Grand Army found itself at last at grips with Russia. In Moscow Tsar and nation had vowed to support their army in its holy war. Kutusov, for the sake of his Russian name, had been sent to take Barclay's place. He could muster 110,000 men to defend a strong position behind the village of Borodino. Napoleon, with some 125,000, counted on a victory that should end the war, and therefore, perhaps, avoided turning movements, which might provoke a fresh retreat. The result was a soldiers' battle, the more chaotic because neither Kutusov nor Napoleon ever approached the field. In such a struggle Russian stubbornness had full play, and Russian guns, as usual, inflicted heavy loss. At last, after ten murderous hours, Murat's cavalry dealt the decisive stroke. Some 90,000 killed and wounded covered the field, but the French army now outnumbered the Russian by two to one, and the Moscow road lay open. A week later, on September 14, Napoleon reached his goal.

The French at Moscow

Moscow, a gigantic village surrounding the domes and spires of the Kremlin, was occupied without a blow. To the amazement of the French, the inhabitants, as well as the garrison, had fled. Kutusov's remnants, passing through the city to the south-east, were accompanied by more than nine-tenths of the civil population. That nearly a quarter of a million Russians should abandon their homes rather than endure his presence showed Napoleon what nationality could mean. The lesson was enforced when some of those who remained fired their houses, and a vast conflagration drove the Emperor himself outside the town. Meanwhile in Spain Wellington enjoyed a momentary triumph, and Joseph again fled from Madrid. While Moscow was burning, Wellington began the siege of Burgos. Vastly outnumbered as he was by the French and feebly aided by the Spaniards, failure to capture the fortress must compel him to retreat once more towards Portugal. Napoleon, however, was in a far more critical condition. Master of empty and half-ruined Moscow, to what profit could he turn his triumph ? For him at least the eastward march was over. Murat pursued Kutusov, but the Emperor in the Kremlin, surrounded by 100,000 men, remained to organize, negotiate and plan. Almost automatically he gave orders to widen his conquests in Russia and to bring up the necessary reinforcements from the west. The vital task, however, was to induce Alexander to regain his realm by arranging terms of peace. Here he was foiled by forces which he could not understand. Russian horror at the profanation of the churches and at the destruction of hallowed Moscow ranked high among them. Only by slow degrees could he convince himself that when the Tsar proclaimed "No peace while a single foreign soldier remains in Russia," he was in earnest. Such, indeed, was Alexander's high resolve. It was strengthened by pride, by religion, by the counsels of Russian patriots, French *emigrés*, his British allies, statesmen like Stein and Hardenberg, and not least by the dawning perception that even Napoleon had shot his bolt and must soon see his advantage dwindle.

Napoleon's Dilemma at Moscow

If, then, the march to Moscow was not to bring peace, how could the war be won ? Could Napoleon hold and gradually enlarge a vast wedge of Russian territory with Moscow at its apex ? Kutusov was moving south of the city with forces nearing 100,000, while Napoleon's moral base was half a continent away. To hold Moscow, Europe must be kept under arms, and its autocrat marooned in Russia. Above all, the garrison could not be fed. For the men the existing stores of food were small; for the horses, wholly inadequate; and there was no way of making good. A four-hundred-mile march to St. Petersburg for victory was for like reasons too desperate a gambler's throw. Even withdrawal to Smolensk involved great risk and hardship, with no certainty that from that point Russia could be subdued. As in Spain, guerrillas were already showing what it cost to hold down an unwilling country.

The Retreat from Moscow

After nearly five weeks in Moscow, however, Napoleon could find no better course than to winter between the Dnieper and the Dwina. On October 19 he left the city, ordering a lieutenant to destroy the public buildings in which the Grand Army had found shelter. Marching south-west, he hoped to crush Kutusov and to attain Smolensk by way of undevastated country far to the south of Borodino. Five days later, the armies met at Malo-Jaroslavetz. As always, the French had the advantage, but the fighting was again severe. Kutusov, although he had lost 4,000 men and made a short retreat, remained too formidable for Napoleon to continue on the southern route. While the Russian, as it proved, was resolving on retirement, Napoleon ordered his own retreat to the devastated route by Borodino. There winter found what had been the Grand Army but was soon a hunted mob. Kutusov made it his object to keep his main force intact and distant, thus preventing any pause in the retreat. His vanguard harried the French left, while Cossacks with light artillery cut off stragglers and attacked the rear. Ney, who commanded the rear-guard, earned the title of " bravest of the brave " by desperate valour in a wellnigh desperate task. With little to eat save horseflesh, the troops could not withstand the Russian cold. After three weeks' torture, less than one-half of those who set out from Moscow reached Smolensk. Five days later the march continued, and conflicts with Kutusov's troops still left the French victorious. Their losses in men, horses and equipment, however, by mid-November had wrecked Napoleon's plan. He now sought winter quarters behind the Beresina, but a Russian advance from the south frustrated him. He was threatened, indeed, with the capture of his bridge-head across the river by one Russian force while two others converged upon his rear. The bridge-head went, and the encircling enemy were three to one. By November 29, none the less, Napoleon had found means to cross the river and to clear a way to Vilna. For the second time since quitting Moscow, he had lost half his surviving men. But this passage of the Beresina prolonged the belief that he was invincible, and saved the staff, on which his power depended. The victory, indeed, was due as much to his name as to his dispositions. In all Europe, Blücher alone desired to meet him in the field. Wellington frankly owned his pleasure at having escaped the test. Happily for Russia, Kutusov and his colleagues knew their own limitations.

Napoleon returns to Paris 1812

Three weeks after his rearguard crossed the Beresina, Napoleon himself reached Paris. He had learned that the news of his death, spread by the Republican plotter, General Malet, had roused no demonstration of loyalty to his wife and son. The Empire, it was clear, needed a cordial which he alone could give. While a few thousand men, in name the Grand Army under Murat, fled across the Niemen into Prussia, Napoleon drove rapidly by Warsaw and Dresden to ask France for a new levy of 350,000 men. The capture of Kovno from Ney fulfilled the Tsar's promise to his people. Perhaps 200,000 of the invaders remained on Russian soil, but all were casualties or stragglers. Alexander none the less had bought his victory dearly, for his loss exceeded the whole strength of the armies which at the outset faced Napoleon.

Russia and Europe

In December, therefore, the future of Europe rested in Alexander's hands. Russia could make almost what terms she pleased with France, provided that the Empire was respected. Many Russians, Kutusov among them, held that the well-being of their nation was best served by holding aloof from western politics. If Russia did not attack, Napoleon stood in little danger from partial and isolated rebellions. If, on the other hand, the Tsar resolved on a crusade, Prussia and even Austria might join in. Britain and all Iberia were already in the field, and Sweden was about to move. Frederick William hesitated, but Yorck, who commanded the Prussian contingent in Napoleon's army, actually undertook by the Convention of Tauroggen to remain neutral while Alexander struck at France (Dec. 30). Although the Prussian King, upon whom Napoleon called for help, convinced him of his loyalty, the Prussian government gave underhand encouragement to Yorck, and the Prussian people longed to rise.

BIBLIOGRAPHICAL NOTE

See the Bibliographical Note at the end of Chapter I and the bibliographies to Chapters XV, XVII, XVIII, XIX.

Add :—

A

H. Belloc : *The Campaign of 1812 and the Retreat from Moscow* (1924).

C. R. S. Buckland : *Metternich and the British Government from 1807 to 1813* (1932).

C. R. S. Buckland : *F. von Gentz's Relations with the British Government, 1809–1812* (1933).

H. Butterfield : *Napoleon* (1939).

K. von Clausewitz : *La Campagne de 1812 en Russie* (trans. 1900).

E. Dard : *Napoléon et Talleyrand* (1935, trans. 1937).

A. Duff Cooper : *Talleyrand* (1932, repr. 1945).

A. Fugier : *La Révolution française et l'empire napoléonien* (1954).

P. Guedalla : *The Duke* (1931).

A. Heath : *Napoleon and the Origins of the War of 1812* (1915).

R. B. Mowat : *The Diplomacy of Napoleon* (1924).

C. Oman : *Studies in the Napoleonic Wars* (1929).

C. Oman : *History of the Peninsular War.* 7 vols. (1902–30).

J. H. Rose : " Napoleon and Sea-Power," *Camb. Hist. Jour.* I (1924), pp. 138–57.

Lord Rosebery : *Napoleon, The Last Phase* (1900).

E. H. Stuart-Jones : *The Invasion that Failed* (1950).

E. Tarlé : *Napoleon's Invasion of Russia in 1812* (trans. 1942).

A. Thomazi : *Napoléon et ses Marins* (1950).

J. M. Thompson : *Napoleon Bonaparte : his Rise and Fall* (1952).

A. Vandal : *Napoleon et Alexandre I.* 3 vols. (1891–96).

A. Vandal : *L'Avènement de Bonaparte.* 2 vols. (1903).

B

R. K. Porter : *Campaign in Russia, 1812.*

Tolstoy : *War and Peace.*

CHAPTER XXI

THE FALL OF NAPOLEON, 1813–14

WHEN 1812 ended, Alexander had determined to march from Russia towards the west in order to destroy Napoleon's power over eastern Europe. The *rôle* of champion of the Christian world against its enslaver was great enough to fire the impressionable Tsar, while the chance of enormous conquests might well sway Catherine's grandson. At the moment, however, a balanced calculation yielded dubious results. The Grand Army, indeed, had been destroyed, and with it those devoted Polish, German and Italian soldiers who, in their several countries, formed the main pillars of Napoleon's power. But Napoleon still held the fortresses: the sovereigns were still nominally his allies: his Viceroy was assembling a considerable force at Posen: he himself was hurrying into existence a vast host which he like none other could inspire and use. The Russians, on the other hand, had shown little capacity in the field, and no new Suvorov had arisen. Ill-trained and ill-found, they must march through regions inhabited by their bitterest enemies, the Warsaw Poles. Alexander's friends of 1812, moreover, were all confronted with a novel situation. Against Britain the United States had lately launched a war. She must send troops to Canada and meet a formidable series of attacks by sea. In the Peninsula her success had proved evanescent. With Napoleon and Joseph once again in Paris and Madrid, Wellington's campaign of 1813 might be fought for nothing greater than the doorway into Portugal. The Spanish rebels, moreover, had proclaimed themselves upholders of everything most abhorrent to a Russian Tsar. Early in 1812, the extraordinary Cortes of Cadiz, while maintaining Catholicism, claimed sovereignty for the nation, limited the monarchy, confiscated the Church lands, freed the press and established a social and legal order in accordance with the Revolution. At that very time Alexander

The Chances in 1813

drove from office Speransky, the greatest of Russian ministers, who was tainted with similar ideas. On the Oder as on the Ebro, a crusade against Napoleon might involve alliance with the Revolution. There remained Sweden, which was secretly Russia's ally, and the Turks, whose behaviour must influence Austria and Russia. Of the former it was hardly possible to be sure of more than that Bernadotte's hopes of Norway would influence her course of action. To the Turks the Peace of Bucharest had given an opportunity to reduce Serbia to obedience and this they did. If Alexander were at death-grips with Napoleon, trouble might easily arise upon the Danube. Only the moderation shown at Bucharest prevented this from being almost certain.

Prussian Policy and Feeling

With so dubious a horizon, it would have been madness for the Tsar to march unless assured of Prussia. The secret convention with Yorck concluded at Tauroggen on the northern Prussian frontier allowed the Russians to traverse Prussia unopposed by the Prussian section of Napoleon's army. As the left wing, to which this section belonged, could not in any case have maintained its ground against the Russians, a local arrangement to avoid unnecessary slaughter was not unnatural. An *entente* between the Prussians and Russians already existed, as between Russians and Austrians on the right. But a Prussian general would hardly have signed such a convention had he believed it displeasing to his King. Timid and agitated as he was, Frederick William waited only for a safe occasion to renounce his allegiance to Napoleon, and this he had himself confided to Yorck before the fall of Moscow. Now he dismissed the general and annulled the Convention, but its effects he could neither destroy nor in the end regret.

The immediate military effect of the Convention, combined with the betrayal of Warsaw by the Austrians, was that the French fell back before the Russians to the Oder. The political effects proved infinitely more far-reaching. Stirred by soldiers, professors, poets, the Prussian nation swept away both the adherents of the revolutionary ideas and the politic hesitations of the King. Stein actually summoned a Diet at Königsberg, but lately the headquarters of a French marshal. The Diet called on all able-bodied Prussians to take up arms. Meanwhile the King, still professedly loyal to Napoleon, had quitted Berlin for Breslau, observing the demeanour of his people on the way. Convinced that the danger of dethronement was greater from them than from the French, he sought only an ally before yielding openly to their wishes. Austria, to which he first turned, continued to caress Napoleon, and of all statesmen Metternich was the least likely to defer to mobs. Five-and-thirty years later, when the Viennese were howling for his blood, an Archduke asked him what the noise was. "Sir," he replied, "it is what the Liberals call the voice of God." While he bided his time Russia alone remained. As the price of her alliance she demanded much of the so-called New East Prussia, Polish lands gained in 1795. On the last day of February, however, Alexander and Frederick William came to terms at Kalisch in western Warsaw. To free Germany and restore Prussia to her boundaries of 1806, Russia would furnish 150,000 men and Prussia 80,000, both abjuring any separate peace. On March 15, Alexander entered Breslau in triumph, the French falling back from the Oder upon the Elbe. Frederick William then threw off the mask. The negotiations with which Prussia had tried to hoodwink Napoleon were ended. Her new defence force was openly proclaimed, and the people summoned to support the crown. The Tsar and the King of Prussia even demanded that every German prince should join them or forfeit his dominions. Soon Blücher, the hero of the former German rising, found himself at the head of 25,000 men, with Scharnhorst, the creator of the new army, as his Chief of Staff. Thanks to Scharnhorst's short service system, nearly 150,000 Prussians had been trained in arms. After six years of Napoleonic rule, the nation was prepared to end it at any sacrifice of gold and blood. Blücher therefore at once pushed forward to the Elbe, and the French fell back upon the Saale. At this point, however, Napoleon reappeared and the real campaign of 1813 began.

Prusso-Russian Alliance 1813

The Campaign of 1813. Napoleon's Preparations

In four winter months at Paris Napoleon had done wonders. His first thought, as always, was for his dynasty. France, it was clear, cared little for his wife, his brothers or his son. But so far as law could secure the succession, it was accomplished. If Napoleon fell, the Empress was to be regent for the infant King of Rome, with a Council headed by Cambacères, the former Second Consul. To strengthen his hold upon France and every other Catholic land, he patched up a new Concordat with the Pope. Since their inevitable conflict had made the Emperor Gallican, while the divorce caused half the cardinals to absent themselves from the second marriage, Pius VII had become a prisoner at Fontainebleau. Now he substantially consented to accept Napoleon's nominees as bishops, and to surrender the Papal States. These concessions, indeed, he soon afterwards refused to confirm, but the reconciliation between Pope and Emperor was publicly proclaimed.

Napoleon's main task, however, was to create an army strong enough to regain every inch of his former conquests. Whether blinded to political realities by flatterers and by his long career of victory, or justified in assuming that any breach would cause the whole structure to collapse, he made "No concession" his watchword in 1813. By selling the communal lands he acquired money without increasing the taxes or incurring debt. To fill the ranks he recalled 100,000 men from Spain and 30,000 from the fleet. Some 140,000 young conscripts were already trained, and 100,000 formerly exempted could be called up. A thousand guns stood ready in the arsenals. French war-industry could provide arms and munitions for the half-million to which the fighting strength was raised. The Grand Army of 1812 had been half foreign, that of 1813 was mainly French, and France stood solidly behind it. Its great lack was that of cavalry trained to turn victory into triumph, for the least reparable losses of the Grand Army had been in horses. The marshals, moreover, included war-weary and disaffected men, with some of inferior calibre. Where Napoleon could be present in person his fame and skill promised victory against troops led by Kutusov and Wittgenstein, men whose inferiority had been amply displayed in Russia. Blücher, however, though no strategist, could inspire the energetic fulfilment of the designs of others. The Allies were perhaps best aided by Napoleon's imperfect perception of the fact that his lieutenants were not quite what they had been, and that they lacked his own power of inspiring young and ill-trained soldiers.

On what allies could Russia and Prussia count for help?

The German struggle of 1813

Sweden alone had answered the call to take up arms against Napoleon. Even the loss of Dresden had failed to move the Saxon King. The sandy plain west of Leipzig, where Gustavus Adolphus fell and where Frederick routed the French at Rossbach, therefore became the scene of a conflict for the allegiance of the German princes. At Lützen, on May 3, under the eyes of Napoleon and of Ney, the Young Guard received its baptism of fire and helped to win a costly victory. Blücher was wounded, Scharnhorst killed, and western Saxony reconquered. Frederick William was with difficulty prevailed upon not to retreat to Berlin. On May 19, near Bautzen, the armies met again, contending this time for eastern Saxony and the line of the Spree. After three days' fighting, this battle, like that of Lützen, ended in an indecisive victory for Napoleon. His losses were great: among them that of Duroc, his companion since Toulon. While the French, with Denmark their ally, regained Hamburg and the Elbe, the Prussians defended Berlin and clung resolutely to Silesia. The war of liberation, however, was feebly waged. Northern Silesia passed to the enemy: Prussian and Russian generals were at feud: the allied troops were dispirited and far worse provided than the French. Although Napoleon's army was battered and weary, it would be strange indeed if it did not respond to one more call from him, and if one more battle did not dissolve the Coalition. On the eve of Bautzen, he had declared to his father-in-law, Francis II, that he would consent to a congress for peace, and to the Tsar that he would give good terms to Prussia.

Austrian Intervention

Peace talk, of course, is often a mere *ruse de guerre* intended to confuse and weaken the enemy. It is certain that Napoleon feared and suspected Austria, and with good reason. While flattering him, Metternich had assured Alexander that as soon as she was strong enough, Austria would strike. Campo Formio, Lunéville, Schönbrunn, Pressburg—these formed a sequence of injuries which she must avenge or forfeit her vital pride. The course of the campaign, moreover, had provided Metternich with the best conceivable conditions for her intervention. The weary combatants now faced each other in southern Silesia with Austria on their flank. To avert the armed mediation which he dreaded, Napoleon made an armistice from June 4 to July 20. Before July 20, he calculated, armies too formidable for any coalition would be his.

The Revolt of Europe

His calculations, however, were quickly proved unsound. Historic Europe, against which the Empire had triumphed up to Tilsit, continued to show signs of recovery from the initial shock. In Spain and in Russia, as in Britain, the peoples displayed their allegiance to the older system. They unequivocally preferred the institutions of their fathers to *doctrinaire* Rights of Man which meant the tyranny of Napoleon. The popular resentment which had carried Prussia into war was still spreading, none could predict how far. At the same time new diplomats and soldiers were serving Europe with greater skill than their predecessors had ever shown. Sweden handled by Bernadotte, Austria by Metternich, the Prussian army by Blücher and Gneisenau, the Peninsular army by Wellington—all these threw fresh weight into the scales against Napoleon. In Alexander Russia now possessed the incarnation of the force that had shattered the Grand Army. Castlereagh revived the England of William III and Marlborough—a power tactful, astute, sympathetic, labouring with sincere devotion to free Europe from the tyrant. Served by such men as these, historic Europe might generate a strength surpassing even that of Napoleon. Her deep-seated jealousies and divisions, however, had by no means lost their force. If Sweden joined the Allies, Denmark clung the closer to France; if the King of Prussia fought against Napoleon, the King of Saxony stood the more firmly by his side. Above all, Austria could not forget her past spoliation by Prussia, or the threat to her power, perhaps to her existence, that the rise of Russia implied. Metternich was a diplomatist, not a fanatic, and Francis was far from desiring to dethrone his own daughter. Expanded France and the Rhenish Confederation could produce armies which under Napoleon made the victory of the strongest coalition doubtful. Had the Emperor been a statesman, and had he trusted France to forgive him peace on moderate terms, Bautzen might have ended the war.

Intransigence of Napoleon

As Napoleon was determined to yield nothing, the history of the negotiations during the armistice is of little moment. If, however, a new coalition were formed, it was by no means unimportant that it should be able to plead clear necessity.

Metternich himself presented to Napoleon at Dresden the conditions on which Austria was prepared to mediate between the warring powers. These made an end of the expanded Empire, but left France her " natural frontiers " with much of Italy and Spain. In their eight hours' interview of June 28, Napoleon bent all his energies to terrify Austria through her spokesman. " What are the lives of a million men to such a man as myself ? " he stormed, flinging his hat upon the ground, where Metternich let it lie. Meanwhile Britain had become the paymaster of the Russians and Prussians, and Wellington, triumphant at Vittoria (June 21), was shattering Joseph's throne and threatening France. A sham congress at Prague prolonged the armistice until August 10, while France trifled with Austria and Austria with France. On August 9, Napoleon offered to surrender Warsaw, Illyria and Danzig. Before Metternich received the offer, Austria's hour had struck. At midnight on August 10 a chain of bonfires carried from Prague to Silesia the signal that the Congress was at an end and that the march into Bohemia might begin. Two days later, Austria formally joined the Coalition.

The Later Campaign of 1813

The Coalition which took the field in August 1813 disposed of half a million men and handled them according to a formidable plan. The experience of 1812 and 1813 in Russia, Spain and Germany taught that Napoleon's lieutenants were often beaten ; Napoleon, never. Bernadotte now urged that the Allies should fight only with the lieutenants and thus gradually encircle and crush the Emperor. Napoleon, on the other hand, calculated that as, with a firm base at Dresden, he was better placed than the straggling Coalition, he could catch them at a disadvantage if they crossed the Elbe.

When the autumn campaign began, Napoleon found three great allied armies moving against him. The furthest north was that of Bernadotte, who would probably promenade for his own glory while avoiding battle. The Prussians with him, however, were firmly resolved that he should not pursue political ends to the length of sacrificing Berlin. Further south, in Silesia, stood Blücher, with both Prussians and Russians under him. The Austrians in Bohemia were commanded by Prince Carl von Schwarzenberg, a cautious diplomatist who was hampered by the presence at his headquarters of the Tsar, the Austrian Emperor and the King of Prussia. Napoleon, with sound instinct, if with imperfect information, struck at Blücher first, counting on being able to crush him before the Austrians could capture Dresden. His presence brought advantage but not victory, and on August 23 he was compelled to hand over the command to Macdonald and hurry back to Dresden. There on the 27th he won perhaps the most illustrious of all his victories. Though heavily outnumbered, he drove the Allies from their positions, took 15,000 prisoners and flung Schwarzenberg's masses into the Bohemian mountains in headlong flight. The pursuit, however, ended in the crushing defeat of Vandamme at Kulm on August 30. Meanwhile at Gross-Beeren Oudinot had been defeated while endeavouring to take Berlin, and on the Katzbach Blücher had routed Macdonald with heavy loss. Napoleon marched to the rescue, but Blücher avoided battle. The return of the Austrians then compelled Napoleon to rescue Dresden. There he learned that on September 6 Ney had been beaten at Dennewitz and that his army had lost its *moral.* Within three weeks France had sacrificed 100,000 men, while the Coalition was more united and more confident than before. It was of high moment that, in each of the three theatres of war, Prussians had shown great determination and no little skill. If the 300,000 Prussians fought like their grandfathers in Frederick's day, the three great military powers, aided by British gold, must beat the French in Germany. Already Soult was compelled to summon thousands of conscripts to defend south-western France against Wellington. Napoleon recognized the danger by sending home secret orders to prepare against invasion from the east.

The Allies and Germany

The second campaign of 1813 had further encouraged the Allies by revealing signs of disaffection towards Napoleon. Under his lieutenants, Dutch and Saxon troops had refused to do their duty. If only the German princes could be induced to desert a tottering cause, allied success might well be swift and easy. At Teplitz, on September 9, the allied sovereigns renewed their alliance and provided for the division of the spoil. While Prussia and Austria were to be restored to their boundaries of 1805 and Napoleonic

Germany dissolved, Austria now dictated German reconstruction in accordance with Metternich's ideas. Centralization, as Stein envisaged it, must give place to the absolute independence of the several princes. To attract them to the Coalition, the dignities which they owed to Napoleon were recognized by the two great German powers. Early in October, upon those terms, the King of Bavaria changed sides. The steady ally of France since 1806 now bound himself to help Austria with 36,000 men. Only an amazing victory could warrant Napoleon in remaining beyond the Rhine.

Meanwhile the energy of Blücher and the impossibility of forcing any of the allied armies to give battle gradually brought about Napoleon's retreat to Leipzig. Blücher, regardless of his losses, had forced the line of the Elbe. His was the courage that framed a stroke which Napoleon believed impossible, and his the will-power that brought the reluctant co-operation of Bernadotte. Dominated by him, the northern armies foiled the counter-stroke on which Napoleon built his hopes—their separate defeat by his marshals, union with Davoust at Hamburg and the capture of Berlin. As Blücher and Bernadotte evaded battle, Schwarzenberg advanced towards Leipzig and Russian reserves came up. To uphold Napoleonic Germany, Leipzig must be saved from an overwhelming concentration. If the northern forces could not be crushed before Schwarzenberg arrived, Schwarzenberg must be crushed before they could interfere. With Bernadotte supreme the calculation would have held good, but not, as it proved, with Blücher.

On October 14 Napoleon and the Saxon royal pair arrived **Leipzig** at Leipzig. Posting Marmont and Ney at Möckern, northwest of the city, to guard against the northern army, Napoleon with the main force opposed Schwarzenberg on the southeast. Blücher hurried on, but Napoleon, grown arbitrary even towards facts, refused to believe Marmont's report of his approach. The Emperor had chosen his position with no thought of retreat. Master of more than 170,000 men and rightly despising Schwarzenberg, he counted on victory in the great battle which began on October 16. Actually, on that day he gained a considerable success against the Austrians and Russians, while the defeat of Marmont by the Prussians cost the victors dear. Had Ney been either left with Marmont or summoned earlier against Schwarzenberg, the defeat might have been averted or the success turned into a triumph. As it proved, however, some 60,000 men had fallen to achieve but little. The result of the day was that if the battle should be resumed on the same ground Napoleon's chance of victory had vanished. Möckern was lost, and the northern army, reinforced by Bernadotte, must soon outflank the Emperor and imperil his retreat. Schwarzenberg's attack had failed, but his army remained unbroken, while vast reinforcements were drawing near. On Sunday, October 17, none the less, Napoleon resolved on one more bid for victory. He offered an armistice to his father-in-law, but received no answer. Designating Britain the implacable enemy, he talked of yielding northern Germany in return for the conquered islands. By concentration, moreover, he lessened the impediments to his eventual retreat. On the 18th, "the battle of the nations" took the form of an attack by 300,000 allies upon a force one-half as strong. Napoleon's troops, the Poles conspicuous among them, once more showed skill and valour. Even the desertion of a Saxon corps with nineteen guns did not break the defence. The casualties on both sides were less than on the 16th, and again the Allies suffered most. But loss of ground and men, their utter weariness and failure of munitions made it impossible for Napoleon to renew the fight. On October 19, the French retreat began, the rearguard struggling with the enemy in the streets of Leipzig. Over the Elster, west of Leipzig, there was but a single bridge; at the Beresina a far smaller force had two. By a fatal error this sole avenue of escape was blown up, and many thousands perished or surrendered. It was an army weak in everything—health, numbers, guns, munitions, transport—that began the long march through central Germany, from Leipzig to the Rhine.

Napoleon's Prospects after Leipzig

In Germany outside Prussia, however, Napoleon need fear nothing from the countryside. The Bavarian army, indeed, disputed the Main crossing at Hanau, but their cavalry were shattered by the guns. Three days later, on November 2, some 70,000 fever-stricken men reached Mainz. Napoleon found his authority unquestioned in France, but the army of his Empire had vanished. Some 170,000 veterans still held the German fortresses from Hamburg and Danzig to Glogau. The remnants of the army of Spain faced Wellington in the Pyrenees. Something could doubtless still be yielded by France, but two-and-twenty years of almost incessant war had overtaxed the man-power of the nation. Between midsummer 1812 and his arrival at Mainz, Napoleon had lost a million men, of whom half at least were French. On what terms could the war be ended?

The collapse of Napoleon's Empire had been so swift as gravely to threaten the new-found unity of the Allies. The sovereigns and statesmen who gathered at Frankfort while their armies lay along the Rhine were faced with a double task—to plan a reconstructed Europe and to convince or coerce Napoleon. Aided by his own bad strategy they had dislodged him from the heart of Germany and had largely destroyed his empire beyond the Rhine. The loss of all his allies was the penalty of defeat. But success shook the disjointed Coalition. As soon as the tyrant of Europe was overthrown, the several powers began to grudge their sacrifices, to grasp at compensations and to revive their old dissensions. Unless they could agree that Napoleon was to be dethroned, and by what means, they might fall to quarrelling among themselves, while he rebuilt his army.

The Coalition and Europe

One fact, indeed, distinguished this Coalition from any of its predecessors. Hampering at times its military movements, but vastly augmenting its political strength, the three eastern autocrats followed the army in a group. When the representative of the Tory government of Britain attended on Alexander, Francis and Frederick William, Europe in essence could be found in a single room. Castlereagh was one of the few British statesmen who have been genuine "Europeans," and his high character and obvious sincerity did much to reconcile the sovereigns. The task was far from easy, for while the Tsar was bent on entering Paris, Austria feared the unbalanced power of Russia, and Frederick William wished his army back in Prussia to defend monarchy against the Revolution.

The outcome in mid-November was an offer to make peace with a France reduced to the boundaries of 1797. This would have left her the dominions of the old monarchy together with Belgium, the German lands to the Rhine,

Savoy and even Nice—the "natural frontiers" and the revolutionary dynasty being thus accepted by the legitimate sovereigns of other lands. For Napoleon to say "Yes" was to place French interests above his own ambitions; while his "No" would invite Europe to attack him, and France to accept his deposition. Napoleon therefore, as in the summer, temporized, and sought a Congress, endeavouring to revive the old disunion between Britain and the Tsar.

The war renewed

The Allies' rejoinder took the form of a public appeal to Europe and a quadruple invasion of France. While Wellington made for Bayonne, Blücher moved from Mainz towards the Ardennes, Schwarzenberg, marching from Basel into Alsace, took the plateau of Langres as his objective, and Bubna, seizing the Rhône, attacked the French communications with Italy.

From the North Sea to the Mediterranean, the ruins of the Napoleonic system were being swiftly cleared away. Napoleon himself resolved to free Pius VII and Ferdinand VII, thus renouncing the Papal States and Spain. Denmark abandoned the French alliance by making peace with Sweden and with Britain. In Holland, the Orange line reappeared in the somewhat degenerate person of William I.

The Rhenish Confederation gave place to a group of German princes fighting against France. The Swiss threw off the Constitution of 1803 and provided the invaders of France with a base. In Italy, the Viceroy, Eugène, fought a losing battle against the Austrians, while Murat, King of Naples, joined the Allies in the hope of a widened kingdom. One short campaign, it seemed, must convince the French that Napoleon was impossible.

The Coalition and France

Former coalitions, indeed, had found it hard to teach Frenchmen their duty by invading France. But in December 1813, the allied troops were five to one, with both sea-power and financial power behind them, and, as they believed, an exhausted and divided nation to coerce. Their propaganda was, perhaps, more powerful than their arms. They could, and did, indict Napoleon before his subjects as the sole cause of the sufferings which they were reluctantly inflicting upon France. The indictment was formidable, because it could not be gainsaid. The kings and peoples had in truth joined against France to free themselves from intolerable oppression. The former, however reluctantly, had unequivocally accepted the new dynasty, while the latter rose against a tyrant, not against the Rights of Man. Within France, disaffection found a dangerous focus in Talleyrand. That prince of diplomatists had long believed that Napoleon's rule was fatal to his country, and his anti-Napoleonic zeal was heightened by all that the Peninsula and Moscow revealed. After Leipzig his efforts increased and bore abundant fruit. Before the spring of 1814 set in, he had come to be regarded by the Allies as the spokesman of the French, and Napoleon feared that the Allies were right. The fundamental differences between the Powers, however, revealed themselves more clearly as the armies neared their goal. Tory or Liberal, legitimacy or nationality, Austria or Russia, which was to prevail? The answer would determine both the person to be placed upon the throne of France and the frontiers to be assigned her. French resistance, again, must vary with the Allies' terms of peace. When the new year began, the majority of Frenchmen would probably have welcomed a Napoleonic kingdom with the boundaries of 1789, while a large and ardent minority would have sacrificed their Emperor to save Belgium and the left bank of the Rhine. Thirteen years of Napoleon, however, had lowered the spirit of the nation. The civil population had been taught to leave all to him and would now make any sacrifice for peace.

Talleyrand

He, on the other hand, was a soldier, prepared to fight on as long as he could find an army to command. France of the "natural frontiers" and Italy formed the minimum which he would accept. Forced by public opinion to negotiate, he bargained as ambiguously as at Prague, clutching at any hope of a victory which might end the negotiations. With 70,000 men he defied Europe and her boasted million, aided as they were by traitors within France. Fighting for two months in the heart of his kingdom, he gave the world a sublime spectacle of courage, and proved the error of those who declared that years, success and flattery had quenched his genius and relaxed his fibre. During January, indeed, the sole hope of averting disaster seemed to be afforded by the dissensions of the Allies. France, it appeared, lay at their mercy, and French prisoners or deserters were merely bidden to go home. Masking the eastern for-

Attitude of Napoleon

The Campaign of 1814

tresses, Blücher, with the army of Silesia, and Schwarzenberg, with the main army, advanced each in his own fashion into the easy rolling country of Champagne. Napoleon himself then took the field, and immediately gained two successes against the army of Silesia. On February 1, however, he was sharply defeated by Blücher and his Russians at La Rothière, near his own old military school. Four days later, a peace congress opened at Châtillon. By this time, however, success was disintegrating the Coalition and only the devoted labours of Castlereagh kept Austria and Russia in league. Metternich, rightly fearing Russia more than France, had no mind to instal Alexander in Paris by Austrian arms, there to charm the French with revolutionary doctrine while he annexed Poland and gave Prussia Saxony in compensation. He therefore drew closer to Britain, whose chief concern was that Antwerp should not be French, nor France left dangerous to her neighbour. Since Austria was prepared to withdraw her troops rather than unleash the Tsar, the forward movement of the main army ceased while the Congress argued. To defeated France the Allies offered the boundaries of 1791. Blücher, meanwhile, was marching upon Paris. Napoleon, who regarded congresses only as pauses for military preparation, had vaguely countenanced acceptance of the terms offered him at Frankfort. The new proposals he described as a disgrace. Divining Blücher's rash errors, he resolved to annihilate the army of Silesia, to drive off the Austrians, and to save her " natural frontiers " for France.

While Napoleon lay at Nogent, south-east of Paris, facing Schwarzenberg and protected by the Seine, Blücher drove westwards from Châlons towards the capital. A swift and daring movement north from Nogent might therefore take him in flank. Napoleon seized the opportunity. On February 10 he crushed a Russian corps at Champaubert ; on the 11th, moving west, a larger Russian force at Montmirail ; on the 12th, the fugitives of Montmirail and their Prussian saviours at Château-Thierry, whence they sought safety across the Marne. Next day, marching south once more, he came upon Blücher himself near Vauchamps, striving with Prussians and Russians to break down the resistance of Marmont. At the cry of "*Vive l'Empereur*," Blücher

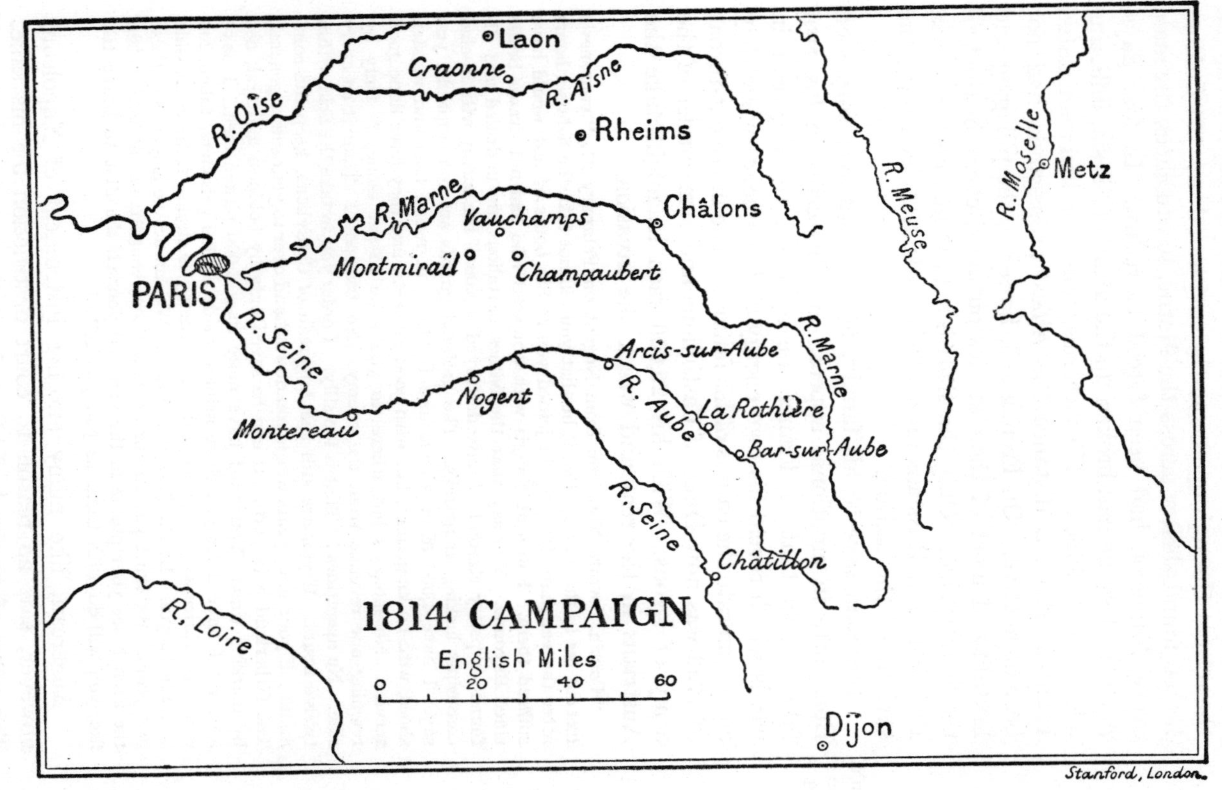
Laon
Craonne
R. Aisne
R. Oise
Rheims
R. Marne
Vauchamps
Châlons
Montmirail
Champaubert
PARIS
R. Seine
R. Meuse
R. Moselle
Metz
Arcis-sur-Aube
R. Marne
Nogent
R. Aube
La Rothière
Montereau
Bar-sur-Aube
R. Seine
Châtillon
R. Loire
1814 CAMPAIGN
English Miles
0
20
40
60
Dijon
Stanford, London.

repeated his tactics of Silesia. His troops fought well, but the retreat through open country cost him dear. At Châlons he too found shelter across the Marne, for, to check the main army, Napoleon had been forced to return. In four days, none the less, he had broken up the army of Silesia, inflicting a loss of 16,000 men. His victories, moreover, had reanimated France. From a distance the Allies' propaganda had not been ineffective. On French soil, however, the pillaging and brutality of most of their armies outraged every instinct of the countryside. Only the British held themselves in check. Prussians and Russians most of all made Napoleon seem the saviour of the nation.

Napoleon's Appeal to Augereau

Inhuman save to his family, no man has ever surpassed Bonaparte in emotional appeal. At this crisis in his own fate and in that of France, he appealed to Augereau in words which reveal his own energy and eloquence while they commemorate the causes of his failure. The brave cut-throat of 1796 was now Duke of Castiglione and commander of the army of Lyons. With his 25,000 men he might take the Austrians in the rear and wreck the invasion.

> "Cousin," wrote Napoleon from Nogent on February 21, "your news has cut me to the quick. Can it be that you did not take the field six hours after the vanguard from Spain joined you? Six hours of rest would have sufficed them. I won at Nangis with dragoons who had not drawn bridle since Bayonne. You say that the Nîmes battalions are undrilled and ill-found—a paltry reason! I have destroyed 80,000 of the enemy with ill-clad conscripts lacking knapsacks. The national guards are contemptible, you say. I have 4,000 from Angers and Brittany, in round hats and wooden shoes, with no knapsacks, but with good muskets, and they have done good service. No money! but where do you hope to get money? Only by rescuing our revenue from the enemy. No transport! Take it on every side. No magazines! That is too silly. I order you to take the field within twelve hours. If you are still the Augereau of Castiglione, keep the command; if your sixty years weigh you down, hand over to your senior general. The fatherland is in peril. It can be saved only by boldness and zeal, not by marking time. You must have more than 6,000 picked men. I have less, yet I have destroyed three armies, made 40,000 prisoners, taken 200 guns and thrice saved the capital. The enemy is fleeing from every side towards Troyes. Be the first at the ball. We can act no longer as in these last years. We must put on our boots and our countenance of '93. When the French see your plume in the van and yourself the first to brave the fire, you will do with them as you please."

Augereau, like many another instrument of Napoleon, however, saw no reason to court destruction for his sake. Ten years of empire had blunted the Emperor's appeal save to those under his immediate command, while they had raised up countless foes abroad. His personal offensiveness now turned the scales against him. For a critical fortnight Augereau stood inactive.

After four days of victory over Blücher, as we have seen, Napoleon had been compelled to break off the pursuit and to return from the Marne to the Seine. Instead of threatening Paris, however, Schwarzenberg was driven to retreat by the news of Blücher's failure. On February 18, Napoleon regained Montereau with its important bridge and Schwarzenberg summoned Blücher to his aid. Blücher complied, having treated Napoleon after Vauchamps as Frederick treated the victorious Austrians after Hochkirch. Within five days of their defeat, the Prussians boasted, their offensive was resumed. But Schwarzenberg, now fearing for his communications, continued his retreat, vigorously pressed by Napoleon. On the 25th, however, Blücher was reinforced and authorized to take independent action.

Victory of the Coalition

Meanwhile Napoleon's victories had worked powerfully to his disadvantage. When he could hope to rouse France, to save Belgium and to drive his foes beyond the Rhine, he had invited Francis to make peace on the terms of Frankfort. This unyielding attitude and his renewed prestige consolidated anew the league of Europe. Despite his local successes, moreover, it was difficult on a calm review of the situation to doubt the issue. Blücher and Schwarzenberg had been beaten, but by February 27 both had resumed the offensive. Belgium had been won, and its conquerors were on their way to join Blücher. Wellington had crossed the southern frontier. Alexander was determined to go on, and it was safer for Austria that Russia and Prussia should not share between themselves the spoils of a victory which now seemed certain.

Ten days more, therefore, saw Napoleon himself checkmated and the doom of France pronounced. Neither by fiercely attacking the Russians at Craonne nor the whole of Blücher's force at Laon could the Emperor dissipate the danger from the north (March 8 and 9). While the battle raged round Laon, the Allies signed the Treaty of Chaumont, dictated by Castlereagh. At a time when the mobile troops of France were barely 100,000 strong, each of the four Great Powers pledged itself to maintain 150,000 in the field.

Britain, moreover, promised £5,000,000 to subsidize Austria, Prussia and Russia for the campaign. For twenty years, if need be, they would maintain the war in common to reduce France to her old frontiers and to render the nations beyond them independent.

The struggle to which the Allies were pledged for twenty years came to an end within three weeks. Although the illness of Blücher and the timidity of other generals hampered the Allies, Napoleon's failure at Laon left them practically invincible. Only by a revival of their dissensions, which could hardly come at once, or by a national uprising in France, which was still less possible, might they be robbed of victory. The Emperor, feeling himself once more the Corsican revolutionary of 1792, fought on with courage, resource and power of inspiration, but the odds were now too great. Breaking away from the enemy at Laon, he captured Rheims, and attempted to capitalize this success and the terror of his name into the acceptance of his new terms of peace. But without confessing his own weakness and alienating the French, he could no longer offer anything worthy of notice. His proposals were not even considered by the Allies. At Arcis, moreover, he failed to drive Schwarzenberg from his position on the Aube. From north-east and from south-east irresistible forces threatened Paris. Moving eastwards, the Emperor menaced their communications, but they masked his slender forces and pressed on. When Napoleon was treated as negligible in diplomacy and in the field, Marmont and Mortier might well fail to check 180,000 men, both in Champagne and beneath the ramparts of Paris. Before the Emperor could ride to their assistance all was over. On March 30, Paris fell. Next day, Alexander and Frederick William rode into the city, and on April 2, Napoleon was deposed by the representatives of France. It seemed that his ingrained suspicions of the French were justified. The civil population, which he had endowed with so many splendid institutions, made no gesture of resentment at his fall. In the army, whatever might be the feelings of the rank and file, the chief officers were unwilling to fight on. It was they who prevented Napoleon from leading a forlorn hope, and who procured his abdication in favour of the King of Rome.

The submission of Napoleon, of the army and of France, however, was far from ending the difficulties of the Allies. The men who had entered Paris must propose, and that immediately, some substitute for the Empire, and one which would neither revolt Paris, the army and the nation, nor blight the prospect of an abiding peace. Napoleon and his family had been proscribed. The *ancien régime* must not return: foreign domination was impossible. By the common law of Europe, a Bourbon should be King of France, but to most Frenchmen the Bourbons were tyrants and traitors whose installation would mean the restitution of the confiscated land, and the ultimate loss of equality before the law. So difficult was the problem that Bernadotte, as a Frenchman of the royal caste, might cherish hopes of the French crown. Alexander and Talleyrand, however, found a solution from which the history of Europe derived for fifteen years. The Bourbons as the legitimate dynasty were to return, but "legitimate" was to receive a new meaning. That limited monarchy, with much of the English Revolution in its being, which Frenchmen had desired in 1789 was now prescribed by the Allies. By swearing to rule with limitations, the Bourbons regained their throne. In four days, by a triumph of Russian influence, France received a Liberal constitution. The Senate accepted a so-called Constitutional Charter which the nation was to endorse by a popular vote and Louis XVIII to acknowledge as a Bill of Rights. The restored King of France would therefore rule in virtue of a contract which he had sworn to carry out. The executive power would be his, and King, Senate and Chamber of Deputies would share in making laws. But his ministers would be responsible to the two Chambers, while the King must promise to respect the chief changes made since 1789. The Church lands were to be enjoyed by those who had bought them, and the new organization of France was sacrosanct. Even the Napoleonic officers and nobles were to remain. The taxpayer was secured against unparliamentary taxation and the jury system upheld. So far as constitutional laws could protect the French, they were safeguarded against the return of the old *régime* or a White revenge.

Consequences of Napoleon's Abdication

The Constitution of 1814

On these terms the Bourbon restoration was accomplished. While at Fontainebleau Napoleon hesitated between sub-

The Bourbon Restoration

mission and suicide, the future Charles X made a ceremonial entry into Paris. His elder brother, Louis XVIII, lay ill in England, the asylum of every French monarch who reigned in the nineteenth century. Louis' tolerant temper and Charles' regal grace mitigated the abasement of a nation forced by its conquerors to obey a dynasty which it had exiled and detested for more than twenty years. In the capital at least, the new constitutional *régime* dawned hopefully. Next day, on April 13, Napoleon accepted the Allies' terms. He received Elba in full sovereignty with an ample revenue, while Marie Louise was to rule Parma, Piacenza and Guastalla, with the young Napoleon as her heir. Before the end of April, the ex-Emperor had departed for his southern island, where he found vent for his inexhaustible vitality in headlong rides and fruitful labours of reorganization. There young Lord John Russell found him "very fat and very gay," studying Europe so profoundly as to divine that Wellington was undoubtedly aiming at the British crown. Meanwhile, in regions where collective Europe did not interfere, the Restoration seemed bent on gilding the memory of Napoleon and the Revolution. In Spain and Italy, the Inquisition was set up anew. The Pope restored the Jesuits and the Index. Some returning tyrants banished such revolutionary innovations as vaccination and public lighting. The Bourbons and the Allies, however, combined to forbid such reaction in France.

Early in May, Louis XVIII himself came to preside over the reorganization of the government. The outline drawn under Russian influence was now filled in, and the new constitution embodied in a Charter which the King "granted" to his people. Like Charles II of England, moreover, he dated his reign from the day on which his legitimate predecessor died. But France gained a genuine constitution under a king whose sincerity and wisdom were unquestionable. Catholicism became once more the religion of the State, but full religious toleration was proclaimed. France thus acquired a limited monarchy, which was to serve her for a generation. While no Liberal casting back his eyes to 1789 could doubt that much had been gained, no Conservative could doubt that much had been recovered. The Empire was quietly but none the less effectively superseded by a constitutional *régime*. Next year, when Napoleon returned to Paris, he could not pose as Emperor. An acute observer then insisted that he was a stuffed figure rather than the Man. The Constitution helped to turn the scale at Waterloo.

The Peace of Paris

At the same time as this domestic settlement was accomplished, France came to terms with the Allies regarding the outcome of her twenty years of war. Unhappily, however, the settlement proclaimed early in June, and now known as the First Peace of Paris, could not possibly satisfy either the French or the conquering powers. Throughout Europe, the revolutionary and Napoleonic wars had inflicted losses which the total wealth of France could not repair. On the other hand, the French armies had made conquests which France could not cheerfully relinquish. The French in 1814, moreover, like the Germans in 1919, could not regard themselves as a standing danger against which all their neighbours must insure. Chief among those who then steered Europe, however, were Castlereagh, Metternich and Alexander—men who realized that if the Restoration was to make France moderate the Bourbons must not be pressed too hard. The Allies therefore consented to forego monetary indemnities, although Napoleon had left France free from debt. They even forbore to seize in Paris the works of art which had been looted from their capitals. Their armies were to evacuate the country, and many of the French munitions and ships, notably the Texel fleet, were to be returned. The French frontiers of January 1, 1792, were rounded off with many small additions which increased the population by some 450,000 souls. But this seemed trifling by comparison with the 15,360,000 which the Empire stood to lose as soon as hereditary right rather than conquest or "natural frontiers" should prevail. Overseas, Malta became British, Mauritius (Île de France) with Tobago and Santa Lucia must be ceded to Britain, and ex-Spanish San Domingo to Spain, while France could not escape from an undertaking to collaborate with Britain against the slave trade. She must, moreover, accept the Allies' ideas of a new Europe so organized as to hem her in. The House of Orange was to rule over an aggrandized Holland of which Belgium was to form a part. The German states were to unite in a vast federation. Switzerland remained an independent state and

Politic Moderation of the Allies

Prussia recovered Neuchâtel. France must also promise to accept the disposition of conquered or ceded lands which the Allies might make, and in particular the aggrandizement of Sardinia at the expense of the Genoese.

The Allies and Security

Mild as were the terms of the First Paris treaty in comparison with those of the Second (1815), they were galling to a proud nation whose provinces had been but little despoiled by the invaders. Pending the congress which was to complete the reorganization of Europe at Vienna, the four powers who had allied themselves at Chaumont agreed at London to keep at least 225,000 men under arms. Negotiations, moreover, went on briskly for the establishment of the new Europe. Austria and Bavaria revised their mutual frontiers and became allies. Britain gained the Cape of Good Hope from the Dutch. Every preparation was made for the august assembly which was designed to establish Austria and Prussia as strong powers supported by their mighty neighbour, Russia. If the work of the Vienna Congress answered expectations, Europe would emerge as a harmonious and stable structure which no future Napoleon could ever overthrow. It was at least hopeful for the new order that France was not to be excluded from the assembly of the Powers.

In the west, the new European order was, however, exposed to a twofold danger. Napoleon's *parvenu* status, the collapse of his power and the hatred towards him which had been shown in parts of France, blinded the Allies to the possibility that he might rise once more. On paper, he had abdicated in the interest of France. By word of mouth, he declared that he yielded nothing. His Guards, less than 10,000 strong, had demanded to be led against all Europe. Strewn over the Continent were perhaps twenty times as many veterans who would gladly join them. Much turned upon the happiness or woe of France under his successor. Could the Bourbons and their "Charta" satisfy the people of humiliated France?

France and the Charta

The Charta of 1814, like the Edict of Nantes or Magna Carta itself, though in form a grant, was in fact a treaty. The parties to that treaty were substantially the restored monarchy in France, the allied powers, who had restored it, and the French people, without whose favour it could in future years be overthrown. Like most bargains, the Charta enshrined a compromise, in this case between those to whom the Rights of Man and their historic consequences were disgusting and those to whom they were vital. The first party included the *emigrés* and some of the Powers; the second, Alexander and, in varying degrees, the French nation. The words employed were moderate and tactful. Louis XVIII, recalled by Divine Providence, recognized that peace and a constitutional charter were the pressing needs of France. He declared that all authority resided entirely in the King, and that in the interest of the people autocracy should be maintained. Like his predecessors, however, he was prepared to modify its exercise to suit the times. He therefore granted for ever the equality of all Frenchmen before the law, the liability of all to pay taxes according to their wealth, their equal admissibility to office, and such liberty as the Revolution had proclaimed with regard to arrest, worship and the expression of opinion. Conscription was abolished and the Legion of Honour maintained. Ministers became responsible, and judges irremovable from office. The King was the sole executive, the fountain of justice and of honour, and the proposer of new laws. He shared the legislative power with the Peers and Deputies. No Frenchman was called upon to renounce his new freedom of cultivation, or to give up the nationalized lands that he had purchased, or to resume payment of those feudal dues which the Revolution had swept away. The Charta, therefore, might well seem to concede all the chief benefits of the Revolution. Yet "to make justice, concord and peace reign among men is never easy." The weakness of the Charta lay in the claim that it was "granted." What autocracy had granted, autocracy could take away, and some of those who might sway the autocracy made no secret that they wished to do so. The King's health was frail, while the future Charles X and many of the *emigrés* were royalist *doctrinaires*. Not a few had entered Paris through a mob which had massacred their kinsmen and which perhaps now occupied their own estates. The Edict of Nantes is most famous for its Revocation. How could the Charta ensure justice, concord and peace? The principle of the Balance of Power, indeed, had gained in authority from its subversion by Napoleon. The

Powers were about to restore a balanced Europe, and to take it under their protection. So long as France was their associate and *protégé* the Charta might be secure. The loosening of the concert, however, would jeopardize the French settlement, and so it proved in 1830. Before 1814 was at an end, a discord far greater than that of 1830 was apparent.

BIBLIOGRAPHICAL NOTE

See the Bibliographical Note at the end of Chapter I and the bibliographies to Chapters XIX and XX.

Add :—

A

A. Cecil : *Metternich, 1773–1859* (1935).

H. du Coudray : *Metternich* (1935).

P. Geyl : *Napoleon : For and Against* (trans. 1949).

C. de Grunwald : *Metternich* (trans. 1953).

H. Houssaye : *1814* (1888, 67th ed. rev. 1911).

F. M. Kircheisen : *Napoleon I, sein Leben und seine Zeit.* 9 vols. (1911–34).

G. Lefebvre : *Napoléon.* (4th ed. 1953).

F. D. Scott : *Bernadotte and the Fall of Napoleon* (1935).

H. von Srbik : *Metternich, der Staatsmann und der Mensch.* 3 vols. (1925–54).

F. Stählin : *Napoleons Glanz und Fall im deutschen Urteil : Wandlungen des deutschen Napoleonbildes* (1952).

H. W. V. Temperley and L. M. Penson : *Foundations of British Foreign Policy from Pitt (1792) to Salisbury (1902)* (1938).

C. K. Webster : *The Foreign Policy of Castlereagh, 1812–1815* (1925).

B

O. Sjögren : *Charles John and the Scandinavian Peninsula* (Stockholm).

CHAPTER XXII

EUROPE AFTER THE FALL OF NAPOLEON

Peace Prospects April 1814

IN April 1814, when, " as by the stroke of an enchanter's wand, the revolutionary government of France, after tormenting the world for nearly twenty-five years . . . quietly yielded up its breath," the diarist H. C. Robinson thus appraised the European situation. Premising that, if honourably feasible, the Allies should " break the treaty so imprudently made with that arch-knave Murat," and that Norwegian emancipation from the dominion of Bernadotte, " so unworthily obtained," would be welcome, he urged that

" Saxony ought to revert to the House which lost it during the wars produced by the Reformation." " Poland," he declared, " has no chance of regaining her independence, and perhaps would not be able to make use of it. Russia will descend deeper into Europe than I can contemplate without anxiety. . . . Prussia I wish to see mistress of all Protestant Germany and . . . the rest of Germany swallowed up by Austria ; but this will not be. . . . This is the one evil I apprehend from the restoration of the Bourbons—that the jealousy which ought to survive against France, as France, will sleep in the ashes of the Napoleon dynasty."

Robinson's clear-sighted analysis was at the same moment confirmed and amplified by Gentz, " a prince of publicists," and the spokesman of Austrian moderation.

" 'Tis a great mistake," he warned the Hospodar of Wallachia, " to believe that with the destruction of Napoleon's power, peace and happiness will be re-born all over Europe. . . . Storms of every kind still threaten us. The fear of endangering the Allies' union is for ever causing critical questions to be adjourned. Nothing, absolutely nothing, therefore, has yet been decided about the future lot of Germany, Italy and Poland."

Under the weak Bourbons, he foresaw, exhausted France would for many years be unable to balance triumphant Russia, which would threaten the Turks and keep Austria in perpetual apprehension.

The public, none the less, rejoiced in a new freedom. At midsummer, when Napoleon, though scarcely past his prime, was caged in Elba, civilians were once more set free

Public Rejoicings

to travel, and to observe a Europe which had conquered the Revolution. After a winter severe almost beyond precedent, the nations prepared to celebrate "the present brilliant epocha—when through the providential and signal interposition of the Almighty Disposer of events, the deliverance of the Continent of Europe from a system inimical to the repose of mankind had been gloriously effected." As the two Emperors and the King of Prussia formed a coterie which continued to move about outside their own dominions, it was left to London to rehearse in June what Vienna was to eclipse in October—a series of impressive *fêtes*. During the early summer, the south of England and the capital were for ever being stirred by the comings and goings of the great. Louis XVIII had been sped to his new dominions with splendid processions: Wellington was to be carried in triumph by the people of Dover, and escorted by the Prince Regent to St. Paul's. In the meantime whatever the court, the city, and the University of Oxford could devise to impress Francis, Alexander, Frederick William and their glittering suites was done without regard to cost or labour. When the royal guests had returned to France, the London populace, not without fear of what the mob might do, was entertained with an elaborate though somewhat pointless exhibition. The war had sunk into the past, and, until the Congress met, the expected benefits were relegated to the future.

Economic Strain

In Britain the rejoicings passed off well, but the strained economy of the nation showed itself before winter came and the troops returned from America and France to be disbanded. Only by importing French supplies of food could prices be made reasonable in the south. Luddites and frame-breakers committed outrages with impunity. Near Nottingham they formed committees which met by daylight to prescribe both work and wages, and to requisition funds for strikers. At the same time the manufacturers on the Continent were being freed from their war-time handicaps. "To the inexpressible joy of the inhabitants," the Hamburg Exchange was reopened. Trade prepared to flow in its accustomed channels, for little had occurred to change them. The populations had neither moved from their old homes, nor greatly changed their way of living. Peasant emancipation in France and Prussia had exalted man without greatly improving tillage, and industry shed its medieval fetters without at first radically altering its methods. Neither the loss due to the cessation of war expenditure nor the gain due to the Revolution and to British inventions was clearly perceptible in 1814.

Meanwhile, in the presence of the Allied armies, the Peace of Paris was duly carried out. Its terms included liberal provision for the Bonapartes at the expense of France. When Louis XVIII returned to Paris, Josephine was being carried to her grave.

France and the Empire

The Empress and her son remained at Parma, with Count Neipperg, her lover, in attendance. Napoleon's mother came to his side with the vast fortune that she had saved. His sister Pauline, and for a time the Countess Waleska with their son, were also there. The Man of Destiny, it seemed, had become an obscure Italian prince. His mushroom empire had already shrivelled into the France of 1792, a France now exhausted by adventure and longing for peace and rest. There, as in allied Europe, the elders had grasped the reins anew. While the young marshals and Bonapartes returned to their former insignificance, veteran diplomats prepared to assemble at Vienna and to purge Europe from the poison of 1789.

Restoration in Europe

The counter-revolution, indeed, promised to be neither indiscriminate nor insane. Only a few fanatics traced back national sentiment to sin and to the fall of man. Although some princes, Italians and Spanish Bourbons high among them, might restore the Inquisition and attempt to set back the clock, few uncrowned statesmen were so blind. The Tsar himself declared that he had lived and would die a Republican. Metternich, Talleyrand, Castlereagh, Wellington, whatever their political doctrines, were men of high ability and vast experience of affairs.

Europeans such as these would not provoke unnecessary resentment or triumph meanly. Of kings they had seen too much to be fanatics for Divine Right. If they restored Legitimacy, it would be with the implied condition of ruling well, while Privilege could hope for only a partial restoration. The King might come back; the *grand seigneur* would not.

Throughout Europe, none the less, Restoration was a reality. Kings and statesmen feared the mob, but they meant to rule, and to rule without its aid. When they met at Vienna it would be to reconstruct that historic Europe which for a quarter of a century had been buffeted and mauled by Revolution. Their task was not to construct a new edifice based on the Rights of Man but to repair the damage done by misguided upstarts since 1789. They must also buttress the building so that no second Napoleon should ever ruin it anew. What were the prospects of success?

Prospects for the future of Europe

A horoscope of Europe cast on the eve of the Vienna Congress must be the outcome of both politics and civilization. It is for us to sum up first the changes among states produced by two decades of general overthrow, and, second, the progress of man during the half-century since America had claimed her independence. Given these, we may assess the legacy of the eighteenth century to the nineteenth and attempt to forecast the future.

Results of the War Period

Looking back across the chaos which had enveloped Europe since 1792, three outstanding facts compel attention. (1) Among the important Powers, Britain and Russia alone had escaped the sway of France. Thus the two states whose history and composition differed most from those of the rest of Europe had again experienced a peculiar fate. (2) All others had submitted to French hegemony, and several had been comprised in the French Empire. Revolutionary doctrine had therefore been taught by practice over the greater part of Europe. (3) At a full month's distance from the nearest European shore, a new Power of European origin was now firmly established—the United States of America. The distracting war of 1812–14 had already shown how the New World might disturb the politics of the Old. The American rejection of monarchy at a time when Europe looked to its monarchs for salvation pointed the contrast of ideals between the Old World and the New. While in 1814 the United States appeared to Europe primarily as a potential enemy or ally, their commercial and cultural influence could hardly fail to become important. Even the poverty and the remoteness of the new Power would not blind Europeans to the importance of its experiments in democracy and education. Seven million white men of the new type on or near the Atlantic sea-board must inevitably influence Europe.

Leadership of Britain

Among the European states, Britain, although still distracted by the American struggle, was for the moment unquestionably the first. While the French were marching into almost every continental capital, London had remained inviolate. Which of the Powers save Britain had never been Napoleon's ally ? British diplomacy had formed the Coalitions, British gold had sustained them, and the armies of the Continent had marched to battle clad in British cloth. It was the efforts of Britain in the common cause, not less than their own character and talents, that gave Castlereagh and Wellington unique influence in Europe. The cause and the crown of British prestige was her fleet, which completely subverted the balance of power without arousing what might seem the inevitable protests. But British wealth appeared even more impressive. While the war had called upon Britain for an immense output of goods it had prevented foreigners from copying her processes and had crippled her potential rivals. Manufactures called for fresh hands, and the consequent rise of population favoured the farmers who provided it with food. Since foreign supplies were naturally checked by war, England was cultivated to her very hill-tops. Despite innumerable taxes, government loans could be raised from the unwonted profits of both industry and agriculture, and the national debt reached unheard-of heights. Doubled by the American war, but in 1793 still under £250,000,000, it now exceeded thrice that sum. For two-and-twenty years Britain had spent on the average several times her normal income. Napoleon consoled himself with the reflection that he had doomed his enemy to sink under her debt. In 1814 a nation which could pay interest on more than £800,000,000 and yet could seem to thrive was the wonder of exhausted Europe.

The appearance of prosperity, it is true, was largely a war-time illusion. When the next year closed, a dispassionate chronicler recorded in the *Annual Register* that there had rarely been an epoch of more widely diffused complaint. " All the triumphant sensations of national glory," he declared, " seem almost obliterated by general depression. Peace, although a consummation long anxiously looked for, was scarcely welcomed. . . . The public feelings were nearly concentrated upon private and personal distress." Although

Britain had escaped invasion and had gained empire, such feelings increased the fears of her statesmen that "the whole thing might break up." Within five years of the fall of Napoleon, Shelley dared to indict "an old, mad, blind, despised and dying King; rulers who neither feel nor see nor know; a senate—time's worst statute unrepealed," and the public danger visible a century later in the General Strike was present in a grimmer form. In the summer of 1814, however, the feeling resembled that which was roused by the Armistice of 1918, rather than that which followed the Second Peace of Paris (1815), or the Treaties of Versailles (1919). "The rejoicings," wrote a contemporary, "frequently offered very pleasing displays of coalescence between the superior and inferior ranks, marked by bounty in the former, and decency in the latter." Having dethroned Napoleon and defeated the Americans, Britain turned with enthusiasm and self-complacency to put down the slave trade. The fall of Napoleon, indeed, had not ended Britain's effort upon the Continent. Apart from his resurrection, a miracle which none could then foresee, the problem of France was far from fully solved. In 1814, as in 1918, Britain must expect to continue her assistance to the common cause until her late opponent could regain stability and Europe therefore might disarm. When the last campaign ended, however, her insularity was bound to make itself felt anew. She was unravaged, industrial, free, and mistress of the seas—advantages which no nation of the Continent could claim.

Influence of Russia

In the reconstruction of France, none the less, British influence was at first surpassed by that of Russia. As Cæsar, Alexander I ranked above a mere king or minister, and the legions which he had led to Paris across all Europe seemed to signify irresistible power. Russia had suffered grievously from the devastation of her finest districts and from the slaughter of her sons. Her reward might well be a great expansion westwards at the expense of Napoleon's friends. Take Norway from the King of Denmark and give it to the Swede in exchange for Finland; take Warsaw from the ruling Bonaparte and carve from it a Polish Kingdom; give both Finland and Poland to Alexander; aggrandize Prussia, virtually his protectorate since Tilsit—Russia would thus receive her due reward and boundless influence over continental Europe. A century after Poltava (1709) the army created by Peter enabled his successor to dictate a constitution to France, to annex Poland, and to establish something like a dictatorship over Germany. The loyalty shown for a century to Russia by the German Baltic Barons who ruled the sea-board countries south of the Gulf of Finland made it possible to hope that the inhabitants of Finland and of Poland might likewise prove elements of strength. Even if these lay passive, the new power of Russia seemed overwhelming. German by blood and marriage, the Tsar could count on allies among the Germans while his dominions flanked and protruded into Germany. His predominance in Poland tightened his hold upon Austria and Prussia, which were also Polish powers. He could set up a two-power standard and maintain an army equal to those of Prussia and Austria combined. A few weeks would suffice to transport into the heart of Germany a Russian force from seventy to eighty thousand strong, supported, as men believed, by almost unlimited reserves. After 1812, to invade Russia passed for madness, while, alone among continental powers, Russia need have no anxiety about her rear. Against her, sea-power could hardly turn the scale. As history had proved, the economic bonds that linked her to Britain were strong. If they were broken, a huge, remote and agricultural empire offered no vital spot for maritime attack.

Internal Problems of Russia

The revolutionary and Napoleonic wars, it is clear, had contributed not a little to advance the power of Russia. They had also strengthened two Russian currents which were powerfully to affect the future. Slavophils, who adored "Holy Russia," were bound to regard the triumph over Napoleon as the resplendent glory of a chosen people. The overweening national pride which all observers remarked was by some ascribed to the oriental origin of the race, by others, to their ignorance and isolation, to the vastness of their land, or even to their secret self-distrust. Whatever its cause or causes, it could not but be swelled when the Russians single-handed vanquished French, Germans, Poles and Italians led by Napoleon himself. As the self-consciousness of the Slavs increased, therefore, an important section of the chief Slavonic race was inspired by the history of 1812–1814 to believe that God destined that race to perform wonders upon earth under the leadership of Russia. While, in the words of the Holy Synod,

"the French nation, bewildered by a demoniac phantom of liberty, overthrew the altars of God, and trampled on the throne of His anointed," corrupting other nations, "the Church and the Empire of Russia, preserved by the goodness of God as witnesses of His glory and mercy, have long been compassionate witnesses of the miseries plucked by the nations on their own heads, by having deserted the protection of the Most High. Awful is the spectacle."

The fall of Napoleon strengthened Russia's pride in protecting thrones and altars.

At the same time the victory of Russia and the contact of her young officers with the west deepened the suspicion of some native thinkers that since Peter's time she had been steering a mistaken course. Conquest had followed conquest, but the masses had become ever more and more deeply enslaved. The peasant who escaped conscription, which the people regarded as equivalent to a sentence of death, usually remained tied to an estate, and his human rights were of the scantiest. The Church was dominated by the State. Thought and the press enjoyed no freedom, and the crown was uncontrolled. Now that the lost Russian lands had been regained from Poland, and the Swede and Turk had become incapable of offence, it was time for the tsardom to restore to the people rights which they had sacrificed only for the sake of its accomplished mission. Such reasoning inspired the so-called Decabrists, gentlemen revolutionaries who rebelled a decade later. Throughout the century it arrayed enlightened classes against the government. Charging in effect the tsars with fraud, it conduced to terror and counter-terror, and darkened the whole history of the Russian people for a hundred years.

It was for the future. however, to ripen what the preceding age had sown. In 1814 it was of first importance that Russia more fully than ever before belonged to Europe. Not content to repudiate and to repel Napoleon, she had assisted Germany and the west to destroy his power. She had reconstructed France and was about to take the lead in reconstructing Europe—a continent over which she intended to preside. The genuine and progressive Europeanization of the Russian court and policy must be, for good or evil, of immense import for Europe.

France at the Fall of Napoleon

When Napoleon abdicated, he left France the most uncertain factor in Europe. For the moment at least, the French were exhausted and defenceless, with the flower of their armies cooped up in foreign lands. They had displayed little eagerness to uphold Napoleon, who, indeed, claimed that for three years he alone had saved them from civil war. A republic, history seemed to show, had proved unsuitable to the genius of the nation, but what king would command their allegiance? Forgotten by Frenchmen, the Bourbons had never been proclaimed the heirs of France by the Allies. When Britain and Russia, swayed by Talleyrand, pressed the claims of Louis XVIII upon the conquered capital, the Senate decreed that he should be proclaimed king of the French as soon as he had sworn to uphold the new and liberal constitution. None save the *emigrés*, however, thought of the gouty exile with enthusiasm, and no one supposed that he still had eleven years to live. It was hard to predict who would or could reconcile the returning aristocrats to their former serfs. How could proud France, moreover, accept the startling inferiority of her colonial empire beside that of England? With more than double the British population at home, she retained, as her statisticians reckoned, little more than one-sixtieth the number of subjects overseas.

Financially, indeed, France emerged from the long contest far less heavily burdened than her rival. Even Napoleon's enemies could not charge him with the addition of as much as £200,000,000 to the French public debt. Against this the new treasures which he had bestowed on France in the shape of roads and harbours and public buildings were visible to every eye. Talleyrand claimed that while each French subject paid less than twenty-two francs yearly in taxes the Briton paid 120. He might have added that the abandonment of the Continental System and the re-opening of the seas to trade must benefit France far more than the mistress of the ocean. Louis XVIII, therefore, might count on the absence of any rival candidate for his throne and on such popularity, or at least such acquiescence, as falls to a government when the times are palpably improving. He could reasonably hope that the Tsar, the champion of Legitimacy, who had sheltered him for many years, and

Prospects of the French Monarchy

who had done most to place him on the throne, would still remain his friend. The common interests of France and Britain, moreover, pointed to an *entente* between them which might well prove better based than its precursor in the days of Walpole. It was perhaps impossible that the French should love the victors in the struggle of four generations. But history had taught them that without such an *entente* they could not prosper, and they too had become constitutional like Britain. The King's task, none the less, might well perplex the most consummate royal statesman. He must return to his fatherland in the train of foreign armies. Himself sincerely moderate, he must submit to be hampered and discredited by an extremist heir and by extremist and perhaps revengeful friends—the men and women who re-entered Paris through a crowd of their parents' murderers. The Duchess d'Angoulême, on her way to the Tuileries, fainted in the arms of her servants when she saw the gratings of her mother's dungeon. It was for her uncle, the successor of his murdered brother, Louis XVI, to uphold the social system introduced by the Revolution and the laws and institutions which Napoleon had devised. To accept the tricolour and the *Marseillaise*, those symbols of French glory, demanded more moral flexibility than the Bourbons possessed. Their government, moreover, might easily become too clerical for urban France. Above all, the new king was required to exercise an exotic form of kingship—that "constitutional" or "limited" monarchy which had flourished only in Britain. Among the logical, uncompromising French, an institution which depends for its success upon good temper and tradition was unlikely to succeed. In France, either the King or the Parliament must undisguisedly prevail. The Bourbon Restoration of 1814 was obviously hedged round with peril.

The Restoration in Spain

On every side, sovereigns less wise and moderate than Louis XVIII were being restored to their dominions. In Spain, the Bourbon Ferdinand VII, whom Napoleon had expelled, reclaimed his kingdom and his autocratic power. The Cortes were simply directed to disperse, and the adherents of the ex-King, Joseph Bonaparte, to remain outside the kingdom. While isolated voices were raised on behalf of the new constitutional liberties, and the revolt of Spanish

America continued, Spanish nationalism was flattered by Ferdinand's return. The people of Madrid drew their sovereign's carriage for seven leagues in triumph, and he marked his home-coming by wandering through every street of the capital on foot. The convents were restored; the Inquisition, re-established; many Liberals, flung into prison; and all that had happened since 1808, so far as possible erased. Having thus purged Old Spain of revolutionary taint, the restored monarchy, careless of blood and treasure, prepared to attempt the reconquest of its American dominions.

Restoration in Italy

In Italy the returning sovereigns had greater difficulties to face. The French Empire had for a decade ruled unchallenged beyond the Alps and had left its mark for all time upon the rising Italian middle class. Under the influence of Napoleon, the citizens of the petty states had learned wider ways of thinking. Local customs and allegiances had been dissolved by the mighty Code and Empire. Even the memories of ancient Rome might be blurred when the city found itself in a realm stretching from the frontiers of Naples to those of Spain and Denmark and dominating all Europe save only Britain. In such an atmosphere the old parochialism withered away. Young Florentines and Venetians began to think of themselves as Italians and to dream of delivering Italy from the sway of France. To the last moment Napoleon, Italian by descent and by cast of mind, had clung to his Italian throne. Now, at Elba, he was to rule a corner of Italy with imperial state, while throughout that peninsula, the dynasties deposed by him expected to return. If King Joachim Murat could be disposed of, the Bourbons of Naples would no longer have ceased to reign. Thanks to the British fleet, indeed, Ferdinand III already ruled as a constitutional king in Sicily. The ancient House of Savoy, now Kings of Sardinia, undistinguished but practical as of old, regained Turin, and were soon to be rewarded with Genoa, a city of palaces and merchant princes. The remainder of the north, indeed, was still occupied by Austrian troops, and not all its former governments could hope for restoration. Venice, as a non-dynastic power, invaluable to Austria both by her wealth and by her strategic position, had but the faintest prospect of regaining independence. "No obstacle," the Emperor Francis proclaimed in August to the Venetians, " can interpose to prevent the execution of the plans for your happiness which I have formed. Your provinces will always be one of the brightest gems in my crown." In the hymn of 1841, "*Deutschland, Deutschland über alles*, from the Adige to the Belt," the accomplishment of his designs on Venice was recalled.

Restoration in the Papal States

In 1814, the only restored Italian sovereign who was free to legislate as he pleased was the ruler of the Papal States, Pius VII. A septuagenarian who had witnessed the rise and fall of many worldly empires, he boldly styled himself " God's Vicar on Earth," and hastened to cleanse his dominions from the stains inflicted by the French. The *Code Napoléon* and the lay budget vanished. All monasteries and converts were, so far as possible, re-endowed, and the Pope called upon the Catholic sovereigns to make similar restitution to the Church. Ecclesiastical restoration extended even to the lighting of the streets of Rome. This was abandoned by the government and left once more to the efforts of householders and of those who placed votive lanterns before the wayside images and crosses. Secret societies, especially Freemasons, were forbidden to meet. Above all, since its effect must be felt throughout the world, Pius VII abrogated the bull of 1773 and restored the Jesuit Order. " The Catholic World," he declared, " demands with unanimous voice the re-establishment of the Company of Jesus." On the application of Paul of Russia and of Ferdinand of Sicily, he had previously sanctioned Jesuit congregations in their dominions. He now extended the same concession to his own and all other states. So far as papal power could prevail, the Order might live and teach and minister as in the days of Loyola.

Restoration in the Low Countries

On the northern frontier of Napoleon's former empire, Europe was faced with problems no less complex and vital. Whereas Italy resembled a pier thrust out into the Mediterranean, the Low Countries formed a broad esplanade coveted by many neighbours and flanking a more important sea. Careless of history and checked by no natural frontier, the France of 1810 comprised Münster and Bremen and Hamburg beyond what could ever be called the Netherlands. From the dynastic standpoint, moreover, Holland and Belgium were two heterogeneous aggregates, while the differences between Dutch, Walloons and Flemings increased the difficulties of forming a united state. A kingdom of the Netherlands must include the most Catholic and the most Protestant of populations. Men accustomed to obey Roman law would be fellow-citizens of men whose legal concepts were Teutonic. The doctrines of the Revolution had penetrated deeply into the minds of many among them. Europe, indeed, required a northern bulwark against France which the amalgamated Dutch and Belgians might perhaps supply. But it might be doubted whether French-speaking Catholics, including not a few immigrants from France, formed the best material from which to build it, or whether the House of Orange, which had frequently proved impotent among the Dutch, would be welcomed by the Belgians as their ruler.

The Netherlands United

Events moved steadily, however, towards the establishment of an Orange dynasty over the United Netherlands. Napoleon's ebb had left the way clear for Prince William VI, leaning upon Britain, to return to Holland as William I, a constitutional sovereign. Dutch notables were summoned to Amsterdam, and in March an overwhelming majority approved the new constitution. In May, the sixth article of the Treaty of Paris placed the sanction of the Powers, including France, behind the Dutch dynasty and promised an undefined increase of its territory. To the eastward, at least, the boundaries of the new kingdom were suggested by the declaration of the German right to federate. Hamburg and its neighbours, now rejoicing at the departure of the French, had never been anything but German. To the south, the decision lay in the hands of Austria, since Utrecht the overlord of Belgium, and now once again in military occupation of the country. Belgium, indeed, like Holland had been conquered in France, and the French garrisons departed slowly. The announcement of Carnot that he would hold Antwerp for Louis XVIII formed a romantic incident in the sullen course of the imperial collapse. As the Austrians, however, had always found, the ten distant Belgic provinces were hard to defend and unprofitable to govern. Joseph II had bargained them away for Bavaria, and Francis hoped to exchange them for Lombardy and Venice. Early in August, with the full consent of the Allies,

William of Orange took the place of their Austrian governor, publicly informing the Belgians that their own interests and those of Europe required a change of status. Within two months, superfluous French immigrants were being replaced by Belgians, the most severe French restrictions on the press were done away, and the establishment of a native Belgian army was set on foot. Meanwhile the Dutch colonies which Britain had conquered during the war were returned to the mother country, and, by reducing expenditure and continuing war taxation, Holland achieved a surplus. The experiment of a United Netherlands guaranteed by Europe did not lack elements of hope.

The Rearrangement of Scandinavia

At the same time, another of the great territorial bargains whereby the Europe of 1814 hoped to secure future harmony was being negotiated in the north. During the twenty years which followed the assassination of Gustavus III of Sweden (1792), the two Scandinavian autocrats had been faced with problems too great for either their mind or their might to solve. In 1807, the seizure of his fleet by Britain threw Frederick VI of Denmark-Norway into the arms of Napoleon. His decision to support the tyrant of Europe against the mistress of the seas inevitably accentuated the difference between the interests of his Norwegian and of his Danish subjects. While the French could not march to Christiania or Bergen, the British could immediately destroy Norwegian trade. A Danish war with both Britain and Sweden even meant that Norway would go short of food. At that moment, indeed, Sweden still suffered under the rule of a monarch far less endurable than Frederick VI. This was Gustavus IV, whose frenzied hero-worship of Charles XII led him to defy any and every adverse combination in the field. Confronting Napoleon, Alexander and Frederick at once, he lost Swedish Pomerania in 1807, and, two years later, Finland fell to Russia. Even against the Norwegians Gustavus failed. In 1809 he was deposed, and Sweden reverted to that constitutional monarchy from the degenerate form of which she had been rescued by Gustavus' father (1772). In 1810 Marshal Bernadotte suddenly found himself transformed into Charles John, the Lutheran Crown Prince of Sweden, with unbounded influence over his new country so long as Europe remained at war. In spite of a Gascon imagination which betrayed him into believing himself destined to supplant Napoleon, Bernadotte proved a most competent and cautious prince. His martial renown, his heroic stature and friendly, helpful ways won the hearts of his northern subjects, and to serve the crown of Sweden he shrank from no exertion. He first made the Swedish army efficient, and then used it as a pawn to win Norway from the Allies.

The severance of that kingdom from Denmark, indeed, was facilitated by the rising self-consciousness of the Norwegians, to which the foundation of the University of Christiania (1811) bore witness. Though less than a million strong, they were a proud nation, always, after a colonial fashion, independent, and for a century unravaged by foreign or by civil war. A semi-federal union with constitutional Sweden might well be more to their taste than continued subservience to autocratic Denmark. In January 1814, however, when Frederick VI simply ceded Norway to the King of Sweden by the Treaty of Kiel, they had no thought of tamely accepting such a veiled conquest by their hereditary foe. Their mood was heightened by the presence among them of Prince Christian Frederick, the heir to Denmark, their viceroy and would-be king. Borrowing principles of national freedom from the Americans of 1776, the French of 1791 and the Spaniards of 1812, the notables met in May at Eidsvold and declared Norway independent. Christian accepted a Fundamental Law which provided for a single chamber (Storting) which the King could not dissolve. Men talked of defending Norway free and independent to the last drop of their blood. The unanimous election of Christian Frederick, the later Christian VIII of Denmark, by a poor and unarmed people could not, of course, annul a treaty which four Great Powers had guaranteed and which Bernadotte was ready to uphold. A fortnight's military promenade—"Pussyfoot Warfare" as the soldiers sneered—disposed of Norwegian separation though not of Norwegian constitutional independence. The Swedes prudently accepted the Fundamental Law, and in November Norway was proclaimed "a free independent and indivisible kingdom, united with Sweden under one King." All the Danish fetters—monopolies, privileges, censorship of the press—had thus been abolished without sacrifice, and a constitution gained, yet Norway began her new career in the gloomiest disappointment and depression. Europe, however, had achieved a settlement of the Scandinavian question which contributed not a little to the prospects of general peace. Russia, which had gained Finland; Sweden, now compensated with Norway; and Denmark, soon to be forgiven and enriched with Lauenburg, could all become cheerful members of post-war Europe, while the abandonment of the Swedish bastion in Germany removed an obsolete complication from the map.

South-eastern Europe in 1814

Of the regional arrangements which have already been sketched those of Spain and France offered no marked defiance to the potent principle of nationality, while in Italy, the Low Countries and Scandinavia national feelings were violated cautiously and from necessity. In south-eastern Europe, on the other hand, naked legitimacy achieved its most fragrant triumphs, and nationality continued to meet with the most reckless disregard. The Austrian Emperor did not shrink from forcing into one realm provinces inhabited by Poles, Czechs and Germans, Magyars and Italians, Croats, Slovaks and Slovenes. For the most part, as later history has shown, these were united by mutual economic and military convenience, while all owed allegiance to the Roman Catholic Church. In half a century, indeed, this Habsburg aggregate would ferment into a "European Turkey," but for the moment its vast and fertile area made it a leading state. Far more anomalous and lamentable was Turkey in Europe, the region which the Turks had conquered from Europe and were still allowed to hold. Perhaps the gravest indictment of the statesmanship of the Allies is that in 1814 they devised no plan for ridding Europe of the Turk. The Sultan, it is true, was a "legitimate" sovereign in the fourth century of the exercise of his hereditary rights. With his subjects' religion he did not interfere, and their social sufferings only seldom became known abroad. He was, moreover, a sincere reformer, in an age which had not acquired the conviction of its great-grandsons that the Turk could never become European. Europe, again, was still grateful for the peace of Bucharest. Although the Sultan had fought against Russia (1806–12), his refusal to join with France had contributed immensely to the downfall of Napoleon. At the same time the remaining Allies could not dream of coercing Russia, and

Russia stood to gain more from uncontrolled relations with the Turk than from any scheme devised by Europe as a whole. The Sultan was thus protected partly by his weakness, partly by the possibility, always present in a vast military and largely Asiatic empire, of his unsuspected strength, and chiefly by his inaccessibility to any European power save Russia. Turkey in Europe therefore remained, as the fall of Napoleon had left it, a power comprising some 215,000 square miles of European soil, inhabited by perhaps 10,000,000 people, of whom the vast majority were Christians.

Mahmoud II, Sultan since 1808, had, as it proved, still a quarter of a century before him, and his desires were all in favour of reform. But the janissaries had not ceased to be a powerful obstacle to progress, while since the Austrian occupation of Serbia in the war of 1788–91 the Serbs had gained at least a semi-independence. A like status had been enjoyed by Moldavia and Wallachia since 1774. The Greeks, who had risen in rebellion more than forty years before Napoleon fell, only waited for an opportunity to throw off the yoke. Whether these Christian races should be held captive by the Sultan's Africans and Asiatics, whether Russia should be allowed to emancipate them to her own advantage, what part Austria and the Western Powers should play in the disintegration or preservation of Turkey —these were among the problems which followed hard upon the inaction of Europe in 1814.

The Problems of Central Europe in 1814

Inaction in Turkey might perhaps be condoned, because in the vast and complex region of central Europe inaction was impossible. Between a line west of the Rhine and Adige and a line east of the Vistula and upper Dniester a few harassed and often ignorant statesmen must invent political forms and allot dominions. The eastern frontier of France, indeed, had been fixed by the Peace of Paris. While the constitution and the neutral status conferred upon Switzerland by Bonaparte in 1803 fell with his empire, the boundaries of the Swiss Confederation admitted of little dispute. Prussia and Austria, of course, must remain Great Powers, however their rewards and exchanges might modify the list of the provinces over which they ruled. But what of the geographical and historical terms Germany and Saxony and Poland ? In deciding the political fate of these three, years might well be spent, and, as events were soon to show, it would be fortunate if a new war were avoided.

During the summer of 1814, indeed, no one could say with confidence what arrangements for maintaining the balance of power would be made by the Allies. One scheme, which came from a reputable British source, envisaged the restoration of Norway to Denmark and of Poland to the heir of Poniatowski, the cession of Galicia by Spain to Portugal, the consolidation of northern Italy into one kingdom, and the establishment of another west of the Mississippi.

Reorganization of Germany

Since 1806, when the Holy Roman Empire was formally abolished, Napoleon had organized non-Austrian Germany in the interest of his own empire. The creation of a kingdom of Westphalia for his brother Jerome, the annexation of the north coast as far eastward as the Elbe, the partition of Prussia, the creation of a dependent Confederation of the Rhine, which included Bavaria and Saxony—all this, like the promotion of Bavaria and Würtemberg to be kingdoms, showed that he despised nationality and legitimacy alike. In so far as legitimacy rested on unbroken tradition, however, it could not but be weakened by the upheaval which the Revolution began and Napoleon continued. A ruler who is restored by his former subjects because they wish to be rid of a foreign usurper rules on a very different basis from one who is God's deputy, the immemorial father and owner of the state. Thanks to the extension of the boundaries and influence of France, the empire of reason had been enlarged, and reason upheld nationality, that child of the right of self-determination. The German idea, hallowed by such poets as Klopstock and Schiller, and by new heroes like Hofer and Schill, had grown too strong to be wholly overcome. Direct force might accomplish some repression; statecraft, perhaps much more; but Germans were on the way to regard themselves as brethren, and to wish to express that brotherhood by uniting themselves within a single state. Their ideal fatherland was widening from a town or district into a great country.

In 1814 this mighty but immature nationalism turned chiefly against the French, to whose challenge its development was largely due. By enforcing the frontiers of 1792, the Allies had compelled France to abjure districts which she needed and which needed her, but which, like some of her most loyal provinces, were racially and historically German. Legitimacy and nationality combined to dictate the surrender of Mainz, although the loss of territories on her own bank of the Rhine was likely to rouse the French as their retention of Alsace and Lorraine the Germans. Legitimacy and nationality combined also, it may fairly be said, to uphold that simplification in the constituents of the Holy Roman Empire which had been effected in the preceding twenty years. The number of sovereign persons or bodies in Germany had been reduced from over 300 to 39, and the nation was now united in opposing restitution. As Napoleon's kings in Bavaria and Würtemberg remained, Hanover likewise assumed the royal status. A single Germany, therefore, must be federal, since kings could not be made dependants.

Rivalry between Austria and Prussia

A single German state, or even a purely German federation, however, seemed to be vetoed by the continued existence of Austria and Prussia. Two great German dynasties, the Habsburgs and the Hohenzollerns, each ruled a powerful empire comprising several non-German provinces. Until the Congress met, indeed, it was impossible to predict what their future boundaries would be. But one fact was assured, that neither would submerge itself in a German empire unless that empire was its own. Federation, administered, it might be hoped, by a "friendly dualism" between Austria and Prussia, formed the only possible solution, and at Chaumont (March 1, 1814) the Allies had agreed on federation. It was clear that to round off the individual German states and to combine them in a federal system would tax the statesmanship of Europe. If it could be accomplished, however, it would place central Europe under a government which might well be slow to attack, but which in defence would be invincible. At the same time a federation offered to every German a wide fatherland, together with that homely feeling which the citizen of a small state enjoys. The members of the federation, it might reasonably be supposed, would give their subjects reasonable freedom. Hanover, indeed, forthwith summoned representatives of its constituent provinces to a general diet. Nassau, a duchy not much larger than Gloucestershire, but including portions of seven-

Reform and Reconstruction in Germany

and-thirty powers once sovereign, followed by establishing a legislature copied from that of Britain. The Nassauers received by charter freedom of religious worship, the abolition of forced labour, eligibility to the highest offices without regard to birth, and judicial independence of the English type. Could the Prussians, who to restore their kingdom had defied Napoleon, be denied similar rights? and what important German state would proclaim itself less liberal than Hanover and Prussia? In their Rhineland provinces, Bavaria and Prussia preserved the *Code Napoléon.* With what show of reason could a Prussian subject enjoy Revolutionary liberty at Bonn, and at Berlin be treated as a child?

Both the organization of Germany as a whole and the determination of the form of government within her component parts were in 1814 eclipsed, however, by problems of more immediately vital import. Prussia must be restored forthwith to her former population, and Russia compensated for her efforts in the common cause. Two regions before all others lay at the disposal of Europe for this purpose—Saxony and Poland. Both had condemned themselves by their adhesion to Napoleon, and both were so situated that, if Prussia and Russia continued to claim them, they could hardly be rescued by other powers. Prussia, of course, desired all Saxony, offering in the first instance to make it an independent kingdom under Frederick William. To this Alexander would consent, provided that his own new realm of Poland might include the regions known as New East Prussia, South Prussia and Posen, Hohenzollern gains from the Second and Third Partition. Prussia, however, was not prepared for such a sacrifice, while Austria would resist to the utmost the aggrandizement of her old rival which the absorption of Saxony must involve. It was significant that, in September 1814, Prussia proclaimed the principle of universal military service for men of twenty. At the same time the Saxons, who had lived for a year under an Allied administration improvised by Stein, were informed by the Russian governor of Dresden that they were thenceforward to be ruled as a separate kingdom by the Prussian King. It was in a spirit of unrestricted freedom to dispose of Saxony and Poland in the interest of Europe that the statesmen proceeded to Vienna.

BIBLIOGRAPHICAL NOTE

See the Bibliographical Note at the end of Chapter I, the bibliographies to Chapters XXI and XXIII, and the books named in the text.
Add :—

A

B. King: *A History of Italian Unity.* 2 vols. (1899).

A. de Lamartine: *History of the Restoration of Monarchy in France* (1851–52, trans. 1854).

G. Mann: *Secretary of Europe: The Life of Friedrich Gentz* (1946).

H. Nicolson: *The Congress of Vienna* (1946).

C. Seignobos: *History of the Nineteenth Century* (1897, trans. 2 vols. 1901).

H. W. V. Temperley *The Foreign Policy of Canning* (1925).

C. K. Webster: *The Congress of Vienna, 1814–15* (2nd ed. 1934).

B

Countess Brownlow: *Reminiscences of a Septuagenarian, 1802–34* (1940).

F. Gentz: *On the State of Europe before and after the French Revolution* (trans. 1802).

The Pamphleteer, No. VII, for August 1814.

Prokesch-Osten: *Dépêches inédites du chevalier de Gentz.* I (1876).

T. Sadler (ed.): *Henry Crabb Robinson: Diary, Reminiscences and Correspondence.* 3 vols. (1869).

Frances, Lady Shelley: *Diary, 1787–1817* (1912).

CHAPTER XXIII

EUROPEAN PROGRESS 1774–1814

Progress of Civilization 1774–1814

EUROPE in 1814 looked to the coming Congress to draw such frontiers and to establish such a public law that she might in future enjoy unbroken peace. Her future progress undoubtedly depended in large measure upon the success or failure of her statesmen at Vienna. But, bloody and exhausting as the interminable wars had been, they had retarded rather than stopped the advance of European civilization. With all their lawlessness and pillage, the Revolutionary and Napoleonic struggles had nowhere produced such devastation as that which had ruined great parts of Germany between 1618 and 1648. Since 1792, Britain, France and the Rhine valley, the leaders in the arts of peace, had seldom been wholly paralysed by their warfare, while in general the armies had suffered far more than the civil population. "War," it has been said, "is cruelty, and you cannot refine it." Foreign invaders, plundering for their daily bread, often evaded or defied their leaders. Some, seeking fodder, tore the thatch from their own general's temporary quarters. But law existed; some armies were strict in its observance; and, despite the *levées en masse*, the doctrine that war was a transaction between states rather than between individuals widely prevailed. While whole contingents perished in 1812 there were no abductions or massacres of civilians. A brief review of the four decades between the outbreak of the American rebellion and the meeting of the Vienna Congress serves to show the new power that the European had gained to cope with the tasks of life.

Life in 1814

When the statesmen assembled at Vienna, the great-grandson of the youth with whose investigations this book began would find himself in an England modified but by no means transformed since 1715. The English landed gentry still held sway in a countryside of villages and domestic industries, of manor-houses and cottages, whose inhabitants depended upon the horse and the sailing-ship for transport and chiefly upon the sun and moon for light. Agriculture remained by far their chief preoccupation, and local isolation was still profound. Some students of history find English social life almost stationary from the Revolution of 1688 to the Reform Bill of 1832.

"Nothing is harder," writes Earl Baldwin, who was born in 1867, "for the post-motor generation to realize than that in an age of horse-drawn vehicles you lived at the centre of a circle with a six-mile radius, or on special occasions one of twice that length."

To appreciate the local isolation which restricted the men of 1814, the post-motor generation must remember that by 1880 railways, steamships and telegraphs existed almost as they do to-day. The improvement of the bicycle and of the telephone were soon to increase beyond all precedent the range of man's activity, and to be followed by the motor-car, the gramophone, the aeroplane, the cinema and the radio, which have further transformed daily life. The local isolation of the England of 1814 has been imperishably recorded by Jane Austen; the slowness of communications, with a few adjustments to mark the passage of twenty years, in *Pickwick* and in *Tom Brown.* Its life, however, was already beginning to be changed by a discovery more revolutionary than any of those that have been lately named, that of gas as a practical means of illumination. In 1814 the streets of Westminster were lighted by gas derived from coal, and a thousand new possibilities for labour immediately opened up. The preceding half-century, however, had been limited to natural light and that of fires, rushlights, candles and feeble lamps. After sundown, the vast majority must choose between semi-darkness and their beds. Candle-light might suffice to sing, or drink, or dance, or even read by, but it was wholly inadequate to illuminate factories or towns. Without gas or some equivalent, a real industrial revolution was impossible.

Progress of Agriculture 1715–1814

Every English village, however stolid its population, none the less bore witness to the progress made by three generations which had hardly known invasion or civil war. Agriculture gained, moreover, by that diffused talent and spirit of enterprise which made the age most memorable in the industrial history of Britain. The continuous rise in population assured the food-grower of an expanding market.

The wars handicapped his competitors from abroad, and from 1797, when the Bank of England suspended cash payments, he gained the further stimulus which comes from cheap money and inflation. The legislature, moreover, helped by passing thousands of enclosure acts and by sanctioning a system of poor relief which kept his wage bill low. Larger farms, better stocked with implements and animals, better drained, better cultivated and better manured —the concurrence of manifold improvement rather than any startling invention constituted something like an agricultural revolution. At the same time the means of transport were improving, particularly in Scotland. To further agriculture, high and low, learned and ignorant co-operated. The Royal Society in science found its parallel in various voluntary organizations, culminating in the National Board of Agriculture (1793). On the Continent of Europe progress was far slower than in Britain. Communications were indeed improved, and war occasioned some fresh substitutes for produce from overseas, sugar from beet in France being the most notable among them. The revolutionary growth of peasant proprietorship in France, the primogeniture of the *Code Napoléon*, and the emancipation of the Prussian serfs were changes which must affect the future, but which influenced immediate production but little. In the United States, on the other hand, progress in agriculture was rapid. Men of energy, talent and education were yearly adding vast tracts to the area under cultivation, in order to supply their yearly advancing numbers. They did not as yet farm high, but they foreshadowed both an immense addition to the world's acreage of arable and pasture, and a labour force unhampered by tradition.

Growth of Population in Britain

Although it is difficult to secure accurate figures of population and easy to interpret wrongly such data as exist, the increase of the English people was no less significant than striking. It may be assumed that between 1700 and 1750 a moderate growth had taken place—perhaps of about half a million, or one in twelve during fifty years. It is certain that between 1801 and 1811 the population of England and Wales rose by a million and a quarter, and that of Scotland by nearly 200,000, the rate of increase having reached about one in seven during ten years. Great Britain, with over twelve million people, was in 1814 practically twice as populous as she had been in 1715. The annual rate of increase had become six times as great. Her additional six million were accounted for partly by new families, which were being formed at the rate of nearly 30,000 a year, and partly by the enlargement of the existing families, the increase averaging as much as one person in twenty years. Thus although the former homes generally became more crowded, more than 231,000 new inhabited houses were registered in 1811 than ten years before, and the rate of new building was rising.

Making due allowance for the facts that a rise in population of 150,000 in any year may mean that thousands of aged men and women are being preserved a little longer from the grave and that thousands of helpless infants also tax the existing workers, the British figures still connote an impressive growth of power. Wherever the new-comers were employed, whether in the villages, to raise the necessary food, or in towns to meet their wants by manufacture, they were bound to require the services and thereby to increase the numbers of educated men. Doctors, lawyers, schoolmasters, architects, ministers of religion, bankers, surveyors, civil servants and many more must be trained to provide for this new multitude. Such men diffused throughout the country the best antidote to that isolation and mental inertia which in an age of rudimentary communications must keep back a rural nation. The rise of the middle classes must transform Europe, and here once again Britain stood pre-eminent.

Britain's growth, especially within the middle class, removed from her the danger of the fate which had overtaken Portugal and Holland, that of becoming too small a nation to bear the weight of empire. The large families of educated men furnished the necessary recruits for governing and developing her overseas possessions, while the teeming lower ranks manned the mines and factories at home. Both high and low supplied the navy, that great connecting link between Britain and her dominions and between class and class.

Population on the Continent

During the Napoleonic wars, the rate of increase within Britain far exceeded that upon the Continent. Between 1800 and 1810 the British population grew almost thrice as fast as did the French. In the next decade a still greater difference in the rate of growth prevailed. The French increased at first slightly and afterwards considerably slower than the average for Europe. Only in a few states were figures obtainable which could compare in accuracy with those of modern times. But it may be roughly estimated that of the states which emerged from the Vienna Congress, Russia to the Urals with Poland and Finland considerably exceeded forty-five million souls, and that France and the Austrian Empire, each with more than thirty million, came next. Italy, excluding the four million Austrian Italians, was credited with more than twenty million, the United Kingdom with some nineteen. Prussia approached twelve million, and the lesser German states about the same, while Spain reckoned some fourteen and Portugal five. The United Netherlands comprised some six millions; all Scandinavia, barely five; the Swiss, two; and Turkey in Europe, perhaps nine.

Industrial Progress

If the peace which was being made in 1814 could be preserved, the Continent, as history has shown, stood on the verge of an era of progress such as had been but faintly indicated during the past forty years. In spite of the interruption whose climax was Waterloo, this era may be said to have begun in 1830. Industry, commerce, population, wealth—all these from that time forward may be accounted modern. Between 1774 and 1814 their clearest forerunner may be seen in the cotton trade. In cotton, at least throughout those decades, England led the world, France followed, and save the then unchanging East, no serious competitor existed. European countries, drawing from America supplies of the raw material, began to furnish the Old World and the New with a fabric which every human being needed. Thereby they might enrich themselves beyond all precedent, at the same time augmenting their population, changing its habits and its distribution, and preparing many far-reaching social problems which still remain unsolved. But for the predominance of the landed and moneyed interests, and but for the universal preoccupation with the war, this side of the industrial revolution might have received attention before carelessness had produced disease.

Before the close of the eighteenth century Lancashire

The Cotton Trade in Britain and France

had dedicated herself to cotton. For many years the cleansing and spinning of the raw material and its weaving into cloth had gone on there by the side of other industries. But the peculiar fitness of her climate for the manufacture of an ever more popular fabric brought cotton operatives higher gains than those made by their fellow-workers in wool and flax, so that these migrated elsewhere or turned to cotton. At the same time new inventions tended to concentrate the industry, to increase and improve its products beyond all calculation, and to lower their price. High wages for hand labour stimulated the invention of machinery, and the redundant workers could only hope for such an expansion of demand as to restore their occupation. The earlier cotton operatives in England wove cotton cloth on hand-looms within their homes, cultivating also small holdings or working for farmers during harvest. John Kay's flying shuttle (1738), however, at once halved the weavers' work and increased their efficiency, thereby creating a great demand for the warps of wool or linen which gave the necessary strength to cotton cloth. This was met by the invention of spinning machines which enabled the warps themselves to be made of cotton. While Hargreaves, a weaver, devised a spinning-jenny with eight spindles in place of one (1764), Arkwright, a barber, produced about the same time a water-frame, in which a great number of spindles were driven by water-power and strong warps were spun from cotton. Although these new machines were only hand-made contrivances of wood with metal fittings, they must inevitably grow in size and power. Two dozen spindles might be worked by hand, but the spinning-jennies soon passed the hundred. Such growth doomed the domestic industry, substituting for it great buildings situated on rivers. In these, far more refined and uniform products could be made, and regimented operatives called on to fulfil large and distant orders. As early as 1785, steam-power was applied to cotton, and concentration of all branches of the industry in "cotton towns" inevitably followed. In France, although British warships cut off the raw material and hindered export, while Napoleon attempted to make France self-sufficient, this industrial revolution found an echo. Both Alsace and the region around Lille had cotton mills in 1814. Given peace and steam-power, French taste and skill could not fail to develop a great industry. The spinner Crompton's mule (1779), combining the merits of the Arkwright and the Hargreaves machines, had already shaped the future of the manufacture. The next in the strange series of inventors, Edmund Cartwright, a country rector, patented his power-loom in 1785. Like all the rest save Arkwright, he failed to gain wealth in business, and his invention, like theirs, needed supplementing by other men. The value even of their uncompleted work, however, was made evident by the growth of the industry. In the 'seventies the imports of raw cotton into England had averaged some $5\frac{3}{4}$ million pounds a year. In 1790 it exceeded 30 million. In 1805 this amount was doubled, and five years later the imports had reached 120 million pounds. Peace brought a momentary check, but by 1830 no less than 270 million pounds were imported, to be spun into yarns far finer than those of the earliest days. In 1764 the exports of cotton goods were valued at a mere £200,000; in the year of Waterloo, at £22,000,000. This startling rise in total value was accompanied by an equally startling fall in individual price. On the morrow of Trafalgar, yarn could be bought for a tenth of what it had cost on the eve of the Revolution.

The Cotton-gin

The manifest enrichment of Europe by means of cotton was assisted by a characteristic invention which equally enriched the United States. Eli Whitney, who graduated at Yale in 1792, soon afterwards devised his cotton-gin for separating the lint from the seeds by a roller furnished with spikes and bars and brushes. This hand-operated machine, some fifty times as effective as the unaided hand, enriched the Southern States, committed them to negro slavery, and shaped the commercial relationship between Europe and America for nearly seventy years.

Iron

While in 1814 cotton formed an important modern addition to man's comforts, iron has ranked for thousands of years among the chief necessities of human life. During the eighteenth century mankind was always struggling with the problem of increasing its supply, whether in the form of wrought iron, cast iron or steel. Iron ore could be found in many lands, but the existing means of transport were inadequate to connect it in bulk with the supplies of fuel, while, when the connexion had been made, the smelting processes were costly and far from perfect. In many parts, as conspicuously in Sussex, the supply of wood for the charcoal furnaces had failed, and efforts to make use of coal had had but small success until 1735. In that year Abraham Darby of Coalbrookdale showed that by first turning coal into coke it was possible to make cast iron in blast furnaces without contaminating it with sulphur. In the next decade, however, the watchful Swedish metallurgists reported adversely upon Darby's process, and for the remainder of the century Britain remained an iron-importing country. Russia and Sweden, lands where charcoal abounded, still supplied the chief part of her needs. These were, of course, greatly increased by the invention of the steam-engine, itself an iron product creating iron tools. The first steam-hammer was made in 1781.

Steam-driven machines

In 1784, however, the industry took a great step forward, and coal-bearing Britain came in sight of primacy within it. Henry Cort, a Lancashire man (1740–1800), then devised the "reverberatory" puddling furnace which enabled wrought iron to be produced without contamination from the coke. Britain almost doubled her output of pig-iron between 1788 and 1796 and redoubled it within the next ten years. In the new iron age of the world she continued indeed to import from other lands, but her imports soon became a mere fraction of her native production. This, it became clear, would be concentrated near her coalfields, and another portent of the greatness of the north of England thus appeared.

Already, thanks to Britain, the Continent was moving towards the wider use of metal machines. The famous Belgian firm of Cockerill owes its origin to a Lancashire mechanic who brought over a steam-engine in 1813. France, meanwhile, spared by her vast forests from the fuel difficulties of England, made some small imitative progress in smelting with coal and coke. Germany, on the other hand, remained a land of charcoal-smelting and small establishments. Through a German born in England, Benjamin Huntsman (1704–76), toolmaker and amateur surgeon, an approach had in fact been made towards the solution of one of the major problems which survived this period.

The world needed cheap steel: Huntsman cast steel of surpassing purity and hardness: Sheffield at first denied its value and then pillaged the invention.

European Cultural Progress 1774–1814

When we turn to survey the gains that Europe had made in the forty years preceding 1814, and to estimate her increase in moral and intellectual power, our first thought must be of her new allies—Russia and the United States. The triumphant Peace of Kainardji (1774) meant that the Russian sceptre was firmly grasped by an Empress among whose chief ambitions lay that of advancing culture. Under her rule the classic land of barbarism afforded shelter and support to the boldest thinkers from western lands. The former nickname of Holland—"the Noah's ark of refugees"—seemed now to be deserved by Russia. There the creative Swiss mathematician Euler, defying his blindness, worked and died, there Diderot and Grimm sojourned for awhile, and there d'Alembert and a host of other Philosophers knew that they could find shelter in case of need. The career of Lomonosov, a typical Russian giant of limitless and versatile power, proved that much might be hoped from native sources. Speransky, Alexander's minister, succeeded him. Catherine's manifold efforts to educate her people promised at least an indefinite extension of their demand for the products and ideas of Europe. Her grandson Alexander was no less susceptible to western culture. The ignorance and inertia of the peasants counted for less in an age when European culture was in almost every country the private possession of a few. In 1814, when Speransky had already displayed his encyclopædic powers and Pushkin was about to write, it was clear that in culture at least Russia had widened and strengthened Europe.

Influence of the United States

The same was no less obviously true of the United States. In the political world, and especially towards Britain, the new power was a rival and a perennial source of peril. The British went to Vienna all the weaker because their ships and soldiers were absorbed by the war with the United States. For many years to come they must regard Canada and the West Indies as hostages in the hands of a potential foe. Spain and Portugal, France and Holland, Russia and even Denmark, moreover, were still colonial powers, and the United States ranked as the pioneers and patrons of colonial rebellion. Although their constitution has been ascribed to Montesquieu's mistaken notions of Blackstone's errors about that of Britain, as a nation they were proud of rejecting the political ideas of Europe. In culture as distinct from politics, however, America had already proved herself a powerful ally of Europe. Free from monopoly and privilege, from illiteracy and grinding poverty, from militarism, heavy taxation, stupefying tradition and disabilities of creed and sex, the new race must surely quicken the advance of man. In Franklin the philosopher and in Washington the hero it had already produced men whom Europe could not but admire. Whatever the defects of its constitution, the Union secured liberties which millions of Europeans still desired in vain. While in the Old World the growing middle class painfully struggled for its due share in power, in the New it ruled the State. The zeal of Europe for progress was still damped by notions of degeneration from a former golden age. The Americans, building a new structure in an empty continent, were immune from such illusions. Undistracted by the complexities of courts and capitals, they could the better homage literature and learning. In astronomy and in medicine they had already taught Europe not a little. Within twenty years Poe was to demonstrate that across the Atlantic the seeds of classical culture might produce luscious fruit. The contribution of the United States to European progress, however, might well depend less upon individual men of genius than upon the mass. The existence of a virile kindred community overseas must enlarge the horizon of every European nation. Already many sects or schools of thought in the Old World were strengthened by disciples in the New. The chance of emigrating thither gave hope to many an European. And the confidence in human progress which America inspired was augmented by her own unparalleled increase. In 1760 the Thirteen Colonies comprised some 1,600,000 souls, of whom nearly one-fifth were negroes. Thirty years later the number approached 4,000,000. In 1800 it had reached 5,300,000, and in 1810, almost 7,240,000. During the sixty years of George III the inhabitants of Britain doubled their numbers, but the Americans, aided by gains in Florida, multiplied sixfold. In 1820, the straggling Union could show nearly 9,640,000 citizens,

Progress of the United States

against some 14,000,000 within this island. Since the organized States were soon to extend beyond the Mississippi, these figures suggest the contrast between a land of contiguous cities, like the Rhine Valley, and a land of scattered rural communities which might appreciate civilization without contributing much to its advance. In 1814, however, Boston, New York and Philadelphia with their varied and boundless hinterland assured progressive Europe of a new and vigorous ally. Britain, which politically had most to fear from the Americans, stood to gain most from them in culture by the dissemination of her language and the easy interchange of new ideas. Steam transport, which would abolish three-fourths of the distance between the two continents, was already under trial. Robert Fulton (1765–1815), a Pennsylvanian of Irish descent, who had studied and made experiments in England and in France, joined with the statesman and scientist, Robert Livingston, to establish the first steamboat service on the Hudson in 1807. Thanks to American versatility, it would soon be possible to cross from Dover to Calais with a more exact time table than the " possibly three hours and probably not more than twelve " which in 1814 still held good. Fulton's engines were made by Boulton and Watt, and next year a steamship service united Liverpool and Glasgow. The path of progress was thus defined which was to bring Europe into swift, easy and regular connexion with North and South America. No change in human arrangements promised to affect her more.

European Progress

To measure the advance of man by enumerating his mechanical contrivances is, however, one of the most natural of vulgar errors. Fulton's invention certainly gave mankind a greater command over winds and waves. By improving communications, it increased wealth, thus enabling more people to exist and that in greater comfort. Easier intercourse, moreover, might reduce those international misunderstandings which create tension and sometimes explode in war. Such an invention, on the other hand, leaves the intellectual stature of a Newton or a Darwin unchanged, and it may merely bewilder and distract a Coleridge or a Wordsworth. Only chance, moreover, prevented Fulton from cursing Europe with the submarine a century before its time. Common sense would perhaps decide that the

Relativity and Specialization

steamship contributed to help man forward and that the submarine, except as counteracting some greater evil, contributed to set him back. To find some general criterion of progress, however, is not easy. One of the most conspicuous achievements of the eighteenth century was to undermine that faith in absolute truth or value which ruled when it began. Its own philosophers were at one with those of the seventeen preceding centuries in believing that all things human were bound by the same rules of truth. Their contribution was to find out these rules by reason, not from tradition. But by seeking truth from science, they helped to loosen men's minds, so that Clapham could regard its own crimes as chaste at Martaban and Relativity prevail in every field. Throughout the century, moreover, the growth of learning had not yet crushed independence. Increase of knowledge is doubtless generally to be desired. But the existence of more knowledge than any man can master compels him to guess his way towards wisdom with the aid of specialists, renouncing the robust and pugnacious omniscience which animated a Wesley or a Johnson. Some indeed may find Newton's preoccupation with Daniel and the Apocalypse incongruous. But would not the anomaly be greater if the foremost human mind were debarred from forming an opinion upon topics which his age believed essential to salvation? The years 1774–1814 witnessed the growth of a tendency to put "man of science" in the place of "man of letters," but at their close the intelligent amateur still held sway. The annals of Europe bristle with the names of clergymen who contributed to scientific knowledge. Malthus, who argued that population must be restricted, was a clerical master at Haileybury; Cartwright, who invented a power-loom, was a Fellow of Magdalen and Doctor of Divinity; White, of Selborne, was likewise an Oxford clergyman; Priestley, one of the greatest chemists of the century, acted as pastor of several Nonconformist Churches and wrote much ecclesiastical history; Price, another dissenting minister, wrote on theology and on finance with equal distinction. At the other extremity of northern Europe, in the Scandinavian Peninsula, in Finland, in the Baltic Provinces, the pastors were advancing the arts of life and staffing the universities and the civil service with their sons.

International Scientific Co-operation

Although these forty years were years of almost incessant warfare, they are conspicuous for the achievements of the informal Grand Alliance for the advancement of human knowledge. This tacit pact carried on the traditions of the preceding age, when the thermometer was brought to perfection by Fahrenheit, a German working in Holland, Réaumur, a French noble who served the State, and Celsius, a Swede. At the height of the Seven Years War, a French astronomical mission passed safely to and from Tobolsk, while when France was wresting America from Britain, Priestley was expounding oxygen, then called "dephlogisticated air," in Paris. Napoleon, with his own hand, authorized his enemy Davy to enter France, and the discovery of iodine resulted from Franco-British conference during war. The Law of Nations firmly forbade interference by belligerents with vessels engaged in scientific expeditions.

The Explorers

Favoured both by international zeal for knowledge and by national hopes of acquiring new dominions, new resources or new trade, the exploration of the unknown world went briskly on. The supreme discoverer, Captain Cook (1728–1779) received his first commission at the instance of the Royal Society and in connexion with that transit of Venus in 1769 which linked all Europe in pursuit of truth. In three great voyages he taught mankind a method of averting the waste of life which had hitherto attended such expeditions, as well as the vanity of hoping for a great new continent in the south Pacific or Atlantic and the impracticability of the so-called north-west passage. At the same time he surveyed and mapped the southern seas and, in part, the northern, and secured for Britain her claims to Australasia. On the mainland of North America, explorers were likewise commissioned by Russia and the United States. Corporal Ledyard, who had sailed with Cook, set out with ten guineas in his purse to cross Arctic America from Kamschatka to the Atlantic, and reached the Black Sea from Torneå before he was arrested.

It was another of Cook's pupils, George Vancouver, who made the greatest contribution to the survey of the western coast (1792). Four years later, commissioned by the African Association, which was formed in 1788 for the purpose of "rescuing the age from a charge of ignorance," the Scottish surgeon Mungo Park penetrated alone to the Niger, which he traced for some 300 miles. In 1806, having led a disastrous government expedition to the same river, he fulfilled his vow to die there if he could not reach its mouth. While Cook and his successors explored, the military surveyor, Rennell, invalided from Bengal, published maps and charts which helped to make both Asia and Africa better known and ocean travel possible. Continuing the work of his French predecessors through a long and active life, Rennell became the supreme geographer which he still remains. To him mankind already owed in 1814 much of its understanding of winds and currents at sea.

Thanks to the labours of the explorers and of the geographers, the major part of the surface of the globe was known and mapped. Of the four great continents, Africa alone remained largely unexplored. There the map-maker traced a great range, the mountains of the Moon, across almost its whole breadth, and made Egypt almost identical with the river Nile. South of the mountain barrier, all save the coastal lands lay blank. Of the western half of North America little more was known, while the presentment of Amazonia and Brazil could inspire but little confidence. With these exceptions, and, of course, much of the arctic and antarctic regions and of Thibet, the earth at last lay plain before men's eyes.

Scientific Progress

Meanwhile learning was being advanced by discoveries which claimed less immediate practical importance. If the human race was still engulfed in darkness, western men at least were thrusting torches on every side. New elements were discovered on the earth and new worlds within the heavens. Scheele (1742–86), a Swedish chemist who died at forty-four, within twelve years observed or obtained chlorine, uric acid, tungsten, oxygen and many other substances hitherto unknown. The versatile philosopher Lavoisier, whom the Republic guillotined as a farmer-general, rendered unique service to progress by destroying false theories which kept it back. His demonstrations that water boiled in glass is not converted into earth, and that phlogiston, the raw material of fire, had been the product of a mistaken imagination paved the way for the true knowledge of gases and for correct analysis. The self-taught Cornishman,

Humphry Davy (1778–1829), with Thompson, an American who served Britain and became Count of the Holy Roman Empire, could then go on to show that heat was not a material substance but a mode of motion, and to startle the newly founded Royal Institution by melting lumps of ice by friction within a freezing vacuum (1799).

" Science " in 1774 and in 1814

When the forty years which ended in 1814 were beginning, Linguet, a severe critic, complained that in the eighteenth century science had made but little progress. In astronomy, he urged, the disciples of Newton and his contemporaries were merely stammering out the catechism which those masters had drawn up. Petty experiments made with loud acclaim at the equator and the poles had merely confirmed Newton's deductions and attested the superiority of his mind. In geometry, likewise, men were only squabbling over the leavings of the seventeenth century. Although the possibilities of the steam pump were enormous, the 'seventies could neither bring them to fruition nor make more than a child's toy of electricity, which obviously was the key to nature. Medicine and chemistry, he declared, were no less languid. Their exponents discoursed with perspicuity and grace, but without advancing science. Collectors lavished wealth on things curious and rare, but natural history made little progress.

During the years 1774–1814, it is true, no master comparable with Newton appeared, and no discovery like his advanced mankind. Despite the freemasonry between philosophers which even war did not entirely interrupt, research as yet had not become sufficiently co-operative and systematic for the labours of the many to compensate for the lack of an outstanding genius. None the less, widespread curiosity and experience combined to bring about much incidental progress. In 1786–7, for instance, " chemical philosophy " gained greatly from the accident that a close-packed burial ground in Paris was laid out for building. A pit in which more than a thousand coffins of the poor had reposed for only fifteen years afforded the starved scientists an incomparable opportunity for study. In some respects, indeed, these forty years brought mankind within sight of some of the greatest triumphs of modern times. Fulton's steamboat, the latest application of Watt's steam-engine of 1765, preceded by only seven years George Stephenson's invention of the locomotive (1814). Eleven years later, the Stockton–Darlington Railway was in being. The electric telegraph, though perfected more slowly, was brought by Sömmering of Munich in 1809 to a state in which it could be offered to Napoleon. Aerial navigation was begun by the Montgolfier brothers in 1783, and the balloon quickly developed towards perfection. As the outcome of work by scientists of many nations, photographs could be imprinted, though as yet they quickly faded. In 1778, when the Austrian physician Mesmer began to cure the ailments of fashionable Paris, a long step forward was taken towards the hypnotism and spiritualism which thrilled later generations.

Medicine

The critic's strictures on medicine were met in part by the Scotch Professor Cullen and his pupil William Hunter. These men at least stimulated many students and threw out many ideas. John Hunter (1728–93), William's younger brother, raised the whole status of surgery. Jenner armed Europe against one of the most deadly of its diseases. The French master, Bichat, who died at thirty-one, was conspicuous for methodical research. The age may at least claim to have broadened the foundations upon which medical men could build in future. After the middle of the nineteenth century, none the less, Sidney Herbert could declare that " sanitary science is looked upon as mere humbug by the mass of mankind," while all the medical candidates for professorships in the Army Medical School stated that they were ready and qualified to fill every chair.

Progress in the Theory of Education

The medical profession, perhaps most of all, stood to gain from an advance in general education. In 1774, the year of Samuel Butler's birth, revolt incarnate had appeared in Basedow of Hamburg. He had already gained the support of the enlightened grandees for a rational system which should not neglect physical training and instruction in the mother tongue. He introduced into the curriculum pictures, models, samples, tools, conversation classes, every practical and natural device to fill six hours of study and two of manual labour daily to the best advantage. Reform was widened and inspired by the epoch-making work of Pestalozzi, a Zurich doctor's son, and of his pupil, the North German Herbart. Their work, like that of the Jesuits in an earlier age, humanized the instruction of the young. Sharing in Rousseau's championship of the child, but rejecting the fantastic precepts of his *Emile*, they based education upon the five ideals of freedom, perfection, rectitude, equity and benevolence. The teacher must become his pupil's friend and must base his training upon religion. The whole being, mind, body and character alike, must be developed. Towards such development the pupil is the teacher's best ally, and he must therefore be taught to help himself. In particular, he must learn to observe, to describe what he has observed, and to frame definitions.

The appointment in 1814 of Froebel as professor at the new university of Berlin guaranteed the future progress of educational theory along the lines laid down by Pestalozzi. The Kindergarten would not be long delayed.

The Romantic Revival

Romanticism, the triumphant "assault of neglected emotions" upon the rational system of the eighteenth century, formed another new and powerful current which in 1814 bade fair to carry educated Europe into uncharted seas. Reaction had indeed become inevitable against a society beyond all precedent artificial. Rousseau had cried, "Back to Nature," while the younger men and women were gaining a new faith in progress and a new sympathy both for the European past and for the world beyond the bounds of Europe. China, at once too remote for criticism and the creator of a captivating art, particularly stirred their minds. A new literature in many lands nourished the revolt. *Waverley* (1814) forms a milestone in an already considerable march. It came just forty years after Goethe's *Sorrows of Werther* had given sentiment and German prose a new appeal. German folk-songs were studied, while Schiller spread the romantic drama. In France and throughout Europe, *Paul et Virginie* (1788) with its shipwrecked heroine's refusal to be saved by a naked sailor, seemed to attain sentimental perfection. The extraordinary "sensibility" of the later eighteenth century found vent in enthusiasm for Scott and those whom he inspired. Grimm, for example, had gained much fame by his conduct when rejected by an opera girl. He "was entirely overset and fell into a sort of catalepsy which continued for several days. . . . His friends believed him dead; the Abbé Raynal and Rousseau watched by his bed for several nights successively." One morning he suddenly recovered, having furnished history with a valuable instance of contemporary affectation.

Evolution Foreshadowed

At the time that the idea of man as a machine-like being seemed strongest, it was about to be undermined by that of his kinship with animals and plants. Philosophers began to appreciate the progressive development in nature. The theory of evolution, indeed, was not fully formulated until 1859. But in 1778 the Prussian King's librarian at Neuchâtel, characteristically defining true philosophy as that which respected religion and contributed by research to the progress of the sciences and of virtue, dedicated to the Landgrave of Hesse an edition of the works of Charles Bonnet, a Geneva scientist honoured by all the Academies in Europe. Bonnet, a keen student of insects, represented man as standing at the summit of a "ladder of natural beings." Below him appear successively the orang-outang, the ape, quadrupeds, the flying squirrel, the bat, the ostrich, ordinary birds, aquatic birds, amphibious birds, flying fish, ordinary fish, climbing fish, eels, water-snakes, and ordinary snakes. Descending yet three dozen rungs, through snails, insects, plants, stones, salts, metals, semi-metals, sulphurs, earths, water and air, the searcher into nature arrived at fire, and finally at "more subtle substances." In 1814, indeed, evolutionary ideas had been making their way in Europe for two generations. Formidable obstacles, however, still hindered the attainment of final truth. In the Age of Reason thinkers preferred imagination to observation. They therefore produced neat theories which over-simplified their conclusions and which could not stand the test of further facts. At the same time, for many reasons, they incurred almost everywhere the hostility of the Church.

Religion and Political Theory

In the political world the authority of religion had long been invoked to render sacrosanct conditions difficult to defend on grounds of reason. The omnipotence and the frailty of kings had alike been shielded thus against criticism from their subjects. God, His spokesmen declared, had commissioned the great as His deputies, and, they sometimes added, it was to Him alone that the great must give account for their private lives. The anomalies in the social world were often defended by appeals to scripture and to the teachings of the Church. " The poor ye have always with you " carried more conviction to the rich than the doctrine that for themselves it was hard to enter the Kingdom of Heaven. Among Catholics, an unbroken tradition extolled the holiness of poverty, giving opportunity as it did for the acquisition of merit by bestowing alms. The monarchs everywhere, and in some countries those wealthy classes who had become the real masters of the State, therefore viewed suspiciously any tampering with religion. Even if they discredited its tenets for themselves, they held it necessary for the disciplining of the people.

The Church and Learning

The Church, though naturally inclined to claim for itself the foremost place in education, could not as a whole be charged with hostility to learning. Of some branches, indeed, the indictment that to an ecclesiastic *le bien pensant* meant *cela qui pensait le moins possible* might be true. But what bodies of teachers and scholars rivalled the Jesuits and the Benedictines in well-deserved renown ? In Protestant lands such as England and Denmark the universities were almost wholly clerical. A foreign visitor to England described the dons, in the intervals between their convivialities, as " educating, clumsily enough, a parcel of lads for the Church." Throughout the eighteenth century British divines played a leading part in lightening the burdens which the supernatural element in religion made on conscience. *The Natural History of Selborne* was produced in the year of the Fall of the Bastille, while Mendel, a biologist worthy to be named with Darwin, was a monk born within seven years of Waterloo.

Science and Religion

The advance of science, however, challenged two great loyalties of the churchmen, to divine revelation and to Christian morality respectively. By Catholic and Protestant alike, Genesis was held to provide an indisputable record of creation. While the eighteenth century was still young, two hundred scholars, Isaac Newton among the number, had deduced as many dates of the creation from Holy Writ. Such labour was pious, while to quote geological research against the Bible had an impious taint. The faithful would bring fossils within the lawful six thousand years from the creation by declaring that God had placed them in the rocks to test belief. The same spirit prompted many to oppose the invocation of science to check afflictions which might be ascribed to the providence of God. If the Almighty had fixed His canon 'gainst self-slaughter, must not disease be regarded as His chastisement and meekly borne ? Many Europeans, like the court of Spain, abhorred inoculation, which came from Turkey, and when in 1796 Dr. Jenner engrafted a boy with an infectious disease derived from cows he encountered no little opposition. Within a few years, however, the modernization of men's minds during the eighteenth century was to receive conspicuous illustration. Most divines now acclaimed the medicine, not the disease, as the gift of God, and Spain dispatched a mission to vaccinate throughout her empire.

Religion and Morality

To look to sources other than God for rules of conduct, on the other hand, could not be tolerated by the Church. The ten commandments gave clear and authoritative moral laws upon which Christian society had been built up. Deists, who placed God at an infinite distance from man, atheists, who denied that He had ever existed, and sceptics, who declared that man could not know whether He did or could exist—all these compelled society to invent fresh rules of life. Scientists therefore became associated with that unprecedented revolt against Christian morality which marked the age. When men ceased to believe in witchcraft and began to jeer at priestcraft, while their fear of eternal torment faded, they caught eagerly at the notion that they might seek pleasure where they could find it, guided by the light of reason. They were discarding torture and acquiring a new tenderness towards the poor and weak—why should they remain harsh towards themselves ? A widespread revolt against the churches was accompanied by sexual laxity on a scale which no earlier age in modern history had seen.

The Mass Mind

Another current of modernity visible in 1814 owed its rise in great part to the Neapolitan jurist and philosopher Vico, who had died, little heeded, seventy years before. Hampered by grinding poverty, working without colleagues, knowing no history well save that of Rome, misled by the attitude of his age towards the Chosen People and by its appetite for cast-iron theories, Vico was yet so fertile, courageous and sincere as to take an outstanding place in intellectual progress. This he did by insisting on the creative value of the masses, whose work, as he showed, both preceded and supplemented that of the individual givers of laws. In his view, God ruled not by recurrent miracles, as even Newton believed, but by natural laws, having implanted a sentiment of justice in the mind of man. Later ages ascribed to heroic law-givers that inseparable blend of law, morality and religion which composes primitive custom, and which, according to Vico, arose from the application of man's inborn sentiment of justice to his affairs. As the race progressed towards civilization it naturally produced more conscious and philosophic legislation. Its law thus reflected its personality and recorded its historic growth. This growth proceeds in every nation through successive cycles—an alluring dogma which perhaps rather evades the notion of progress than denies its possibility. Vico at least portrays civilization as in constant motion, " dialectic " in modern phrase, and finds its motive power not in outstanding heroes but in the collective mind. Like Leibnitz, who died in 1716, his greatness was perceived more clearly by later centuries than by his own. Though he founded no school, he influenced Comte and Hegel, and his insistence on a sympathetic study of the mind of earlier races helped to make the nineteenth century a historically-minded age. Earlier ages, as Acton taught, cared little for an opponent's point of view. In them " a man was occupied in making out his own meaning, with the help of his friends."

Religion in 1814: its Strength and the Attacks upon it

It is impossible for the historian either to calculate exactly the strength of the religious force in the Europe of 1814 or to omit it from consideration. In the social and economic life of the masses, religion was still a force to be ranked with government and daily bread. To them the Christian faith, which in some form embraced all save a handful of Europeans, afforded guidance and comfort in this life and offered redress and happiness in the hereafter. Not until 1886, it is said, did fiction surpass theology in the yearly output of English printed books. In many lands, moreover, laymen of influence and education were preoccupied with questions of religion, whether for the sake of their own souls or for the good governance of their respective countries. Not for the first time nor the last, some philosophers proclaimed that the advance of man had cut the roots of faith. Hume deemed religion only fit for monkeys. Tom Paine denounced Jehovah for immorality. Voltaire had deftly made the current beliefs about Abraham and David incredible. Many divines stripped religion of its supernatural elements, and not a few thinkers argued that no man could know the nature or the ordering of the universe. From Britain and France to Russia, the intelligentsia was prone to despise the priest and to hold that he was suborned by the State to keep the down-trodden classes in subjection. In 1814 many were already bold enough to regard religion as the opium of the people.

Beyond all doubt, many priests and laymen in every land were at heart indifferent to religion. It is no less certain that in every land many found in it the inspiration of their lives. The long wars, it seems, had neither driven the masses out of the fold nor had they compelled them to come in. In so far as religion depended on mere habit, campaigns, industrial changes, new knowledge and the Revolution could not but relax its sway. The new philanthropy might either quicken Christianity or become its rival. But during these four decades (1774–1814) theology had steadily advanced, many ecclesiastical abuses had been purged away and religious zeal had given birth to new organizations. The year 1814, which saw the restoration of the Jesuits, and, beyond the Alps and Pyrenees, the restoration of the Inquisition, saw also a mighty outburst of missionary work among the Protestants and of evangelism by the Tsar himself. But the Church Missionary Society had already been established for thirteen years and the Bible Society for ten. In the darkest hour of the British struggle with Napoleon (1810) the National Society prepared to give religious education to the poor. At the same time, fifty years after Count Zinzendorf's death, his disciples at Geneva began a new Protestant revival.

Religious Advance

The fervour that as soon as peace opened foreign fields sent missionaries to the heathen had found vent since 1774 in the foundation of new churches. The Shakers in New England, communists who revered the daughter of an English blacksmith as a female manifestation of the Christ, the Countess of Huntingdon's Connexion, the Swedenborgians, the Theophilanthropists, the Methodist New Connexion, the New Israelites—all these severed themselves from the existing Protestant bodies to emphasize some new source or aspect of truth. The new foundations were contemporary with far more important developments within the old. In 1780 Raikes founded Sunday Schools at Gloucester. Soon afterwards, at Cambridge, Simeon became the leader of the Evangelical movement in the English Church, a movement which captured many notable philanthropists and gave birth to the so-called Clapham sect. Philanthropy without proselytism was the hall-mark of the Quakers, or Society of Friends, who led the world during these years in efforts for the suppression of the slave trade and worked for the reform of prisons and asylums and for popular education. The Quaker tenets, however, influenced few save Anglo-Saxons, and the loss of their control over Pennsylvania (1776) narrowed what had earlier seemed an almost boundless horizon in the New World. Meanwhile the Roman Church was braced by successive struggles with Joseph II, with the Revolution, and with Napoleon. Catholic Ordinands fled from the Low Countries to St. Edmund's, Ware, and Maynooth was founded to make Ireland independent of revolutionary Paris.

Toleration 1774–1814

How far had forty years brought the Philosophers the prize that they most desired—the extirpation of intolerance? In the nature of things, toleration could within that time become complete only in the domain of law, which might give citizens of every creed or of none the right to live and to worship where they pleased. If the law granted such toleration, indeed, it would in time affect practice and opinion. Absence from church when attendance was a legal duty was far less venial than it has since become. More than a single generation must grow up and die, however, before a rural community would not in some degree resent the presence in its midst of unbelievers. Whether in the higher form of "frank respect for the freedom of indwelling conscience" or in that of contemptuous indifference to old wives' tales, full tolerance has hardly yet conquered any nation. In Europe, none the less, the generation which followed the deaths of Voltaire and Rousseau (1778) witnessed in this field also an unmistakable advance. Persecution by the State became rare, while concession after concession was made to subjects outside the established churches.

It is significant that Poland and Sweden, which were among the least tolerant of powers, declined, while the most tolerant, Russia, Prussia, Britain and Napoleonic France, increased in strength. No less significant were the successive failures of religious or anti-religious aggression by the State. Within five years (1788–93) Prussia strove to make the clergy more orthodox by force of law and France to abolish Christianity. Before 1802 both had retraced their steps. In religion, while the blood of martyrs is the seed of the Church, persecution by state churches creates sects and scoffers. The Revolutionary age, on balance, attacked religion, and thus increased mutual toleration by the religious and the compassion of society for those attacked.

The masses, moreover, became more tolerant as they became less fearful. As the history of trials for witchcraft shows, the Devil and eternal torment were losing their hold upon men's minds. Communities no longer feared the vengeance of a deity outraged by the presence of an unbeliever in their midst. Many inevitably lost their faith in God when they saw Antichrist unchecked for twenty years. If the Lisbon earthquake had made men infidels, what of the Terror and of Napoleon?

The effects of seemingly unending war upon the growth of toleration were necessarily twofold and contradictory. Wars of peoples, then a new thing, must generate far more hatred than wars of kings, thus making men less tolerant. Nelson, swearing that he would like to hang every Frenchman that came near him, may stand for an emblem of the time. When a Catholic and a Protestant nation are at war, each inevitably suspects the co-religionists of the enemy who live within its borders. Napoleon, however, marshalled soldiers of every faith, while the Greeks and Latins, the Jews and Lutherans, the Anglicans and Dissenters who combined against him could not but grow more tolerant of one another. When Europe was not fighting, her increased preoccupation with commerce learning and philanthropy lessened her capacity for religious strife. New philosophers arose who taught that religion lay outside the province of the State. Thinkers like Kant and Humboldt, Godwin and Condorcet created an atmosphere in which persecution seemed an absurdity. Some strove to demonstrate that Christianity was not even the best among religions. Intolerance, none the less, marked all save the rarest minds.

BIBLIOGRAPHICAL NOTE

See the Bibliographical Note at the end of Chapter I, the bibliography to Chapter IX and the books named in the text.
Add :—

A

T. S. Ashton : *The Industrial Revolution, 1760–1830* (repr. 1955).

E. Baines : *History of the Cotton Manufacture in England* (1835).

J. N. L. Baker : *A History of Geographical Discovery and Exploration* (rev. ed. 1937).

T. C. Barker and J. R. Harris : *A Merseyside Town in the Industrial Revolution—St. Helen's, 1750–1900* (1954).

W. Boyd : *The History of Western Education* (3rd ed. 1932).

J. B. Bury : *The Idea of Progress* (1920, new ed. 1932).

E. A. Burtt : *The Metaphysical Foundations of Modern Physical Science* (1925).

J. D. Chambers : *Nottinghamshire in the Eighteenth Century* (1932).

J. H. Clapham : *Economic Development of France and Germany* (2nd ed. 1923).

J. H. Clapham : *The Bank of England, a history, 1694–1914.* 2 vols. (1944).

H. W. Dickinson : *A Short History of the Steam Engine* (1938).

G. T. Griffith : *Population Problems of the Age of Malthus* (1926).

E. Halévy : *A History of the English People in 1815* (1924).

K. S. Latourette : *A History of the Expansion of Christianity.* III (1943).

W. R. Le Fanu : *A Bio-Bibliography of Edward Jenner, 1749–1823* (1951).

C. R. Markham : *Major James Rennell* (1895).

F. M. H. Markham : *Napoleon and the Awakening of Europe* (1954).

P. Mantoux : *The Industrial Revolution in the Eighteenth Century* (1928, rev. ed. 1947).

D. McKie : *Antoine Lavoisier* (1952).

B. Russell : *History of Western Philosophy* (1946).

H. Sée : *Les Origines du capitalisme moderne* (5th ed. 1946, trans. 1928).

H. Sée : *Esquisse d'une histoire du régime agraire en Europe aux XVIIIe et XIXe siècles* (1921).

G. Stanhope and G. P. Gooch : *The Life of Charles, Third Earl Stanhope* (1914).

J. A. Williamson : *Cook and the Opening of the Pacific* (1946).

B

E. Heckscher : *World History*, ed. Tunberg and Bring, XIII (Stockholm).

M. Linguet : *Annales politiques, civiles et littéraires du dix-huitième siècle.* I (1777).

Rees's Cyclopaedia (1820).

CHAPTER XXIV

DIPLOMACY, 1715–1814

The Family of Nations, c. 1715

THE history of Europe is in great part a record of the official intercourse between its constituent states. Their wars, the alliances which they made to avert or to profit by wars, the treaties of peace which brought those wars to an end—these public acts have rightly received the foremost place, for they determine the conditions of human life and work. With wars and treaties should be ranked diplomacy, the art of managing peaceful exchange of views between the states. By 1715, Christian Europe had become a true society, whose constituent members, however jealous and distrustful, accepted one another as friends, with common customs and common aims. Mutual succour against the worst calamities, facilities for mutual trade, continent-wide protection for travellers, punctilious courtesy towards the representatives of other states—such were the badges of the family of nations. For two generations, it had been recognized that Europe was made up of independent sovereign states which no new empire or papacy might subdue. Between such, a balance of power had been reached, which any state might lawfully uphold by force.

The Balance of Power

The balance of power, indeed, was rather a principle than a cast-iron system. A contemporary defined it, not inaptly, as "the Art requisite for preserving the European states independent, by forming Confederacies against any Potentate or Commonwealth, formidable by its Power and Conduct towards many of its Neighbours." The balance of Europe necessitated a balance in each of several European regions. Russia, Sweden and Denmark must, if possible, be kept at peace so as to form a group strong enough to shield Europe against Asia. Meanwhile they must not themselves create a threatening northern Colossus. Men thought that Italy, a rich and populous country, should be cantoned out amongst many princes and free states, lest if united, it should humble other European powers, particularly those which lived by trade. The balance between Bourbon and Habsburg was still a necessity for Europe, and that among the states of Germany grew more important every day. No power felt any disturbance of the balance more quickly than Holland. None was so ambitious to hold it as was France, and perhaps none so competent as Britain.

For a quarter of a century (1689–1713), Britain had marshalled Europe against the subversive claims of France. When at last the Allies had forced back France into her place, the European society could develop. A strong feeling generally prevailed that territories should not be wrested by force from their lawful sovereigns. The deeper instinct that wars should not be ended by the annihilation of the vanquished state—that Europe needed France and Spain and Austria and Holland—was already being born. As the Dutch, the Swiss, the Venetians, and the Genoese bore witness, monarchy did not embrace all Europe. Most states, however, were personified by their kings, who seldom crossed their frontiers in time of peace. To maintain easy intercourse with other states, these kings must exchange representatives. As intercourse grew, the need for permanent representation increased. Hence the diplomatic service gradually took shape. In France, then the leader of the world in diplomacy, experts held that the best diplomatist would normally be a man of good birth and perhaps one trained to arms. Of the three great professions, that of the Church no longer ordinarily served to provide permanent residents abroad. Lawyers might be sent to countries like England, Holland, and Poland, where policy was determined by assemblies whom they might address. But advocates trained "to split hairs about nothing" and judges trained to dictate with dignity, were equally undiplomatic. There remained the Gentry of the Sword, among whose number Marlborough and Eugene had both gained triumphs in negotiation. Diplomacy, however, must not be linked with war, "for although war arises out of policy, it should be only a means to an end" (De Callières). The day of special envoys, dispatched only when special business made them necessary, was giving place to the maintenance by every important prince of a minister at the court of every other. In an age

Diplomatic Agents.

of sails, horses and bad roads, the peace of Europe often depended upon a diplomat's tact and skill. On the other hand, a rash diplomatist could often create the risk of war. In 1720, one British Minister threatened Genoa with bombardment if certain Jacobites were not expelled. In 1772, another denounced war on Denmark if she molested her English queen. Ambassadors, it was held, should not go into mourning for their own relatives "by reason they represent the persons of their prince, and must conform and keep pace with him." Their duty towards their master was to conciliate the court to which each was sent, to uphold the honour of their nation and its trade, to protect their fellow-countrymen within the country, to avert international incidents, especially in cases of desertion from the army, to give passports for entering their own land, to report everything of interest that might happen, to keep an eye on colleagues from other countries with a view to frustrating the knavish tricks of the unfriendly, and, of course, to act as the official mouthpiece of their own sovereign and the licensed auditor of whatever the local sovereign or his ministers might wish to say to him. To succeed, they must neglect no advantage that study or the social arts could give. Kings and ministers, being surfeited with daily flattery, must be flattered with discretion, not praised for defects of which they were aware or riches which they could not help possessing. Refined diplomatists allowed them unobtrusively to win at cards, the constant occupation of eighteenth-century courts. An ambassador, held Choiseul, should always be pleasant, even when he has to declare war. "Nothing," he held, "is more injurious than lying (*fausseté*) in business; true finesse is truth, spoken sometimes with force and always with grace."

Diplomatic Difficulties

In theory, therefore, and often in practice, the diplomat abroad was the guardian angel of peace. Yet on countless occasions his presence led to strife. Marooned in a foreign capital, perhaps deprived of intercourse with men speaking his own language and practising his own religion, he often fell ill, or turned to drinking and gambling, or otherwise occasioned scandal. Not seldom he libelled the government to which he was accredited, or was convicted of spying, or even of plotting against it. As few governments could pay their servants well, diplomatic posts often fell to men whose chief qualification was their private fortune. Bribery likewise played its part in confusing the relations between states. Some envoys were corrupt, and the most scrupulous among them had to pay spies and bribe officials.

Worst of all, however, was the friction arising from a cause for which individual diplomatists were not to blame—the jealousy between states with regard to precedence. Some sovereigns gave themselves titles which others could not hear unmoved. George I claimed to be King of France. Although Poland comprised several provinces called Russia, Red, Black or White, Peter the Great styled himself Tsar of all the Russias. France declared that, except indeed at a price, her language would not allow the expression *Majesté impériale*, which the Russian Empress demanded. As diplomats represented their masters, they used and were used with all imaginable pomp. In 1715 the Venetian spent ten hours in making a public entry into London. At the same time, their own conflicting claims tended to become affairs of state. If a princess did not dance with one of them as early or as often as his "character" required, good relations between their respective nations were jeopardized or suspended. The envoys' servants took up such quarrels, and brawls resulted in which the diplomats themselves might be engaged. The pomp that an ambassador might assume or exact when he appeared in public formed another cause of quarrel. Treatises were composed on such rights as that of driving with six horses.

Instructions

His original Instructions, signed by his master, formed the rule of life of everyone appointed to represent a state abroad. These were kept secret, save on occasion, when by express command they might be divulged to prove the royal friendship. Sometimes indeed, "ostensible" Instructions were drawn up to trick the foreign state. These Instructions contained in the case of Britain meticulous rules for the observance of "the ceremonial." Since 1668, they were informed, Ambassadors might not give the hand in their own houses to Envoys, but, to mark the difference in rank, must take the hand.

Sovereigns might send to represent them ministers of the first class, who were styled Ambassadors, or of the second which comprised Envoys Extraordinary and Residents. Ambassadors might be Ordinary or Extraordinary. The latter were in France entitled to three days' hospitality from the King. All Ambassadors wore their hats in the King's presence—the highest dignity to which a human being could attain. Envoys made no state entry, and stood uncovered before the seated and covered King. As among themselves, hardly anything was certain save that Ambassadors preceded Envoys, whatever their masters' rank. What grade of minister should be sent was the subject of negotiation between the princes, and their failure to agree might result in sending none.

The veteran diplomat Horace Walpole urged in 1736 that Titley should be made Envoy, not Resident, at Copenhagen, for "nothing less . . . will put him in a condition to watch the motions of the French and to make an interest with the ladies who govern that court."

Conferences

The "very puzzling and awkward ceremonial" which it would involve was even adduced as a reason for declining a royal visit. Ceremonial did its worst when it was necessary for powers to meet in conference with a view to ending or averting war. The difficulty of agreeing on a mediator or convener sometimes proved insuperable and almost always caused delay. The choice of meeting-place was also highly controversial. The vast cavalcades by which embassies expressed their sovereign's sense of his importance, made it impossible for them to meet except where food and lodging could be had in plenty. Such a place, moreover, must be so situated that no power might humiliate itself by taking a much longer journey than some rival. When these obstacles had been overcome, no embassy would willingly precede the others to the place of meeting, or seem to defer to another when on the spot. It was a Russian who had triumphed over an English diplomat by arranging that they should descend from their carriages at the same moment but bidding his servants hold him up so that the Englishman's feet first touched Russian soil. Sometimes a pavilion was set up with a door for every representative, and all entered at the same time. The smallest affront might cause a member of the conference to withdraw until his sovereign, after an elaborate exchange of dispatches, instructed him to resume his place. Hence it came about that although armies went into winter quarters and would-be peacemakers could labour for months together without the complications of hostilities, negotiations frequently went on for several years.

Diplomatic Privileges

In the ordinary course, an envoy was at once a sacred guest and a suspected semi-spy. His house was regarded as a detached portion of his sovereign's territory, to be interfered with by the police only in necessary self-defence. There the envoy, his staff, and his servants might follow their own worship and mode of life. There, as was universally agreed, fugitive debtors, perhaps even malefactors, might seek shelter from the local sovereign. Diplomatists might in general import commodities duty free for the use of their households. For those who abused this privilege by selling them, no condemnation could be too strong, but no punishment from the injured state could follow. An ambassador who plotted was merely escorted towards his own country. For the local state to punish him for this or any other crime would be the equivalent of an act of war. Representing his own sovereign, he could claim easy access to the local sovereign or his ministers, and the most unfettered communication with his own. If he were a "family ambassador," coming, for instance, from the country of the local queen, his rights of access were much enlarged. At the same time

Routine Duties

it was his duty to penetrate the secrets of those about him, and they spied upon him in return. Each party knew that such must be the case, and that without private "channels of intelligence," no embassy could do its duty. All the friars at Madrid who said masses for the dead in great houses were at one time said to be in the pay of the British ambassador. Fifty pistoles sufficed to buy the Russian despatches to their envoy in Spain from his secretary, a Frenchman with six children and a salary of three shillings a day. A minister sent home at least two reports each month, often many more. Some of these were plain to read, others in "cipher," a string of numbers which could be retranslated into words by those who possessed the special code used by the writer. A really effective cipher was regarded as worth more than its weight in gold. Some dispatches went by special courier, others by the ordinary post. Both were exposed to the attention of the local power. Couriers were trusty officers, but means might be found of securing from some spy or traitor an account of what had been put into the diplomatic bag, or, through the state's own representative abroad, what had come out of it. Despatches sent by post, however carefully sealed, were opened, copied, and if possible deciphered. Well aware of this practice, a wily diplomatist sometimes wrote what he wished the local power to read, apprising his own court, by some safer conveyance, of the true state of affairs.

Although the life of a diplomat abroad comprised many hardships and much chicane, it was not seldom embraced by patriotic and devoted men. The spectacle of an honest gentleman profusely assuring a kind host that his own master's sentiments were what both knew they could not be—this, though curious to the layman, was too commonplace to excite contemporary remark. Not a few envoys became sincere well-wishers of the nation in whose midst they exercised their office. Such creditable human weakness was recognized by their masters as a danger against which the State must guard. On balance the whole system probably averted more friction than it caused. As a quiet but potent and omnipresent force it must be taken into account when the biography of Europe is traced.

Ripperda and Diplomacy

The possibilities and the technique of contemporary diplomacy in the years which followed Utrecht (1713) were vividly illustrated by the career of Baron Ripperda (*c.* 1680–1737). In Hervey's eyes "a projecting, speculating, enterprising, inconsiderate, hot-headed fellow, with great views rather than great parts," he achieved impressive, even dazzling, results by his negotiations. Son of an ancient Spanish family in Holland, he was educated by the Jesuits at Cologne, and became a colonel in the Dutch army and the husband of an heiress. He next turned Protestant and was chosen deputy in the States-General. Military men, no less than ecclesiastics, like Alberoni, or University dons, like Robinson, were eligible for diplomatic posts, and Ripperda had brushed shoulders with the negotiators at Utrecht. In 1715, therefore, the States-General sent him as envoy to the Court of Spain. It was the moment when a *rapprochement* with Britain seemed essential to the revival of Spanish prosperity. At the same time two foreigners from Parma, Alberoni and the new Queen, Elizabeth, were exercising supreme influence in affairs of state. Ripperda, with his vivid imagination and inborn feeling for commerce, saw what Spain and himself might accomplish. He turned Catholic, renounced his Dutch commission, and produced abundant schemes for the political and industrial advancement of his adopted country. With the aid of artisans and machinery from Holland, a busy cloth-factory was set up at Segovia, in the hope of delivering the Spanish empire from dependence upon British goods. After Alberoni's fall, Ripperda became inspector-general of Spanish manufactures, and, though not proof against bribes, the trusted agent of the Queen. The occasion was eloquent both of the royal diplomacy and of the clumsy congresses in which the age abounded. In June 1720, Alberoni's war with the Emperor had been brought to an end by the Treaty of Madrid. This provided that a Congress should meet forthwith to settle outstanding questions between the late belligerents—Spain, the Emperor and Savoy. Britain and France, who were to act as mediators, knew full well that, if anything were to come of it, the parties to such a conference must agree in advance upon its resolutions. In this case such agreement was not easy, for the two proudest of monarchs claimed not only the same realm but the same title, that of Most Catholic King. The Emperor therefore demanded that King Philip's renunciation of Italy should be confirmed by the Cortes of Spain. The King could only reply by demanding that the Emperor's renunciation of Spain should be confirmed by the Estates of the Empire, who had no more to do with Spain than with the moon. A deadlock was averted by the mediators, who went bail for the fulfilment of the two renunciations.

Congress of Cambrai

Meanwhile, however, the Emperor had established his famous Ostend Company for transoceanic trade (December 1722). This outraged those mediators and others who enjoyed the monopoly of that trade and claimed that they were secured in it by treaties. The Emperor, moreover, now repented of his undertaking to invest a Spanish prince with Tuscany and Parma, though with this also the mediators were concerned. When the Pope and the rulers of Tuscany and Parma were loud in protest, while Spain objected to the forms which France proposed, the prospects of a successful European congress paled. In 1722, none the less, ministers from the three belligerent and the two mediating powers actually presented themselves at Cambrai, and in April 1724 the obstacles were so far surmounted that the formal sessions could begin.

The appointment of Ripperda had startled Madrid, but it was thought that his love of magnificence and contempt of money rendered him extremely fit to deal with the Germans. During the long delay, however, the several claimants had hardened in their demands. Questions of ceremonial, of history, of law, and of politics, questions in Belgium, Savoy, Sardinia, Italy, and Germany overwhelmed the half-hearted plenipotentiaries. The term Congress in the diplomatic game has been compared with the cry of General Post at a children's party. "Each power left its former place, and each was nervous lest it alone should be excluded from the new settlement" (Armstrong). Spain, not without reason, lost confidence in the Cambrai conferences, and at the instance of the Queen, Ripperda was secretly sent to negotiate at Vienna. The interests of his own career had now made him the enemy of Britain. The Dutchman and Spaniard within him conspired against a rival commercial nation which held Spain in thrall. Ferrol was to wrest from her the lucrative trade in salted fish. Spanish America must be closed to her manufactures, cleansed of her smugglers, and so organized as to render her aid unnecessary. The future of our trade and empire, therefore, might be swayed by the diplomat's use of the opportunity of 1725. Catholic feeling and the private interest of the Duke of Bourbon and of the Queen of Spain combined with the Emperor's commercial aspirations to produce a European situation from which a French insult to Spain enabled Ripperda to extract a dazzling fortune. Although a notorious drinker, who conspicuously lacked that discretion which is the first essential for a diplomat, he swiftly achieved four treaties of immense importance. From seemingly irreconcilable enemies Spain and the Emperor became warm allies. Britain, in effect, was offered a choice between surrendering Gibraltar or her American trade, and Europe found herself threatened with immediate and general war. Ripperda's combination was far more formidable than that with which Alberoni had threatened to turn Europe upside down.

Secret Mission to Vienna

Ripperda's Triumph and Fall

A diplomat who negotiated any treaty expected a rich reward. Ripperda, who had compelled the powers to form league and counter-league, and had prospectively rearranged the map of Europe, became duke, grandee and virtually premier in the proudest of all the realms. His fall, however, was even more swift and startling than his rise. The war which followed on his treaty proved small and futile, and Spain turned against its author. After one year of power, he fled to the British Embassy for shelter against the threatening storm. Thence, " abandoning his papers," sneered the wits, " but taking a bottle in either hand," " we see him pursued by the merciless Rage of a distracted people, hurried to a prison, and forgotten there by his Friends, his Wife, and even Justice herself. Escaping by the aid of a lovesick woman, flying with the Dart of Revenge sticking in his heart to England, Holland, Barbary." In Africa he became —so the world believed—a Mohammedan, fought against Spain, offered his aid to a Prussian would-be King of Corsica, and dreamed of reconciling the Jewish, Christian and Mohammedan systems of religion. Whether or no on his death-bed he became for the third time a Catholic, it is certain that he died in poverty without re-entering Europe.

Notable Diplomatic Victories

No period has surpassed the middle eighteenth century in the variety or brilliance of its diplomatic triumphs. In 1739 the astuteness of Villeneuve apparently reversed the main current of east European history. For more than forty years it had seemed clear that progressive Europe must gain at the expense of stationary Asia, and that Russia was the rising and Turkey the declining power. Yet thanks to Fleury's strategy and Villeneuve's tactics, the Treaty of Belgrade baulked Russia of the fruits of victory and restored Ottoman rule over broad Christian countries. Belgrade was swiftly followed by the great Coalition against Austria which was created by the personal negotiations of Marshal Belleisle.

After the war thus produced had proved fruitless, the Revolution in Alliances *par excellence* owed its consummation to the vision and subtlety of Kaunitz. For forty years Frederick the Great acted as his own Foreign Secretary and chief diplomatist. The retention of Silesia, the alliances with Russia and the *entente* with Austria were all in great part due to his personal labours in negotiation. Meanwhile the character and skill of Keene had perhaps as much to do with restraining Spain from striking at Britain in one war as the character and skill of Franklin with inciting France to participate in the next.

Envoys and Home Policy

So long as a few men and women steer the State, their regard for those about them cannot fail to influence their course. The wariest sovereigns avoid dangerous intimacy with the diplomatic *corps*.

That *corps* at any court, however, of necessity lived much together. Human need often determined that political opponents should be private friends, and *vice versa*. These relationships inevitably affected their reports and counsels to their respective governments, thus exercising a subtle, intermittent and often impalpable influence on politics.

Racial Talent for Diplomacy

In his work on the *Art of Negociating with Sovereigns*, published in 1716, François de Callières, who had won diplomatic laurels at Ryswick (1697), gave out that in diplomacy the Spaniards and Italians bore the palm. The Russians, of course, had not yet shown that eminence in the art which was notorious a century later. His fellow-countrymen, the French, he deemed too restless for prolonged negotiation, and so fond of war as to find it almost inconceivable that glory could be won in peace. Yet as diplomatists he held them superior to the other northern nations. Intelligence in Europe, he concluded, varied with the warmth of climate. Two generations after De Callières wrote, however, Britain shook his conclusions by producing one of the foremost among all diplomatists, an artist whom Talleyrand himself admired. This was James Harris (1746–1820), from 1788 Lord Malmesbury. A strikingly handsome youth, son of a scholarly and musical man of fortune, Harris by his own account "did nearly what he liked" at Winchester, and to Oxford "carried no great propensity to attend lectures and conform to college rules." In 1765 he began to educate himself, by studying among the Dutch and by travelling as far afield as Poland. At twenty-four, when a mere *chargé d'affaires* at Madrid, he took a tone of the utmost firmness with regard to that Falkland Islands expedition which brought Spain and Britain to the verge of war. His merit then lay in forming and in relying on his just impression that the minister, Grimaldi, feared a struggle for which Spain

Harris

possessed neither ships, nor money, nor allies, while her troops were needed to keep down the people. After Harris had actually been recalled, Spain yielded and abandoned the expedition (Jan. 1771). Early in 1772, at twenty-five, he found himself British Minister at Berlin. The post was chiefly one of education. It is significant that those from whom Europe had most to fear found the *surveillance* by foreign diplomats most irksome.

Harris and Diplomacy

" Most kings," Frederick the Great instructed his successor, " often groan under the weight of chains which they themselves have forged. My father was bold enough to break his, and I have sedulously kept the freedom which he bequeathed to me. I have even increased it by keeping foreign ministers as far as possible from my person. Here we have no rank, no ceremonial, no ambassadors. Thus we escape those disputes about precedence and all the chicanery of royal pride which in other courts require serious attention and steal time which could be better spent for the common weal."

Though no man could play it better, Frederick deliberately banished from Berlin the " game of wits played in a narrow circle " (Phillips) in which much of eighteenth-century diplomacy consisted.

At Berlin

This Harris perfectly understood. Berlin too he found corrupted by the success and renown of a King who displayed " irreligious neglect of all moral and social duties," and the city afforded him no enjoyment of social life. Yet, like many another diplomat, he bore all for the sake of his career. " I rise early," he informed his closest friend, " see nobody till dinner, generally dine at home with two or three of my acquaintances, go to the French play or to Court, and sup generally abroad, except once a month, when I have a supper of twenty-four or thirty covers at home." With Frederick, his ministers and the Berlin public he stood well, and life was tolerable.

Close study of the foremost prince in Europe convinced him that " immediate gain, however small, will always preponderate with him," and that his principles were so narrow that the Polish provinces brought him no real profit. At the same time, so Harris judged, " his views . . . rove from one side of the Continent to the other, and as long as he has the means . . . no alliance, however close, no convention, however sacred, will be able to place bounds to his ambition." A few years later, thanks to Frederick, he could speak of " this treaty-breaking age."

Frederick William II

In 1774 Harris found himself involved in a frequent but delicate species of negotiation, that of purchasing future advantages for his country by subsidizing the heir to a throne. A dandy, lavish towards his mistresses, forced to bribe Frederick's spies, the future Frederick William II "lacked cash to pay his laundress." His agent pleaded that he had drained the merchants dry, that the Prince of Orange, his son-in-law, had not a penny, that Joseph II did not hold the purse, and that Maria Theresa would give only to churches. Catherine, if approached, would at once let Frederick know. A mere £20,000, he urged, would buy Prussia away from France, for the French would be delighted to serve His Royal Highness. At that moment, however, Britain could not afford to speculate, and Harris skilfully evaded the request. While Frederick reigned and was assured of Russia, the most skilful and experienced British minister could do little at Berlin. There, as in many missions, the sovereign's illnesses kept the diplomatic *corps* on the *qui vive*. Harris was no wiser than many others in predicting an early end to Frederick's reign.

Harris and Catherine the Great

January 1778 found him in perhaps the most arduous of diplomatic posts, that of St. Petersburg. There any British minister must be prepared to spend a fortune beyond his pay, to jeopardize his health, and to encounter endless disorder, falsehood and delay. Harris, beyond this, had to contend with Frederick's predominance and hatred of Lord North's ministry as well as with a steady decline in Britain's prestige as the American war went on. Catherine's sincere regard for England, whose laws and constitution she knew well, offered some slight hope of Russian assistance, if not of that alliance which Britain now once more proposed. Failing a guarantee of help, a demonstration of friendship may be of value, and a Declaration from Catherine might have restrained some enemies of Britain. With natural insight, aided by study of previous Anglo-Russian negotiations, Harris soon divined that, for all his seeming friendliness, Panin was helping Frederick to block the way, and that his best hope lay in Potemkin. A violent man of wild ambition and spasmodic conversation, so rich that only an enormous sum could influence him—Catherine's Petruchio was no easy instrument to wield, but Harris handled him with great resource. To reach the Empress he must contrive, if possible, to put his views on paper, to induce Panin to let this pass, and to find out by "a channel" what arguments Panin had resolved to marshal against his. He might then compose an effective counter-argument, and, if possible, make the counter-argument reach Catherine before Panin's memorial could arrive. Unhappily for him, no favour to Russian ships could avert Catherine's Armed Neutrality Convention, and, while he fought his losing battle, "those profligate rascally patriots at home" launched the Gordon riots and further humbled Britain. When at last the Armed Neutrality was agreed on (June 1780), he asked for his own recall, the admission of a diplomatist's defeat. The Government, however, refused to give his enemies such a triumph, and the success of Joseph's meeting with Catherine at Mohilev amounted to a British victory. Frederick, employing "every trick the black art of politics is capable of," encouraged the rumour that Harris had fired the Russian fleet, but in vain. A visit from the tedious heir of Prussia failed and the Austrians triumphed.

The Armed Neutrality of 1780

When in December Britain acquired a fourth enemy in the "ungrateful, dirty, senseless boors" of Holland, Harris rendered priceless service to his country by proving that the Anglo-Dutch War was independent of the Armed Neutrality. He failed, however, to induce the Empress to accept Minorca as the price of procuring a peace with France, Spain and Holland which should leave the Americans in the lurch. These struggles, in which the foremost diplomats in Europe took part, were fought with little regard for morals. Bribes, of course, flowed freely, and Harris confessed that his opponents "are much more adroit at this dirty business than I am, who cannot help despising the person I corrupt." Panin, he declared, spent whole nights in concocting copies of imaginary British dispatches, and persuaded Paul that Harris had tried to poison the royal family by a present of geraniums and other plants. To checkmate spies, Harris must leave his secretary under lock and key. The Empress wrote an important communication in Russian and authorized Potemkin to give only a *viva voce* French translation, which could be afterwards denied. "The pains he takes to deceive me," Harris reported, "are not greater than those I take to make him believe I am deceived by him." "You are employed," he wrote in words with his own hand to a colleague at Berlin, "near the person of the greatest monarch that perhaps ever reigned." "Guard against his wiles, suspect his professions, and subtract a large portion from his fair words," he added in cipher. "Fighting, not negotiating *est notre fort*," he modestly professed, but the Government yielded most reluctantly to the claims of his injured health and recalled him in 1783.

Harris and the Dutch

Within a year Pitt found the presence of Sir James Harris at the Hague very essential. There he fought a diplomatic battle which deserves to rank with that by which thirty years later Talleyrand rescued France from ostracism at the Vienna Congress. Britain, it seemed, had a vital interest at stake and no weapon with which to defend it. The Low Countries must not be French, but the Emperor's claim to open the Scheldt threatened to lay Holland at the feet of France. The Hereditary Lieutenant (Stadholder), William of Orange, stood on the verge of illegal deposition for supposedly mismanaging the recent war with England. His consort, a virile Prussian princess, seemed to be guided by Frederick in the interest of a Prusso-French alliance. No vigorous or united English party existed, while the omnipotent Patriots or Democrats looked to France. Britain, where Pitt was about to nurse the finances and the navy, shunned any risk of hostilities, but France was reported ready to move her armies in support of her Dutch clients, and to make a perfect democracy of the Republic. Harris could at least enjoy detecting and frustrating their spies, among them "a link-boy who most assiduously lighted me whenever I went out in the evening, although I had two flambeaux, and this without asking fee or reward." The British Minister at once set to work to win friends among the Dutch and to encourage every element of discontent with Patriot policy. Show affability; they have not been used to it from Britain; and keep a good cook, "Dutch hearts lie to leeward of their stomachs,"—such were the first among his rules. He was helped when the Emperor substituted the plan of exchanging the Austrian Netherlands against Bavaria for that of enriching them under his own rule. The project threatened to result in Imperial control of southern and western Germany and probably in French control of Belgium. But for those very reasons it conduced to action by the threatened parties, Frederick and Pitt. Harris was fighting with tied hands so long as the Ministry clung at any price to peace.

The battle, none the less, proved long, and more than once seemed hopeless. Early in 1785, Harris invaded Amsterdam. In that hostile centre he "endeavoured to appear rather addicted to dissipation than business," and at least succeeded in forming a rallying-point for a future Opposition. His plan was to divide the Seven United Provinces, and in Holland, the chief of them, to set other towns against Amsterdam, working meanwhile to strengthen the Orange party and to prevent the fatal Franco-Dutch alliance. "My life," he said, "is a perpetual canvass," and he employed many secret agents. Without the support of Britain, however, the task was impossible, and unless Prussia concurred, Britain must be less powerful than the French.

Before 1785 was out, Harris had the satisfaction of winning from the Cabinet a Memorial to the Dutch which assured them that Britain remained their friend. Thus heartened, three Provinces refused their consent to the peace with the Emperor which France procured, but that treaty and a second for a French alliance were adopted. Zealand, however, offered to put itself under the protection of England. If Sweden, it was argued, could lend the port of Gothenburg to France, Zealand could lend Flushing to England. England, however, dared not take such a risk. Early in 1786 the French influence at the Hague was bearing down everything before it. To check the scheme for a Franco-Dutch conquest of British India, Harris was compelled to excite the Dutch East India Company against the Patriots and their allies. Meanwhile his work and the natural swing of the pendulum were not without effect. The pro-Orange upper classes trembled, but among the people a strong current began to run against the French. In July 1786, Britain made representations in favour of the established constitution. Next month, Frederick William ascended the throne of Prussia, and a new phase of Harris's work began. The most vital of his many labours became that of penetrating Frederick William's designs and of inducing him, if possible, to act with Britain. So long as Pitt's system remained resolutely pacific, however, progress either in Berlin or at the Hague could not be great. At this juncture Pitt achieved the free-trade Treaty of Versailles—" a landmark in human progress " (Rose). Harris could hardly expect to accomplish more than to make the Dutch an unserviceable ally to France.

Convinced that the French were our natural enemies, he laboured unceasingly to spike their guns. Early in 1787, 8,000 men of Rotterdam " by different means " were brought to remonstrate against the proceedings of the Patriots in that town, while the Princess of Orange sanctioned an Association to uphold the Hereditary Lieutenancy. Harris repeatedly assured Ministers of the potential strength of his party, and declared himself certain that " if we begin to roar, France will shrink before us." With the then system in Europe, France stood to dominate the Low Countries and Russia to partition Turkey. In May he was summoned to the Cabinet and had the joy of carrying his point. Britain resolved on an active policy, shown in the first instance by devoting up to £20,000 to promote Dutch opposition. The French none the less gained further successes, but in June when civil war broke out their partisans seized the Princess of Orange on her way to the Hague. This blunder was destined to decide everything. " Notwithstanding the importance of the object," wrote the indignant Harris, " not a single Deputy would leave their beds before the usual hour." " Don't be disheartened by a check to the Queen," replied the Foreign Secretary. " Let her be covered by the Knight, and all's safe." " The Knight " meant Frederick William, her brother, and, largely by Harris's influence with England, he was induced to make his move. The Turkish declaration of war on Russia (August) lessened the Prussian fears. Forty British ships demonstrated in support of the Prussian army which in October entered Holland.

Prussian Intervention

France had neither the men nor the money to take up the challenge, and the rest was triumph. The diplomat, as all agreed, had manipulated the balance of Europe. In August 1787 he had sent all his public papers to England, two hours before they might have been seized at the Hague itself. Within five weeks the Dutch were on their knees

Triumph of Harris

to the Princess of Orange. Another fortnight brought the submission of Amsterdam. In October the Triple Alliance between Britain, Prussia and Holland was on the way, to be signed in June 1788. It followed on the Anglo-Dutch treaty of April, which Harris negotiated. By that time his grateful country had raised him to the dignity of Ambassador Extraordinary, bringing "the whole Hague" to congratulate him in person. As Baron Malmesbury, which he became forthwith, he was honoured by Frederick William with the Prussian eagle upon his shield, and by the Prince with the Orange motto. In twenty years he had displayed all the technique of diplomacy and all the strength and weakness, the possibilities and the limitations of the diplomatic art.

Harris, now a tutor in statesmanship, lived on and through the Revolutionary and Napoleonic years in which diplomacy became rather the agent of war than the guardian of peace. Again, as in the days of William III and Marlborough, sovereigns, generals and statesmen negotiated in person, eclipsing the ablest of the diplomats by profession. In Talleyrand the age produced an ambassador as subtle as Harris, perhaps his superior in self-control, and endowed with the added strength and weakness that lack of principle provides.

Stratford Canning

Harris's true successor, Stratford Canning, a Minister Plenipotentiary at twenty-three, made his mark in that Treaty of Bucharest (1812) which proved what diplomacy could accomplish towards turning the balance of the forces that were about to shake the world. Wellington even described it as "the most important service that ever fell to the lot of any individual to perform." Canning was to be the last of those great diplomatists who spoke for their country in some sphere so distant that they often must, or might, act without special instructions. These men, it must not be forgotten, were not seldom responsible to Foreign Secretaries who were ignorant and careless of their special field.

Meanwhile the world had at least been growing wiser with regard to the machinery of intercourse between the nations. The nineteenth century opened with a growing determination that states should no longer baulk themselves

Precedence Determined

in business by their failure to agree in what order the parties should be named or their representatives appear at a reception. The dissolution of the Holy Roman Empire, the appearance of the Russian Emperor in Paris, and the good sense of Britain towards provocative claims all helped the Europe which emerged from the Napoleonic deluge to forego some traditional absurdities. In the hour of victory over France, the powers agreed to determine precedence by the alphabetical order of their names in French. A few years later, they adopted a cast-iron classification which prevented a thousand disputes about precedence between their representatives. These were in 1818 definitely divided into four classes, the highest, that of ambassadors, legates and nuncios, being reserved for persons so commissioned by the greater powers. Apart from the special honour which a Catholic court may pay to the legate or nuncio, precedence between diplomats of any rank at any court incontrovertibly came to depend upon priority in the date of their official reception there.

Diplomacy and the General Good

Before the eighteenth century closed, the notion that every independent state must further the common weal had found expression. The Kaunitz circular of July 17, 1791, has been designated by high authority as the first official recognition that the duty of watching over the common interests of Europe or of the world had become a function of diplomacy (Alison Phillips). Common action, it is true, could only be taken as the result of diplomatic negotiations. The eighteenth century, however, received from earlier times and transmitted to later the two chief defects in the diplomat if regarded as a champion of mankind. The first, which is as old as *Utopia*, arises from the dissonances between states, "they must be called friends but had in suspicion as enemies." The second, perhaps reduced but seldom if ever abolished when a statesman represents his country at a congress, consists in the position of a diplomat as an attorney of the State which instructs him, concerned with its success and blind to abstract justice. The history of the eighteenth century proved that trained negotiators were indispensable to the conduct of business between states. It proved also that whatever might be the case among men, among states natural appetites led to anarchy, not to social order. Silesia,

Poland, Europe in 1792, the swollen France of 1810—all indicated that without a public law supported by irresistible force no country could feel secure.

BIBLIOGRAPHICAL NOTE

See the Bibliographical Note at the end of Chapter I, the bibliography to Chapter II, and the books mentioned in the text.
Add :—

A

E. B. F. D'Auvergne : *Envoys extraordinary* (1937).

J. L. Brierly : *The Law of Nations* (5th ed. 1955).

A. Cobban : *Ambassadors and Secret Agents. The Diplomacy of the First Earl of Malmesbury at the Hague* (1954).

W. E. Hall : *International Law* (1924).

J. W. Headlam-Morley : *Studies in Diplomatic History* (1930).

D. P. Heatley : *Diplomacy and the Study of International Relations* (1919).

E. Lehr : *Manuel théorique et practique des agents diplomatiques et consulaires français et étrangers* (1888).

L. F. A. Oppenheim : *International Law.* 2 vols. (6th rev. ed. 1940).

E. Satow : *A Guide to Diplomatic Practice.* 2 vols. (2nd rev. ed. 1922).

T. A. Walker : *History of the Law of Nations* (1899).

H. Wheaton : *Commentaire* (1868).

B

Third Earl of Malmesbury (ed.) : *Diaries and Correspondence of James Harris, First Earl of Malmesbury.* 4 vols. (1844).

G. Smyth (ed.) : *Memoirs and Correspondence of Sir Robert Murray Keith, 1762–1792.* 2 vols. (1849).

A. Wicquefort : *L'ambassadeur et ses fonctions* (1681, new ed. 1730).

CHAPTER XXV

WAR, 1715–1814

War as a Remedy

TO the century which closed with 1914 the preceding hundred years seemed to constitute a bloody age. War or wars continued from 1715 to 1721. From 1733 to 1748 no year was peaceful and the scope of the chief wars was wide. Between 1755 and 1763 world-war raged. The next quarter of a century was disturbed four times at least by widespread war. From 1792 to 1814, war on a scale beyond all precedent darkened the history of Europe. Battle as a means of attempting to decide international disputes consistently deserved the poignant satire of Carlyle (1831) on the sixty brisk useful craftsmen transported at the public charges from a French and an English village to be blasted into sixty dead carcasses in the south of Spain.

> "Had these men any quarrel? Busy as the Devil is, not the smallest. . . . Nay, in so wide a universe there was even, unconsciously by commerce, some mutual helpfulness between them. . . . Their governors had fallen out; and, instead of shooting one another, had the cunning to make these poor blockheads shoot."

Seldom, if ever, during the century did any war provide a clear-cut answer to the questions which were supposed to have occasioned it. Never, it may be safely said, were the gains to the victor worth the cost in blood and treasure. Yet nations on the whole went cheerfully to war, loved their commanders, and refrained from attempting to organize any better system of settling their disputes. The British merchants whose spokesman in 1742 declared in the face of Parliament that they were "proud to be esteemed the authors of a just and necessary war" probably represented their nation and their age. The war was proved to be just and necessary because it aimed at restoring the freedom of navigation and vindicating British honour. This acquiescence in warfare appears to have been due to many causes, immemorial tradition and inborn pugnacity perhaps the chief. Mass warfare was long in coming, and when it came, it was slow to develop into mass-wastage without decision. When bloodletting was the chief resort of surgery, it seemed natural to treat the body politic in like manner. Undoubtedly the elements dangerous to a state were thus employed and reduced. By comparison with the hundred years which came to an end at Utrecht, moreover, the eighteenth century seemed almost peaceful. The Thirty Years War, its continuance between France and Spain, the wars of Louis XIV—these, with a background of Dutch wars, Scandinavian wars, and wars with the Turks and Russians, formed a dark mass against which the Regency shone resplendent as an age of peace. If the rape of Silesia convulsed the world, the Silesian wars were followed by nearly thirty years without a similar convulsion. It cannot be denied, however, that in the century which began with Marlborough and Eugene and ended with Suvorov and Bonaparte, Europe seldom enjoyed unbroken peace. Nearly two-thirds of the years between 1700 and 1800 were disturbed by widespread war. In the next fifteen, Blenheim, Gibraltar, Narva and Denain paled before Austerlitz, Trafalgar, Borodino and Leipzig. In the eighteenth century, moreover, the wars of Europe tended to become worldwide. Only after Trafalgar, as Bonaparte's conquest of Egypt went to prove, did the growth of British sea-power limit the customary battlefield to the Continent. Europe meanwhile was taught by her colonists in South and North America that the spread of civilization had created secondary foci of war. Without some consideration of the warfare that Europeans waged so earnestly and so often, a history of the century before Waterloo would be incomplete.

Wars of the Eighteenth Century

The French Revolution and Warfare

Although the Revolution and Bonaparte made wars shorter and more violent rather than changed their principles, those of the years 1715 to 1791 form one chapter; those of the next quarter of a century, another. Louis XIV left wars professional; the Republic began to make them national. In the former phase, the gentry of a country, aided perhaps by volunteers from abroad, commanded standing armies of conscripts from their own land, while similar forces were supplied by allied princes. These were eked out by mercenaries and by fresh levies from the nation. After the

Revolution, however, the *levée en masse* appears; men rise from the ranks to high command; allies begin either to fight as principals or not at all; on land the mercenary almost becomes extinct. Curiously enough, while the rank and file tended to change from the professional to the amateur, among the officers a converse development took place. When the century began, the higher grades were often occupied by grandees with no military training. These might be unpaid, save, perhaps, by profits from government allowances, sometimes for non-existent soldiers. The influence of Frederick and Bonaparte, however, gradually compelled even sovereigns to leave the conduct of the campaign to those who had studied war. This tendency was aided by the ever-increasing importance of artillery, an arm which no amateur could suppose himself fit to handle. Cannon, indeed, still fired bullets of iron, lead, or stone, and the largest were forty-eight-pounders, some twelve feet long, weighing 8,000 lb., and requiring 24 lb. of powder. It was still possible for a master of the ordnance to hold that, with the heaviest, accurate aiming was impossible. But cannon, Frederick the Great could declare, decided everything, and so long as soldiers charged in column this might well be true.

Marshal Saxe

Between 1715 and 1792, warfare on land may best be understood by studying a great commander. Perhaps their most accomplished and distinguished soldier was neither Eugene nor Frederick nor Suvorov, but a German Elector's son, who chose to serve France—Maurice, Marshal Saxe. An Englishman, who, in 1900, gained distinction in actual warfare by studying what Saxe published in 1740, argued powerfully that the Marshal was the first scientific soldier. Genius supplied the place of books, for Saxe found writing and arithmetic so difficult that his tutors proposed making a machine to close up his skull. Before the war of the Polish succession broke out (1733), however, he had demanded eleven "modern" military improvements, from breech-loading rifles to an organized general staff. Charles XII and Frederick the Great, being kings, could count upon the filial devotion and self-sacrifice of half their soldiers, and on instant obedience from all. Saxe was an alien who could safeguard his post only by threatening to resign it. His stature, strength and daring, however, commended him to fighting men, whose taste for drinking, gambling and debauchery he fully shared. When a Londoner jeered at him, he seized the man by the breeches and flung him into a mud-cart. Women by scores found him irresistible.

Saxe's Pre-French Period

In its fantastic adventurousness, his career was typical of the early eighteenth century. He was a royal bastard whom the famous Swedish beauty, Aurora von Königsmarck, bore, in 1696, to Augustus the Strong of Saxony, soon to be King of Poland. At twelve, he served against the French, and next year distinguished himself at Malplaquet. In 1710, he played a brave part in the siege of Stralsund, where the Swedes fought desperately for the last of their German dominions. At fifteen, the young veteran married a great heiress, whom he treated with infidelity worthy of his royal father, whose bastards numbered 354. In 1712, for the second time he had a horse killed under him, while rallying his cavalry against the victorious Swedes. When the Spanish Succession War was over, and his father had finally regained the Polish throne, he turned to serve under Eugene against the Turks. The peace of 1718 impelled him towards France, the classic land of war and pleasure. Orleans allowed him to buy a regiment, and he proved himself as vigorous in military study and manœuvres as in the field.

Saxe and the Slavonic Powers

Having fought against French, Swedes, and Turks, Saxe turned to politics, in the vast theatre of Russia. Despite his birth, he was elected Duke of Courland, a Polish fief largely controlled by the Tsar. Although Catherine I drove him thence, in 1736 he might have shared Anne's throne at Petersburg but for an intrigue with a lady of her court. In the Polish Succession War he chose to serve France against his half-brother, Augustus III, instead of accepting the chief command of the Saxon forces. In this war (1733–1736), as always, he distinguished himself both in open and in siege warfare, beating Eugene and rising to lieutenant-general in the foremost army of the world. When the Emperor's death in 1740 occasioned the war of the Austrian Succession, Saxe gained the opportunity of his career. Next year it fell to him to command the left wing of the army which Belleisle sent to Bohemia. Again he showed himself a skilful leader and a rare adventurer. The man who had twice defended a house against enormous odds, the first

Saxe in the War of 1740–8

time eighteen against some eight hundred, now scaled the walls of Prague and took the city. The result was that, in 1744, having meanwhile failed to marry Elizabeth of Russia, he was appointed to command the army which was designed to make the Young Pretender King of Britain. The wind frustrated the expedition, but Saxe declared that he must have the highest military rank or quit French service. At forty-eight, therefore, he triumphed over every rule. A bastard German Protestant became Marshal of France and the official cousin of the King.

Saxe and the Netherlands

From 1744 to the peace in 1748, the biography of the new Marshal becomes one of the chief threads in the history of Europe. Here it must be described only so far as is necessary to illustrate one side of war. The accident which brought this adventurer to the side of France, together with the skill of Louis XV and his mistress which kept him there, doubled the effectiveness of the French army and enabled it to conquer the Netherlands. Victory every year was the work of a warrior swollen with dropsy who yet remained an author and a man of pleasure. To the labours of the campaign Saxe added those of negotiating the marriage of his niece with the Dauphin and of overthrowing the chief minister, d'Argenson. In 1747 he gained a yet higher title, that of Marshal-General of the armies and camps of France. Aided by another adventurer, Löwendahl, he made the last campaigns of the war as brilliant as that of Fontenoy. The two years by which he survived the peace were passed in a half-royal, half-military and wholly sinful life at Chambord. They were enlivened by schemes for winning a crown—in Courland, in Tobago, perhaps in Corsica or Madagascar. In 1750, since he died outside the faith of France, he could not be buried with due pomp nearer than at Strasburg. There Frenchmen setting out to conquer his native Germany were wont to sharpen their swords upon his tomb.

Military and Civilians

In 1750 as in 1715, warfare remained professional in the sense that it was left chiefly to fleets and armies, while the bulk of the population continued to follow their normal life. Both by land and sea, however, fighting men were not yet a separate caste. In an age when every gentleman might be called on at any moment to draw his sword in defence of his personal honour, most were deemed fit to serve the King at the head of their dependants. Even for high command, birth often counted for more than brains or training. Only a soldier of Saxe's originality could argue that garrisons should have a military library and a school for young officers, who usually wasted their time in ignorance and idleness. Cumberland, the brave commander whom Horace Walpole deemed a great man, and whose popularity the sweet william still recalls, was said to have no better idea of tactics than to lead his men into the hottest fire and keep them there as long as possible. French courtiers, Austrian archdukes, Russian gentry, too often made the description "lions led by asses" appropriate to eighteenth-century armies. Among their juniors, birth and valour ranked above drill and study, and the success of the more professional Prussian armies proves how deficient was the training that such men received and gave.

Military Equipment

The amateur character of many of the fighting forces was reflected in their garb. Except for the leather jerkin, which was especially popular among cavalry, soldiers and sailors had not yet departed far from the comfortable dress of the civilian. A seaman in the British navy might wear a flat three-cornered hat, or a leather cap faced with red cotton, a jacket and stockings of grey, with shoes and gay shirt, waistcoat and breeches.

Gallants who could imagine no more delightful life than seven months in Flanders followed by five in Paris continued into the Seven Years War the decorative traditions of the aggressive wars of Louis XIV. Among such, powdering the head ranked high, and the whiteness of the powder called for rouge to save the face from looking ghastly. English newspapers often advertised "campaign boxes for officers, fitted with eau-de-luce, rouge, perfumed pomatum, powder-puffs, lip salve, and ivory eyebrow combs" (Richardson). The broad brim which made the felt hat useful against sun or rain might be looped up, first on one side, then on both, or at the front and back, without essential alteration. The grenadier, it is true, needed some headgear over which he could swiftly pass his musket-strap so as to free his hands for the "anarchistic bombs" which hung beside him. Hence arose his plated cap, heightened perhaps that his stature might impress the enemy, like the bearskin or shako which the Hungarians and Croatians rendered popular in later years. But whether grenadier, musketeer or trooper, officer or private, the soldier's chief covering was the loose long coat of the ordinary civilian, with breeches, and, if a foot-soldier, with buckled shoes. The officer wore his curling full-bottomed wig, while the rank and file protected their necks with hair so long that on the march it became necessary to enclose it in a bag or plait it into a pigtail. Between 1713 and 1740 Frederick William I of Prussia proved himself "the Sergeant-King" towards the soldier's clothing, as well as towards his drill. Under his supervision, coats were shortened, clothing grew tight and stiff, pigtails, with the aid of horsehair, reached the waist, and Prussian soldiers became conspicuously a class apart.

Arms and Tactics

The wars of Louis XIV, which had taught regiments uniformity in dress, left arms and tactics more simple than before. The socket bayonet made the pikeman obsolete, though the notion of winning battles "by push of pike" influenced the use of the new weapon. When the seventeenth century began, the musket was a clumsy tool with a barrel three feet eight inches in length, firing a ball an ounce in weight. Throughout the eighteenth century all infantrymen carried flintlocks, shorter and thicker weapons charged with five ounces of iron or seven and a half of lead and an equal quantity of powder.

Tactics were murderously simple. A thick phalanx of infantry marched towards the enemy until well within musket-shot. The distance between the opposing hosts was small, for even by the year of Waterloo a musketeer at the foot of Ludgate Hill could not have been sure of hitting the dome of St. Paul's. They then halted, fired, and charged with the bayonet. The cavalry completed their victory or covered their retreat. The appalling slaughter caused by such warfare and their proved inferiority to the British and Germans in waging it, impelled the French to think out a better system and Fontenoy resulted. There, as Mark Sykes records, after the Dutch had given way, the British and Hanoverians charged with irresistible weight and fury.

Fontenoy a Turning Point

"Line after line pressed closely together, like one great red brick. Never . . . had so strange a thing been seen on a battlefield as this vast heavy mass of angry men. . . . The French fired salvoes of artillery at it, rent bloody gaps in its sides, but still it advanced . . . ploughing a course through the very centre of the French army. . . . The wild Irish Brigade darted howling at its head ; whole batteries of artillery charged with round shot, bullets, stones, broken glass or anything that could be crammed down the heated muzzles, belched their contents into its side at point-blank range. . . . It was because the British broke through the French centre that they were utterly routed."

For Saxe had grasped the fact that "a phalangeal army is incapable of maintaining its cohesion over obstructed ground," and had duly prepared defensive posts and masses of artillery. Many of these, indeed, were swept away, but at last the guns fired down the whole length of the advancing column and no valour could avail. Twelve thousand of the beaten force remained on the field, and, as Napoleon said, "experience shows that three months after a battle only one-sixth of the wounded remain." Thanks to Saxe, the Netherlands lay open to conquest and the Pretender shook King George's throne. As Fontenoy had shown, while the principles of war remain unchanged, the methods by which one side is forced to submit to the will of the other progress, albeit slowly. Their advance is usually made by jerks, each due to the brain of an outstanding leader. According to the judgment of Napoleon, whom all nations ever since he lived have regarded as the greatest master of the art of war, the chief among his precursors was Frederick the Great. "His own personal presence," wrote the British Minister who was with him in 1759, "I reckon equal to 30,000 men." That of Napoleon was currently estimated at 40,000. Attempts to analyse Frederick's methods and to account for Prussian success suggest that he relied upon combining several distinct factors of superiority to his opponents. Mobility, choice of ground, armament and tactics must each yield him an advantage.

Methods of Frederick the Great

From the days of the Sergeant-King (1712–40), the Prussian infantry had been famous for the thoroughness of their drill. This gave them speed in manœuvring, especially when their king was in command. Frederick himself had perfected the cavalry and the artillery, and had co-ordinated the three several arms. A Prussian force of moderate size could therefore be moved by him so quickly as usually to outpace the enemy. Many armies at that time, moreover, endeavoured to out-manœuvre their opponents by occupying successive positions which were too strong to be attacked, while their antagonist, unless he could dispossess them, must himself abandon his objective. Frederick and his staff excelled in rapid appraisement of the value of a position, either for occupation or attack. The King had also a lively sense of the power of heavy guns, and as an autocrat could secure for himself a superiority in gun-power by drawing freely upon the Prussian store. His peculiar secret, however, lay in his appreciation of the fact that superior numbers used as his opponents used them might be made to contribute to his own success. The enemy usually took up a fixed position which was strong against frontal attack, and which barred Frederick's direct road to his objective. If, therefore, the King could swiftly assail one flank with a part of his troops while employing the remainder so as to convince his opponent that he was about to attack elsewhere, he might roll up the whole line and win the victory. While his purposeful onslaught was swiftly reinforced from the wing which he did not intend to engage, the puzzled enemy might be too late in forming a fresh front and in bringing reinforcements from a distance. Of ten great battles in the Seven Years War, six were thus won. Three were lost by imprudent departures from the accustomed plan. At Zorndorf, the Russian formation in a square and the tenacity of the Russian rank and file discounted the Prussian tactics and qualified Frederick's victory. Although the subsequent expansion of the armies must render the plan obsolete, the principle of attacking, and if possible of attacking in flank, was consecrated by his success.

The French Revolution and Change

As the war of the Bavarian Succession (1778–9) and the first engagements of the Revolution (1792) amply proved, the art of war developed little in three decades from the Peace of Paris (1763). A long-service army of between one and two hundred thousand men, of which the infantry marched at seventy-six paces to the minute and attacked in line—such remained the ideal. The first years after the outbreak of war in 1792, however, produced in France a change like that in Britain after the outbreak in 1914. Regulars and National Guard became fused together ; citizens flocked to the colours ; in tactics, the new wine burst the old bottles ; in strategy, the will of the rank and file became a factor of more account. By 1795 the French forces exceeded half a million. Such a mass could not be quickly drilled to keep a perfect alignment on the field of battle, or to risk their lives willingly in adventures of which they disapproved. On the other hand, they fought with conviction, especially in defending their fatherland, or in seeking the means of living. If they could not be counted on to retreat in good order, they could be taught to march fast, to dispense with the tents and supply-services of the old army, and to attack in masses with enthusiasm. Taught by necessity and by experience, the French formed army corps, for the rapid communication of orders, and infantry whose step was quickened by one-third or even more. Five years of war hardened the troops and revealed the gifts of many leaders.

Napoleon Bonaparte

Among the new men there chanced to be the greatest military genius of all time. Bonaparte had been professionally trained and at first made no revolutionary changes in the art of war. From the first, however, he raised the *tempo* of the French machine. Where he commanded, unwilling conscripts were soon turned into soldiers, and soldiers became heroes. In a degree which few historic generals have approached, Bonaparte knew his own mind, took risks without suffering from mental strain, and instantly adapted his plans to fresh emergencies. No man, with the means of communication that then existed, could make an army move like a machine.

"Certain canons of practice," Mr. Jeudwine ironically remarks, "vary little throughout the century. For an assault on a fortified position the ladders were either forgotten, or they were too short, or they were thrown away in the advance of the men. If the attack was made at night . . . the troops did not arrive at the position until morning and the guides led the attacking force to the most unassailable position. The ammunition did not fit the guns, the men in charge of the horses bolted."

But no commander in history rivalled Bonaparte in foresight and co-ordination. For swift and sustained labour, and for the power of calling out the energies of his subordinates, he was, and is, unequalled. As, unwounded and unexhausted, he gathered in victory after victory, both his own men and the enemy could not but credit him with almost superhuman powers, and thus fresh victory became more sure. For some seven campaigns, however, he rendered known tactics irresistible rather than invented new. Then, in 1806, he produced a formation, till then unknown, but in his hands brilliantly successful. Always seeking out his enemy and purposing to destroy him by a battle, he covered his own advance by a line of skirmishers followed closely by a force of all arms sufficient to pin down the enemy when found. Then, a day's march behind, came a great army which could be hurled at his opponents in whichever direction the best judgment in the world dictated. This army marched like a great lozenge, sixty to seventy miles wide at its greatest breadth. If the lozenge was moving due north and A designated the foremost of the equal squares composing it, B and C followed side by side and D brought up the rear. It was thus possible, according as the situation required, to form a front of A and B facing north-west or of A and C facing north-east, or of B, A and C facing due north, D in all cases acting as reserve.

Napoleon's Failure

So long as this method of warfare was applied to a continent of moderate size inhabited by men who did not detest the political system which it supported, Napoleon might be accounted invincible. Beyond the European mainland, however, sea-power must be reckoned with. From 1803 onwards, therefore, Napoleon, when not immediately threatened, must bend all his energies to conquer Britain. At first he hoped to evade her navy and to slip an irresistible army across the Channel. When the British cruisers promised to make this impossible, he planned to fend them off for the necessary time by a strong convoying force. In 1804 he supposed that six hours would suffice, but next year the estimate had risen to a fortnight. The plan of a great French and Spanish concentration which should bring a sufficient convoying fleet to Boulogne was that which produced Trafalgar. The British navy had not been so mishandled as to permit the concentration without a battle. Some future combination of fleets, indeed, might make it possible to carry out the plan of invasion. Meanwhile the only possibility of breaking Britain's will lay in a partial blockade or siege directed principally against her commerce. In essence, the Continental System resembled the German blockade during the Great War. Although the German submarines were infinitely more dangerous than the French cruisers or privateers, Napoleon, after 1807, was master of almost the whole of Europe at a time when intercourse with any other continent was comparatively small. In attempting to win a war without defeating either the land or the sea forces of his enemy he was perhaps involuntarily recognizing the fact that the will of the people is the ultimate spring of combat, and that to break or exhaust that will by any means may be to gain the victory. All nations, whether autocracies, democracies or intermediate governments, have their breaking-point, and the Continental System was by no means ill-devised to find the breaking-point of Britain. The trade which was threatened included imports of necessary food, and a hungry people with no hope of victory may rise against those who demand that they should struggle on for problematical gains beyond the seas.

As all the world knows, the patience of Napoleon's allies expired before that of his opponent. In 1812 and in 1813 he waged war on a scale the most colossal ever known. In 1814 he made incomparable use of small resources. To the art of war, however, these campaigns added nothing, save perhaps the plan of evading battle with Napoleon himself while seeking to overthrow him by crushing his lieutenants. This desperate expedient, which was practised rather than formally resolved on, attests the unique character of the military history of an era which may fairly be called unique. "Never before had the fortunes of all the nations of the West depended upon the fate of one man." Since that man was pre-eminently a soldier, the history of Europe in the age of Napoleon has more than a military tinge. With his withdrawal, this would pass away, leaving the art of warfare not much advanced.

Within five years of Leipzig, the diplomats had reorganized and stereotyped their profession (1818). The soldiers, however, developed theirs but little until half a century had passed. Then, in the days of Lincoln and of Moltke, men found that the growth of population, wealth and railways had changed both the scale of warfare and its strategy. Fifty years more made weapons far more deadly, while extending the area of strife to the air, the depths of the sea and the homes of the unwarlike masses. Then and only then did the nations set themselves in earnest to replace war by justice and to organize a commonwealth of mankind.

BIBLIOGRAPHICAL NOTE

See the Bibliographical Note at the end of Chapter I and the bibliographies to Chapters VII, X, XVI, XVIII and XX.
Add :—

A

J. H. Anderson : *The Napoleonic Campaign of 1805* (1912).

H. Camon : *Maurice de Saxe, maréchal de France* (1934).

W. L. Clowes : *The Royal Navy : A History from the Earliest Times to the Present.* 7 vols. (1897–1903).

J. Colin : *Les campagnes du Maréchal de Saxe.* 3 vols. (1901–6).

J. S. Corbett : *England in the Seven Years' War.* 2 vols. (1907).

J. S. Corbett : *Some Principles of Maritime Strategy* (1911).

R. Custance : *A Study of War* (1924, 2nd ed. 1927).

E. B. F. D'Auvergen : *The Prodigious Marshal.* (1930).

E. M. Earle (ed.) : *Makers of Modern Strategy.* (1943).

J. W. Fortescue : *History of the British Army.* I–X (13 vols. 1899–1931).

J. W. Fortescue : *The British Army, 1783–1802* (1905).

W. Görlitz : *The German General Staff* (trans. 1953).

R. A. Hall : *Frederick the Great and the Seven Years' War* (1915).

E. D. B. Hamley : *The Operations of War* (7th ed. rev. 1923).

C. Jany : *Geschichte der Königlich-Preussischen Armee.* 4 vols. (1928–33).

R. Jouan : *Histoire de la marine française.* 2 vols. (1932).

B. H. Liddell Hart : *The Ghost of Napoleon* (1933).

C. R. Low : *History of the Indian Navy, 1613–1863.* 2 vols. (1877).

H. W. Richmond : *The Navy in the War of 1739–1748.* 3 vols. (1920).

H. W. Richmond : *Statesmen and Sea Power* (2nd ed. 1947).

R. Sauliol : *Frédéric le grand : la campagne de 1757* (1934).

F. H. Skrine : *Fontenoy and Great Britain's Share in the War of Austrian Succession* (1906).

C. Oman : *Studies in the Napoleonic Wars* (1929).

H. Pichat : *La campagne du Maréchal de Saxe dans les Flandres, de Fontenoy (mai 1745) à la prise de Bruxelles (février 1746)* (1909).

J. H. Rose : *The Indecisiveness of Modern War, and other essays* (1927).

B

K. von Clausewitz : *On War* (trans. 3 vols. rev. ed. 1908 ; another trans. 1943).

J. S. Corbett (ed.) : *Fighting Instructions, 1530–1816* (1905).

Journals of the Hon. William Hervey, in North America and Europe, from 1755 to 1814 ; with order books at Montreal, 1760–1763 (1906).

G. Monck : *Observations upon Military and Political Affairs* (1671).

Maurice, Comte de Saxe : *Memoirs upon the Art of War* (trans. 1757).

S. Pargellis (ed.) : *Military affairs in North America, 1748–1765 ; selected documents from the Cumberland papers in Windsor castle* (1936).

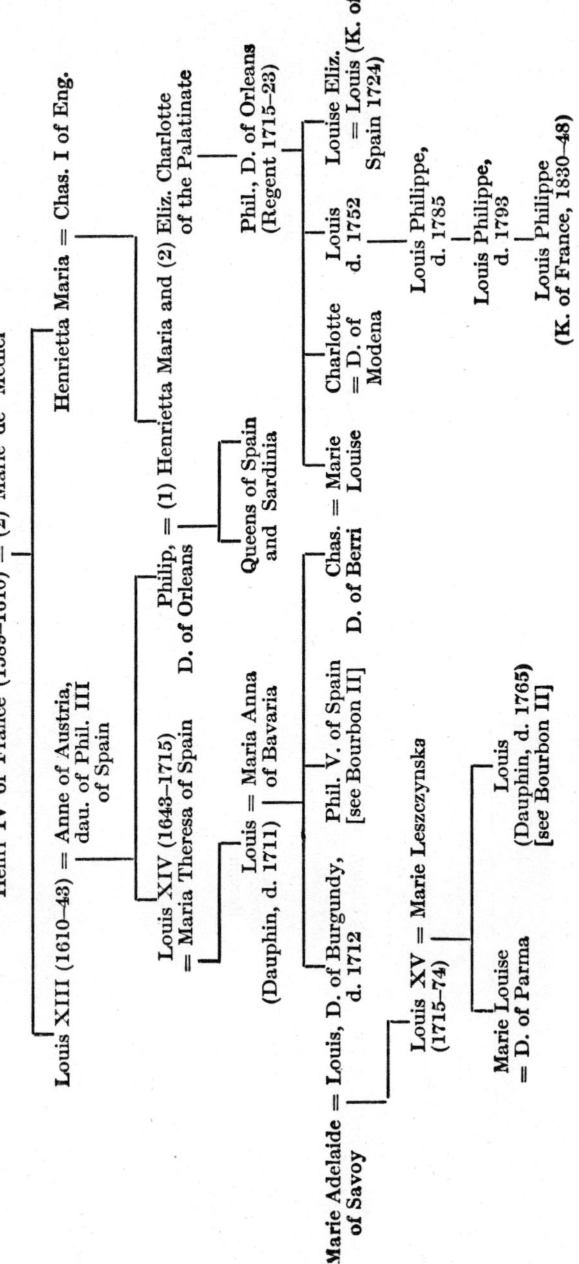
THE HOUSE OF BOURBON. I
Henri IV of France (1589–1610) = (2) Marie de' Medici
Louis XIII (1610–43) = Anne of Austria, dau. of Phil. III of Spain
Henrietta Maria = Chas. I of Eng.
Louis XIV (1643–1715) = Maria Theresa of Spain
Philip, D. of Orleans = (1) Henrietta Maria and (2) Eliz. Charlotte of the Palatinate
Louis (Dauphin, d. 1711) = Maria Anna of Bavaria
Queens of Spain and Sardinia
Phil., D. of Orleans (Regent 1715–23)
Marie Adelaide of Savoy = Louis, D. of Burgundy, d. 1712
Phil. V. of Spain [see Bourbon II]
Chas. D. of Berri = Marie Louise
Charlotte = D. of Modena
Louis d. 1752
Louise Eliz. = Louis (K. of Spain 1724)
Louis XV (1715–74) = Marie Leszczynska
Louis Philippe, d. 1785
Louis Philippe, d. 1793
Louis Philippe (K. of France, 1830–48)
Marie Louise = D. of Parma
Louis (Dauphin, d. 1765) [see Bourbon II]

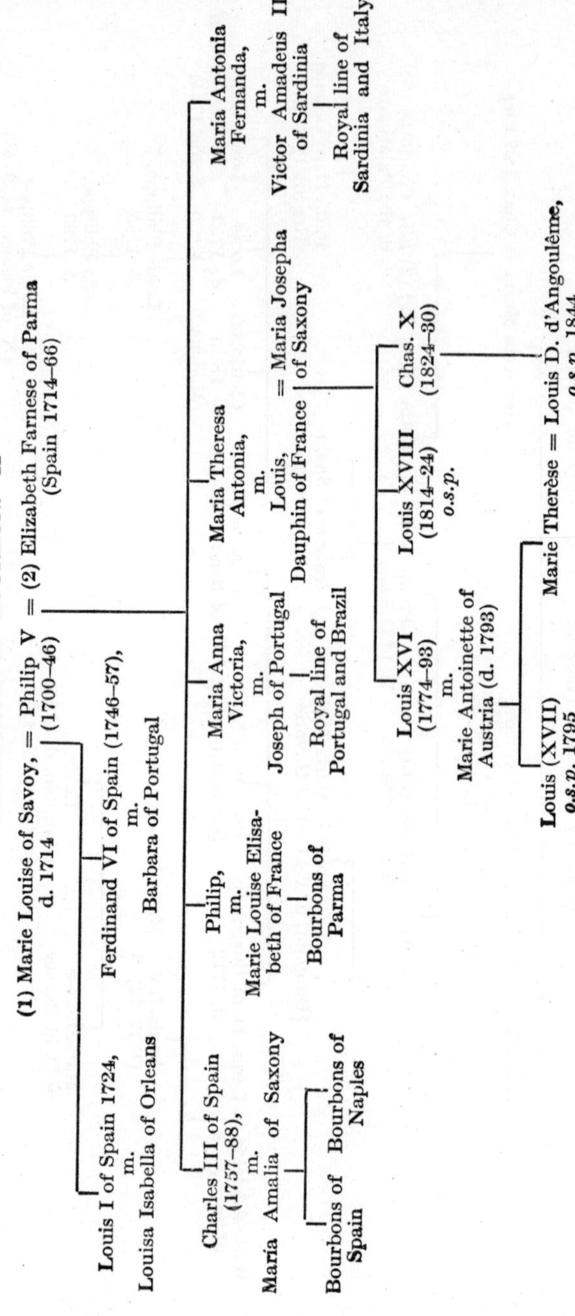
THE HOUSE OF BOURBON. II
(1) Marie Louise of Savoy, = Philip V = (2) Elizabeth Farnese of Parma
d. 1714
(1700–46)
(Spain 1714–66)
Louis I of Spain 1724,
m.
Louisa Isabella of Orleans
Ferdinand VI of Spain (1746–57),
m.
Barbara of Portugal
Charles III of Spain
(1757–88),
m.
Maria Amalia of Saxony
Bourbons of Spain
Bourbons of Naples
Philip,
m.
Marie Louise Elisabeth of France
Bourbons of Parma
Maria Anna Victoria,
m.
Joseph of Portugal
Royal line of Portugal and Brazil
Maria Theresa Antonia,
m.
Louis, Dauphin of France = Maria Josepha of Saxony
Maria Antonia Fernanda,
m.
Victor Amadeus II of Sardinia
Royal line of Sardinia and Italy
Louis XVI
(1774–93)
m.
Marie Antoinette of Austria (d. 1793)
Louis XVIII
(1814–24)
o.s.p.
Chas. X
(1824–30)
Louis (XVII)
o.s.p. 1795
Marie Therèse = Louis D. d'Angoulême,
o.s.p. 1844

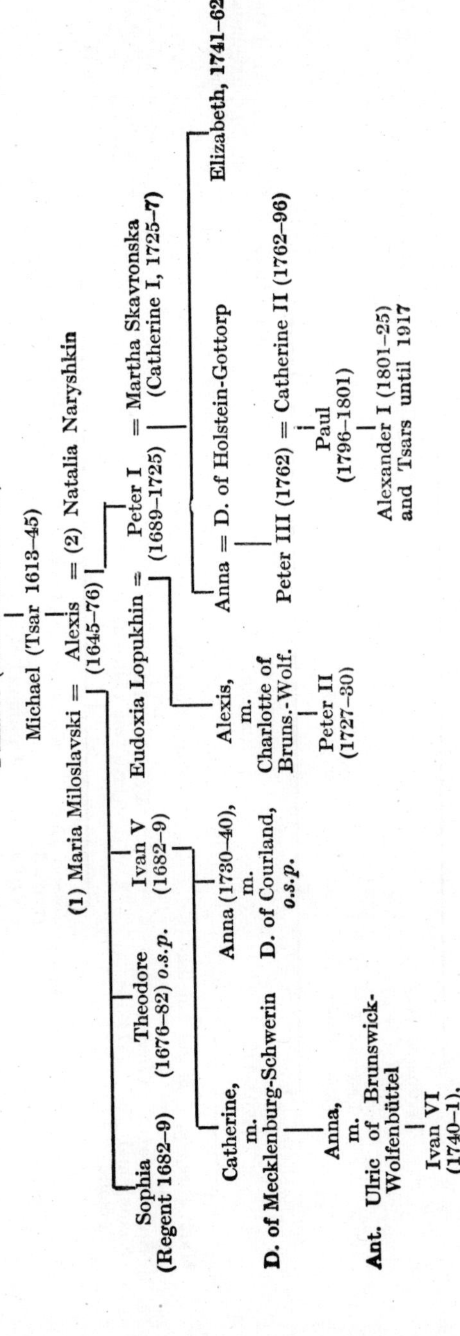
THE HOUSE OF ROMANOV
Nicetas
(bro.-in-law of Ivan the Terrible, 1533–84)
Philaret (Patriarch 1619–33)
Michael (Tsar 1613–45)
(1) Maria Miloslavski = Alexis = (2) Natalia Naryshkin
(1645–76)
Sophia
(Regent 1682–9)
Theodore
(1676–82) o.s.p.
Ivan V
(1682–9)
Eudoxia Lopukhin = Peter I = Martha Skavronska
(1689–1725)
(Catherine I, 1725–7)
Catherine,
m.
D. of Mecklenburg-Schwerin
Anna (1730–40),
m.
D. of Courland,
o.s.p.
Alexis,
m.
Charlotte of
Bruns.-Wolf.
Anna = D. of Holstein-Gottorp
Elizabeth, 1741–62
Anna,
m.
Ant. Ulric of Brunswick-
Wolfenbüttel
Peter II
(1727–30)
Peter III (1762) = Catherine II (1762–96)
Paul
(1796–1801)
Ivan VI
(1740–1),
o.s.p. 1764
Alexander I (1801–25)
and Tsars until 1917

THE AUSTRIAN SUCCESSION

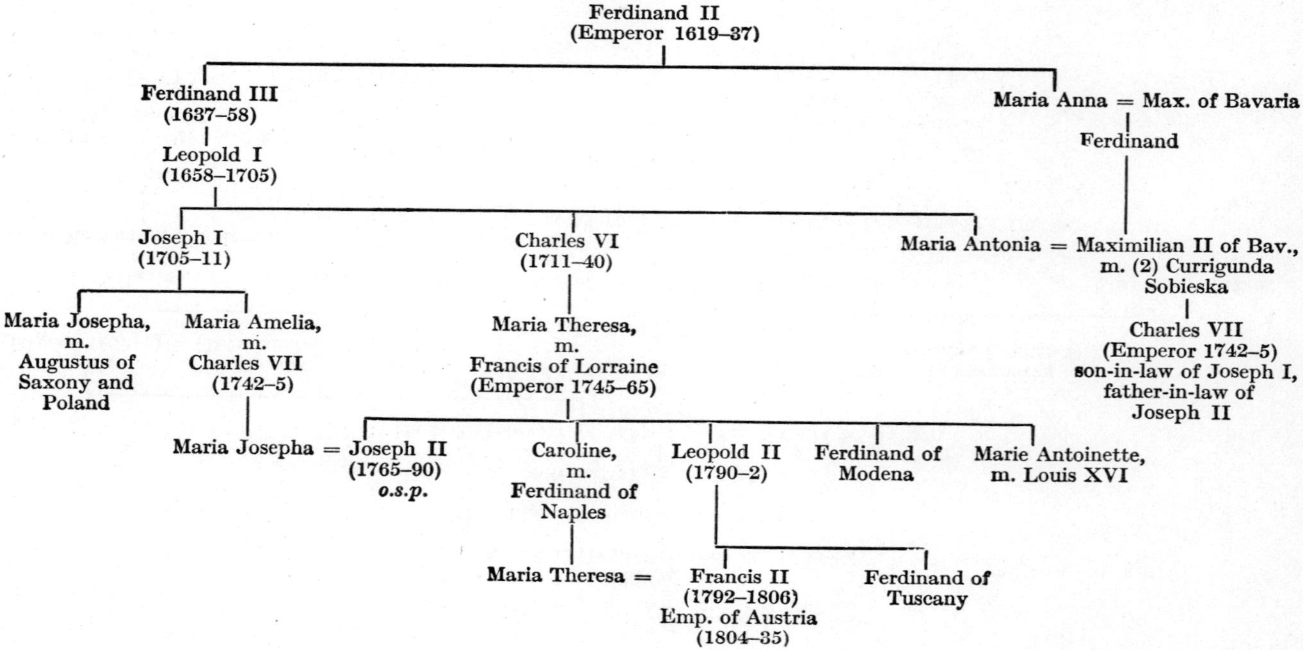

Ferdinand II (Emperor 1619–37)

- Ferdinand III (1637–58)
  - Leopold I (1658–1705)
    - Joseph I (1705–11)
      - Maria Josepha, m. Augustus of Saxony and Poland
      - Maria Amelia, m. Charles VII (1742–5)
        - Maria Josepha = Joseph II (1765–90) *o.s.p.*
    - Charles VI (1711–40)
      - Maria Theresa, m. Francis of Lorraine (Emperor 1745–65)
        - Joseph II (1765–90) *o.s.p.*
        - Caroline, m. Ferdinand of Naples
          - Maria Theresa = Francis II
        - Leopold II (1790–2)
          - Francis II (1792–1806) Emp. of Austria (1804–35)
          - Ferdinand of Tuscany
        - Ferdinand of Modena
        - Marie Antoinette, m. Louis XVI
    - Maria Antonia = Maximilian II of Bav., m. (2) Currigunda Sobieska
      - Charles VII (Emperor 1742–5) son-in-law of Joseph I, father-in-law of Joseph II
- Maria Anna = Max. of Bavaria
  - Ferdinand
    - Maximilian II of Bav.

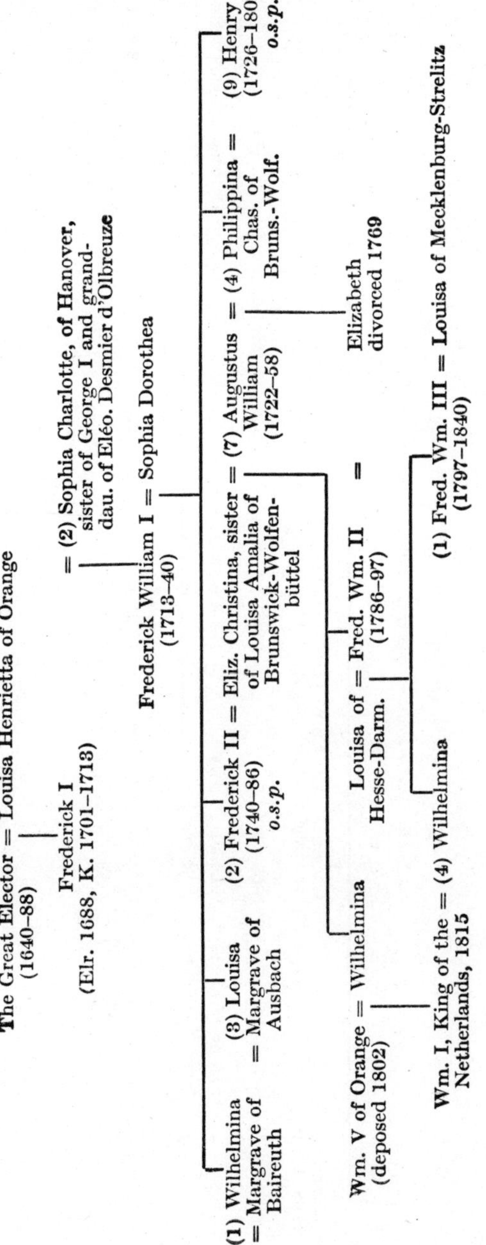
THE PRUSSIAN ROYAL HOUSE (1701–1815)
The Great Elector = Louisa Henrietta of Orange
(1640–88)
Frederick I
(Elr. 1688, K. 1701–1713)
= (2) Sophia Charlotte, of Hanover,
sister of George I and grand-
dau. of Eléo. Desmier d'Olbreuze
Frederick William I = Sophia Dorothea
(1713–40)
(1) Wilhelmina
= Margrave of
Baireuth
(3) Louisa
= Margrave of
Ausbach
(2) Frederick II = Eliz. Christina, sister
(1740–86)
o.s.p.
of Louisa Amalia of
Brunswick-Wolfen-
büttel
(7) Augustus = (4) Philippina =
William
(1722–58)
Chas. of
Bruns.-Wolf.
(9) Henry
(1726–1802)
o.s.p.
Elizabeth
divorced 1769
Wm. V of Orange = Wilhelmina
(deposed 1802)
Louisa of = Fred. Wm. II =
Hesse-Darm.
(1786–97)
Wm. I, King of the = (4) Wilhelmina
Netherlands, 1815
(1) Fred. Wm. III = Louisa of Mecklenburg-Strelitz
(1797–1840)
Wilhelmina

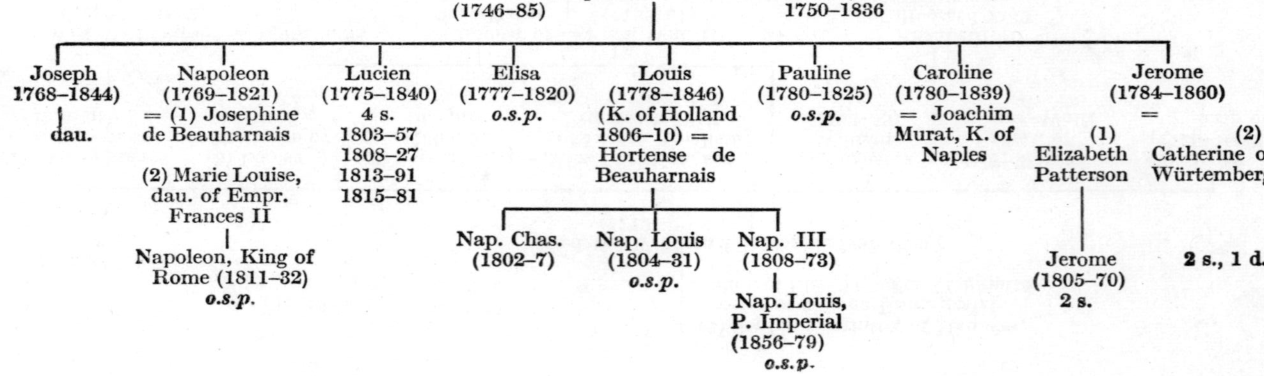
THE HOUSE OF BONAPARTE
Charles Marie de Bonaparte = Letizia Ramolino (*Madame Mère*)
(1746–85)
1750–1836
Joseph
1768–1844)
dau.
Napoleon
(1769–1821)
= (1) Josephine
de Beauharnais
(2) Marie Louise,
dau. of Empr.
Frances II
Napoleon, King of
Rome (1811–32)
o.s.p.
Lucien
(1775–1840)
4 s.
1803–57
1808–27
1813–91
1815–81
Elisa
(1777–1820)
o.s.p.
Louis
(1778–1846)
(K. of Holland
1806–10) =
Hortense de
Beauharnais
Nap. Chas.
(1802–7)
Nap. Louis
(1804–31)
o.s.p.
Nap. III
(1808–73)
Nap. Louis,
P. Imperial
(1856–79)
o.s.p.
Pauline
(1780–1825)
o.s.p.
Caroline
(1780–1839)
= Joachim
Murat, K. of
Naples
Jerome
(1784–1860)
=
(1)
Elizabeth
Patterson
Jerome
(1805–70)
2 s.
(2)
Catherine of
Würtemberg
2 s., 1 d.

INDEX

[Considerations of space have caused the omission of most countries, regions and movements (cp. Table of Contents), together with most persons, places and events mentioned in the text but falling outside the years 1715–1814.]